LUKE CAGE, I[...]

THE Heroes For Hire

John Ostrander & Joe Edkin WRITERS

Pasqual Ferry, Scott Kolins, Martin Egeland,
Mary Mitchell & Derec Aucoin with Chris Renaud PENCILERS

Jaime Mendoza, Dan Panosian, Hector Collazo,
Keith Aiken, Rich Faber & Pascual Ferry with
Mark Lipka, Pond Scum, Harry Candelario & John Floyd INKERS

Joe Rosas with Michael Kraiger & Mike Rockwitz COLORISTS

Jon Babcock and Richard Starkings &
Comicraft's Albert Deschesne LETTERERS

Dan Hosek & Lysa Kraiger ASSISTANT EDITORS

Mark Bernardo EDITOR

Pasqual Ferry & Mark McNabb FRONT COVER ARTISTS

Pasqual Ferry, Bob Wiacek & Mark McNabb BACK COVER ARTISTS

COLLECTION EDITOR Mark D. Beazley
ASSOCIATE EDITOR Sarah Brunstad
ASSOCIATE MANAGER, DIGITAL ASSETS Joe Hochstein
ASSOCIATE MANAGING EDITOR Kateri Woody
SENIOR EDITOR, SPECIAL PROJECTS Jennifer Grünwald

VP PRODUCTION & SPECIAL PROJECTS Jeff Youngquist
RESEARCH & LAYOUT Jeph York
PRODUCTION Ryan Devall, ColorTek & Joe Frontirre
BOOK DESIGNER Adam Del Re
SVP PRINT, SALES & MARKETING David Gabriel

EDITOR IN CHIEF Axel Alonso
CHIEF CREATIVE OFFICER Joe Quesada
PUBLISHER Dan Buckley
EXECUTIVE PRODUCER Alan Fine

LUKE CAGE, IRON FIST & THE HEROES FOR HIRE VOL. 2. Contains material originally published in magazine form as HEROES FOR HIRE #10-19, QUICKSILVER #11-12 and HEROES FOR HIRE/QUICKSILVER ANNUAL 1998. First printing 2017. ISBN# 978-1-302-90418-0. Published by MARVEL WORLDWIDE, INC., a subsidiary of MARVEL ENTERTAINMENT, LLC. OFFICE OF PUBLICATION: 135 West 50th Street, New York, NY 10020. **Printed in the U.S.A.** ALAN FINE, President, Marvel Entertainment; DAN BUCKLEY, President, TV, Publishing & Brand Management; JOE QUESADA, Chief Creative Officer; TOM BREVOORT, SVP of Publishing; DAVID BOGART, SVP of Business Affairs & Operations, Publishing & Partnership; C.B. CEBULSKI, VP of Brand Management & Development, Asia; DAVID GABRIEL, SVP of Sales & Marketing, Publishing; JEFF YOUNGQUIST, VP of Production & Special Projects; DAN CARR, Executive Director of Publishing Technology; ALEX MORALES, Director of Publishing Operations; SUSAN CRESPI, Production Manager; STAN LEE, Chairman Emeritus. For information regarding advertising in Marvel Comics or on Marvel.com, please contact Vit DeBellis, Integrated Sales Manager, at vdebellis@marvel.com. For Marvel subscription inquiries, please call 888-511-5480. **Manufactured between 11/25/2016 and 1/2/2017 by LSC COMMUNICATIONS INC., SALEM, VA, USA.**

10 9 8 7 6 5 4 3 2 1

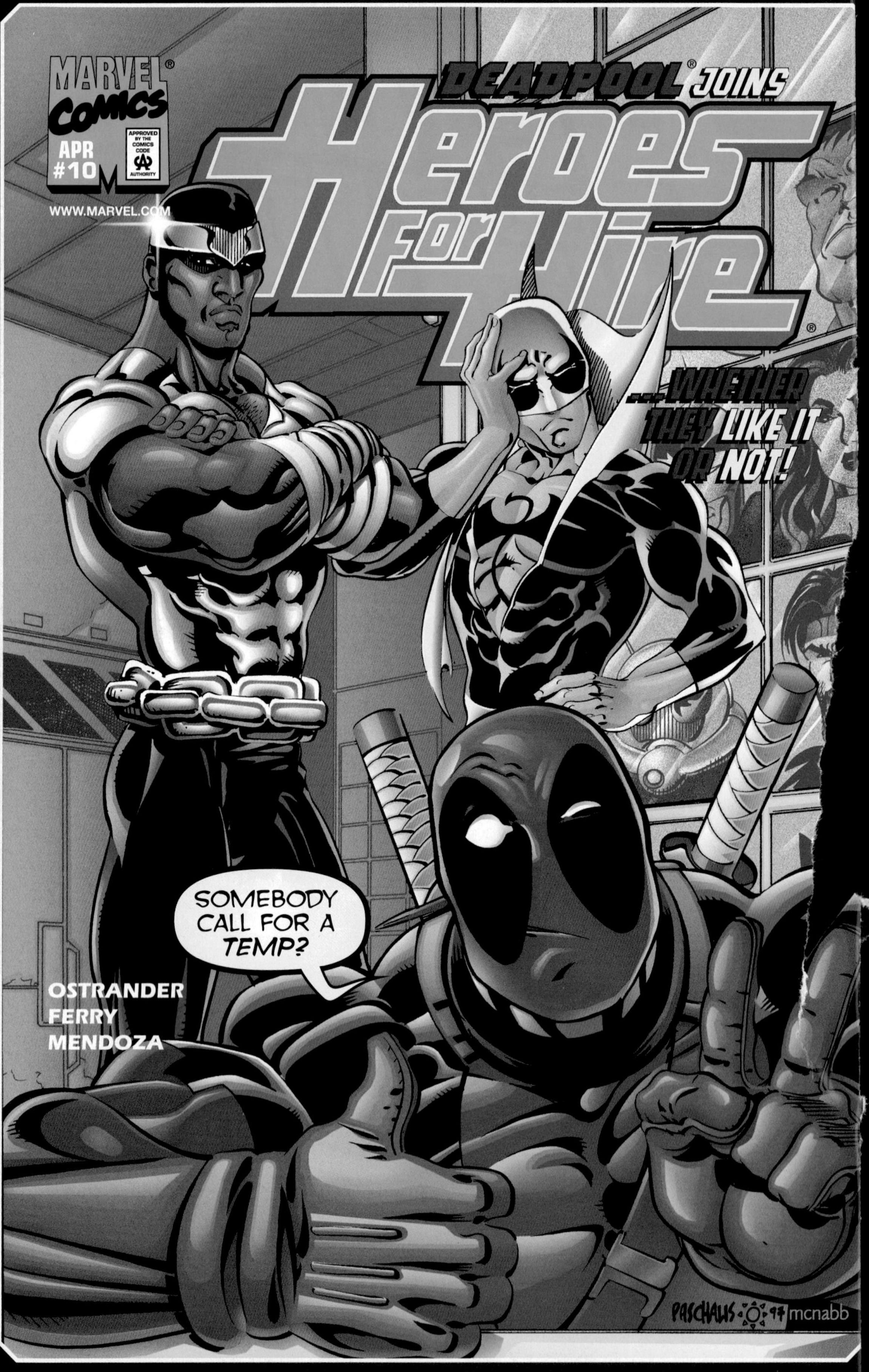
MARVEL COMICS
APR #10
APPROVED BY THE COMICS CODE AUTHORITY
WWW.MARVEL.COM
DEADPOOL JOINS
Heroes For Hire
...WHETHER THEY LIKE IT OR NOT!
SOMEBODY CALL FOR A TEMP?
OSTRANDER
FERRY
MENDOZA
PASCHALIS 97 mcnabb

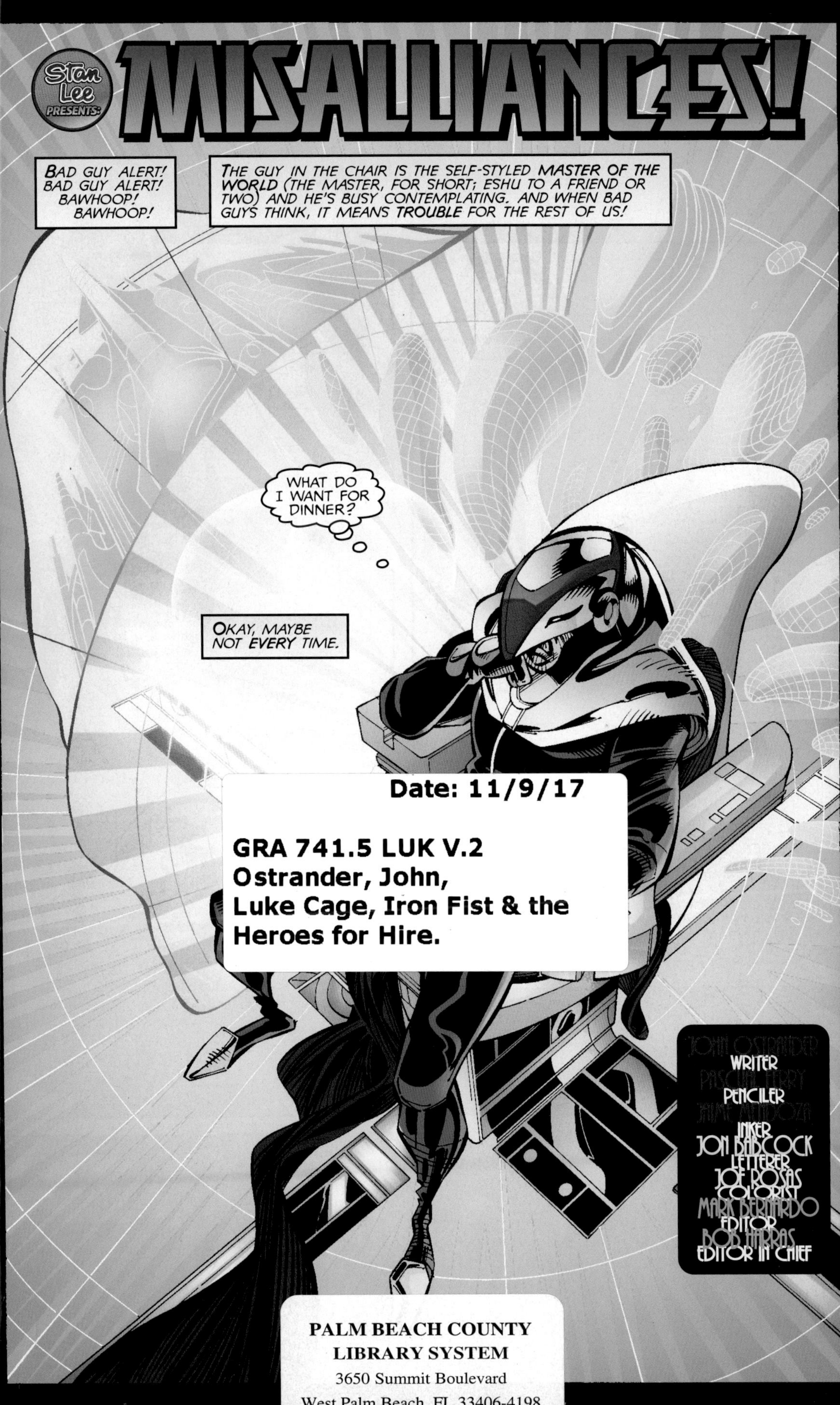
Stan Lee PRESENTS:
MISALLIANCES!
BAD GUY ALERT! BAD GUY ALERT! BAWHOOP! BAWHOOP!
THE GUY IN THE CHAIR IS THE SELF-STYLED MASTER OF THE WORLD (THE MASTER, FOR SHORT; ESHU TO A FRIEND OR TWO) AND HE'S BUSY CONTEMPLATING. AND WHEN BAD GUYS THINK, IT MEANS TROUBLE FOR THE REST OF US!
WHAT DO I WANT FOR DINNER?
OKAY, MAYBE NOT EVERY TIME.
JOHN OSTRANDER WRITER
PASCUAL FERRY PENCILER
JAIME MENDOZA INKER
JON BABCOCK LETTERER
JOE ROSAS COLORIST
MARK BERNARDO EDITOR
BOB HARRAS EDITOR IN CHIEF

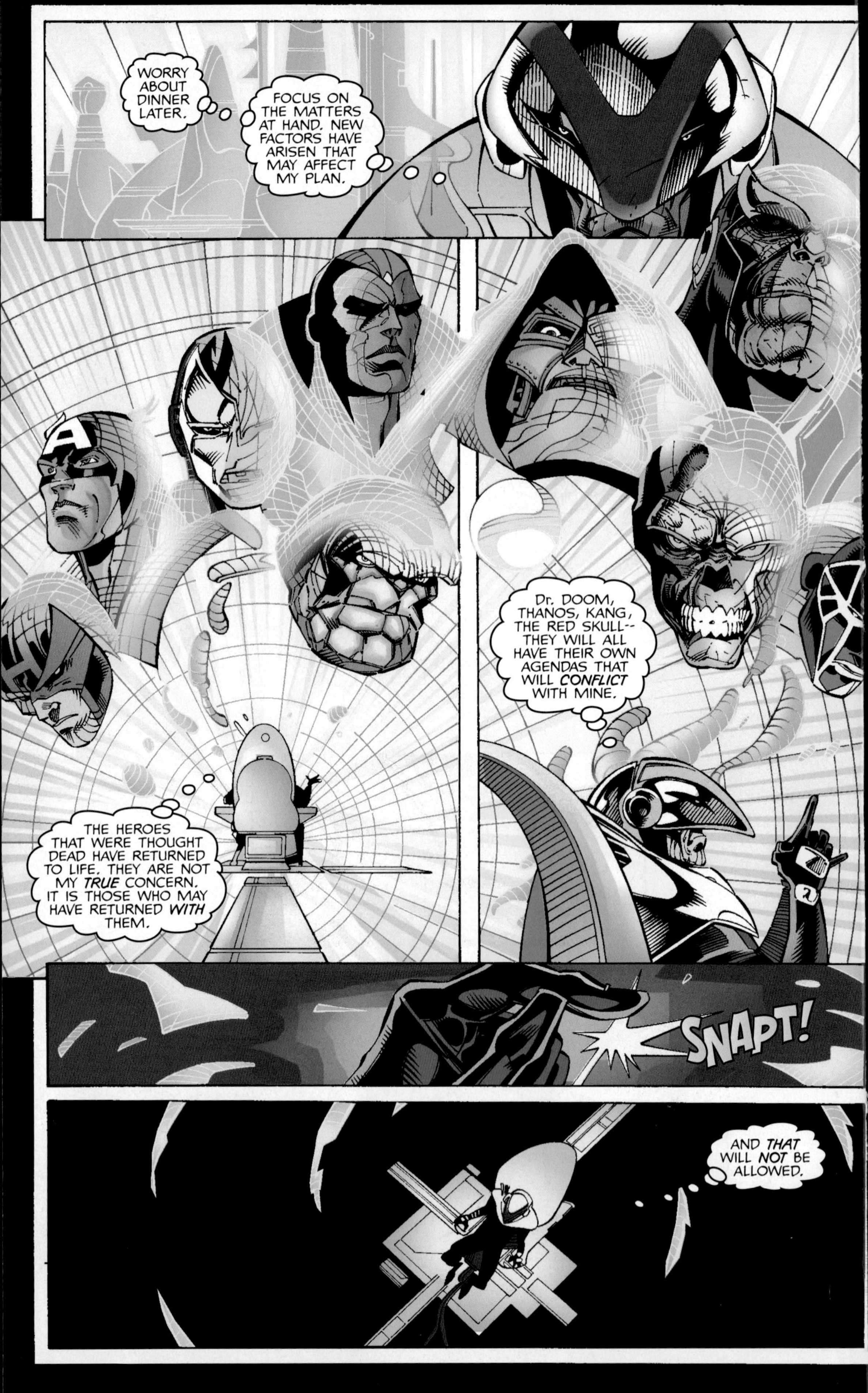
WORRY ABOUT DINNER LATER.
FOCUS ON THE MATTERS AT HAND. NEW FACTORS HAVE ARISEN THAT MAY AFFECT MY PLAN.
THE HEROES THAT WERE THOUGHT DEAD HAVE RETURNED TO LIFE. THEY ARE NOT MY TRUE CONCERN. IT IS THOSE WHO MAY HAVE RETURNED WITH THEM.
Dr. DOOM, THANOS, KANG, THE RED SKULL-- THEY WILL ALL HAVE THEIR OWN AGENDAS THAT WILL CONFLICT WITH MINE.
SNAPT!
AND THAT WILL NOT BE ALLOWED.

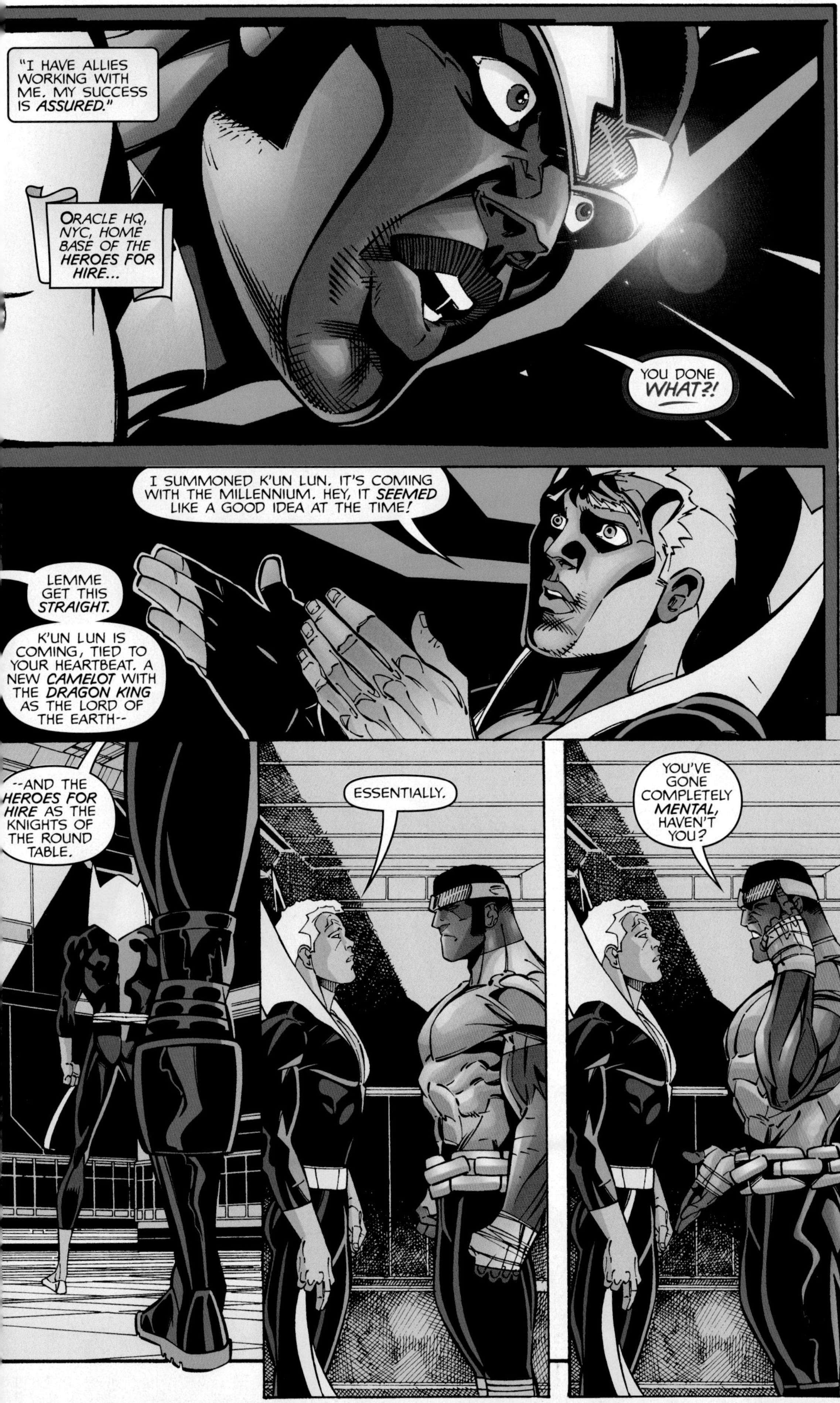
"I HAVE ALLIES WORKING WITH ME. MY SUCCESS IS ASSURED."
ORACLE HQ, NYC, HOME BASE OF THE HEROES FOR HIRE...
YOU DONE WHAT?!
I SUMMONED K'UN LUN. IT'S COMING WITH THE MILLENNIUM. HEY, IT SEEMED LIKE A GOOD IDEA AT THE TIME!
LEMME GET THIS STRAIGHT.
K'UN LUN IS COMING, TIED TO YOUR HEARTBEAT. A NEW CAMELOT WITH THE DRAGON KING AS THE LORD OF THE EARTH--
--AND THE HEROES FOR HIRE AS THE KNIGHTS OF THE ROUND TABLE.
ESSENTIALLY.
YOU'VE GONE COMPLETELY MENTAL, HAVEN'T YOU?

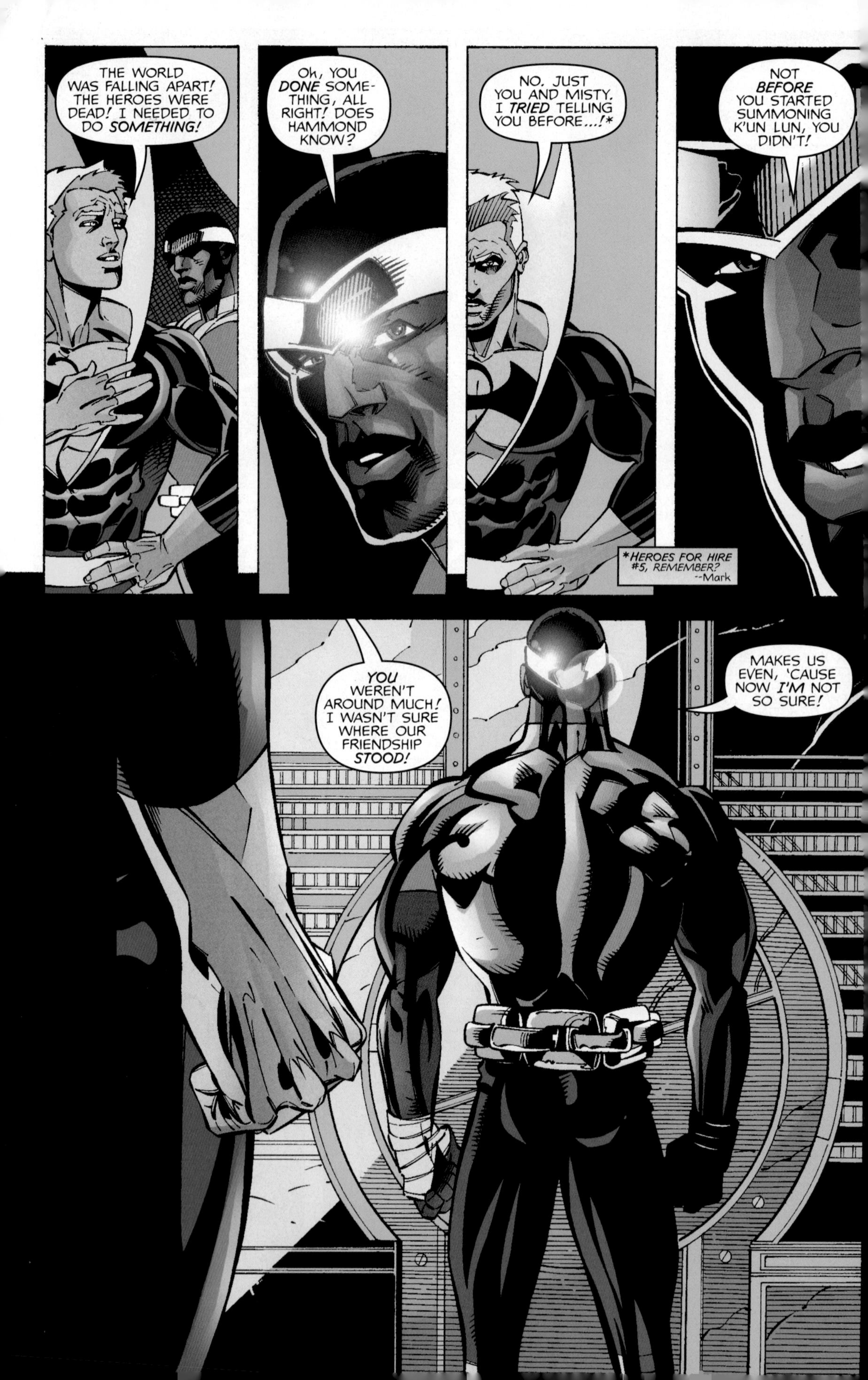
THE WORLD WAS FALLING APART! THE HEROES WERE DEAD! I NEEDED TO DO SOMETHING!
Oh, YOU DONE SOMETHING, ALL RIGHT! DOES HAMMOND KNOW?
NO. JUST YOU AND MISTY. I TRIED TELLING YOU BEFORE...!*
NOT BEFORE YOU STARTED SUMMONING K'UN LUN, YOU DIDN'T!
*HEROES FOR HIRE #5, REMEMBER? --Mark
YOU WEREN'T AROUND MUCH! I WASN'T SURE WHERE OUR FRIENDSHIP STOOD!
MAKES US EVEN, 'CAUSE NOW I'M NOT SO SURE!

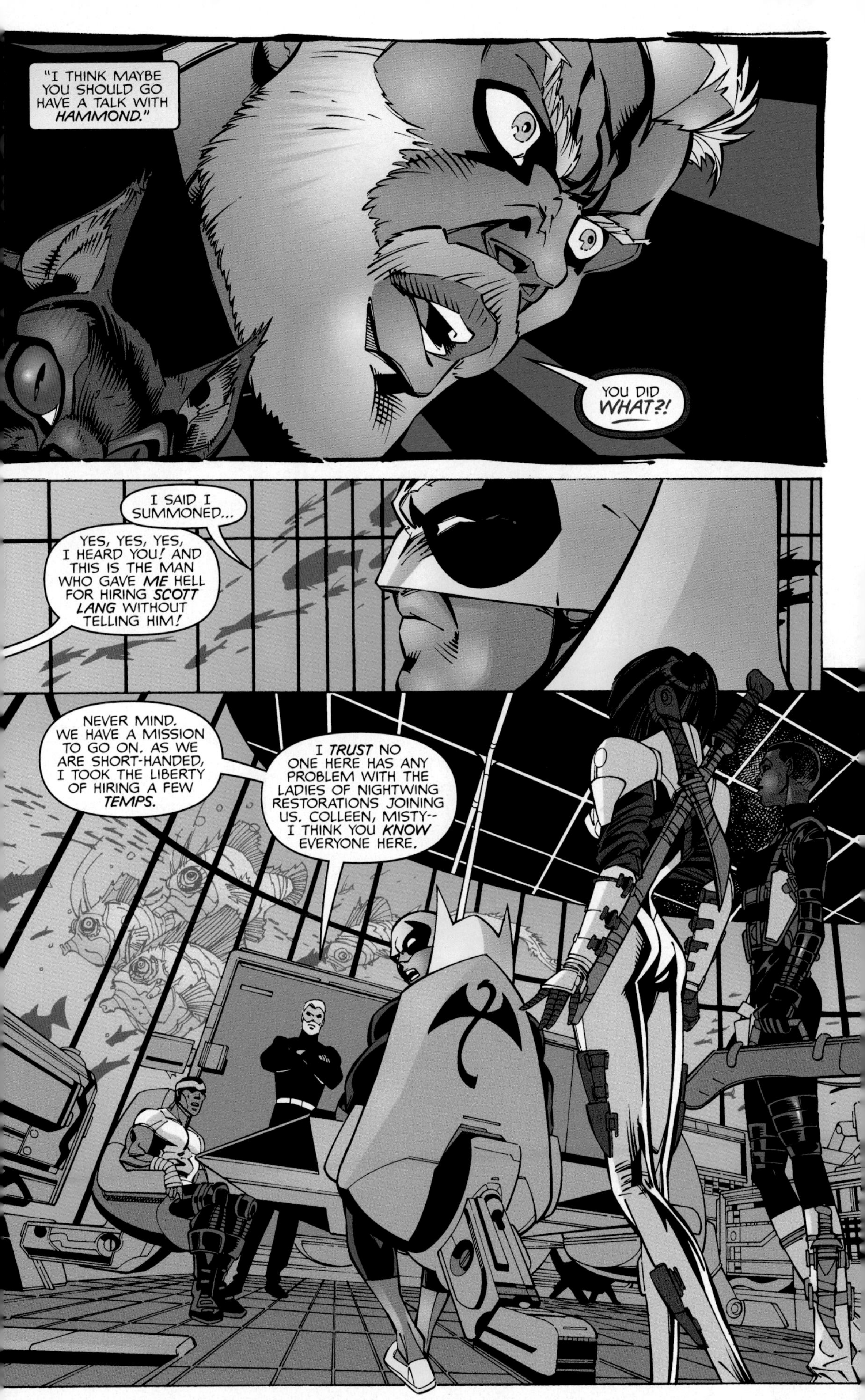
"I THINK MAYBE YOU SHOULD GO HAVE A TALK WITH HAMMOND."
YOU DID WHAT?!
I SAID I SUMMONED...
YES, YES, YES, I HEARD YOU! AND THIS IS THE MAN WHO GAVE ME HELL FOR HIRING SCOTT LANG WITHOUT TELLING HIM!
NEVER MIND. WE HAVE A MISSION TO GO ON. AS WE ARE SHORT-HANDED, I TOOK THE LIBERTY OF HIRING A FEW TEMPS.
I TRUST NO ONE HERE HAS ANY PROBLEM WITH THE LADIES OF NIGHTWING RESTORATIONS JOINING US. COLLEEN, MISTY-- I THINK YOU KNOW EVERYONE HERE.

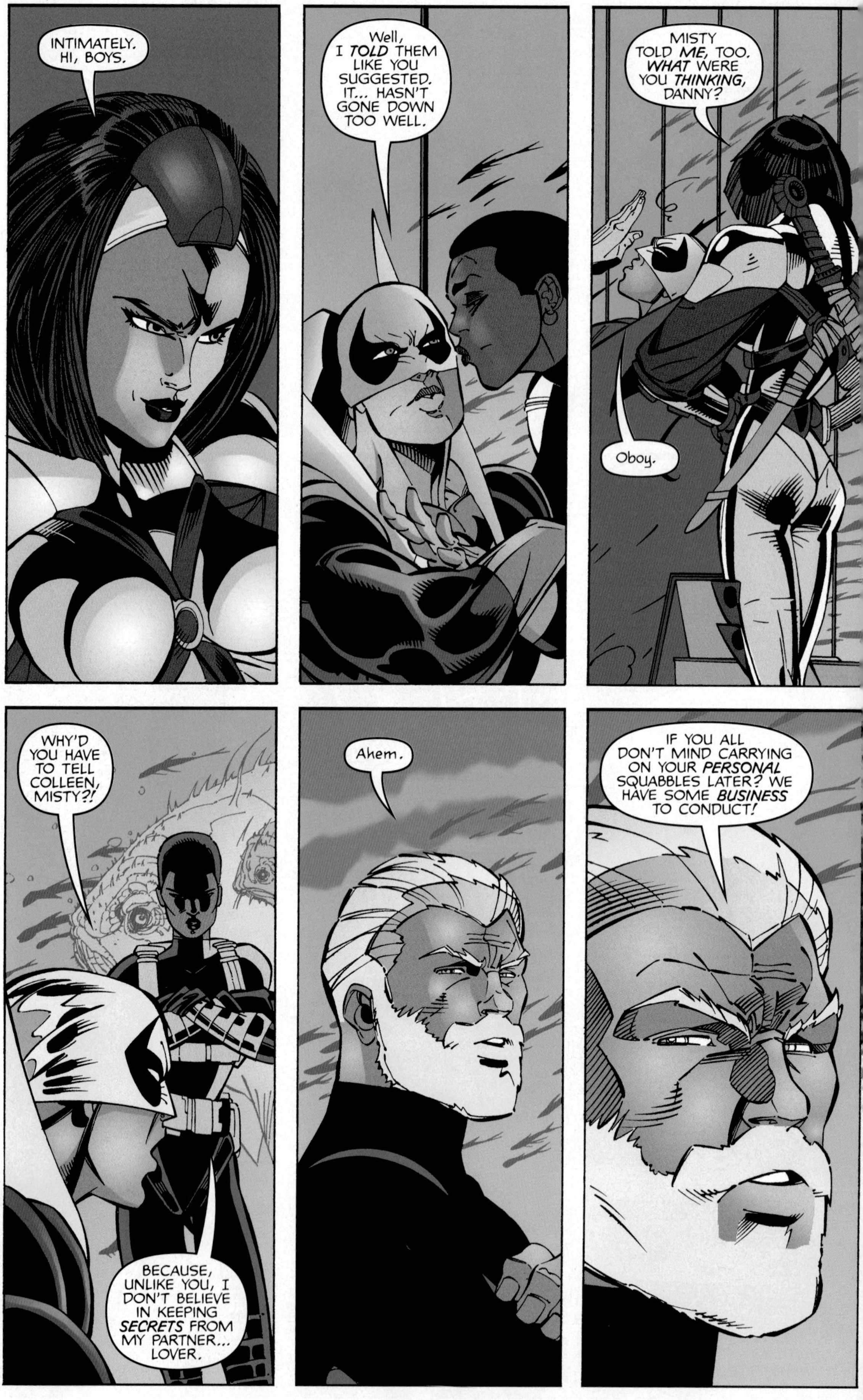
INTIMATELY. HI, BOYS.
Well, I TOLD THEM LIKE YOU SUGGESTED. IT... HASN'T GONE DOWN TOO WELL.
MISTY TOLD ME, TOO. WHAT WERE YOU THINKING, DANNY?
Oboy.
WHY'D YOU HAVE TO TELL COLLEEN, MISTY?!
BECAUSE, UNLIKE YOU, I DON'T BELIEVE IN KEEPING SECRETS FROM MY PARTNER... LOVER.
Ahem.
IF YOU ALL DON'T MIND CARRYING ON YOUR PERSONAL SQUABBLES LATER? WE HAVE SOME BUSINESS TO CONDUCT!

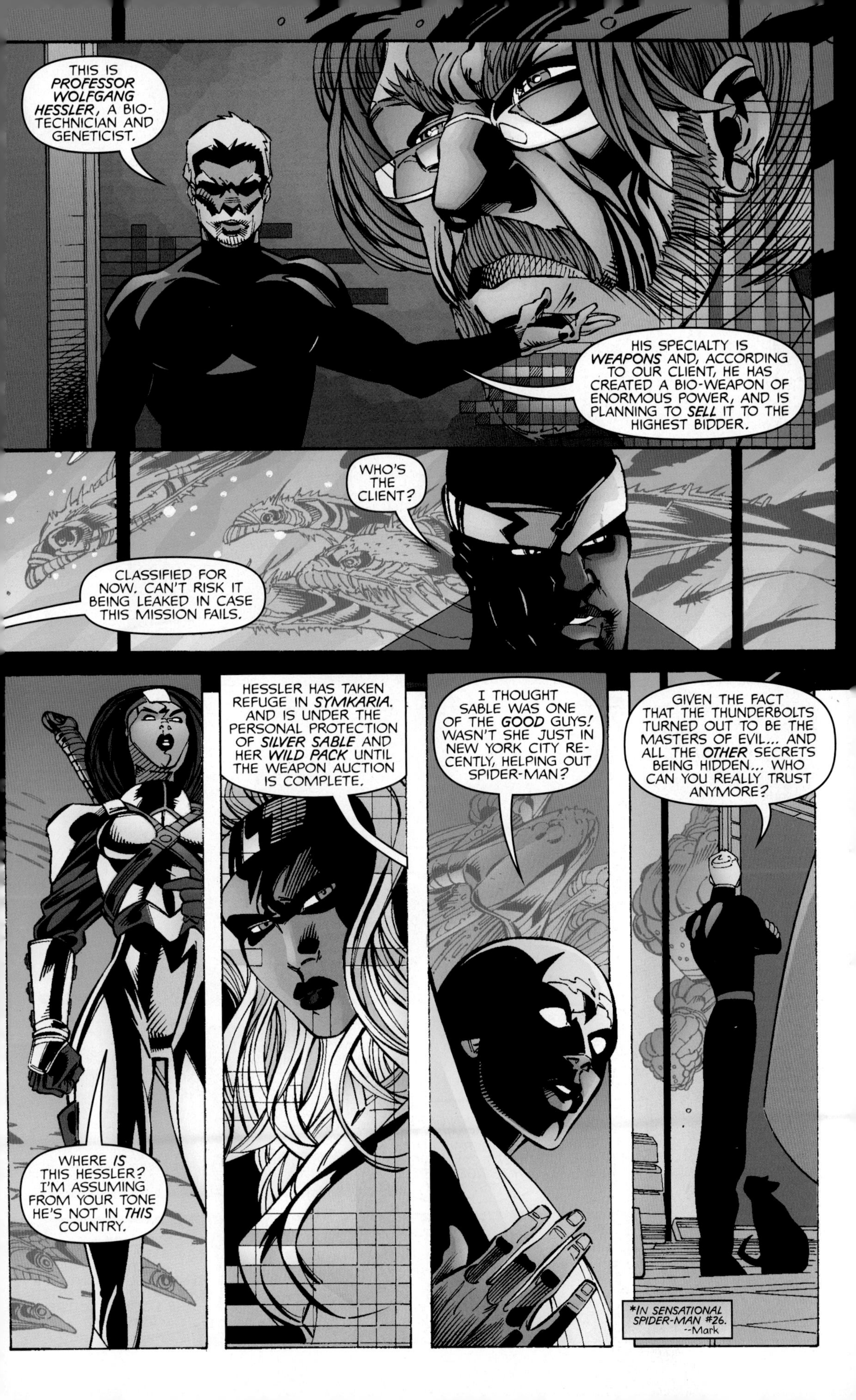
THIS IS *PROFESSOR WOLFGANG HESSLER*, A BIO-TECHNICIAN AND GENETICIST.
HIS SPECIALTY IS *WEAPONS* AND, ACCORDING TO OUR CLIENT, HE HAS CREATED A BIO-WEAPON OF ENORMOUS POWER, AND IS PLANNING TO *SELL* IT TO THE HIGHEST BIDDER.
WHO'S THE CLIENT?
CLASSIFIED FOR NOW. CAN'T RISK IT BEING LEAKED IN CASE THIS MISSION FAILS.
WHERE *IS* THIS HESSLER? I'M ASSUMING FROM YOUR TONE HE'S NOT IN *THIS* COUNTRY.
HESSLER HAS TAKEN REFUGE IN *SYMKARIA*, AND IS UNDER THE PERSONAL PROTECTION OF *SILVER SABLE* AND HER *WILD PACK* UNTIL THE WEAPON AUCTION IS COMPLETE.
I THOUGHT SABLE WAS ONE OF THE *GOOD* GUYS! WASN'T SHE JUST IN NEW YORK CITY RE-CENTLY, HELPING OUT SPIDER-MAN?
GIVEN THE FACT THAT THE THUNDERBOLTS TURNED OUT TO BE THE MASTERS OF EVIL... AND ALL THE *OTHER* SECRETS BEING HIDDEN... WHO CAN YOU REALLY TRUST ANYMORE?
**IN SENSATIONAL SPIDER-MAN #26.* --Mark

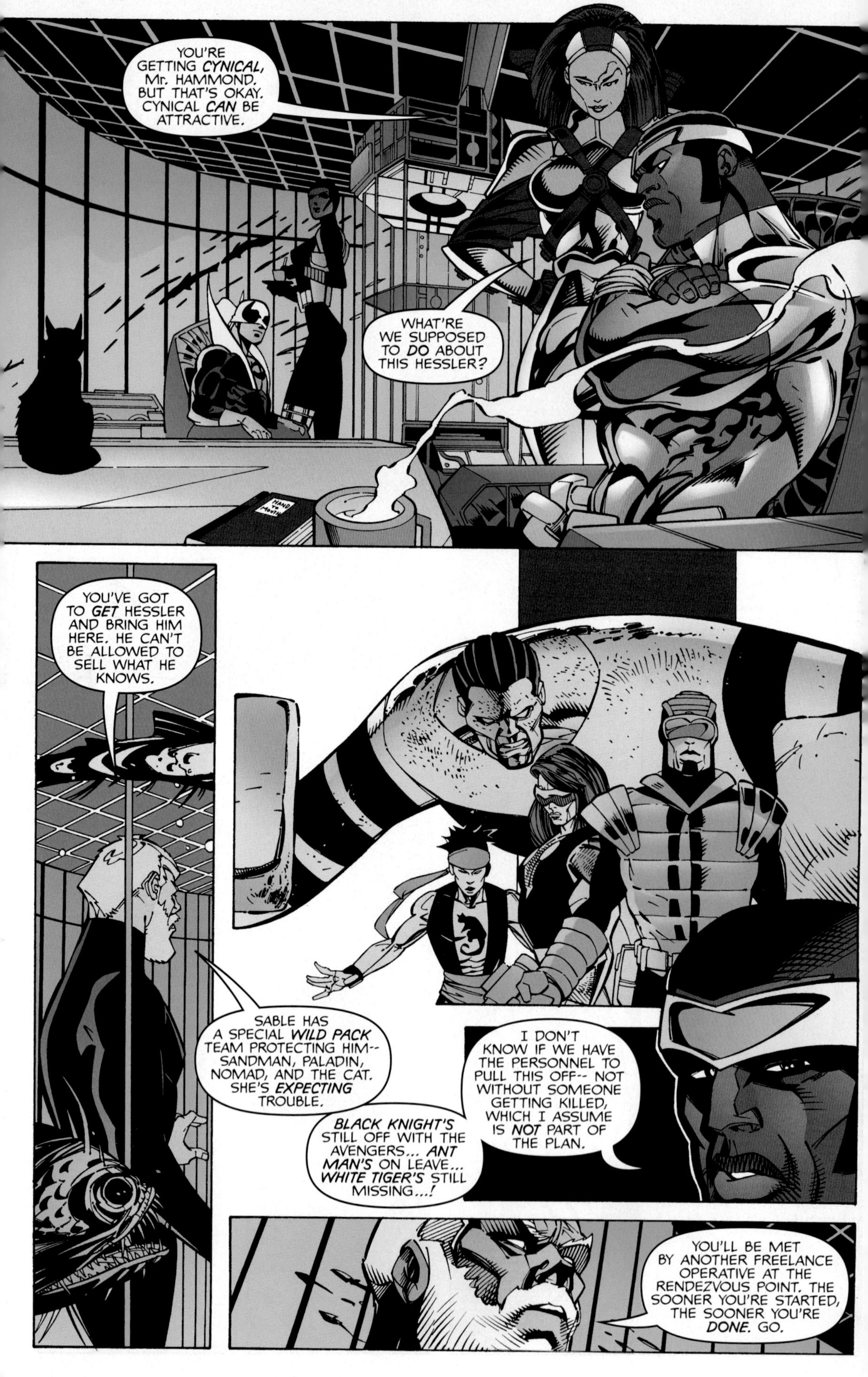
YOU'RE GETTING CYNICAL, Mr. HAMMOND. BUT THAT'S OKAY. CYNICAL CAN BE ATTRACTIVE.
WHAT'RE WE SUPPOSED TO DO ABOUT THIS HESSLER?
YOU'VE GOT TO GET HESSLER AND BRING HIM HERE. HE CAN'T BE ALLOWED TO SELL WHAT HE KNOWS.
SABLE HAS A SPECIAL WILD PACK TEAM PROTECTING HIM-- SANDMAN, PALADIN, NOMAD, AND THE CAT. SHE'S EXPECTING TROUBLE.
I DON'T KNOW IF WE HAVE THE PERSONNEL TO PULL THIS OFF-- NOT WITHOUT SOMEONE GETTING KILLED, WHICH I ASSUME IS NOT PART OF THE PLAN.
BLACK KNIGHT'S STILL OFF WITH THE AVENGERS... ANT MAN'S ON LEAVE... WHITE TIGER'S STILL MISSING...!
YOU'LL BE MET BY ANOTHER FREELANCE OPERATIVE AT THE RENDEZVOUS POINT. THE SOONER YOU'RE STARTED, THE SOONER YOU'RE DONE. GO.

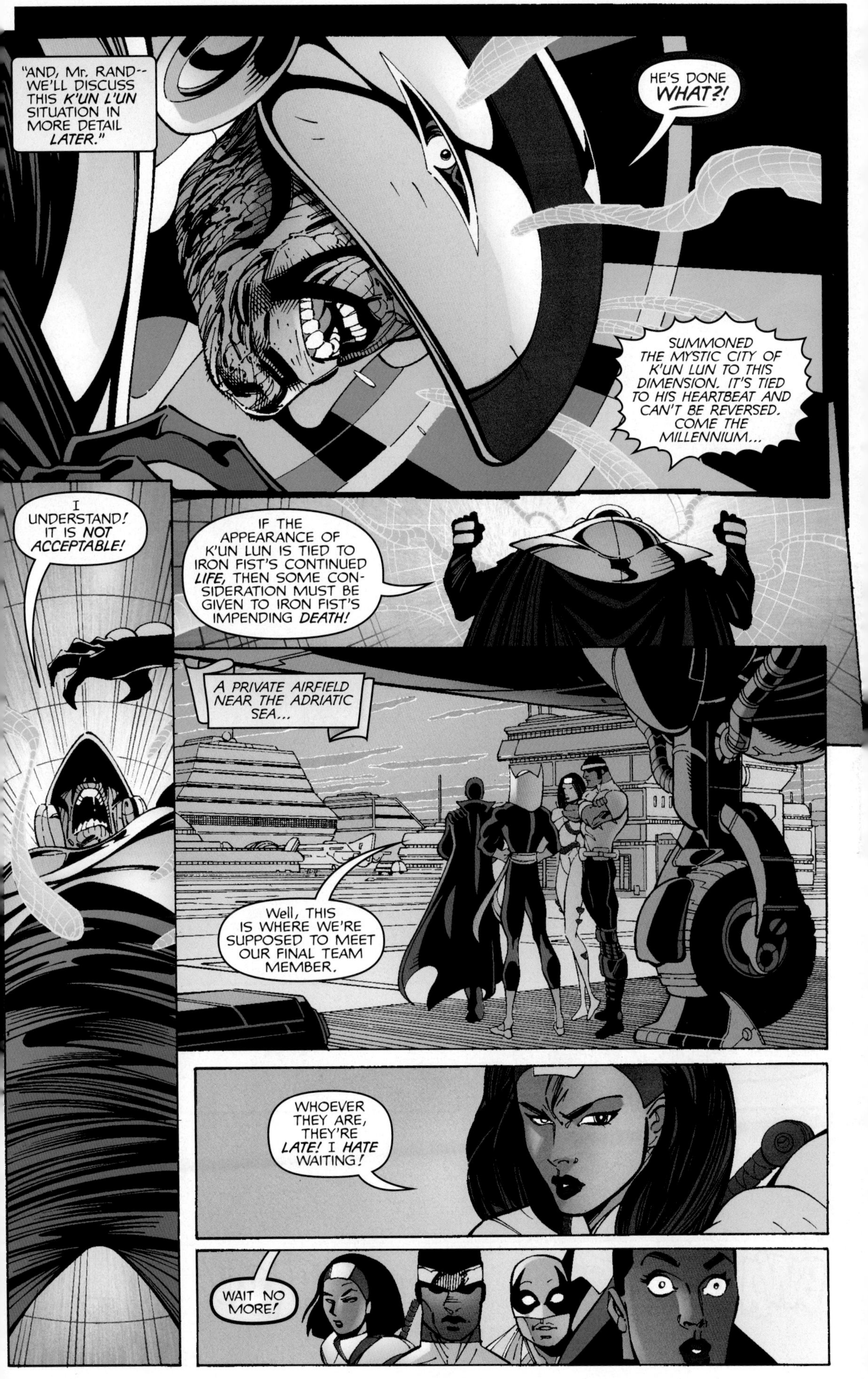
"AND, Mr. RAND-- WE'LL DISCUSS THIS K'UN L'UN SITUATION IN MORE DETAIL LATER."
HE'S DONE WHAT?!
SUMMONED THE MYSTIC CITY OF K'UN LUN TO THIS DIMENSION. IT'S TIED TO HIS HEARTBEAT AND CAN'T BE REVERSED. COME THE MILLENNIUM...
I UNDERSTAND! IT IS NOT ACCEPTABLE!
IF THE APPEARANCE OF K'UN LUN IS TIED TO IRON FIST'S CONTINUED LIFE, THEN SOME CONSIDERATION MUST BE GIVEN TO IRON FIST'S IMPENDING DEATH!
A PRIVATE AIRFIELD NEAR THE ADRIATIC SEA...
Well, THIS IS WHERE WE'RE SUPPOSED TO MEET OUR FINAL TEAM MEMBER.
WHOEVER THEY ARE, THEY'RE LATE! I HATE WAITING!
WAIT NO MORE!

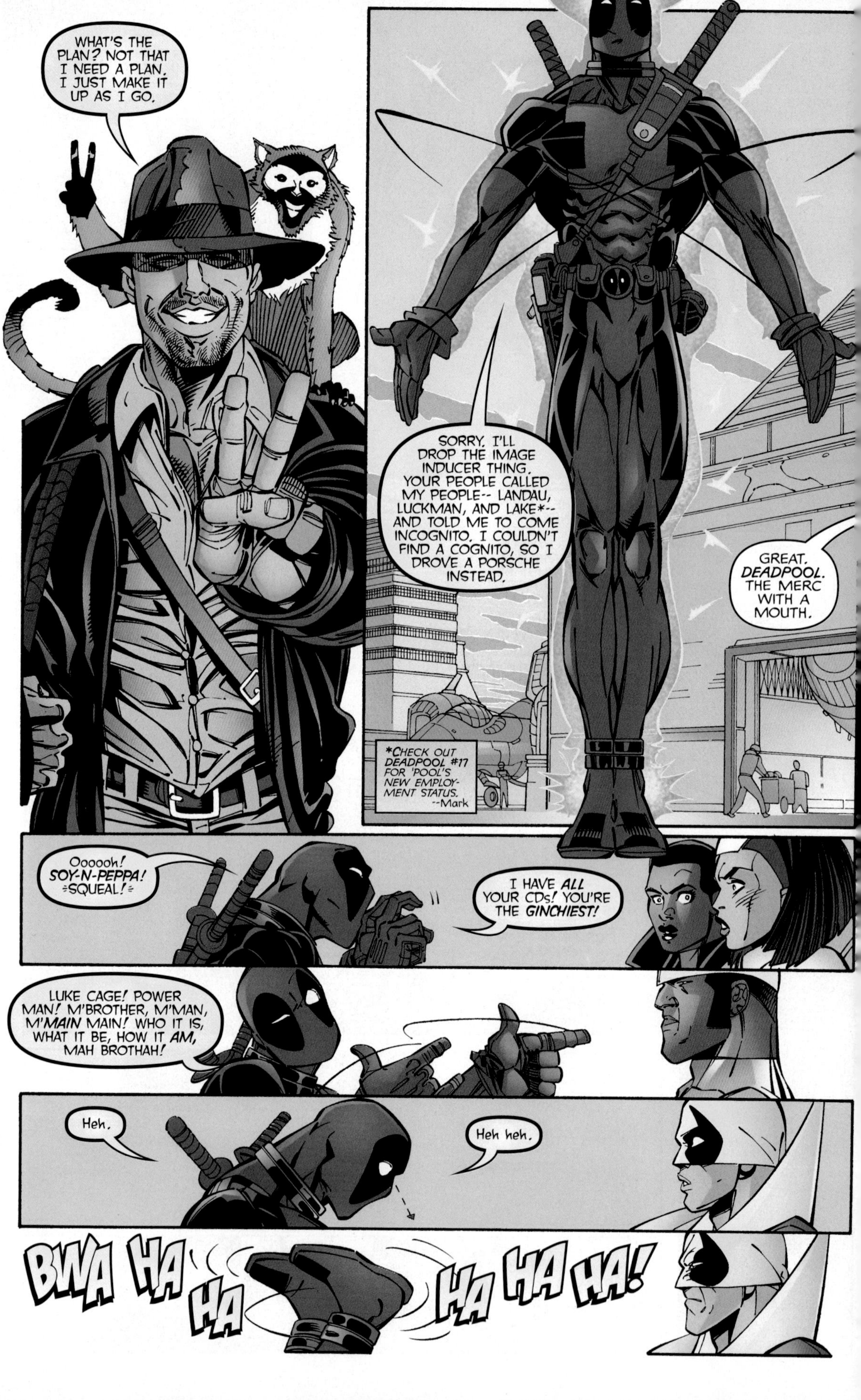
WHAT'S THE PLAN? NOT THAT I NEED A PLAN. I JUST MAKE IT UP AS I GO.
SORRY. I'LL DROP THE IMAGE INDUCER THING. YOUR PEOPLE CALLED MY PEOPLE-- LANDAU, LUCKMAN, AND LAKE*-- AND TOLD ME TO COME INCOGNITO. I COULDN'T FIND A COGNITO, SO I DROVE A PORSCHE INSTEAD.
GREAT. DEADPOOL. THE MERC WITH A MOUTH.
*CHECK OUT DEADPOOL #17 FOR 'POOL'S NEW EMPLOYMENT STATUS. --Mark
Oooooh! SOY-N-PEPPA! SQUEAL!
I HAVE ALL YOUR CDs! YOU'RE THE GINCHIEST!
LUKE CAGE! POWER MAN! M'BROTHER, M'MAN, M'MAIN MAIN! WHO IT IS, WHAT IT BE, HOW IT AM, MAH BROTHAH!
Heh.
Heh heh.
BWA HA HA HA HA HA!

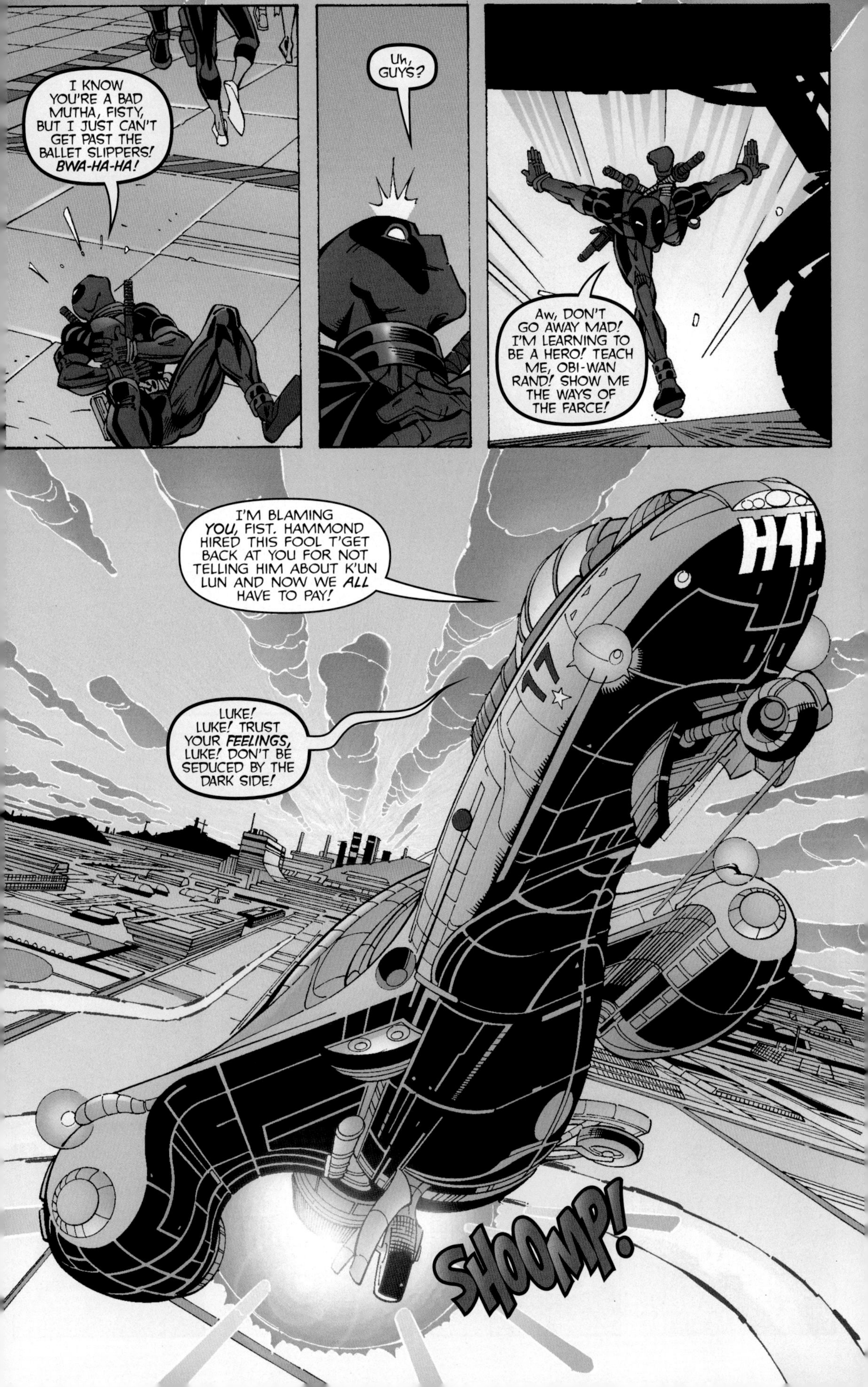
I KNOW YOU'RE A BAD MUTHA, FISTY, BUT I JUST CAN'T GET PAST THE BALLET SLIPPERS! *BWA-HA-HA!*
UH, GUYS?
AW, DON'T GO AWAY MAD! I'M LEARNING TO BE A HERO! TEACH ME, OBI-WAN RAND! SHOW ME THE WAYS OF THE FARCE!
I'M BLAMING *YOU,* FIST. HAMMOND HIRED THIS FOOL T'GET BACK AT YOU FOR NOT TELLING HIM ABOUT K'UN LUN AND NOW WE *ALL* HAVE TO PAY!
LUKE! LUKE! TRUST YOUR *FEELINGS,* LUKE! DON'T BE SEDUCED BY THE DARK SIDE!
H4H
17
SHOOMP!

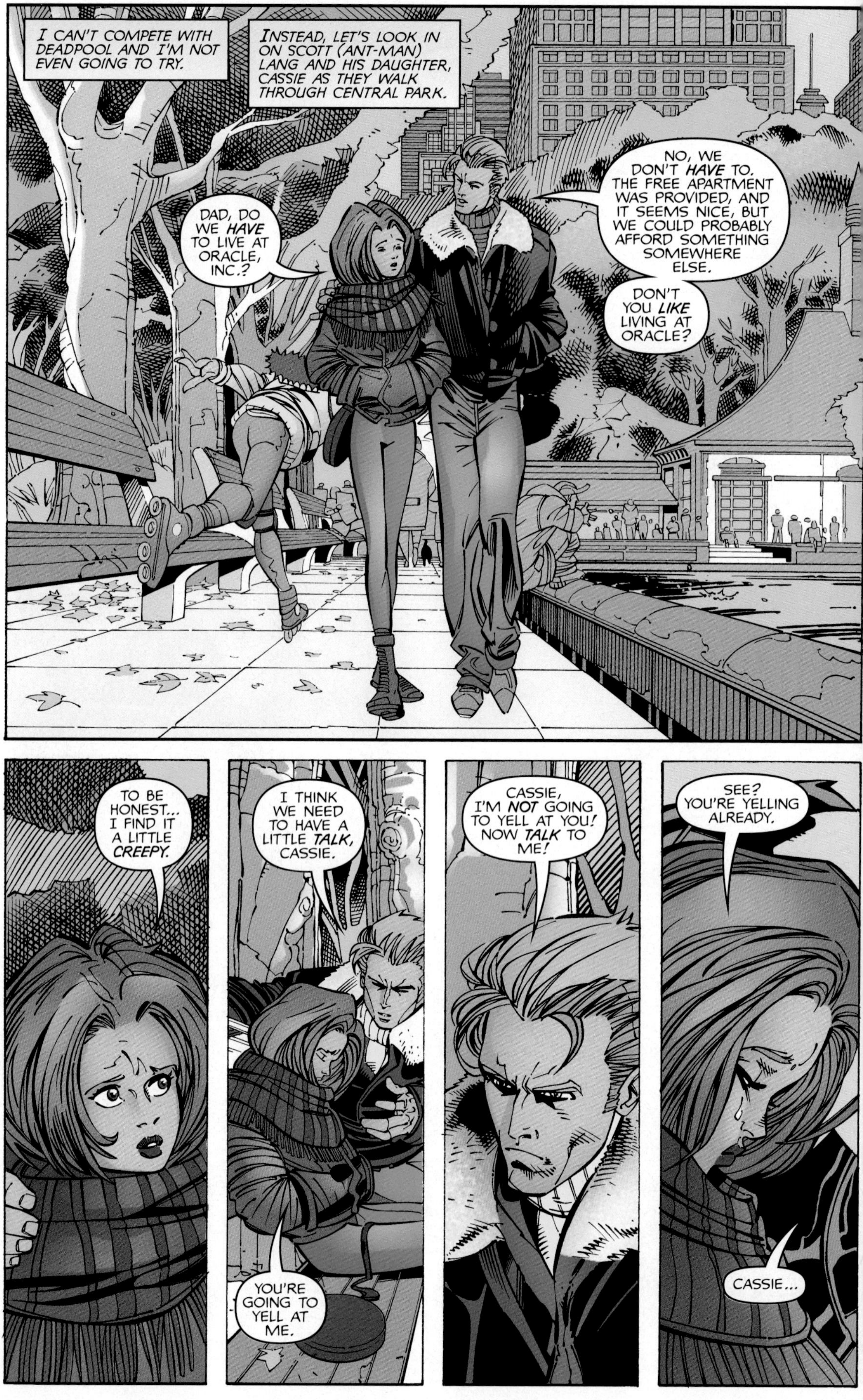
I CAN'T COMPETE WITH DEADPOOL AND I'M NOT EVEN GOING TO TRY.
INSTEAD, LET'S LOOK IN ON SCOTT (ANT-MAN) LANG AND HIS DAUGHTER, CASSIE AS THEY WALK THROUGH CENTRAL PARK.
DAD, DO WE HAVE TO LIVE AT ORACLE, INC.?
NO, WE DON'T HAVE TO. THE FREE APARTMENT WAS PROVIDED, AND IT SEEMS NICE, BUT WE COULD PROBABLY AFFORD SOMETHING SOMEWHERE ELSE.
DON'T YOU LIKE LIVING AT ORACLE?
TO BE HONEST... I FIND IT A LITTLE CREEPY.
I THINK WE NEED TO HAVE A LITTLE TALK, CASSIE.
YOU'RE GOING TO YELL AT ME.
CASSIE, I'M NOT GOING TO YELL AT YOU! NOW TALK TO ME!
SEE? YOU'RE YELLING ALREADY.
CASSIE...

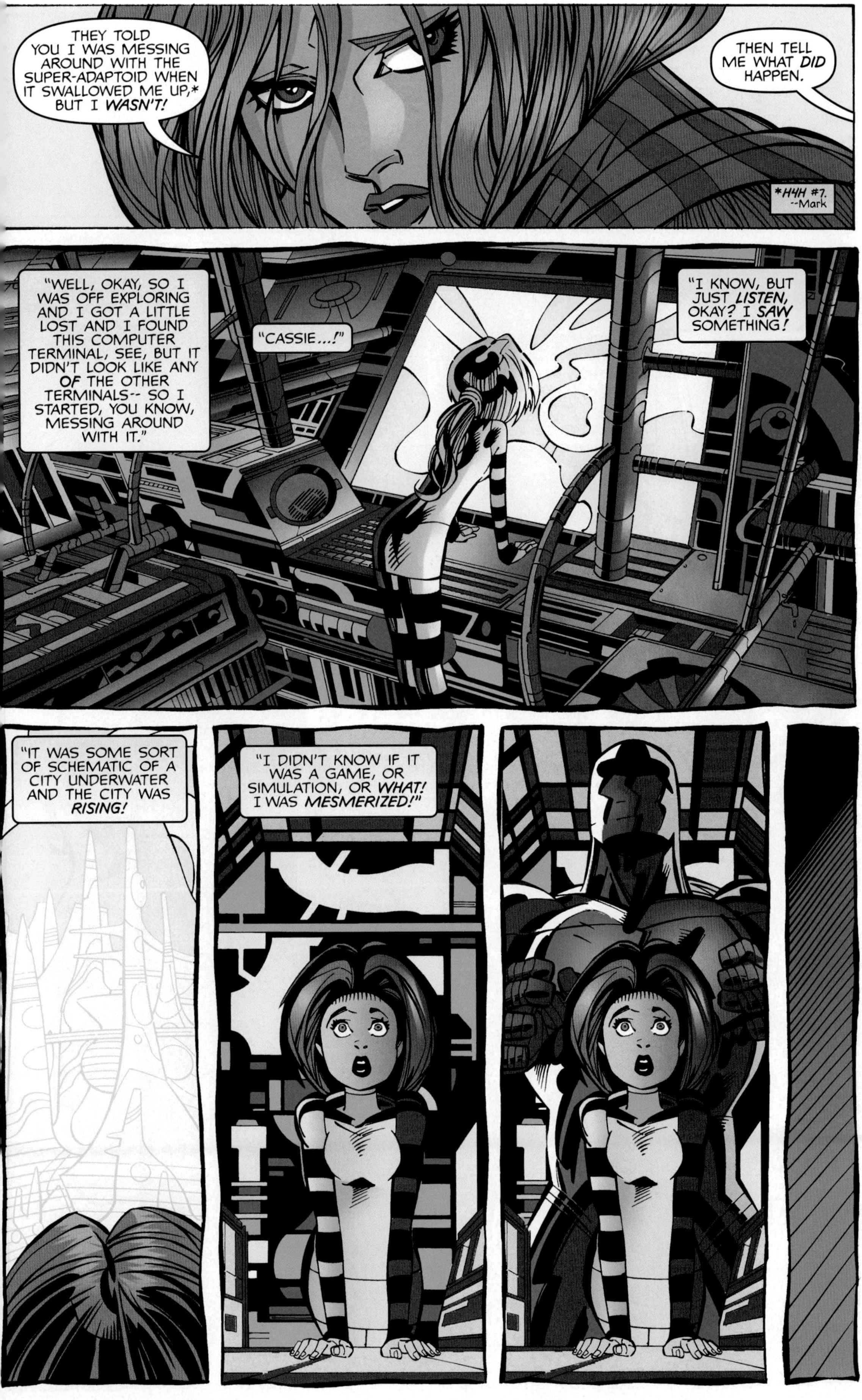
THEY TOLD YOU I WAS MESSING AROUND WITH THE SUPER-ADAPTOID WHEN IT SWALLOWED ME UP,* BUT I WASN'T!
THEN TELL ME WHAT DID HAPPEN.
*H4H #7. --Mark
"WELL, OKAY, SO I WAS OFF EXPLORING AND I GOT A LITTLE LOST AND I FOUND THIS COMPUTER TERMINAL, SEE, BUT IT DIDN'T LOOK LIKE ANY OF THE OTHER TERMINALS-- SO I STARTED, YOU KNOW, MESSING AROUND WITH IT."
"CASSIE...!"
"I KNOW, BUT JUST LISTEN, OKAY? I SAW SOMETHING!
"IT WAS SOME SORT OF SCHEMATIC OF A CITY UNDERWATER AND THE CITY WAS RISING!
"I DIDN'T KNOW IF IT WAS A GAME, OR SIMULATION, OR WHAT! I WAS MESMERIZED!"

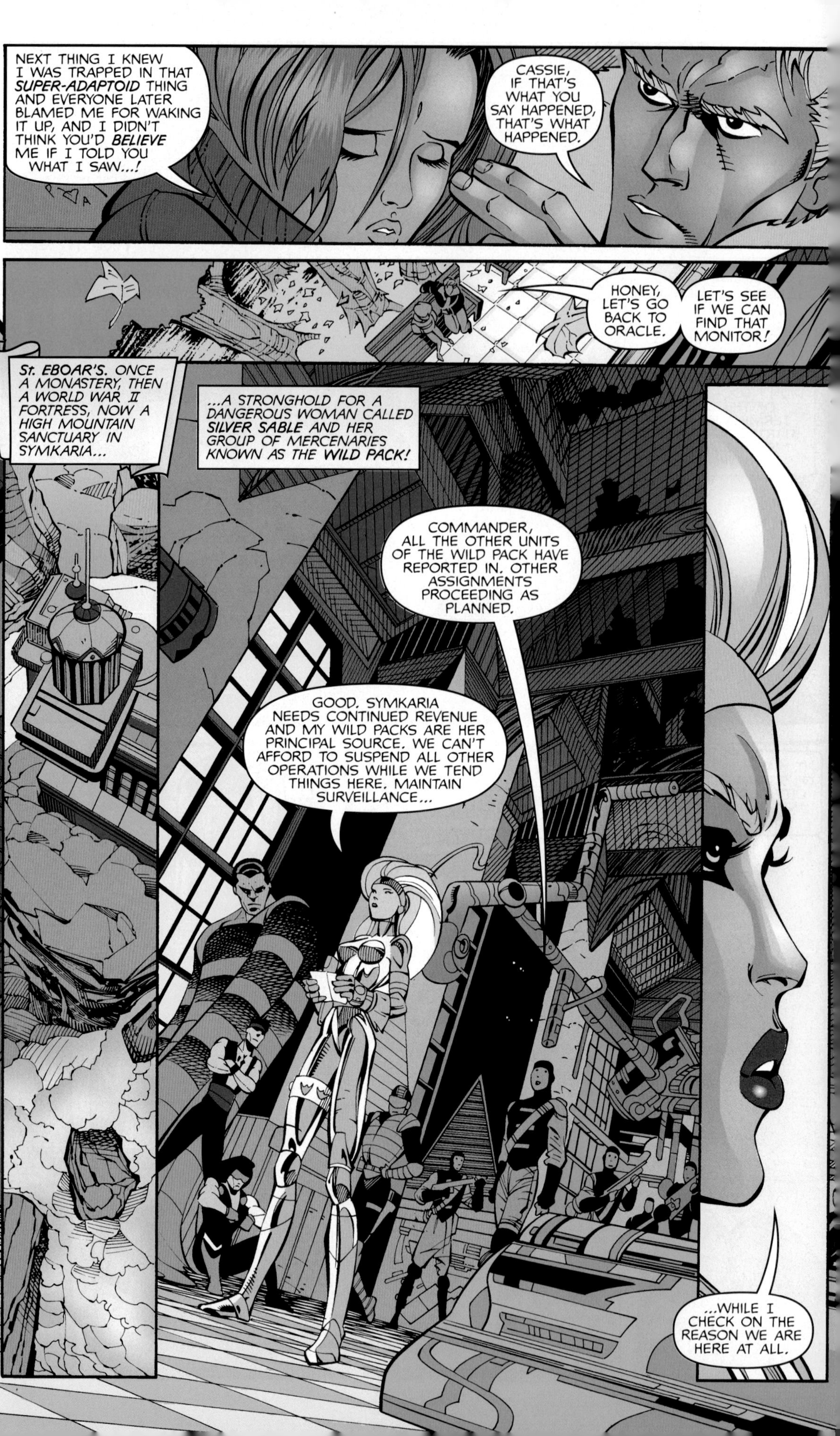
NEXT THING I KNEW I WAS TRAPPED IN THAT SUPER-ADAPTOID THING AND EVERYONE LATER BLAMED ME FOR WAKING IT UP, AND I DIDN'T THINK YOU'D BELIEVE ME IF I TOLD YOU WHAT I SAW...!
CASSIE, IF THAT'S WHAT YOU SAY HAPPENED, THAT'S WHAT HAPPENED.
HONEY, LET'S GO BACK TO ORACLE.
LET'S SEE IF WE CAN FIND THAT MONITOR!
St. EBOAR'S. ONCE A MONASTERY, THEN A WORLD WAR II FORTRESS, NOW A HIGH MOUNTAIN SANCTUARY IN SYMKARIA...
...A STRONGHOLD FOR A DANGEROUS WOMAN CALLED SILVER SABLE AND HER GROUP OF MERCENARIES KNOWN AS THE WILD PACK!
COMMANDER, ALL THE OTHER UNITS OF THE WILD PACK HAVE REPORTED IN. OTHER ASSIGNMENTS PROCEEDING AS PLANNED.
GOOD. SYMKARIA NEEDS CONTINUED REVENUE AND MY WILD PACKS ARE HER PRINCIPAL SOURCE. WE CAN'T AFFORD TO SUSPEND ALL OTHER OPERATIONS WHILE WE TEND THINGS HERE. MAINTAIN SURVEILLANCE...
...WHILE I CHECK ON THE REASON WE ARE HERE AT ALL.

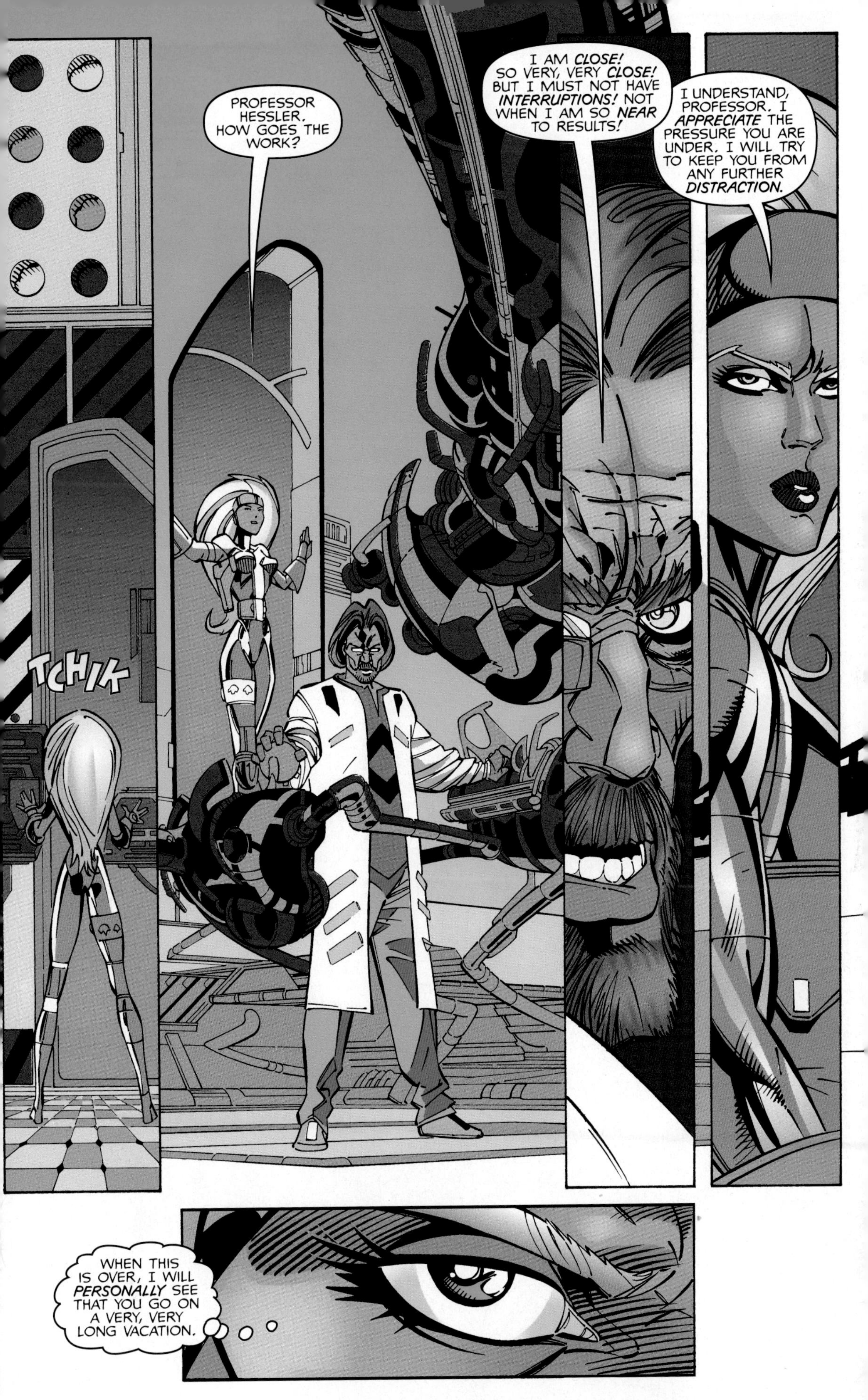
TCHIK
PROFESSOR HESSLER. HOW GOES THE WORK?
I AM CLOSE! SO VERY, VERY CLOSE! BUT I MUST NOT HAVE INTERRUPTIONS! NOT WHEN I AM SO NEAR TO RESULTS!
I UNDERSTAND, PROFESSOR. I APPRECIATE THE PRESSURE YOU ARE UNDER. I WILL TRY TO KEEP YOU FROM ANY FURTHER DISTRACTION.
WHEN THIS IS OVER, I WILL PERSONALLY SEE THAT YOU GO ON A VERY, VERY LONG VACATION.

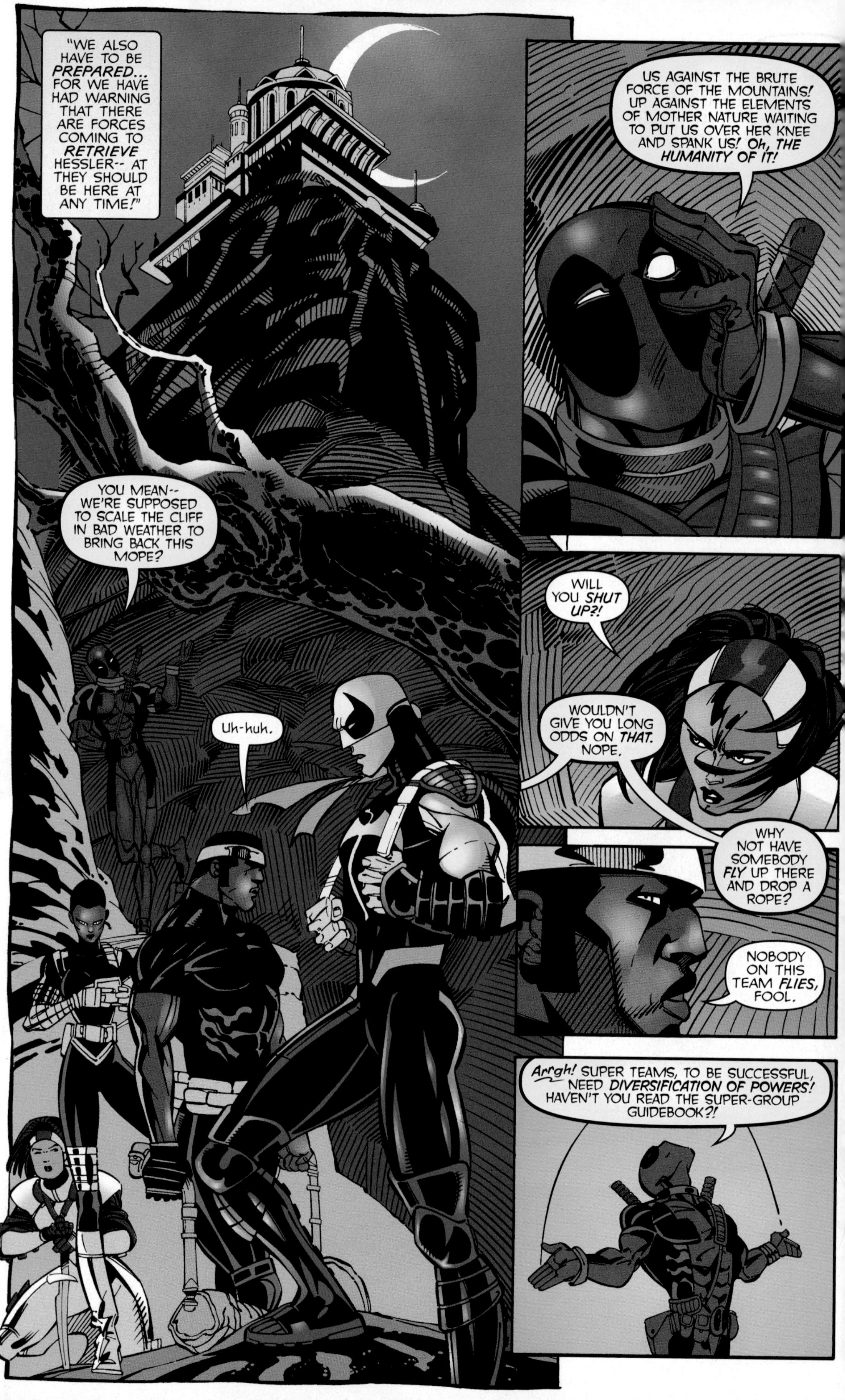
"WE ALSO HAVE TO BE PREPARED... FOR WE HAVE HAD WARNING THAT THERE ARE FORCES COMING TO RETRIEVE HESSLER-- AT THEY SHOULD BE HERE AT ANY TIME!"
YOU MEAN-- WE'RE SUPPOSED TO SCALE THE CLIFF IN BAD WEATHER TO BRING BACK THIS MOPE?
Uh-huh.
US AGAINST THE BRUTE FORCE OF THE MOUNTAINS! UP AGAINST THE ELEMENTS OF MOTHER NATURE WAITING TO PUT US OVER HER KNEE AND SPANK US! Oh, THE HUMANITY OF IT!
WILL YOU SHUT UP?!
WOULDN'T GIVE YOU LONG ODDS ON THAT. NOPE.
WHY NOT HAVE SOMEBODY FLY UP THERE AND DROP A ROPE?
NOBODY ON THIS TEAM FLIES, FOOL.
Arrgh! SUPER TEAMS, TO BE SUCCESSFUL, NEED DIVERSIFICATION OF POWERS! HAVEN'T YOU READ THE SUPER-GROUP GUIDEBOOK?!

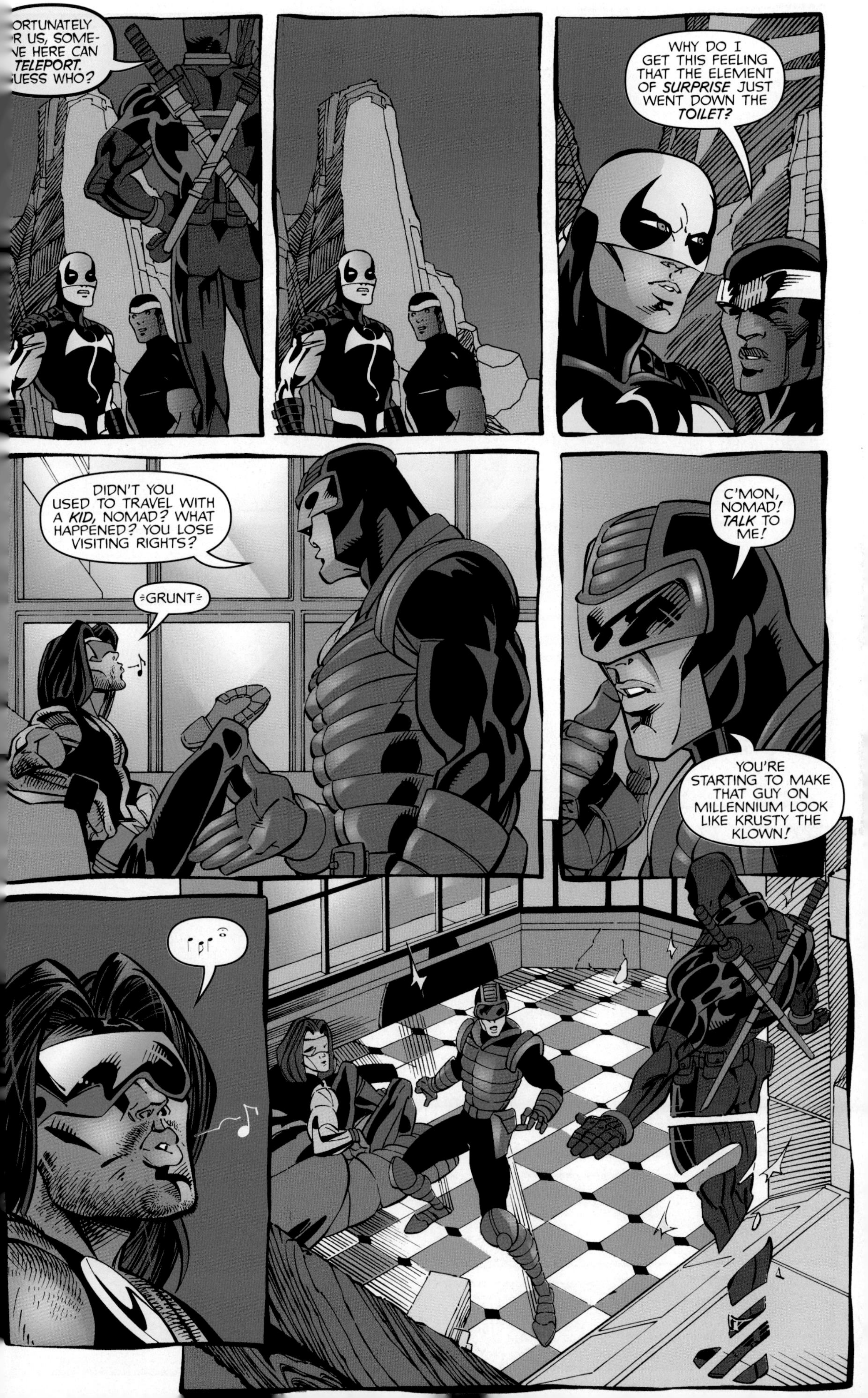
ORTUNATELY
R US, SOME-
NE HERE CAN
TELEPORT.
UESS WHO?
WHY DO I GET THIS FEELING THAT THE ELEMENT OF SURPRISE JUST WENT DOWN THE TOILET?
DIDN'T YOU USED TO TRAVEL WITH A KID, NOMAD? WHAT HAPPENED? YOU LOSE VISITING RIGHTS?
GRUNT
C'MON, NOMAD! TALK TO ME!
YOU'RE STARTING TO MAKE THAT GUY ON MILLENNIUM LOOK LIKE KRUSTY THE KLOWN!

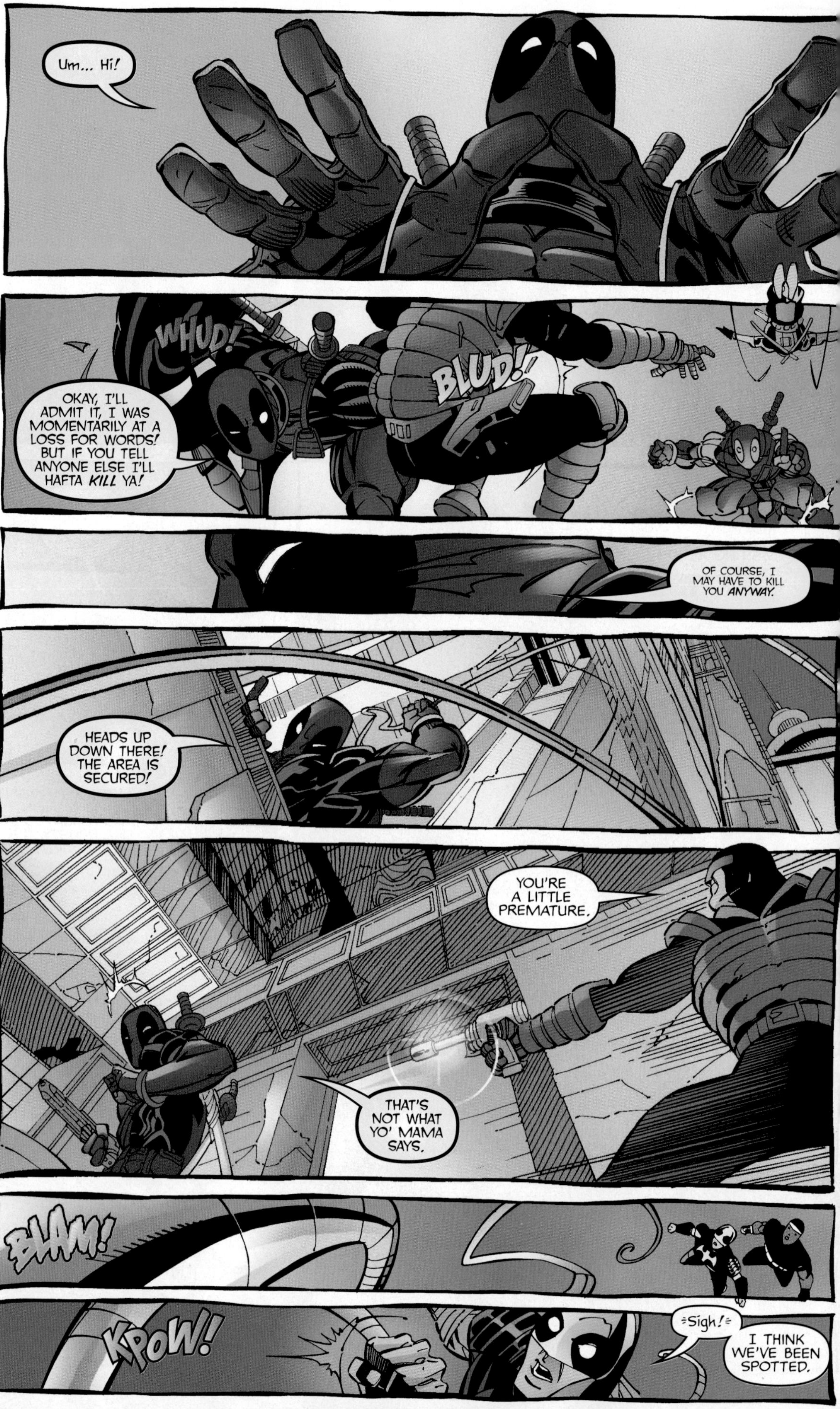

Um... Hi!
WHUD!
BLUD!
OKAY, I'LL ADMIT IT, I WAS MOMENTARILY AT A LOSS FOR WORDS! BUT IF YOU TELL ANYONE ELSE I'LL HAFTA KILL YA!
OF COURSE, I MAY HAVE TO KILL YOU ANYWAY.
HEADS UP DOWN THERE! THE AREA IS SECURED!
YOU'RE A LITTLE PREMATURE.
THAT'S NOT WHAT YO' MAMA SAYS.
BLAM!
KPOW!
Sigh!
I THINK WE'VE BEEN SPOTTED.

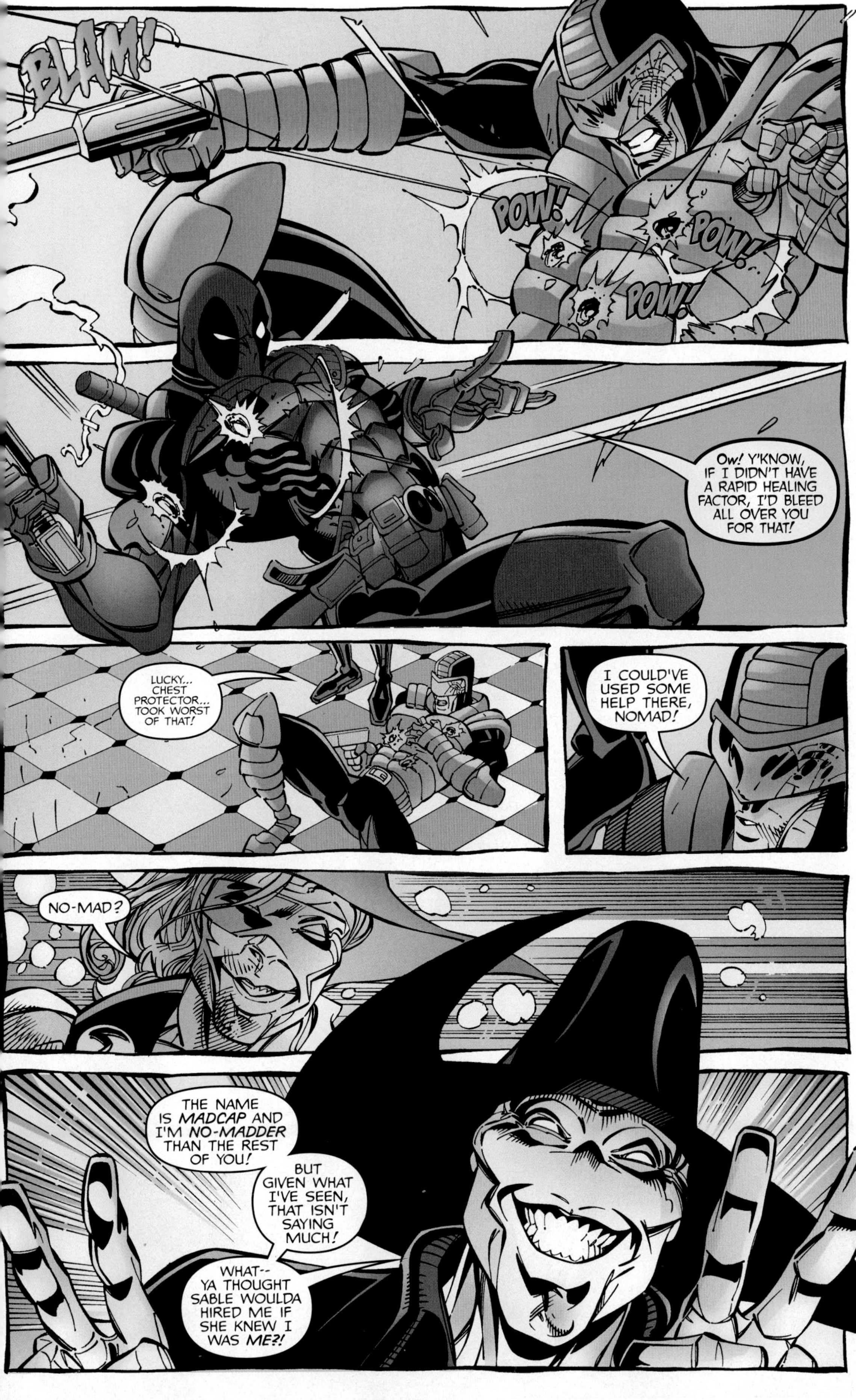
BLAM!
POW!
POW!
POW!
OW! Y'KNOW, IF I DIDN'T HAVE A RAPID HEALING FACTOR, I'D BLEED ALL OVER YOU FOR THAT!
LUCKY... CHEST PROTECTOR... TOOK WORST OF THAT!
I COULD'VE USED SOME HELP THERE, NOMAD!
NO-MAD?
THE NAME IS MADCAP AND I'M NO-MADDER THAN THE REST OF YOU!
BUT GIVEN WHAT I'VE SEEN, THAT ISN'T SAYING MUCH!
WHAT-- YA THOUGHT SABLE WOULDA HIRED ME IF SHE KNEW I WAS ME?!

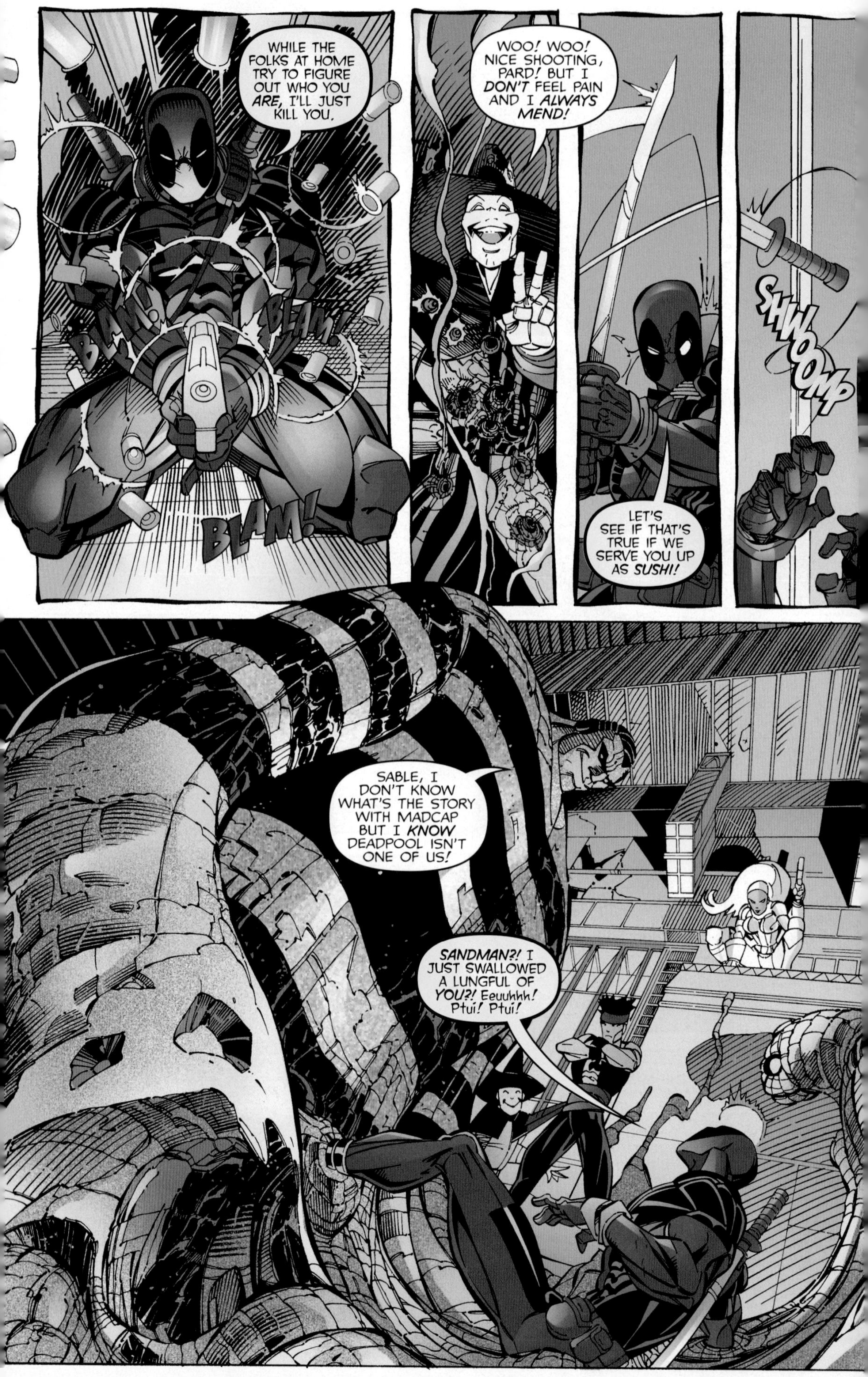
WHILE THE FOLKS AT HOME TRY TO FIGURE OUT WHO YOU ARE, I'LL JUST KILL YOU.
BLAM!
BLAM!
BLAM!
WOO! WOO! NICE SHOOTING, PARD! BUT I DON'T FEEL PAIN AND I ALWAYS MEND!
LET'S SEE IF THAT'S TRUE IF WE SERVE YOU UP AS SUSHI!
SHWOOMP
SABLE, I DON'T KNOW WHAT'S THE STORY WITH MADCAP BUT I KNOW DEADPOOL ISN'T ONE OF US!
SANDMAN?! I JUST SWALLOWED A LUNGFUL OF YOU?! Eeuuhhh! Ptui! Ptui!

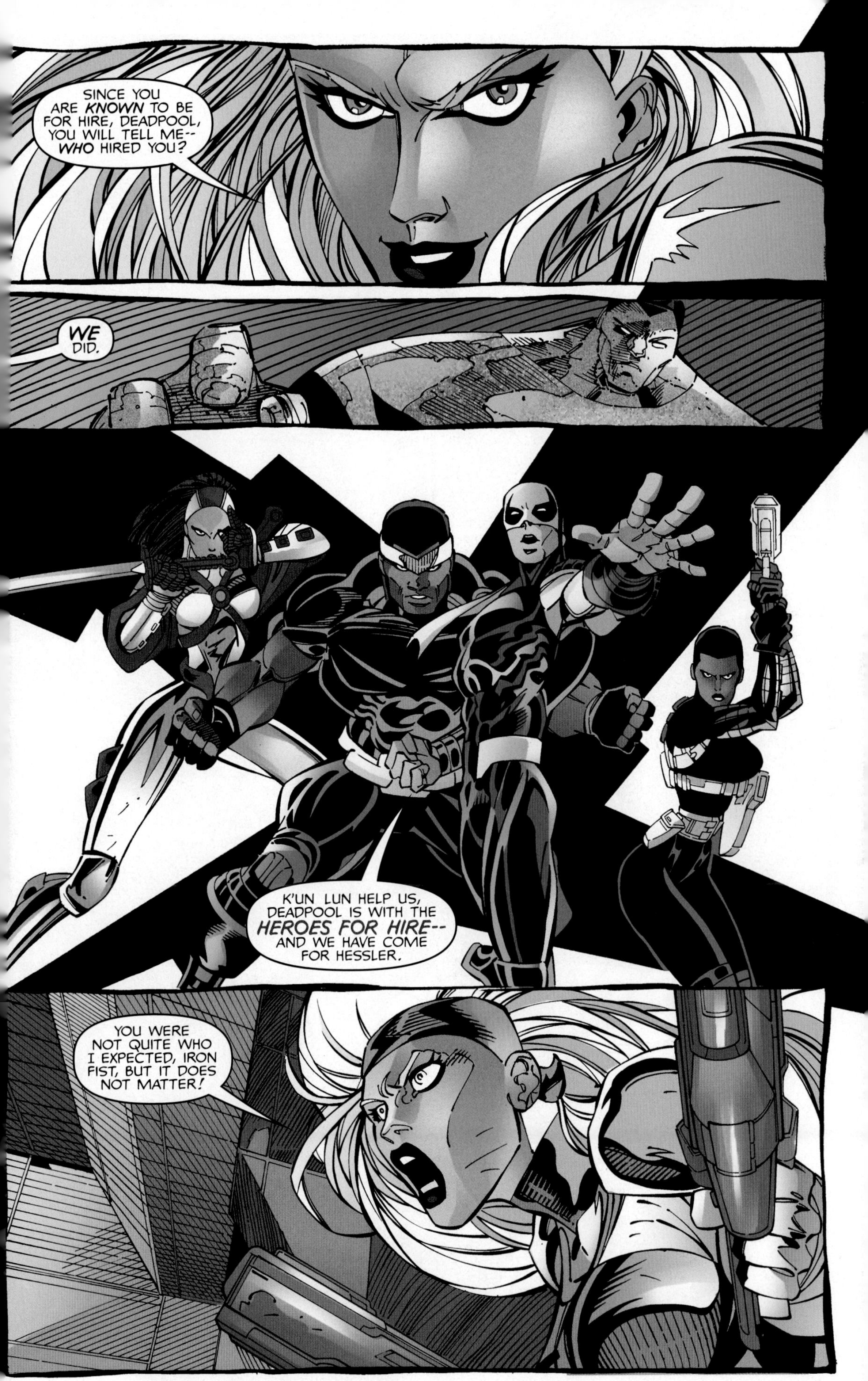
SINCE YOU ARE KNOWN TO BE FOR HIRE, DEADPOOL, YOU WILL TELL ME-- WHO HIRED YOU?
WE DID.
K'UN LUN HELP US, DEADPOOL IS WITH THE HEROES FOR HIRE-- AND WE HAVE COME FOR HESSLER.
YOU WERE NOT QUITE WHO I EXPECTED, IRON FIST, BUT IT DOES NOT MATTER!

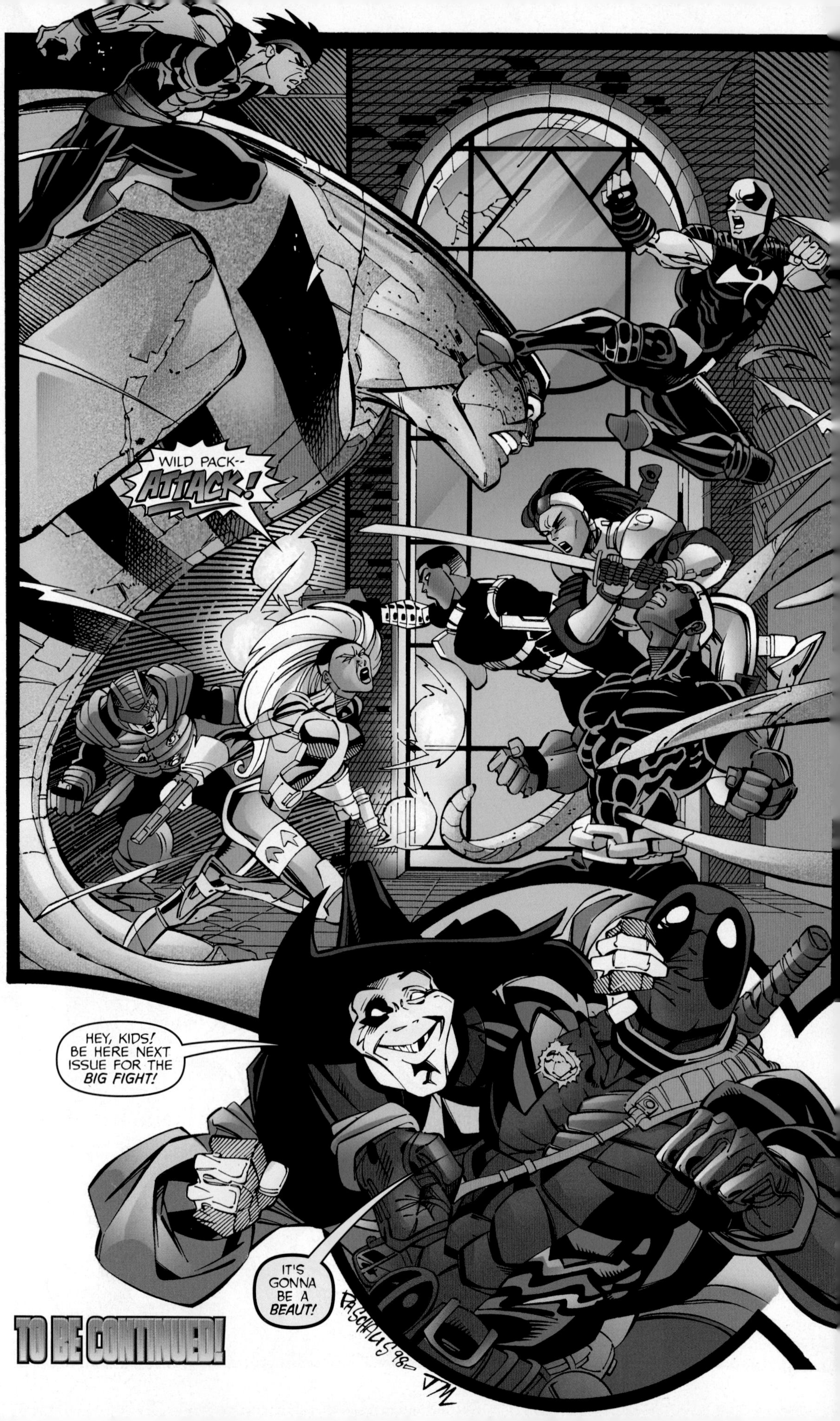
WILD PACK--
ATTACK!
HEY, KIDS! BE HERE NEXT ISSUE FOR THE *BIG FIGHT!*
IT'S GONNA BE A *BEAUT!*
PASCHALIS '98 - JM
TO BE CONTINUED!

DAILY BUGLE®

New York's Finest Daily Newspaper

February 10, 1998

Fifty Cents

Weather
This afternoon unseasonably warm,highs near 50. Tonight mostly cloudy, with a chance of rain, lows in the mid 30's.

IN THIS ISSUE
Excerpt from "Brightest Day, Darkest Hour," the new book by Shard, only in the Bugle.
Page B1

BIO-WEAPONS GO ON THE BLOCK

Jan Parsec -BUGLE

Heroes for Hire members, Powerman and Iron Fist, recently spotted with an unidentified individual

Fear and concern struck an emergency session of the United Nations Security Council yesterday upon receiving news that a stockpile of biological weapons will be auctioned to the highest bidder. "We're very concerned," said one U.N. official. "The threat of biological weapons has always been a great one. In the wrong hands—I just shudder to think what might happen."

Biological weapons returned to prominence in the headlines during the Gulf War when Iraq threatened to use such weaponry against the Allied forces. Biological weapons are considered one of the more heinous weapons of war. The effects of disease unleashed by a bio-bomb are widespread and painful, often affecting non-combatants.

While the various members of the U.N. have been debating a course of action, one super hero group appears to be taken a more offensive stance. Heroes for Hire, a team of super heroes with a shifting roster, recently appeared on the hero scene with a unique twist—you can actually pay them to work for you, for whatever services you require. Formed by the founders of the hired hero business, Iron First and Luke Cage, the team has of late taken on a variety of high-profile missions. While

the team's membership is considered unstable (thereby an appropriate team can be formed for a given assignment), various known members of the hero community including the Black Knight and Ant-Man have been a part of the team. Members such as these lend Heroes for Hire credibility and offset initial public concern that they might be hired by individuals or organizations with a malicious intent. This image was almost instantly confirmed by an unsubstantiated report that a new team member will be the fugitive mercenary, Deadpool, who is still wanted for questioning in connection with an explosion at a research base in the Arctic Circle.

Calls to the Heroes for Hire main office were not returned, so we could not get definite confirmation that the team is indeed headed to Symkaria, as has been rumored, or who has hired them for this mission.

In an alarming development, Silver Sable, who heads a Symkarian-based, world-renowned hired hero organization herself, issued a statement to the United Nations warning that any outside interference in what she termed "a Symkarian internal matter" would be met by "high-powered, highly-trained resistance."

—Continued in HEROES FOR HIRE #10

Staff Photo Chuck Giambalvo

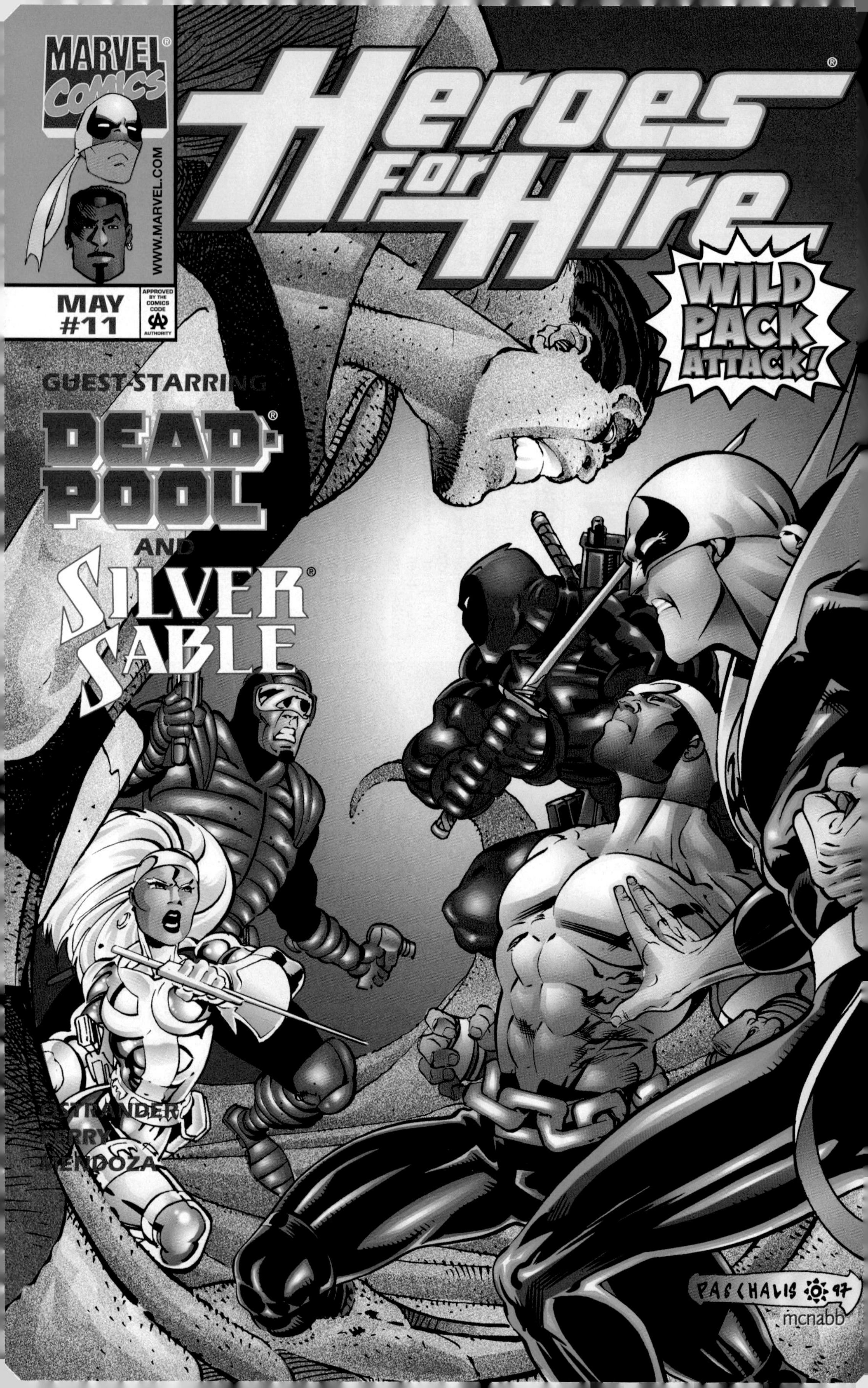
MARVEL COMICS
Heroes For Hire
WWW.MARVEL.COM
MAY #11
APPROVED BY THE COMICS CODE AUTHORITY
WILD PACK ATTACK!
GUEST-STARRING
DEADPOOL
AND
SILVER SABLE
PASCHALIS 97
mcnabb

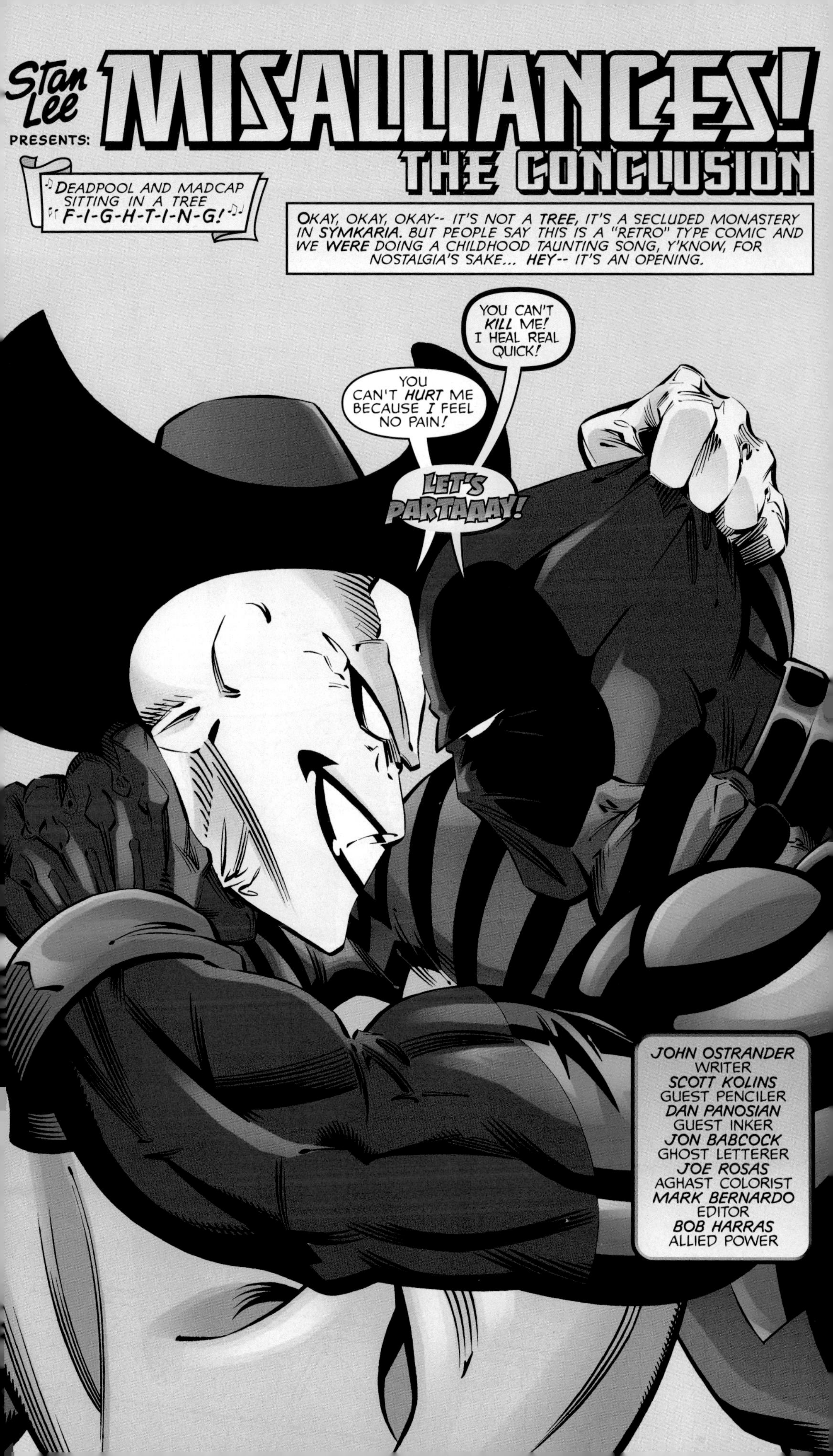
Stan Lee PRESENTS:
MISALLIANCES! THE CONCLUSION
DEADPOOL AND MADCAP SITTING IN A TREE F-I-G-H-T-I-N-G!
OKAY, OKAY, OKAY-- IT'S NOT A TREE, IT'S A SECLUDED MONASTERY IN SYMKARIA. BUT PEOPLE SAY THIS IS A "RETRO" TYPE COMIC AND WE WERE DOING A CHILDHOOD TAUNTING SONG, Y'KNOW, FOR NOSTALGIA'S SAKE... HEY-- IT'S AN OPENING.
YOU CAN'T KILL ME! I HEAL REAL QUICK!
YOU CAN'T HURT ME BECAUSE I FEEL NO PAIN!
LET'S PARTAAAY!
JOHN OSTRANDER WRITER
SCOTT KOLINS GUEST PENCILER
DAN PANOSIAN GUEST INKER
JON BABCOCK GHOST LETTERER
JOE ROSAS AGHAST COLORIST
MARK BERNARDO EDITOR
BOB HARRAS ALLIED POWER

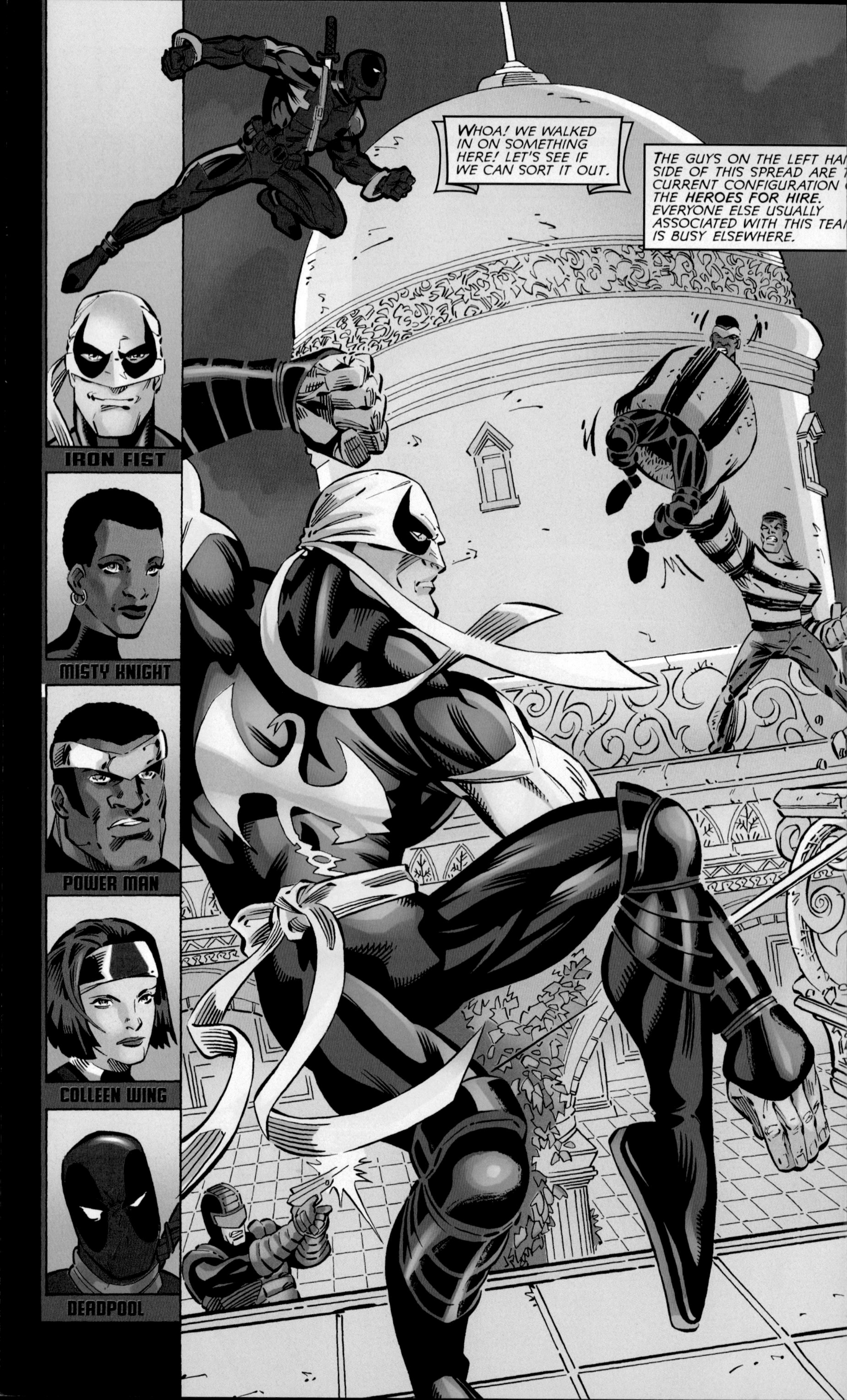
IRON FIST
MISTY KNIGHT
POWER MAN
COLLEEN WING
DEADPOOL
WHOA! WE WALKED IN ON SOMETHING HERE! LET'S SEE IF WE CAN SORT IT OUT.
THE GUYS ON THE LEFT HA SIDE OF THIS SPREAD ARE T CURRENT CONFIGURATION THE HEROES FOR HIRE. EVERYONE ELSE USUALLY ASSOCIATED WITH THIS TEA IS BUSY ELSEWHERE.

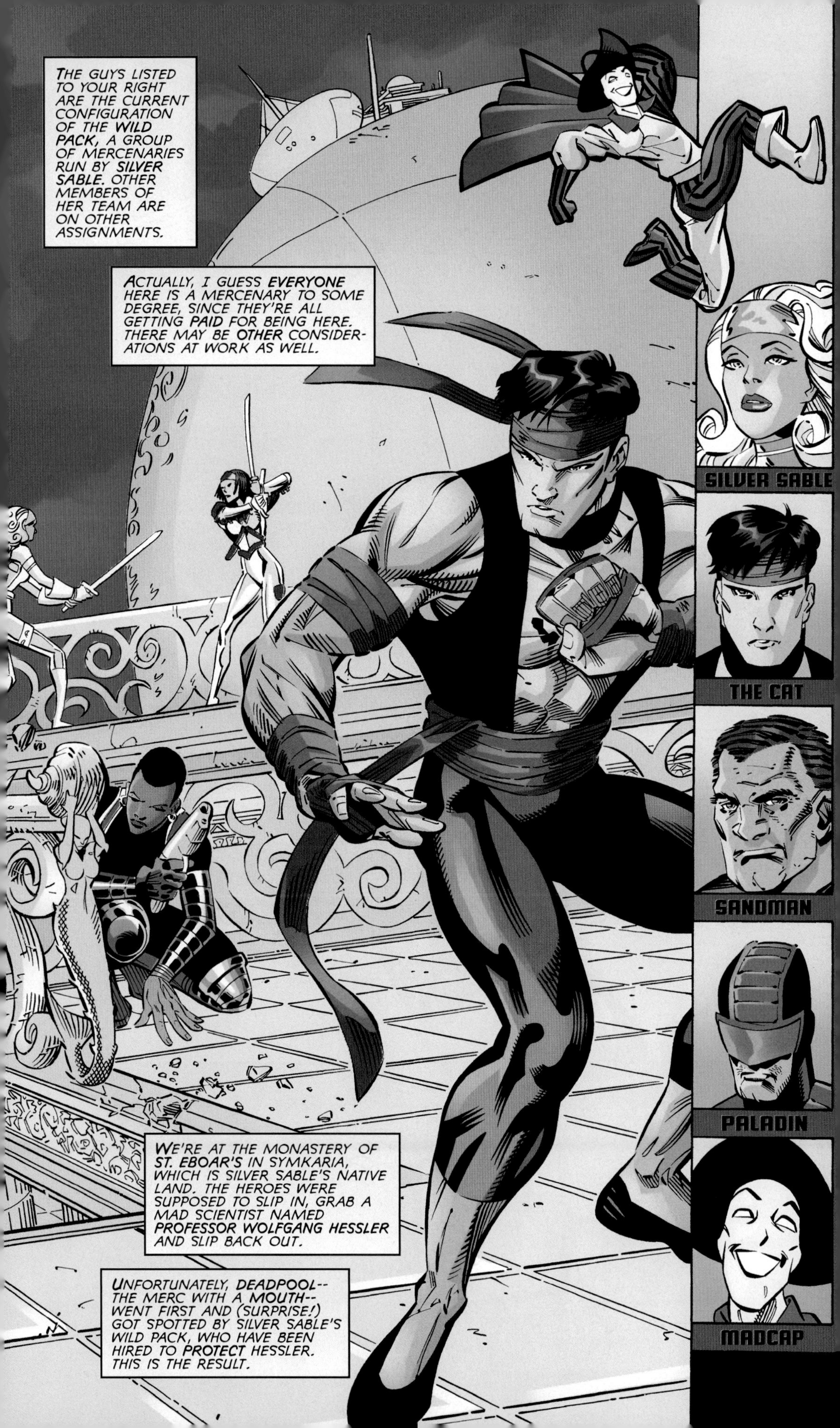
THE GUYS LISTED TO YOUR RIGHT ARE THE CURRENT CONFIGURATION OF THE WILD PACK, A GROUP OF MERCENARIES RUN BY SILVER SABLE. OTHER MEMBERS OF HER TEAM ARE ON OTHER ASSIGNMENTS.
ACTUALLY, I GUESS EVERYONE HERE IS A MERCENARY TO SOME DEGREE, SINCE THEY'RE ALL GETTING PAID FOR BEING HERE. THERE MAY BE OTHER CONSIDERATIONS AT WORK AS WELL.
SILVER SABLE
THE CAT
SANDMAN
PALADIN
MADCAP
WE'RE AT THE MONASTERY OF ST. EBOAR'S IN SYMKARIA, WHICH IS SILVER SABLE'S NATIVE LAND. THE HEROES WERE SUPPOSED TO SLIP IN, GRAB A MAD SCIENTIST NAMED PROFESSOR WOLFGANG HESSLER AND SLIP BACK OUT.
UNFORTUNATELY, DEADPOOL-- THE MERC WITH A MOUTH-- WENT FIRST AND (SURPRISE!) GOT SPOTTED BY SILVER SABLE'S WILD PACK, WHO HAVE BEEN HIRED TO PROTECT HESSLER. THIS IS THE RESULT.

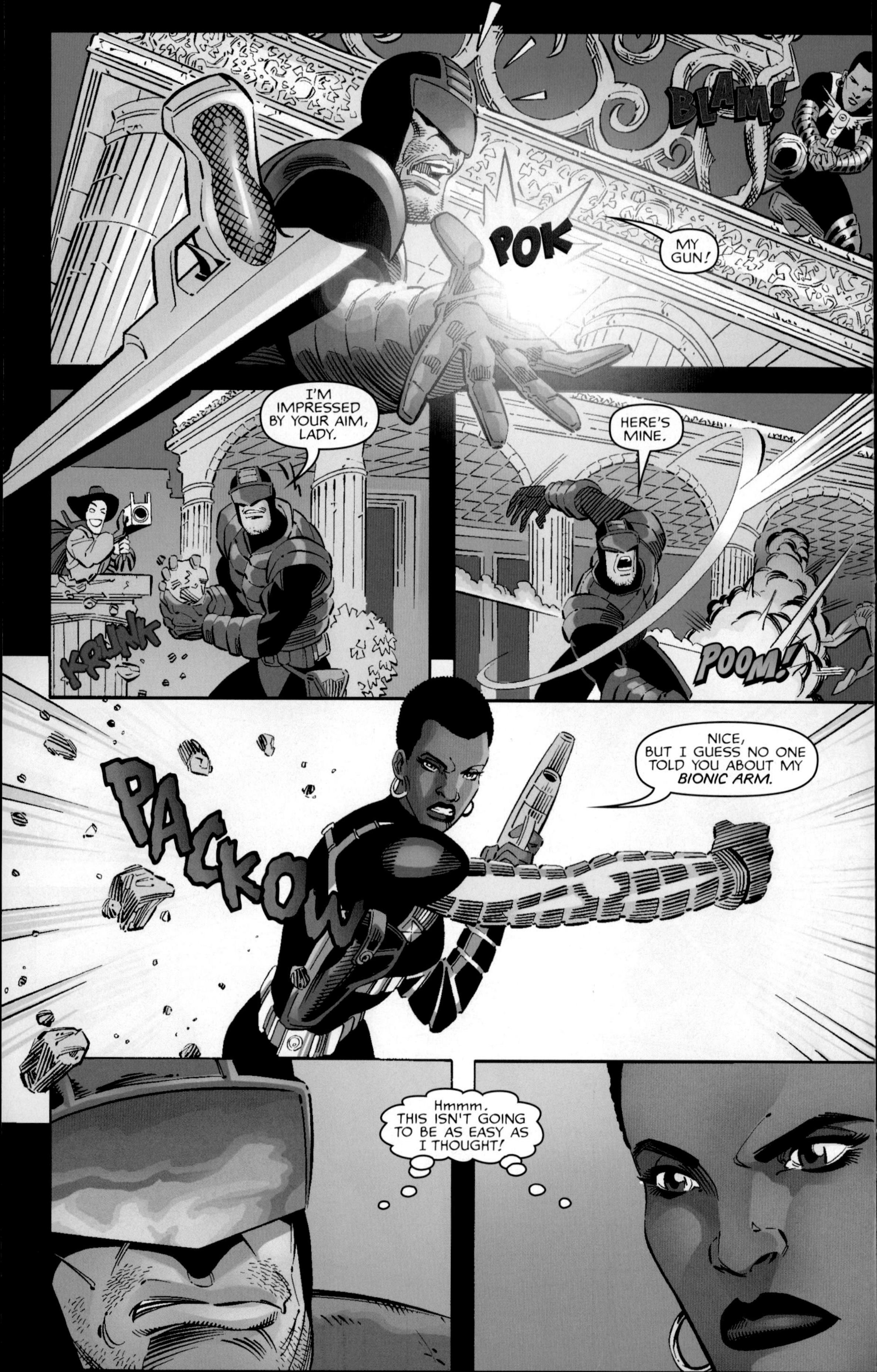
BLAM!
POK
MY GUN!
I'M IMPRESSED BY YOUR AIM, LADY.
KRUNK
HERE'S MINE.
POOM!
PACKOW
NICE, BUT I GUESS NO ONE TOLD YOU ABOUT MY BIONIC ARM.
Hmmm. THIS ISN'T GOING TO BE AS EASY AS I THOUGHT!

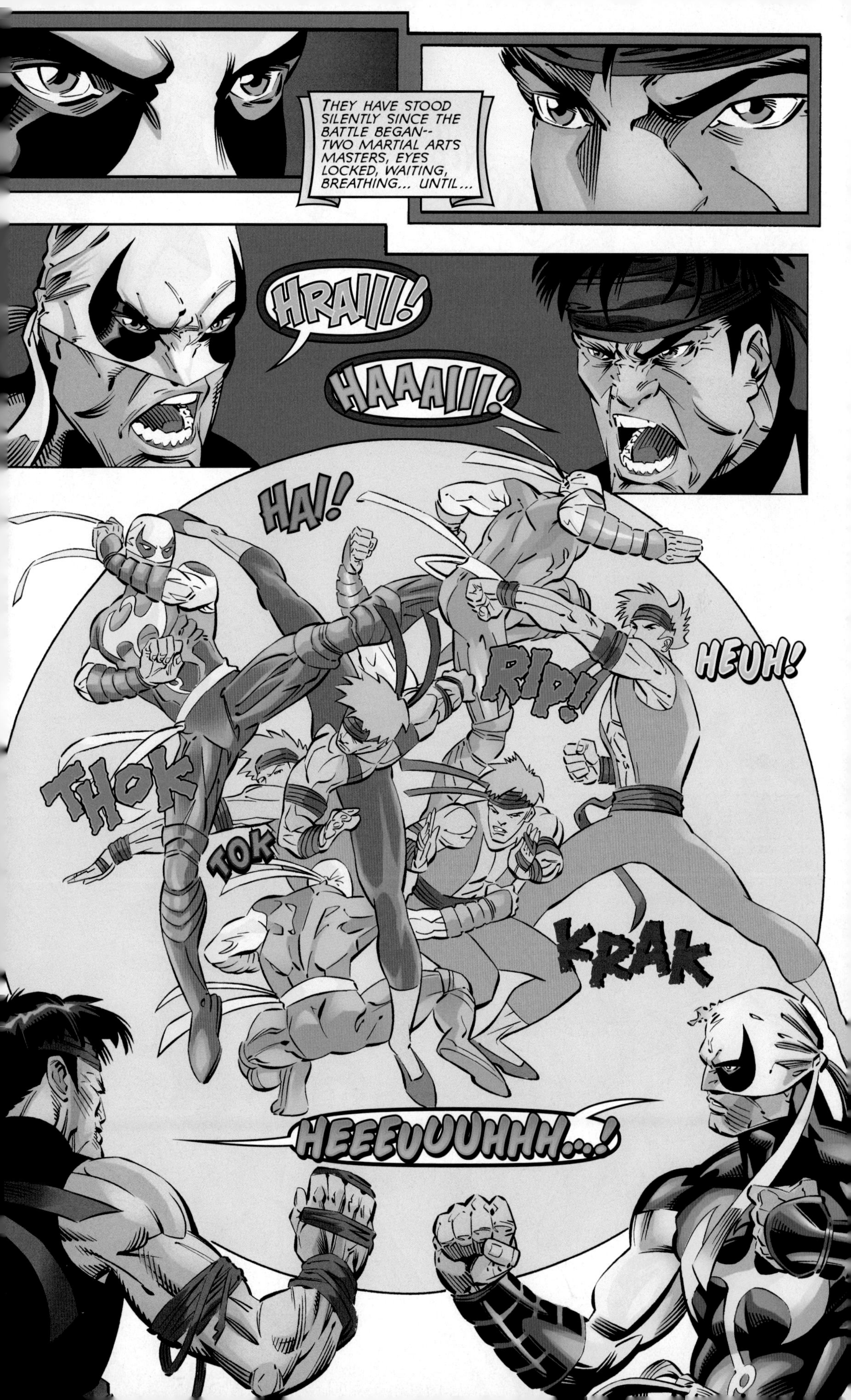
THEY HAVE STOOD SILENTLY SINCE THE BATTLE BEGAN-- TWO MARTIAL ARTS MASTERS, EYES LOCKED, WAITING, BREATHING... UNTIL...
HRAIIII!
HAAAIIII!
HA!
RIP!
HEUH!
THOK
TOK
KRAK
HEEEUUUHHH...!

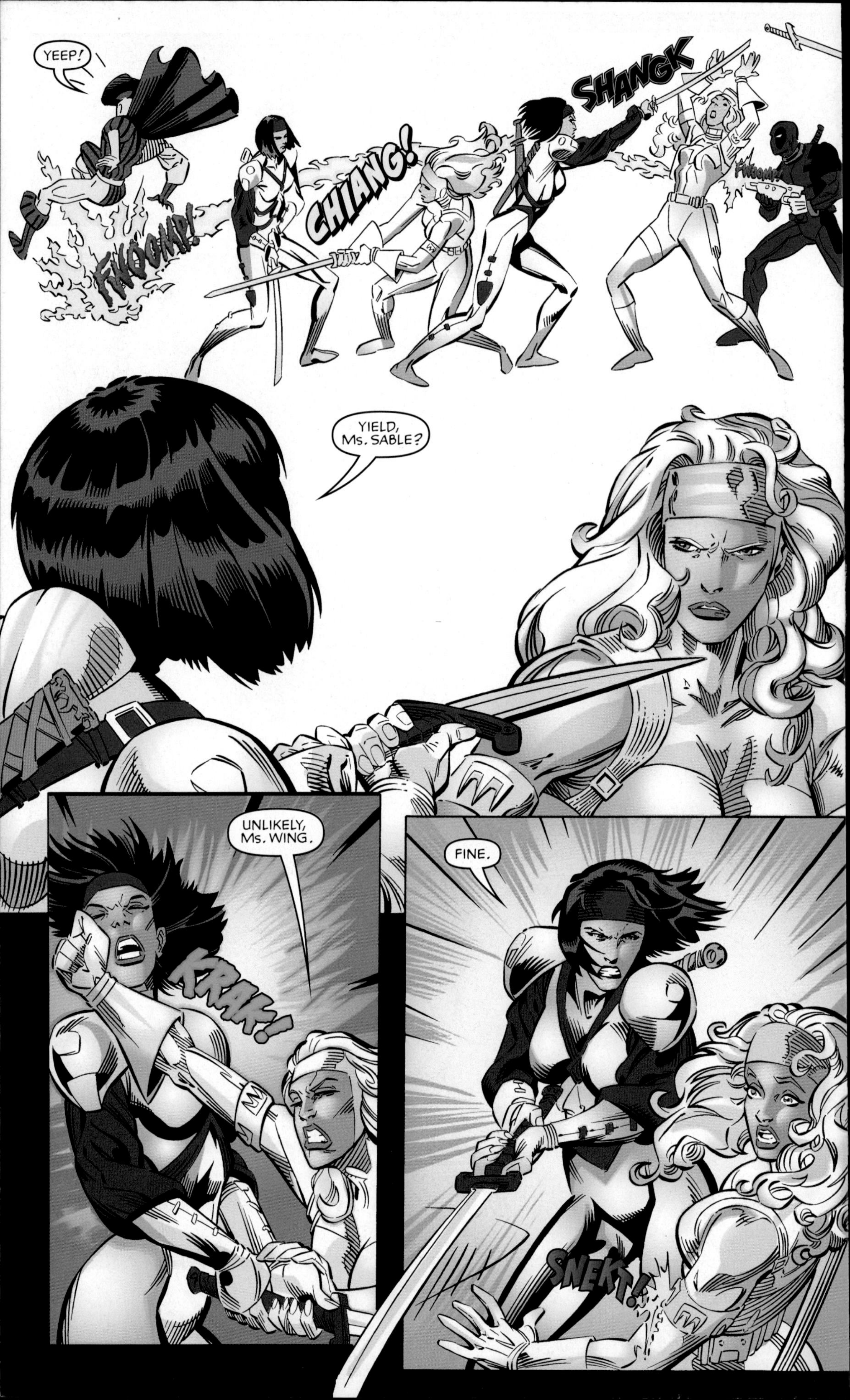
YEEP!
FWOOMP!
CHIANG!
SHANGK
FWOOMP
YIELD, Ms. SABLE?
UNLIKELY, Ms. WING.
KRAK!
FINE.
SNEKT!

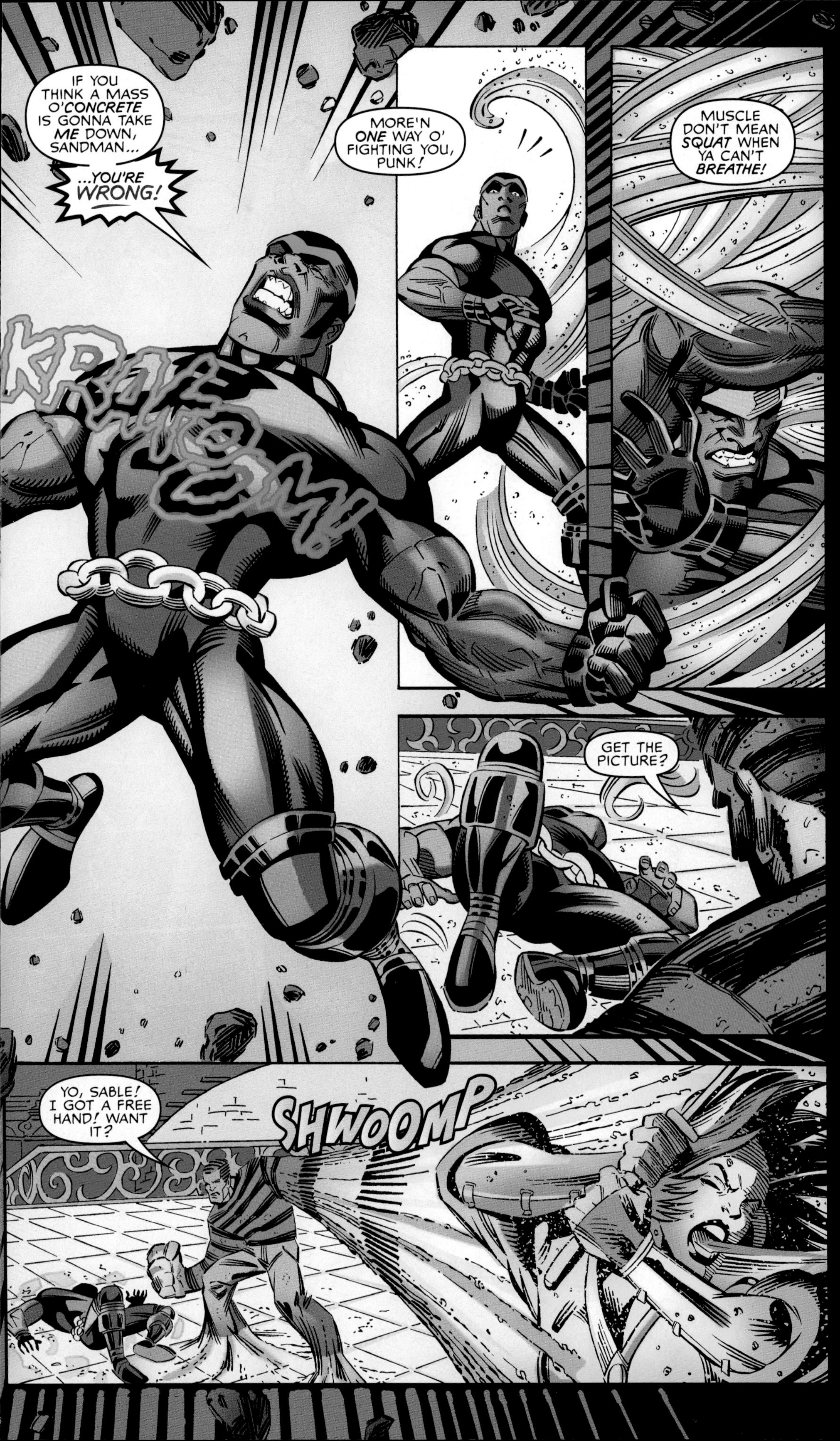

IF YOU THINK A MASS O'CONCRETE IS GONNA TAKE ME DOWN, SANDMAN...
...YOU'RE WRONG!
KRAKOOM!
MORE'N ONE WAY O' FIGHTING YOU, PUNK!
MUSCLE DON'T MEAN SQUAT WHEN YA CAN'T BREATHE!
GET THE PICTURE?
YO, SABLE! I GOT A FREE HAND! WANT IT?
SHWOOMP

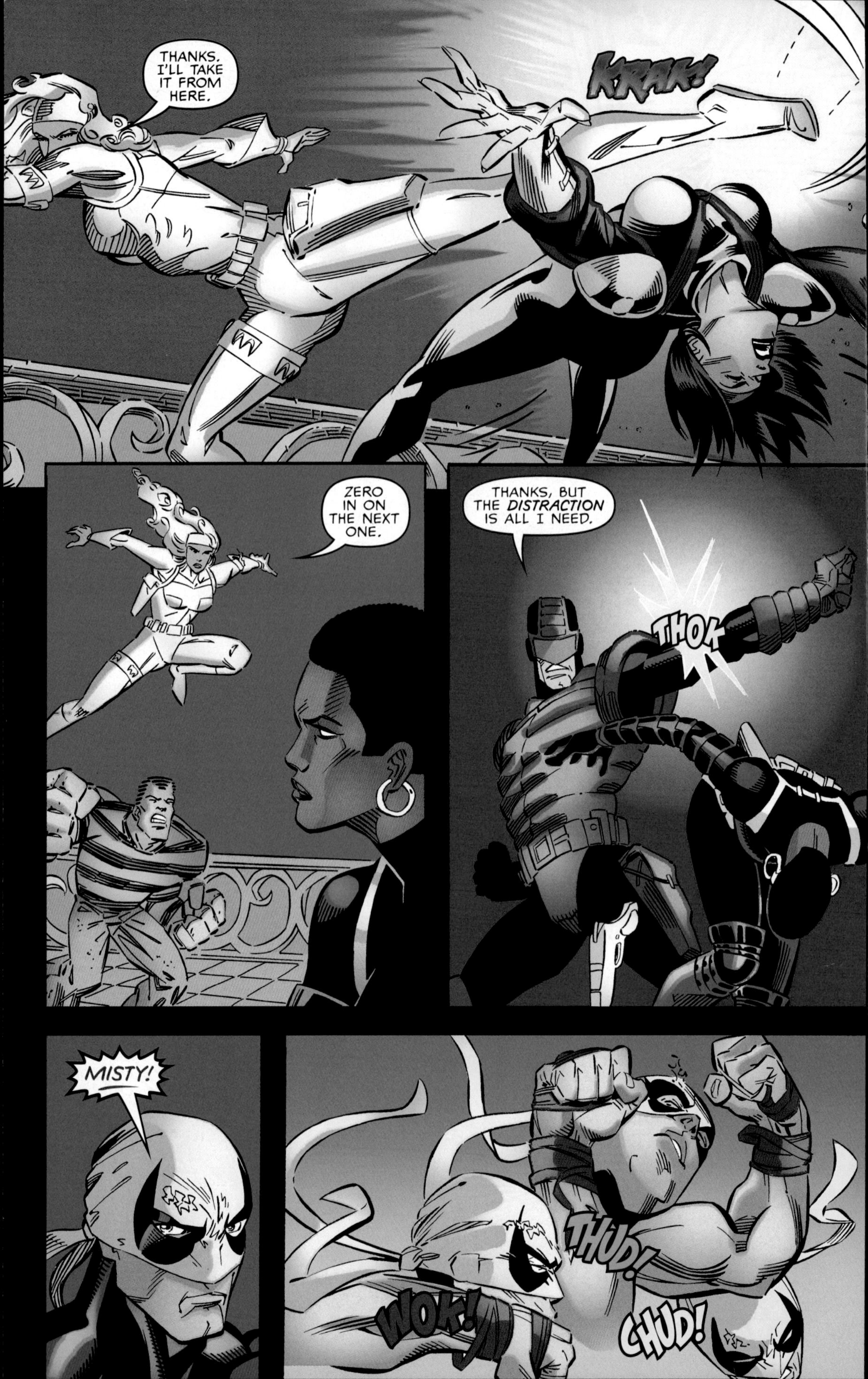
THANKS. I'LL TAKE IT FROM HERE.
KRAK!
ZERO IN ON THE NEXT ONE.
THANKS, BUT THE *DISTRACTION* IS ALL I NEED.
THOK
MISTY!
THUD!
WOK!
CHUD!

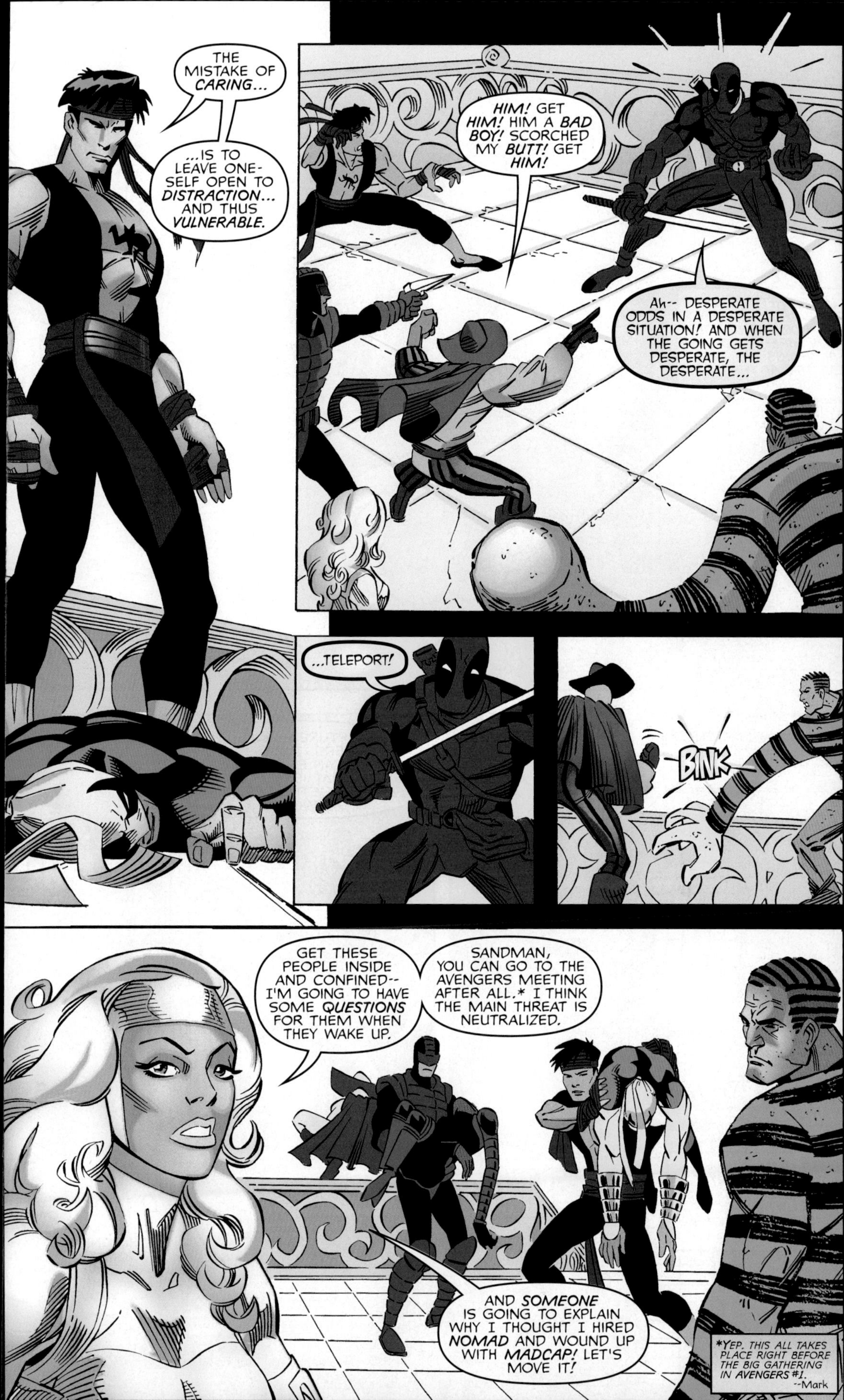
THE MISTAKE OF CARING...
...IS TO LEAVE ONE-SELF OPEN TO DISTRACTION... AND THUS VULNERABLE.
HIM! GET HIM! HIM A BAD BOY! SCORCHED MY BUTT! GET HIM!
Ah-- DESPERATE ODDS IN A DESPERATE SITUATION! AND WHEN THE GOING GETS DESPERATE, THE DESPERATE...
...TELEPORT!
BINK
GET THESE PEOPLE INSIDE AND CONFINED-- I'M GOING TO HAVE SOME QUESTIONS FOR THEM WHEN THEY WAKE UP.
SANDMAN, YOU CAN GO TO THE AVENGERS MEETING AFTER ALL.* I THINK THE MAIN THREAT IS NEUTRALIZED.
AND SOMEONE IS GOING TO EXPLAIN WHY I THOUGHT I HIRED NOMAD AND WOUND UP WITH MADCAP! LET'S MOVE IT!
*YEP. THIS ALL TAKES PLACE RIGHT BEFORE THE BIG GATHERING IN AVENGERS #1. --Mark

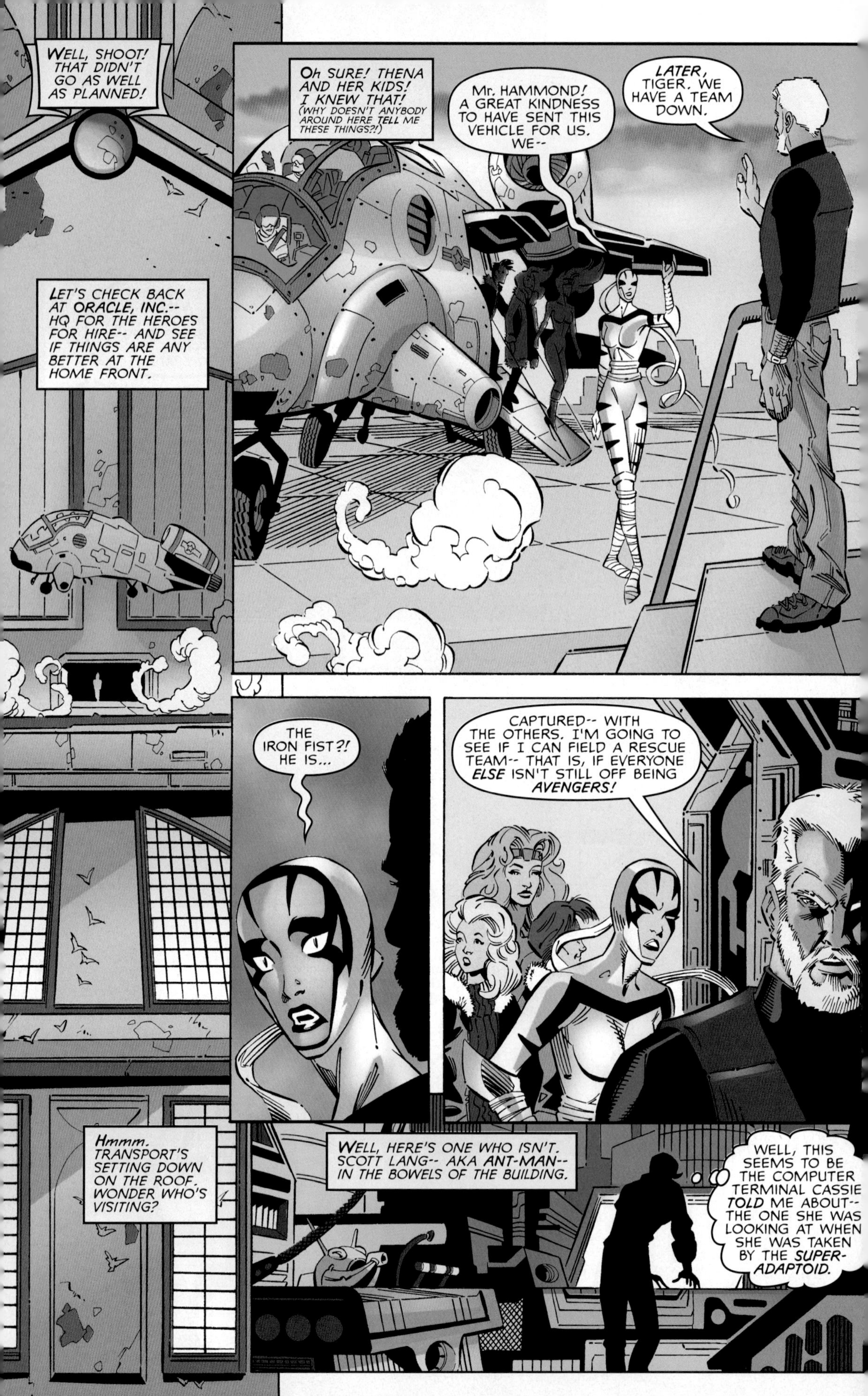
WELL, SHOOT! THAT DIDN'T GO AS WELL AS PLANNED!
LET'S CHECK BACK AT ORACLE, INC.-- HQ FOR THE HEROES FOR HIRE-- AND SEE IF THINGS ARE ANY BETTER AT THE HOME FRONT.
Hmmm. TRANSPORT'S SETTING DOWN ON THE ROOF. WONDER WHO'S VISITING?
Oh SURE! THENA AND HER KIDS! I KNEW THAT! (WHY DOESN'T ANYBODY AROUND HERE TELL ME THESE THINGS?!)
Mr. HAMMOND! A GREAT KINDNESS TO HAVE SENT THIS VEHICLE FOR US. WE--
LATER, TIGER. WE HAVE A TEAM DOWN.
THE IRON FIST?! HE IS...
CAPTURED-- WITH THE OTHERS. I'M GOING TO SEE IF I CAN FIELD A RESCUE TEAM-- THAT IS, IF EVERYONE ELSE ISN'T STILL OFF BEING AVENGERS!
WELL, HERE'S ONE WHO ISN'T. SCOTT LANG-- AKA ANT-MAN-- IN THE BOWELS OF THE BUILDING.
WELL, THIS SEEMS TO BE THE COMPUTER TERMINAL CASSIE TOLD ME ABOUT-- THE ONE SHE WAS LOOKING AT WHEN SHE WAS TAKEN BY THE SUPER-ADAPTOID.

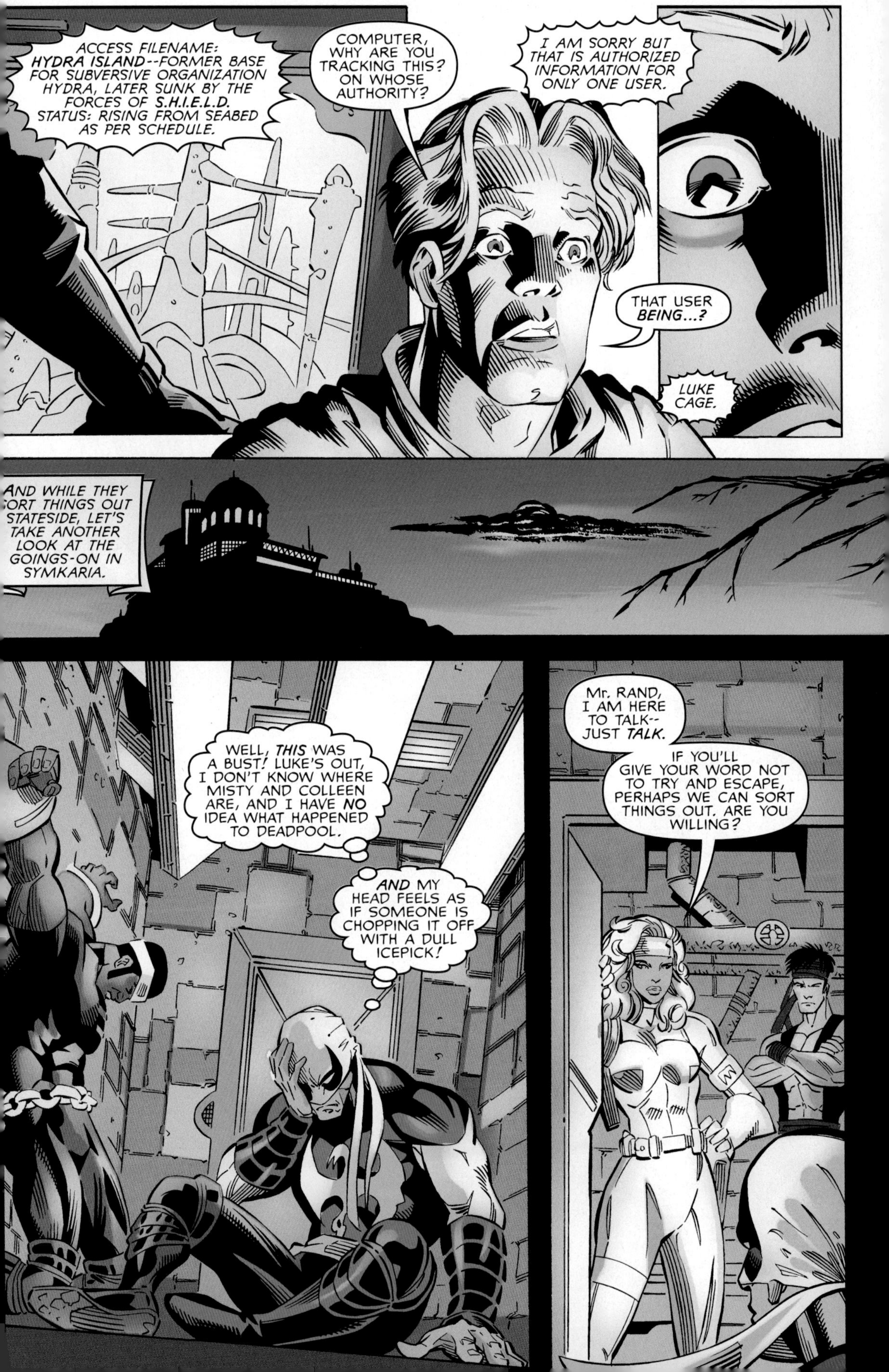
ACCESS FILENAME: HYDRA ISLAND--FORMER BASE FOR SUBVERSIVE ORGANIZATION HYDRA, LATER SUNK BY THE FORCES OF S.H.I.E.L.D. STATUS: RISING FROM SEABED AS PER SCHEDULE.
COMPUTER, WHY ARE YOU TRACKING THIS? ON WHOSE AUTHORITY?
I AM SORRY BUT THAT IS AUTHORIZED INFORMATION FOR ONLY ONE USER.
THAT USER BEING...?
LUKE CAGE.
AND WHILE THEY SORT THINGS OUT STATESIDE, LET'S TAKE ANOTHER LOOK AT THE GOINGS-ON IN SYMKARIA.
WELL, THIS WAS A BUST! LUKE'S OUT, I DON'T KNOW WHERE MISTY AND COLLEEN ARE, AND I HAVE NO IDEA WHAT HAPPENED TO DEADPOOL.
AND MY HEAD FEELS AS IF SOMEONE IS CHOPPING IT OFF WITH A DULL ICEPICK!
Mr. RAND, I AM HERE TO TALK-- JUST TALK.
IF YOU'LL GIVE YOUR WORD NOT TO TRY AND ESCAPE, PERHAPS WE CAN SORT THINGS OUT. ARE YOU WILLING?

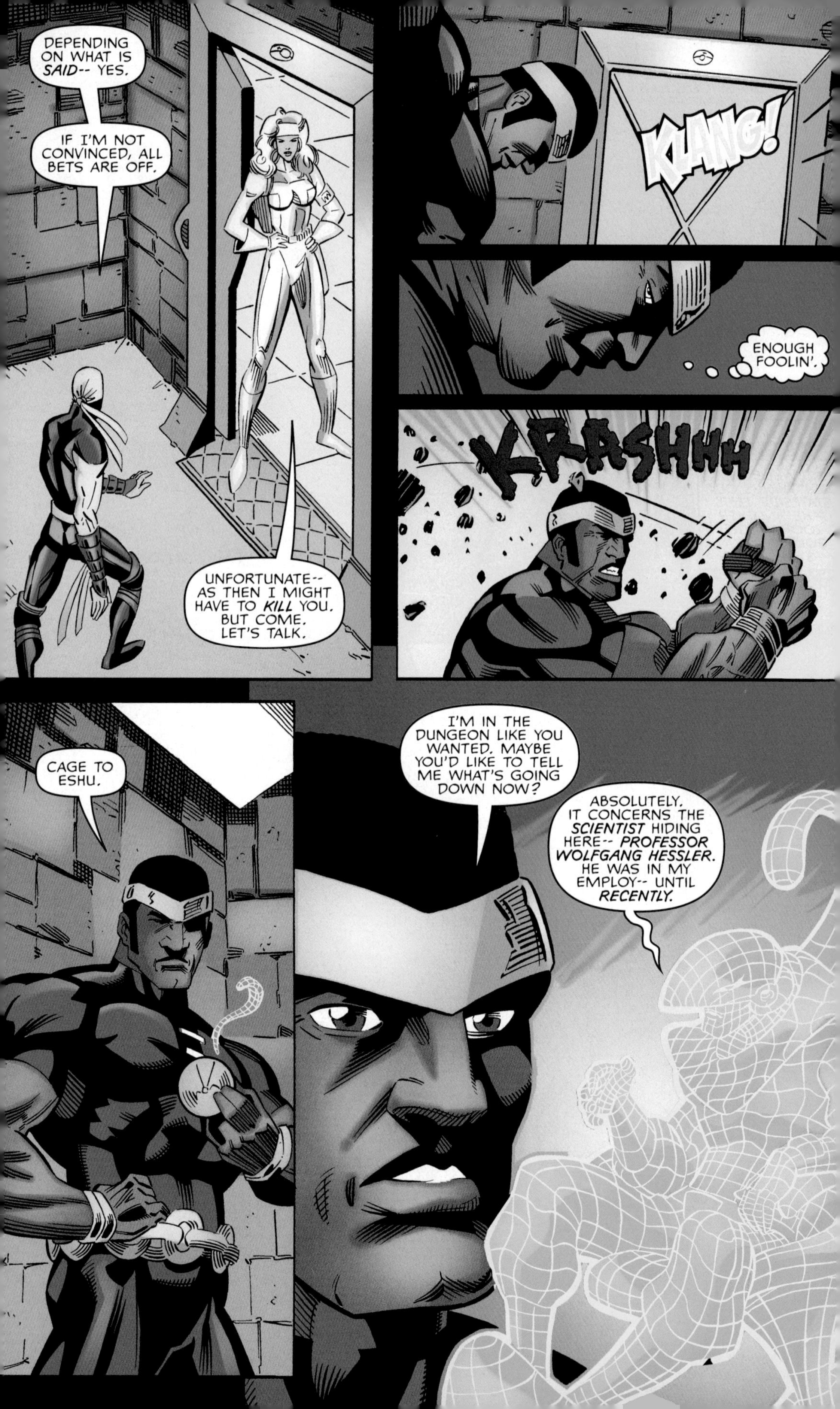
DEPENDING ON WHAT IS SAID-- YES.
IF I'M NOT CONVINCED, ALL BETS ARE OFF.
UNFORTUNATE-- AS THEN I MIGHT HAVE TO KILL YOU. BUT COME. LET'S TALK.
KLANG!
ENOUGH FOOLIN'.
KRASHHH
CAGE TO ESHU.
I'M IN THE DUNGEON LIKE YOU WANTED. MAYBE YOU'D LIKE TO TELL ME WHAT'S GOING DOWN NOW?
ABSOLUTELY. IT CONCERNS THE SCIENTIST HIDING HERE-- PROFESSOR WOLFGANG HESSLER. HE WAS IN MY EMPLOY-- UNTIL RECENTLY.

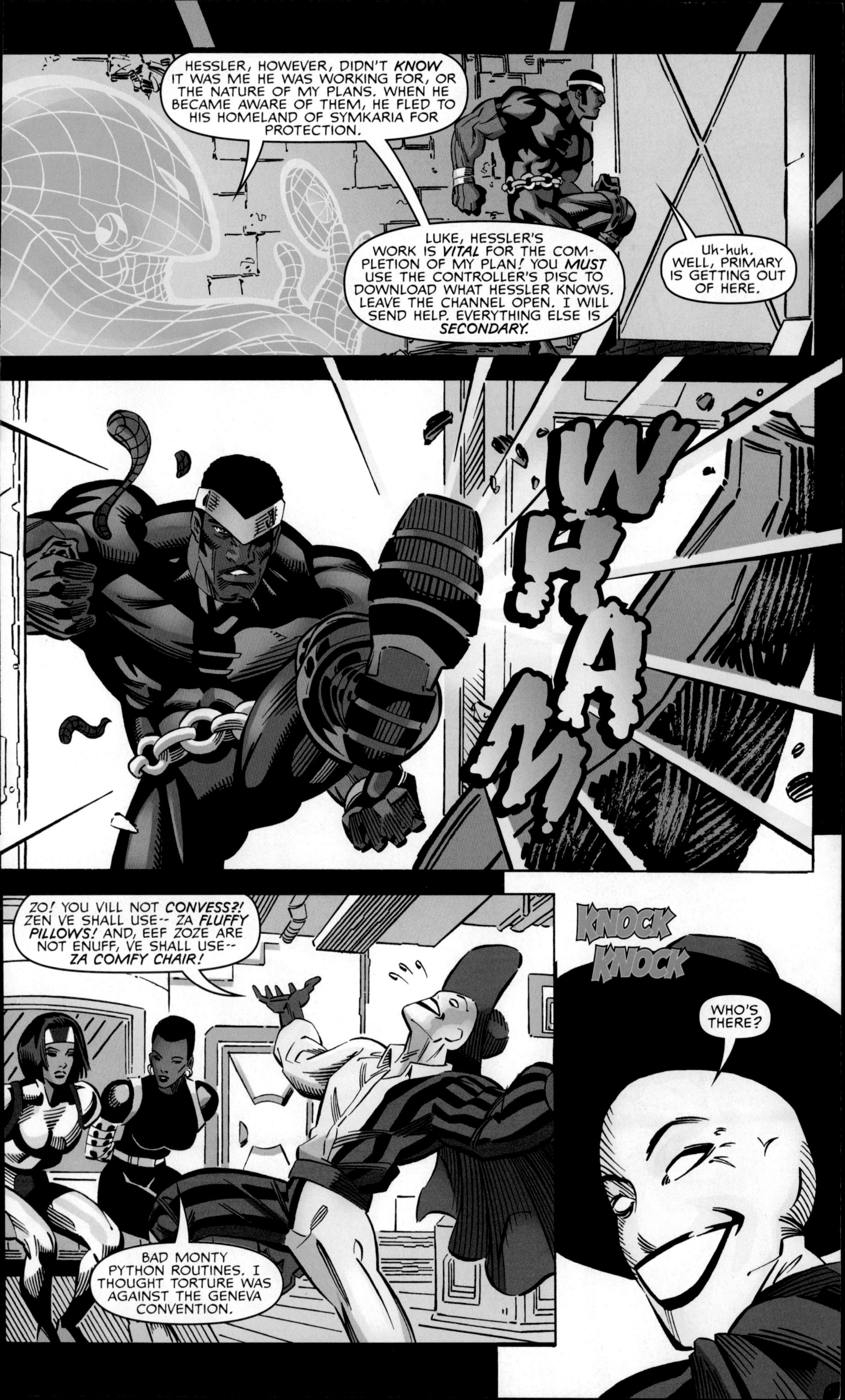
HESSLER, HOWEVER, DIDN'T KNOW IT WAS ME HE WAS WORKING FOR, OR THE NATURE OF MY PLANS. WHEN HE BECAME AWARE OF THEM, HE FLED TO HIS HOMELAND OF SYMKARIA FOR PROTECTION.
LUKE, HESSLER'S WORK IS VITAL FOR THE COMPLETION OF MY PLAN! YOU MUST USE THE CONTROLLER'S DISC TO DOWNLOAD WHAT HESSLER KNOWS. LEAVE THE CHANNEL OPEN. I WILL SEND HELP. EVERYTHING ELSE IS SECONDARY.
Uh-huh. WELL, PRIMARY IS GETTING OUT OF HERE.
WHAM!
ZO! YOU VILL NOT CONVESS?! ZEN VE SHALL USE-- ZA FLUFFY PILLOWS! AND, EEF ZOZE ARE NOT ENUFF, VE SHALL USE-- ZA COMFY CHAIR!
BAD MONTY PYTHON ROUTINES. I THOUGHT TORTURE WAS AGAINST THE GENEVA CONVENTION.
KNOCK KNOCK
WHO'S THERE?

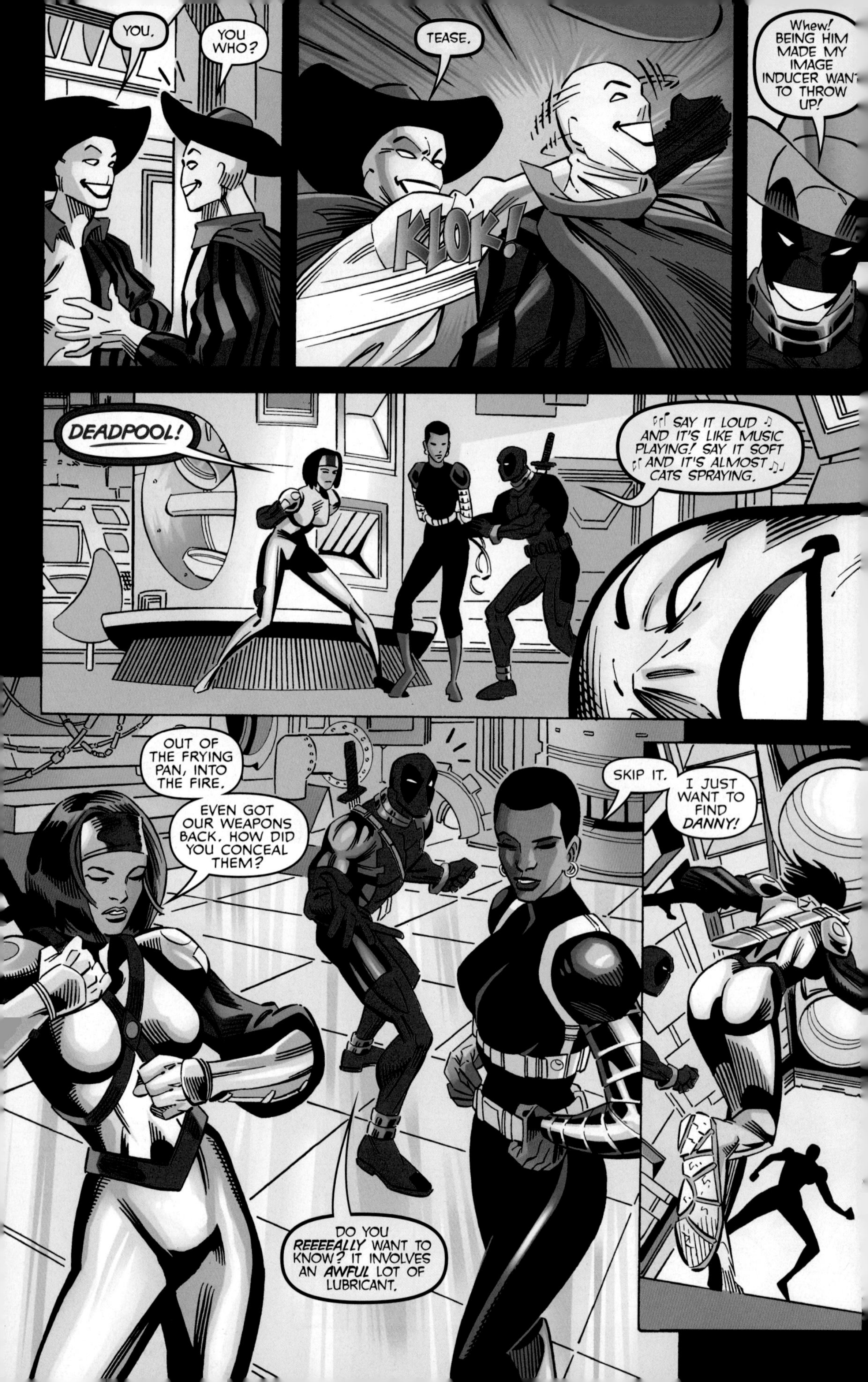
YOU.
YOU WHO?
TEASE.
KLOK!
Whew! BEING HIM MADE MY IMAGE INDUCER WANT TO THROW UP!
DEADPOOL!
SAY IT LOUD AND IT'S LIKE MUSIC PLAYING! SAY IT SOFT AND IT'S ALMOST CATS SPRAYING.
OUT OF THE FRYING PAN, INTO THE FIRE.
EVEN GOT OUR WEAPONS BACK. HOW DID YOU CONCEAL THEM?
DO YOU REEEEALLY WANT TO KNOW? IT INVOLVES AN AWFUL LOT OF LUBRICANT.
SKIP IT.
I JUST WANT TO FIND DANNY!

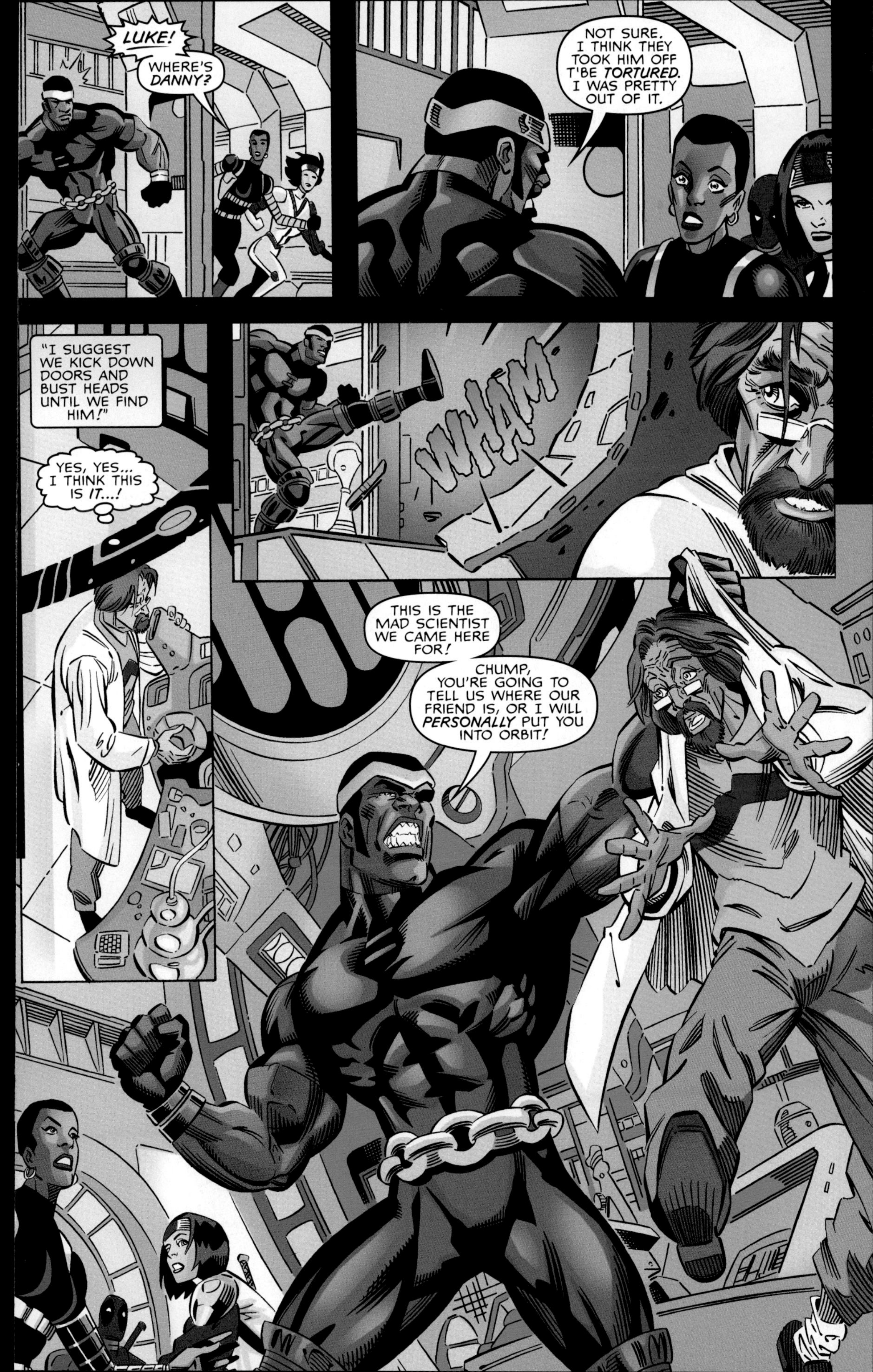
LUKE!
WHERE'S DANNY?
NOT SURE. I THINK THEY TOOK HIM OFF T'BE TORTURED. I WAS PRETTY OUT OF IT.
"I SUGGEST WE KICK DOWN DOORS AND BUST HEADS UNTIL WE FIND HIM!"
YES, YES... I THINK THIS IS IT...!
WHAM
THIS IS THE MAD SCIENTIST WE CAME HERE FOR!
CHUMP, YOU'RE GOING TO TELL US WHERE OUR FRIEND IS, OR I WILL PERSONALLY PUT YOU INTO ORBIT!

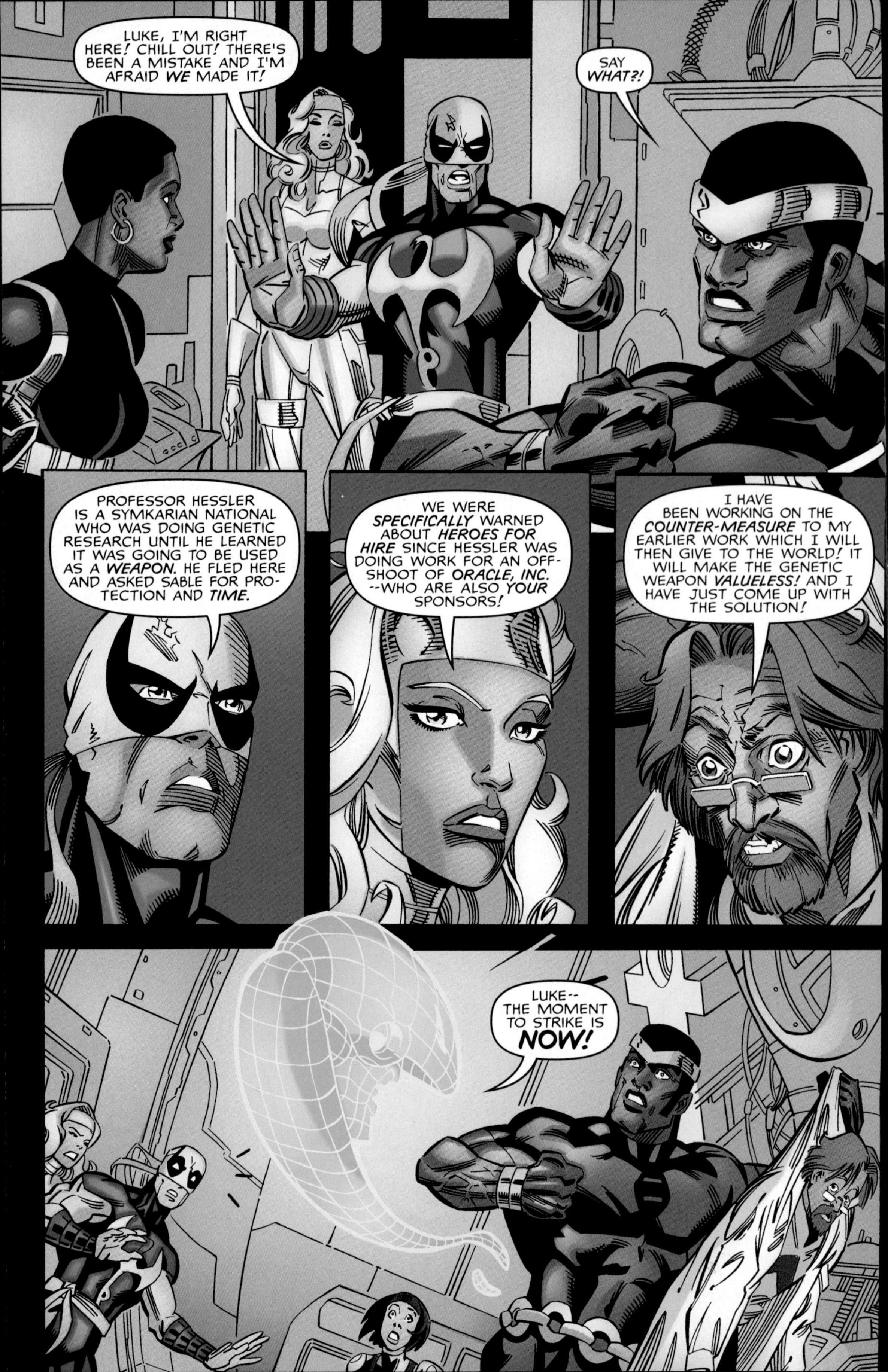
LUKE, I'M RIGHT HERE! CHILL OUT! THERE'S BEEN A MISTAKE AND I'M AFRAID WE MADE IT!
SAY WHAT?!
PROFESSOR HESSLER IS A SYMKARIAN NATIONAL WHO WAS DOING GENETIC RESEARCH UNTIL HE LEARNED IT WAS GOING TO BE USED AS A WEAPON. HE FLED HERE AND ASKED SABLE FOR PROTECTION AND TIME.
WE WERE SPECIFICALLY WARNED ABOUT HEROES FOR HIRE SINCE HESSLER WAS DOING WORK FOR AN OFF-SHOOT OF ORACLE, INC. --WHO ARE ALSO YOUR SPONSORS!
I HAVE BEEN WORKING ON THE COUNTER-MEASURE TO MY EARLIER WORK WHICH I WILL THEN GIVE TO THE WORLD! IT WILL MAKE THE GENETIC WEAPON VALUELESS! AND I HAVE JUST COME UP WITH THE SOLUTION!
LUKE-- THE MOMENT TO STRIKE IS NOW!

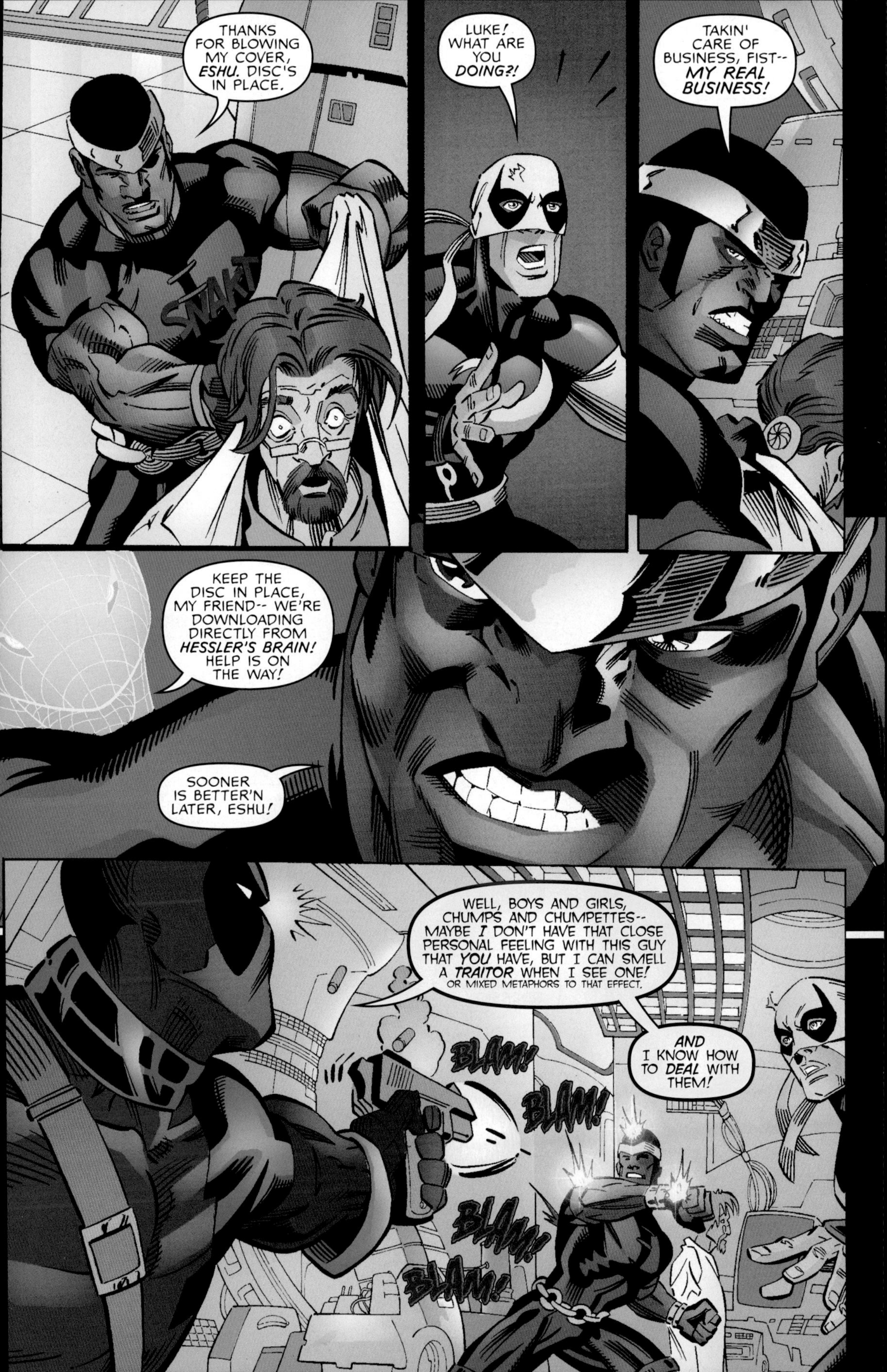
THANKS FOR BLOWING MY COVER, ESHU. DISC'S IN PLACE.
SNAKT
LUKE! WHAT ARE YOU DOING?!
TAKIN' CARE OF BUSINESS, FIST-- MY REAL BUSINESS!
KEEP THE DISC IN PLACE, MY FRIEND-- WE'RE DOWNLOADING DIRECTLY FROM HESSLER'S BRAIN! HELP IS ON THE WAY!
SOONER IS BETTER'N LATER, ESHU!
WELL, BOYS AND GIRLS, CHUMPS AND CHUMPETTES-- MAYBE I DON'T HAVE THAT CLOSE PERSONAL FEELING WITH THIS GUY THAT YOU HAVE, BUT I CAN SMELL A TRAITOR WHEN I SEE ONE! OR MIXED METAPHORS TO THAT EFFECT.
AND I KNOW HOW TO DEAL WITH THEM!
BLAM!
BLAM!
BLAM!
BLAM!

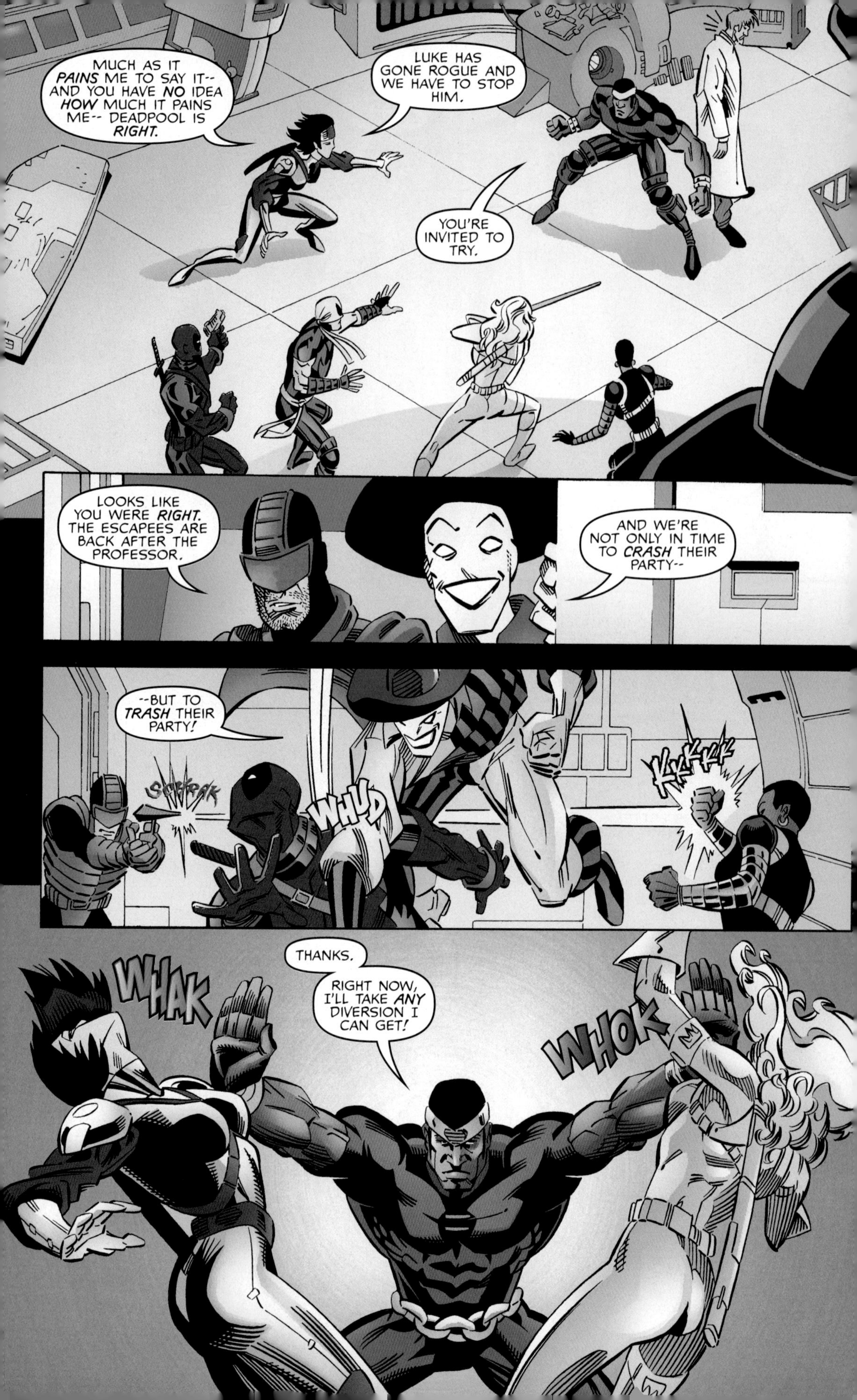
MUCH AS IT *PAINS* ME TO SAY IT-- AND YOU HAVE **NO** IDEA ***HOW*** MUCH IT PAINS ME-- DEADPOOL IS ***RIGHT.***
LUKE HAS GONE ROGUE AND WE HAVE TO STOP HIM.
YOU'RE INVITED TO TRY.
LOOKS LIKE YOU WERE *RIGHT.* THE ESCAPEES ARE BACK AFTER THE PROFESSOR.
AND WE'RE NOT ONLY IN TIME TO *CRASH* THEIR PARTY--
--BUT TO *TRASH* THEIR PARTY!
SCHRAK
WHUD
THANKS.
RIGHT NOW, I'LL TAKE *ANY* DIVERSION I CAN GET!
WHAK
WHOK

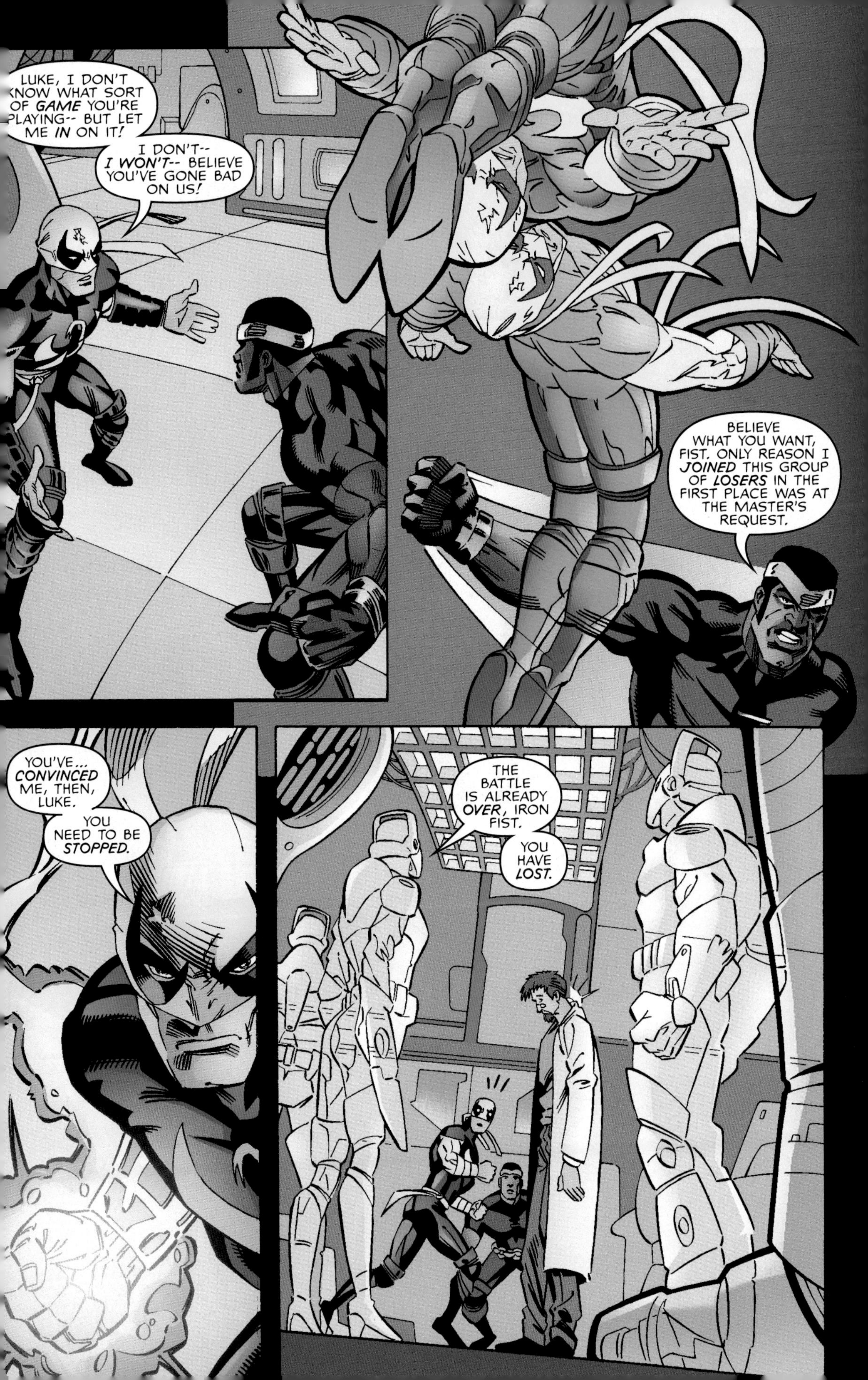
LUKE, I DON'T KNOW WHAT SORT OF GAME YOU'RE PLAYING-- BUT LET ME IN ON IT!
I DON'T-- I WON'T-- BELIEVE YOU'VE GONE BAD ON US!
BELIEVE WHAT YOU WANT, FIST. ONLY REASON I JOINED THIS GROUP OF LOSERS IN THE FIRST PLACE WAS AT THE MASTER'S REQUEST.
YOU'VE... CONVINCED ME, THEN, LUKE.
YOU NEED TO BE STOPPED.
THE BATTLE IS ALREADY OVER, IRON FIST.
YOU HAVE LOST.

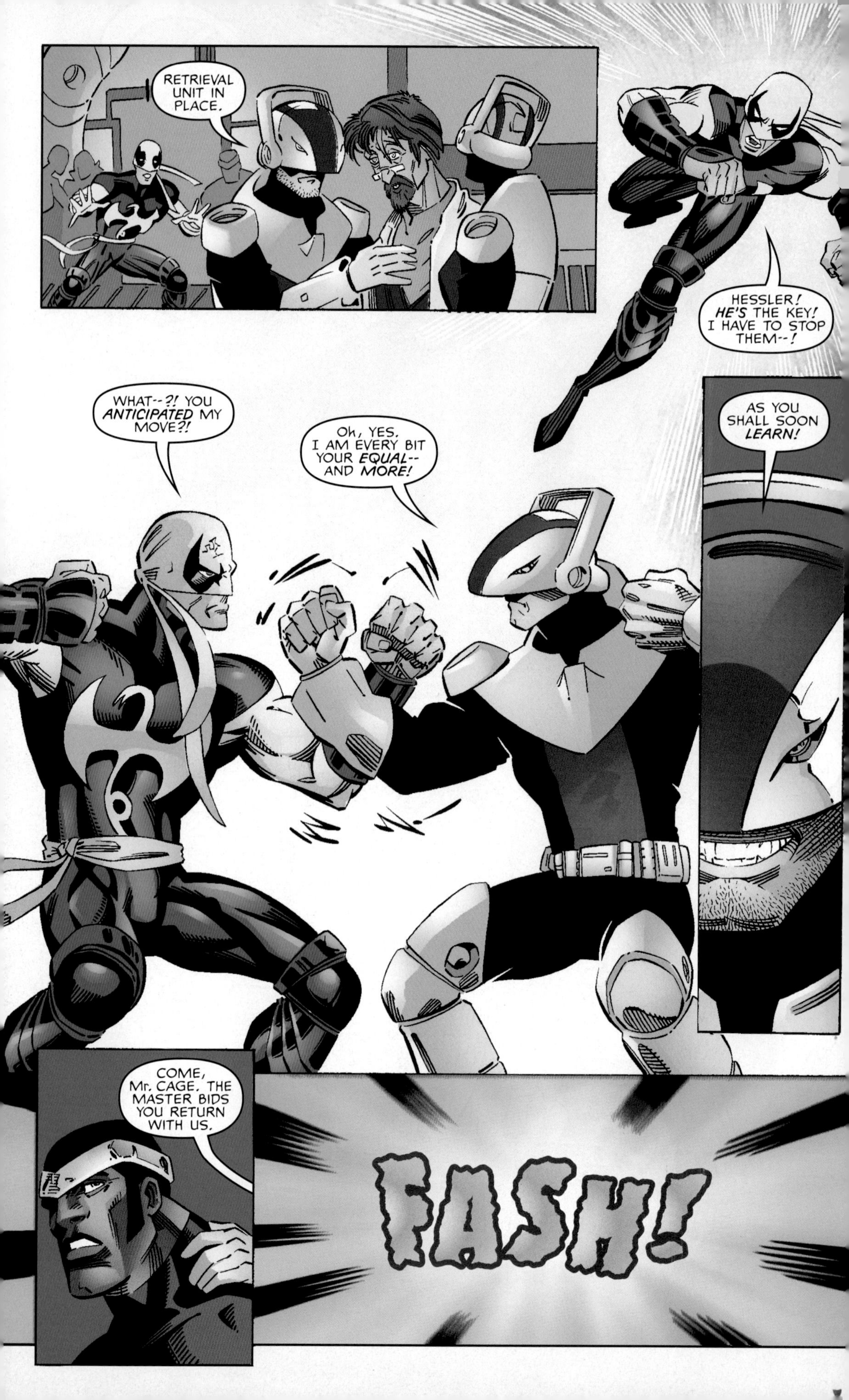
RETRIEVAL UNIT IN PLACE.
HESSLER! HE'S THE KEY! I HAVE TO STOP THEM--!
WHAT--?! YOU ANTICIPATED MY MOVE?!
Oh, YES. I AM EVERY BIT YOUR EQUAL-- AND MORE!
AS YOU SHALL SOON LEARN!
COME, Mr. CAGE. THE MASTER BIDS YOU RETURN WITH US.
FASH!

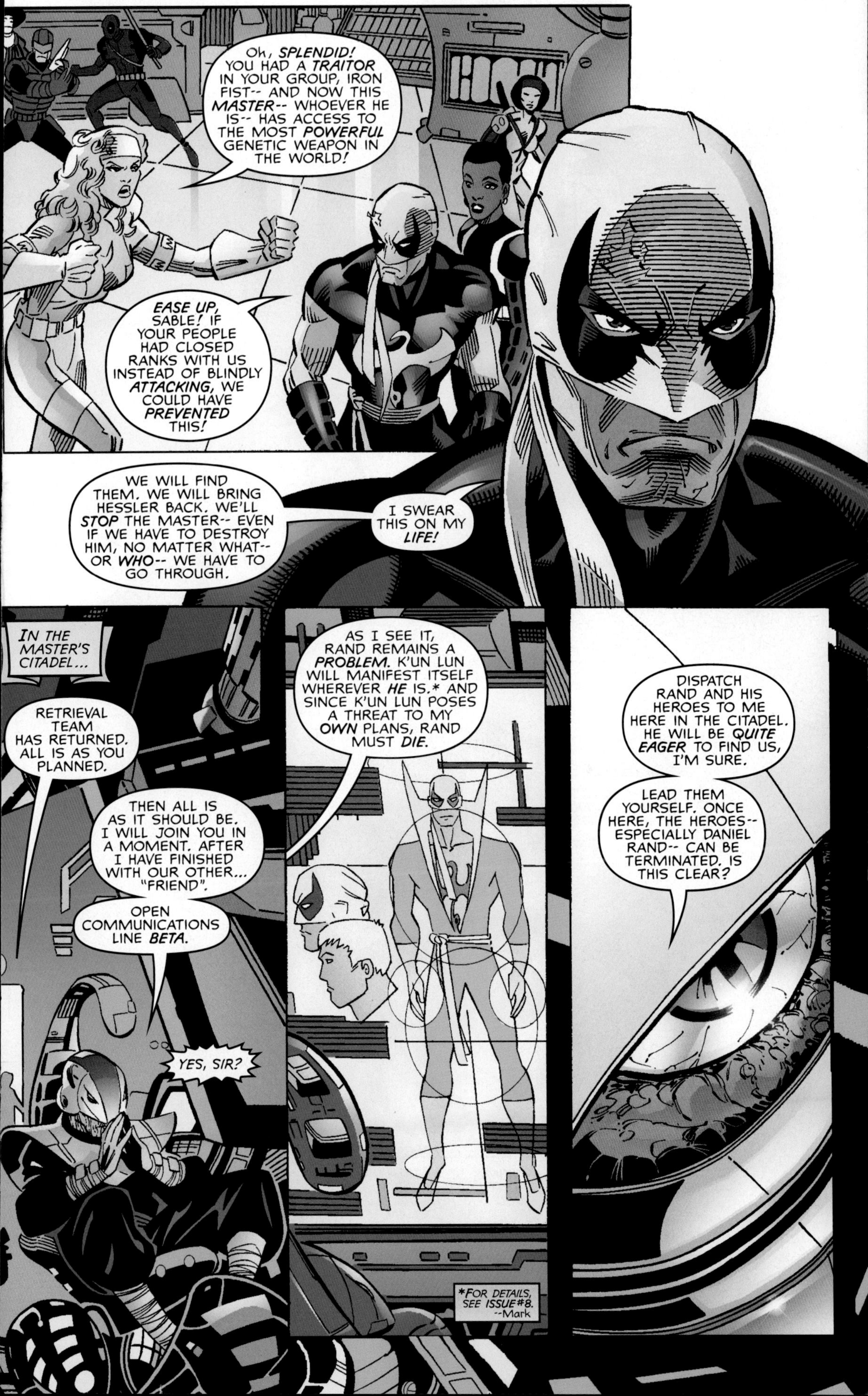
Oh, SPLENDID! YOU HAD A TRAITOR IN YOUR GROUP, IRON FIST-- AND NOW THIS MASTER-- WHOEVER HE IS-- HAS ACCESS TO THE MOST POWERFUL GENETIC WEAPON IN THE WORLD!
EASE UP, SABLE! IF YOUR PEOPLE HAD CLOSED RANKS WITH US INSTEAD OF BLINDLY ATTACKING, WE COULD HAVE PREVENTED THIS!
WE WILL FIND THEM. WE WILL BRING HESSLER BACK. WE'LL STOP THE MASTER-- EVEN IF WE HAVE TO DESTROY HIM, NO MATTER WHAT-- OR WHO-- WE HAVE TO GO THROUGH.
I SWEAR THIS ON MY LIFE!
IN THE MASTER'S CITADEL...
RETRIEVAL TEAM HAS RETURNED. ALL IS AS YOU PLANNED.
THEN ALL IS AS IT SHOULD BE. I WILL JOIN YOU IN A MOMENT. AFTER I HAVE FINISHED WITH OUR OTHER... "FRIEND".
OPEN COMMUNICATIONS LINE BETA.
YES, SIR?
AS I SEE IT, RAND REMAINS A PROBLEM. K'UN LUN WILL MANIFEST ITSELF WHEREVER HE IS.* AND SINCE K'UN LUN POSES A THREAT TO MY OWN PLANS, RAND MUST DIE.
*FOR DETAILS, SEE ISSUE #8. --Mark
DISPATCH RAND AND HIS HEROES TO ME HERE IN THE CITADEL. HE WILL BE QUITE EAGER TO FIND US, I'M SURE.
LEAD THEM YOURSELF. ONCE HERE, THE HEROES-- ESPECIALLY DANIEL RAND-- CAN BE TERMINATED. IS THIS CLEAR?

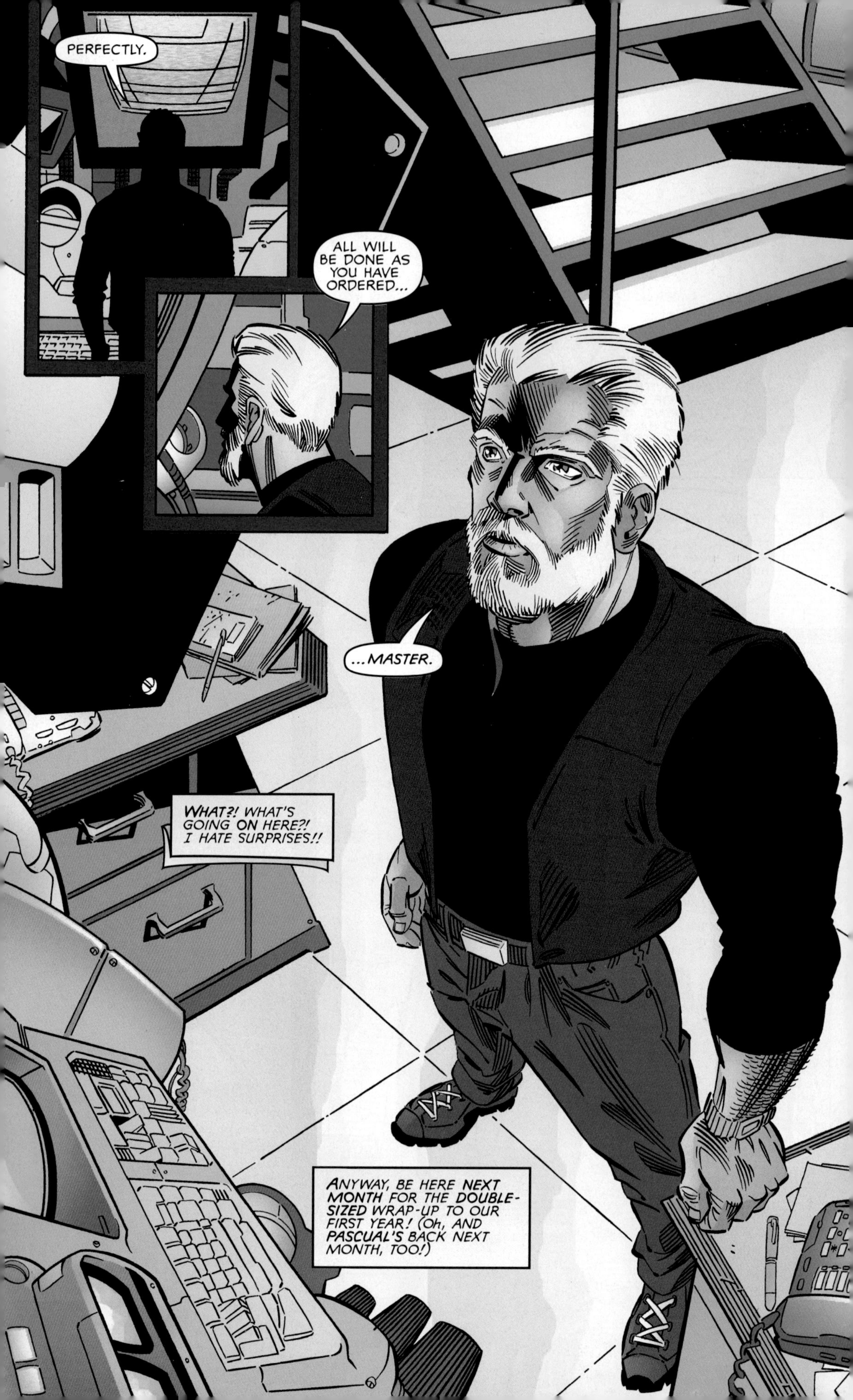
PERFECTLY.
ALL WILL BE DONE AS YOU HAVE ORDERED...
...MASTER.
WHAT?! WHAT'S GOING ON HERE?! I HATE SURPRISES!!
ANYWAY, BE HERE NEXT MONTH FOR THE DOUBLE-SIZED WRAP-UP TO OUR FIRST YEAR! (OH, AND PASCUAL'S BACK NEXT MONTH, TOO!)

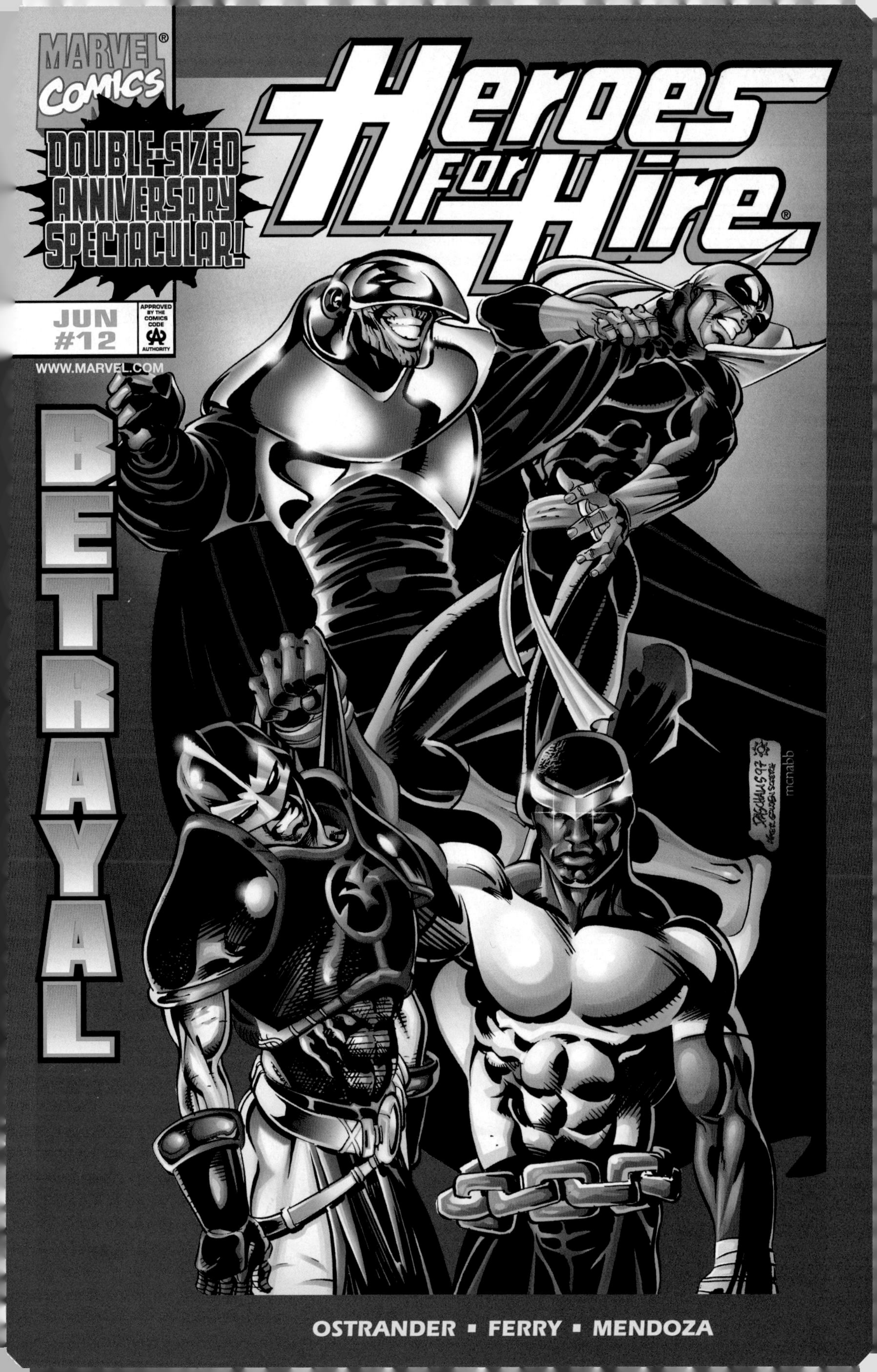

MARVEL COMICS
DOUBLE-SIZED ANNIVERSARY SPECTACULAR!
Heroes for Hire
JUN #12
APPROVED BY THE COMICS CODE AUTHORITY
WWW.MARVEL.COM
BETRAYAL
mcnabb
OSTRANDER ▪ FERRY ▪ MENDOZA

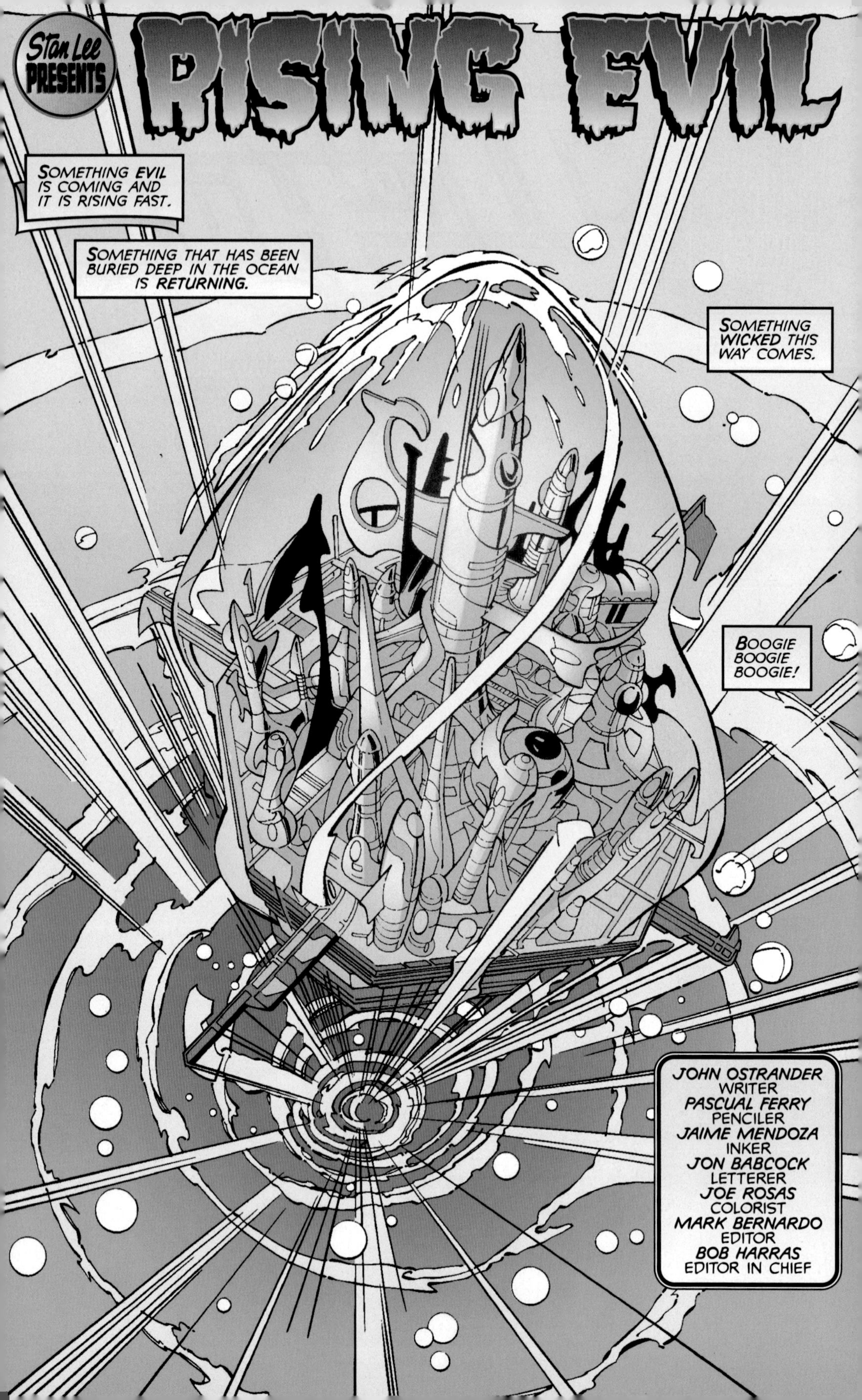

Stan Lee PRESENTS
RISING EVIL
SOMETHING EVIL IS COMING AND IT IS RISING FAST.
SOMETHING THAT HAS BEEN BURIED DEEP IN THE OCEAN IS RETURNING.
SOMETHING WICKED THIS WAY COMES.
BOOGIE BOOGIE BOOGIE!
JOHN OSTRANDER WRITER
PASCUAL FERRY PENCILER
JAIME MENDOZA INKER
JON BABCOCK LETTERER
JOE ROSAS COLORIST
MARK BERNARDO EDITOR
BOB HARRAS EDITOR IN CHIEF

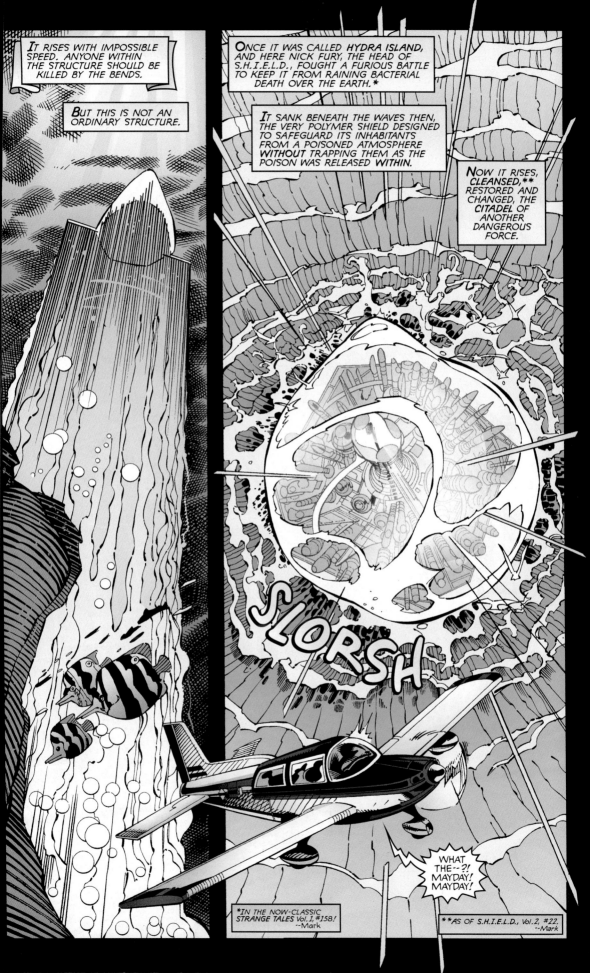

IT RISES WITH IMPOSSIBLE SPEED. ANYONE WITHIN THE STRUCTURE SHOULD BE KILLED BY THE BENDS.

BUT THIS IS NOT AN ORDINARY STRUCTURE.

ONCE IT WAS CALLED HYDRA ISLAND, AND HERE NICK FURY, THE HEAD OF S.H.I.E.L.D., FOUGHT A FURIOUS BATTLE TO KEEP IT FROM RAINING BACTERIAL DEATH OVER THE EARTH.*

IT SANK BENEATH THE WAVES THEN, THE VERY POLYMER SHIELD DESIGNED TO SAFEGUARD ITS INHABITANTS FROM A POISONED ATMOSPHERE WITHOUT TRAPPING THEM AS THE POISON WAS RELEASED WITHIN.

NOW IT RISES, CLEANSED,** RESTORED AND CHANGED, THE CITADEL OF ANOTHER DANGEROUS FORCE.

SLORSH

WHAT THE--?! MAYDAY! MAYDAY!

*IN THE NOW-CLASSIC STRANGE TALES Vol. 1, #158! --Mark

**AS OF S.H.I.E.L.D., Vol. 2, #22. --Mark

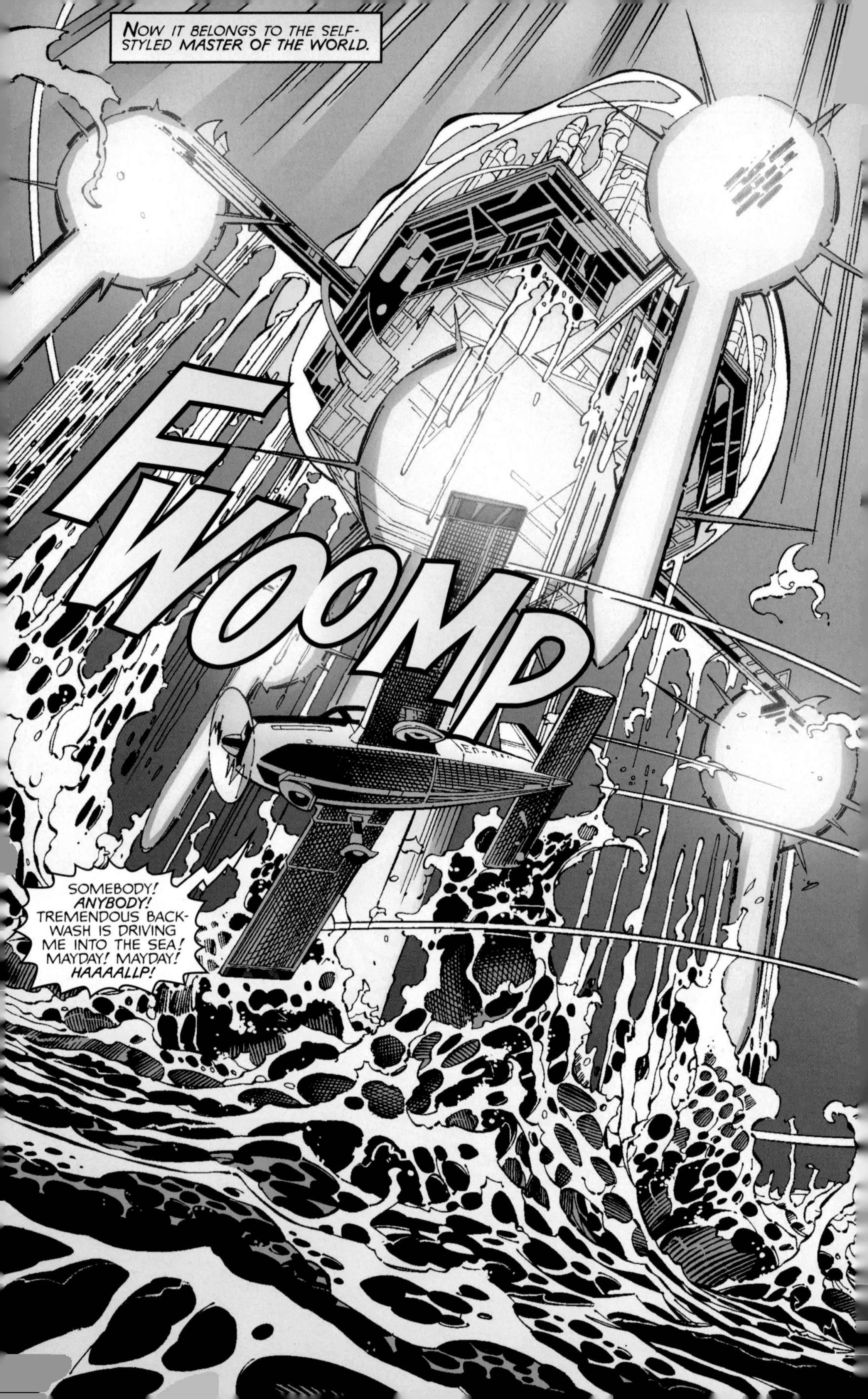
NOW IT BELONGS TO THE SELF-STYLED MASTER OF THE WORLD.
FWOOMP
SOMEBODY! ANYBODY! TREMENDOUS BACKWASH IS DRIVING ME INTO THE SEA! MAYDAY! MAYDAY! HAAAALLP!

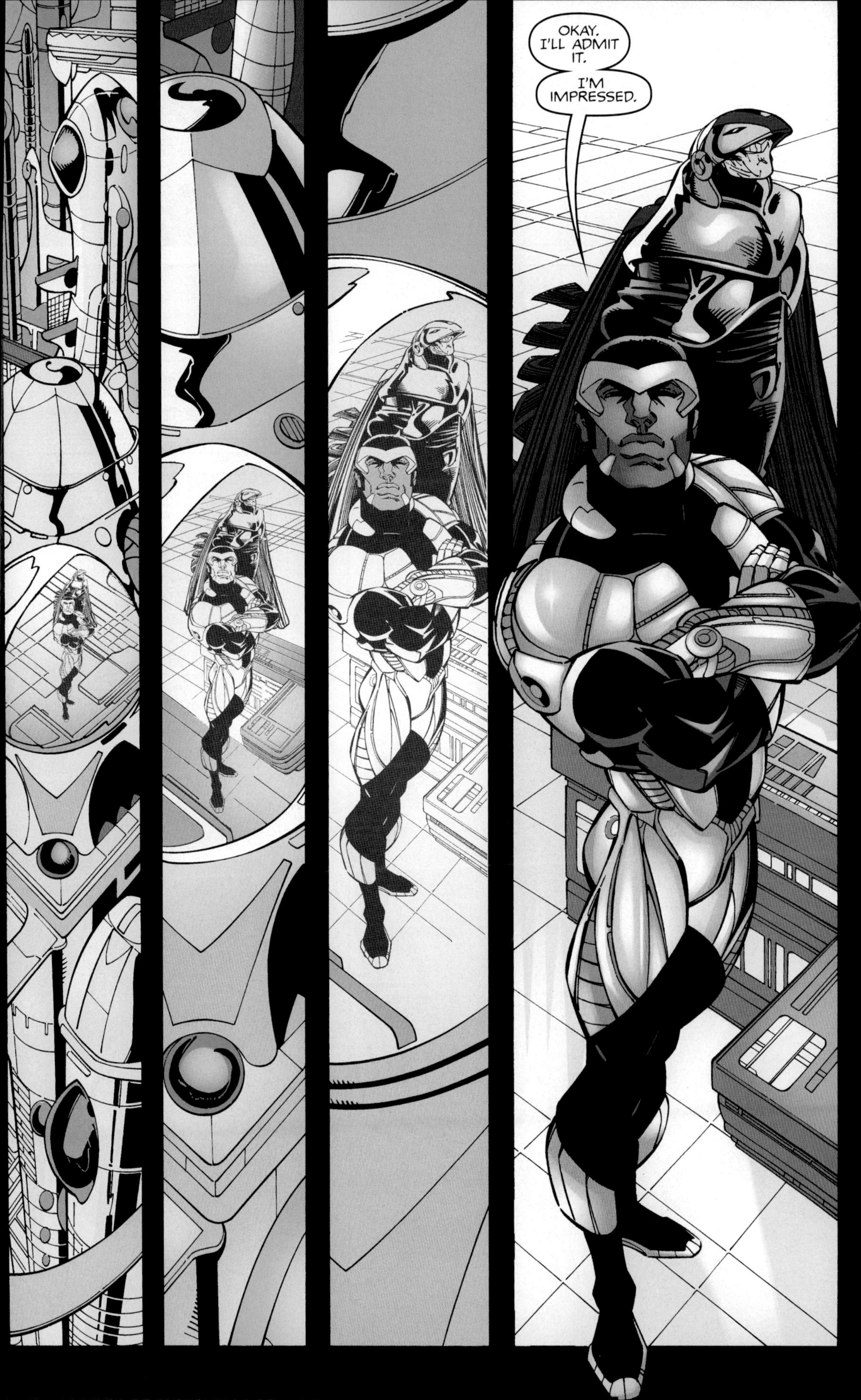
OKAY. I'LL ADMIT IT.
I'M IMPRESSED.

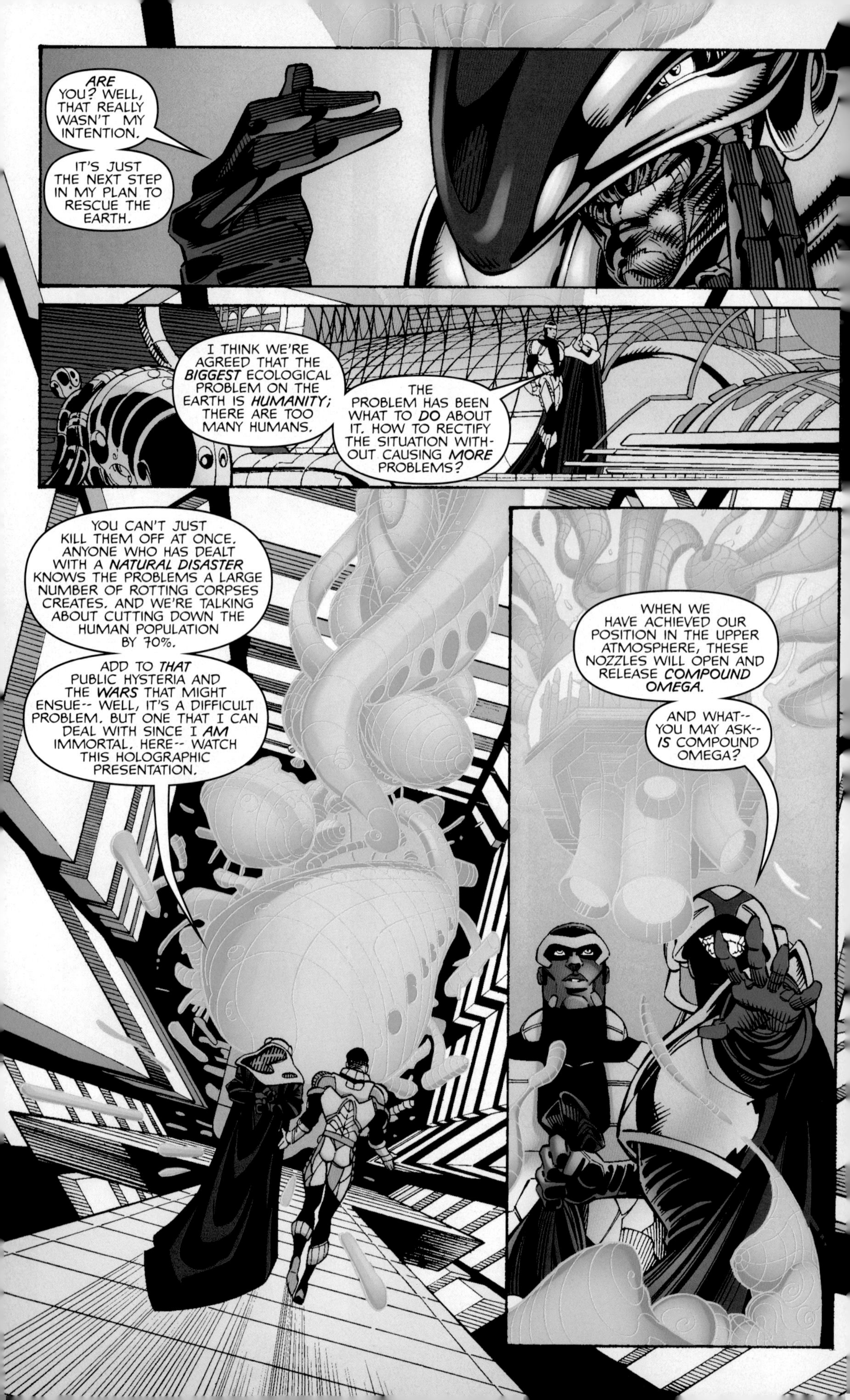

ARE YOU? WELL, THAT REALLY WASN'T MY INTENTION.
IT'S JUST THE NEXT STEP IN MY PLAN TO RESCUE THE EARTH.
I THINK WE'RE AGREED THAT THE *BIGGEST* ECOLOGICAL PROBLEM ON THE EARTH IS *HUMANITY;* THERE ARE TOO MANY HUMANS.
THE PROBLEM HAS BEEN WHAT TO *DO* ABOUT IT. HOW TO RECTIFY THE SITUATION WITH-OUT CAUSING *MORE* PROBLEMS?
YOU CAN'T JUST KILL THEM OFF AT ONCE. ANYONE WHO HAS DEALT WITH A *NATURAL DISASTER* KNOWS THE PROBLEMS A LARGE NUMBER OF ROTTING CORPSES CREATES. AND WE'RE TALKING ABOUT CUTTING DOWN THE HUMAN POPULATION BY 70%.
ADD TO *THAT* PUBLIC HYSTERIA AND THE *WARS* THAT MIGHT ENSUE-- WELL, IT'S A DIFFICULT PROBLEM. BUT ONE THAT I CAN DEAL WITH SINCE I *AM* IMMORTAL. HERE-- WATCH THIS HOLOGRAPHIC PRESENTATION.
WHEN WE HAVE ACHIEVED OUR POSITION IN THE UPPER ATMOSPHERE, THESE NOZZLES WILL OPEN AND RELEASE *COMPOUND OMEGA.*
AND WHAT-- YOU MAY ASK-- *IS* COMPOUND OMEGA?

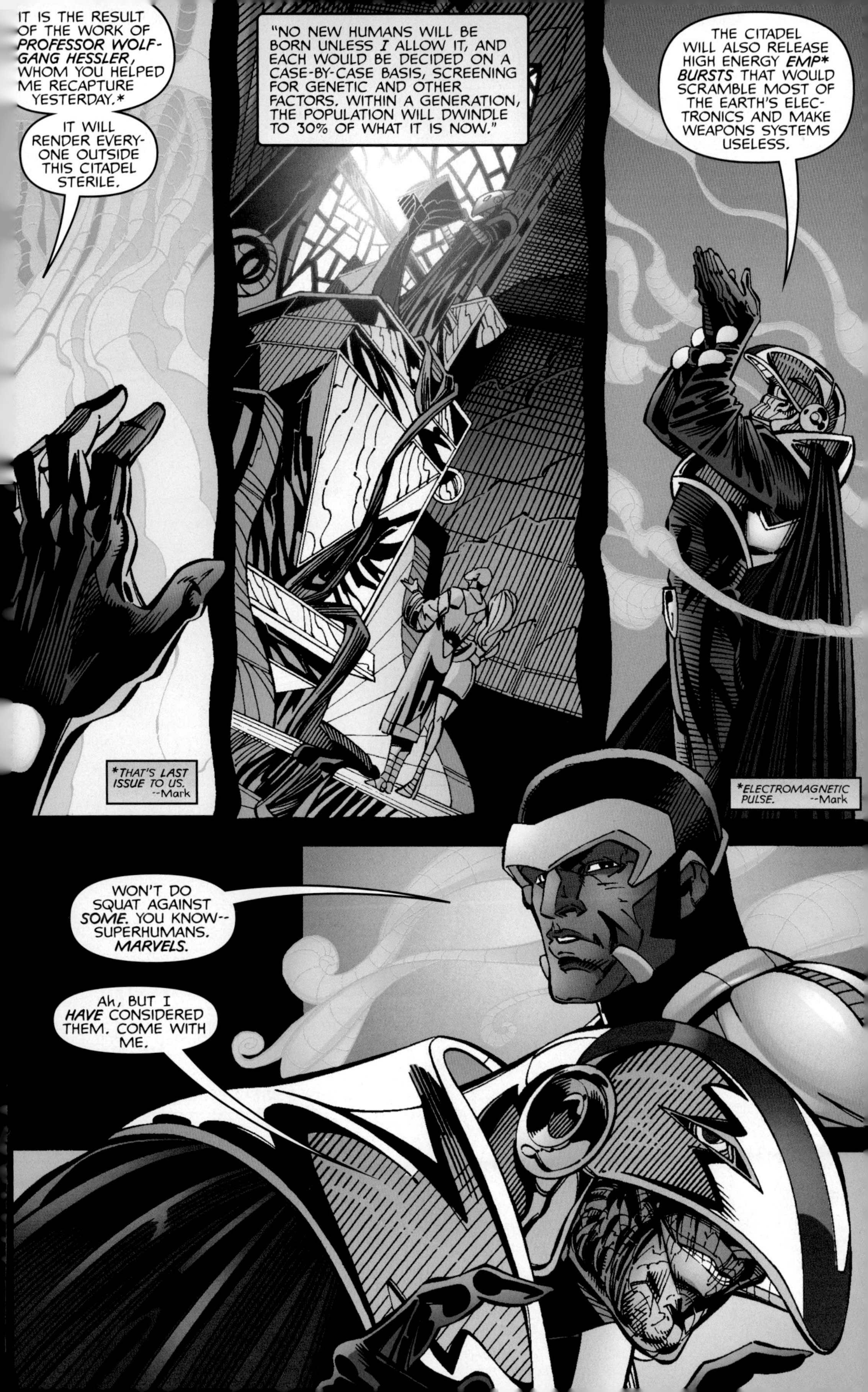

IT IS THE RESULT OF THE WORK OF PROFESSOR WOLFGANG HESSLER, WHOM YOU HELPED ME RECAPTURE YESTERDAY.*
IT WILL RENDER EVERYONE OUTSIDE THIS CITADEL STERILE.
"NO NEW HUMANS WILL BE BORN UNLESS I ALLOW IT, AND EACH WOULD BE DECIDED ON A CASE-BY-CASE BASIS, SCREENING FOR GENETIC AND OTHER FACTORS. WITHIN A GENERATION, THE POPULATION WILL DWINDLE TO 30% OF WHAT IT IS NOW."
*THAT'S LAST ISSUE TO US. --Mark
THE CITADEL WILL ALSO RELEASE HIGH ENERGY EMP* BURSTS THAT WOULD SCRAMBLE MOST OF THE EARTH'S ELECTRONICS AND MAKE WEAPONS SYSTEMS USELESS.
*ELECTROMAGNETIC PULSE. --Mark
WON'T DO SQUAT AGAINST SOME. YOU KNOW-- SUPERHUMANS. MARVELS.
Ah, BUT I HAVE CONSIDERED THEM. COME WITH ME.

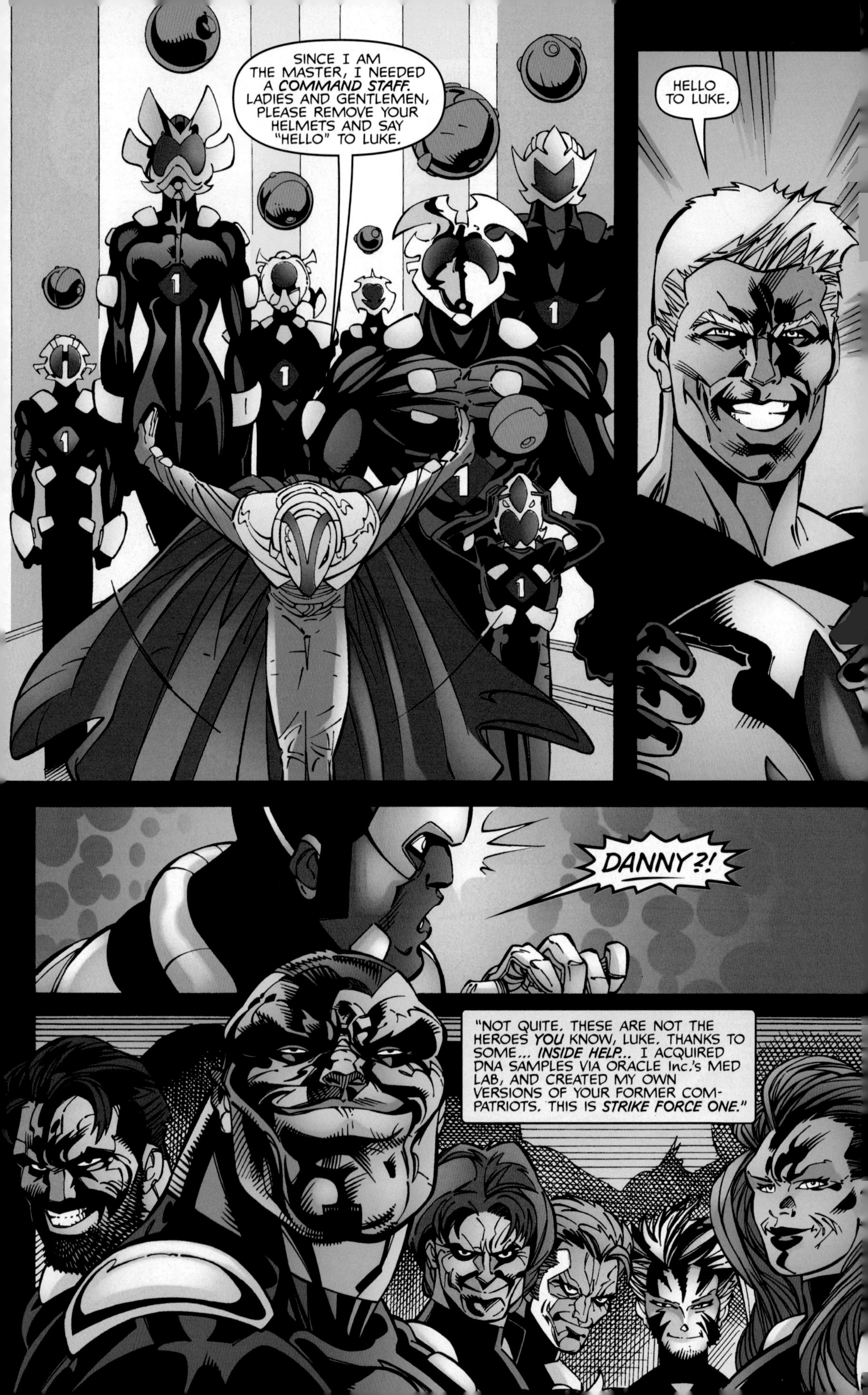
SINCE I AM THE MASTER, I NEEDED A COMMAND STAFF. LADIES AND GENTLEMEN, PLEASE REMOVE YOUR HELMETS AND SAY "HELLO" TO LUKE.
HELLO TO LUKE.
DANNY?!
"NOT QUITE. THESE ARE NOT THE HEROES YOU KNOW, LUKE. THANKS TO SOME... INSIDE HELP... I ACQUIRED DNA SAMPLES VIA ORACLE Inc.'s MED LAB, AND CREATED MY OWN VERSIONS OF YOUR FORMER COMPATRIOTS. THIS IS STRIKE FORCE ONE."

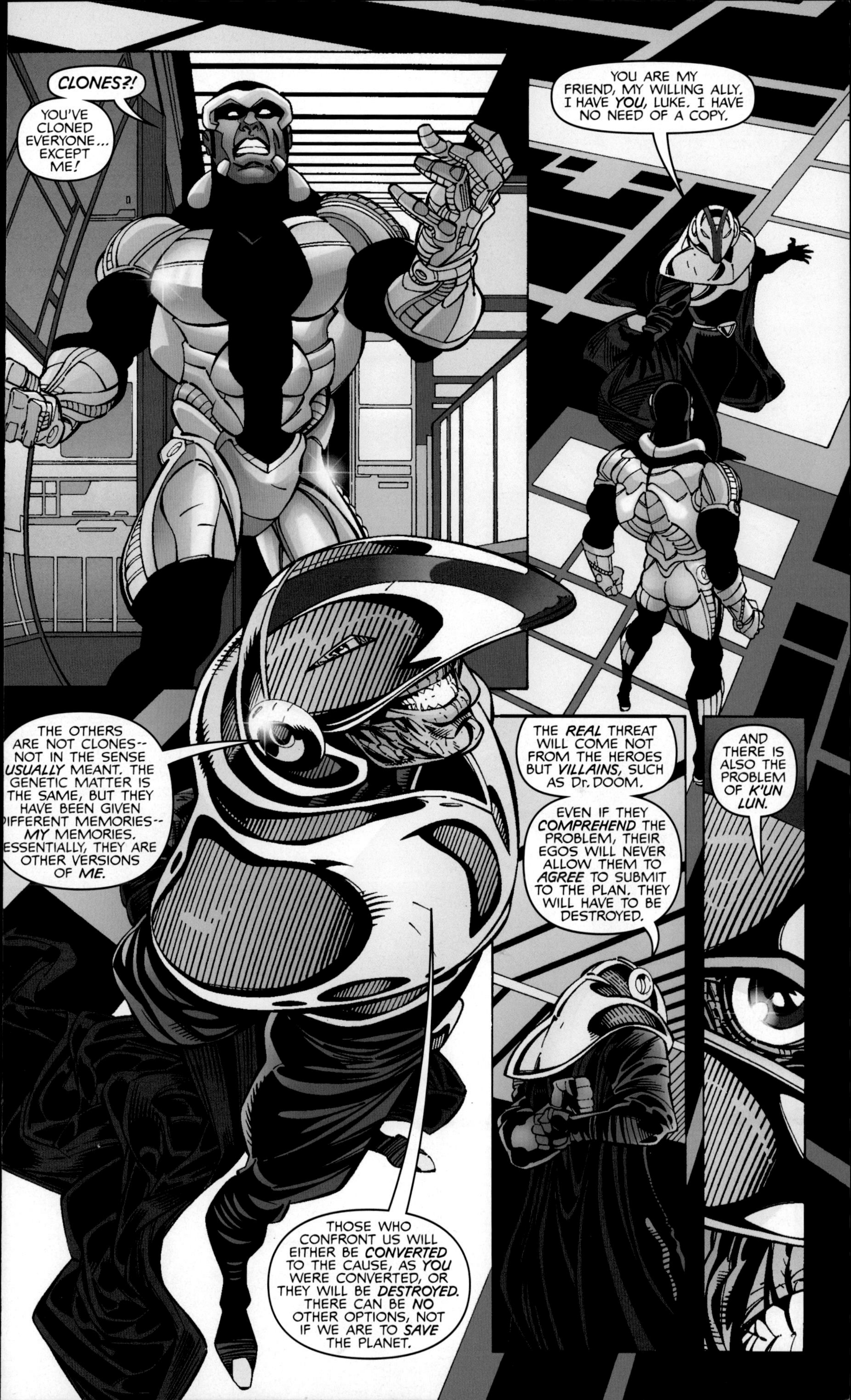

CLONES?!
YOU'VE CLONED EVERYONE... EXCEPT ME!
YOU ARE MY FRIEND, MY WILLING ALLY. I HAVE YOU, LUKE. I HAVE NO NEED OF A COPY.
THE OTHERS ARE NOT CLONES-- NOT IN THE SENSE USUALLY MEANT. THE GENETIC MATTER IS THE SAME, BUT THEY HAVE BEEN GIVEN DIFFERENT MEMORIES-- MY MEMORIES. ESSENTIALLY, THEY ARE OTHER VERSIONS OF ME.
THOSE WHO CONFRONT US WILL EITHER BE CONVERTED TO THE CAUSE, AS YOU WERE CONVERTED, OR THEY WILL BE DESTROYED. THERE CAN BE NO OTHER OPTIONS, NOT IF WE ARE TO SAVE THE PLANET.
THE REAL THREAT WILL COME NOT FROM THE HEROES BUT VILLAINS, SUCH AS Dr. DOOM.
EVEN IF THEY COMPREHEND THE PROBLEM, THEIR EGOS WILL NEVER ALLOW THEM TO AGREE TO SUBMIT TO THE PLAN. THEY WILL HAVE TO BE DESTROYED.
AND THERE IS ALSO THE PROBLEM OF K'UN LUN.

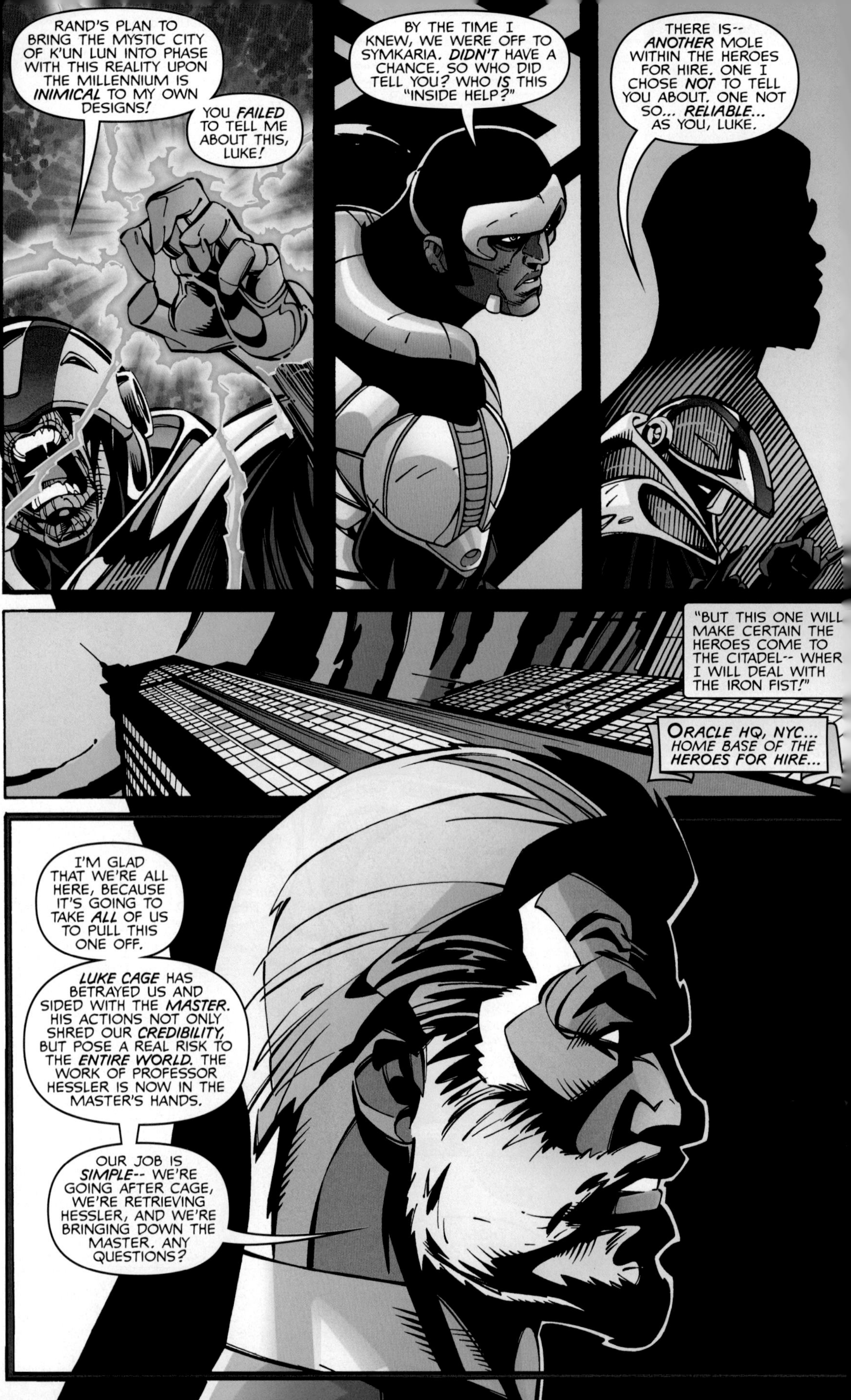
RAND'S PLAN TO BRING THE MYSTIC CITY OF K'UN LUN INTO PHASE WITH THIS REALITY UPON THE MILLENNIUM IS INIMICAL TO MY OWN DESIGNS!
YOU FAILED TO TELL ME ABOUT THIS, LUKE!
BY THE TIME I KNEW, WE WERE OFF TO SYMKARIA. DIDN'T HAVE A CHANCE. SO WHO DID TELL YOU? WHO IS THIS "INSIDE HELP?"
THERE IS-- ANOTHER MOLE WITHIN THE HEROES FOR HIRE. ONE I CHOSE NOT TO TELL YOU ABOUT. ONE NOT SO... RELIABLE... AS YOU, LUKE.
"BUT THIS ONE WILL MAKE CERTAIN THE HEROES COME TO THE CITADEL-- WHER I WILL DEAL WITH THE IRON FIST!"
ORACLE HQ, NYC... HOME BASE OF THE HEROES FOR HIRE...
I'M GLAD THAT WE'RE ALL HERE, BECAUSE IT'S GOING TO TAKE ALL OF US TO PULL THIS ONE OFF.
LUKE CAGE HAS BETRAYED US AND SIDED WITH THE MASTER. HIS ACTIONS NOT ONLY SHRED OUR CREDIBILITY, BUT POSE A REAL RISK TO THE ENTIRE WORLD. THE WORK OF PROFESSOR HESSLER IS NOW IN THE MASTER'S HANDS.
OUR JOB IS SIMPLE-- WE'RE GOING AFTER CAGE, WE'RE RETRIEVING HESSLER, AND WE'RE BRINGING DOWN THE MASTER. ANY QUESTIONS?

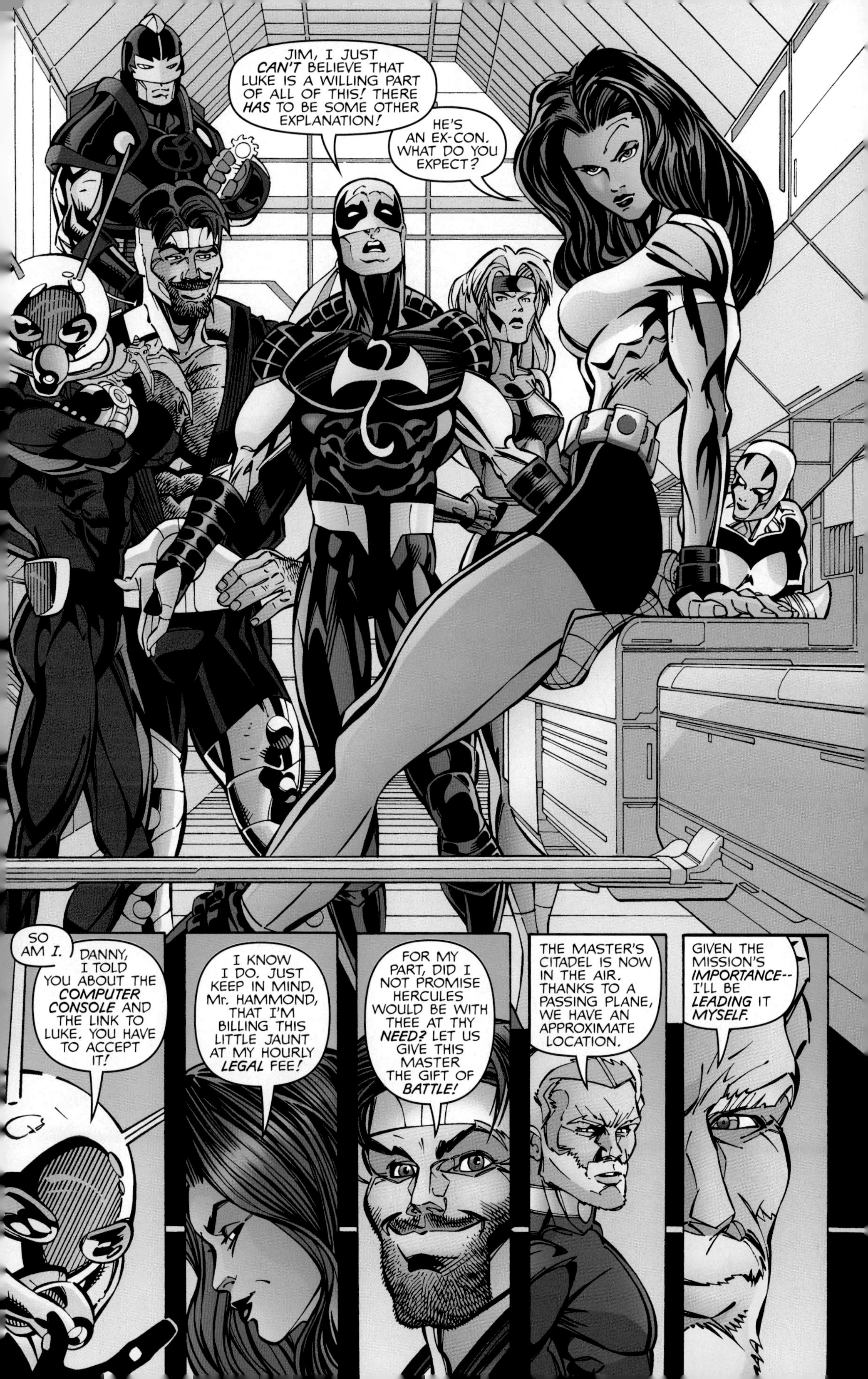
JIM, I JUST *CAN'T* BELIEVE THAT LUKE IS A WILLING PART OF ALL OF THIS! THERE *HAS* TO BE SOME OTHER EXPLANATION!
HE'S AN EX-CON. WHAT DO YOU EXPECT?
SO AM *I*.
DANNY, I TOLD YOU ABOUT THE *COMPUTER CONSOLE* AND THE LINK TO LUKE. YOU HAVE TO ACCEPT IT!
I KNOW I DO. JUST KEEP IN MIND, Mr. HAMMOND, THAT I'M BILLING THIS LITTLE JAUNT AT MY HOURLY *LEGAL* FEE!
FOR MY PART, DID I NOT PROMISE HERCULES WOULD BE WITH THEE AT THY *NEED?* LET US GIVE THIS MASTER THE GIFT OF *BATTLE!*
THE MASTER'S CITADEL IS NOW IN THE AIR. THANKS TO A PASSING PLANE, WE HAVE AN APPROXIMATE LOCATION.
GIVEN THE MISSION'S *IMPORTANCE*-- I'LL BE *LEADING* IT *MYSELF*.

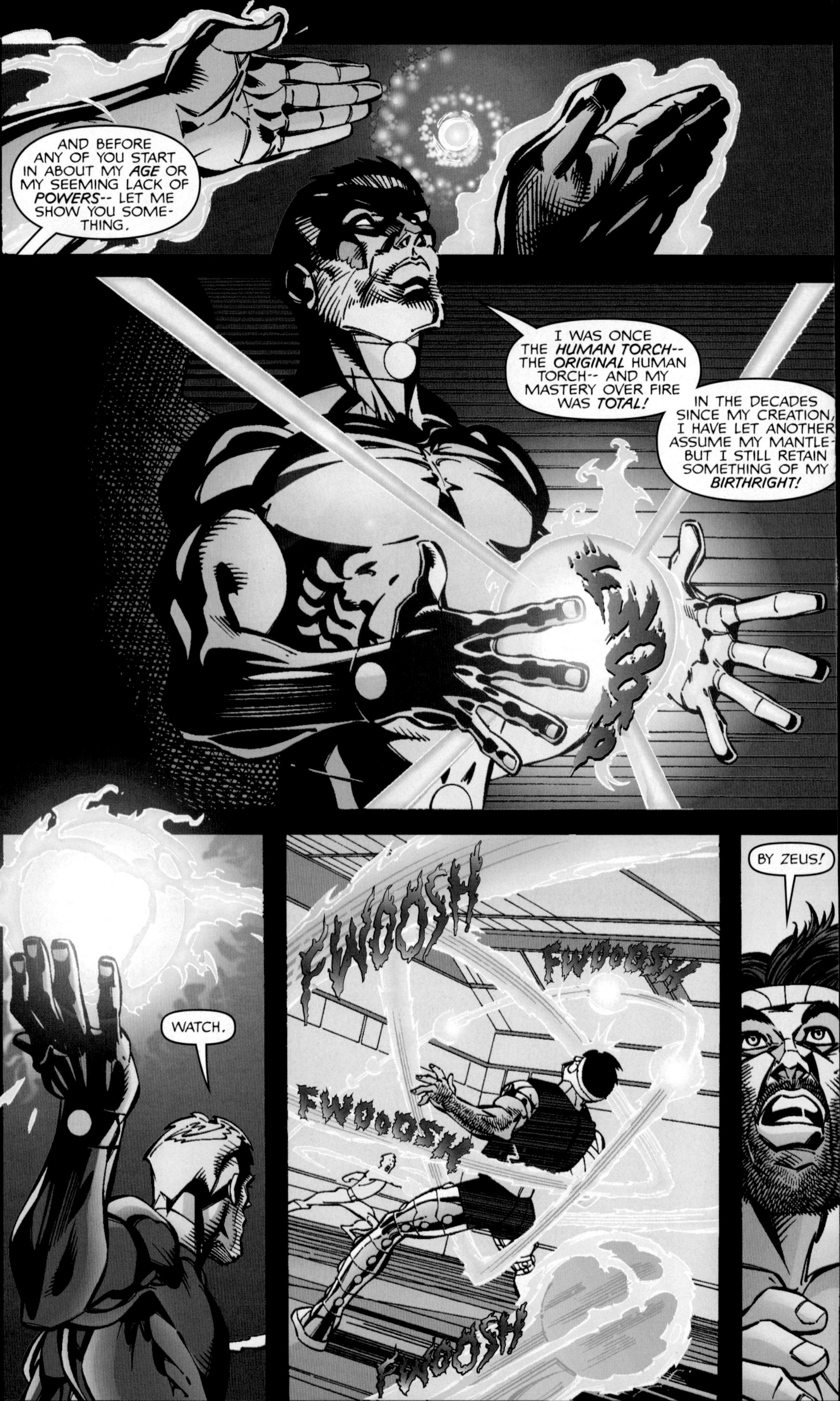
AND BEFORE ANY OF YOU START IN ABOUT MY AGE OR MY SEEMING LACK OF POWERS-- LET ME SHOW YOU SOMETHING.
I WAS ONCE THE HUMAN TORCH-- THE ORIGINAL HUMAN TORCH-- AND MY MASTERY OVER FIRE WAS TOTAL!
IN THE DECADES SINCE MY CREATION, I HAVE LET ANOTHER ASSUME MY MANTLE-- BUT I STILL RETAIN SOMETHING OF MY BIRTHRIGHT!
FWOOMP
WATCH.
FWOOSH
FWOOOSH
FWOOOSH
FWOOSH
BY ZEUS!

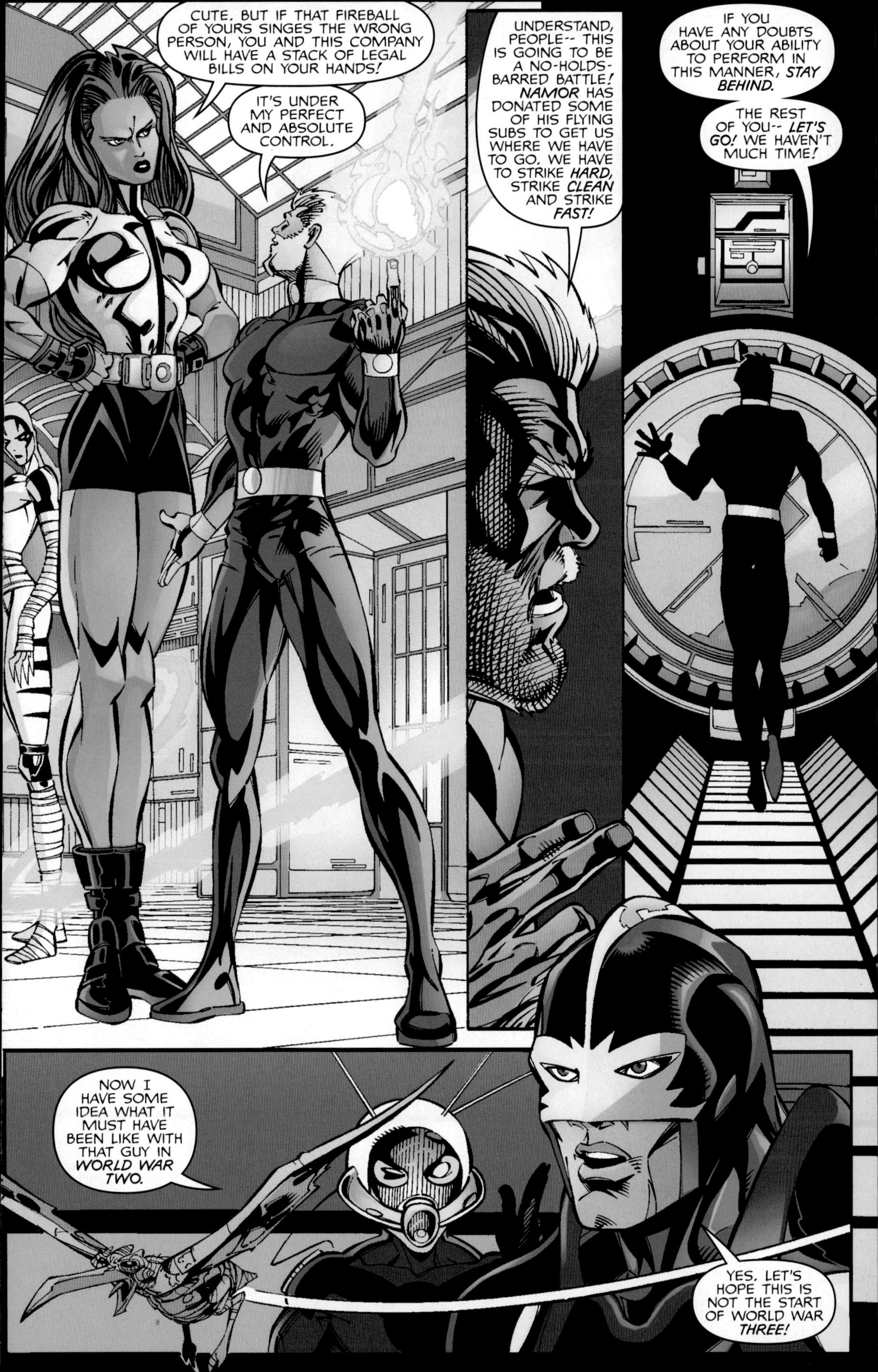
CUTE. BUT IF THAT FIREBALL OF YOURS SINGES THE WRONG PERSON, YOU AND THIS COMPANY WILL HAVE A STACK OF LEGAL BILLS ON YOUR HANDS!
IT'S UNDER MY PERFECT AND ABSOLUTE CONTROL.
UNDERSTAND, PEOPLE-- THIS IS GOING TO BE A NO-HOLDS-BARRED BATTLE! NAMOR HAS DONATED SOME OF HIS FLYING SUBS TO GET US WHERE WE HAVE TO GO. WE HAVE TO STRIKE HARD, STRIKE CLEAN AND STRIKE FAST!
IF YOU HAVE ANY DOUBTS ABOUT YOUR ABILITY TO PERFORM IN THIS MANNER, STAY BEHIND.
THE REST OF YOU-- LET'S GO! WE HAVEN'T MUCH TIME!
NOW I HAVE SOME IDEA WHAT IT MUST HAVE BEEN LIKE WITH THAT GUY IN WORLD WAR TWO.
YES. LET'S HOPE THIS IS NOT THE START OF WORLD WAR THREE!

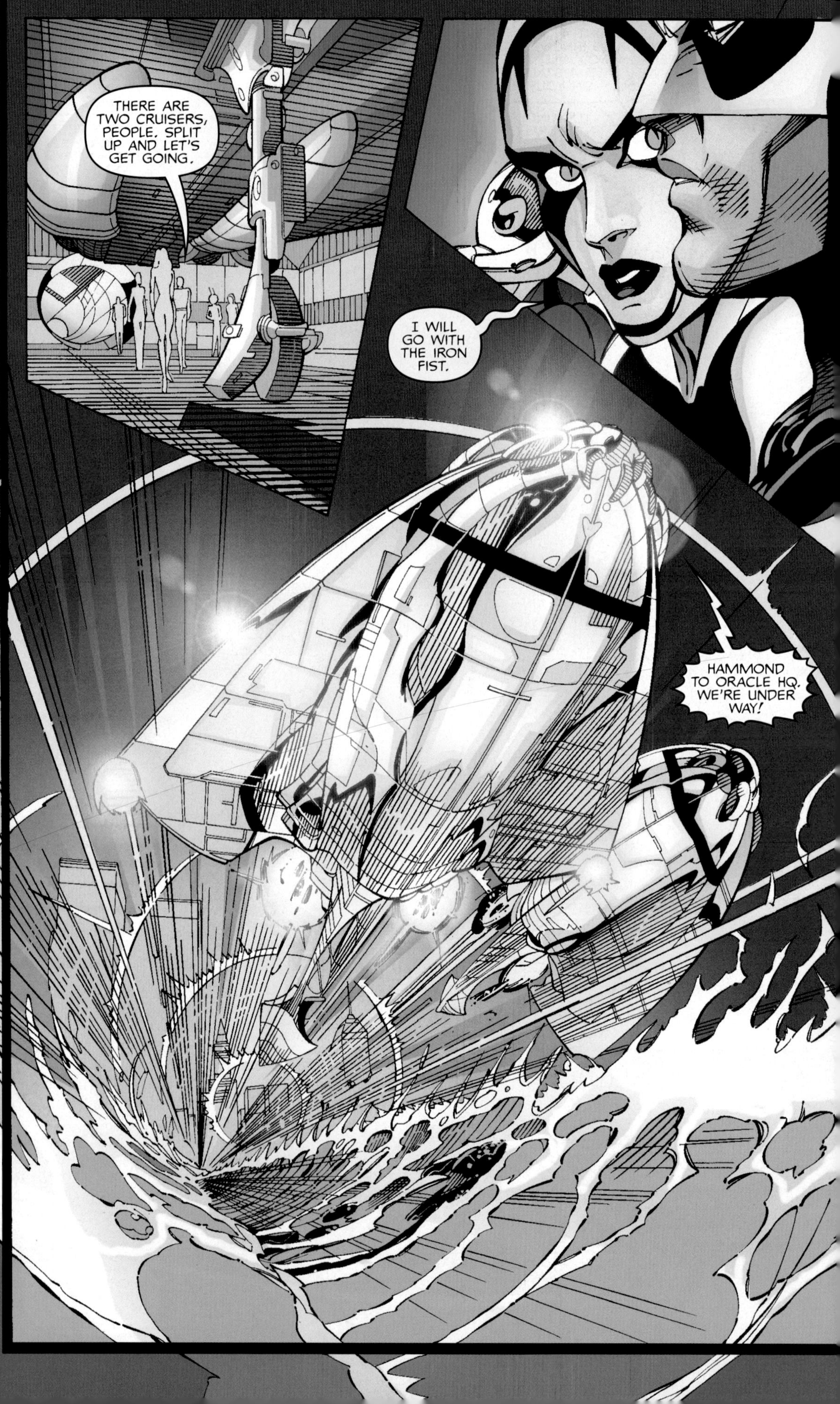
THERE ARE TWO CRUISERS, PEOPLE. SPLIT UP AND LET'S GET GOING.
I WILL GO WITH THE IRON FIST.
HAMMOND TO ORACLE HQ. WE'RE UNDER WAY!

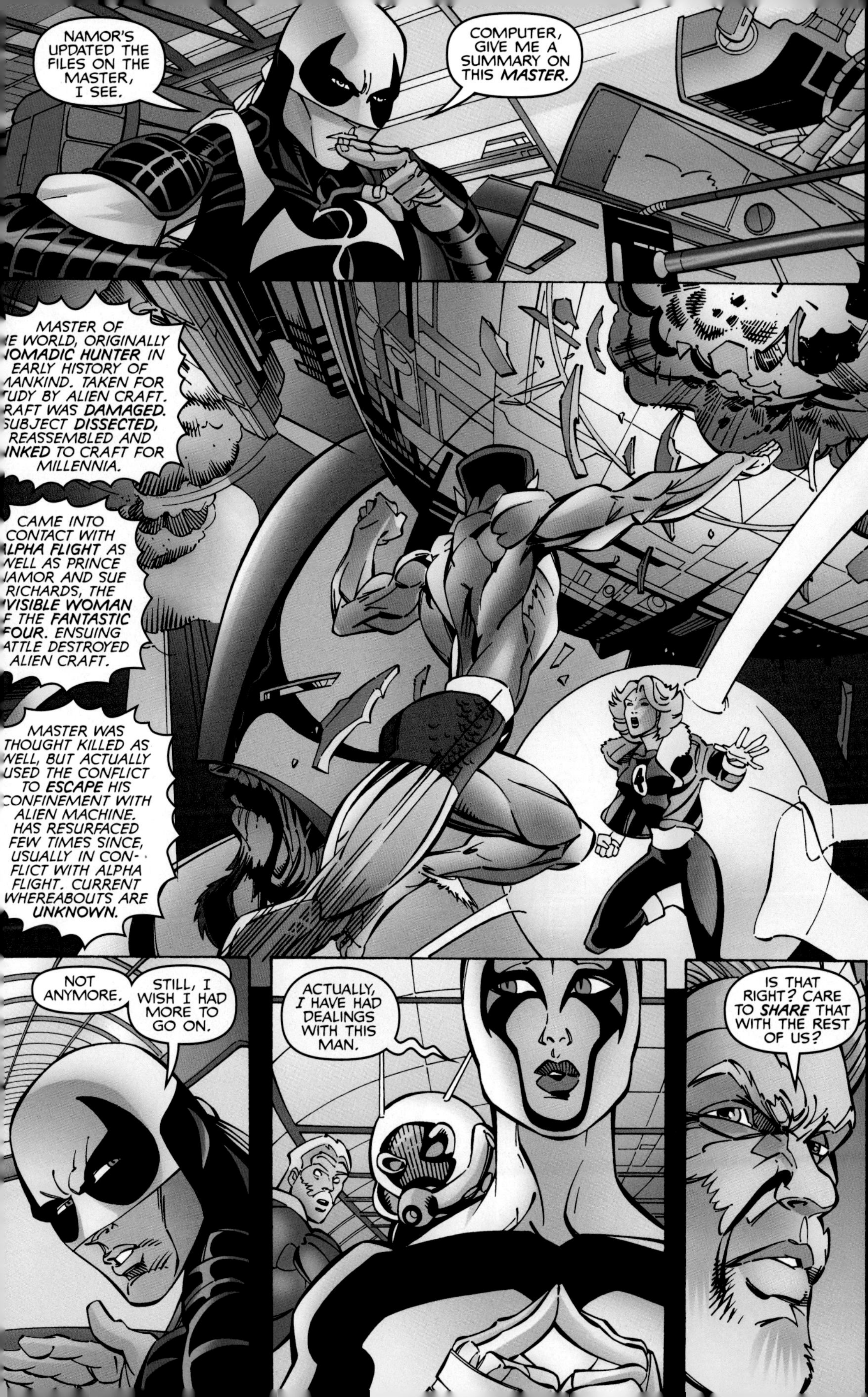
NAMOR'S UPDATED THE FILES ON THE MASTER, I SEE.
COMPUTER, GIVE ME A SUMMARY ON THIS *MASTER*.
MASTER OF THE WORLD, ORIGINALLY NOMADIC HUNTER IN EARLY HISTORY OF MANKIND. TAKEN FOR STUDY BY ALIEN CRAFT. CRAFT WAS **DAMAGED.** SUBJECT **DISSECTED,** REASSEMBLED AND **LINKED** TO CRAFT FOR MILLENNIA.
CAME INTO CONTACT WITH **ALPHA FLIGHT** AS WELL AS PRINCE NAMOR AND SUE RICHARDS, THE **INVISIBLE WOMAN** OF THE **FANTASTIC FOUR.** ENSUING BATTLE DESTROYED ALIEN CRAFT.
MASTER WAS THOUGHT KILLED AS WELL, BUT ACTUALLY USED THE CONFLICT TO **ESCAPE** HIS CONFINEMENT WITH ALIEN MACHINE. HAS RESURFACED FEW TIMES SINCE, USUALLY IN CONFLICT WITH ALPHA FLIGHT. CURRENT WHEREABOUTS ARE **UNKNOWN.**
NOT ANYMORE.
STILL, I WISH I HAD MORE TO GO ON.
ACTUALLY, *I* HAVE HAD DEALINGS WITH THIS MAN.
IS THAT RIGHT? CARE TO *SHARE* THAT WITH THE REST OF US?

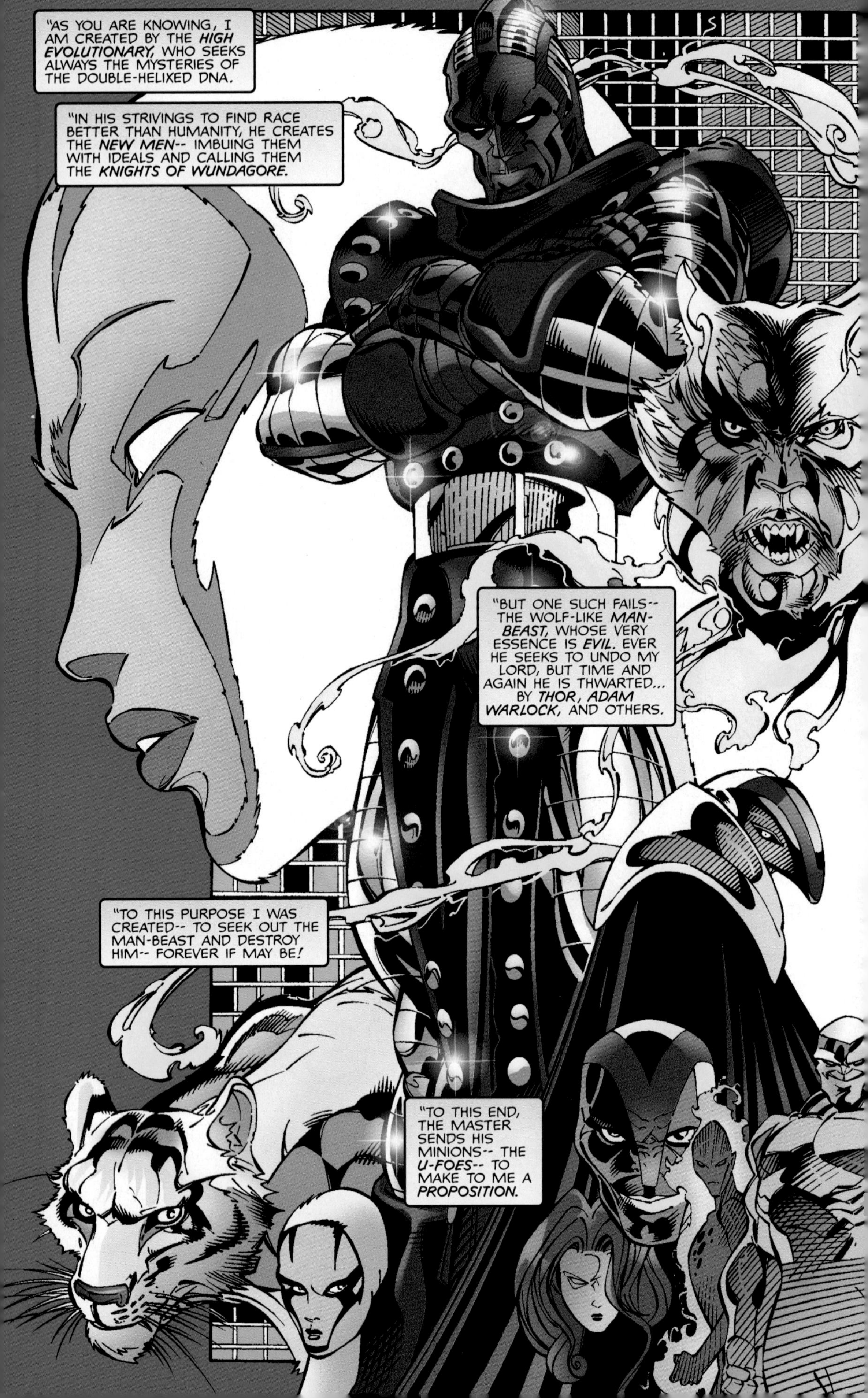
"AS YOU ARE KNOWING, I AM CREATED BY THE HIGH EVOLUTIONARY, WHO SEEKS ALWAYS THE MYSTERIES OF THE DOUBLE-HELIXED DNA.
"IN HIS STRIVINGS TO FIND RACE BETTER THAN HUMANITY, HE CREATES THE NEW MEN-- IMBUING THEM WITH IDEALS AND CALLING THEM THE KNIGHTS OF WUNDAGORE.
"BUT ONE SUCH FAILS-- THE WOLF-LIKE MAN-BEAST, WHOSE VERY ESSENCE IS EVIL. EVER HE SEEKS TO UNDO MY LORD, BUT TIME AND AGAIN HE IS THWARTED... BY THOR, ADAM WARLOCK, AND OTHERS.
"TO THIS PURPOSE I WAS CREATED-- TO SEEK OUT THE MAN-BEAST AND DESTROY HIM-- FOREVER IF MAY BE!
"TO THIS END, THE MASTER SENDS HIS MINIONS-- THE U-FOES-- TO MAKE TO ME A PROPOSITION.

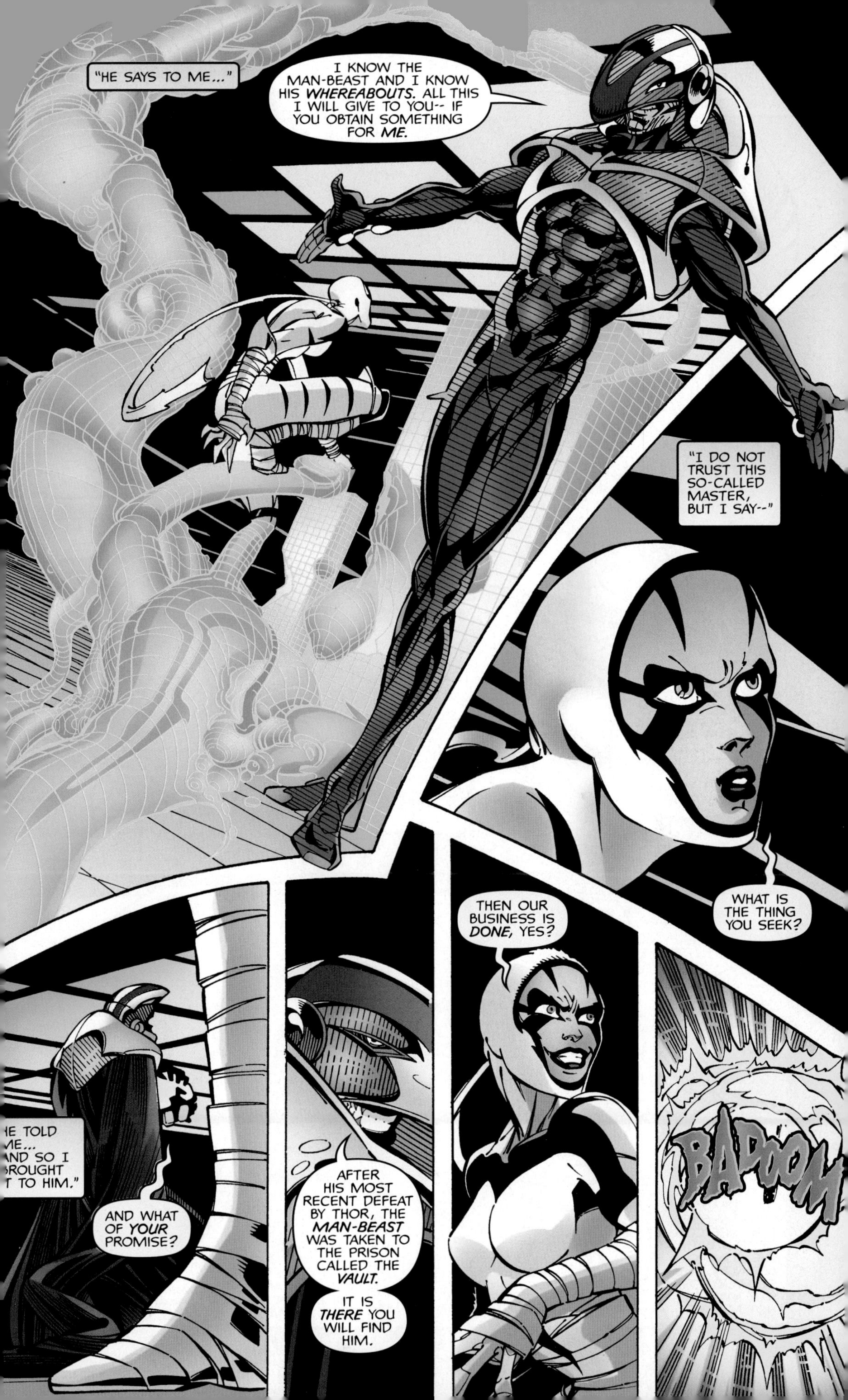
"HE SAYS TO ME..."
I KNOW THE MAN-BEAST AND I KNOW HIS WHEREABOUTS. ALL THIS I WILL GIVE TO YOU-- IF YOU OBTAIN SOMETHING FOR ME.
"I DO NOT TRUST THIS SO-CALLED MASTER, BUT I SAY--"
WHAT IS THE THING YOU SEEK?
HE TOLD ME... AND SO I BROUGHT IT TO HIM."
AND WHAT OF YOUR PROMISE?
AFTER HIS MOST RECENT DEFEAT BY THOR, THE MAN-BEAST WAS TAKEN TO THE PRISON CALLED THE VAULT.
IT IS THERE YOU WILL FIND HIM.
THEN OUR BUSINESS IS DONE, YES?
BADOOM

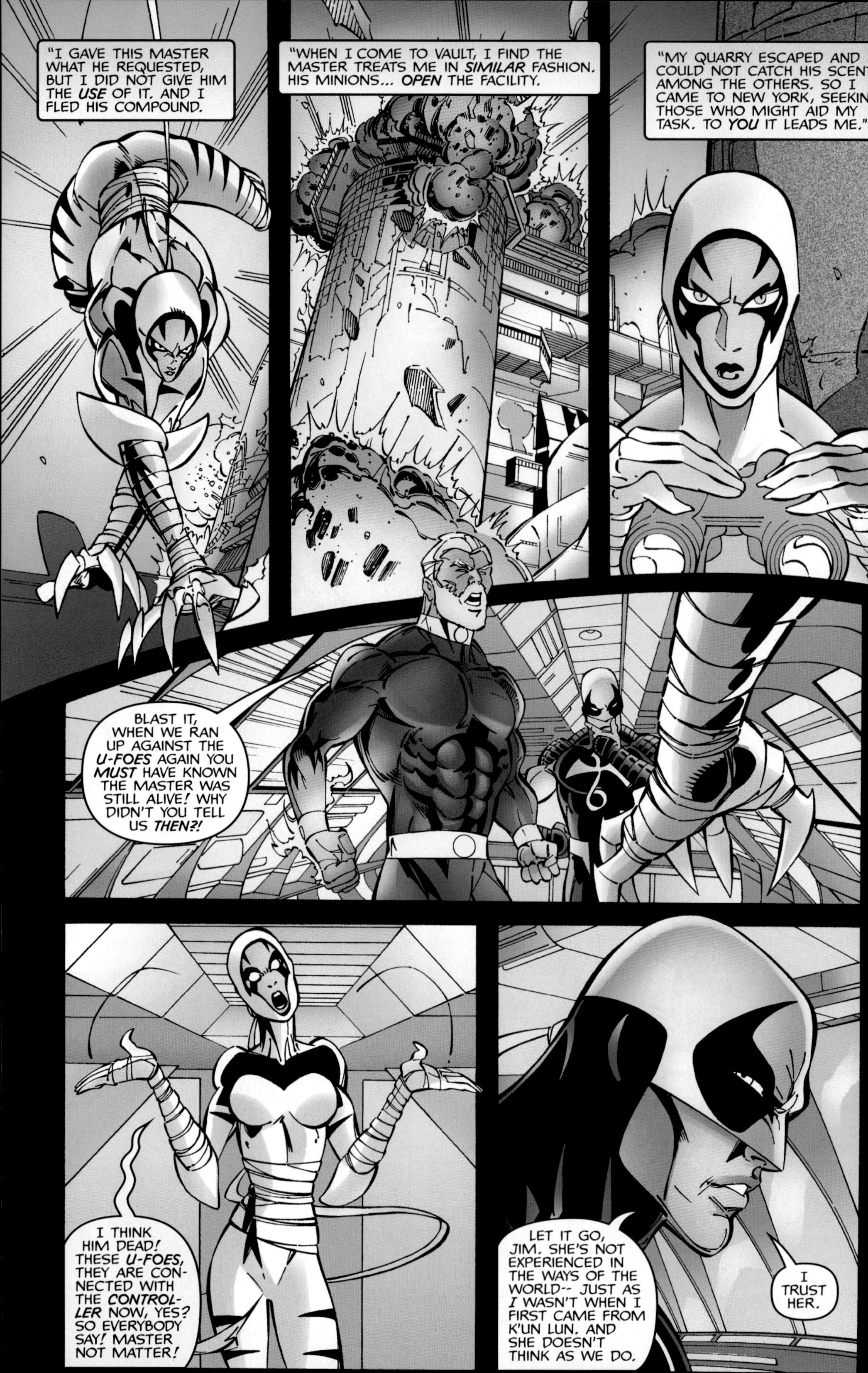
"I GAVE THIS MASTER WHAT HE REQUESTED, BUT I DID NOT GIVE HIM THE USE OF IT. AND I FLED HIS COMPOUND.
"WHEN I COME TO VAULT, I FIND THE MASTER TREATS ME IN SIMILAR FASHION. HIS MINIONS... OPEN THE FACILITY.
"MY QUARRY ESCAPED AND COULD NOT CATCH HIS SCENT AMONG THE OTHERS. SO I CAME TO NEW YORK, SEEKIN THOSE WHO MIGHT AID MY TASK. TO YOU IT LEADS ME."
BLAST IT, WHEN WE RAN UP AGAINST THE U-FOES AGAIN YOU MUST HAVE KNOWN THE MASTER WAS STILL ALIVE! WHY DIDN'T YOU TELL US THEN?!
I THINK HIM DEAD! THESE U-FOES, THEY ARE CONNECTED WITH THE CONTROLLER NOW, YES? SO EVERYBODY SAY! MASTER NOT MATTER!
LET IT GO, JIM. SHE'S NOT EXPERIENCED IN THE WAYS OF THE WORLD-- JUST AS I WASN'T WHEN I FIRST CAME FROM K'UN LUN. AND SHE DOESN'T THINK AS WE DO.
I TRUST HER.

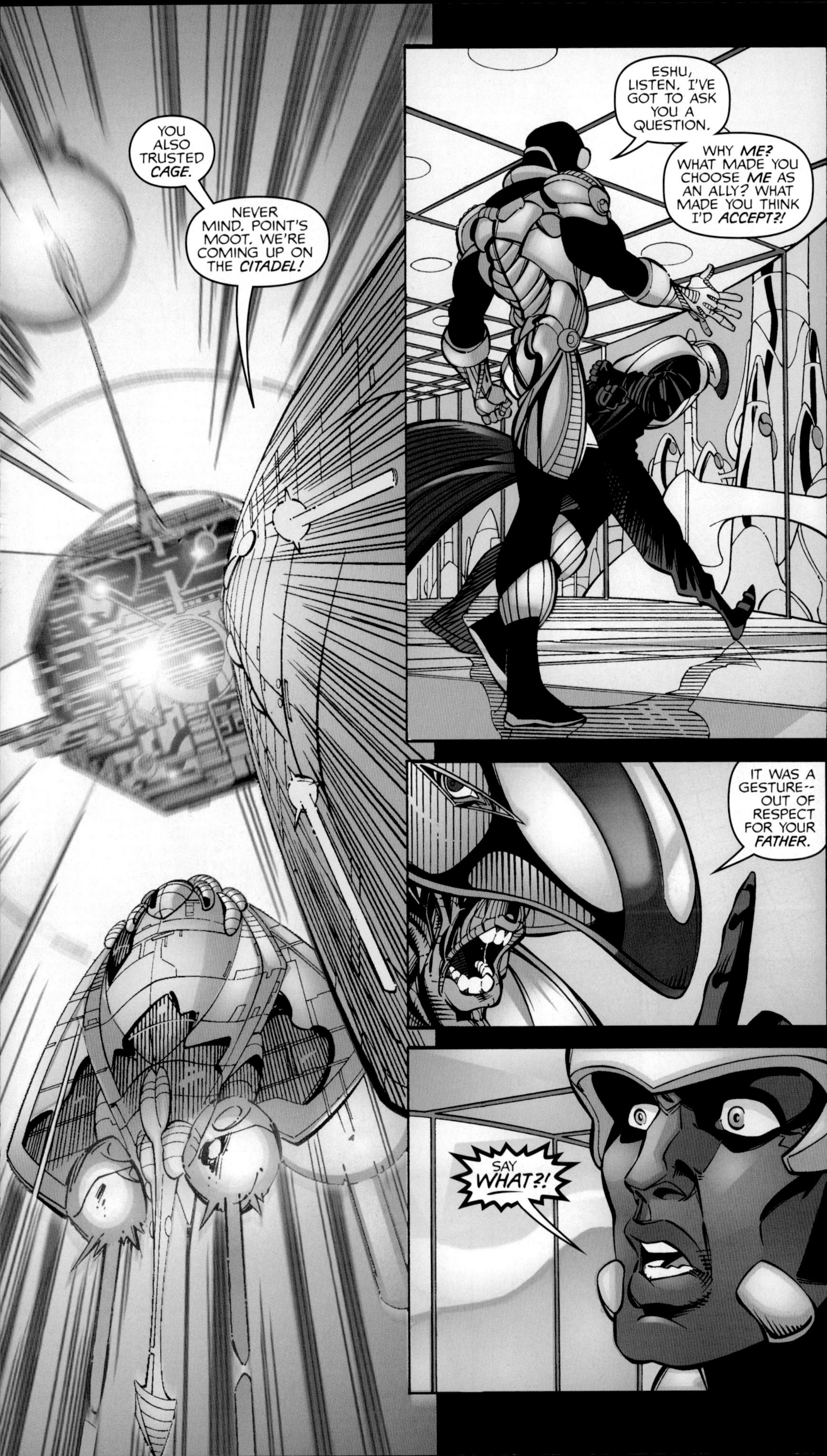
YOU ALSO TRUSTED CAGE.
NEVER MIND. POINT'S MOOT. WE'RE COMING UP ON THE CITADEL!
ESHU, LISTEN. I'VE GOT TO ASK YOU A QUESTION.
WHY ME? WHAT MADE YOU CHOOSE ME AS AN ALLY? WHAT MADE YOU THINK I'D ACCEPT?!
IT WAS A GESTURE-- OUT OF RESPECT FOR YOUR FATHER.
SAY WHAT?!

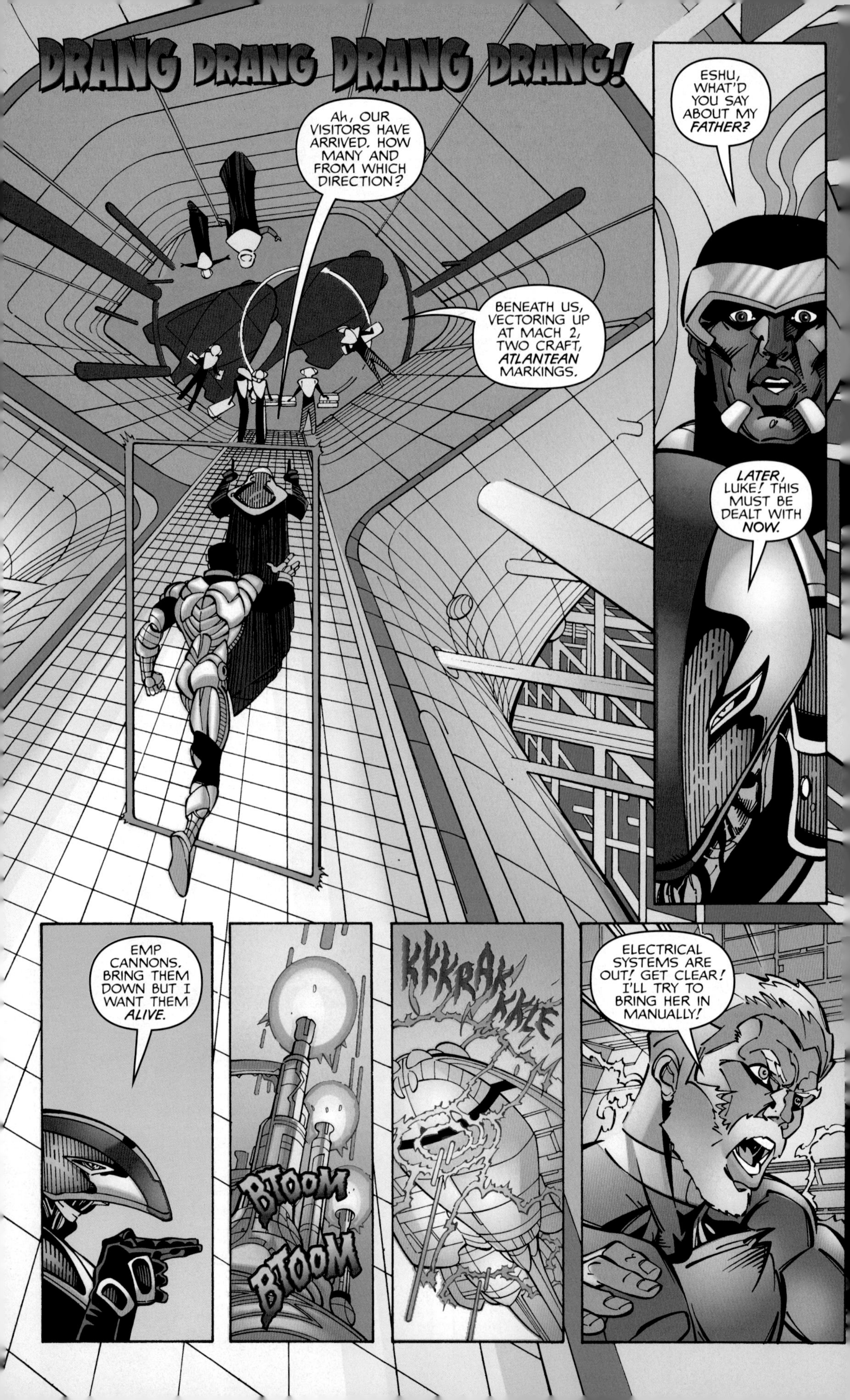
DRANG DRANG DRANG DRANG!
Ah, OUR VISITORS HAVE ARRIVED. HOW MANY AND FROM WHICH DIRECTION?
BENEATH US, VECTORING UP AT MACH 2, TWO CRAFT, *ATLANTEAN* MARKINGS.
ESHU, WHAT'D YOU SAY ABOUT MY *FATHER?*
LATER, LUKE! THIS MUST BE DEALT WITH *NOW.*
EMP CANNONS. BRING THEM DOWN BUT I WANT THEM *ALIVE.*
BTOOM
BTOOM
KKKRAK KAZE
ELECTRICAL SYSTEMS ARE OUT! GET CLEAR! I'LL TRY TO BRING HER IN MANUALLY!

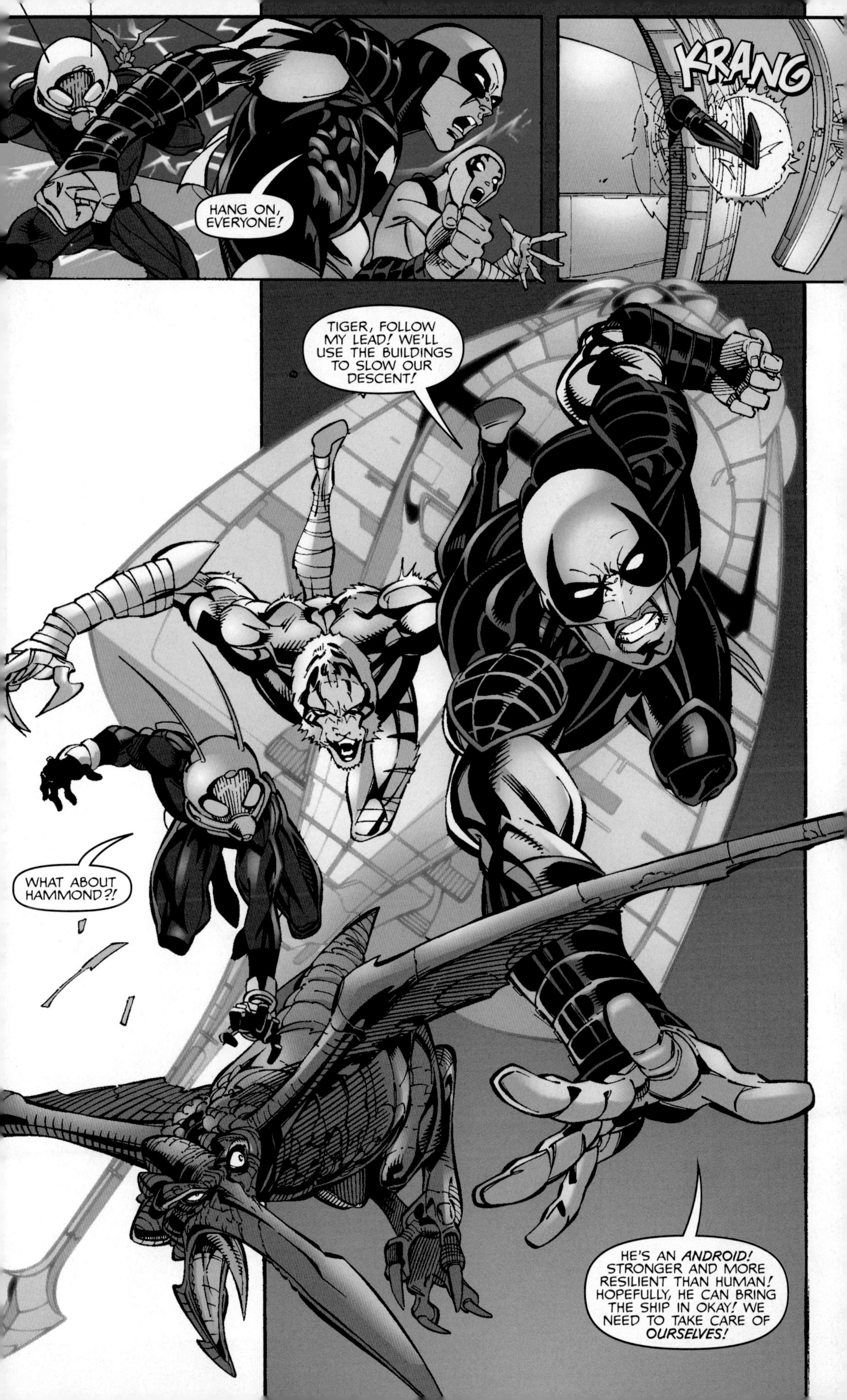
HANG ON, EVERYONE!
KRANG
TIGER, FOLLOW MY LEAD! WE'LL USE THE BUILDINGS TO SLOW OUR DESCENT!
WHAT ABOUT HAMMOND?!
HE'S AN *ANDROID!* STRONGER AND MORE RESILIENT THAN HUMAN! HOPEFULLY, HE CAN BRING THE SHIP IN OKAY! WE NEED TO TAKE CARE OF *OURSELVES!*

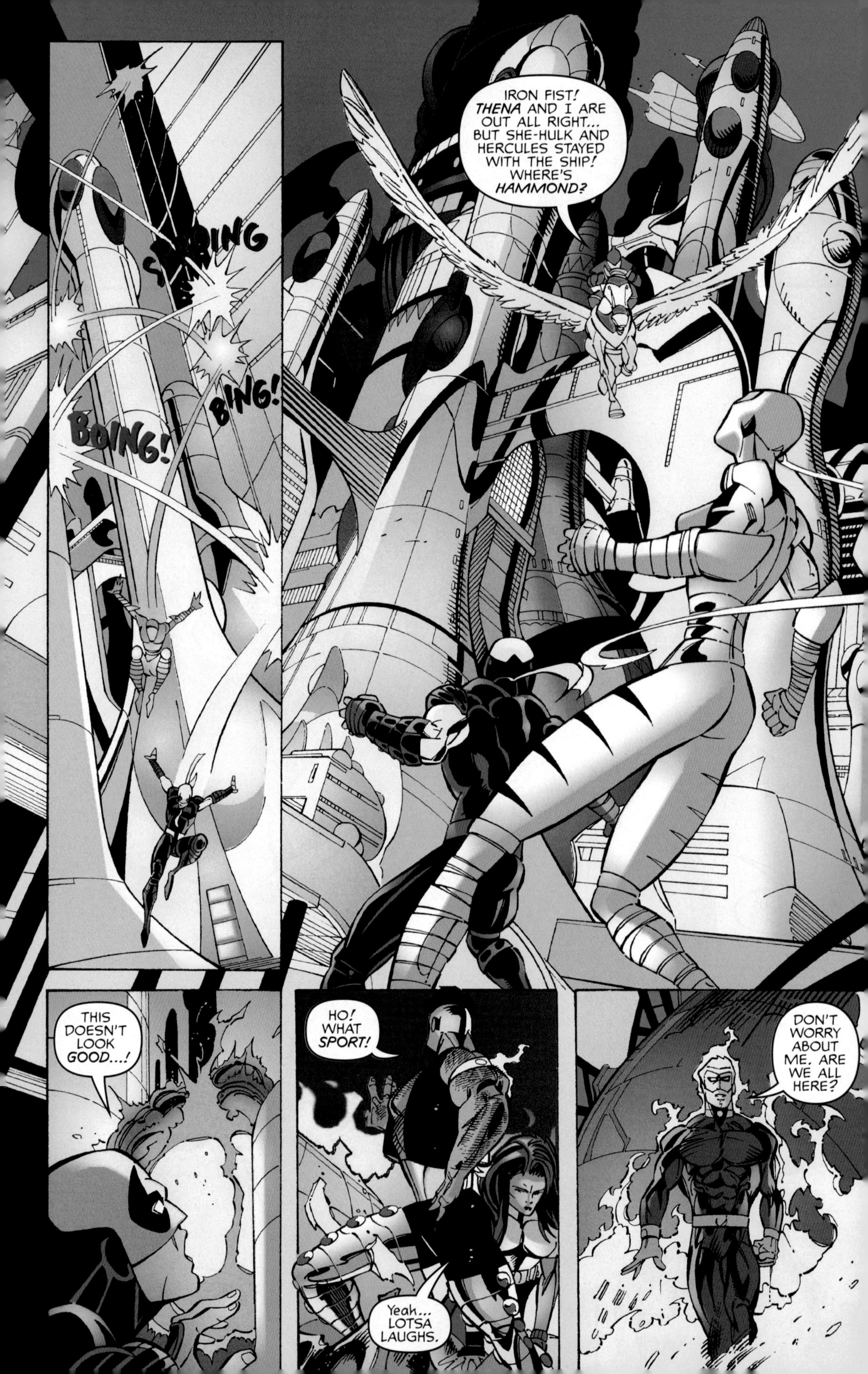
SPROING
BING!
BOING!
IRON FIST! THENA AND I ARE OUT ALL RIGHT... BUT SHE-HULK AND HERCULES STAYED WITH THE SHIP! WHERE'S HAMMOND?
THIS DOESN'T LOOK GOOD...!
HO! WHAT SPORT!
Yeah... LOTSA LAUGHS.
DON'T WORRY ABOUT ME. ARE WE ALL HERE?

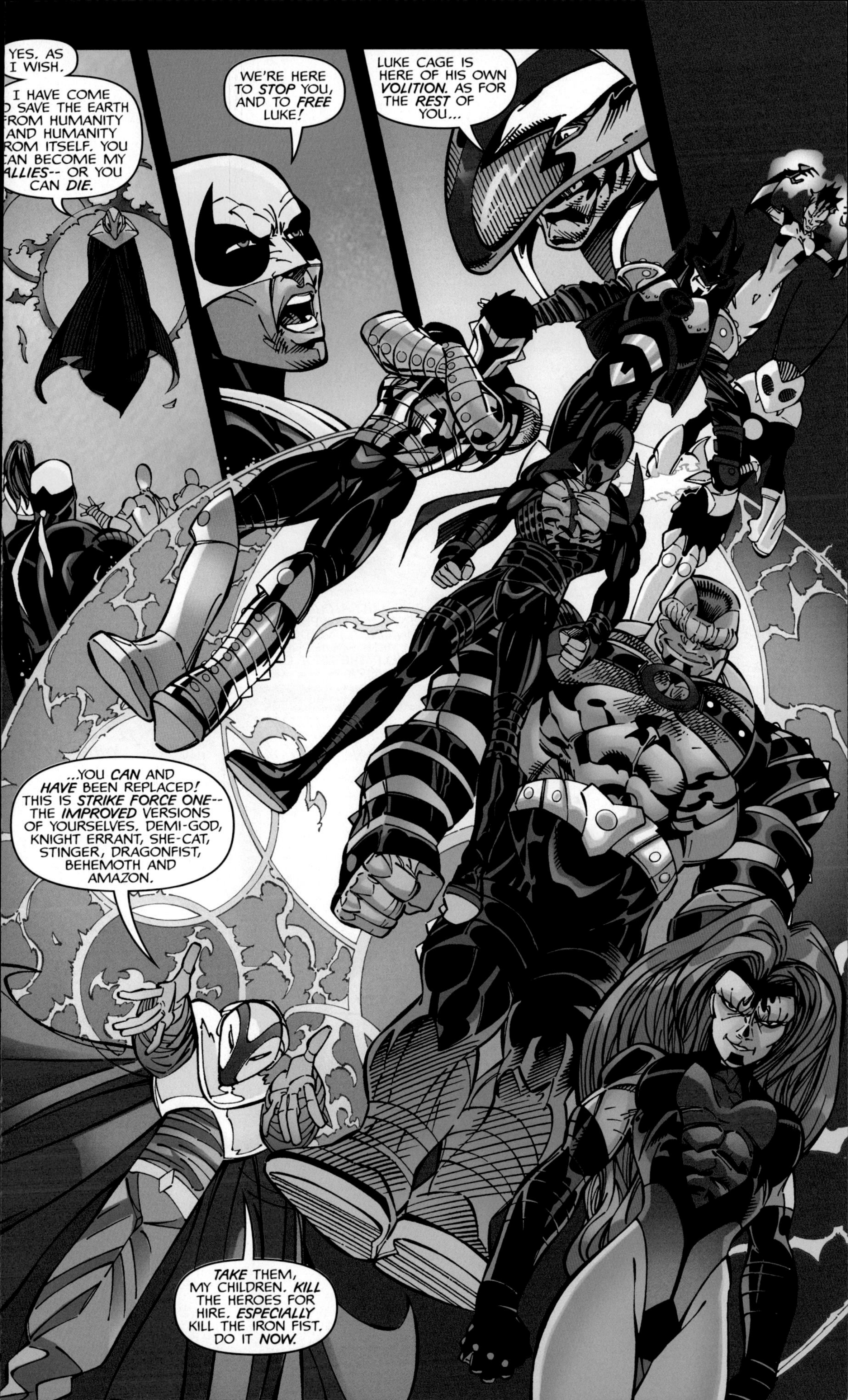
YES. AS I WISH.
I HAVE COME TO SAVE THE EARTH FROM HUMANITY AND HUMANITY FROM ITSELF. YOU CAN BECOME MY ALLIES-- OR YOU CAN DIE.
WE'RE HERE TO STOP YOU, AND TO FREE LUKE!
LUKE CAGE IS HERE OF HIS OWN VOLITION. AS FOR THE REST OF YOU...
...YOU CAN AND HAVE BEEN REPLACED! THIS IS STRIKE FORCE ONE-- THE IMPROVED VERSIONS OF YOURSELVES. DEMI-GOD, KNIGHT ERRANT, SHE-CAT, STINGER, DRAGONFIST, BEHEMOTH AND AMAZON.
TAKE THEM, MY CHILDREN. KILL THE HEROES FOR HIRE. ESPECIALLY KILL THE IRON FIST. DO IT NOW.

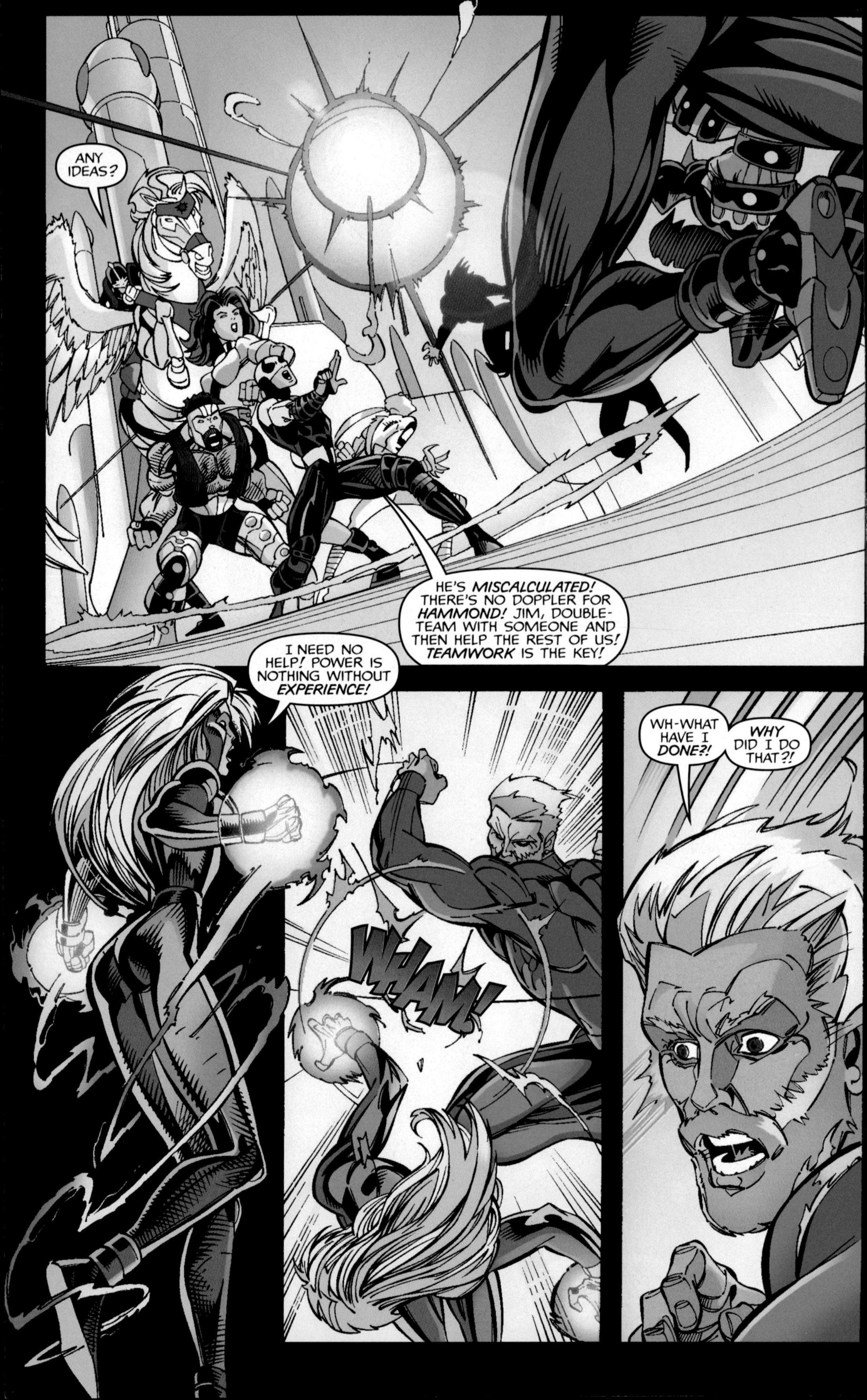
ANY IDEAS?
HE'S MISCALCULATED! THERE'S NO DOPPLER FOR HAMMOND! JIM, DOUBLE-TEAM WITH SOMEONE AND THEN HELP THE REST OF US! TEAMWORK IS THE KEY!
I NEED NO HELP! POWER IS NOTHING WITHOUT EXPERIENCE!
WHAM!
WH-WHAT HAVE I DONE?!
WHY DID I DO THAT?!

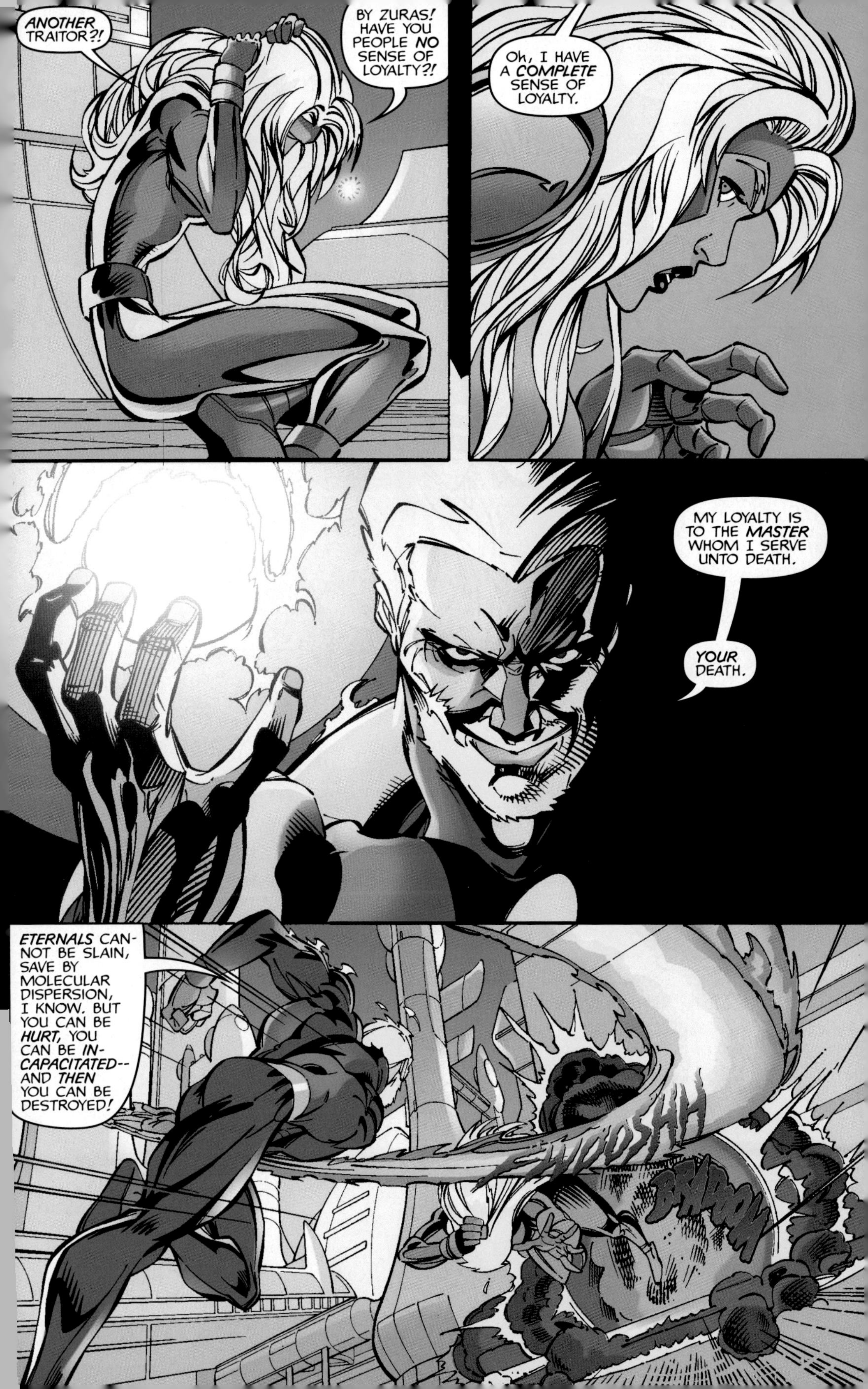
ANOTHER TRAITOR?!
BY ZURAS! HAVE YOU PEOPLE NO SENSE OF LOYALTY?!
Oh, I HAVE A COMPLETE SENSE OF LOYALTY.
MY LOYALTY IS TO THE MASTER WHOM I SERVE UNTO DEATH.
YOUR DEATH.
ETERNALS CAN-NOT BE SLAIN, SAVE BY MOLECULAR DISPERSION, I KNOW. BUT YOU CAN BE HURT, YOU CAN BE IN-CAPACITATED-- AND THEN YOU CAN BE DESTROYED!
FWOOSHH
BRADOOM

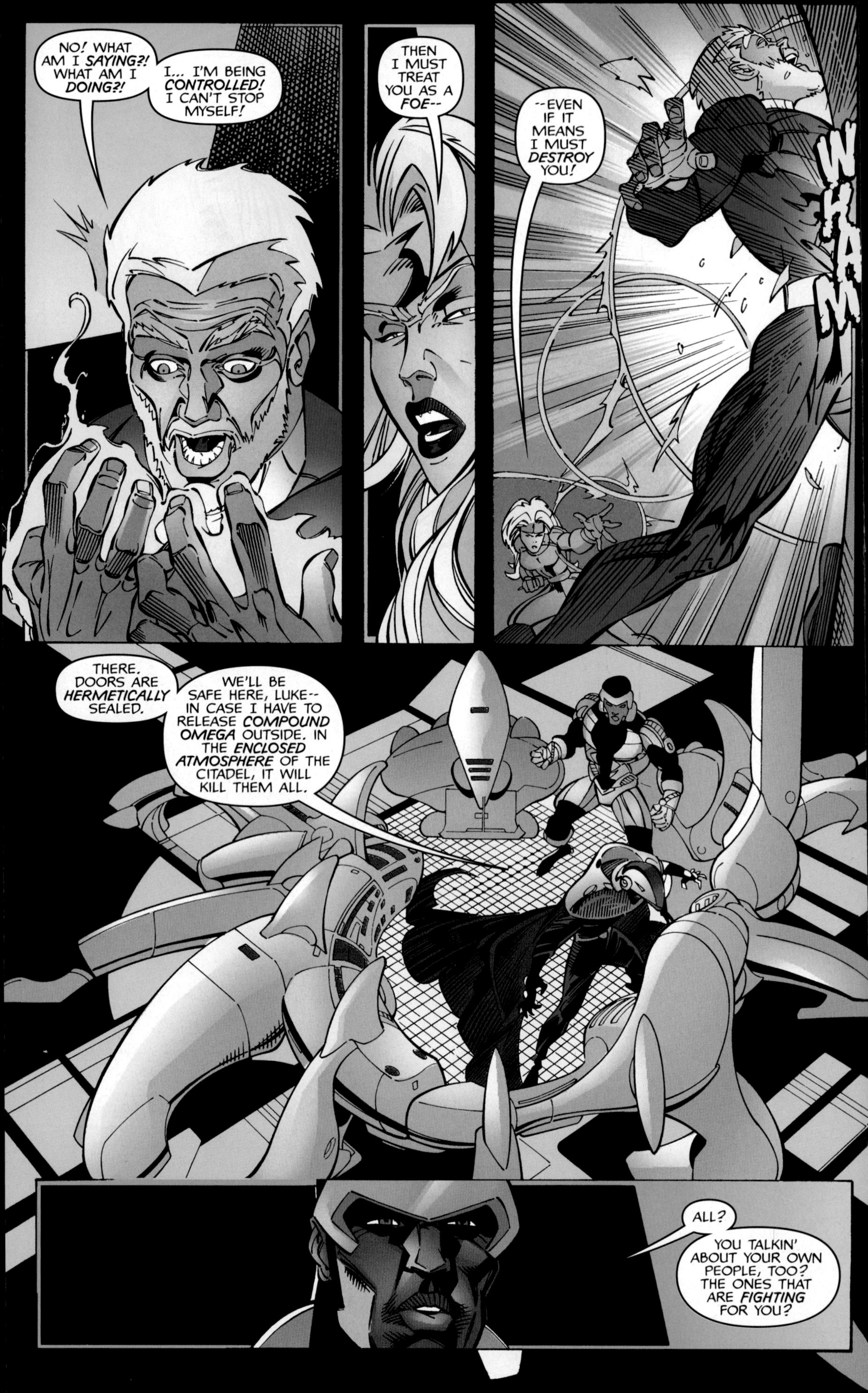
NO! WHAT AM I SAYING?! WHAT AM I DOING?!
I... I'M BEING CONTROLLED! I CAN'T STOP MYSELF!
THEN I MUST TREAT YOU AS A FOE--
--EVEN IF IT MEANS I MUST DESTROY YOU!
WHAM
THERE. DOORS ARE HERMETICALLY SEALED.
WE'LL BE SAFE HERE, LUKE-- IN CASE I HAVE TO RELEASE COMPOUND OMEGA OUTSIDE. IN THE ENCLOSED ATMOSPHERE OF THE CITADEL, IT WILL KILL THEM ALL.
ALL?
YOU TALKIN' ABOUT YOUR OWN PEOPLE, TOO? THE ONES THAT ARE FIGHTING FOR YOU?

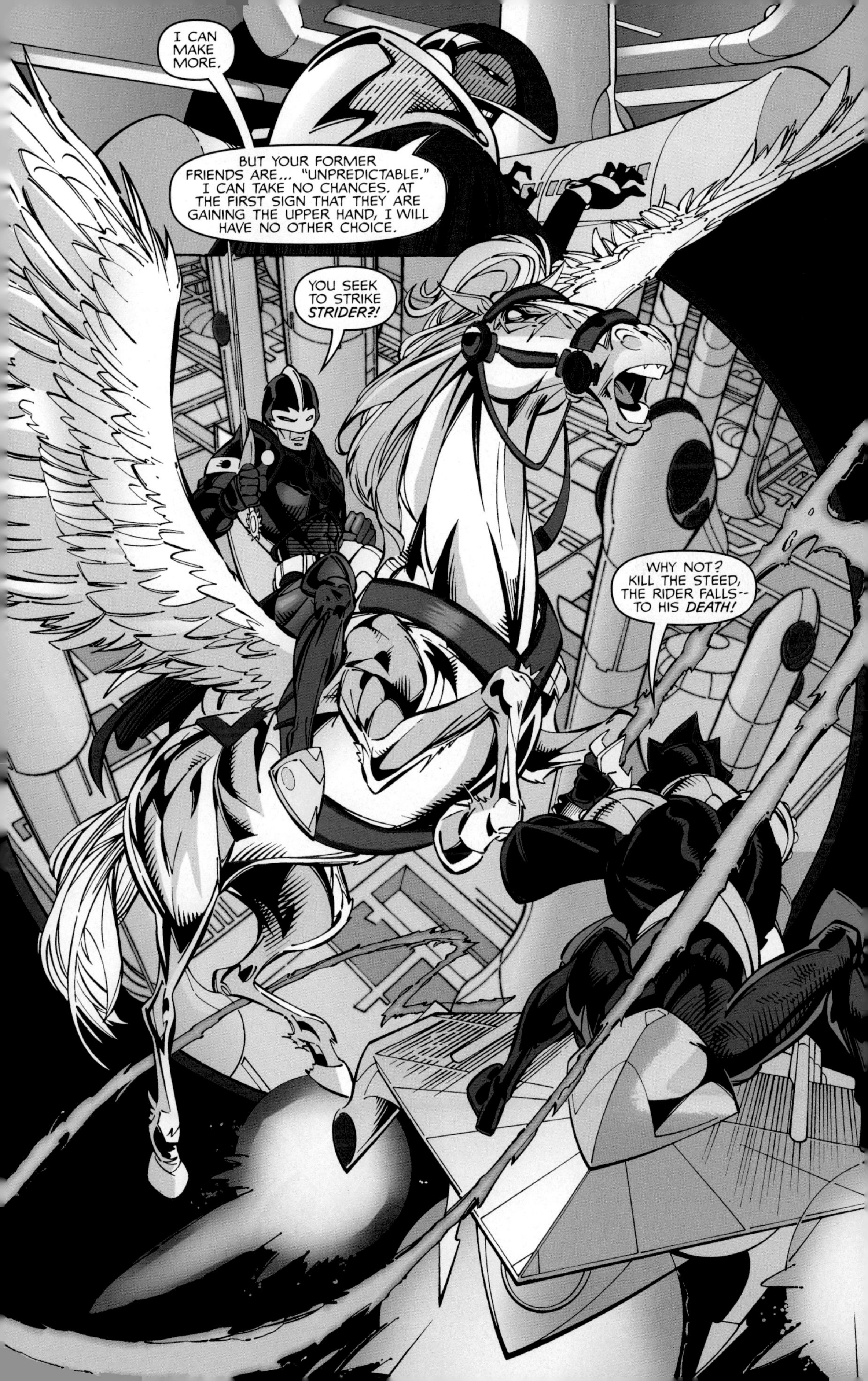
I CAN MAKE MORE.
BUT YOUR FORMER FRIENDS ARE... "UNPREDICTABLE." I CAN TAKE NO CHANCES. AT THE FIRST SIGN THAT THEY ARE GAINING THE UPPER HAND, I WILL HAVE NO OTHER CHOICE.
YOU SEEK TO STRIKE *STRIDER?!*
WHY NOT? KILL THE STEED, THE RIDER FALLS-- TO HIS *DEATH!*

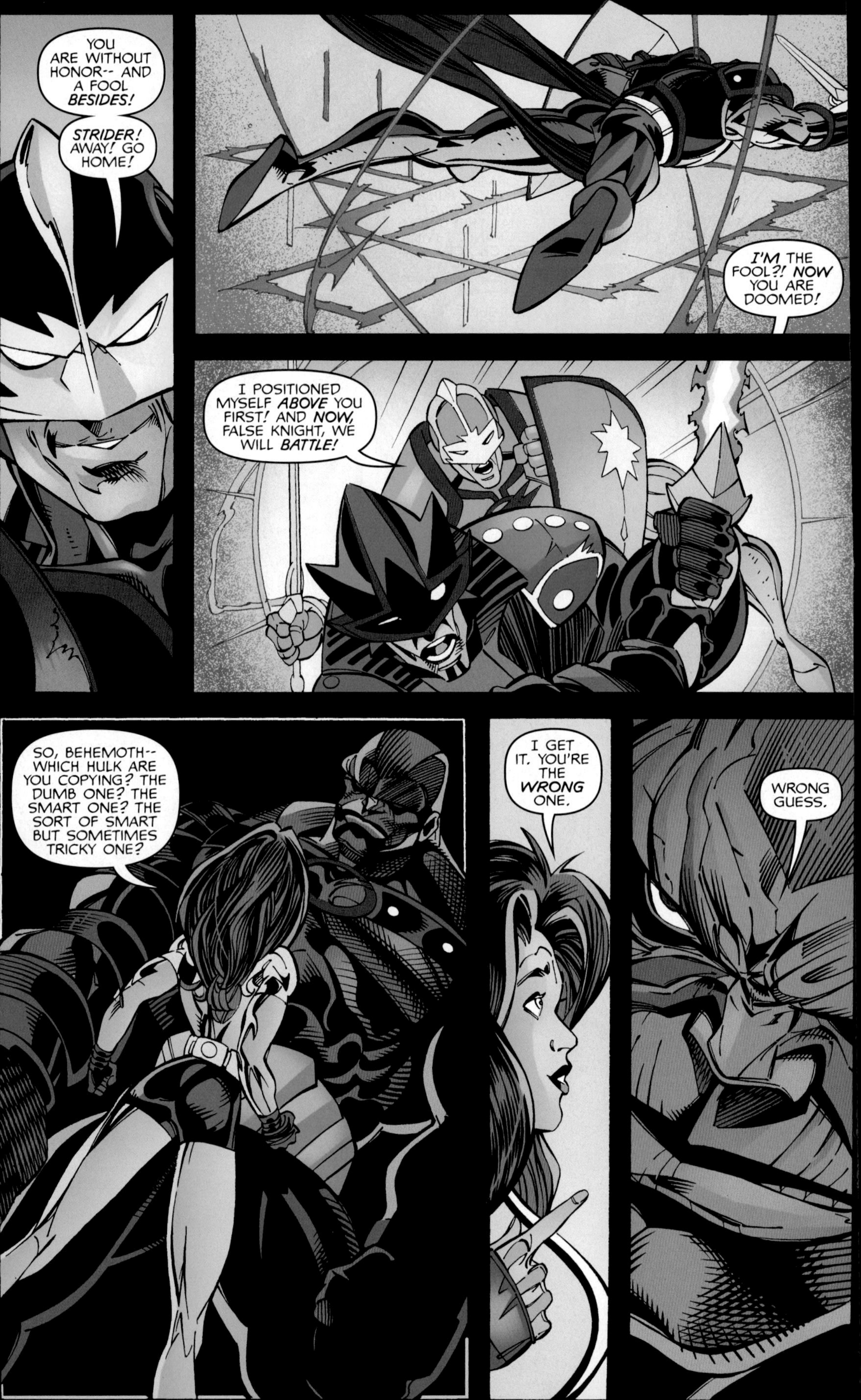
YOU ARE WITHOUT HONOR-- AND A FOOL BESIDES!
STRIDER! AWAY! GO HOME!
I'M THE FOOL?! NOW YOU ARE DOOMED!
I POSITIONED MYSELF ABOVE YOU FIRST! AND NOW, FALSE KNIGHT, WE WILL BATTLE!
SO, BEHEMOTH-- WHICH HULK ARE YOU COPYING? THE DUMB ONE? THE SMART ONE? THE SORT OF SMART BUT SOMETIMES TRICKY ONE?
I GET IT. YOU'RE THE WRONG ONE.
WRONG GUESS.

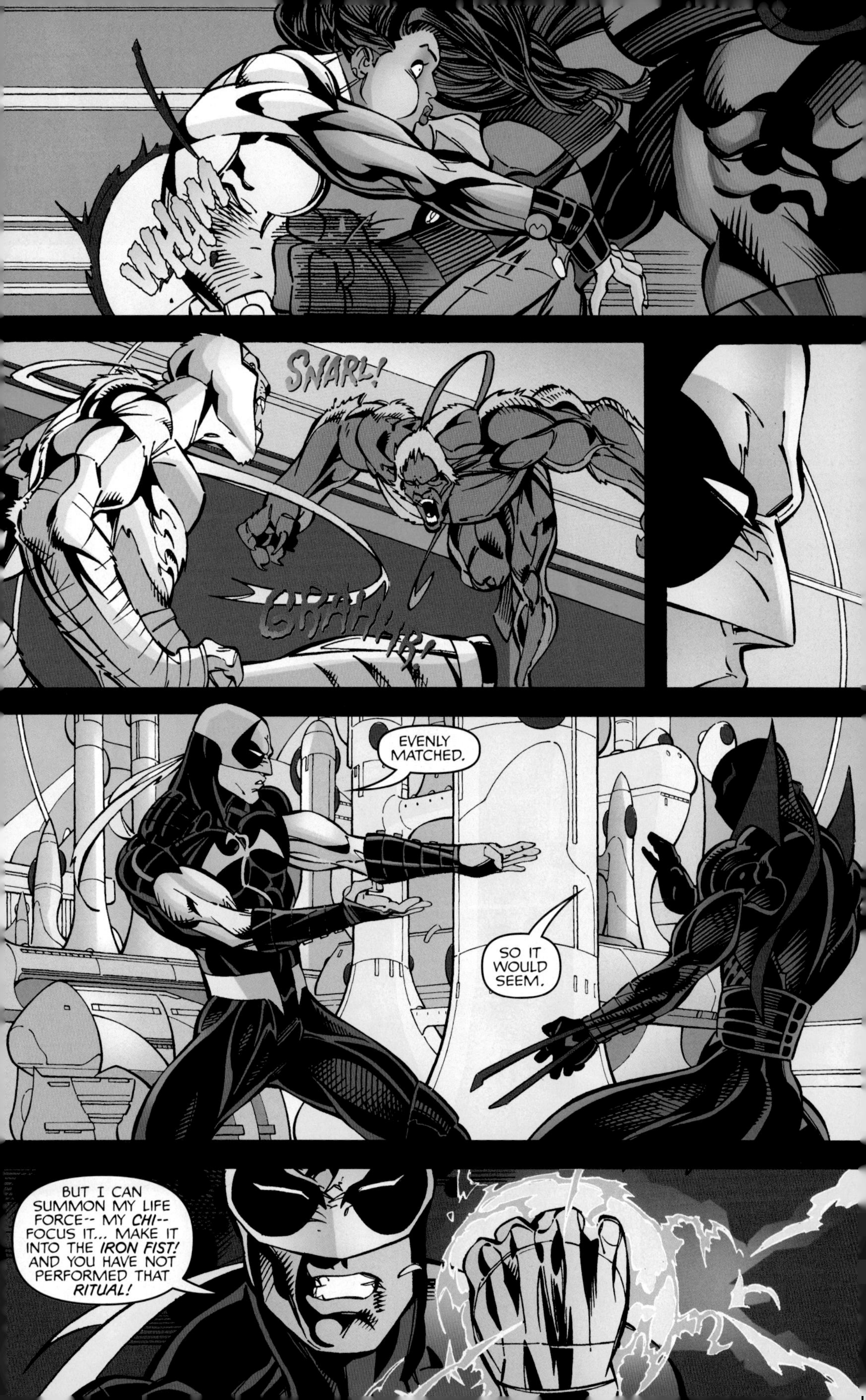
WHAM!
SNARL!
GRAHH-R!
EVENLY MATCHED.
SO IT WOULD SEEM.
BUT I CAN SUMMON MY LIFE FORCE-- MY CHI-- FOCUS IT... MAKE IT INTO THE IRON FIST! AND YOU HAVE NOT PERFORMED THAT RITUAL!

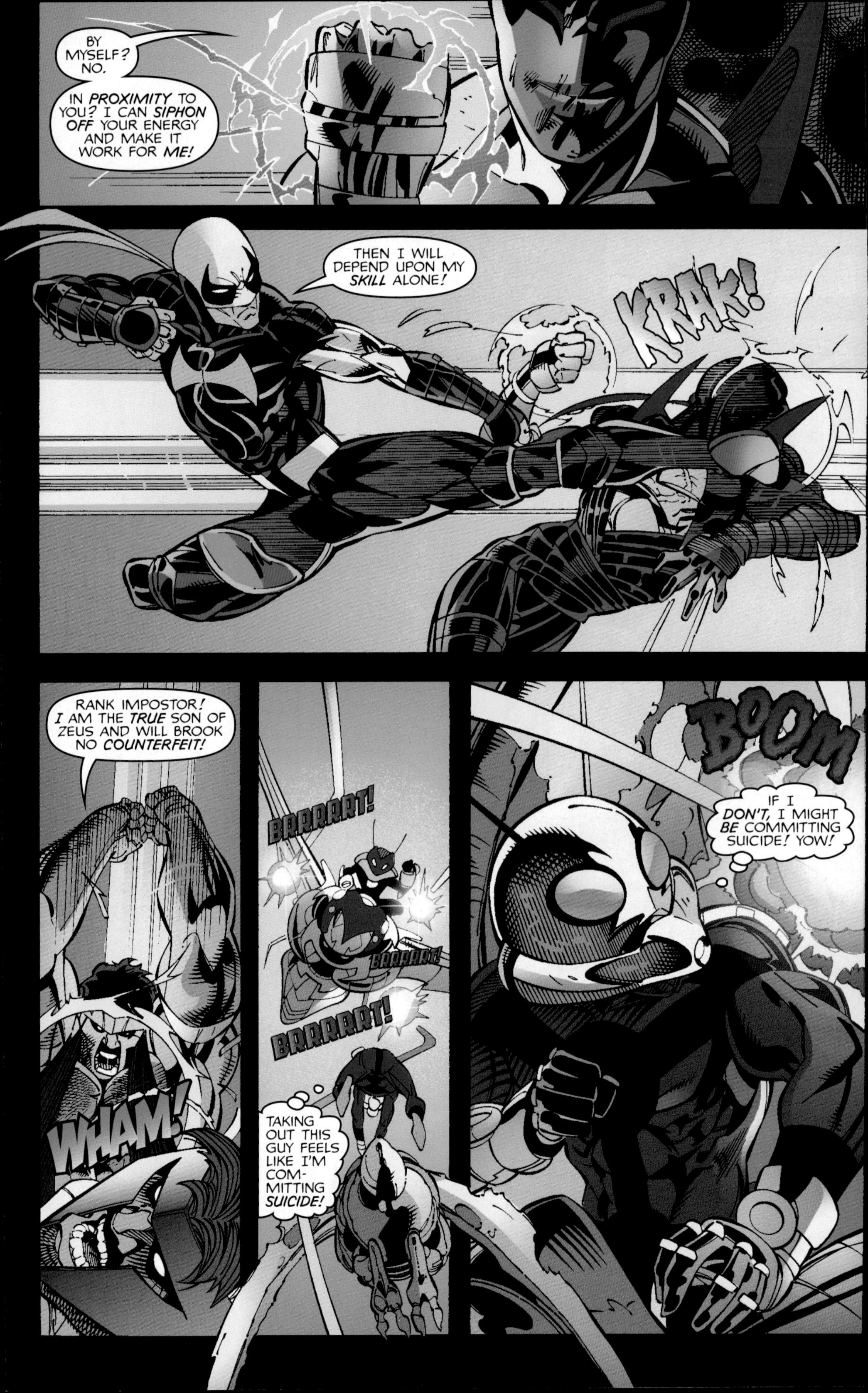
BY MYSELF? NO.
IN PROXIMITY TO YOU? I CAN SIPHON OFF YOUR ENERGY AND MAKE IT WORK FOR ME!
THEN I WILL DEPEND UPON MY SKILL ALONE!
KRAK!
RANK IMPOSTOR! I AM THE TRUE SON OF ZEUS AND WILL BROOK NO COUNTERFEIT!
WHAM!
BRRRRRT!
BRRRRRT!
BRRRRRT!
TAKING OUT THIS GUY FEELS LIKE I'M COM-MITTING SUICIDE!
BOOM
IF I DON'T, I MIGHT BE COMMITTING SUICIDE! YOW!

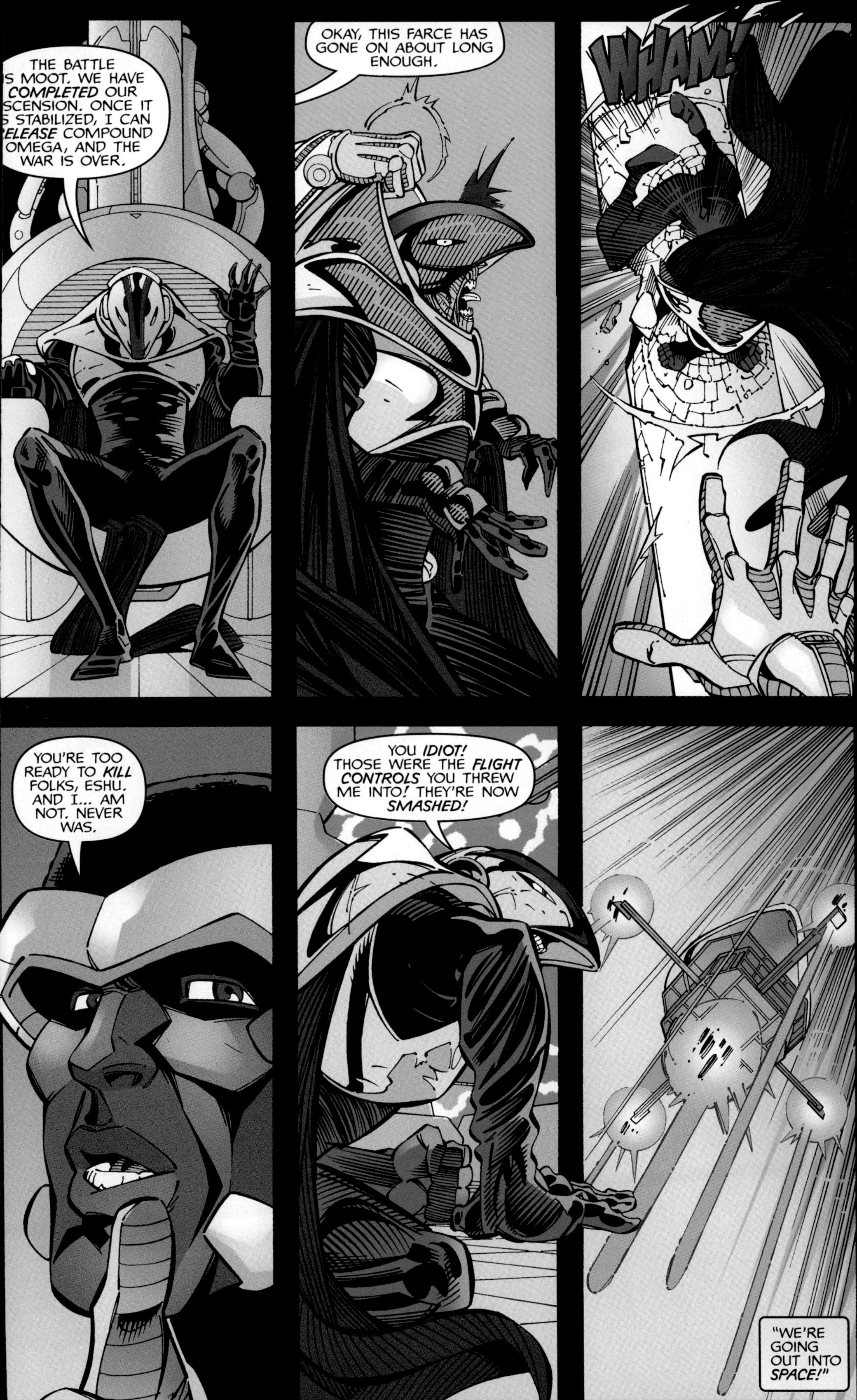
THE BATTLE S MOOT. WE HAVE COMPLETED OUR SCENSION. ONCE IT S STABILIZED, I CAN RELEASE COMPOUND OMEGA, AND THE WAR IS OVER.
OKAY, THIS FARCE HAS GONE ON ABOUT LONG ENOUGH.
WHAM!
YOU'RE TOO READY TO KILL FOLKS, ESHU. AND I... AM NOT. NEVER WAS.
YOU IDIOT! THOSE WERE THE FLIGHT CONTROLS YOU THREW ME INTO! THEY'RE NOW SMASHED!
"WE'RE GOING OUT INTO SPACE!"

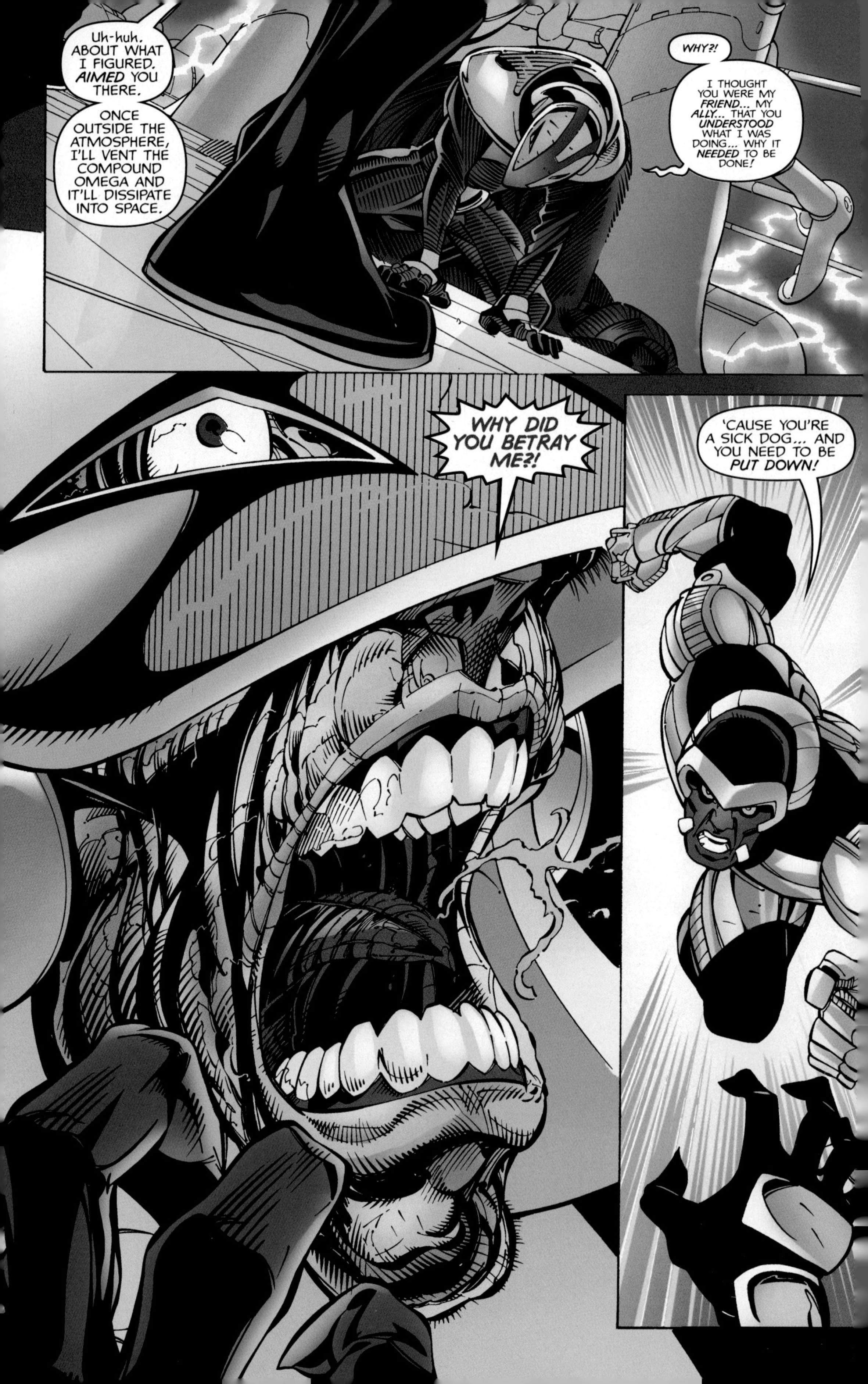
Uh-huh. ABOUT WHAT I FIGURED. AIMED YOU THERE.
ONCE OUTSIDE THE ATMOSPHERE, I'LL VENT THE COMPOUND OMEGA AND IT'LL DISSIPATE INTO SPACE.
WHY?!
I THOUGHT YOU WERE MY FRIEND... MY ALLY... THAT YOU UNDERSTOOD WHAT I WAS DOING... WHY IT NEEDED TO BE DONE!
WHY DID YOU BETRAY ME?!
'CAUSE YOU'RE A SICK DOG... AND YOU NEED TO BE PUT DOWN!

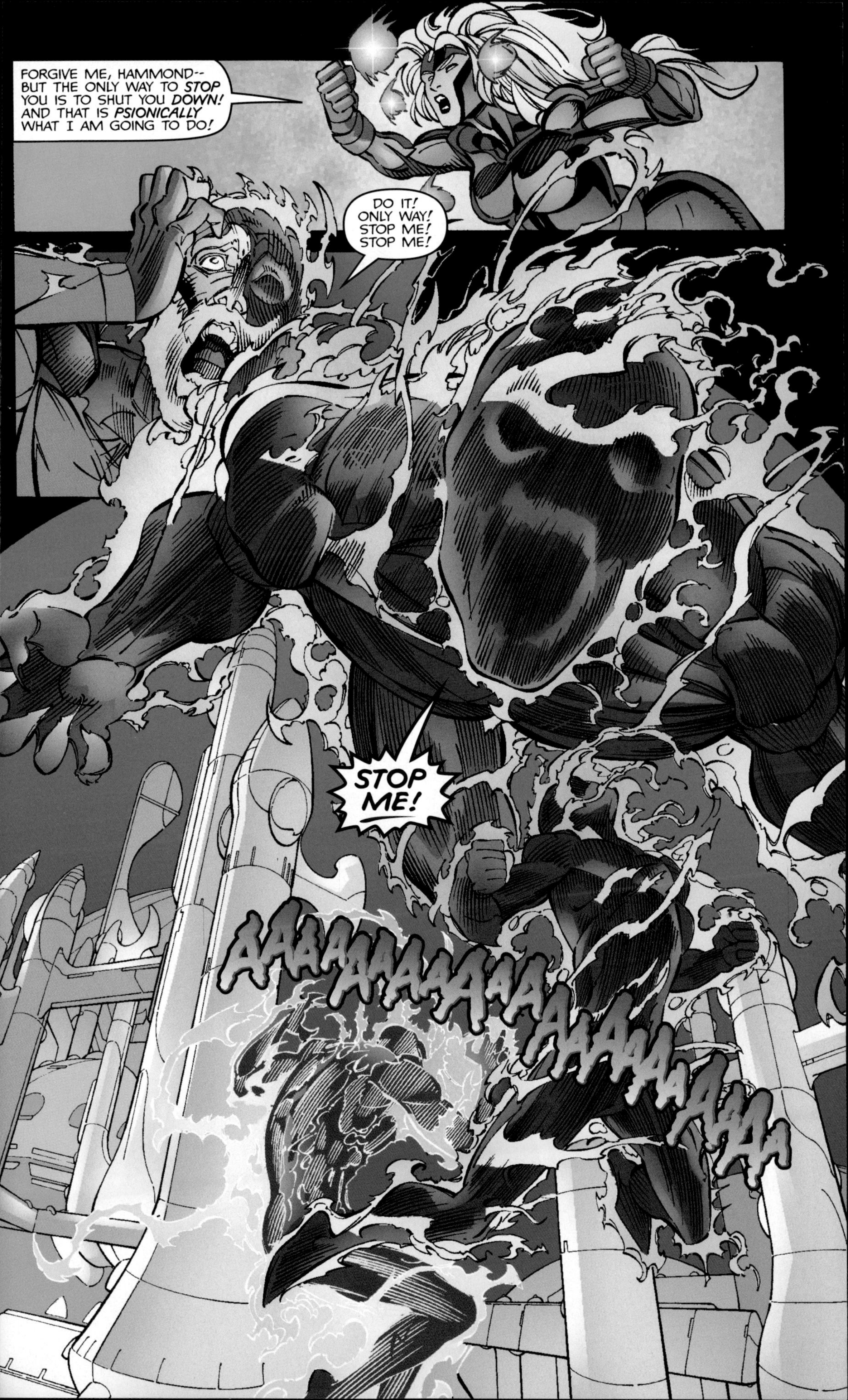
FORGIVE ME, HAMMOND-- BUT THE ONLY WAY TO STOP YOU IS TO SHUT YOU DOWN! AND THAT IS PSIONICALLY WHAT I AM GOING TO DO!
DO IT! ONLY WAY! STOP ME! STOP ME!
STOP ME!
AAAAAAAAAAAAAAAAAAAAAAAAAA

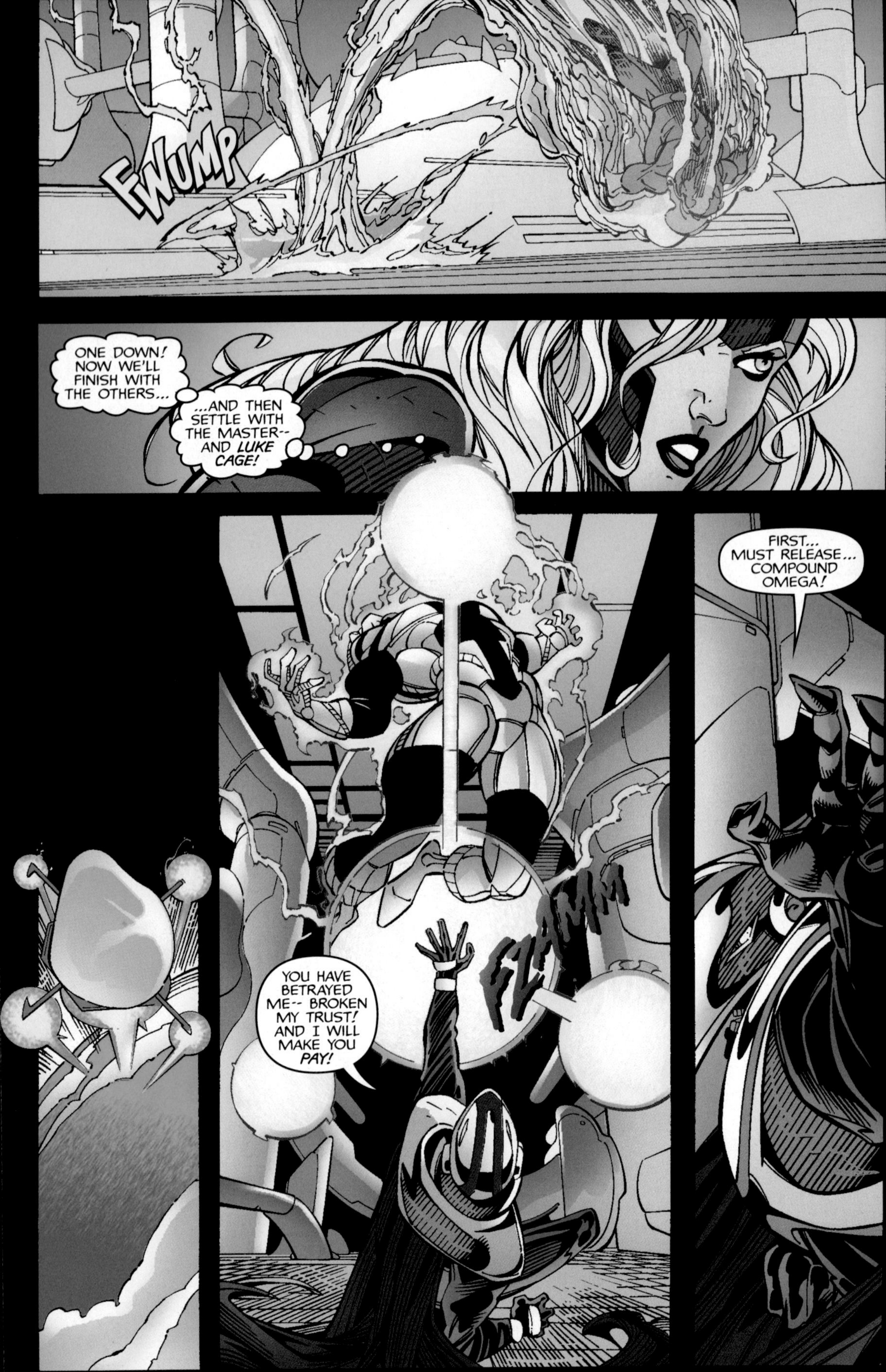
FWUMP
ONE DOWN! NOW WE'LL FINISH WITH THE OTHERS...
...AND THEN SETTLE WITH THE MASTER-- AND LUKE CAGE!
FIRST... MUST RELEASE... COMPOUND OMEGA!
YOU HAVE BETRAYED ME-- BROKEN MY TRUST! AND I WILL MAKE YOU PAY!
FZAMM

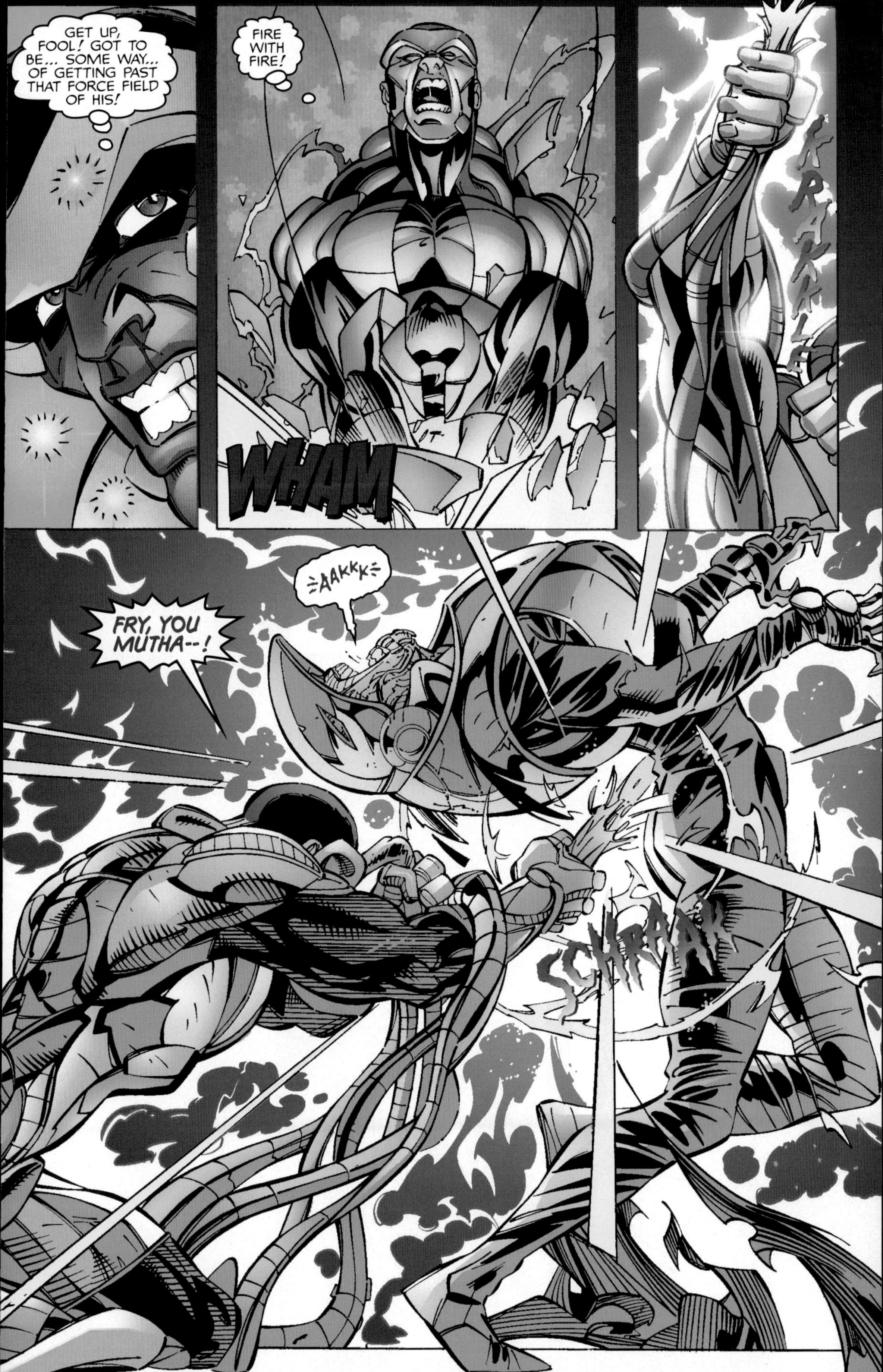
GET UP, FOOL! GOT TO BE... SOME WAY... OF GETTING PAST THAT FORCE FIELD OF HIS!
FIRE WITH FIRE!
WHAM
KRAKKLE
AAKKK
FRY, YOU MUTHA--!
SCHRAAK

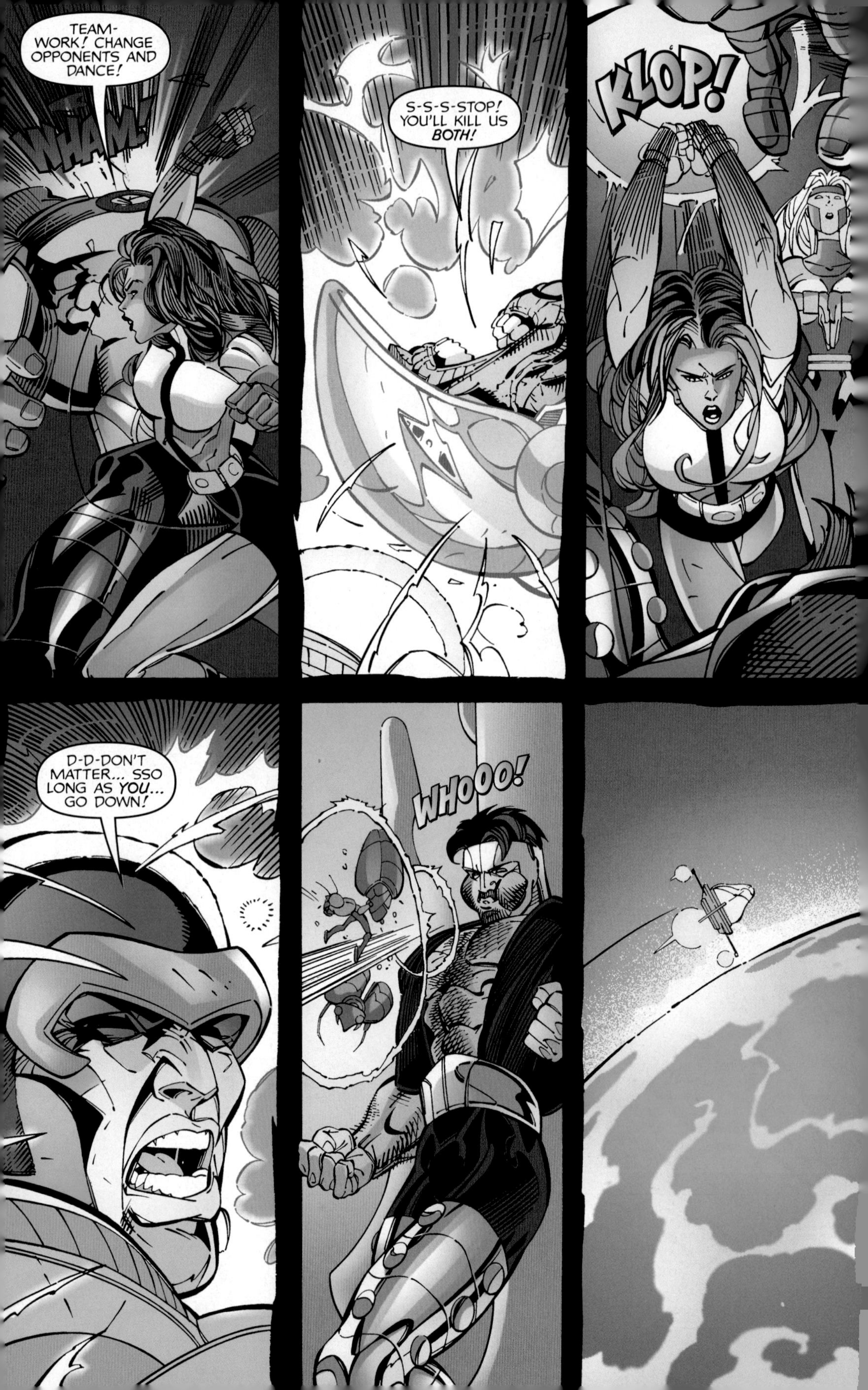
TEAM-WORK! CHANGE OPPONENTS AND DANCE!
WHAM!
S-S-S-STOP! YOU'LL KILL US BOTH!
KLOP!
D-D-DON'T MATTER... SSO LONG AS YOU... GO DOWN!
WHOOO!

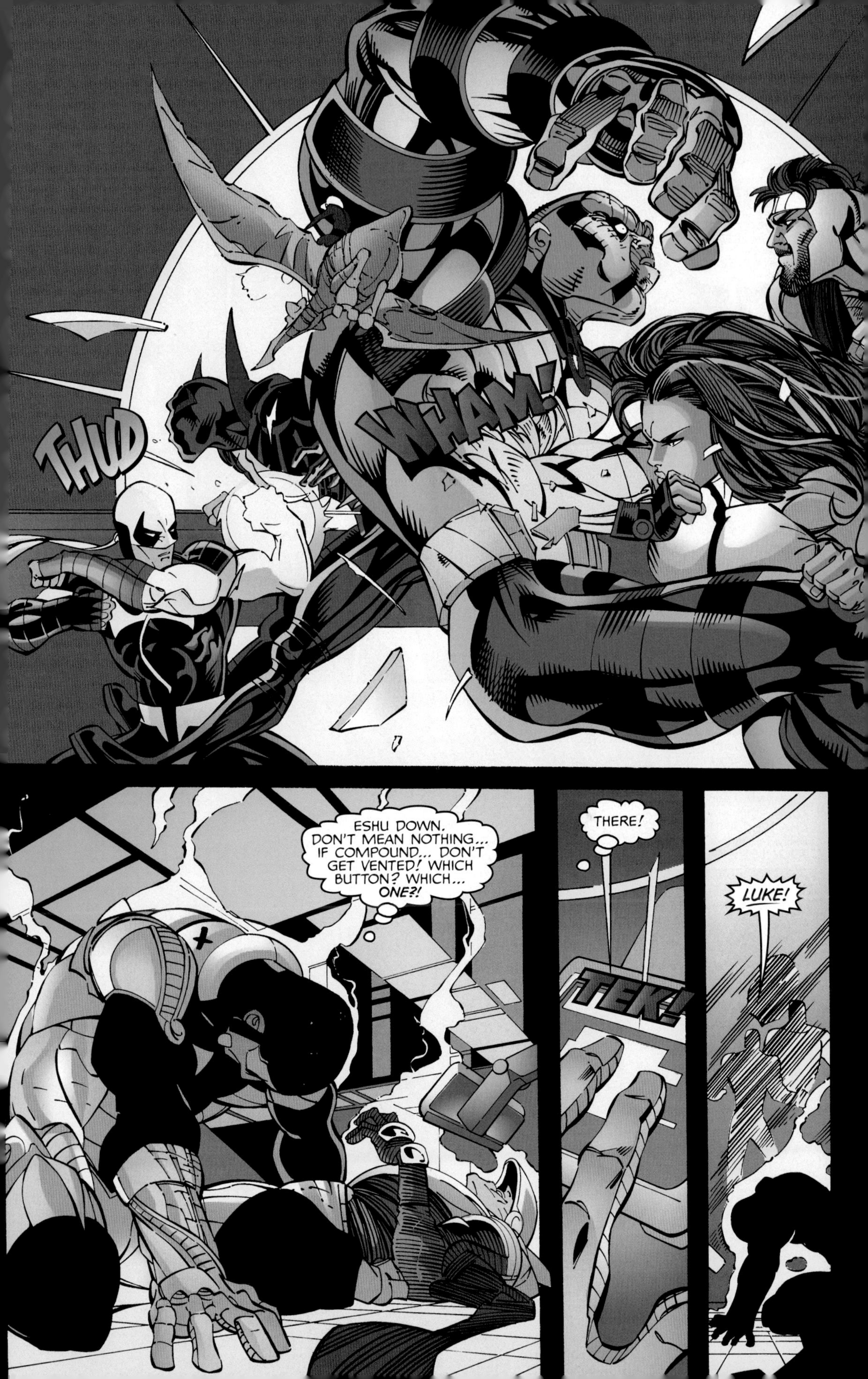
THUD
WHAM!
ESHU DOWN. DON'T MEAN NOTHING... IF COMPOUND... DON'T GET VENTED! WHICH BUTTON? WHICH... ONE?!
THERE!
TEK!
LUKE!

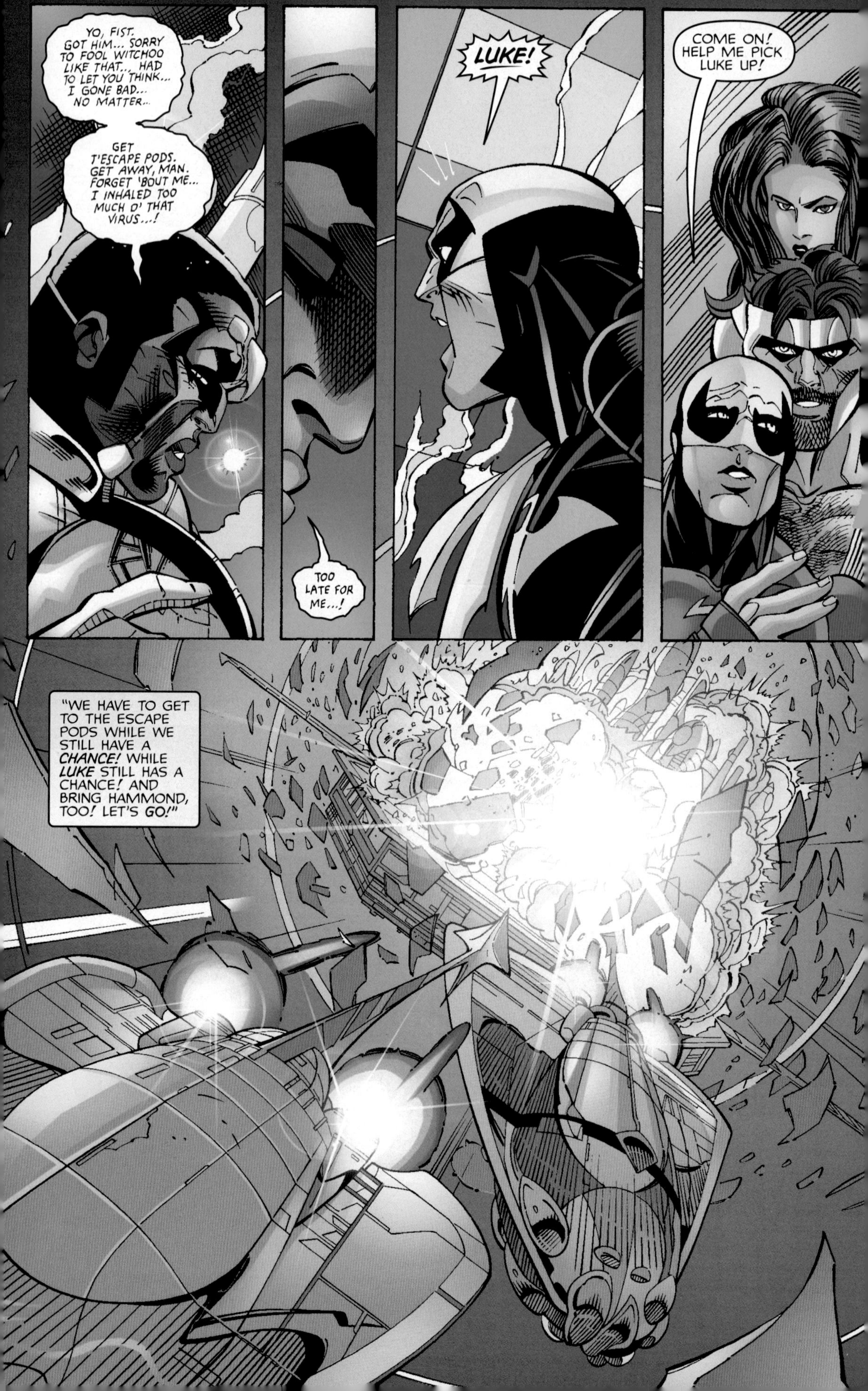
YO, FIST. GOT HIM... SORRY TO FOOL WITCHOO LIKE THAT... HAD TO LET YOU THINK... I GONE BAD... NO MATTER...
GET T'ESCAPE PODS. GET AWAY, MAN. FORGET 'BOUT ME... I INHALED TOO MUCH O' THAT VIRUS...!
TOO LATE FOR ME...!
LUKE!
COME ON! HELP ME PICK LUKE UP!
"WE HAVE TO GET TO THE ESCAPE PODS WHILE WE STILL HAVE A CHANCE! WHILE LUKE STILL HAS A CHANCE! AND BRING HAMMOND, TOO! LET'S GO!"

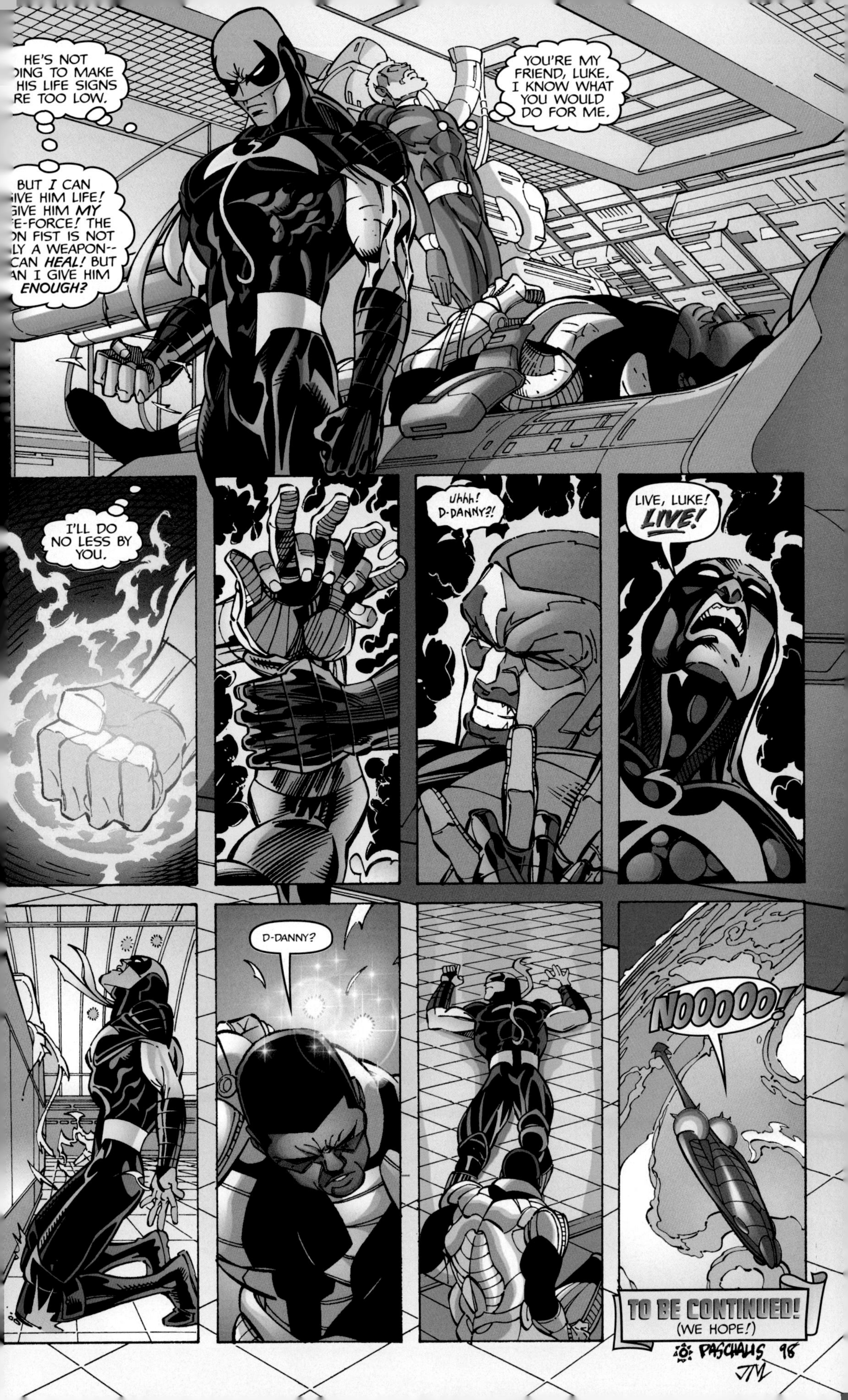
HE'S NOT OING TO MAKE HIS LIFE SIGNS RE TOO LOW.
BUT I CAN IVE HIM LIFE! GIVE HIM MY FE-FORCE! THE ON FIST IS NOT LY A WEAPON-- CAN HEAL! BUT AN I GIVE HIM ENOUGH?
YOU'RE MY FRIEND, LUKE. I KNOW WHAT YOU WOULD DO FOR ME.
I'LL DO NO LESS BY YOU.
Uhhh! D-DANNY?!
LIVE, LUKE! LIVE!
D-DANNY?
NOOOOO!
TO BE CONTINUED!
(WE HOPE!)
PASCHALIS 98

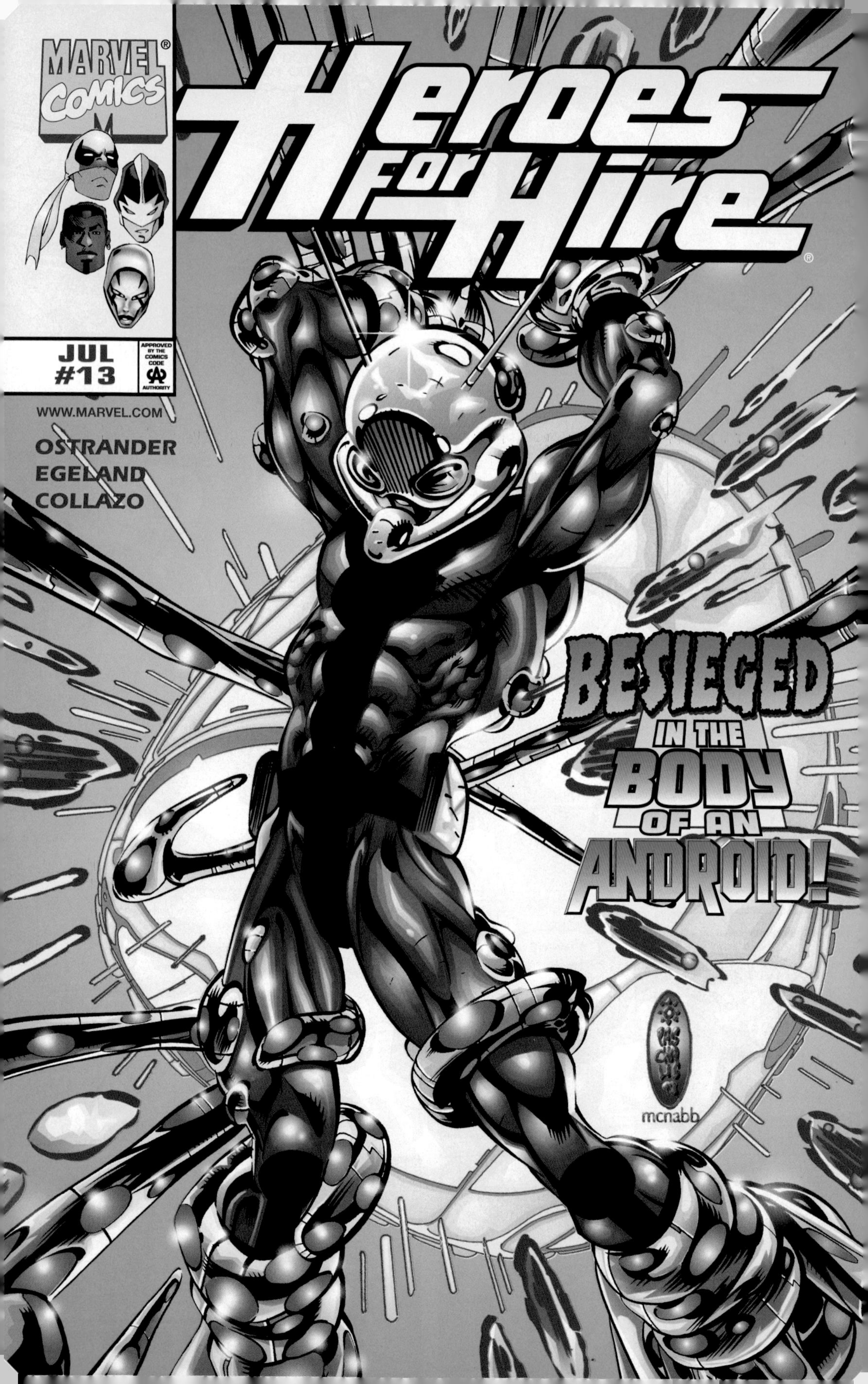
MARVEL COMICS
Heroes for Hire
JUL #13
APPROVED BY THE COMICS CODE AUTHORITY
WWW.MARVEL.COM
OSTRANDER
EGELAND
COLLAZO
BESIEGED IN THE BODY OF AN ANDROID!
mcnabb

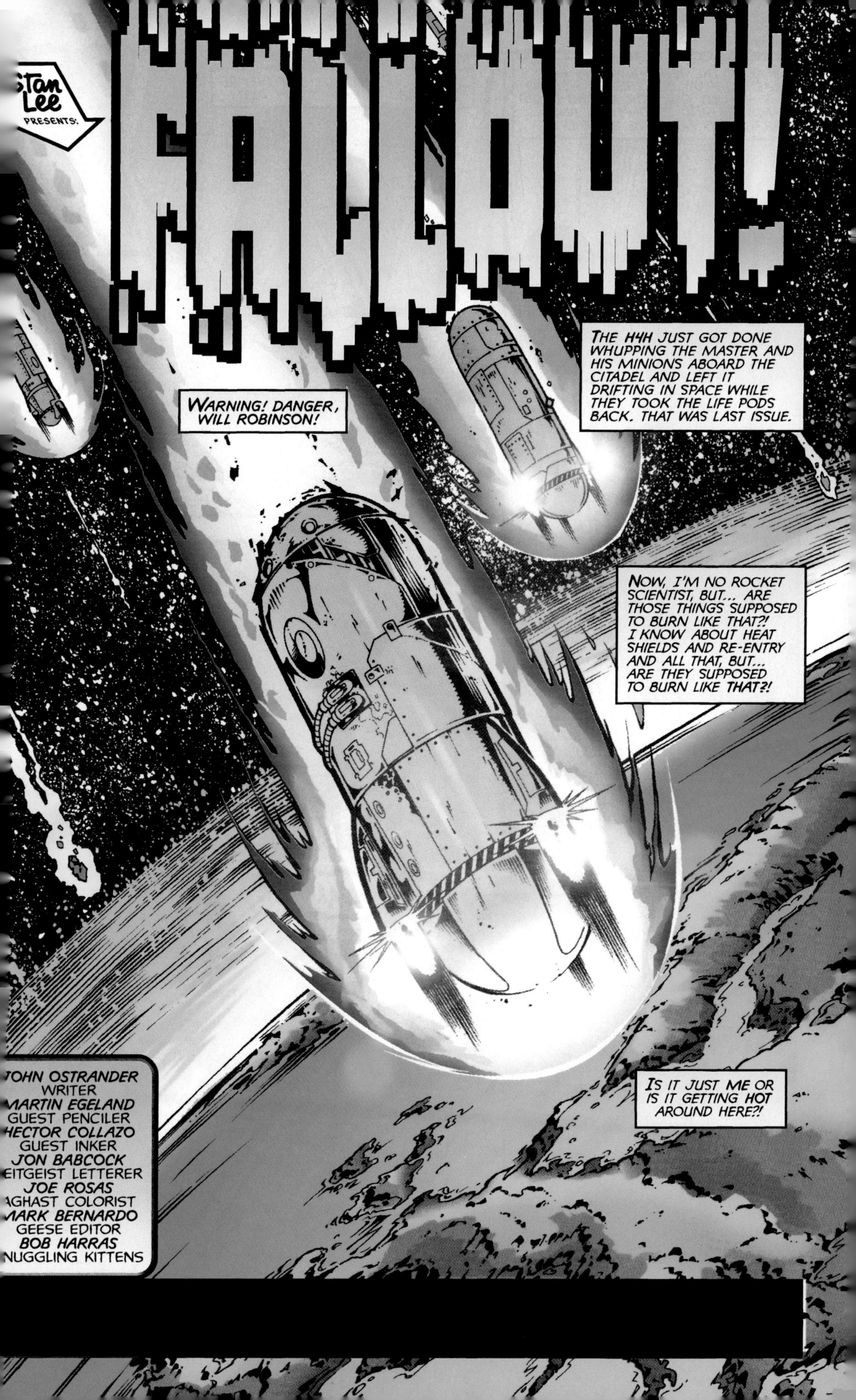

STAN LEE PRESENTS:
FALLOUT!
WARNING! DANGER, WILL ROBINSON!
THE H4H JUST GOT DONE WHUPPING THE MASTER AND HIS MINIONS ABOARD THE CITADEL AND LEFT IT DRIFTING IN SPACE WHILE THEY TOOK THE LIFE PODS BACK. THAT WAS LAST ISSUE.
NOW, I'M NO ROCKET SCIENTIST, BUT... ARE THOSE THINGS SUPPOSED TO BURN LIKE THAT?! I KNOW ABOUT HEAT SHIELDS AND RE-ENTRY AND ALL THAT, BUT... ARE THEY SUPPOSED TO BURN LIKE THAT?!
IS IT JUST ME OR IS IT GETTING HOT AROUND HERE?!
JOHN OSTRANDER WRITER
MARTIN EGELAND GUEST PENCILER
HECTOR COLLAZO GUEST INKER
JON BABCOCK EITGEIST LETTERER
JOE ROSAS AGHAST COLORIST
MARK BERNARDO GEESE EDITOR
BOB HARRAS NUGGLING KITTENS
[redacted]

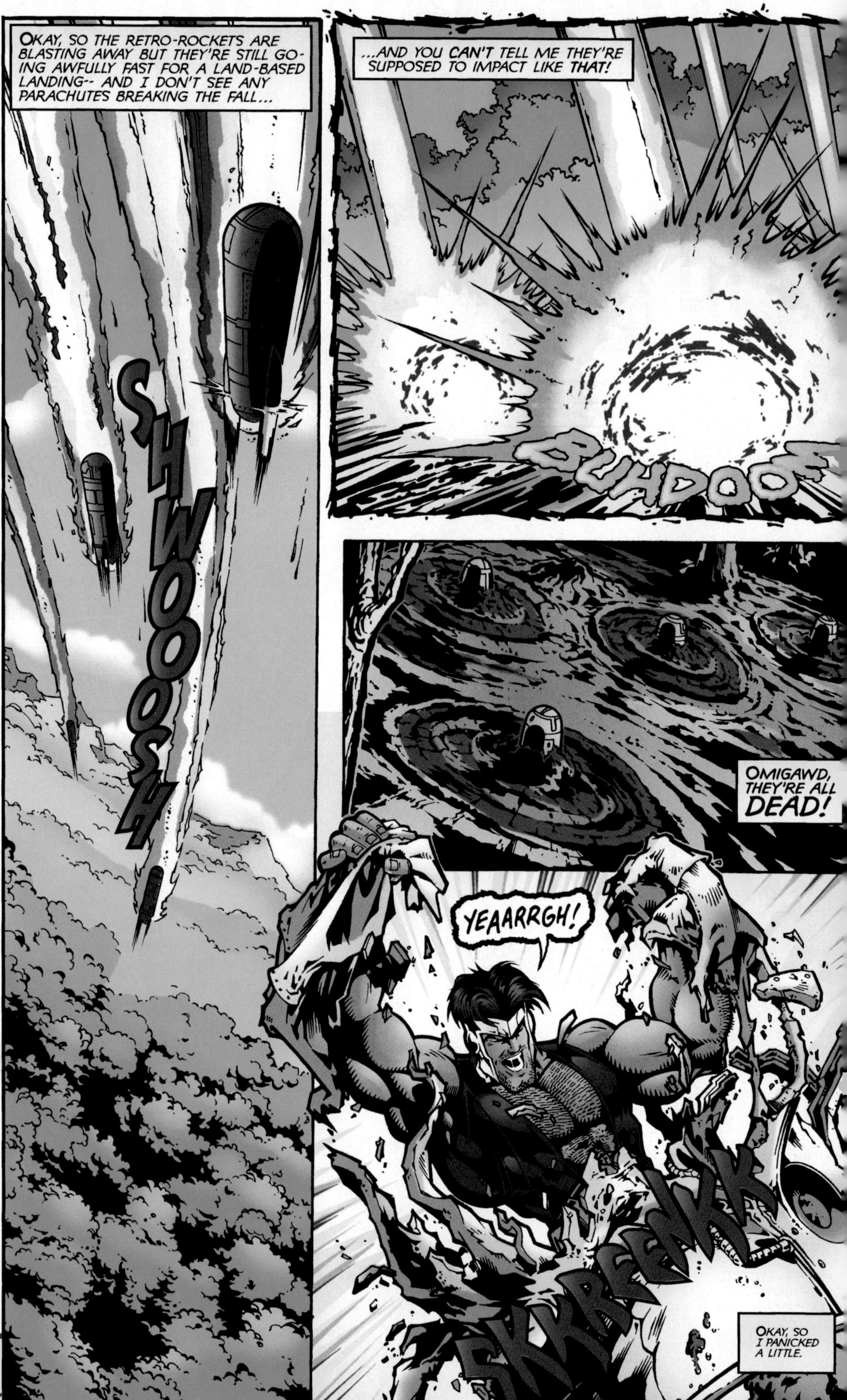
OKAY, SO THE RETRO-ROCKETS ARE BLASTING AWAY BUT THEY'RE STILL GOING AWFULLY FAST FOR A LAND-BASED LANDING-- AND I DON'T SEE ANY PARACHUTES BREAKING THE FALL...
SHWOOOOSH
...AND YOU CAN'T TELL ME THEY'RE SUPPOSED TO IMPACT LIKE THAT!
BUHDOOF
OMIGAWD, THEY'RE ALL DEAD!
YEAARRGH!
SKKREEKKK
OKAY, SO I PANICKED A LITTLE.

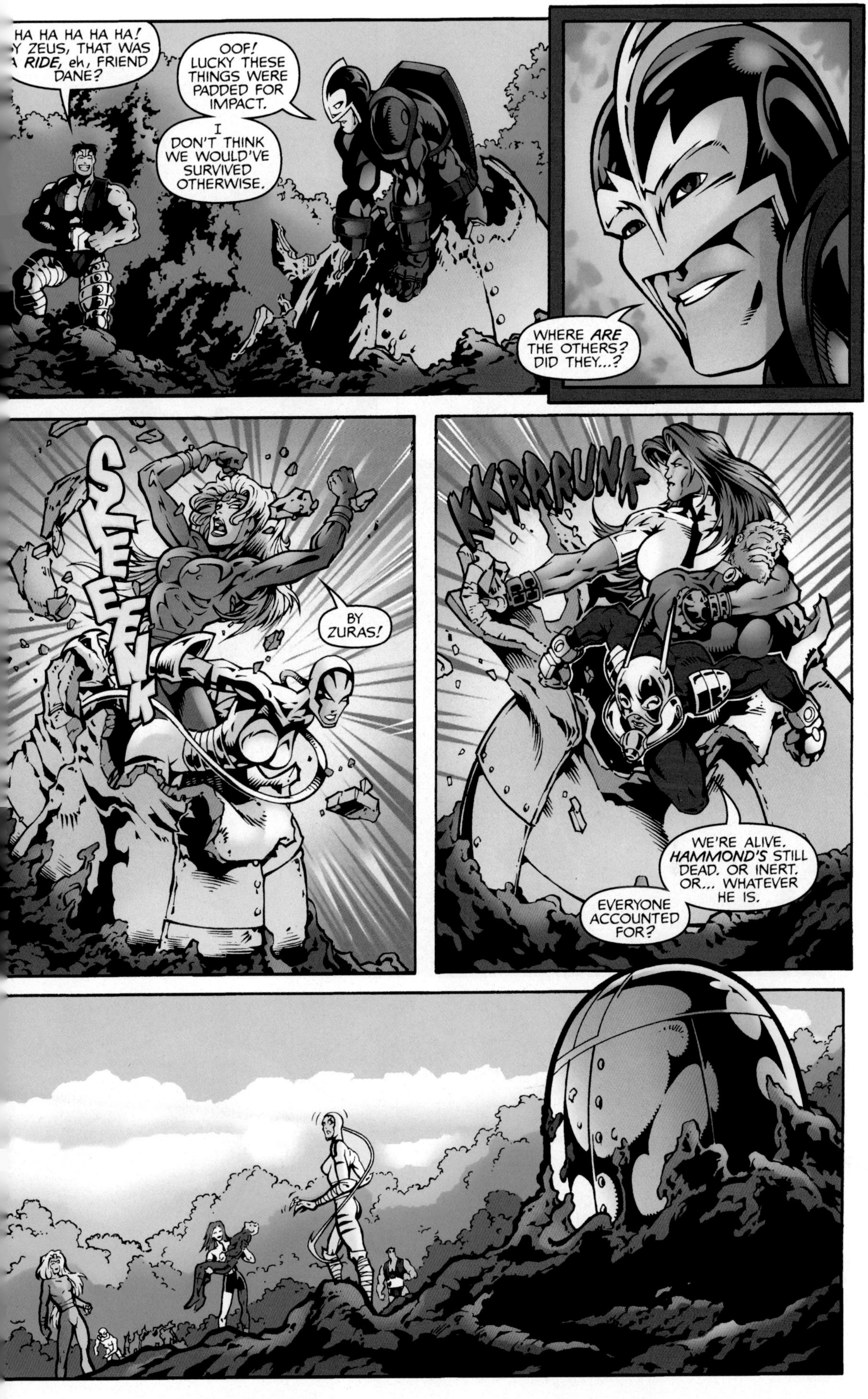
HA HA HA HA HA! BY ZEUS, THAT WAS A RIDE, eh, FRIEND DANE?
OOF! LUCKY THESE THINGS WERE PADDED FOR IMPACT.
I DON'T THINK WE WOULD'VE SURVIVED OTHERWISE.
WHERE ARE THE OTHERS? DID THEY...?
SKEEENK
BY ZURAS!
KKRRRUNK
EVERYONE ACCOUNTED FOR?
WE'RE ALIVE. HAMMOND'S STILL DEAD. OR INERT. OR... WHATEVER HE IS.

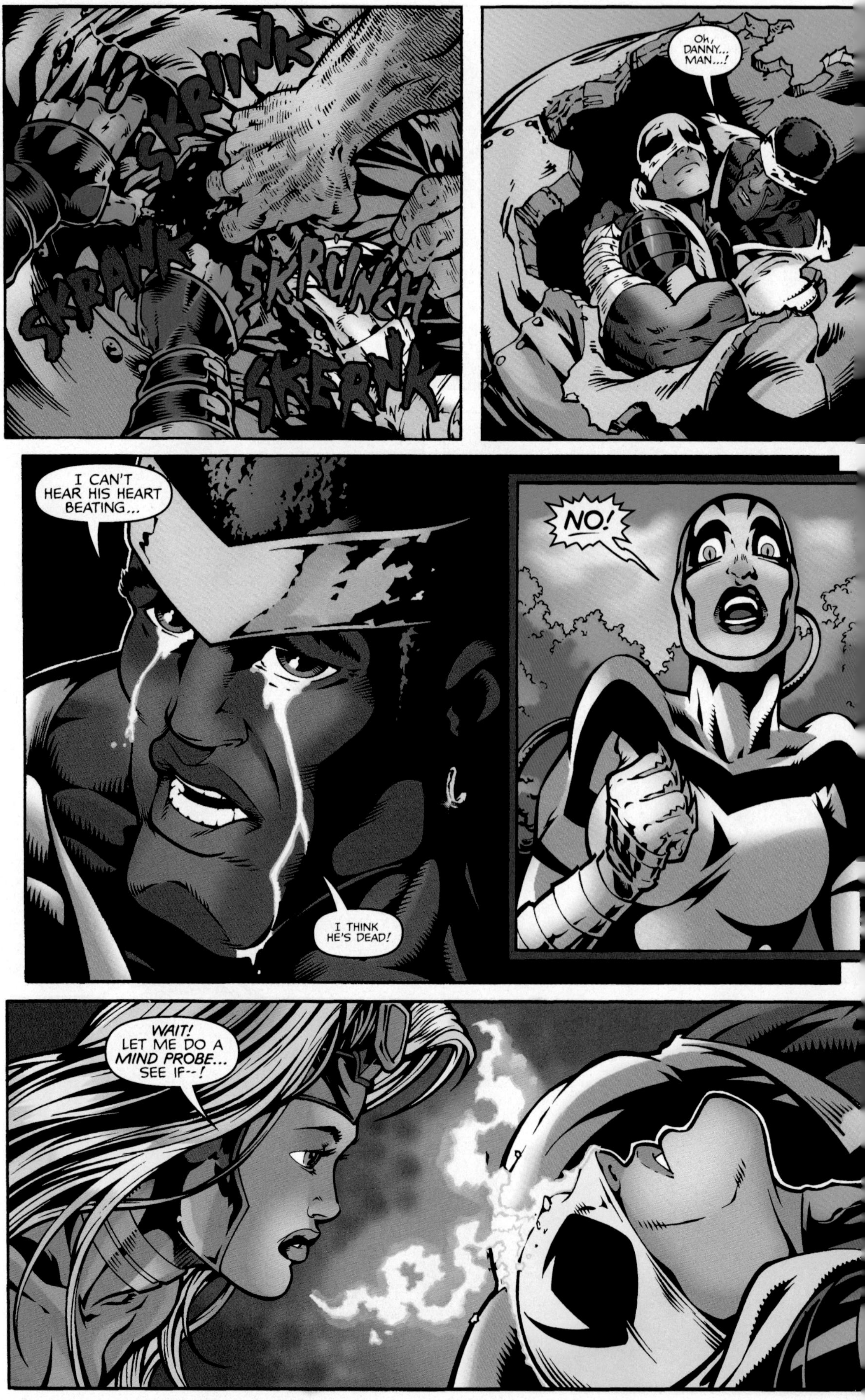
SKRIINK
SKRANK
SKRUNCH
SKERNK
Oh, DANNY... MAN...!
I CAN'T HEAR HIS HEART BEATING...
I THINK HE'S DEAD!
NO!
WAIT! LET ME DO A MIND PROBE... SEE IF--!

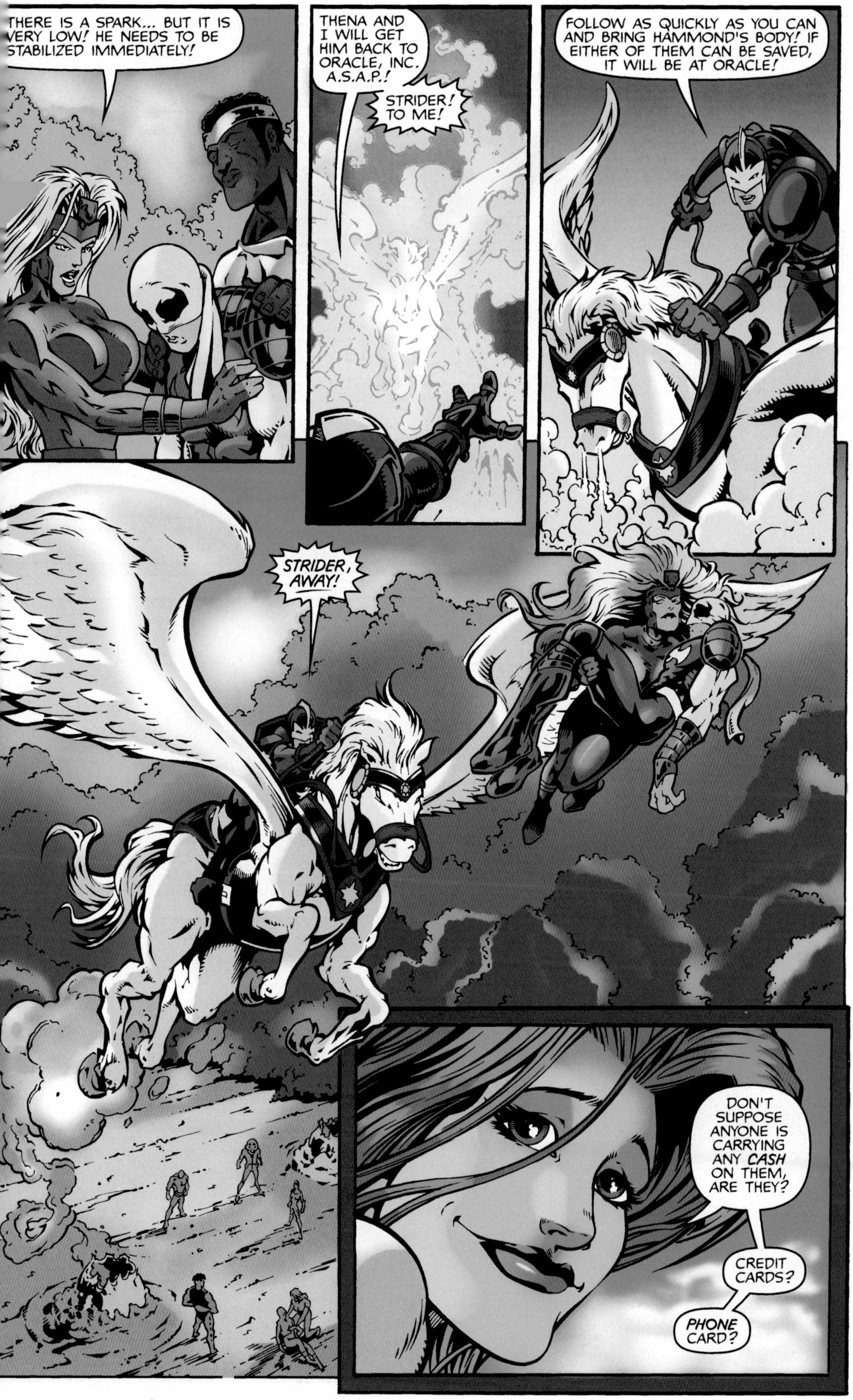
THERE IS A SPARK... BUT IT IS VERY LOW! HE NEEDS TO BE STABILIZED IMMEDIATELY!
THENA AND I WILL GET HIM BACK TO ORACLE, INC. A.S.A.P.!
STRIDER! TO ME!
FOLLOW AS QUICKLY AS YOU CAN AND BRING HAMMOND'S BODY! IF EITHER OF THEM CAN BE SAVED, IT WILL BE AT ORACLE!
STRIDER, AWAY!
DON'T SUPPOSE ANYONE IS CARRYING ANY CASH ON THEM, ARE THEY?
CREDIT CARDS?
PHONE CARD?

ORACLE, INC., HOME AND PARENT ORGANIZATION TO THE HEROES FOR HIRE, A SHORT TIME LATER...

(AND LET'S GET SOMETHING STRAIGHT: ORACLE IS *NOT* THE LADY IN THE WHEELCHAIR WHO TALKS TO A CERTAIN POINTY-EARED DUDE. THAT'S A *DIFFERENT* UNIVERSE.)

HOW IS HE, NURSE-- EXCUSE ME, *DOCTOR* FOSTER?*

WELL, THE DOCTORS HAVE Mr. RAND STABILIZED. HIS *EKG* IS ALL RIGHT BUT HIS *EEG* IS FLAT-LINE.

*THAT'S RIGHT! JANE'S A DOCTOR NOW, AS OF *THOR* #1! --Mark The Medic

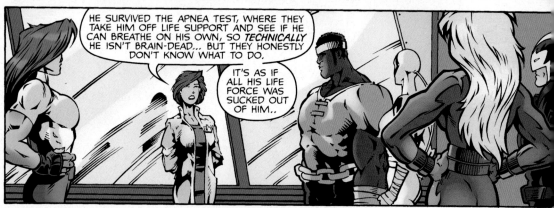

HE SURVIVED THE APNEA TEST, WHERE THEY TAKE HIM OFF LIFE SUPPORT AND SEE IF HE CAN BREATHE ON HIS OWN, SO *TECHNICALLY* HE ISN'T BRAIN-DEAD... BUT THEY HONESTLY DON'T KNOW WHAT TO DO.

IT'S AS IF ALL HIS LIFE FORCE WAS SUCKED OUT OF HIM..

I GUESS IT WAS. I WAS FRIED PRETTY GOOD TAKING DOWN THE MASTER. BEST I CAN RECOLLECT, DANNY SUMMONED HIS CHI... HIS *IRON FIST*... TO PASS ON SOME LIFE-FORCE TO ME!

DAMN FOOL NEVER DID KNOW HOW TO QUIT WHEN HE SHOULD...!

FOR *YOU?!* THE IRON FIST SACRIFICED HIM-SELF FOR *YOU?!* UNDESERVING YOU ARE! TRAITOR YOU ARE!

THIS I SWEAR-- IF *HE* DIES, *YOU* DIE!

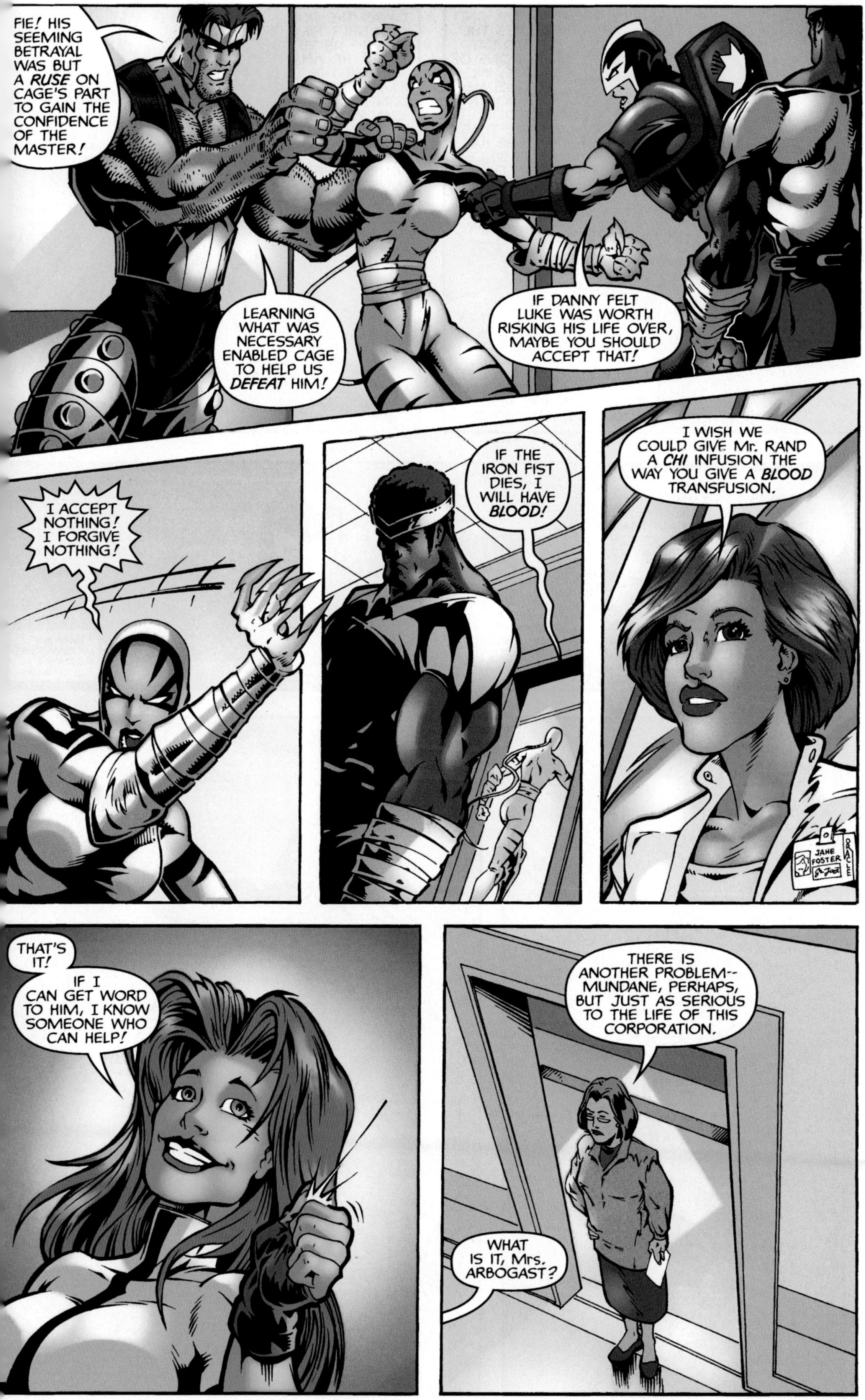
FIE! HIS SEEMING BETRAYAL WAS BUT A RUSE ON CAGE'S PART TO GAIN THE CONFIDENCE OF THE MASTER!
LEARNING WHAT WAS NECESSARY ENABLED CAGE TO HELP US DEFEAT HIM!
IF DANNY FELT LUKE WAS WORTH RISKING HIS LIFE OVER, MAYBE YOU SHOULD ACCEPT THAT!
I ACCEPT NOTHING! I FORGIVE NOTHING!
IF THE IRON FIST DIES, I WILL HAVE BLOOD!
I WISH WE COULD GIVE Mr. RAND A CHI INFUSION THE WAY YOU GIVE A BLOOD TRANSFUSION.
JANE FOSTER
ORACLE
THAT'S IT!
IF I CAN GET WORD TO HIM, I KNOW SOMEONE WHO CAN HELP!
THERE IS ANOTHER PROBLEM-- MUNDANE, PERHAPS, BUT JUST AS SERIOUS TO THE LIFE OF THIS CORPORATION.
WHAT IS IT, Mrs. ARBOGAST?

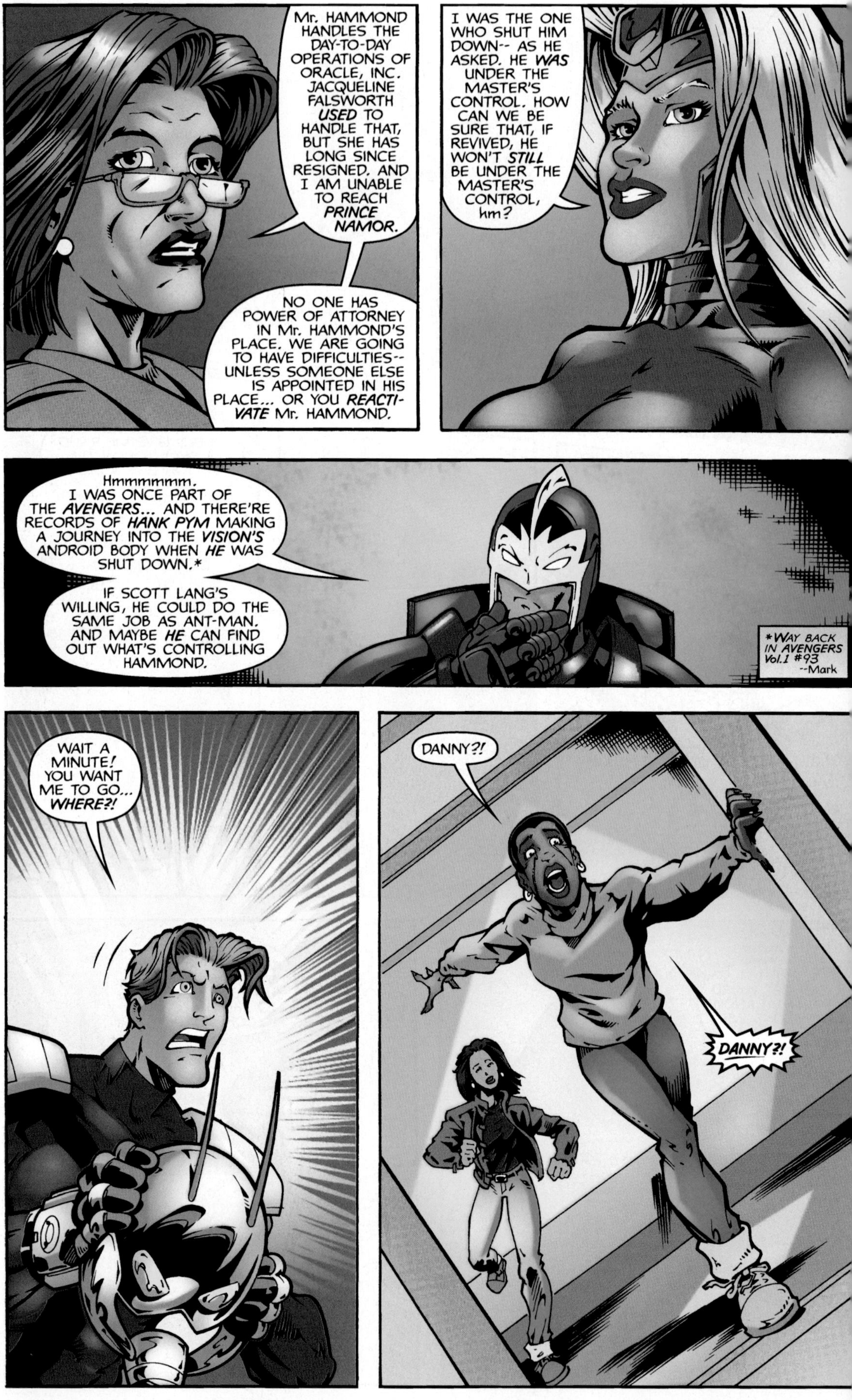
Mr. HAMMOND HANDLES THE DAY-TO-DAY OPERATIONS OF ORACLE, INC. JACQUELINE FALSWORTH USED TO HANDLE THAT, BUT SHE HAS LONG SINCE RESIGNED. AND I AM UNABLE TO REACH PRINCE NAMOR.
NO ONE HAS POWER OF ATTORNEY IN Mr. HAMMOND'S PLACE. WE ARE GOING TO HAVE DIFFICULTIES--UNLESS SOMEONE ELSE IS APPOINTED IN HIS PLACE... OR YOU REACTIVATE Mr. HAMMOND.
I WAS THE ONE WHO SHUT HIM DOWN-- AS HE ASKED. HE WAS UNDER THE MASTER'S CONTROL. HOW CAN WE BE SURE THAT, IF REVIVED, HE WON'T STILL BE UNDER THE MASTER'S CONTROL, hm?
Hmmmmmm. I WAS ONCE PART OF THE AVENGERS... AND THERE'RE RECORDS OF HANK PYM MAKING A JOURNEY INTO THE VISION'S ANDROID BODY WHEN HE WAS SHUT DOWN.*
IF SCOTT LANG'S WILLING, HE COULD DO THE SAME JOB AS ANT-MAN. AND MAYBE HE CAN FIND OUT WHAT'S CONTROLLING HAMMOND.
*WAY BACK IN AVENGERS Vol.1 #93 --Mark
WAIT A MINUTE! YOU WANT ME TO GO... WHERE?!
DANNY?!
DANNY?!

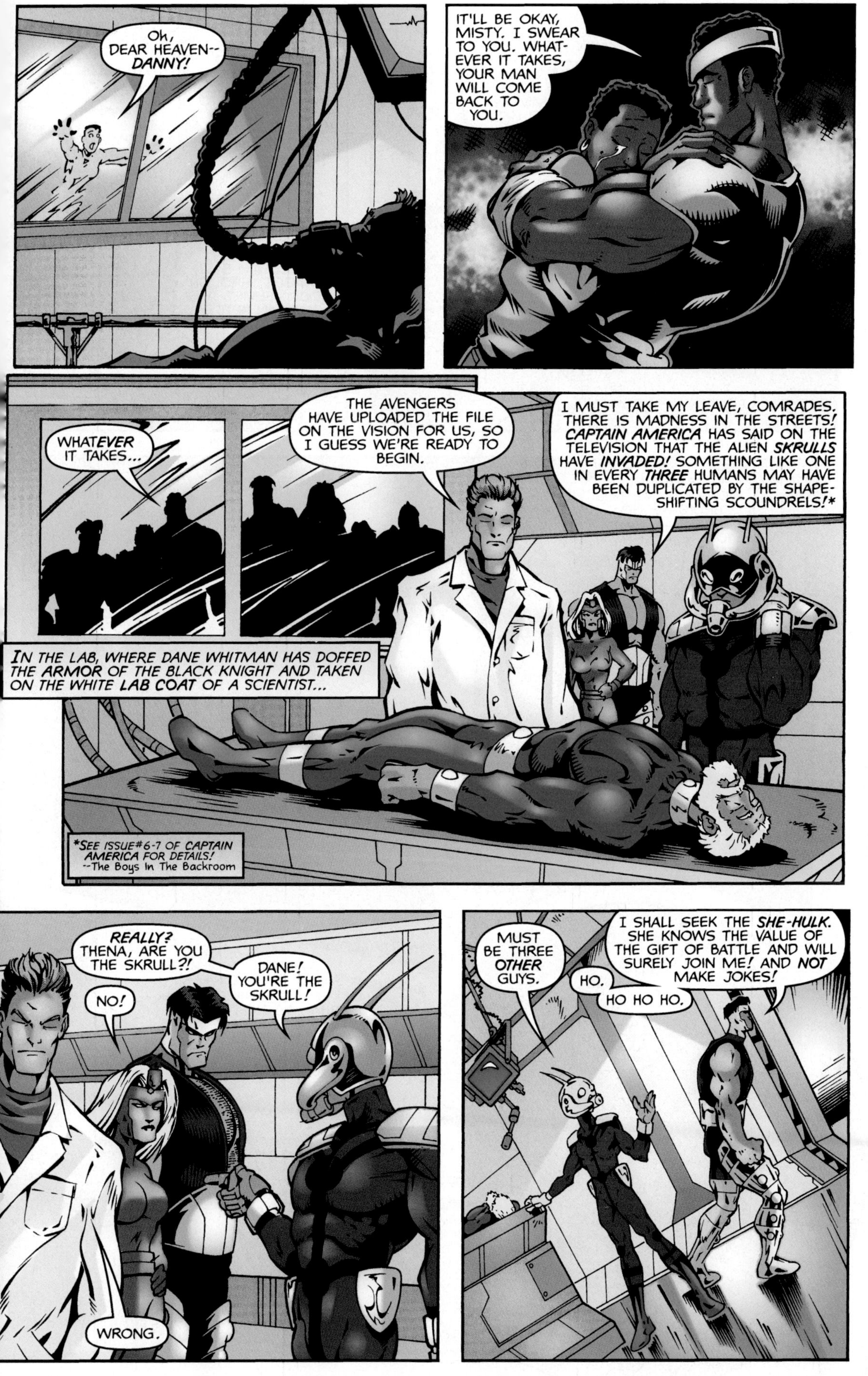
Oh, DEAR HEAVEN-- DANNY!
IT'LL BE OKAY, MISTY. I SWEAR TO YOU. WHATEVER IT TAKES, YOUR MAN WILL COME BACK TO YOU.
WHATEVER IT TAKES...
THE AVENGERS HAVE UPLOADED THE FILE ON THE VISION FOR US, SO I GUESS WE'RE READY TO BEGIN.
I MUST TAKE MY LEAVE, COMRADES. THERE IS MADNESS IN THE STREETS! CAPTAIN AMERICA HAS SAID ON THE TELEVISION THAT THE ALIEN SKRULLS HAVE INVADED! SOMETHING LIKE ONE IN EVERY THREE HUMANS MAY HAVE BEEN DUPLICATED BY THE SHAPE-SHIFTING SCOUNDRELS!*
IN THE LAB, WHERE DANE WHITMAN HAS DOFFED THE ARMOR OF THE BLACK KNIGHT AND TAKEN ON THE WHITE LAB COAT OF A SCIENTIST...
*SEE ISSUE#6-7 OF CAPTAIN AMERICA FOR DETAILS! --The Boys In The Backroom
REALLY? THENA, ARE YOU THE SKRULL?!
NO!
DANE! YOU'RE THE SKRULL!
WRONG.
MUST BE THREE OTHER GUYS.
I SHALL SEEK THE SHE-HULK. SHE KNOWS THE VALUE OF THE GIFT OF BATTLE AND WILL SURELY JOIN ME! AND NOT MAKE JOKES!
HO.
HO HO HO.

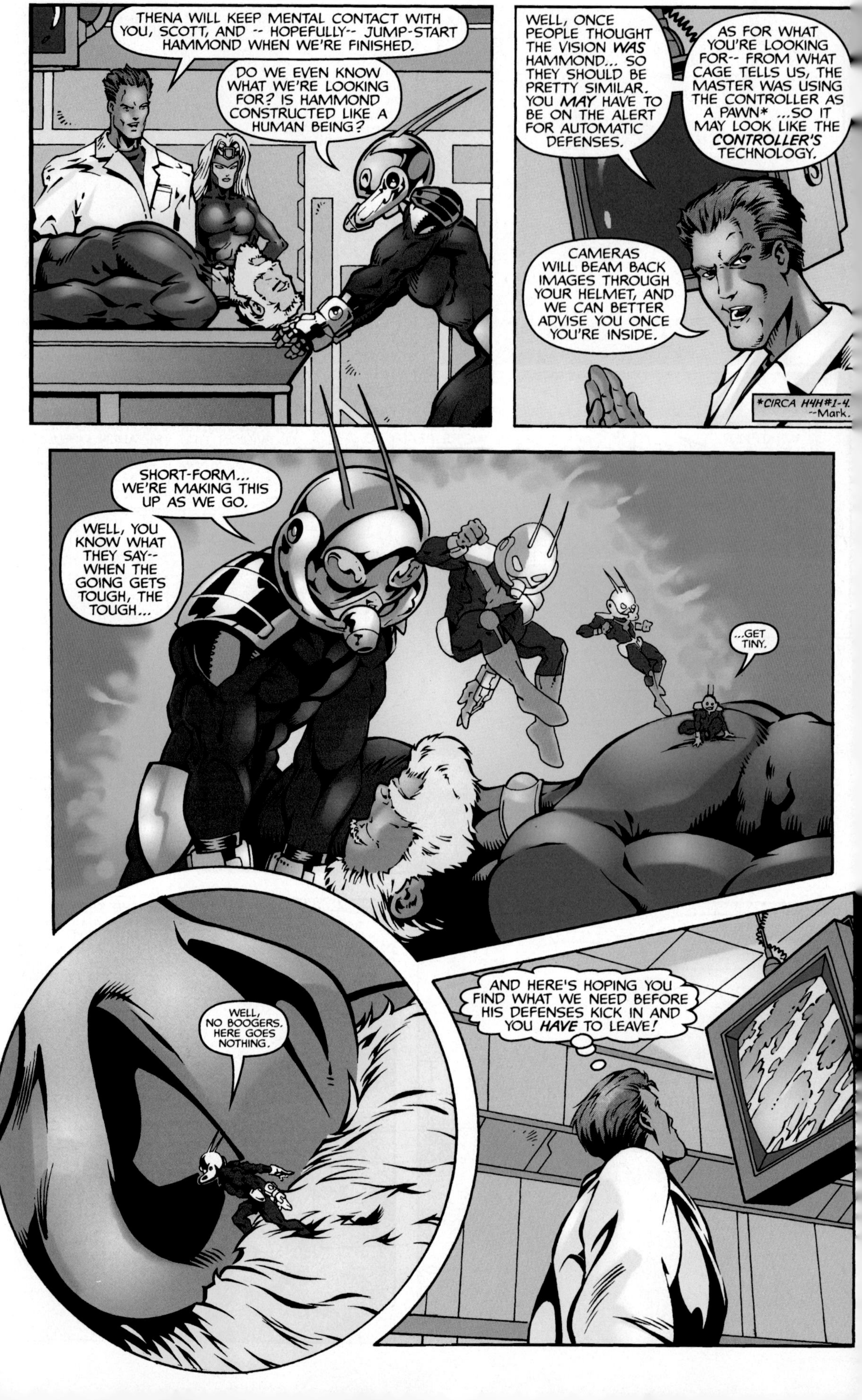
THENA WILL KEEP MENTAL CONTACT WITH YOU, SCOTT, AND -- HOPEFULLY-- JUMP-START HAMMOND WHEN WE'RE FINISHED.
DO WE EVEN KNOW WHAT WE'RE LOOKING FOR? IS HAMMOND CONSTRUCTED LIKE A HUMAN BEING?
WELL, ONCE PEOPLE THOUGHT THE VISION *WAS* HAMMOND... SO THEY SHOULD BE PRETTY SIMILAR. YOU *MAY* HAVE TO BE ON THE ALERT FOR AUTOMATIC DEFENSES.
AS FOR WHAT YOU'RE LOOKING FOR-- FROM WHAT CAGE TELLS US, THE MASTER WAS USING THE CONTROLLER AS A PAWN* ...SO IT MAY LOOK LIKE THE *CONTROLLER'S* TECHNOLOGY.
CAMERAS WILL BEAM BACK IMAGES THROUGH YOUR HELMET, AND WE CAN BETTER ADVISE YOU ONCE YOU'RE INSIDE.
*CIRCA H4H#1-4. --Mark.
SHORT-FORM... WE'RE MAKING THIS UP AS WE GO.
WELL, YOU KNOW WHAT THEY SAY-- WHEN THE GOING GETS TOUGH, THE TOUGH...
...GET TINY.
WELL, NO BOOGERS. HERE GOES NOTHING.
AND HERE'S HOPING YOU FIND WHAT WE NEED BEFORE HIS DEFENSES KICK IN AND YOU *HAVE* TO LEAVE!

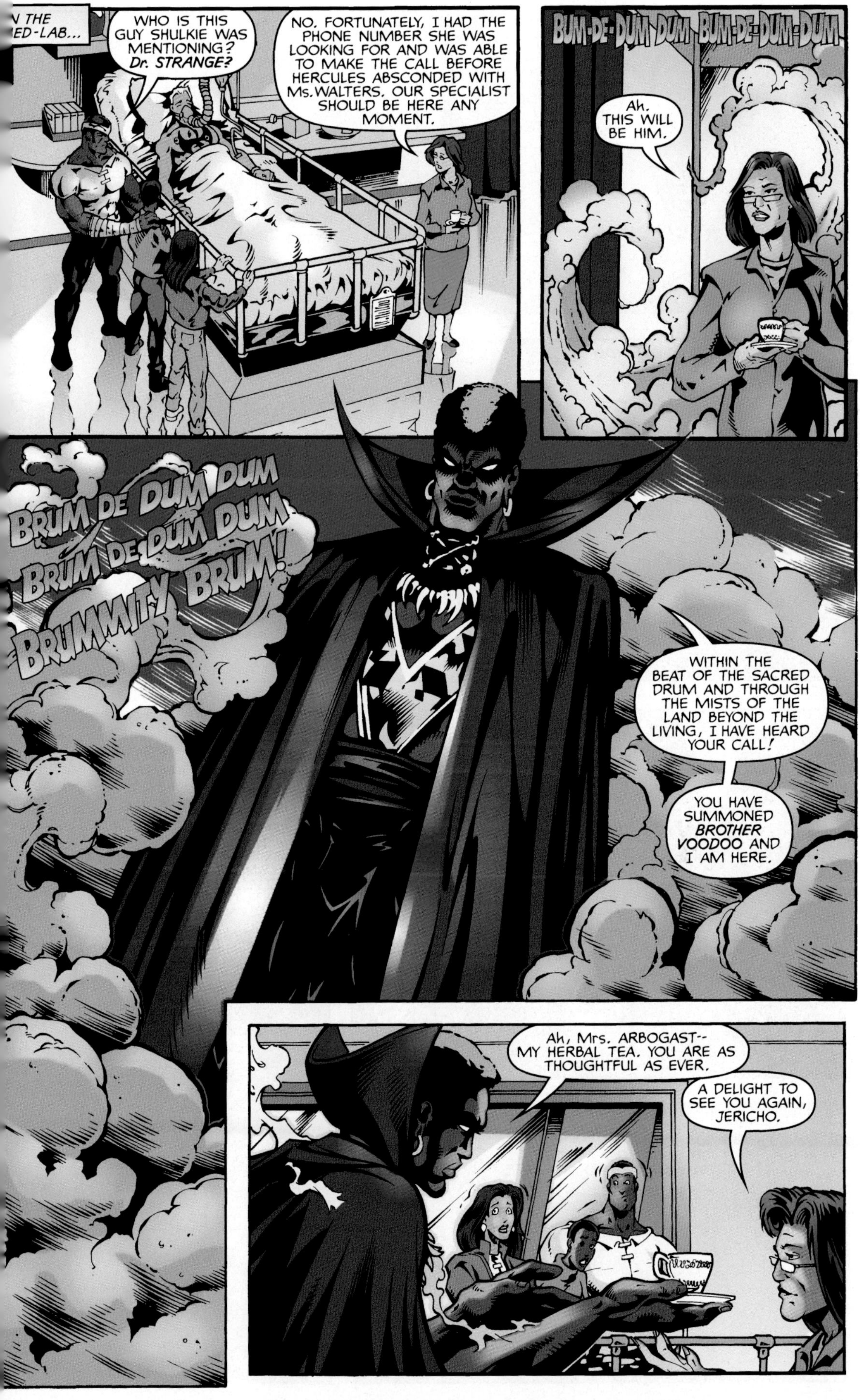

N THE
ED-LAB...
WHO IS THIS GUY SHULKIE WAS MENTIONING? Dr. STRANGE?
NO. FORTUNATELY, I HAD THE PHONE NUMBER SHE WAS LOOKING FOR AND WAS ABLE TO MAKE THE CALL BEFORE HERCULES ABSCONDED WITH Ms. WALTERS. OUR SPECIALIST SHOULD BE HERE ANY MOMENT.
BUM-DE-DUM DUM BUM-DE-DUM-DUM
Ah. THIS WILL BE HIM.
BRUM DE DUM DUM
BRUM DE DUM DUM
BRUMMITY BRUM!
WITHIN THE BEAT OF THE SACRED DRUM AND THROUGH THE MISTS OF THE LAND BEYOND THE LIVING, I HAVE HEARD YOUR CALL!
YOU HAVE SUMMONED BROTHER VOODOO AND I AM HERE.
Ah, Mrs. ARBOGAST-- MY HERBAL TEA. YOU ARE AS THOUGHTFUL AS EVER.
A DELIGHT TO SEE YOU AGAIN, JERICHO.

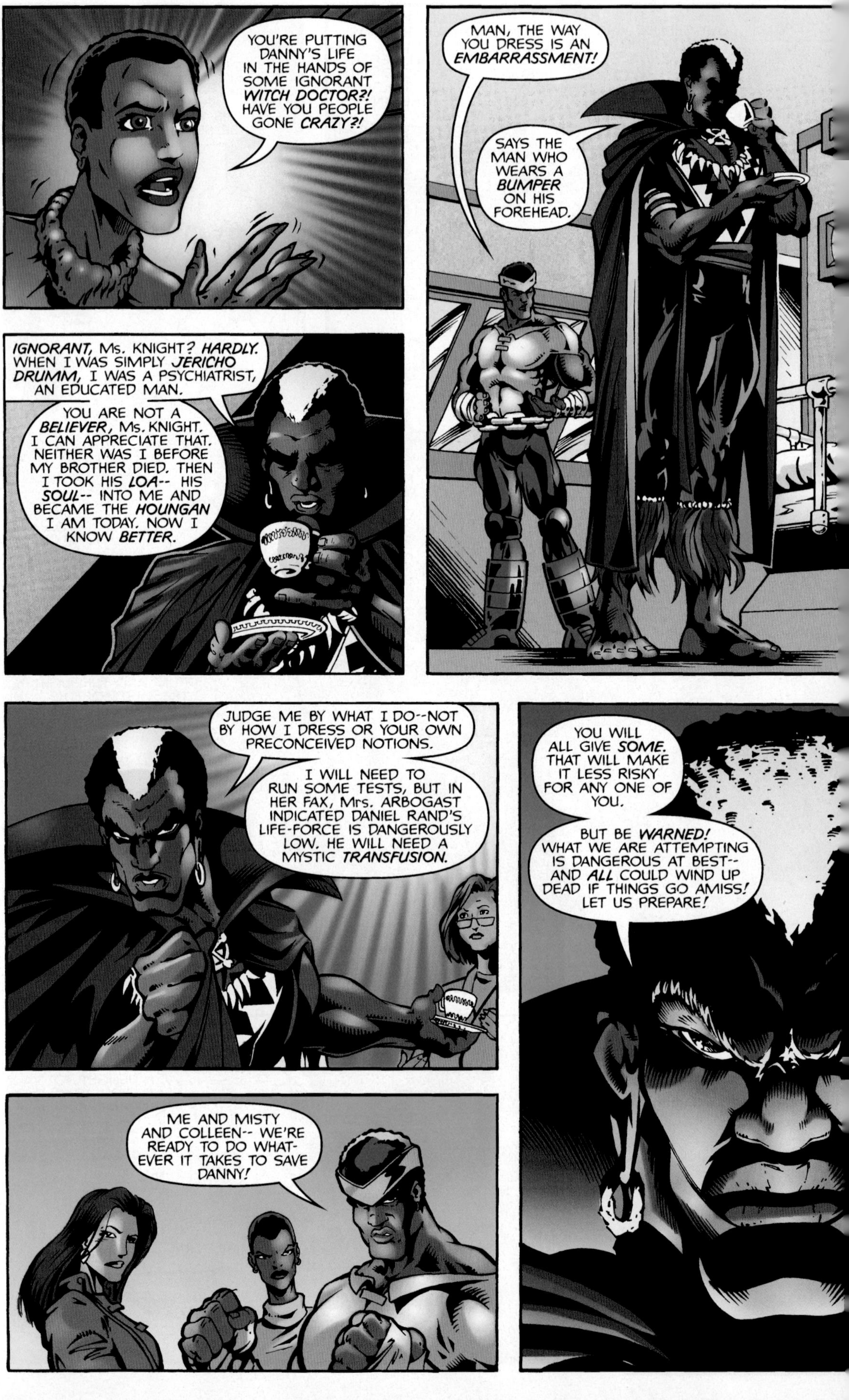
YOU'RE PUTTING DANNY'S LIFE IN THE HANDS OF SOME IGNORANT WITCH DOCTOR?! HAVE YOU PEOPLE GONE CRAZY?!
MAN, THE WAY YOU DRESS IS AN EMBARRASSMENT!
SAYS THE MAN WHO WEARS A BUMPER ON HIS FOREHEAD.
IGNORANT, Ms. KNIGHT? HARDLY. WHEN I WAS SIMPLY JERICHO DRUMM, I WAS A PSYCHIATRIST, AN EDUCATED MAN.
YOU ARE NOT A BELIEVER, Ms. KNIGHT. I CAN APPRECIATE THAT. NEITHER WAS I BEFORE MY BROTHER DIED. THEN I TOOK HIS LOA-- HIS SOUL-- INTO ME AND BECAME THE HOUNGAN I AM TODAY. NOW I KNOW BETTER.
JUDGE ME BY WHAT I DO--NOT BY HOW I DRESS OR YOUR OWN PRECONCEIVED NOTIONS.
I WILL NEED TO RUN SOME TESTS, BUT IN HER FAX, Mrs. ARBOGAST INDICATED DANIEL RAND'S LIFE-FORCE IS DANGEROUSLY LOW. HE WILL NEED A MYSTIC TRANSFUSION.
ME AND MISTY AND COLLEEN-- WE'RE READY TO DO WHAT-EVER IT TAKES TO SAVE DANNY!
YOU WILL ALL GIVE SOME. THAT WILL MAKE IT LESS RISKY FOR ANY ONE OF YOU.
BUT BE WARNED! WHAT WE ARE ATTEMPTING IS DANGEROUS AT BEST-- AND ALL COULD WIND UP DEAD IF THINGS GO AMISS! LET US PREPARE!

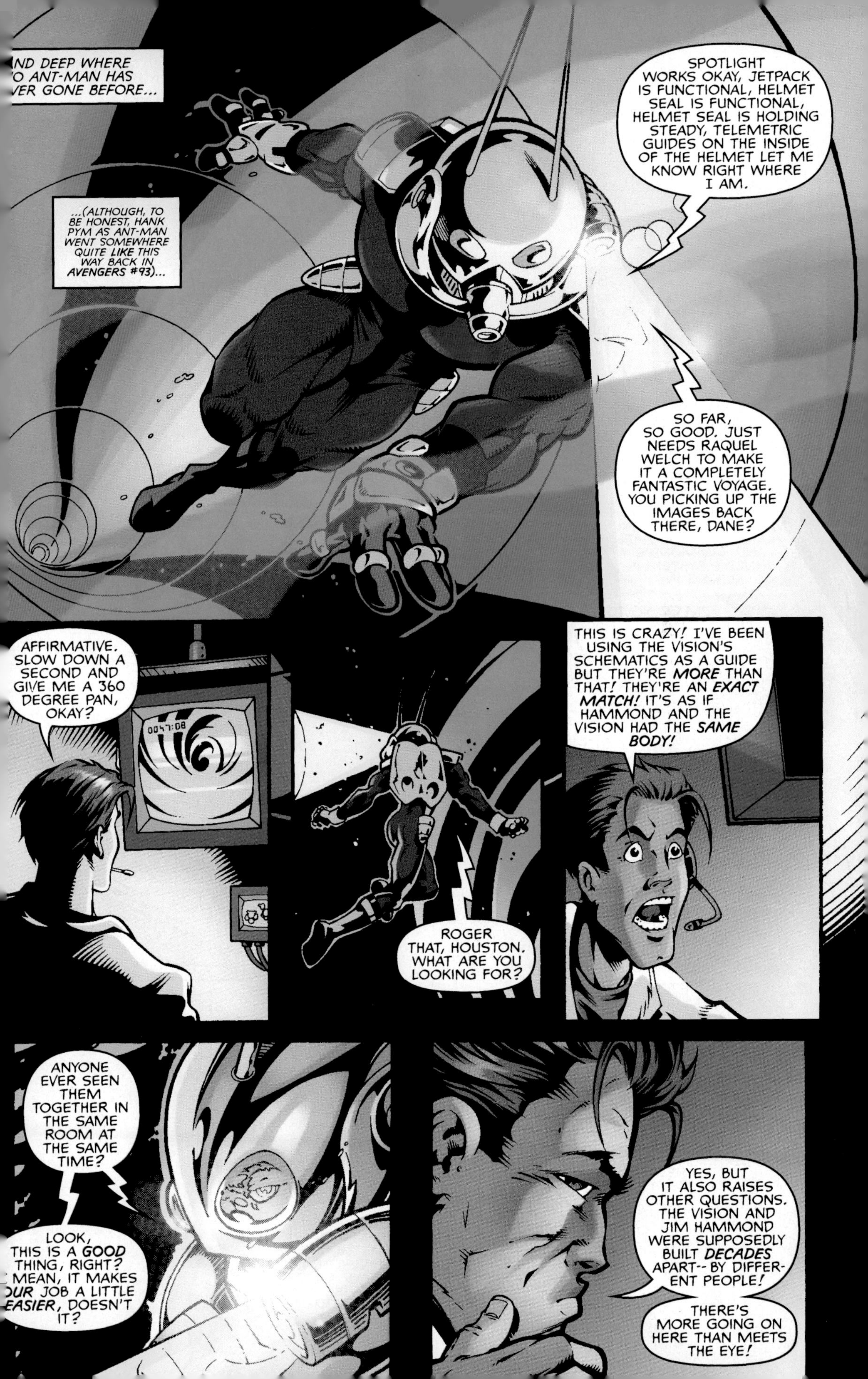

...AND DEEP WHERE NO ANT-MAN HAS EVER GONE BEFORE...
...(ALTHOUGH, TO BE HONEST, HANK PYM AS ANT-MAN WENT SOMEWHERE QUITE LIKE THIS WAY BACK IN AVENGERS #93)...
SPOTLIGHT WORKS OKAY, JETPACK IS FUNCTIONAL, HELMET SEAL IS FUNCTIONAL, HELMET SEAL IS HOLDING STEADY, TELEMETRIC GUIDES ON THE INSIDE OF THE HELMET LET ME KNOW RIGHT WHERE I AM.
SO FAR, SO GOOD. JUST NEEDS RAQUEL WELCH TO MAKE IT A COMPLETELY FANTASTIC VOYAGE. YOU PICKING UP THE IMAGES BACK THERE, DANE?
AFFIRMATIVE. SLOW DOWN A SECOND AND GIVE ME A 360 DEGREE PAN, OKAY?
ROGER THAT, HOUSTON. WHAT ARE YOU LOOKING FOR?
THIS IS CRAZY! I'VE BEEN USING THE VISION'S SCHEMATICS AS A GUIDE BUT THEY'RE MORE THAN THAT! THEY'RE AN EXACT MATCH! IT'S AS IF HAMMOND AND THE VISION HAD THE SAME BODY!
ANYONE EVER SEEN THEM TOGETHER IN THE SAME ROOM AT THE SAME TIME?
LOOK, THIS IS A GOOD THING, RIGHT? I MEAN, IT MAKES OUR JOB A LITTLE EASIER, DOESN'T IT?
YES, BUT IT ALSO RAISES OTHER QUESTIONS. THE VISION AND JIM HAMMOND WERE SUPPOSEDLY BUILT DECADES APART-- BY DIFFERENT PEOPLE!
THERE'S MORE GOING ON HERE THAN MEETS THE EYE!

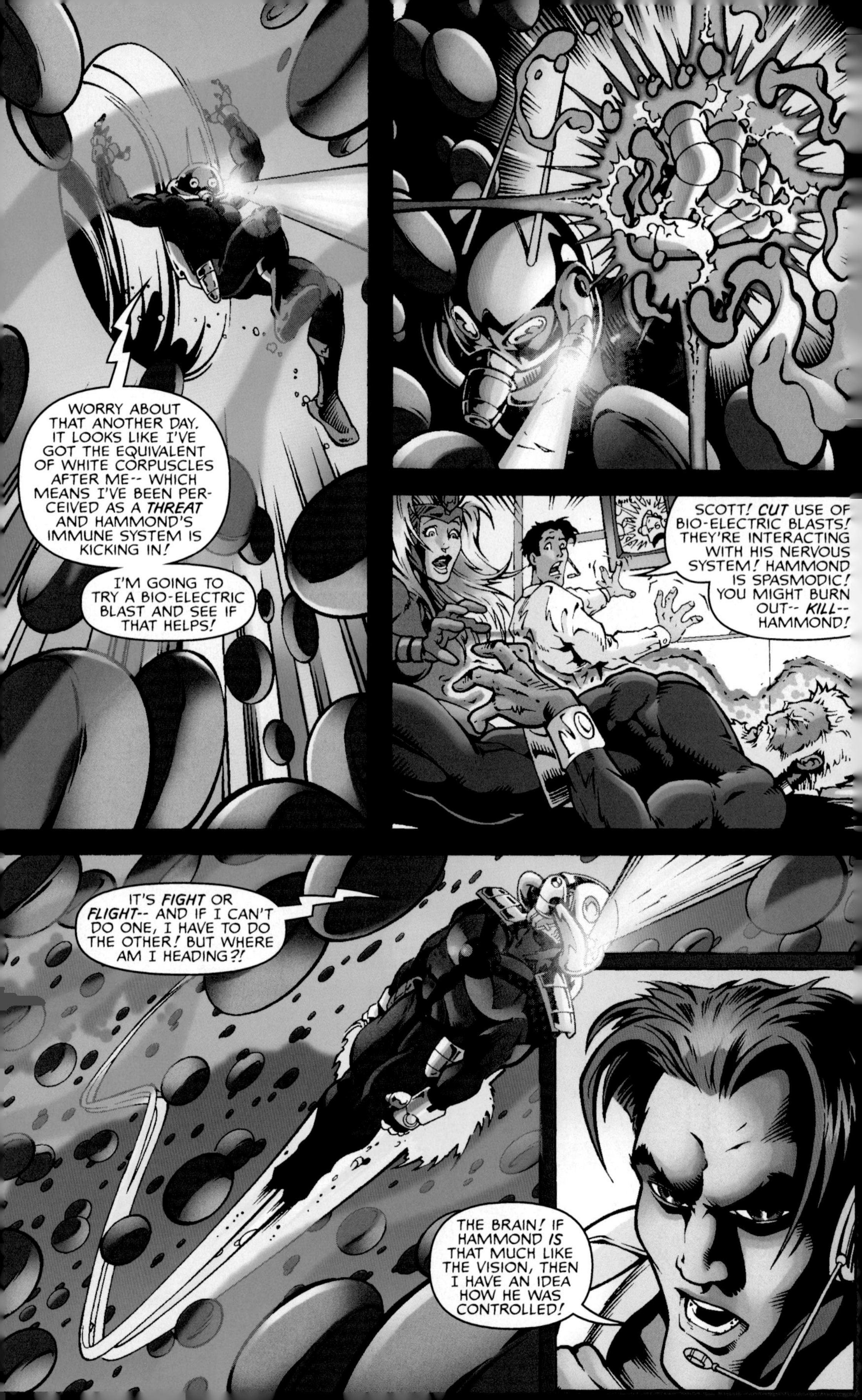
WORRY ABOUT THAT ANOTHER DAY. IT LOOKS LIKE I'VE GOT THE EQUIVALENT OF WHITE CORPUSCLES AFTER ME-- WHICH MEANS I'VE BEEN PERCEIVED AS A *THREAT* AND HAMMOND'S IMMUNE SYSTEM IS KICKING IN!
I'M GOING TO TRY A BIO-ELECTRIC BLAST AND SEE IF THAT HELPS!
SCOTT! *CUT* USE OF BIO-ELECTRIC BLASTS! THEY'RE INTERACTING WITH HIS NERVOUS SYSTEM! HAMMOND IS SPASMODIC! YOU MIGHT BURN OUT-- *KILL*-- HAMMOND!
IT'S *FIGHT* OR *FLIGHT*-- AND IF I CAN'T DO ONE, I HAVE TO DO THE OTHER! BUT WHERE AM I HEADING?!
THE BRAIN! IF HAMMOND *IS* THAT MUCH LIKE THE VISION, THEN I HAVE AN IDEA HOW HE WAS CONTROLLED!

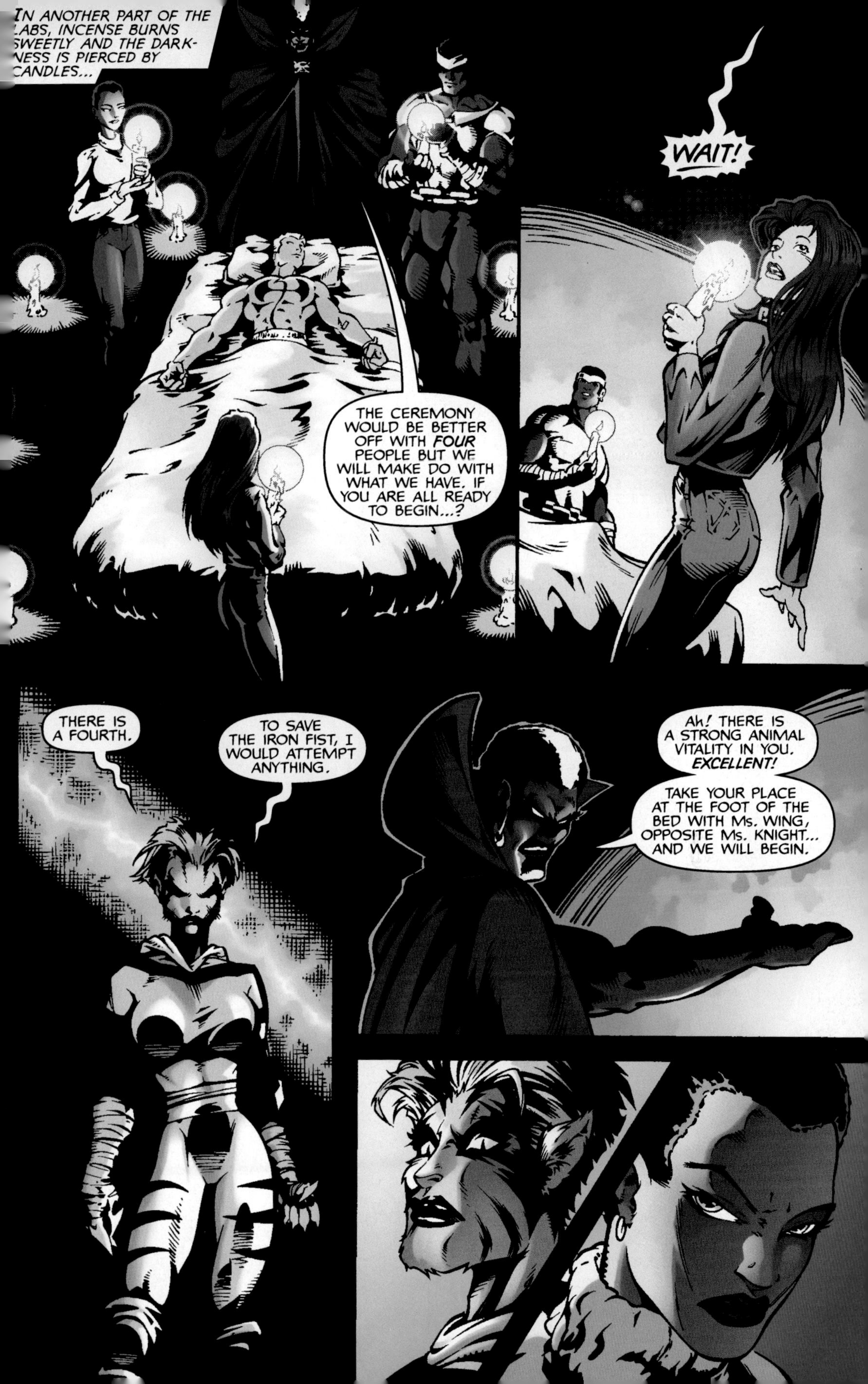
IN ANOTHER PART OF THE LABS, INCENSE BURNS SWEETLY AND THE DARKNESS IS PIERCED BY CANDLES...
THE CEREMONY WOULD BE BETTER OFF WITH *FOUR* PEOPLE BUT WE WILL MAKE DO WITH WHAT WE HAVE. IF YOU ARE ALL READY TO BEGIN...?
WAIT!
THERE IS A FOURTH.
TO SAVE THE IRON FIST, I WOULD ATTEMPT ANYTHING.
AH! THERE IS A STRONG ANIMAL VITALITY IN YOU. *EXCELLENT!*
TAKE YOUR PLACE AT THE FOOT OF THE BED WITH Ms. WING, OPPOSITE Ms. KNIGHT... AND WE WILL BEGIN.

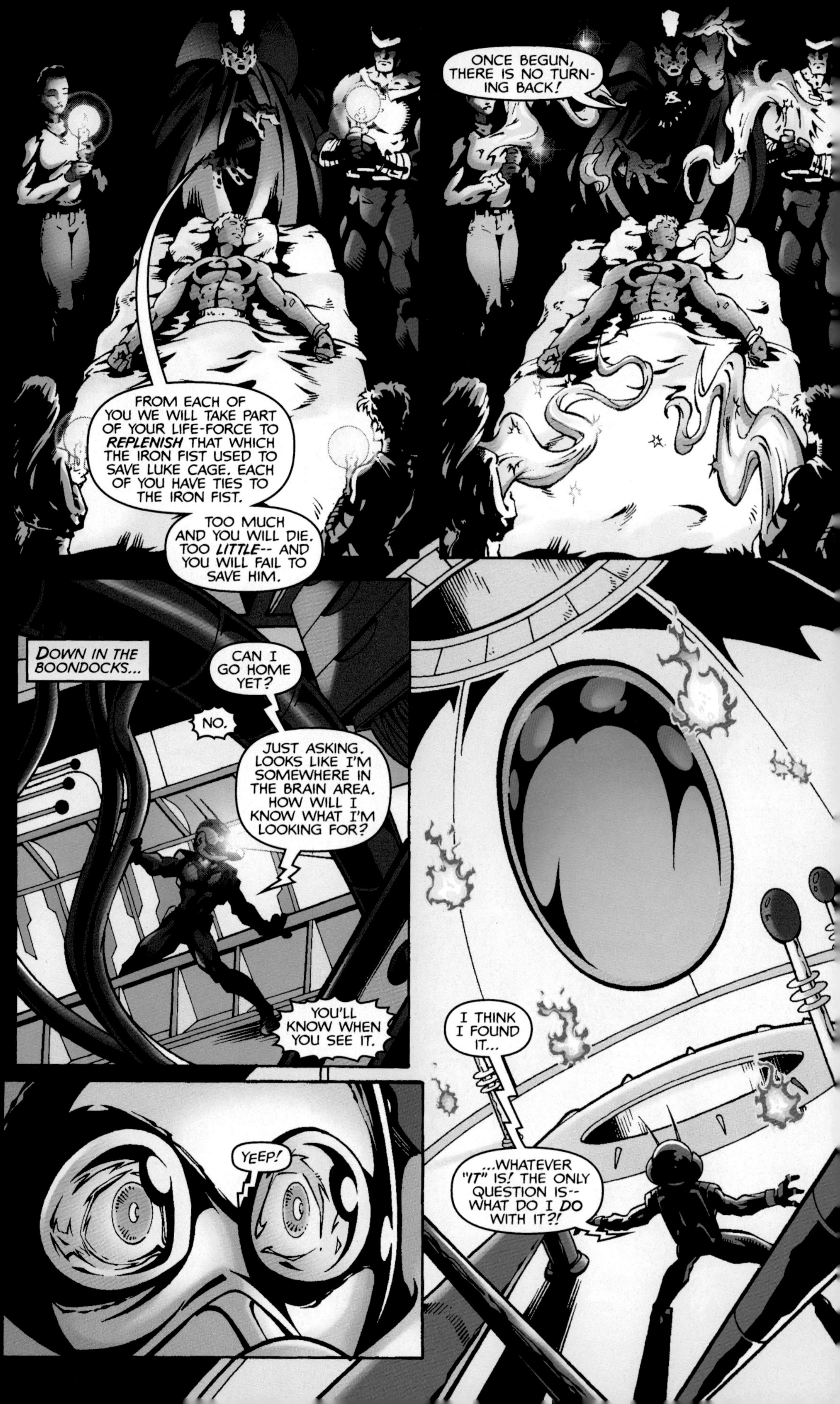
FROM EACH OF YOU WE WILL TAKE PART OF YOUR LIFE-FORCE TO *REPLENISH* THAT WHICH THE IRON FIST USED TO SAVE LUKE CAGE. EACH OF YOU HAVE TIES TO THE IRON FIST.
TOO MUCH AND YOU WILL DIE. TOO *LITTLE*-- AND YOU WILL FAIL TO SAVE HIM.
ONCE BEGUN, THERE IS NO TURNING BACK!
DOWN IN THE BOONDOCKS...
CAN I GO HOME YET?
NO.
JUST ASKING. LOOKS LIKE I'M SOMEWHERE IN THE BRAIN AREA. HOW WILL I KNOW WHAT I'M LOOKING FOR?
YOU'LL KNOW WHEN YOU SEE IT.
YEEP!
I THINK I FOUND IT...
...WHATEVER "*IT*" IS! THE ONLY QUESTION IS-- WHAT DO I *DO* WITH IT?!

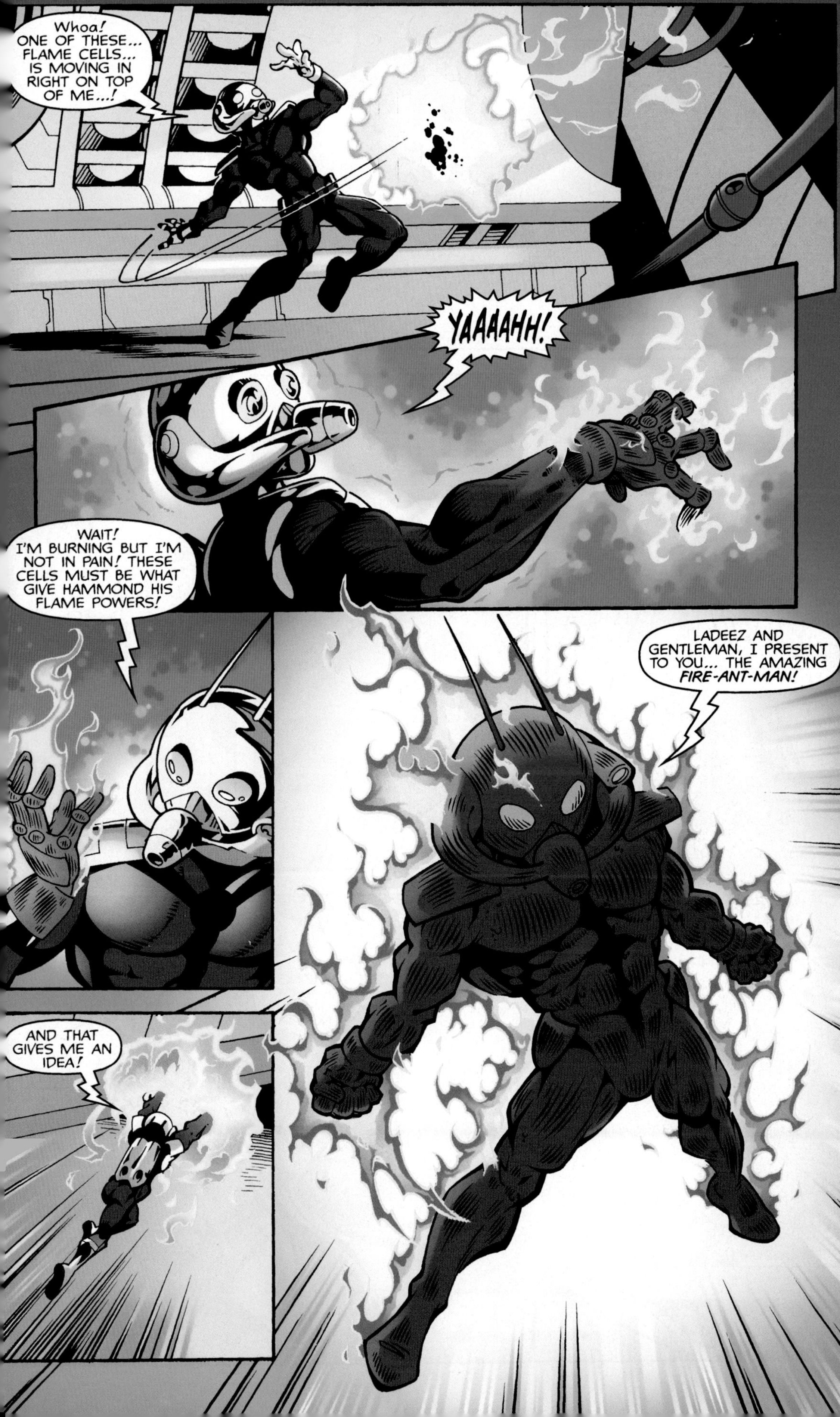
Whoa! ONE OF THESE... FLAME CELLS... IS MOVING IN RIGHT ON TOP OF ME...!
YAAAAHH!
WAIT! I'M BURNING BUT I'M NOT IN PAIN! THESE CELLS MUST BE WHAT GIVE HAMMOND HIS FLAME POWERS!
AND THAT GIVES ME AN IDEA!
LADEEZ AND GENTLEMAN, I PRESENT TO YOU... THE AMAZING FIRE-ANT-MAN!

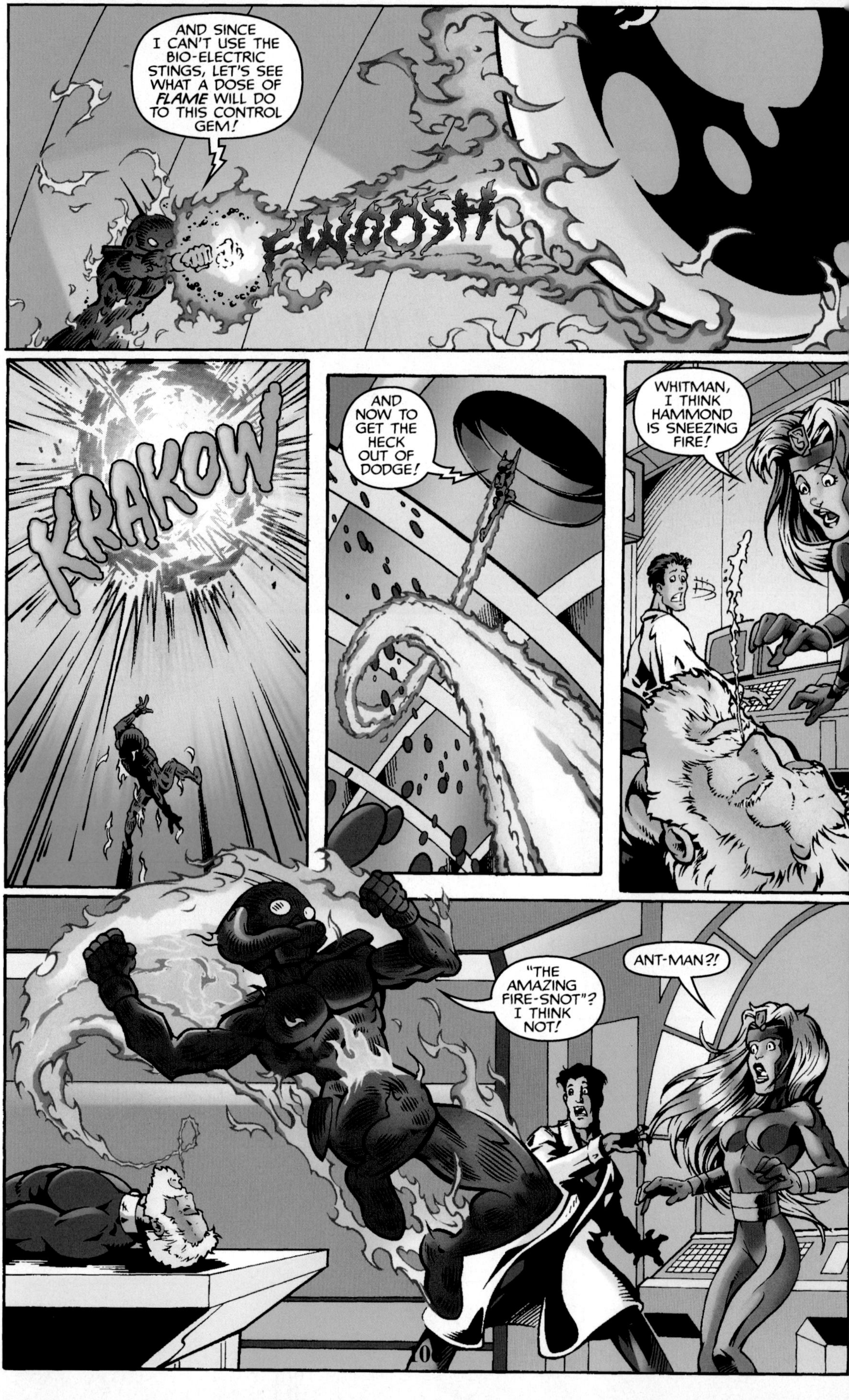
AND SINCE I CAN'T USE THE BIO-ELECTRIC STINGS, LET'S SEE WHAT A DOSE OF *FLAME* WILL DO TO THIS CONTROL GEM!
FWOOSH
KRAKOW
AND NOW TO GET THE HECK OUT OF DODGE!
WHITMAN, I THINK HAMMOND IS SNEEZING FIRE!
"THE AMAZING FIRE-SNOT"? I THINK NOT!
ANT-MAN?!

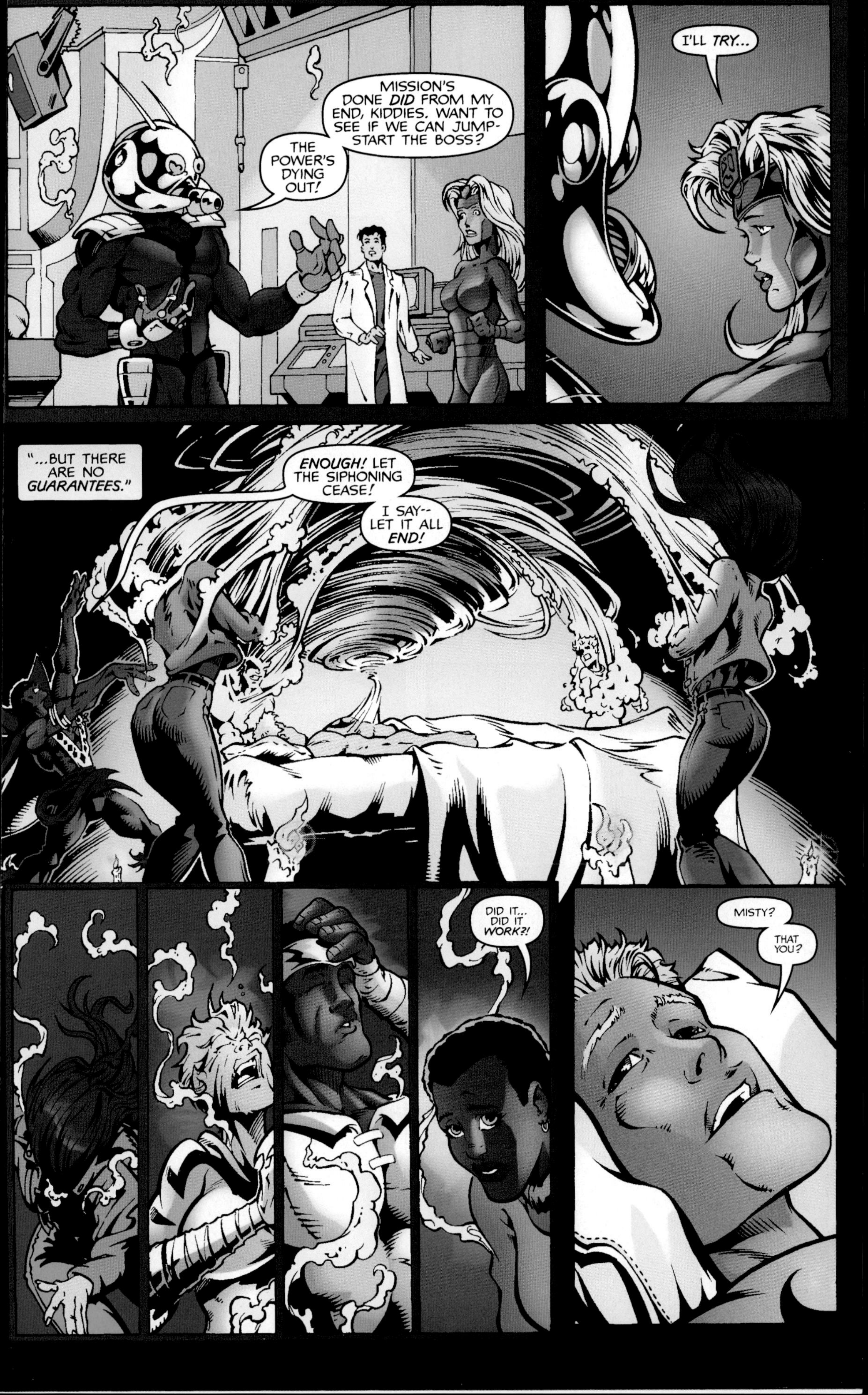
MISSION'S DONE DID FROM MY END, KIDDIES. WANT TO SEE IF WE CAN JUMP-START THE BOSS?
THE POWER'S DYING OUT!
I'LL TRY...
"...BUT THERE ARE NO GUARANTEES."
ENOUGH! LET THE SIPHONING CEASE!
I SAY-- LET IT ALL END!
DID IT... DID IT WORK?!
MISTY?
THAT YOU?

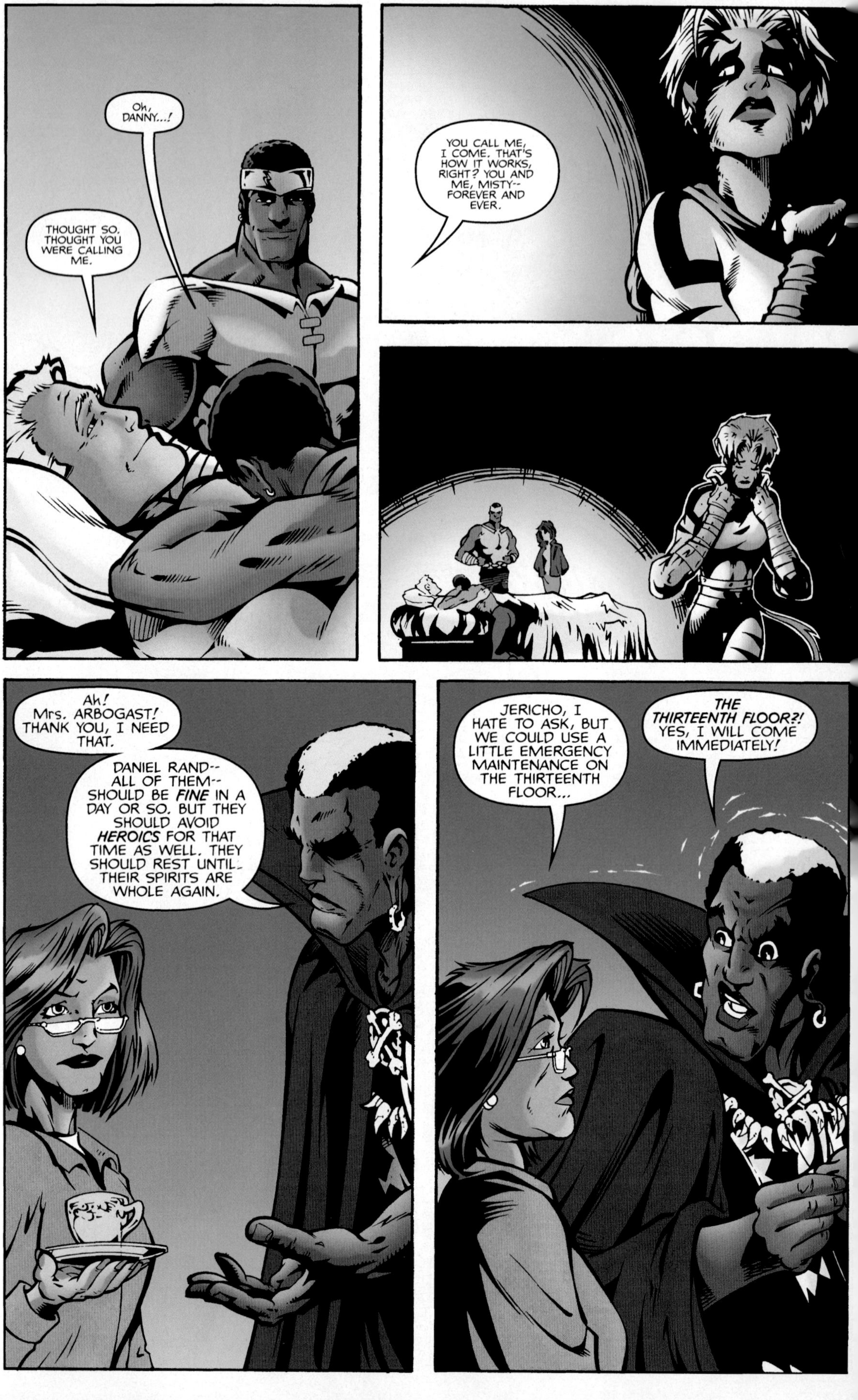
Oh, DANNY...!
THOUGHT SO. THOUGHT YOU WERE CALLING ME.
YOU CALL ME, I COME. THAT'S HOW IT WORKS, RIGHT? YOU AND ME, MISTY-- FOREVER AND EVER.
Ah! Mrs. ARBOGAST! THANK YOU, I NEED THAT.
DANIEL RAND-- ALL OF THEM-- SHOULD BE FINE IN A DAY OR SO, BUT THEY SHOULD AVOID HEROICS FOR THAT TIME AS WELL. THEY SHOULD REST UNTIL THEIR SPIRITS ARE WHOLE AGAIN.
JERICHO, I HATE TO ASK, BUT WE COULD USE A LITTLE EMERGENCY MAINTENANCE ON THE THIRTEENTH FLOOR...
THE THIRTEENTH FLOOR?! YES, I WILL COME IMMEDIATELY!

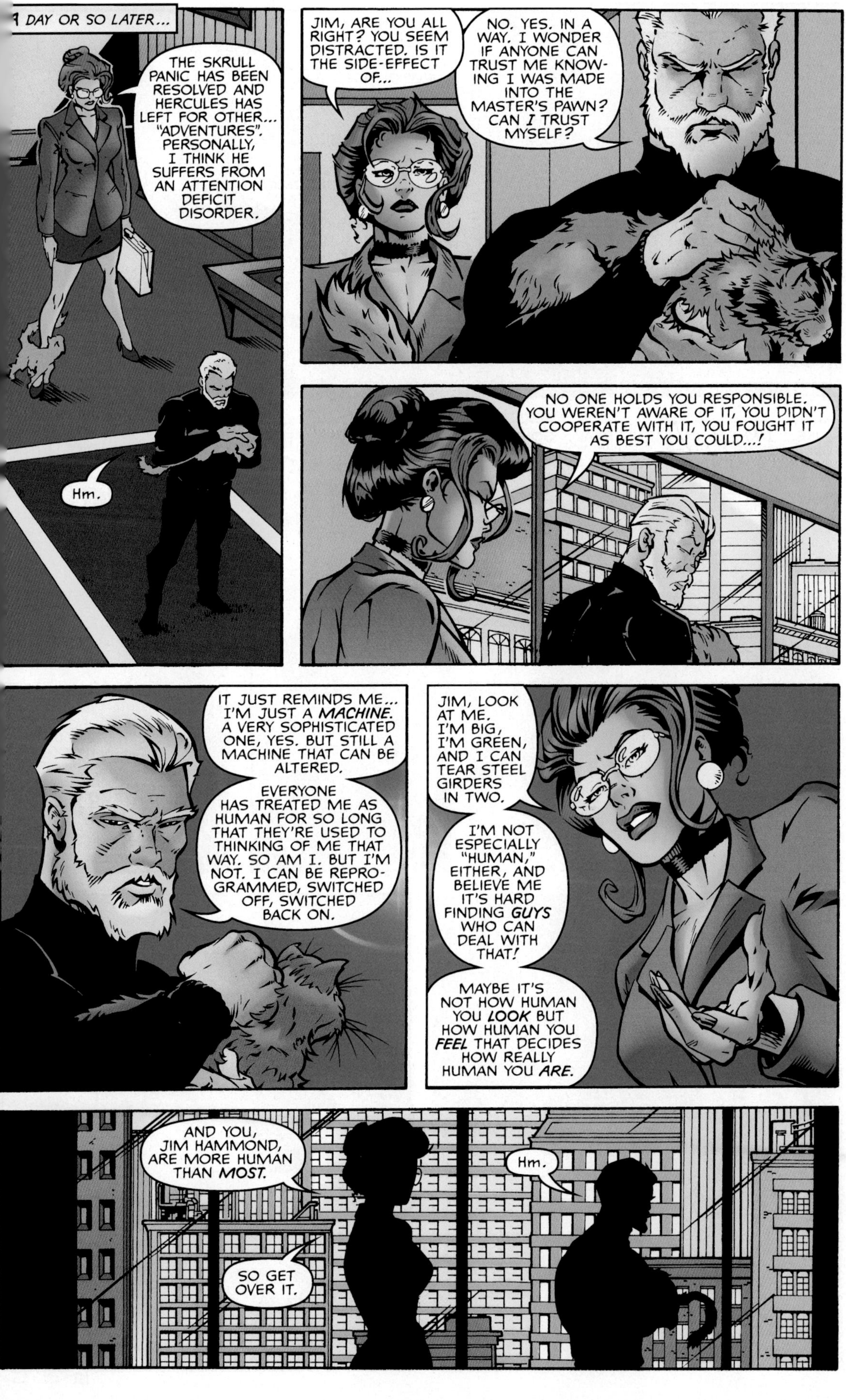
A DAY OR SO LATER...
THE SKRULL PANIC HAS BEEN RESOLVED AND HERCULES HAS LEFT FOR OTHER... "ADVENTURES". PERSONALLY, I THINK HE SUFFERS FROM AN ATTENTION DEFICIT DISORDER.
Hm.
JIM, ARE YOU ALL RIGHT? YOU SEEM DISTRACTED. IS IT THE SIDE-EFFECT OF...
NO. YES. IN A WAY. I WONDER IF ANYONE CAN TRUST ME KNOWING I WAS MADE INTO THE MASTER'S PAWN? CAN *I* TRUST MYSELF?
NO ONE HOLDS YOU RESPONSIBLE. YOU WEREN'T AWARE OF IT, YOU DIDN'T COOPERATE WITH IT, YOU FOUGHT IT AS BEST YOU COULD...!
IT JUST REMINDS ME... I'M JUST A *MACHINE*. A VERY SOPHISTICATED ONE, YES. BUT STILL A MACHINE THAT CAN BE ALTERED.
EVERYONE HAS TREATED ME AS HUMAN FOR SO LONG THAT THEY'RE USED TO THINKING OF ME THAT WAY. SO AM I. BUT I'M NOT. I CAN BE REPROGRAMMED, SWITCHED OFF, SWITCHED BACK ON.
JIM, LOOK AT ME. I'M BIG, I'M GREEN, AND I CAN TEAR STEEL GIRDERS IN TWO.
I'M NOT ESPECIALLY "HUMAN," EITHER, AND BELIEVE ME IT'S HARD FINDING *GUYS* WHO CAN DEAL WITH THAT!
MAYBE IT'S NOT HOW HUMAN YOU *LOOK* BUT HOW HUMAN YOU *FEEL* THAT DECIDES HOW REALLY HUMAN YOU *ARE*.
AND YOU, JIM HAMMOND, ARE MORE HUMAN THAN *MOST*.
Hm.
SO GET OVER IT.

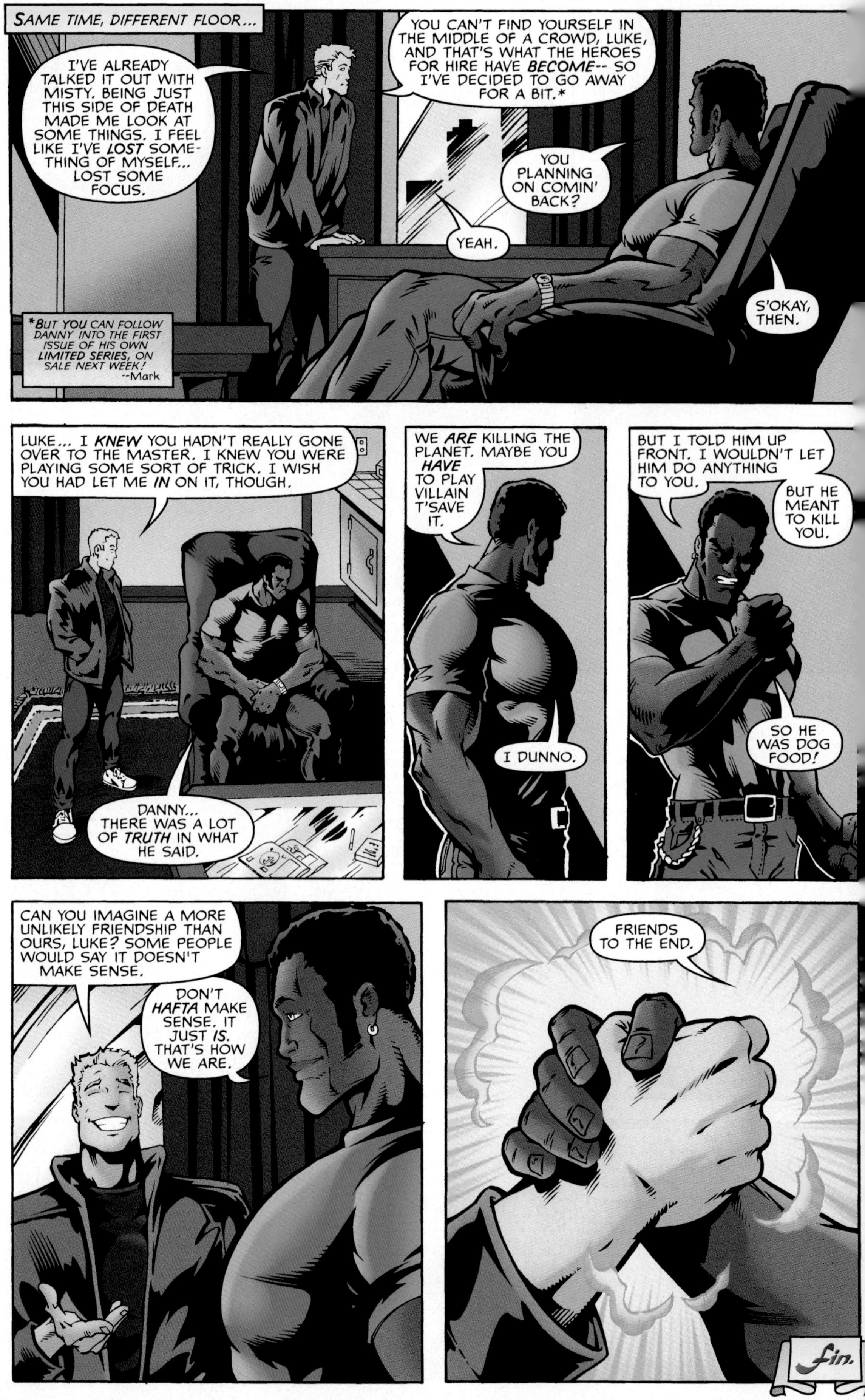
SAME TIME, DIFFERENT FLOOR...
I'VE ALREADY TALKED IT OUT WITH MISTY. BEING JUST THIS SIDE OF DEATH MADE ME LOOK AT SOME THINGS. I FEEL LIKE I'VE LOST SOME-THING OF MYSELF... LOST SOME FOCUS.
YOU CAN'T FIND YOURSELF IN THE MIDDLE OF A CROWD, LUKE, AND THAT'S WHAT THE HEROES FOR HIRE HAVE BECOME-- SO I'VE DECIDED TO GO AWAY FOR A BIT.*
YOU PLANNING ON COMIN' BACK?
YEAH.
S'OKAY, THEN.
*BUT YOU CAN FOLLOW DANNY INTO THE FIRST ISSUE OF HIS OWN LIMITED SERIES, ON SALE NEXT WEEK! --Mark
LUKE... I KNEW YOU HADN'T REALLY GONE OVER TO THE MASTER. I KNEW YOU WERE PLAYING SOME SORT OF TRICK. I WISH YOU HAD LET ME IN ON IT, THOUGH.
DANNY... THERE WAS A LOT OF TRUTH IN WHAT HE SAID.
WE ARE KILLING THE PLANET. MAYBE YOU HAVE TO PLAY VILLAIN T'SAVE IT.
I DUNNO.
BUT I TOLD HIM UP FRONT. I WOULDN'T LET HIM DO ANYTHING TO YOU.
BUT HE MEANT TO KILL YOU.
SO HE WAS DOG FOOD!
CAN YOU IMAGINE A MORE UNLIKELY FRIENDSHIP THAN OURS, LUKE? SOME PEOPLE WOULD SAY IT DOESN'T MAKE SENSE.
DON'T HAFTA MAKE SENSE. IT JUST IS. THAT'S HOW WE ARE.
FRIENDS TO THE END.
fin.

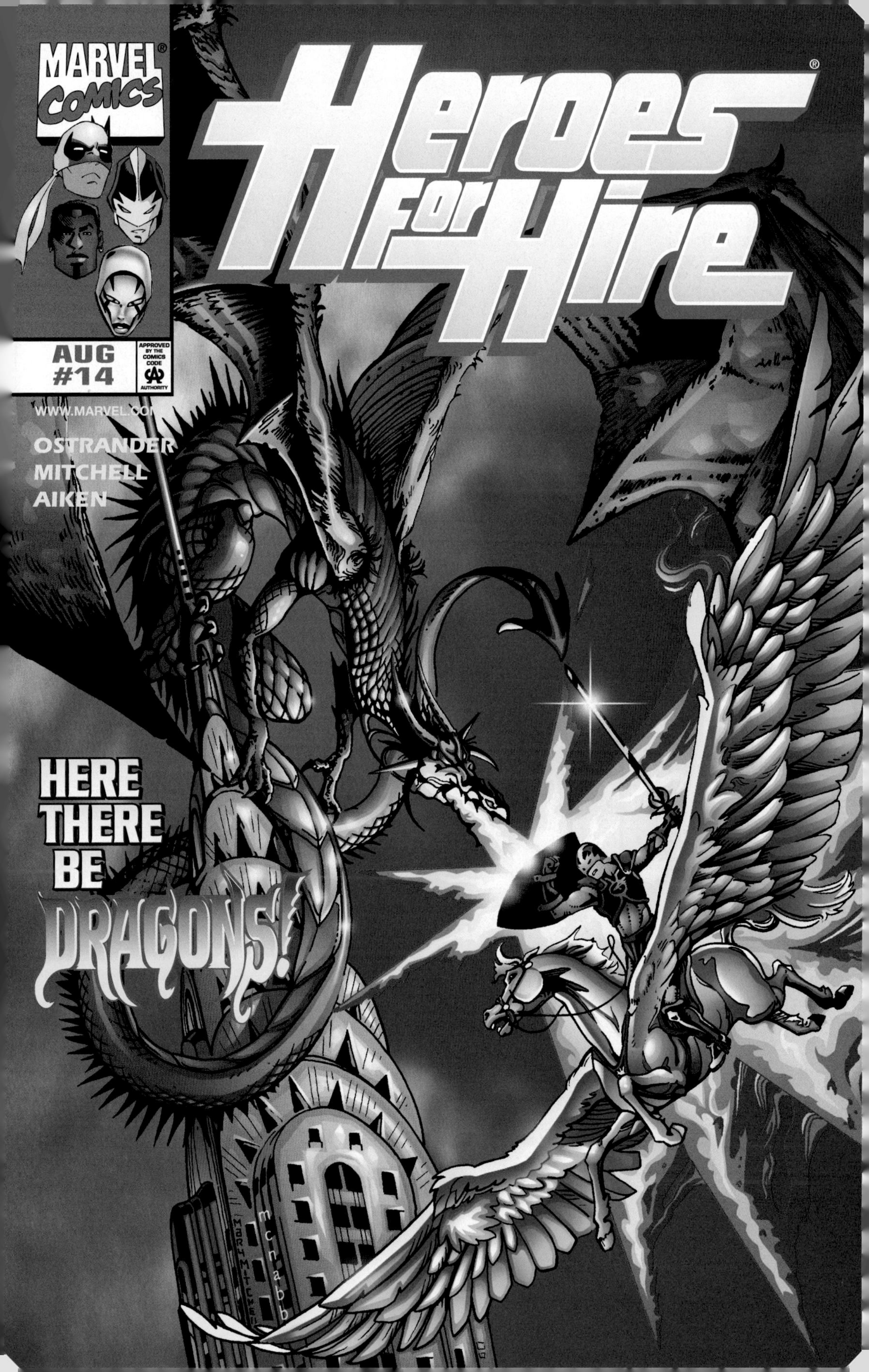

MARVEL COMICS
Heroes For Hire
AUG #14
APPROVED BY THE COMICS CODE AUTHORITY
WWW.MARVEL.COM
OSTRANDER
MITCHELL
AIKEN
HERE THERE BE DRAGONS!

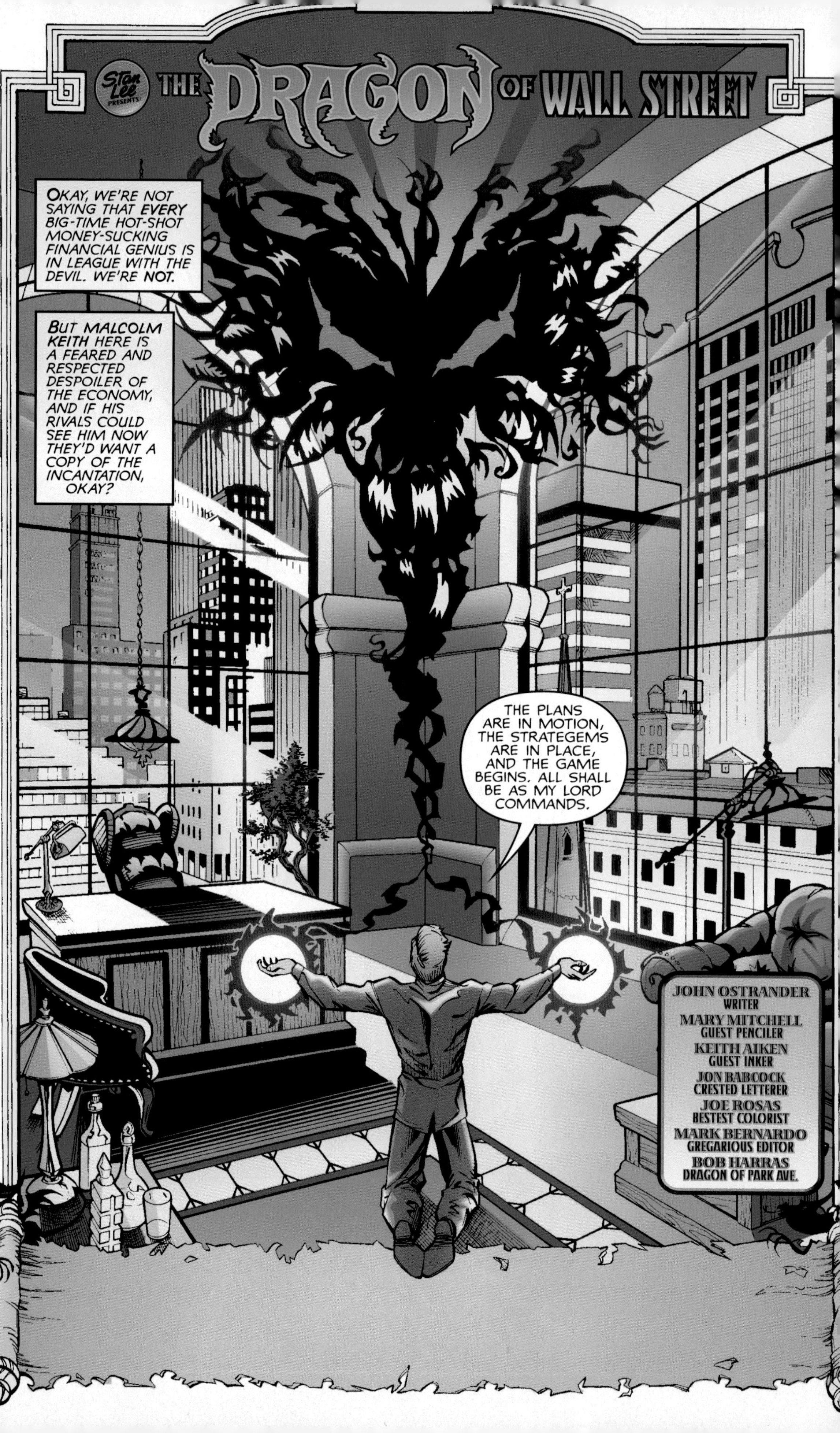

STAN LEE PRESENTS:
THE DRAGON OF WALL STREET
OKAY, WE'RE NOT SAYING THAT EVERY BIG-TIME HOT-SHOT MONEY-SUCKING FINANCIAL GENIUS IS IN LEAGUE WITH THE DEVIL. WE'RE NOT.
BUT MALCOLM KEITH HERE IS A FEARED AND RESPECTED DESPOILER OF THE ECONOMY, AND IF HIS RIVALS COULD SEE HIM NOW THEY'D WANT A COPY OF THE INCANTATION, OKAY?
THE PLANS ARE IN MOTION, THE STRATEGEMS ARE IN PLACE, AND THE GAME BEGINS. ALL SHALL BE AS MY LORD COMMANDS.
JOHN OSTRANDER WRITER
MARY MITCHELL GUEST PENCILER
KEITH AIKEN GUEST INKER
JON BABCOCK CRESTED LETTERER
JOE ROSAS BESTEST COLORIST
MARK BERNARDO GREGARIOUS EDITOR
BOB HARRAS DRAGON OF PARK AVE.

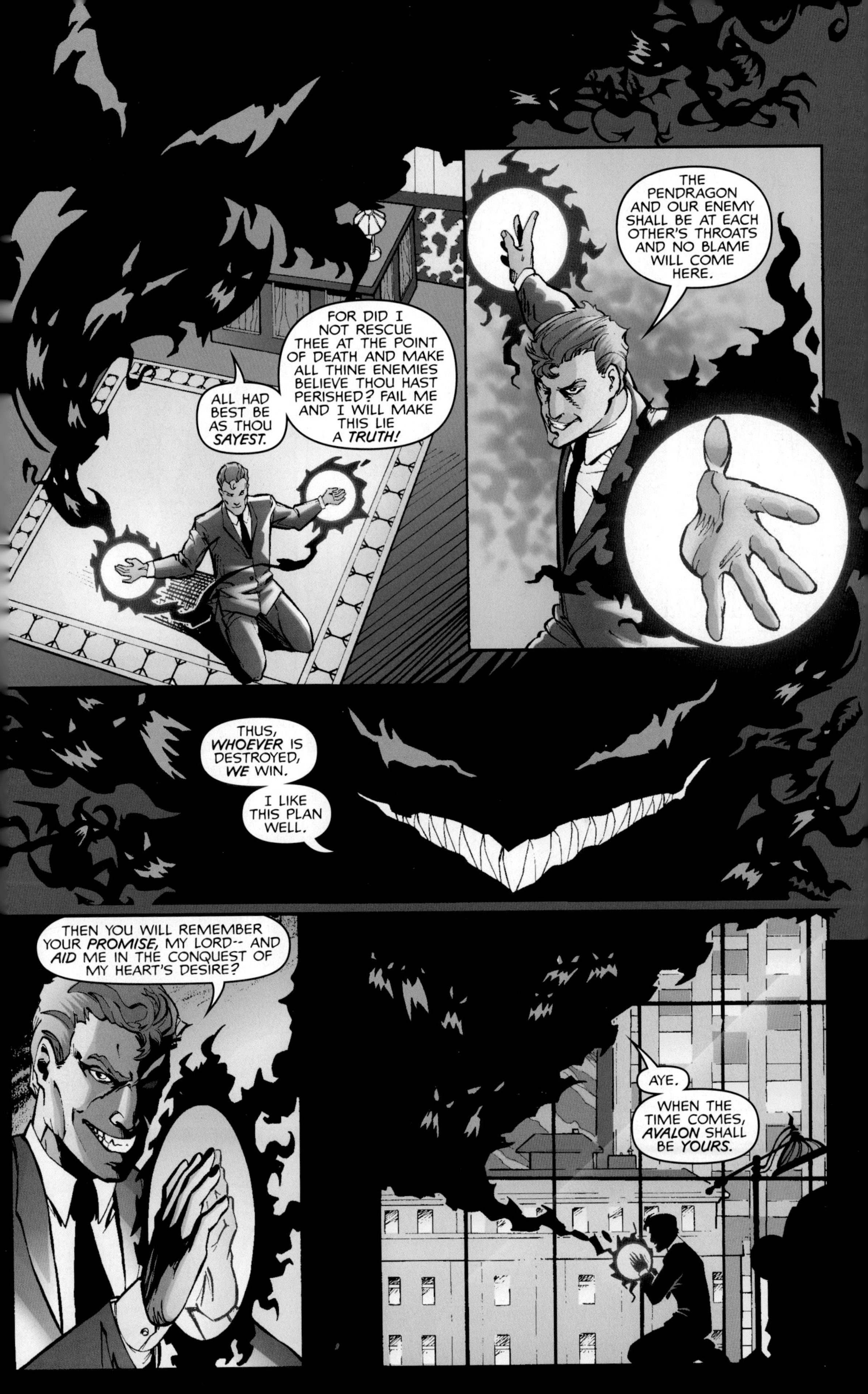
ALL HAD BEST BE AS THOU SAYEST.
FOR DID I NOT RESCUE THEE AT THE POINT OF DEATH AND MAKE ALL THINE ENEMIES BELIEVE THOU HAST PERISHED? FAIL ME AND I WILL MAKE THIS LIE A TRUTH!
THE PENDRAGON AND OUR ENEMY SHALL BE AT EACH OTHER'S THROATS AND NO BLAME WILL COME HERE.
THUS, WHOEVER IS DESTROYED, WE WIN.
I LIKE THIS PLAN WELL.
THEN YOU WILL REMEMBER YOUR PROMISE, MY LORD-- AND AID ME IN THE CONQUEST OF MY HEART'S DESIRE?
AYE.
WHEN THE TIME COMES, AVALON SHALL BE YOURS.

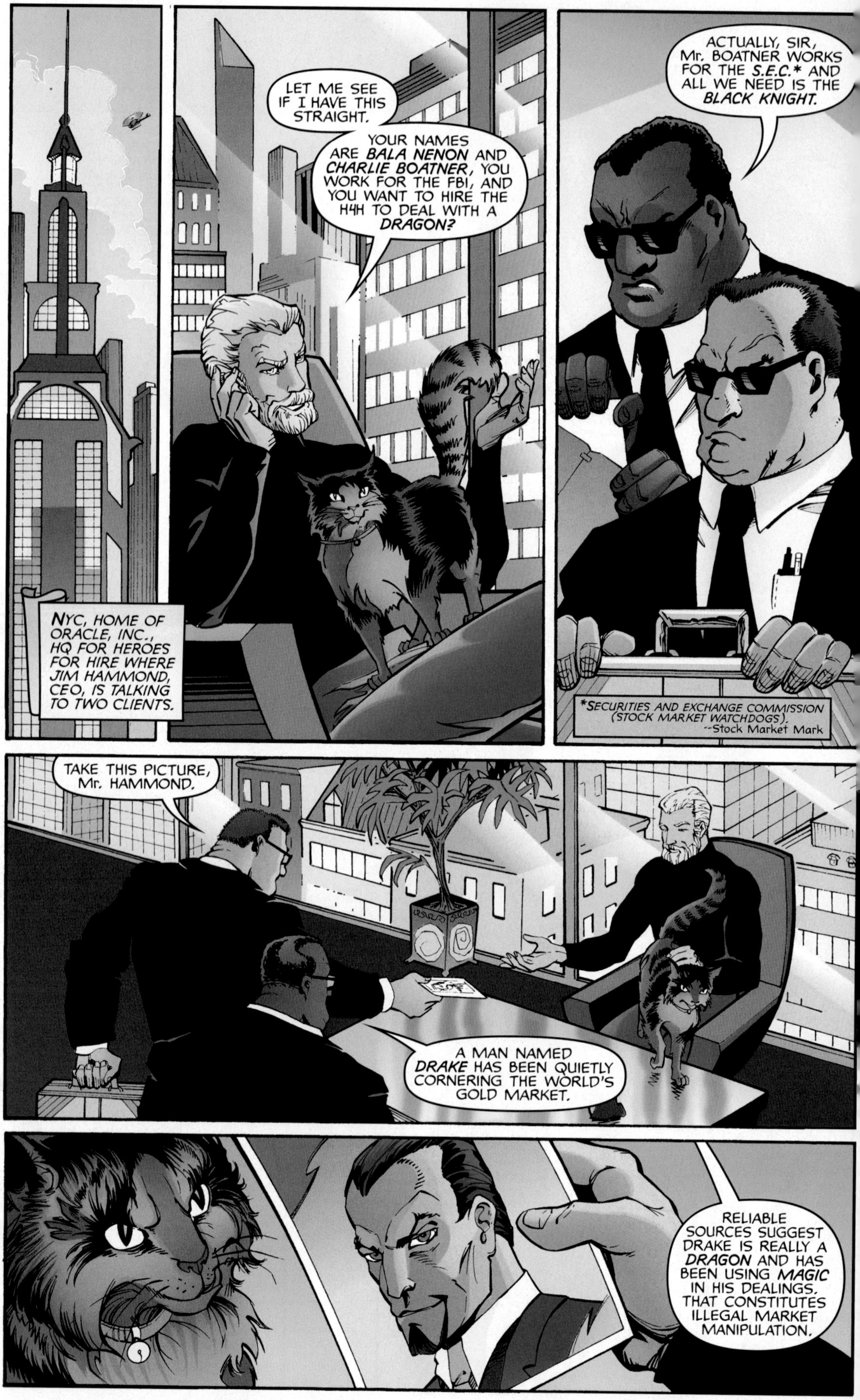
NYC, HOME OF ORACLE, INC., HQ FOR HEROES FOR HIRE WHERE JIM HAMMOND, CEO, IS TALKING TO TWO CLIENTS.
LET ME SEE IF I HAVE THIS STRAIGHT.
YOUR NAMES ARE BALA NENON AND CHARLIE BOATNER, YOU WORK FOR THE FBI, AND YOU WANT TO HIRE THE H4H TO DEAL WITH A DRAGON?
ACTUALLY, SIR, Mr. BOATNER WORKS FOR THE S.E.C.* AND ALL WE NEED IS THE BLACK KNIGHT.
*SECURITIES AND EXCHANGE COMMISSION (STOCK MARKET WATCHDOGS). --Stock Market Mark
TAKE THIS PICTURE, Mr. HAMMOND.
A MAN NAMED DRAKE HAS BEEN QUIETLY CORNERING THE WORLD'S GOLD MARKET.
RELIABLE SOURCES SUGGEST DRAKE IS REALLY A DRAGON AND HAS BEEN USING MAGIC IN HIS DEALINGS. THAT CONSTITUTES ILLEGAL MARKET MANIPULATION.

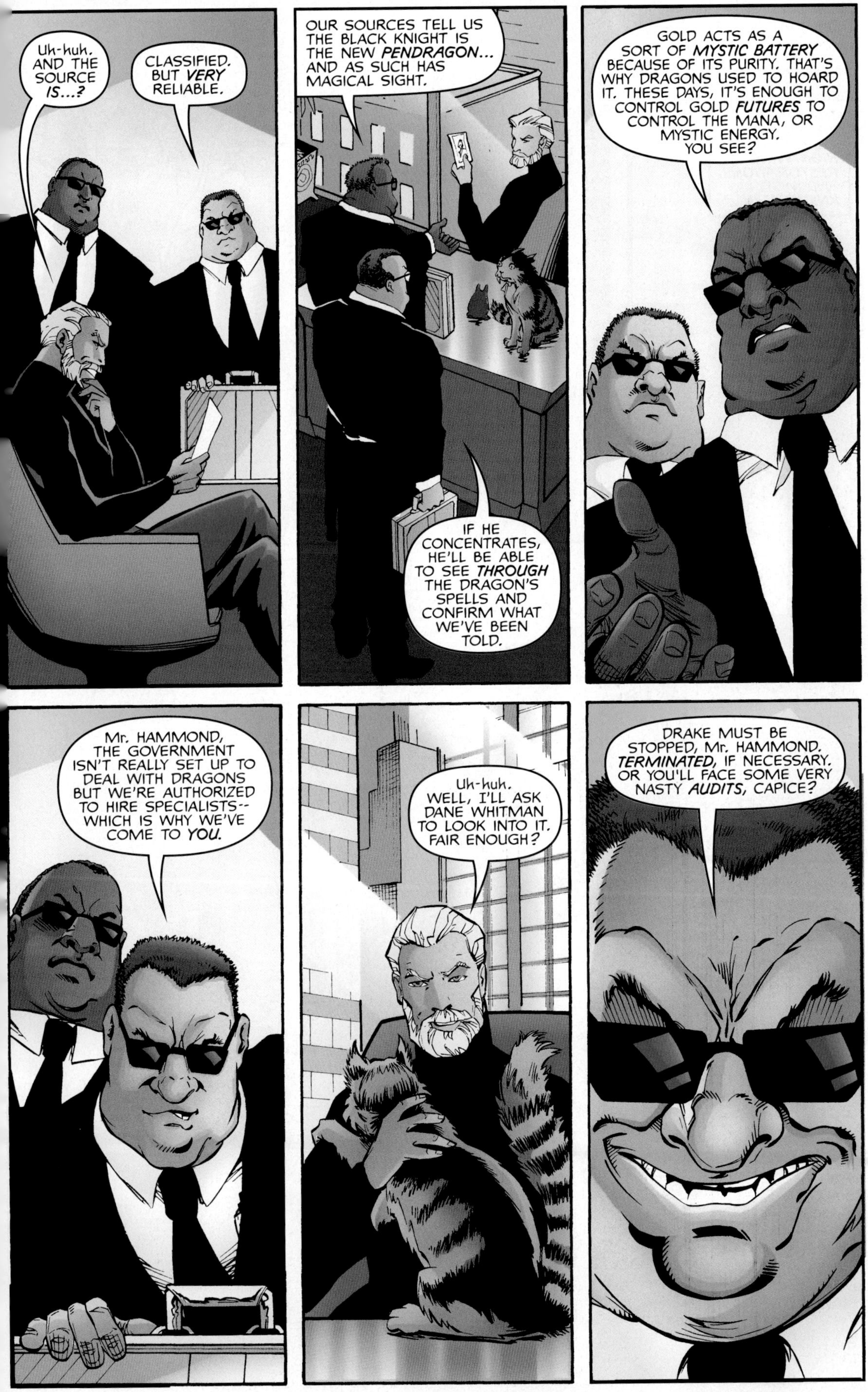
Uh-huh. AND THE SOURCE IS...?
CLASSIFIED. BUT VERY RELIABLE.
OUR SOURCES TELL US THE BLACK KNIGHT IS THE NEW PENDRAGON... AND AS SUCH HAS MAGICAL SIGHT.
IF HE CONCENTRATES, HE'LL BE ABLE TO SEE THROUGH THE DRAGON'S SPELLS AND CONFIRM WHAT WE'VE BEEN TOLD.
GOLD ACTS AS A SORT OF MYSTIC BATTERY BECAUSE OF ITS PURITY. THAT'S WHY DRAGONS USED TO HOARD IT. THESE DAYS, IT'S ENOUGH TO CONTROL GOLD FUTURES TO CONTROL THE MANA, OR MYSTIC ENERGY. YOU SEE?
Mr. HAMMOND, THE GOVERNMENT ISN'T REALLY SET UP TO DEAL WITH DRAGONS BUT WE'RE AUTHORIZED TO HIRE SPECIALISTS-- WHICH IS WHY WE'VE COME TO YOU.
Uh-huh. WELL, I'LL ASK DANE WHITMAN TO LOOK INTO IT. FAIR ENOUGH?
DRAKE MUST BE STOPPED, Mr. HAMMOND. TERMINATED, IF NECESSARY. OR YOU'LL FACE SOME VERY NASTY AUDITS, CAPICE?

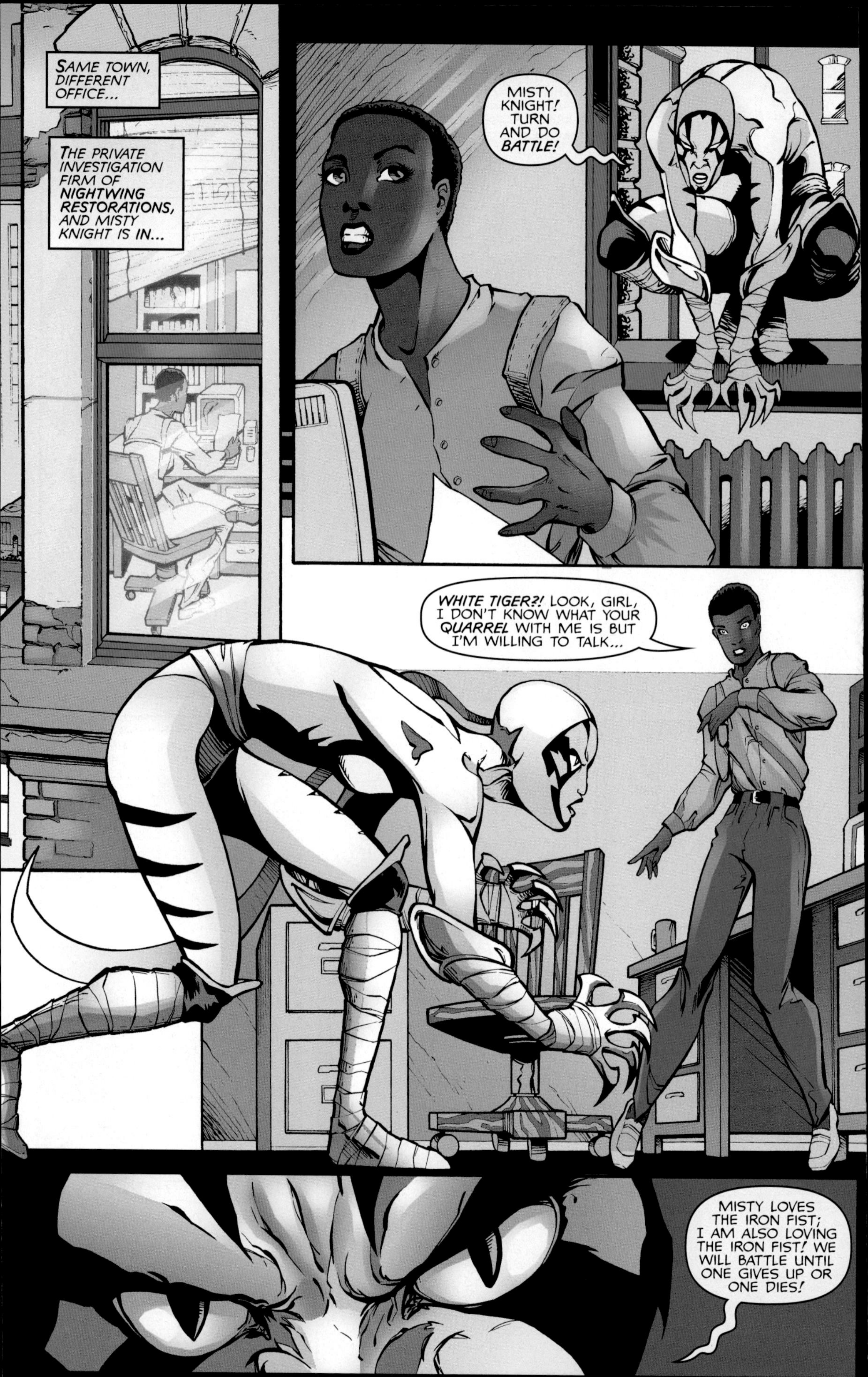
SAME TOWN, DIFFERENT OFFICE...
THE PRIVATE INVESTIGATION FIRM OF NIGHTWING RESTORATIONS, AND MISTY KNIGHT IS IN...
MISTY KNIGHT! TURN AND DO BATTLE!
WHITE TIGER?! LOOK, GIRL, I DON'T KNOW WHAT YOUR QUARREL WITH ME IS BUT I'M WILLING TO TALK...
MISTY LOVES THE IRON FIST; I AM ALSO LOVING THE IRON FIST! WE WILL BATTLE UNTIL ONE GIVES UP OR ONE DIES!

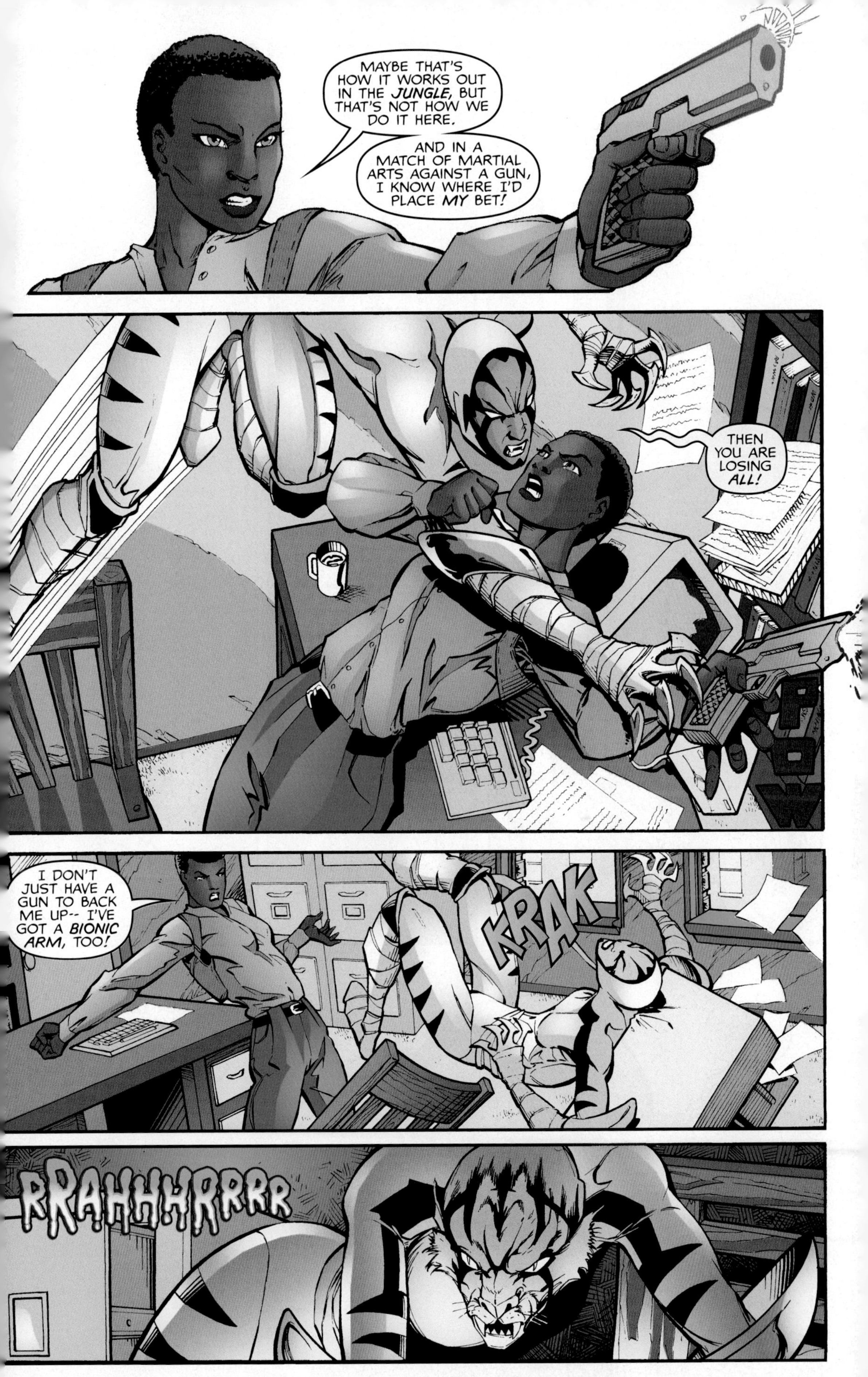
MAYBE THAT'S HOW IT WORKS OUT IN THE *JUNGLE*, BUT THAT'S NOT HOW WE DO IT HERE.
AND IN A MATCH OF MARTIAL ARTS AGAINST A GUN, I KNOW WHERE I'D PLACE *MY* BET!
THEN YOU ARE LOSING *ALL*!
POW
I DON'T JUST HAVE A GUN TO BACK ME UP-- I'VE GOT A *BIONIC ARM*, TOO!
KRAK
RRAHHHRRRR

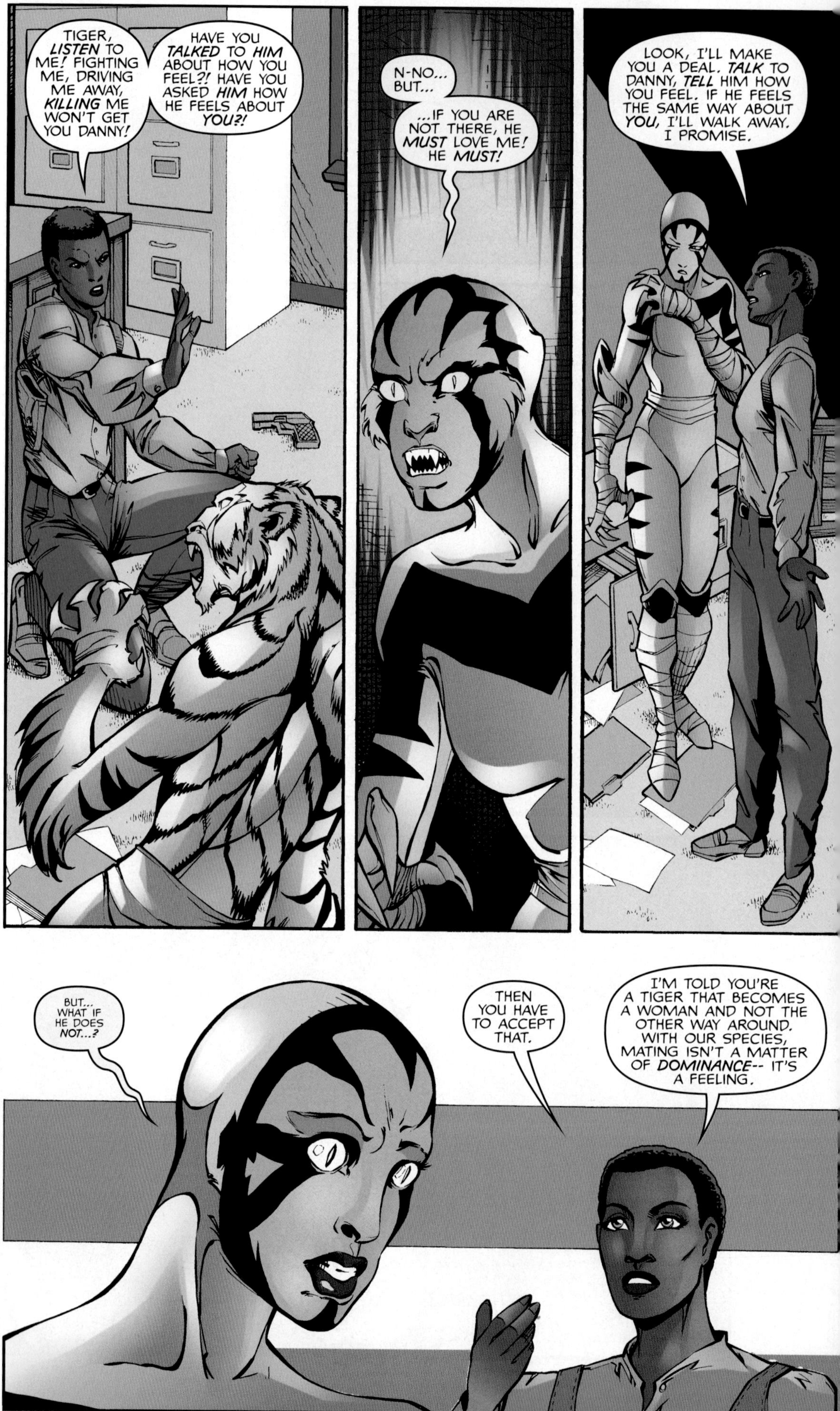
TIGER, LISTEN TO ME! FIGHTING ME, DRIVING ME AWAY, KILLING ME WON'T GET YOU DANNY!
HAVE YOU TALKED TO HIM ABOUT HOW YOU FEEL?! HAVE YOU ASKED HIM HOW HE FEELS ABOUT YOU?!
N-NO... BUT...
...IF YOU ARE NOT THERE, HE MUST LOVE ME! HE MUST!
LOOK, I'LL MAKE YOU A DEAL. TALK TO DANNY, TELL HIM HOW YOU FEEL. IF HE FEELS THE SAME WAY ABOUT YOU, I'LL WALK AWAY. I PROMISE.
BUT... WHAT IF HE DOES NOT...?
THEN YOU HAVE TO ACCEPT THAT.
I'M TOLD YOU'RE A TIGER THAT BECOMES A WOMAN AND NOT THE OTHER WAY AROUND. WITH OUR SPECIES, MATING ISN'T A MATTER OF DOMINANCE-- IT'S A FEELING.

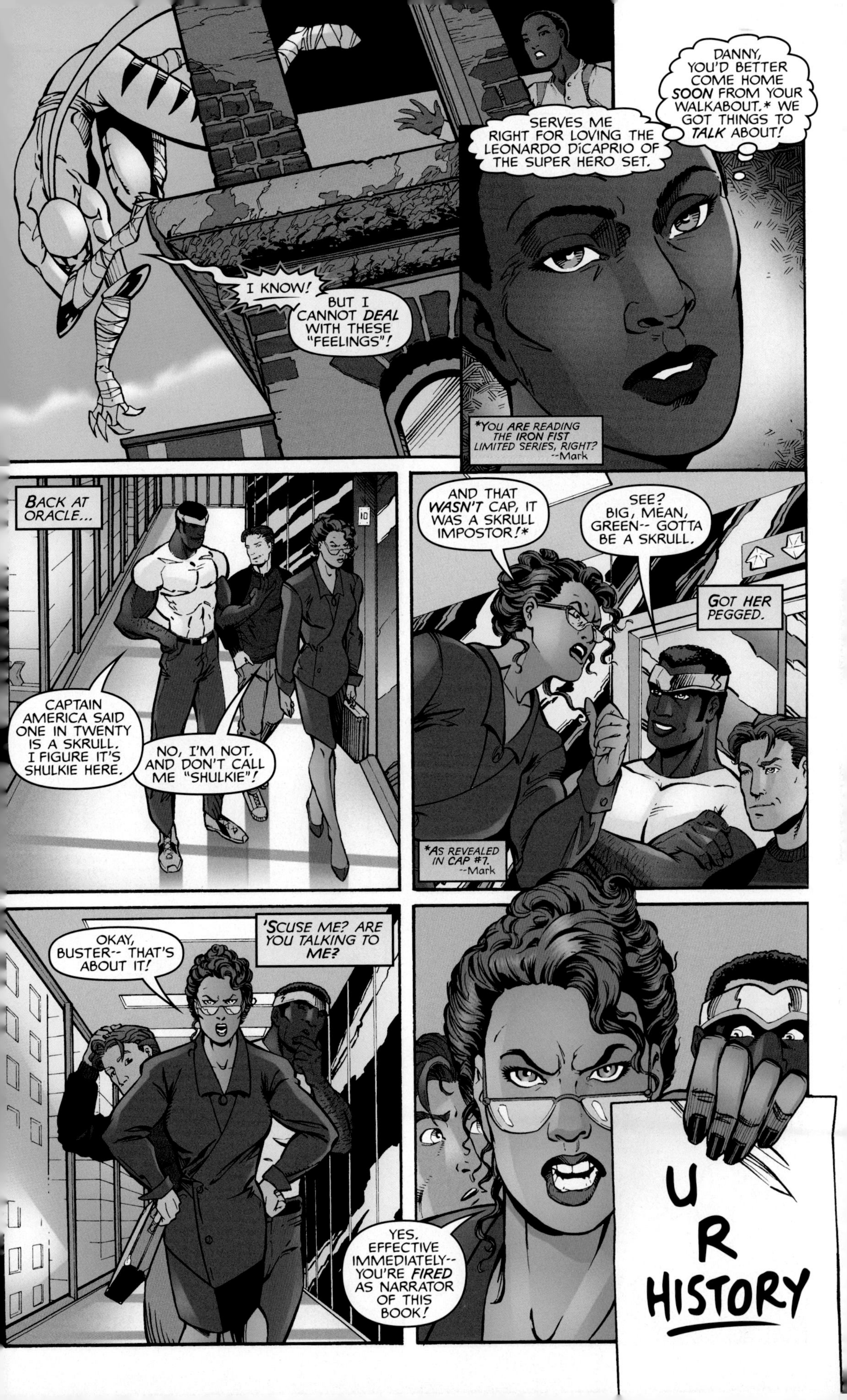
I KNOW!
BUT I CANNOT DEAL WITH THESE "FEELINGS"!
SERVES ME RIGHT FOR LOVING THE LEONARDO DiCAPRIO OF THE SUPER HERO SET.
DANNY, YOU'D BETTER COME HOME SOON FROM YOUR WALKABOUT.* WE GOT THINGS TO TALK ABOUT!
*YOU ARE READING THE IRON FIST LIMITED SERIES, RIGHT? --Mark
BACK AT ORACLE...
CAPTAIN AMERICA SAID ONE IN TWENTY IS A SKRULL. I FIGURE IT'S SHULKIE HERE.
NO, I'M NOT. AND DON'T CALL ME "SHULKIE"!
AND THAT WASN'T CAP, IT WAS A SKRULL IMPOSTOR!*
SEE? BIG, MEAN, GREEN-- GOTTA BE A SKRULL.
GOT HER PEGGED.
*AS REVEALED IN CAP #7. --Mark
OKAY, BUSTER-- THAT'S ABOUT IT!
'SCUSE ME? ARE YOU TALKING TO ME?
YES. EFFECTIVE IMMEDIATELY-- YOU'RE FIRED AS NARRATOR OF THIS BOOK!
U R HISTORY

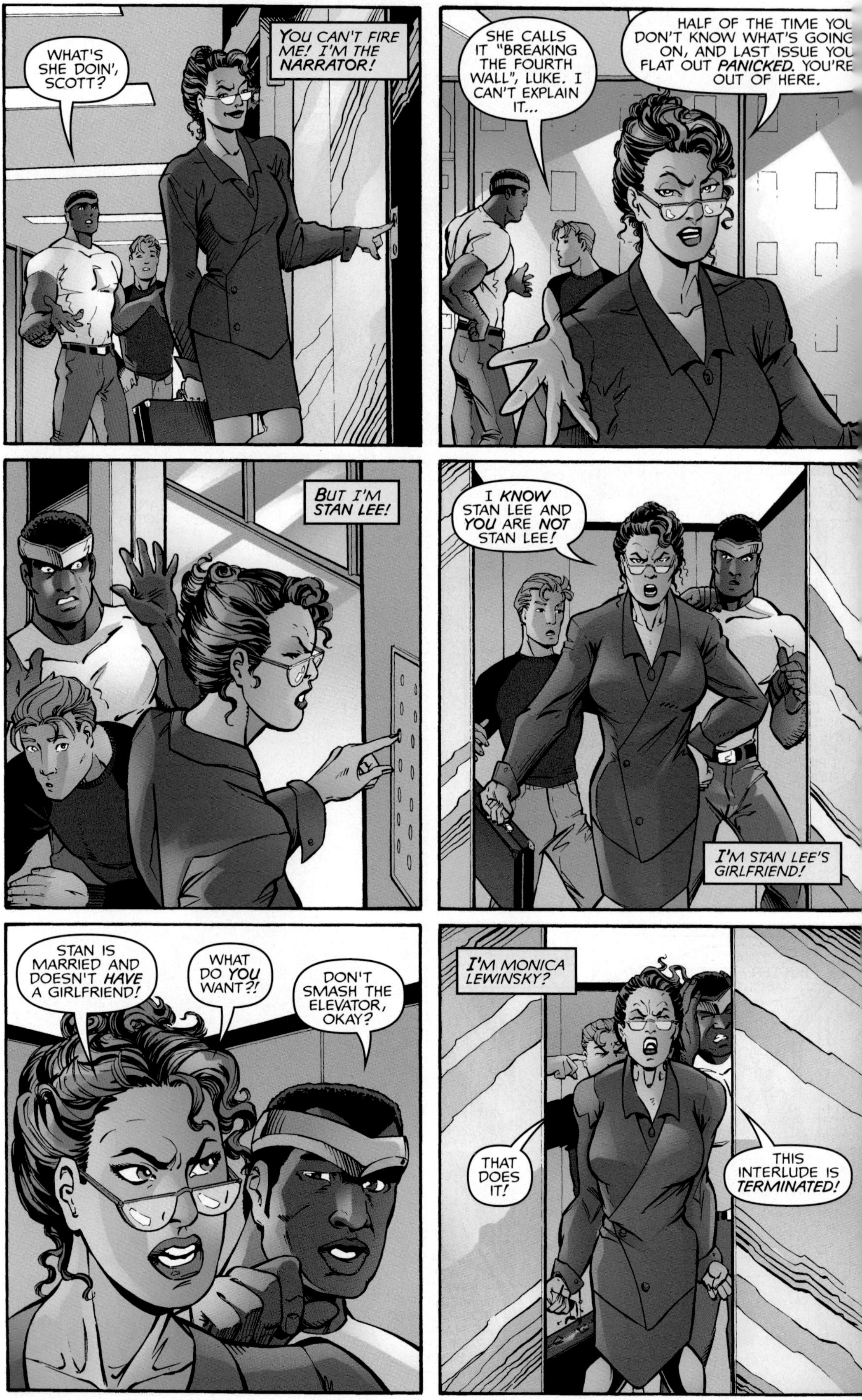
WHAT'S SHE DOIN', SCOTT?
YOU CAN'T FIRE ME! I'M THE NARRATOR!
SHE CALLS IT "BREAKING THE FOURTH WALL", LUKE. I CAN'T EXPLAIN IT...
HALF OF THE TIME YOU DON'T KNOW WHAT'S GOING ON, AND LAST ISSUE YOU FLAT OUT PANICKED. YOU'RE OUT OF HERE.
BUT I'M STAN LEE!
I KNOW STAN LEE AND YOU ARE NOT STAN LEE!
I'M STAN LEE'S GIRLFRIEND!
STAN IS MARRIED AND DOESN'T HAVE A GIRLFRIEND!
WHAT DO YOU WANT?!
DON'T SMASH THE ELEVATOR, OKAY?
I'M MONICA LEWINSKY?
THAT DOES IT!
THIS INTERLUDE IS TERMINATED!

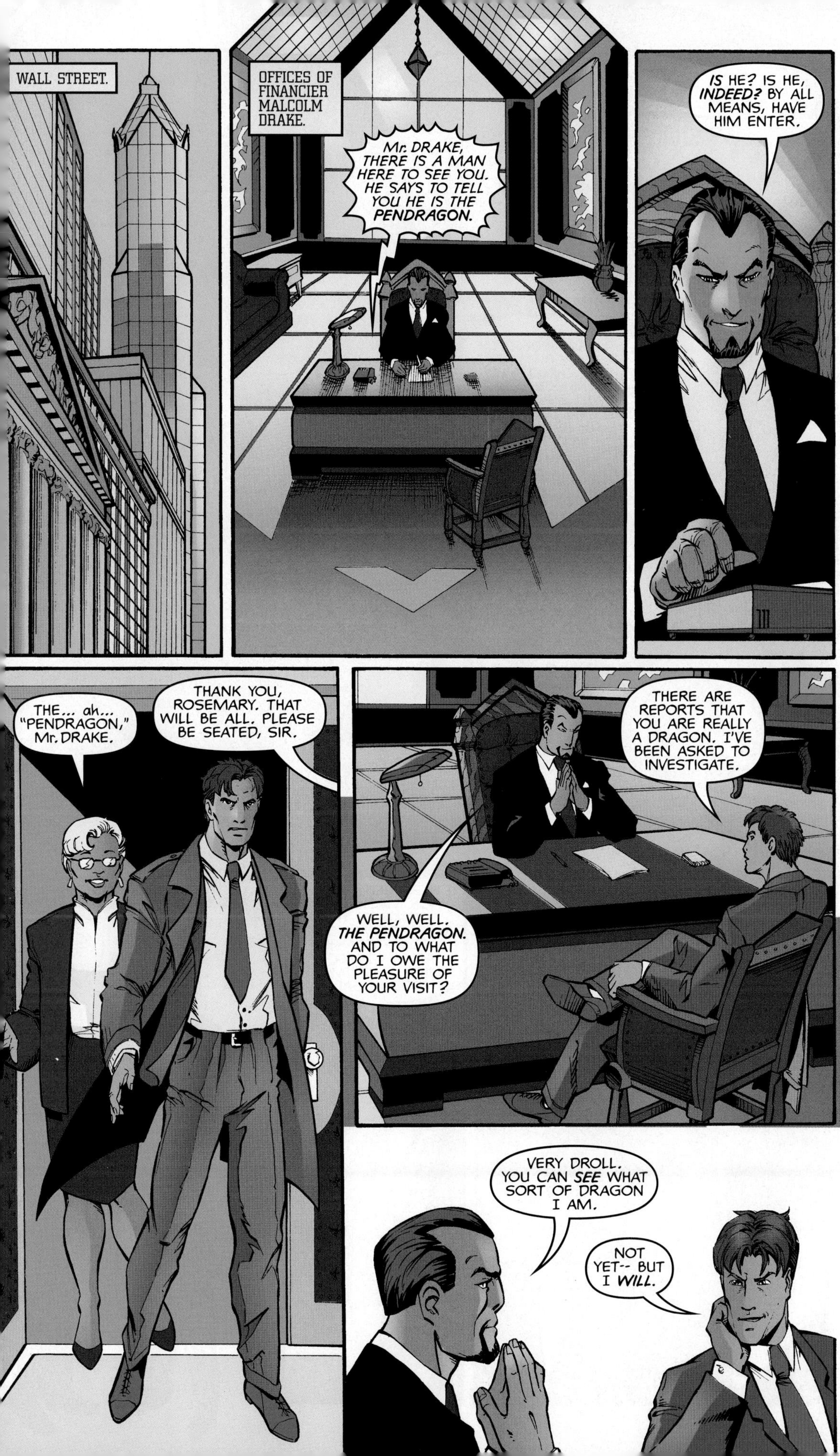
WALL STREET.
OFFICES OF FINANCIER MALCOLM DRAKE.
Mr. DRAKE, THERE IS A MAN HERE TO SEE YOU. HE SAYS TO TELL YOU HE IS THE PENDRAGON.
IS HE? IS HE, INDEED? BY ALL MEANS, HAVE HIM ENTER.
THE... ah... "PENDRAGON," Mr. DRAKE.
THANK YOU, ROSEMARY. THAT WILL BE ALL. PLEASE BE SEATED, SIR.
WELL, WELL. THE PENDRAGON. AND TO WHAT DO I OWE THE PLEASURE OF YOUR VISIT?
THERE ARE REPORTS THAT YOU ARE REALLY A DRAGON. I'VE BEEN ASKED TO INVESTIGATE.
VERY DROLL. YOU CAN SEE WHAT SORT OF DRAGON I AM.
NOT YET-- BUT I WILL.

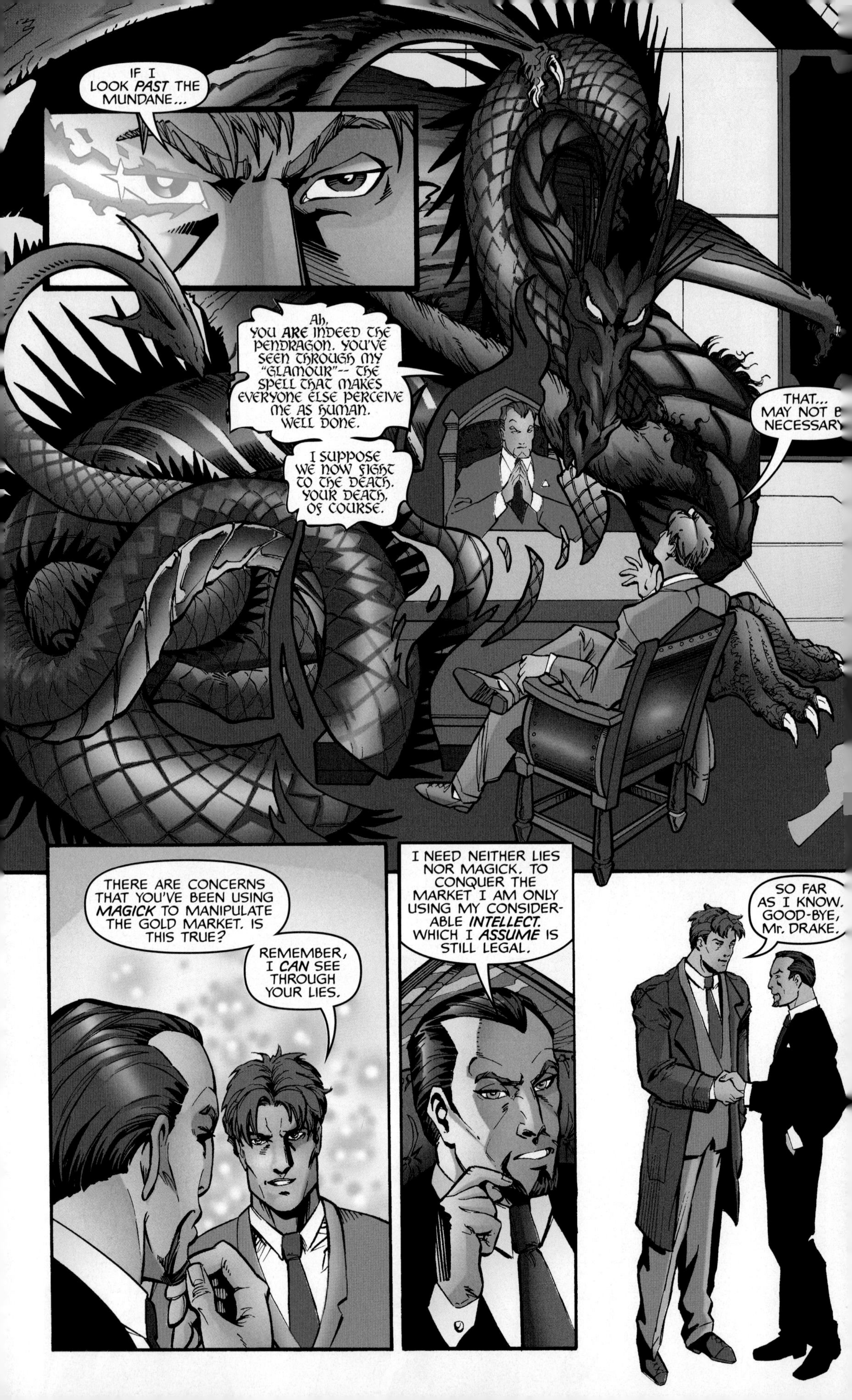
IF I LOOK PAST THE MUNDANE...
Ah, YOU ARE INDEED THE PENDRAGON. YOU'VE SEEN THROUGH MY "GLAMOUR"-- THE SPELL THAT MAKES EVERYONE ELSE PERCEIVE ME AS HUMAN. WELL DONE.
I SUPPOSE WE NOW FIGHT TO THE DEATH. YOUR DEATH, OF COURSE.
THAT... MAY NOT B NECESSARY
THERE ARE CONCERNS THAT YOU'VE BEEN USING MAGICK TO MANIPULATE THE GOLD MARKET. IS THIS TRUE?
REMEMBER, I CAN SEE THROUGH YOUR LIES.
I NEED NEITHER LIES NOR MAGICK. TO CONQUER THE MARKET I AM ONLY USING MY CONSIDERABLE INTELLECT. WHICH I ASSUME IS STILL LEGAL.
SO FAR AS I KNOW. GOOD-BYE, Mr. DRAKE.

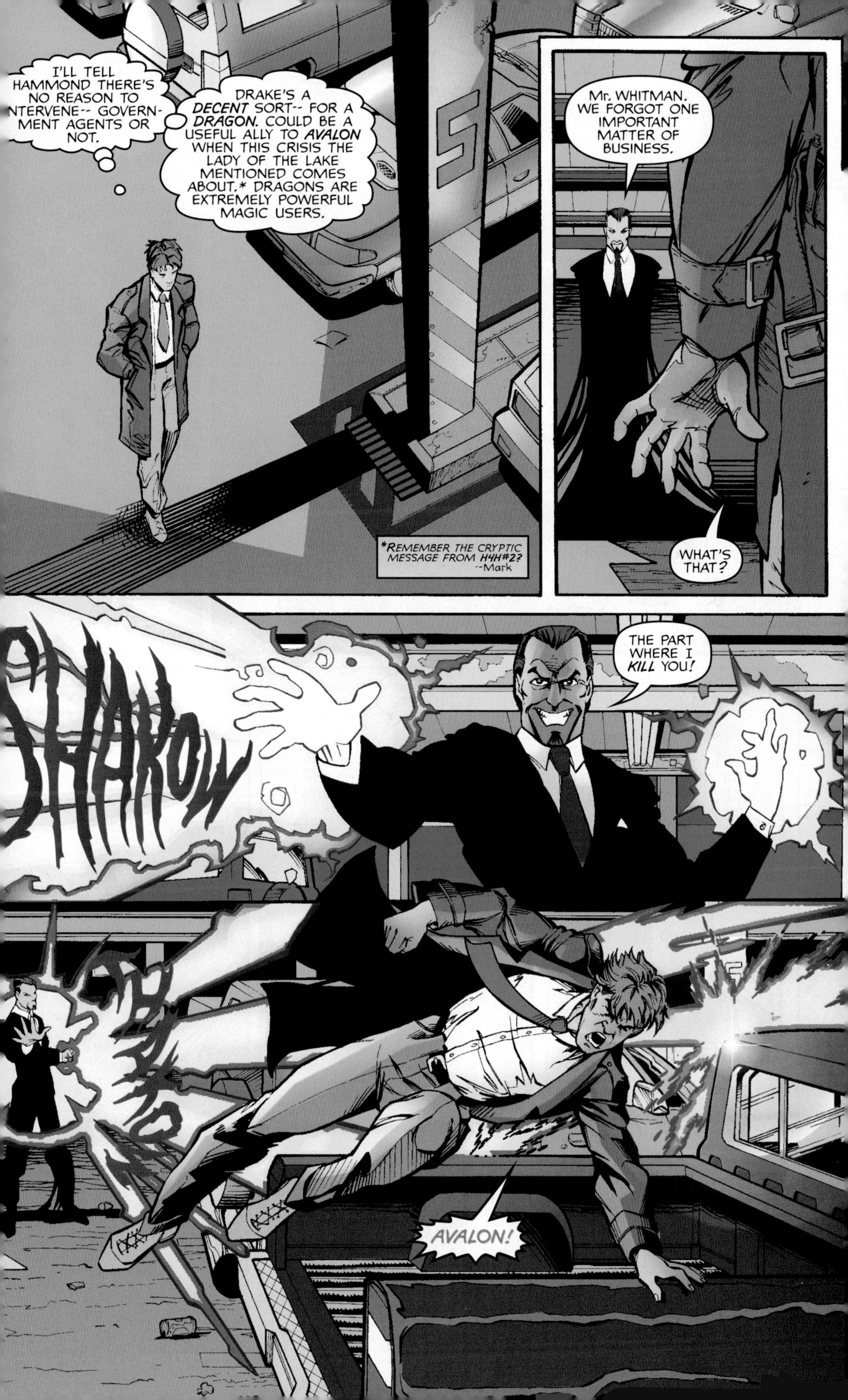
I'LL TELL HAMMOND THERE'S NO REASON TO INTERVENE-- GOVERNMENT AGENTS OR NOT.
DRAKE'S A DECENT SORT-- FOR A DRAGON. COULD BE A USEFUL ALLY TO AVALON WHEN THIS CRISIS THE LADY OF THE LAKE MENTIONED COMES ABOUT.* DRAGONS ARE EXTREMELY POWERFUL MAGIC USERS.
*REMEMBER THE CRYPTIC MESSAGE FROM H4H#2? --Mark
Mr. WHITMAN. WE FORGOT ONE IMPORTANT MATTER OF BUSINESS.
WHAT'S THAT?
THE PART WHERE I KILL YOU!
SHAKOW
AVALON!

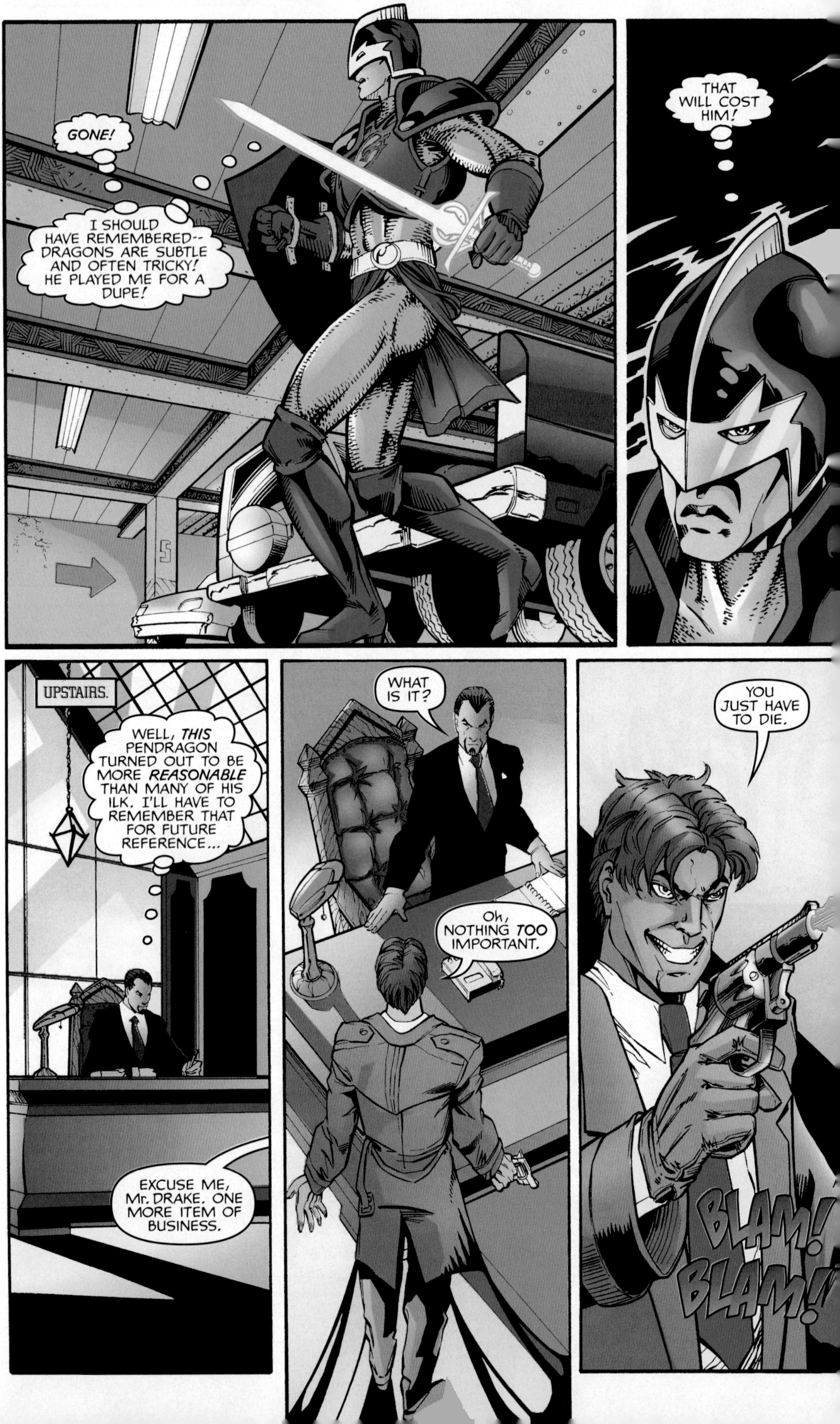
GONE!
I SHOULD HAVE REMEMBERED-- DRAGONS ARE SUBTLE AND OFTEN TRICKY! HE PLAYED ME FOR A DUPE!
THAT WILL COST HIM!
UPSTAIRS.
WELL, THIS PENDRAGON TURNED OUT TO BE MORE REASONABLE THAN MANY OF HIS ILK. I'LL HAVE TO REMEMBER THAT FOR FUTURE REFERENCE...
EXCUSE ME, Mr. DRAKE. ONE MORE ITEM OF BUSINESS.
WHAT IS IT?
Oh, NOTHING TOO IMPORTANT.
YOU JUST HAVE TO DIE.
BLAM! BLAM!!

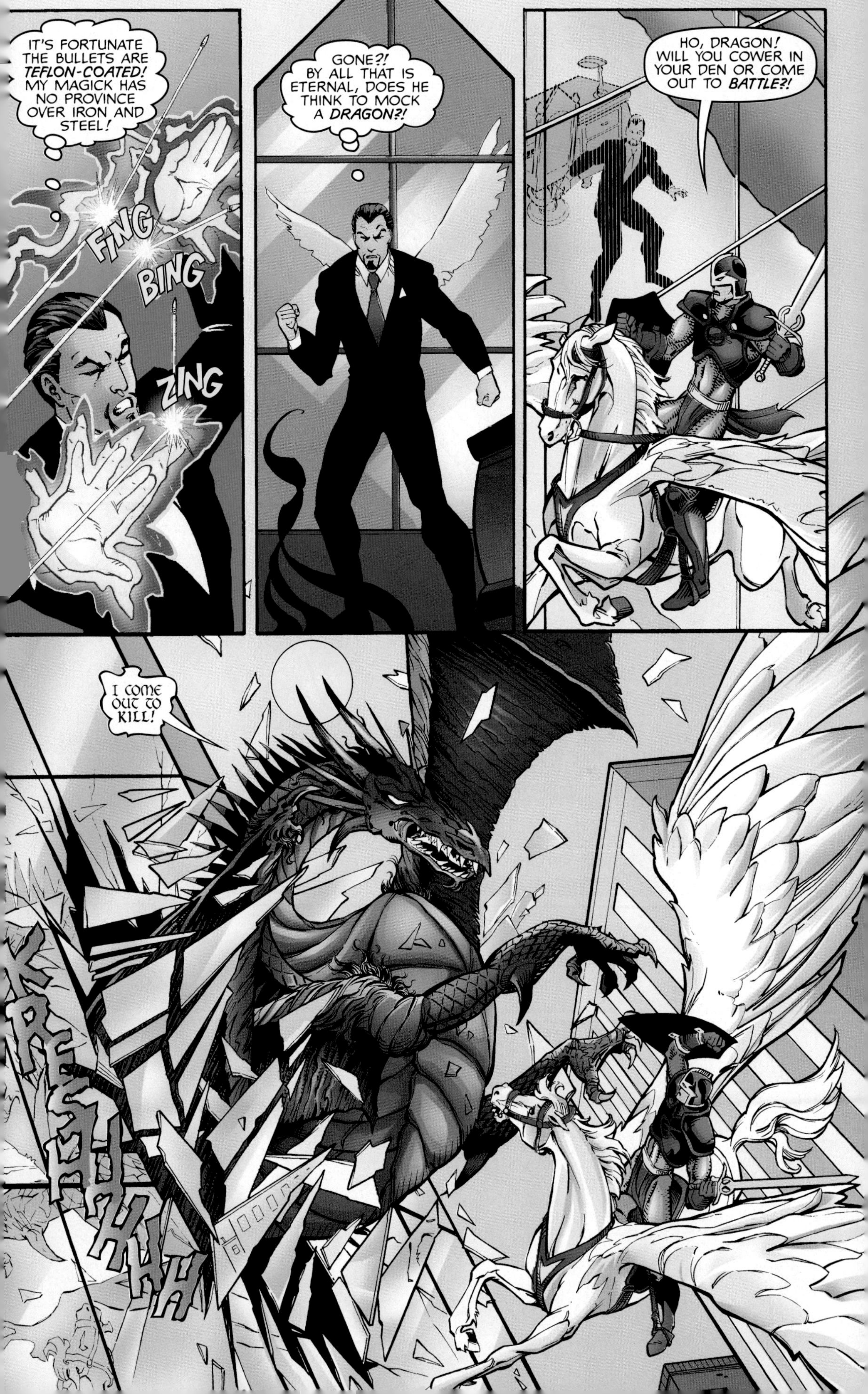
IT'S FORTUNATE THE BULLETS ARE TEFLON-COATED! MY MAGICK HAS NO PROVINCE OVER IRON AND STEEL!
FING
BING
ZING
GONE?! BY ALL THAT IS ETERNAL, DOES HE THINK TO MOCK A DRAGON?!
HO, DRAGON! WILL YOU COWER IN YOUR DEN OR COME OUT TO BATTLE?!
I COME OUT TO KILL!
KRESHHHHH

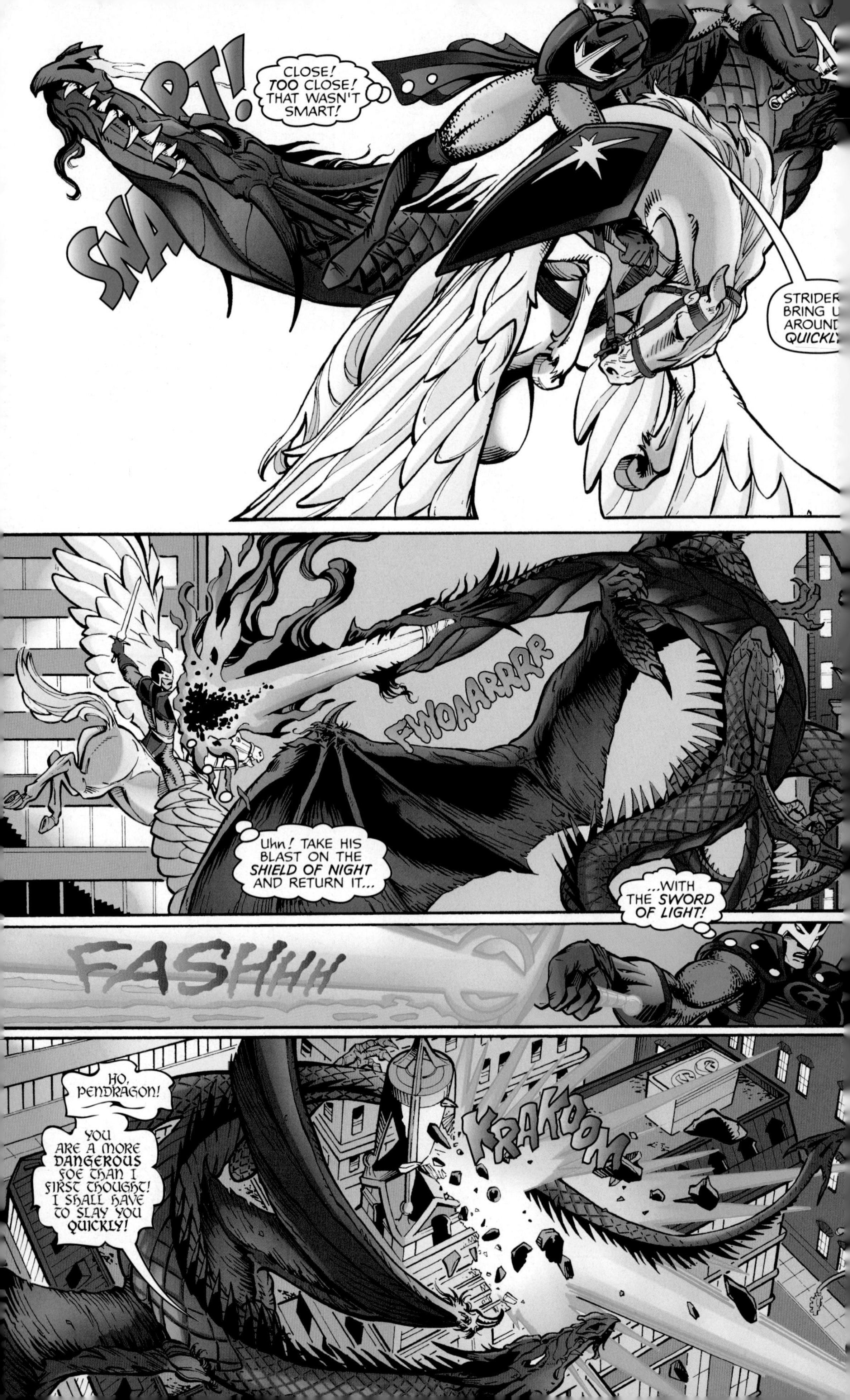
SNAPT!
CLOSE! TOO CLOSE! THAT WASN'T SMART!
STRIDER BRING U AROUND QUICKLY
FWOAARRRR
Uhn! TAKE HIS BLAST ON THE SHIELD OF NIGHT AND RETURN IT...
...WITH THE SWORD OF LIGHT!
FASHHH
HO, PENDRAGON!
YOU ARE A MORE DANGEROUS FOE THAN I FIRST THOUGHT! I SHALL HAVE TO SLAY YOU QUICKLY!
KRAKOOM!

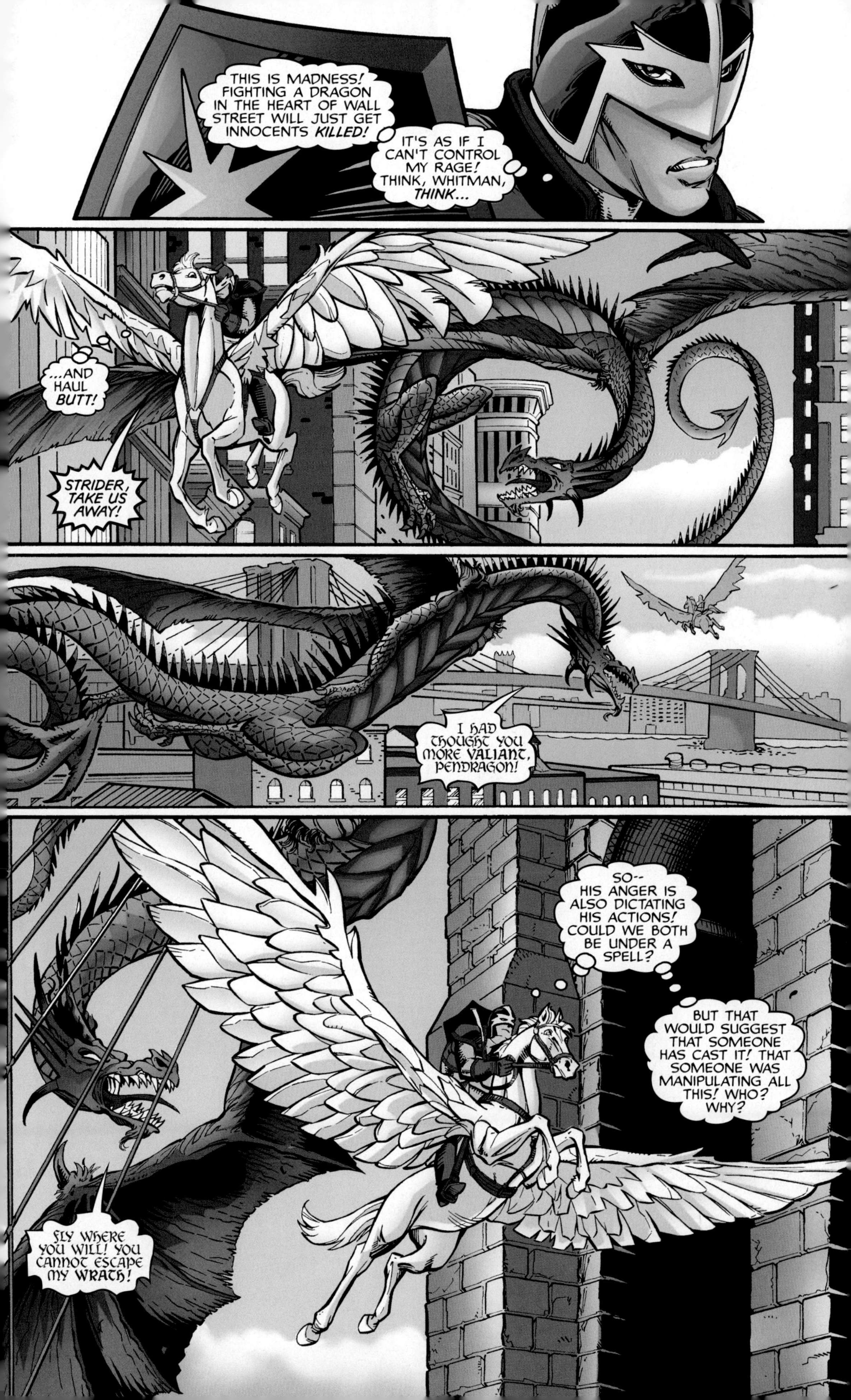
THIS IS MADNESS! FIGHTING A DRAGON IN THE HEART OF WALL STREET WILL JUST GET INNOCENTS KILLED!
IT'S AS IF I CAN'T CONTROL MY RAGE! THINK, WHITMAN, THINK...
...AND HAUL BUTT!
STRIDER, TAKE US AWAY!
I HAD THOUGHT YOU MORE VALIANT, PENDRAGON!
SO-- HIS ANGER IS ALSO DICTATING HIS ACTIONS! COULD WE BOTH BE UNDER A SPELL?
BUT THAT WOULD SUGGEST THAT SOMEONE HAS CAST IT! THAT SOMEONE WAS MANIPULATING ALL THIS! WHO? WHY?
FLY WHERE YOU WILL! YOU CANNOT ESCAPE MY WRATH!

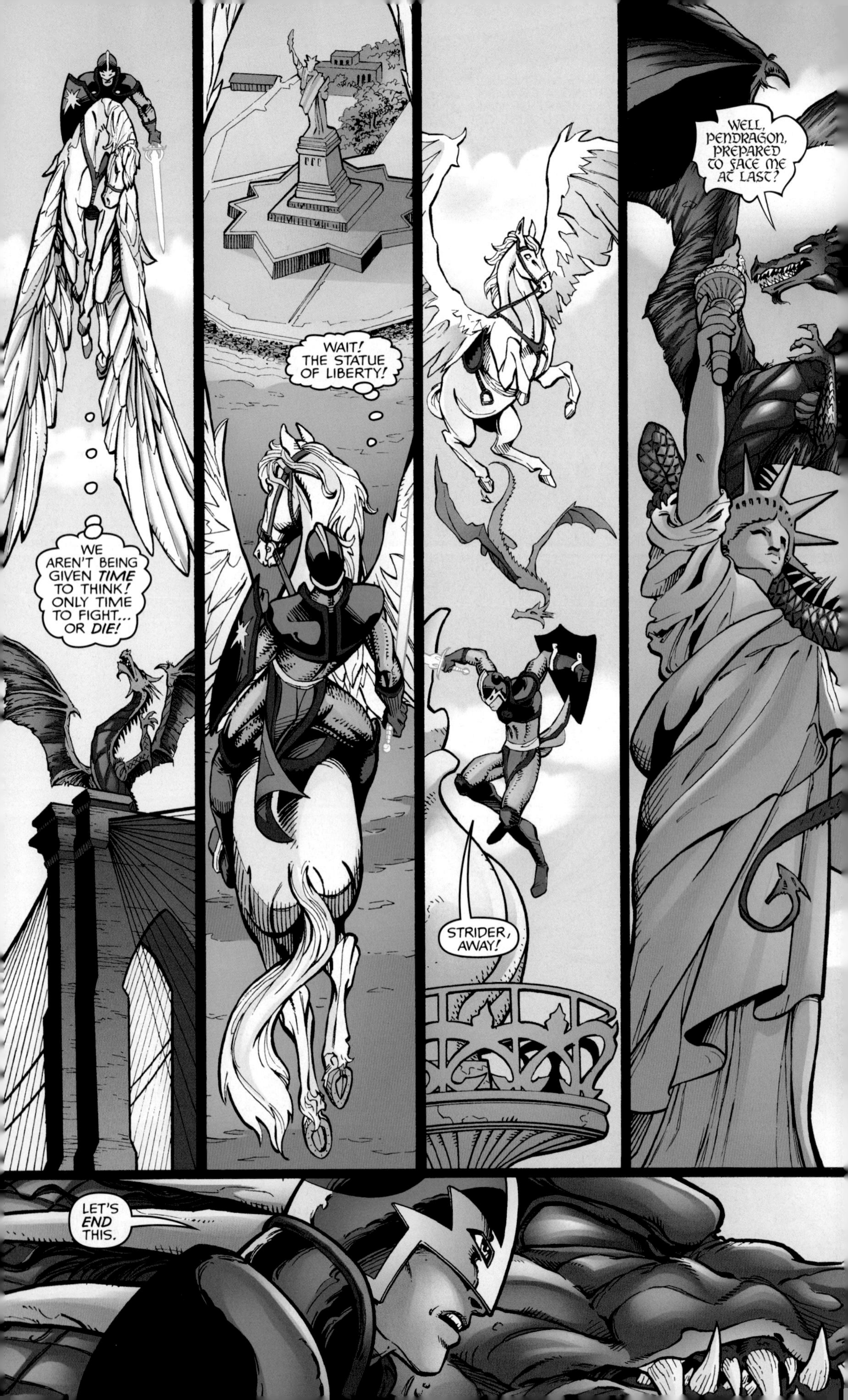
WE AREN'T BEING GIVEN TIME TO THINK! ONLY TIME TO FIGHT... OR DIE!
WAIT! THE STATUE OF LIBERTY!
STRIDER, AWAY!
WELL, PENDRAGON, PREPARED TO FACE ME AT LAST?
LET'S END THIS.

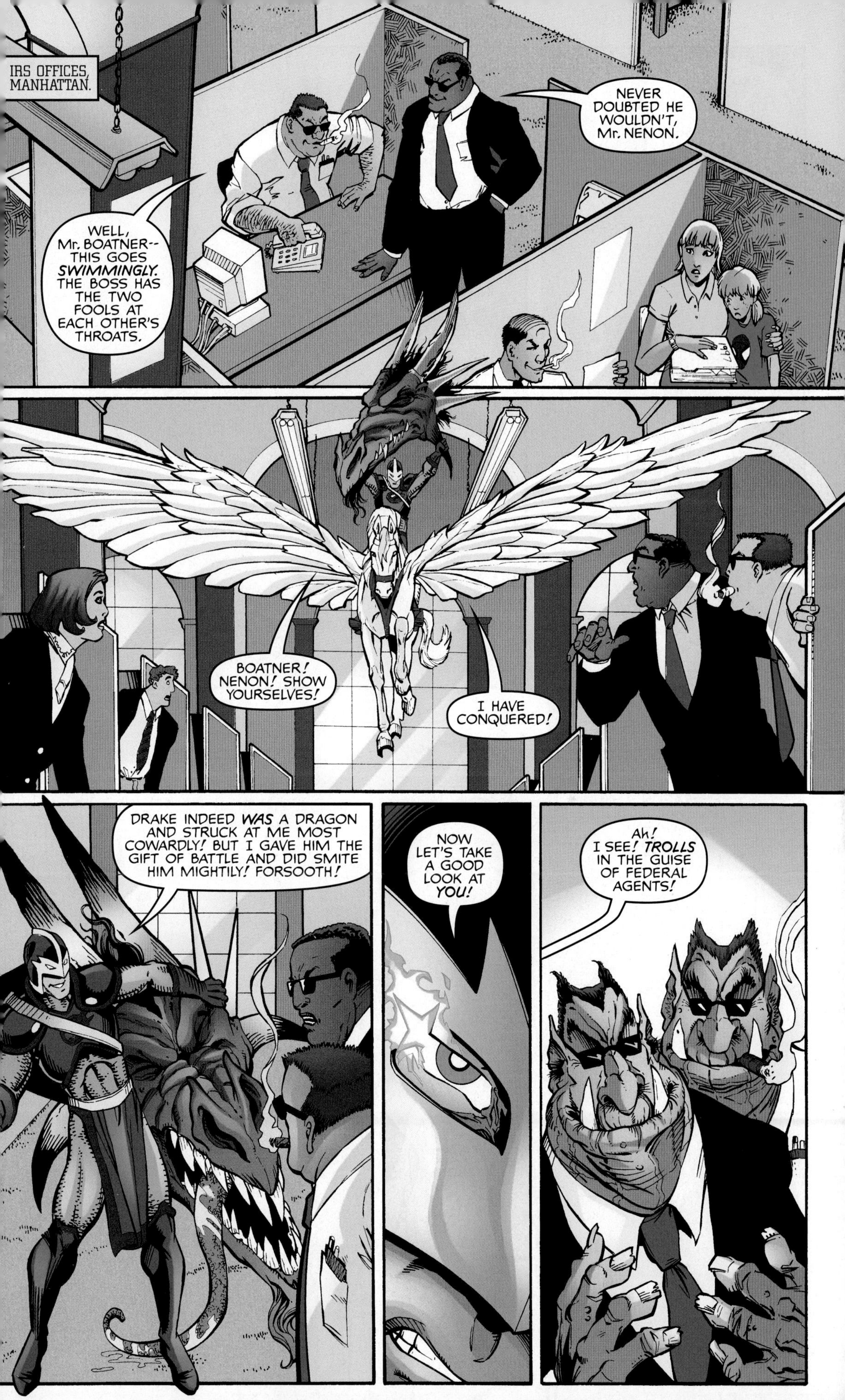
IRS OFFICES, MANHATTAN.
WELL, Mr. BOATNER-- THIS GOES *SWIMMINGLY.* THE BOSS HAS THE TWO FOOLS AT EACH OTHER'S THROATS.
NEVER DOUBTED HE WOULDN'T, Mr. NENON.
BOATNER! NENON! SHOW YOURSELVES!
I HAVE CONQUERED!
DRAKE INDEED *WAS* A DRAGON AND STRUCK AT ME MOST COWARDLY! BUT I GAVE HIM THE GIFT OF BATTLE AND DID SMITE HIM MIGHTILY! FORSOOTH!
NOW LET'S TAKE A GOOD LOOK AT *YOU!*
Ah! I SEE! *TROLLS* IN THE GUISE OF FEDERAL AGENTS!

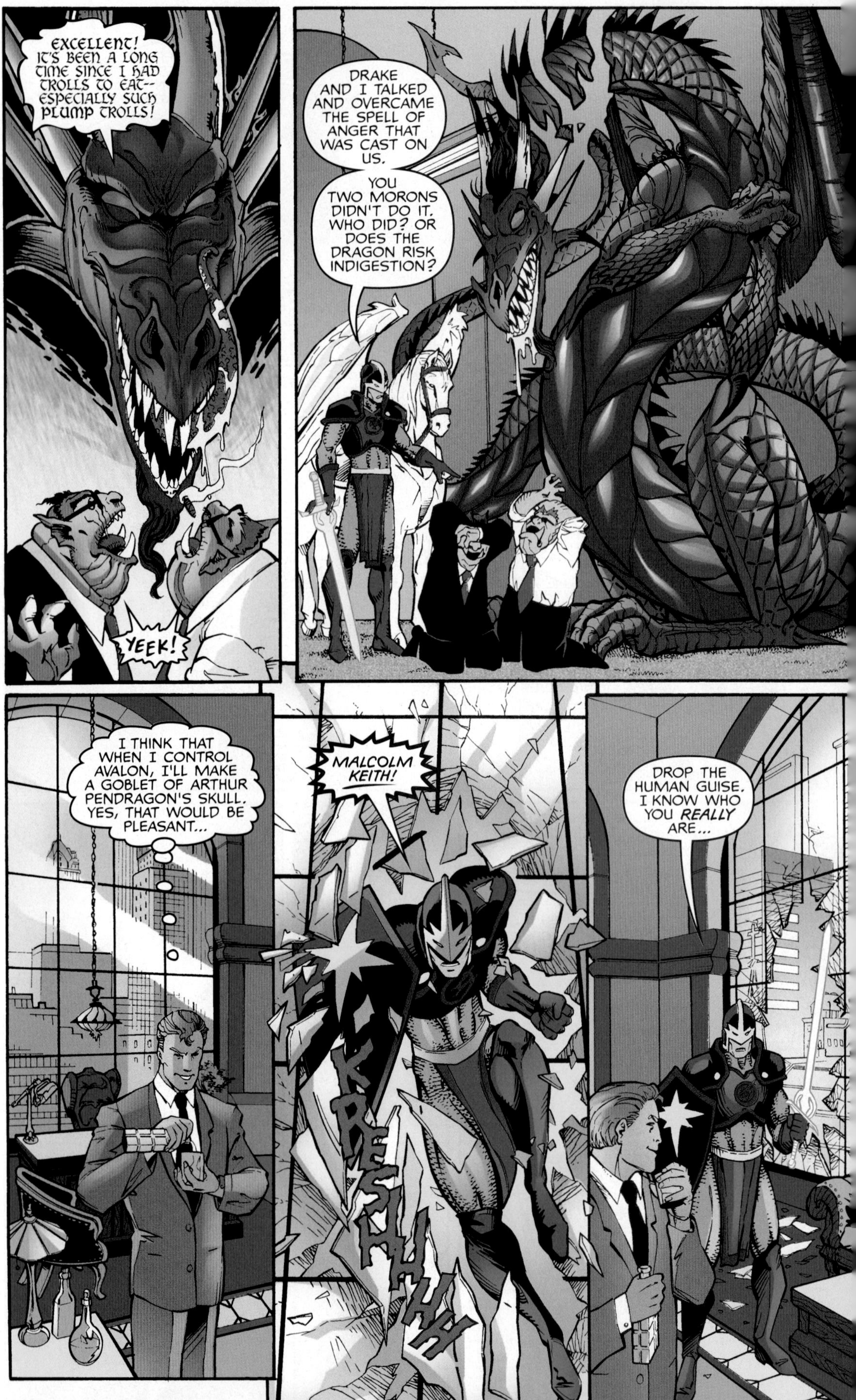
EXCELLENT! IT'S BEEN A LONG TIME SINCE I HAD TROLLS TO EAT-- ESPECIALLY SUCH PLUMP TROLLS!
YEEK!
DRAKE AND I TALKED AND OVERCAME THE SPELL OF ANGER THAT WAS CAST ON US.
YOU TWO MORONS DIDN'T DO IT. WHO DID? OR DOES THE DRAGON RISK INDIGESTION?
I THINK THAT WHEN I CONTROL AVALON, I'LL MAKE A GOBLET OF ARTHUR PENDRAGON'S SKULL. YES, THAT WOULD BE PLEASANT...
MALCOLM KEITH!
KRESHHHH
DROP THE HUMAN GUISE. I KNOW WHO YOU *REALLY* ARE...

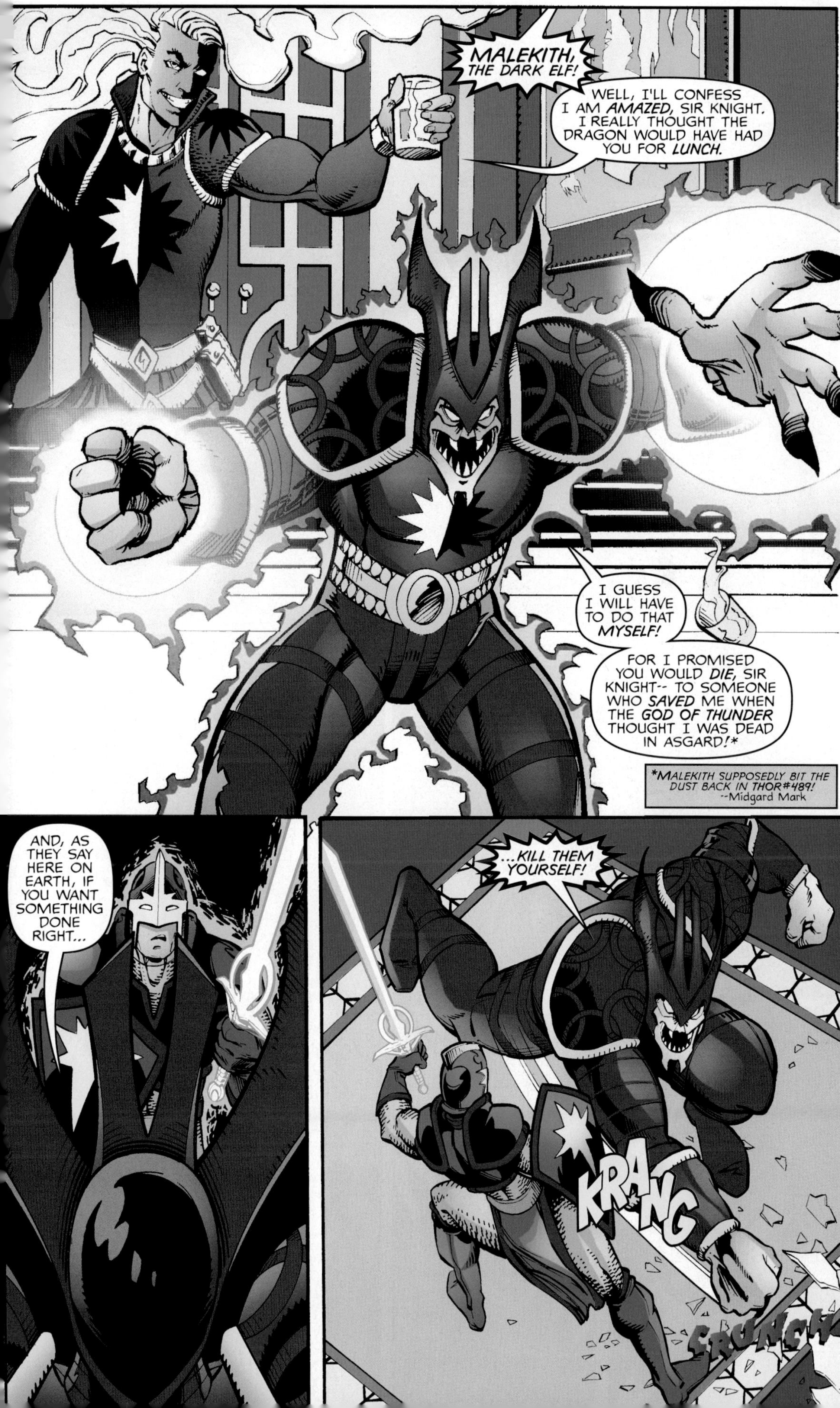
MALEKITH, THE DARK ELF!
WELL, I'LL CONFESS I AM AMAZED, SIR KNIGHT. I REALLY THOUGHT THE DRAGON WOULD HAVE HAD YOU FOR LUNCH.
I GUESS I WILL HAVE TO DO THAT MYSELF!
FOR I PROMISED YOU WOULD DIE, SIR KNIGHT-- TO SOMEONE WHO SAVED ME WHEN THE GOD OF THUNDER THOUGHT I WAS DEAD IN ASGARD!*
*MALEKITH SUPPOSEDLY BIT THE DUST BACK IN THOR#489! --Midgard Mark
AND, AS THEY SAY HERE ON EARTH, IF YOU WANT SOMETHING DONE RIGHT...
...KILL THEM YOURSELF!
KRANG
CRUNCH

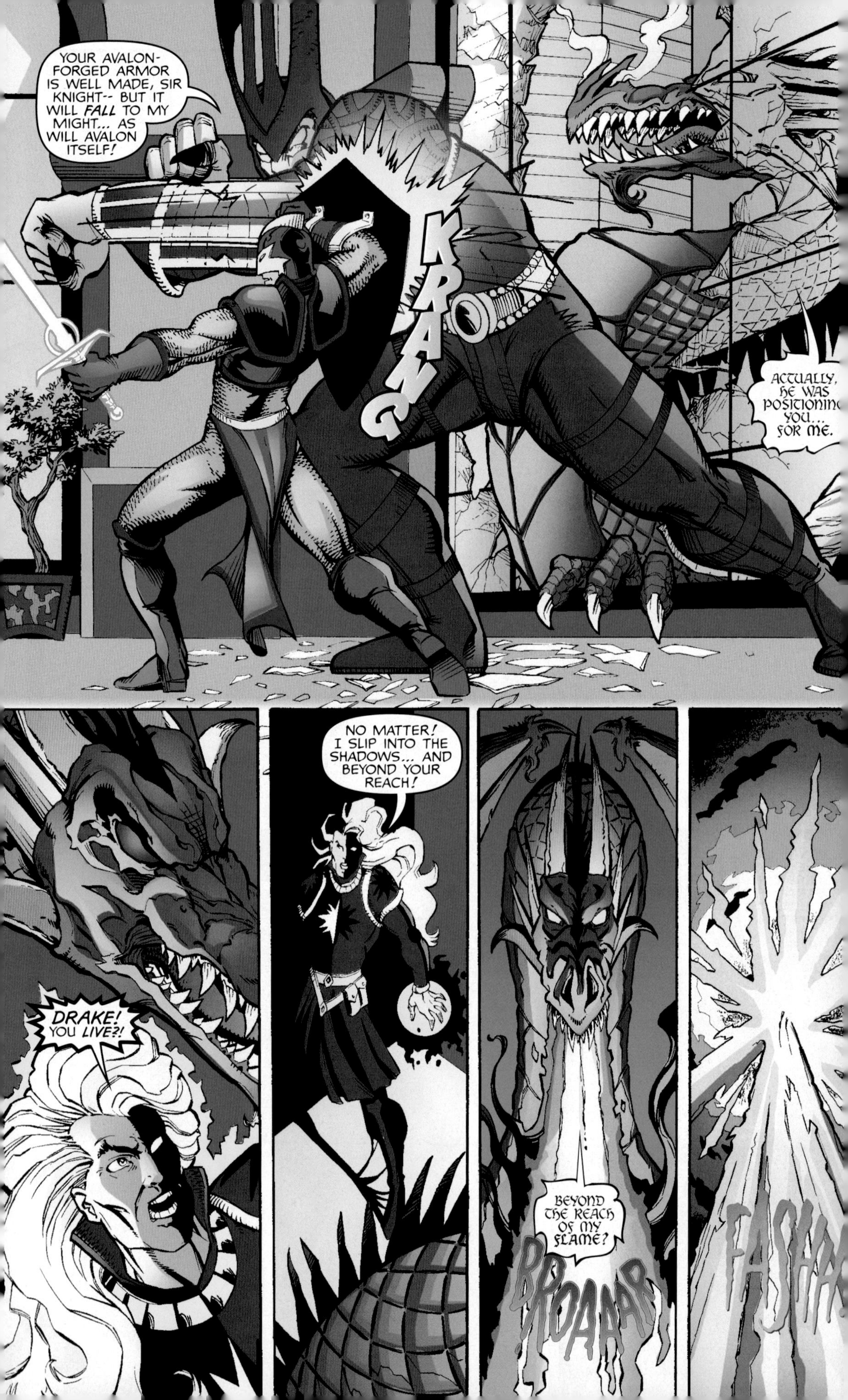
YOUR AVALON-FORGED ARMOR IS WELL MADE, SIR KNIGHT-- BUT IT WILL FALL TO MY MIGHT... AS WILL AVALON ITSELF!
KRANG
ACTUALLY, HE WAS POSITIONING YOU... FOR ME.
DRAKE! YOU LIVE?!
NO MATTER! I SLIP INTO THE SHADOWS... AND BEYOND YOUR REACH!
BEYOND THE REACH OF MY FLAME?
BROAAAR
FASHA

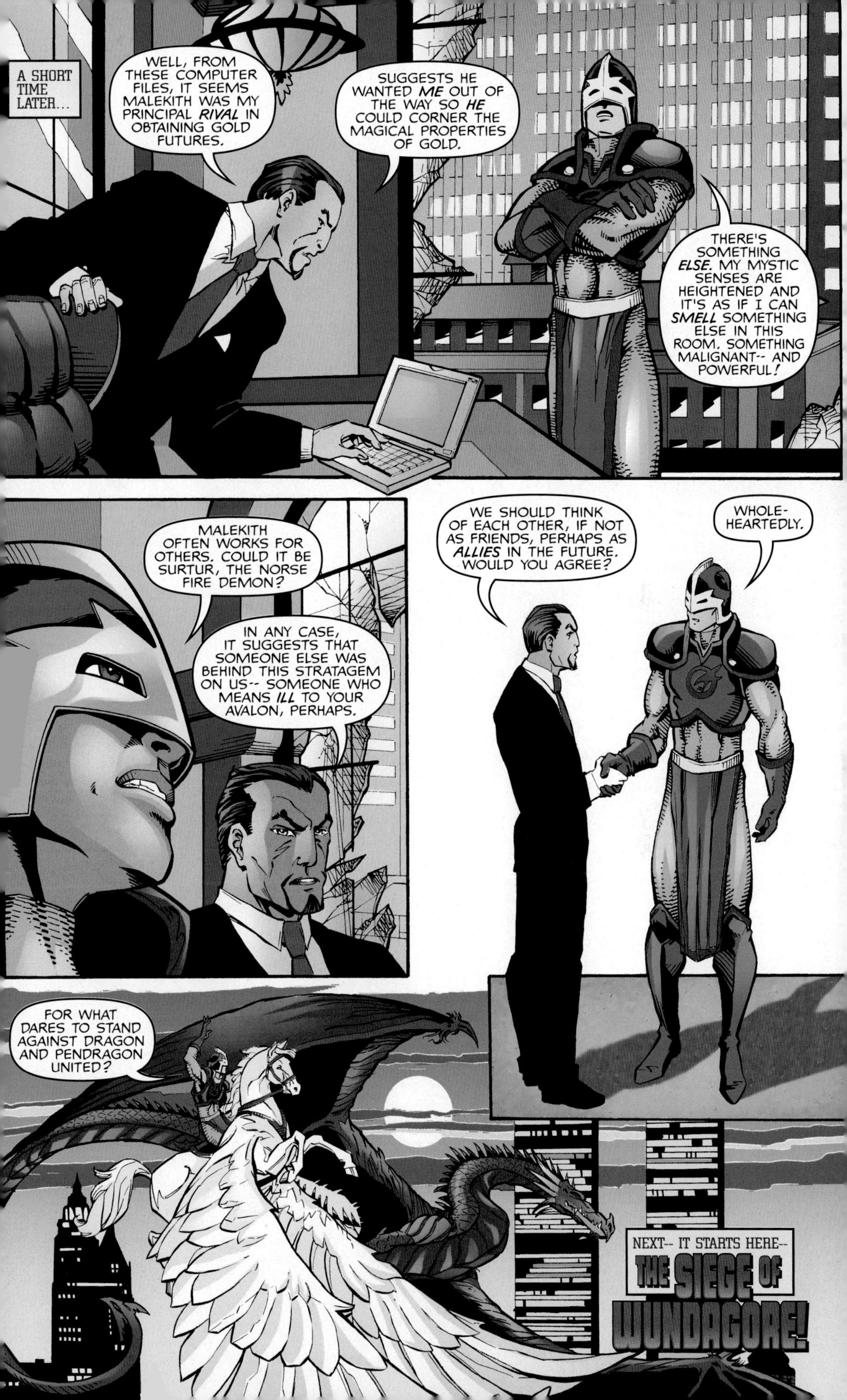

A SHORT TIME LATER...
WELL, FROM THESE COMPUTER FILES, IT SEEMS MALEKITH WAS MY PRINCIPAL RIVAL IN OBTAINING GOLD FUTURES.
SUGGESTS HE WANTED ME OUT OF THE WAY SO HE COULD CORNER THE MAGICAL PROPERTIES OF GOLD.
THERE'S SOMETHING ELSE. MY MYSTIC SENSES ARE HEIGHTENED AND IT'S AS IF I CAN SMELL SOMETHING ELSE IN THIS ROOM. SOMETHING MALIGNANT-- AND POWERFUL!
MALEKITH OFTEN WORKS FOR OTHERS. COULD IT BE SURTUR, THE NORSE FIRE DEMON?
IN ANY CASE, IT SUGGESTS THAT SOMEONE ELSE WAS BEHIND THIS STRATAGEM ON US-- SOMEONE WHO MEANS ILL TO YOUR AVALON, PERHAPS.
WE SHOULD THINK OF EACH OTHER, IF NOT AS FRIENDS, PERHAPS AS ALLIES IN THE FUTURE. WOULD YOU AGREE?
WHOLE-HEARTEDLY.
FOR WHAT DARES TO STAND AGAINST DRAGON AND PENDRAGON UNITED?
NEXT-- IT STARTS HERE--
THE SIEGE OF WUNDAGORE!

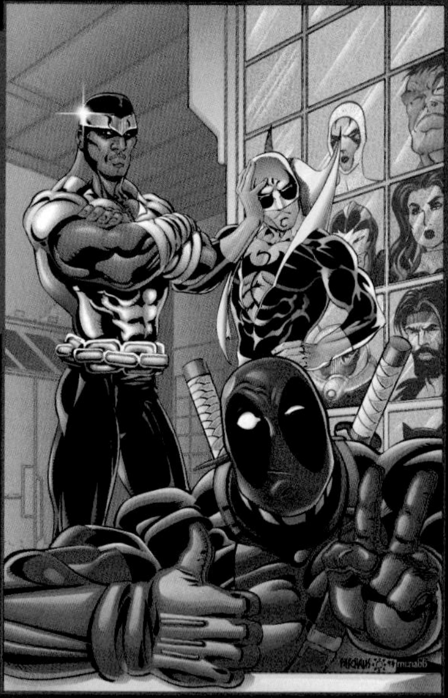
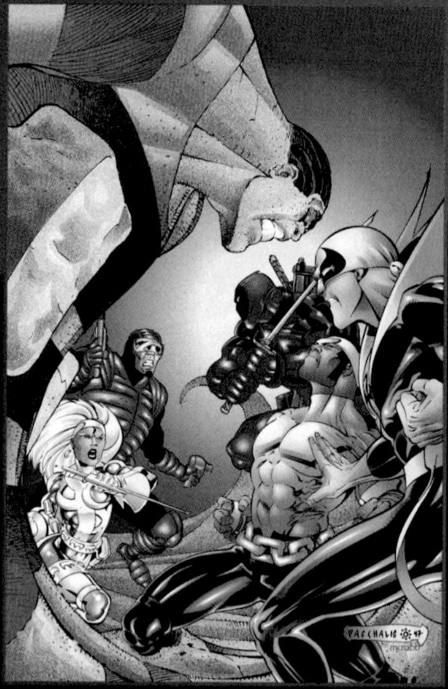
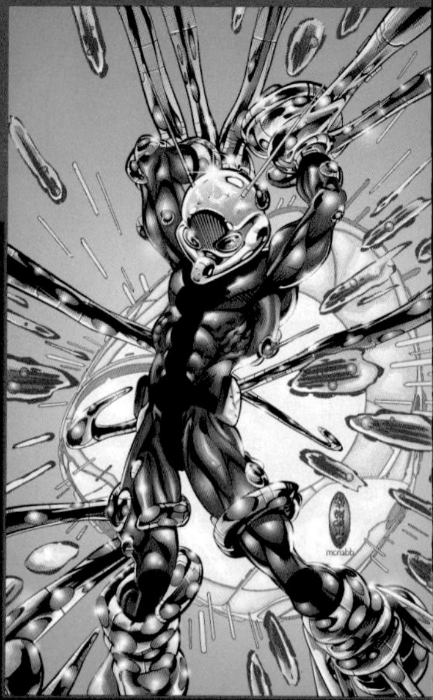
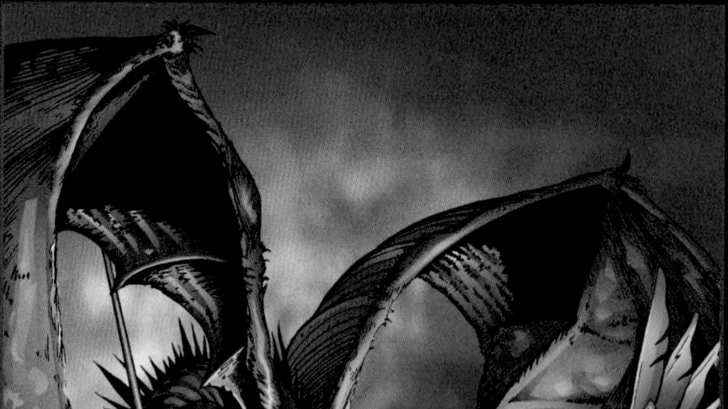
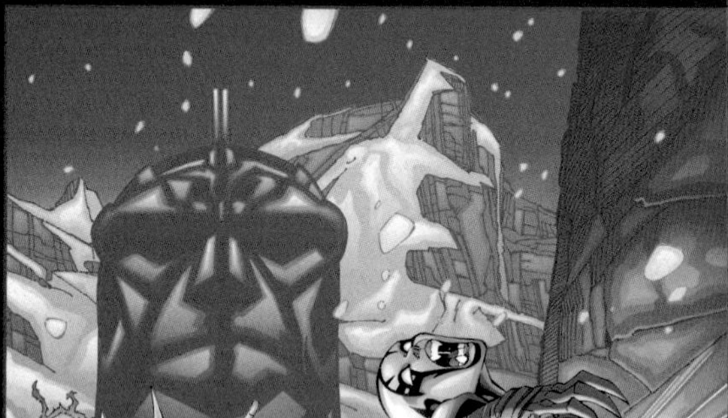

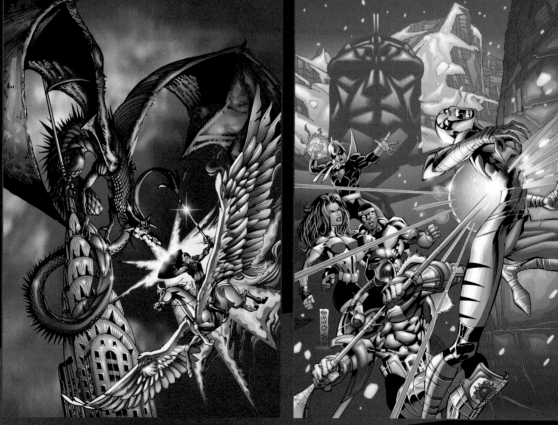

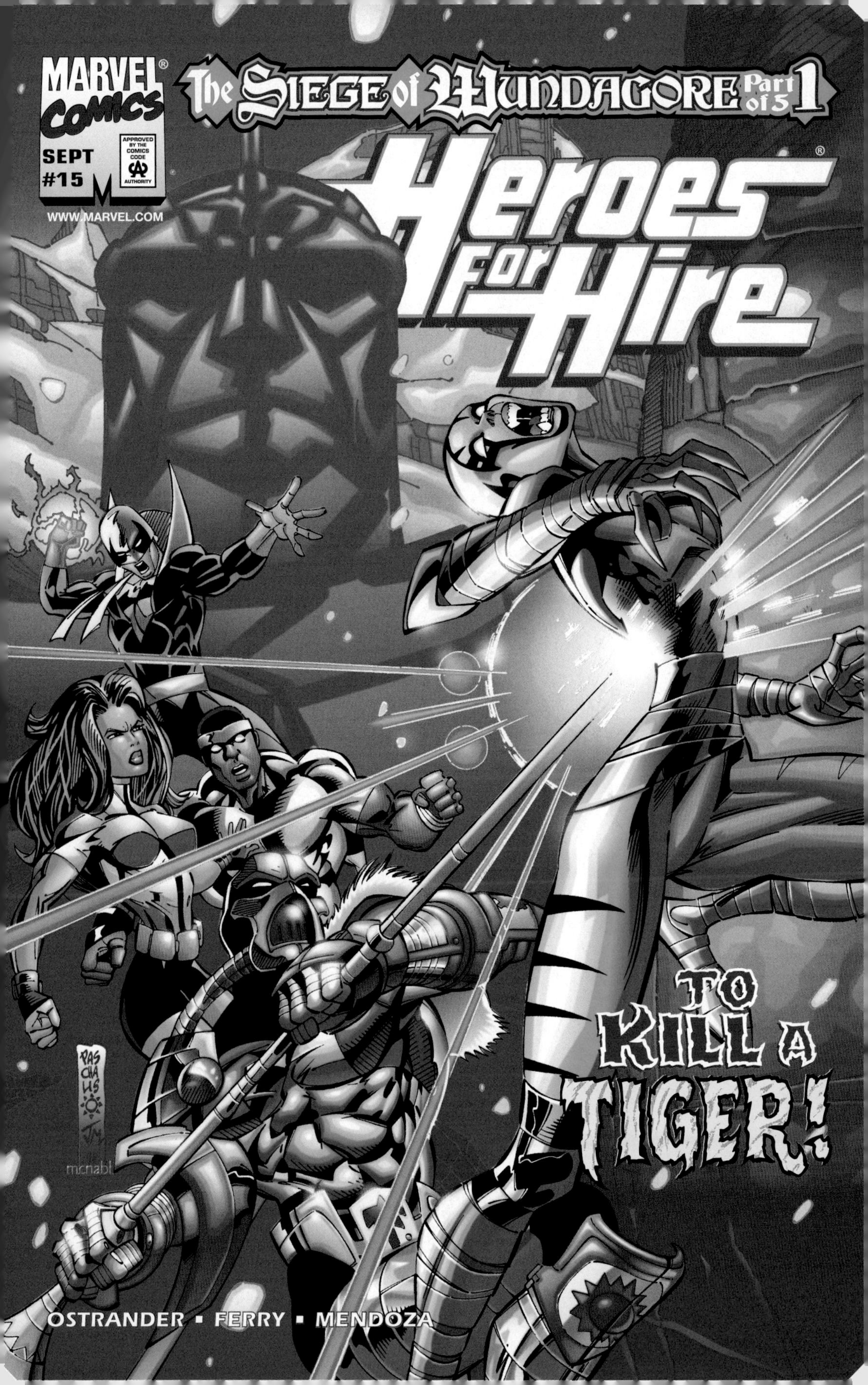

MARVEL COMICS
SEPT #15
APPROVED BY THE COMICS CODE AUTHORITY
WWW.MARVEL.COM
The Siege of Wundagore Part 1 of 5
Heroes For Hire
TO KILL A TIGER!
PASCHALIS JM
mcnabb
OSTRANDER ▪ FERRY ▪ MENDOZA

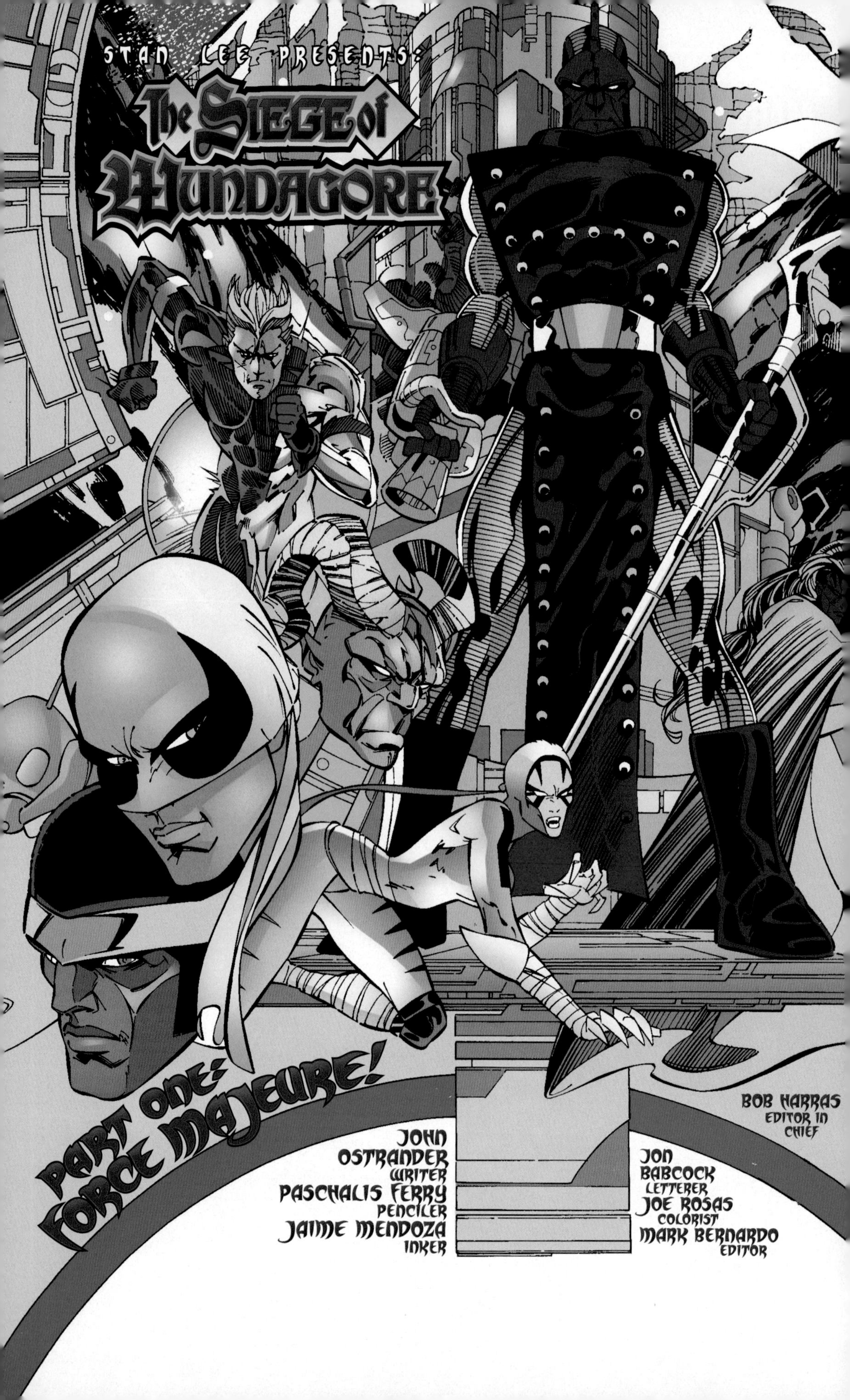
STAN LEE PRESENTS:
The SIEGE of WUNDAGORE
PART ONE: FORCE MAJEURE!
JOHN OSTRANDER WRITER
PASCHALIS FERRY PENCILER
JAIME MENDOZA INKER
JON BABCOCK LETTERER
JOE ROSAS COLORIST
MARK BERNARDO EDITOR
BOB HARRAS EDITOR IN CHIEF

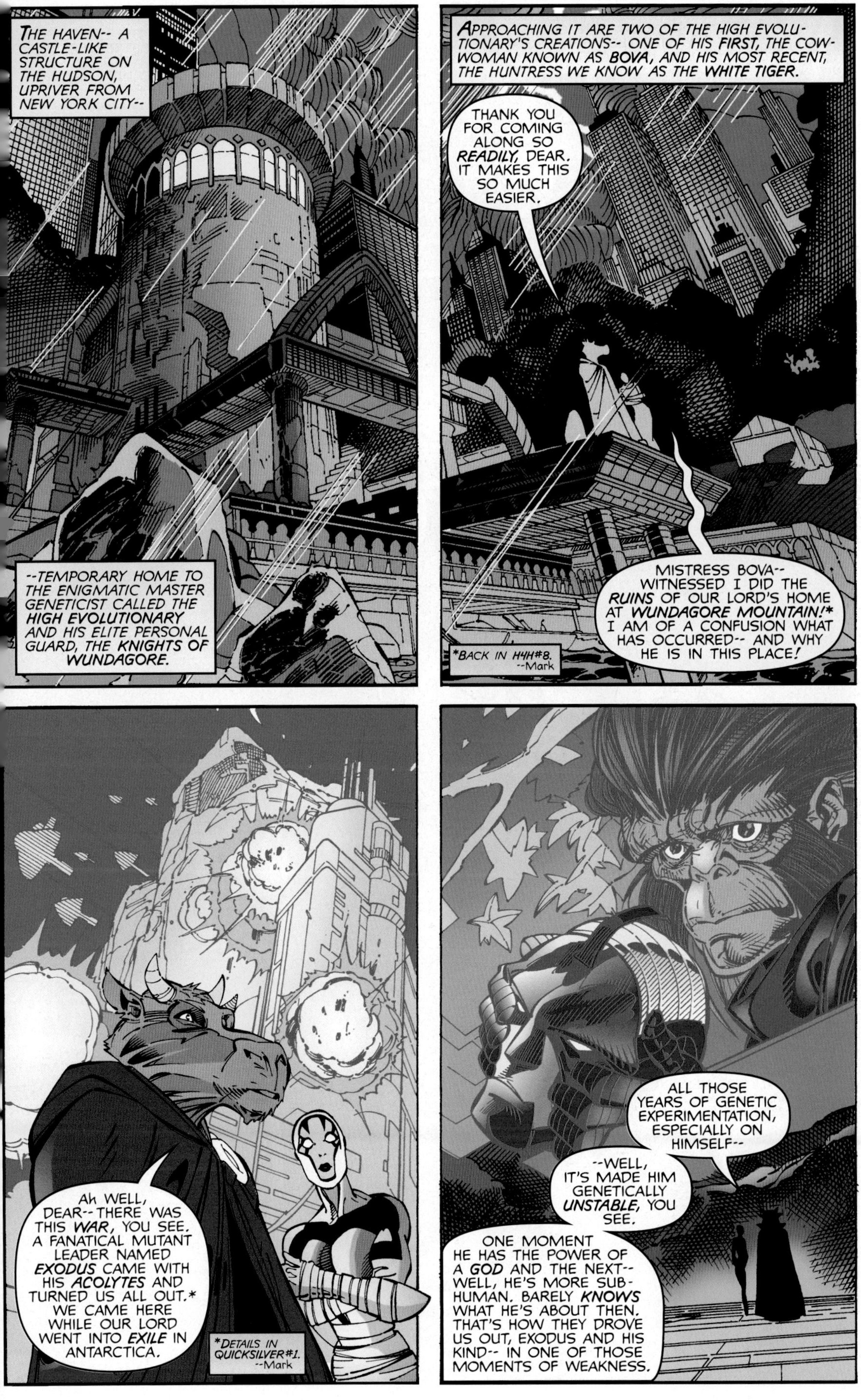
THE HAVEN-- A CASTLE-LIKE STRUCTURE ON THE HUDSON, UPRIVER FROM NEW YORK CITY--
--TEMPORARY HOME TO THE ENIGMATIC MASTER GENETICIST CALLED THE HIGH EVOLUTIONARY AND HIS ELITE PERSONAL GUARD, THE KNIGHTS OF WUNDAGORE.
APPROACHING IT ARE TWO OF THE HIGH EVOLUTIONARY'S CREATIONS-- ONE OF HIS FIRST, THE COW-WOMAN KNOWN AS BOVA, AND HIS MOST RECENT, THE HUNTRESS WE KNOW AS THE WHITE TIGER.
THANK YOU FOR COMING ALONG SO READILY, DEAR. IT MAKES THIS SO MUCH EASIER.
MISTRESS BOVA-- WITNESSED I DID THE RUINS OF OUR LORD'S HOME AT WUNDAGORE MOUNTAIN!* I AM OF A CONFUSION WHAT HAS OCCURRED-- AND WHY HE IS IN THIS PLACE!
*BACK IN H4H#8. --Mark
Ah WELL, DEAR--THERE WAS THIS WAR, YOU SEE. A FANATICAL MUTANT LEADER NAMED EXODUS CAME WITH HIS ACOLYTES AND TURNED US ALL OUT.* WE CAME HERE WHILE OUR LORD WENT INTO EXILE IN ANTARCTICA.
*DETAILS IN QUICKSILVER#1. --Mark
ALL THOSE YEARS OF GENETIC EXPERIMENTATION, ESPECIALLY ON HIMSELF--
--WELL, IT'S MADE HIM GENETICALLY UNSTABLE, YOU SEE.
ONE MOMENT HE HAS THE POWER OF A GOD AND THE NEXT-- WELL, HE'S MORE SUB-HUMAN. BARELY KNOWS WHAT HE'S ABOUT THEN. THAT'S HOW THEY DROVE US OUT, EXODUS AND HIS KIND-- IN ONE OF THOSE MOMENTS OF WEAKNESS.

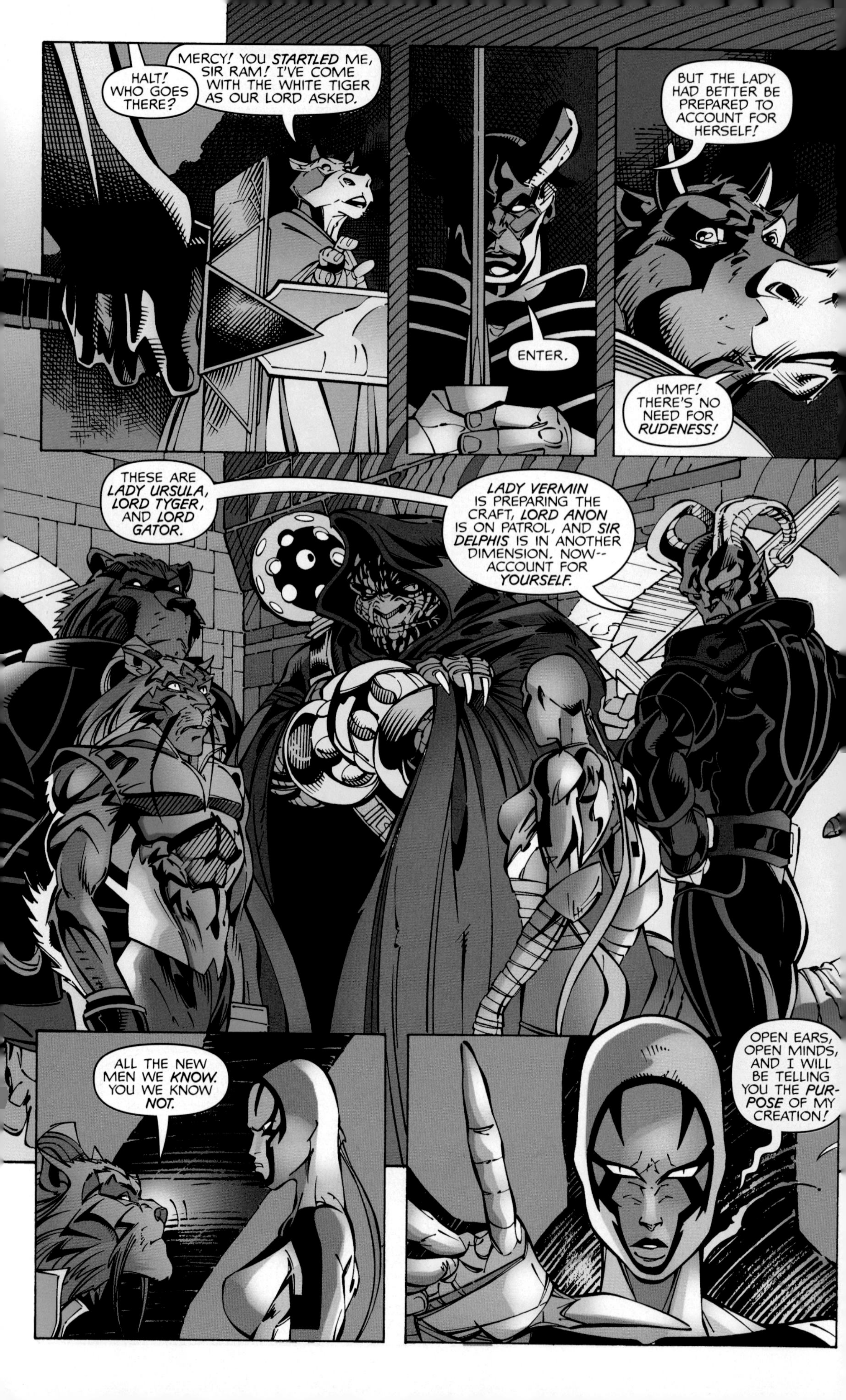
HALT! WHO GOES THERE?
MERCY! YOU STARTLED ME, SIR RAM! I'VE COME WITH THE WHITE TIGER AS OUR LORD ASKED.
ENTER.
BUT THE LADY HAD BETTER BE PREPARED TO ACCOUNT FOR HERSELF!
HMPF! THERE'S NO NEED FOR RUDENESS!
THESE ARE LADY URSULA, LORD TYGER, AND LORD GATOR.
LADY VERMIN IS PREPARING THE CRAFT, LORD ANON IS ON PATROL, AND SIR DELPHIS IS IN ANOTHER DIMENSION. NOW-- ACCOUNT FOR YOURSELF.
ALL THE NEW MEN WE KNOW. YOU WE KNOW NOT.
OPEN EARS, OPEN MINDS, AND I WILL BE TELLING YOU THE PURPOSE OF MY CREATION!

'THE *MAN-BEAST* WAS OUR LORD'S GREAT *FAILURE* AMONG HIS CREATIONS. AS TERRIBLE IT IS TO SAY, MORE TERRIBLE IS THE TRUTH.

"THOUGH AIDED BY SUCH GREAT HEROES AS THE ONE KNOWN AS *THOR*, NEVER HAS OUR LORD, THE HIGH EVOLUTIONARY, BEEN ABLE TO *END* THE MAN-BEAST'S EXISTENCE.

FROM THE WOLF HE WAS DRAWN FORTH-- BUT THERE WAS SOMETHING *MALIGNANT* IN HIS SPIRIT. ALWAYS HE SEEKS TO UNDO OUR LORD'S CREATIONS.

"SO WAS *I* CREATED IN SPECIFIC TO HUNT DOWN AND TO END THE MAN-BEAST-- FOREVER!"

TIGER TO HUNT WOLF-- EXCELLENT IDEA.

BUT WHY NOT MERELY USE *ME?* WHY *YOU* SPECIFICALLY?

BECAUSE IT IS MY *WILL.* IS THAT NOT *ENOUGH* FOR YOU?

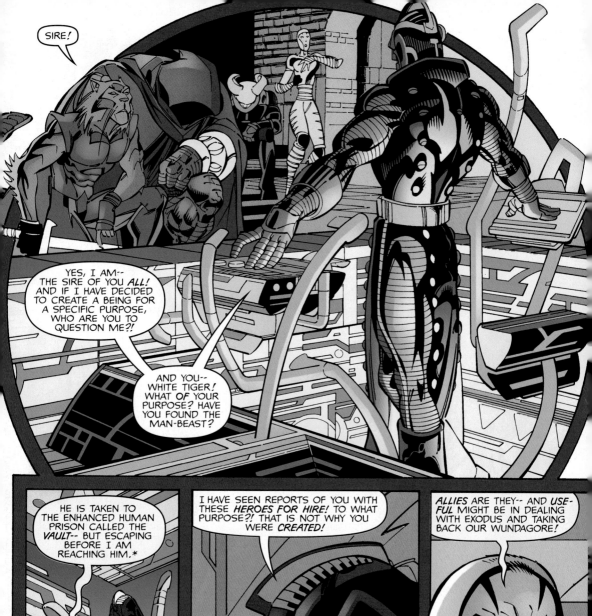

SIRE!

YES, I AM-- THE SIRE OF YOU *ALL!* AND IF I HAVE DECIDED TO CREATE A BEING FOR A SPECIFIC PURPOSE, WHO ARE YOU TO QUESTION ME?!

AND YOU-- WHITE TIGER! WHAT *OF* YOUR PURPOSE? HAVE YOU FOUND THE MAN-BEAST?

HE IS TAKEN TO THE ENHANCED HUMAN PRISON CALLED THE *VAULT*-- BUT ESCAPING BEFORE I AM REACHING HIM.*

*AS SEEN IN H4H #'s 1 & 12. --Mark

I HAVE SEEN REPORTS OF YOU WITH THESE *HEROES FOR HIRE!* TO WHAT PURPOSE?! THAT IS NOT WHY YOU WERE *CREATED!*

ALLIES ARE THEY-- AND *USEFUL* MIGHT BE IN DEALING WITH EXODUS AND TAKING BACK OUR WUNDAGORE!

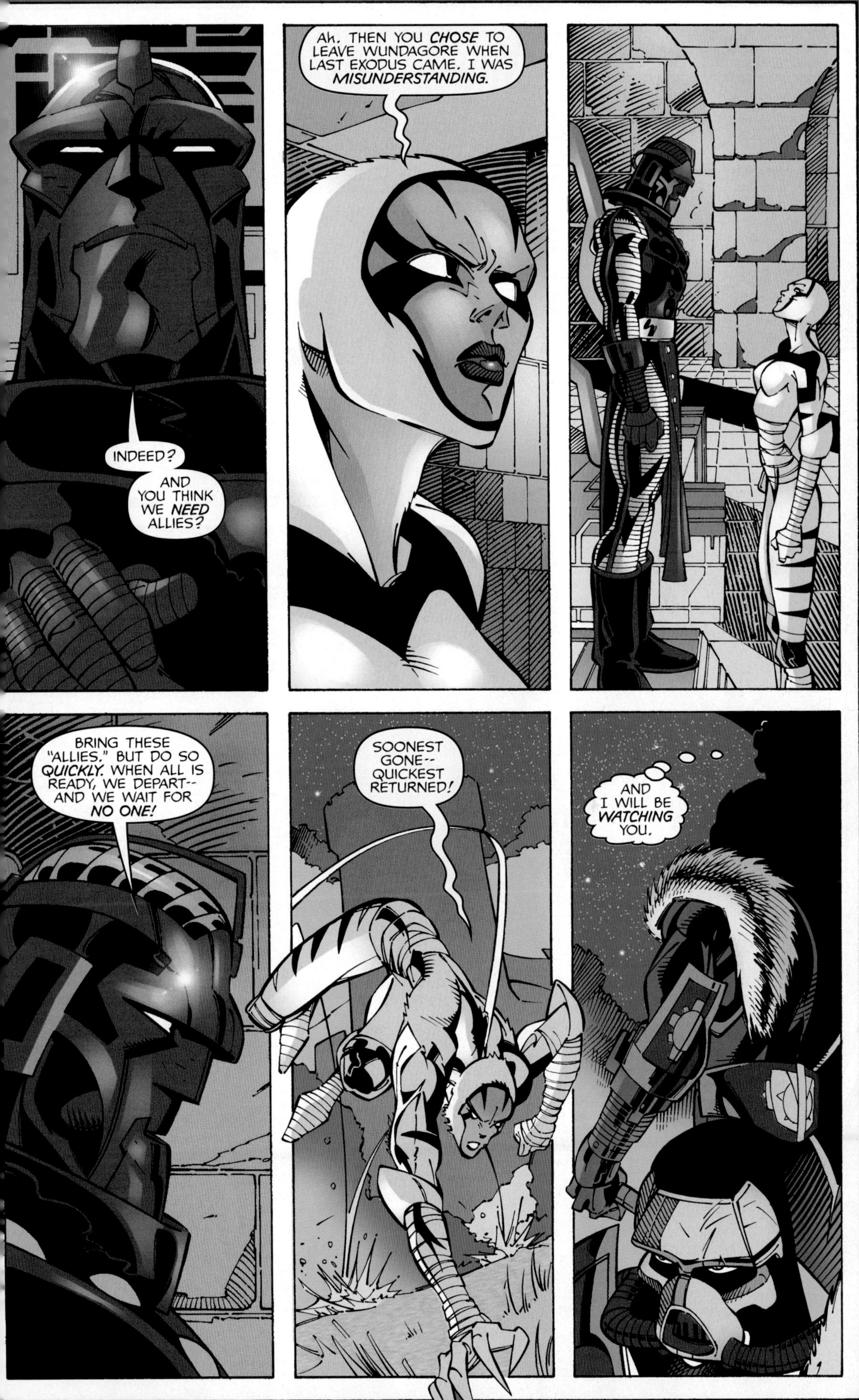
INDEED?
AND YOU THINK WE NEED ALLIES?
Ah. THEN YOU CHOSE TO LEAVE WUNDAGORE WHEN LAST EXODUS CAME. I WAS MISUNDERSTANDING.
BRING THESE "ALLIES." BUT DO SO QUICKLY. WHEN ALL IS READY, WE DEPART-- AND WE WAIT FOR NO ONE!
SOONEST GONE-- QUICKEST RETURNED!
AND I WILL BE WATCHING YOU.

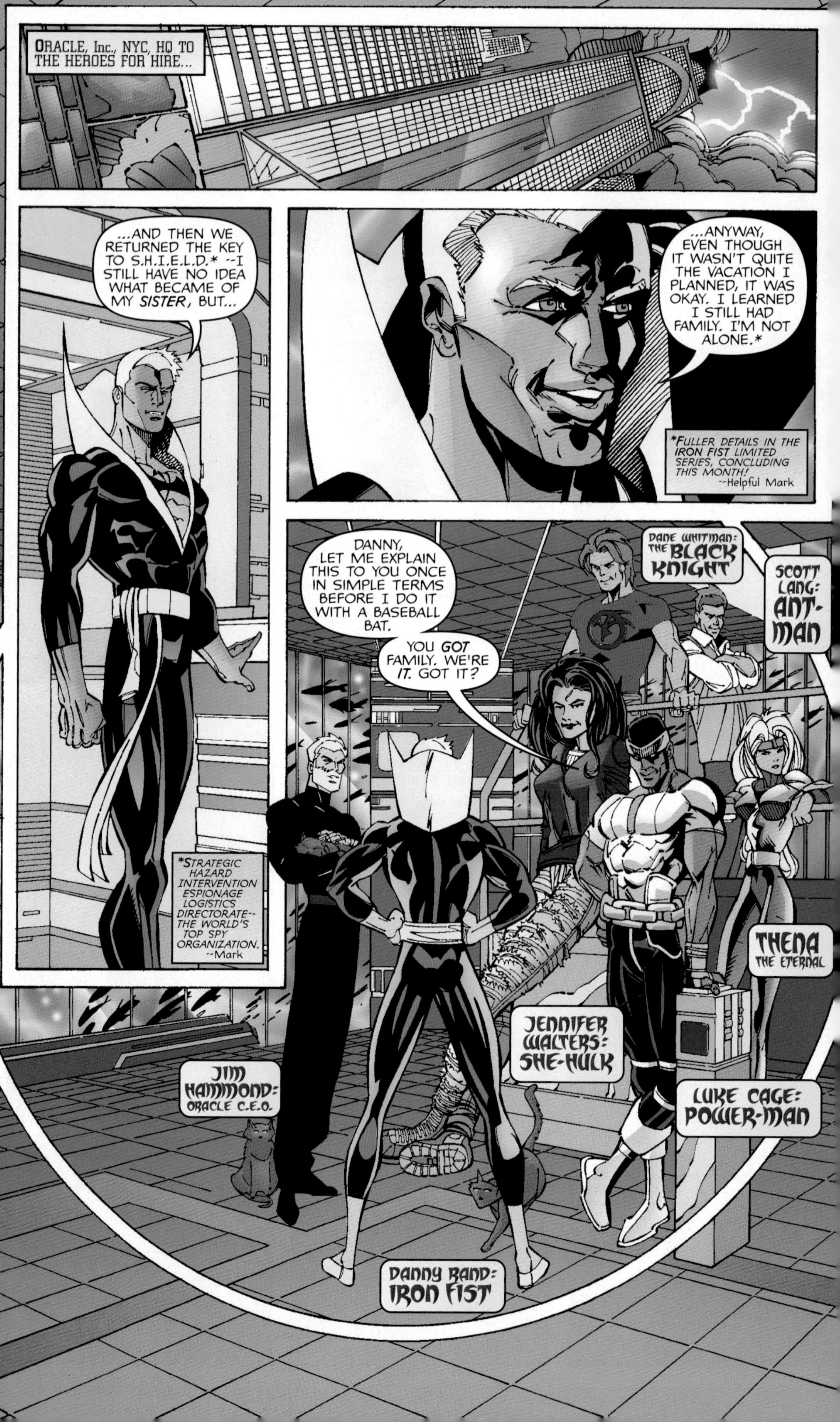

ORACLE, Inc., NYC, HQ TO THE HEROES FOR HIRE...
...AND THEN WE RETURNED THE KEY TO S.H.I.E.L.D.* --I STILL HAVE NO IDEA WHAT BECAME OF MY SISTER, BUT...
*STRATEGIC HAZARD INTERVENTION ESPIONAGE LOGISTICS DIRECTORATE-- THE WORLD'S TOP SPY ORGANIZATION. --Mark
...ANYWAY, EVEN THOUGH IT WASN'T QUITE THE VACATION I PLANNED, IT WAS OKAY. I LEARNED I STILL HAD FAMILY. I'M NOT ALONE.*
*FULLER DETAILS IN THE IRON FIST LIMITED SERIES, CONCLUDING THIS MONTH! --Helpful Mark
DANNY, LET ME EXPLAIN THIS TO YOU ONCE IN SIMPLE TERMS BEFORE I DO IT WITH A BASEBALL BAT.
YOU GOT FAMILY. WE'RE IT. GOT IT?
DANE WHITMAN: THE BLACK KNIGHT
SCOTT LANG: ANT-MAN
THENA THE ETERNAL
JENNIFER WALTERS: SHE-HULK
JIM HAMMOND: ORACLE C.E.O.
LUKE CAGE: POWER-MAN
DANNY RAND: IRON FIST

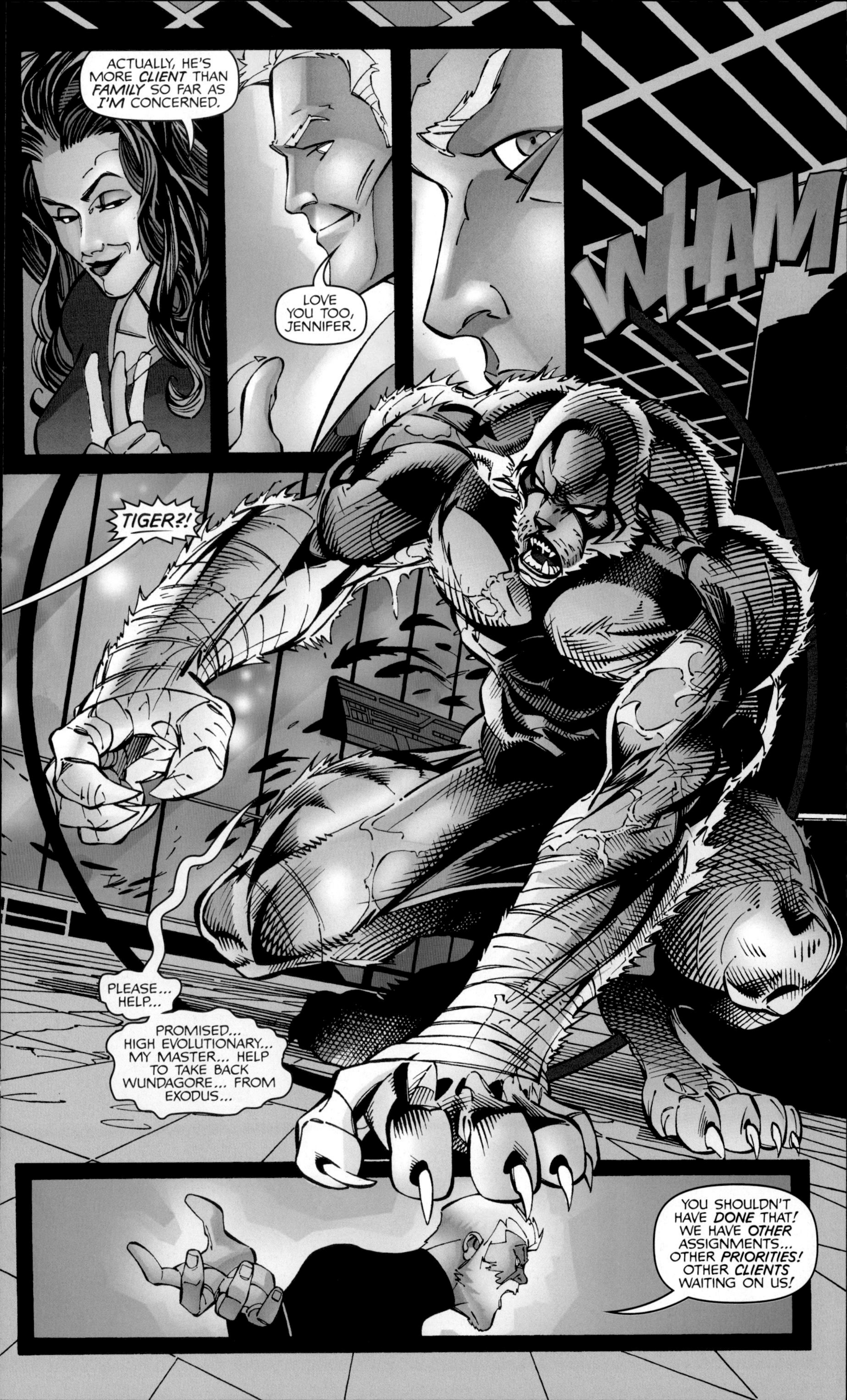
ACTUALLY, HE'S MORE CLIENT THAN FAMILY SO FAR AS I'M CONCERNED.
LOVE YOU TOO, JENNIFER.
WHAM
TIGER?!
PLEASE... HELP...
PROMISED... HIGH EVOLUTIONARY... MY MASTER... HELP TO TAKE BACK WUNDAGORE... FROM EXODUS...
YOU SHOULDN'T HAVE DONE THAT! WE HAVE OTHER ASSIGNMENTS... OTHER PRIORITIES! OTHER CLIENTS WAITING ON US!

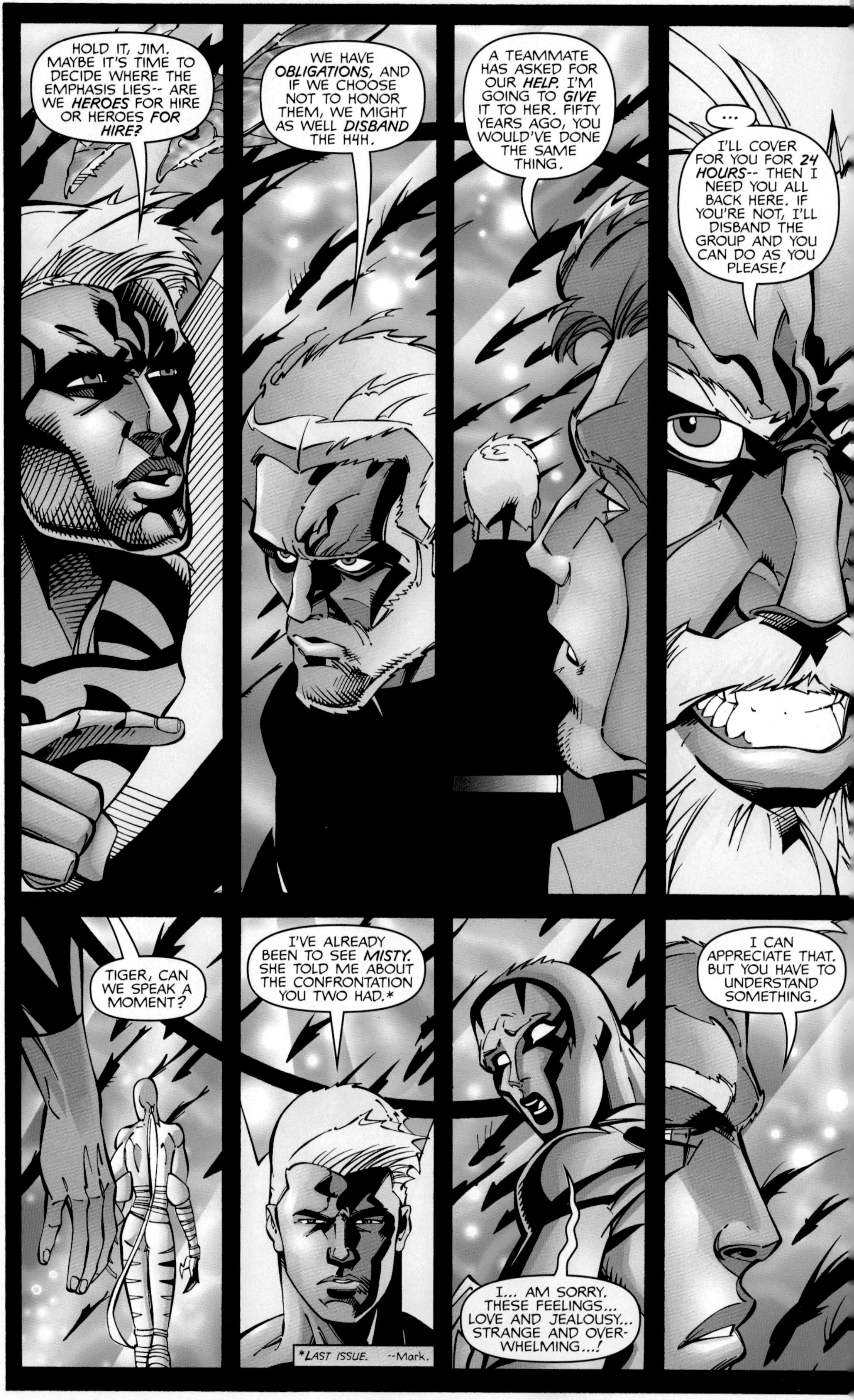
HOLD IT, JIM. MAYBE IT'S TIME TO DECIDE WHERE THE EMPHASIS LIES-- ARE WE HEROES FOR HIRE OR HEROES FOR HIRE?
WE HAVE OBLIGATIONS, AND IF WE CHOOSE NOT TO HONOR THEM, WE MIGHT AS WELL DISBAND THE H4H.
A TEAMMATE HAS ASKED FOR OUR HELP. I'M GOING TO GIVE IT TO HER. FIFTY YEARS AGO, YOU WOULD'VE DONE THE SAME THING.
...
I'LL COVER FOR YOU FOR 24 HOURS-- THEN I NEED YOU ALL BACK HERE. IF YOU'RE NOT, I'LL DISBAND THE GROUP AND YOU CAN DO AS YOU PLEASE!
TIGER, CAN WE SPEAK A MOMENT?
I'VE ALREADY BEEN TO SEE MISTY. SHE TOLD ME ABOUT THE CONFRONTATION YOU TWO HAD.*
*LAST ISSUE. --Mark.
I... AM SORRY. THESE FEELINGS... LOVE AND JEALOUSY... STRANGE AND OVERWHELMING...!
I CAN APPRECIATE THAT. BUT YOU HAVE TO UNDERSTAND SOMETHING.

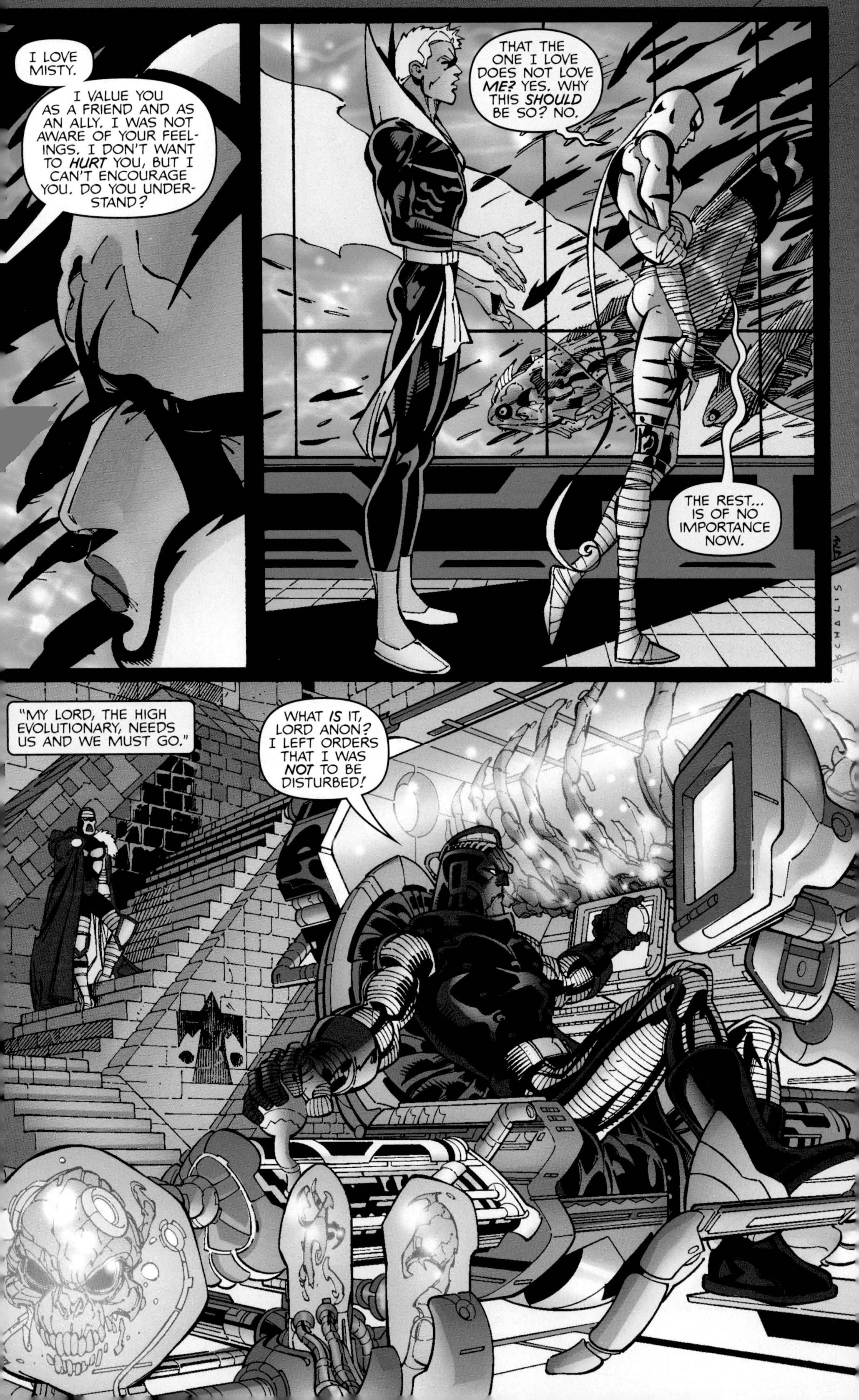
I LOVE MISTY.
I VALUE YOU AS A FRIEND AND AS AN ALLY. I WAS NOT AWARE OF YOUR FEEL-INGS. I DON'T WANT TO *HURT* YOU, BUT I CAN'T ENCOURAGE YOU. DO YOU UNDER-STAND?
THAT THE ONE I LOVE DOES NOT LOVE *ME?* YES. WHY THIS *SHOULD* BE SO? NO.
THE REST... IS OF NO IMPORTANCE NOW.
PASCHALIS
"MY LORD, THE HIGH EVOLUTIONARY, NEEDS US AND WE MUST GO."
WHAT *IS* IT, LORD ANON? I LEFT ORDERS THAT I WAS *NOT* TO BE DISTURBED!

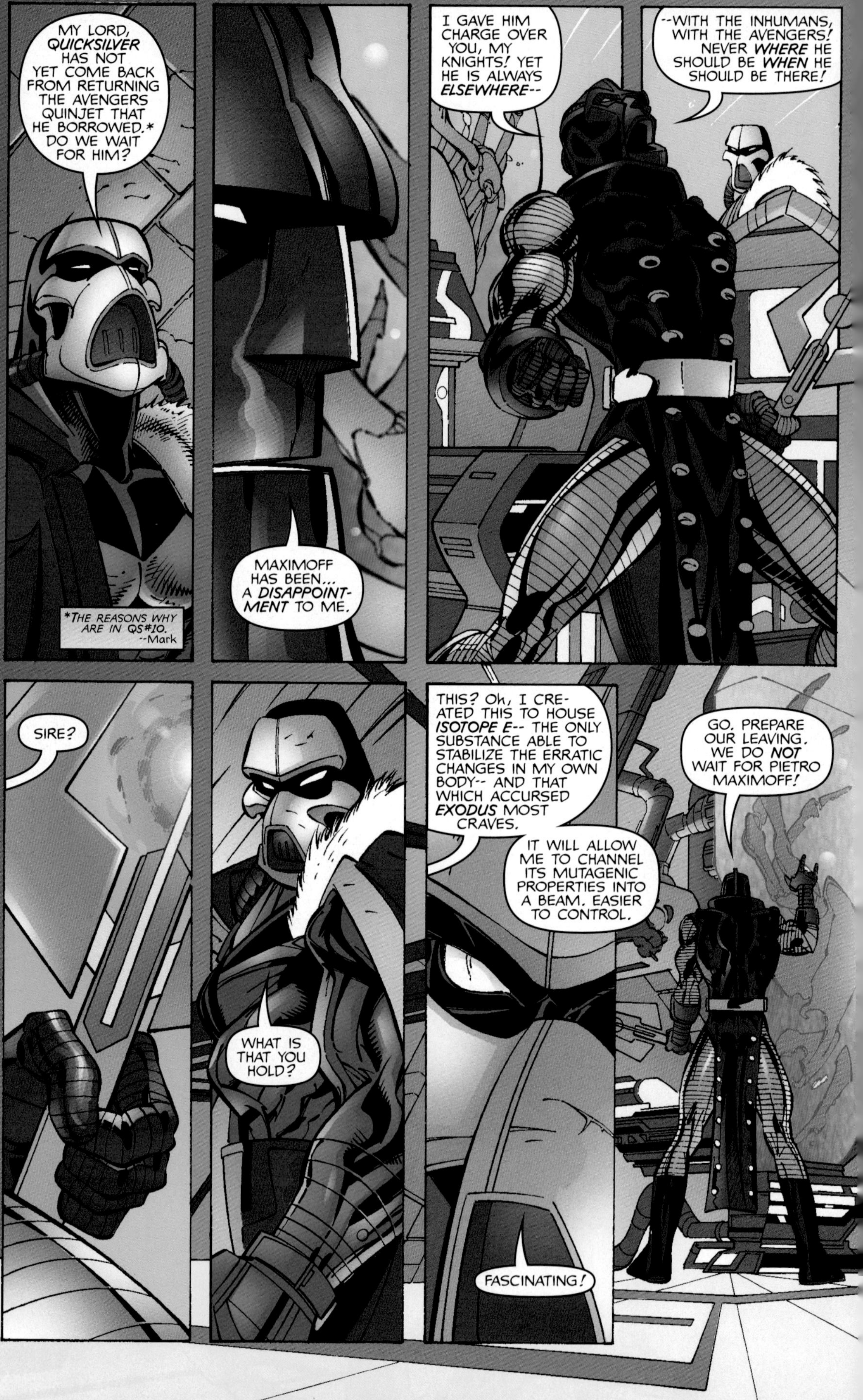
MY LORD, QUICKSILVER HAS NOT YET COME BACK FROM RETURNING THE AVENGERS QUINJET THAT HE BORROWED.* DO WE WAIT FOR HIM?
*THE REASONS WHY ARE IN QS#10. --Mark
MAXIMOFF HAS BEEN... A DISAPPOINTMENT TO ME.
I GAVE HIM CHARGE OVER YOU, MY KNIGHTS! YET HE IS ALWAYS ELSEWHERE--
--WITH THE INHUMANS, WITH THE AVENGERS! NEVER WHERE HE SHOULD BE WHEN HE SHOULD BE THERE!
SIRE?
WHAT IS THAT YOU HOLD?
THIS? Oh, I CREATED THIS TO HOUSE ISOTOPE E-- THE ONLY SUBSTANCE ABLE TO STABILIZE THE ERRATIC CHANGES IN MY OWN BODY-- AND THAT WHICH ACCURSED EXODUS MOST CRAVES.
IT WILL ALLOW ME TO CHANNEL ITS MUTAGENIC PROPERTIES INTO A BEAM. EASIER TO CONTROL.
FASCINATING!
GO. PREPARE OUR LEAVING. WE DO NOT WAIT FOR PIETRO MAXIMOFF!

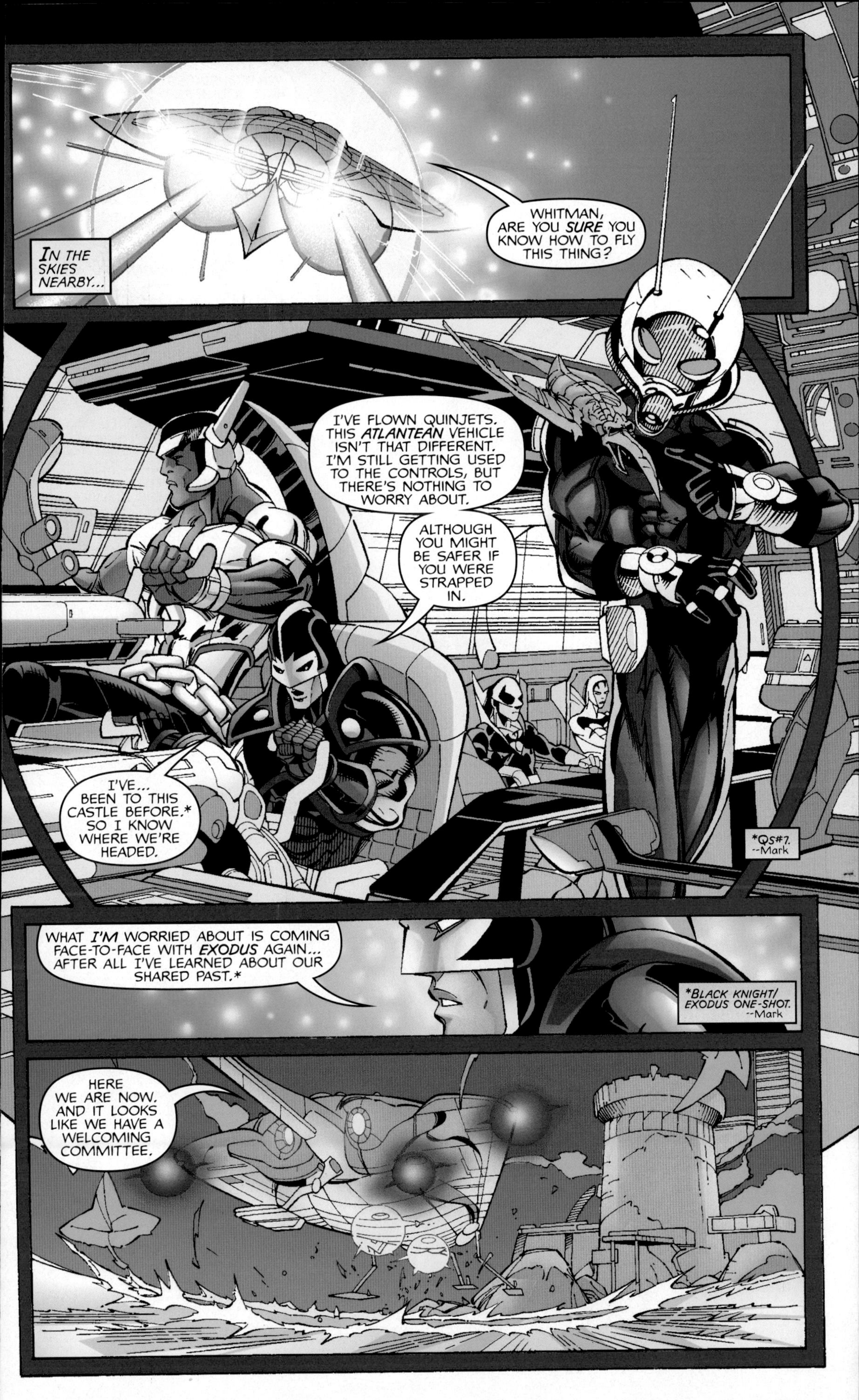
IN THE SKIES NEARBY...
WHITMAN, ARE YOU SURE YOU KNOW HOW TO FLY THIS THING?
I'VE FLOWN QUINJETS. THIS ATLANTEAN VEHICLE ISN'T THAT DIFFERENT. I'M STILL GETTING USED TO THE CONTROLS, BUT THERE'S NOTHING TO WORRY ABOUT.
ALTHOUGH YOU MIGHT BE SAFER IF YOU WERE STRAPPED IN.
I'VE... BEEN TO THIS CASTLE BEFORE.* SO I KNOW WHERE WE'RE HEADED.
*QS#7. --Mark
WHAT I'M WORRIED ABOUT IS COMING FACE-TO-FACE WITH EXODUS AGAIN... AFTER ALL I'VE LEARNED ABOUT OUR SHARED PAST.*
*BLACK KNIGHT/EXODUS ONE-SHOT. --Mark
HERE WE ARE NOW. AND IT LOOKS LIKE WE HAVE A WELCOMING COMMITTEE.

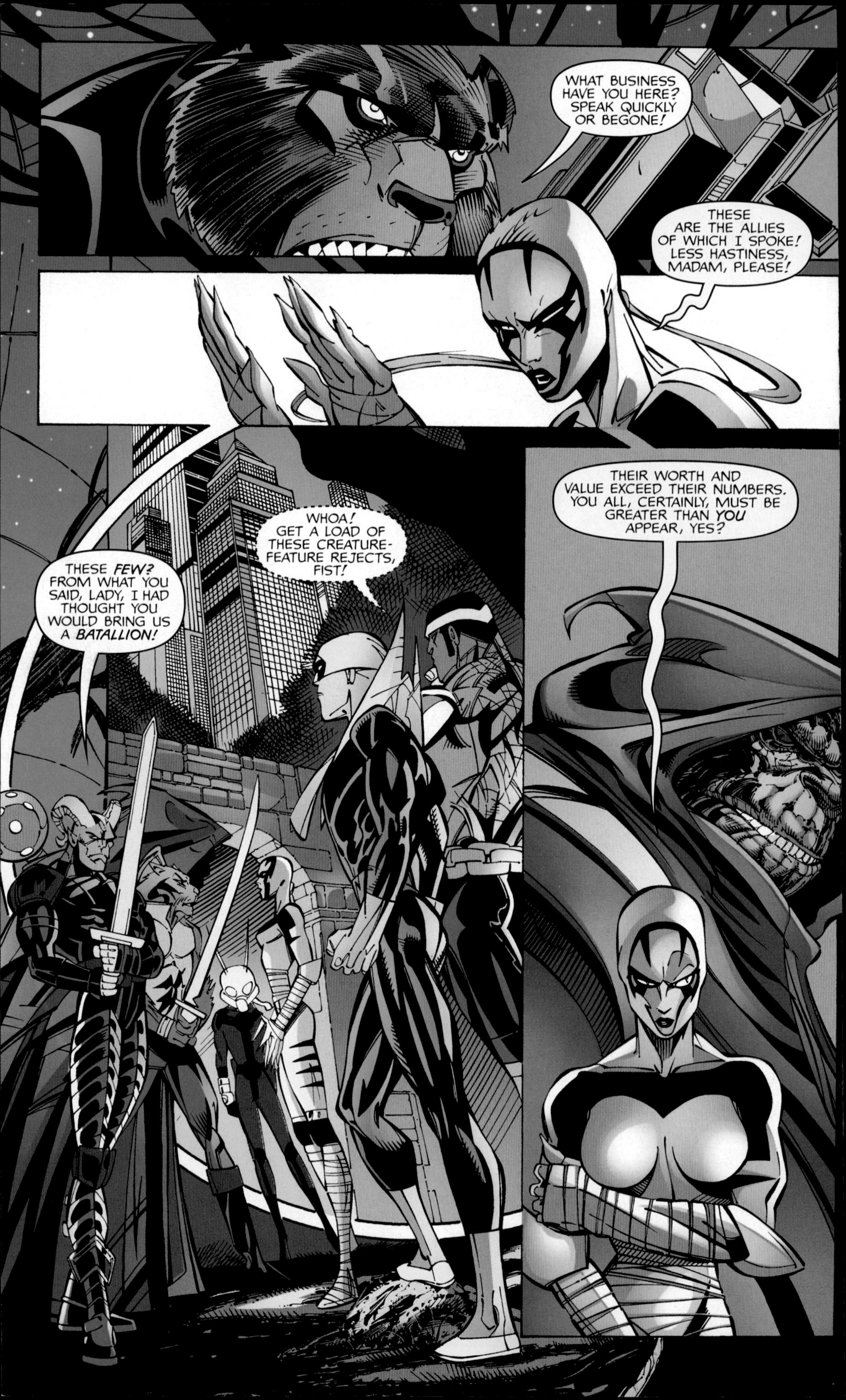
WHAT BUSINESS HAVE YOU HERE? SPEAK QUICKLY OR BEGONE!
THESE ARE THE ALLIES OF WHICH I SPOKE! LESS HASTINESS, MADAM, PLEASE!
THESE FEW? FROM WHAT YOU SAID, LADY, I HAD THOUGHT YOU WOULD BRING US A BATALLION!
WHOA! GET A LOAD OF THESE CREATURE-FEATURE REJECTS, FIST!
THEIR WORTH AND VALUE EXCEED THEIR NUMBERS. YOU ALL, CERTAINLY, MUST BE GREATER THAN YOU APPEAR, YES?

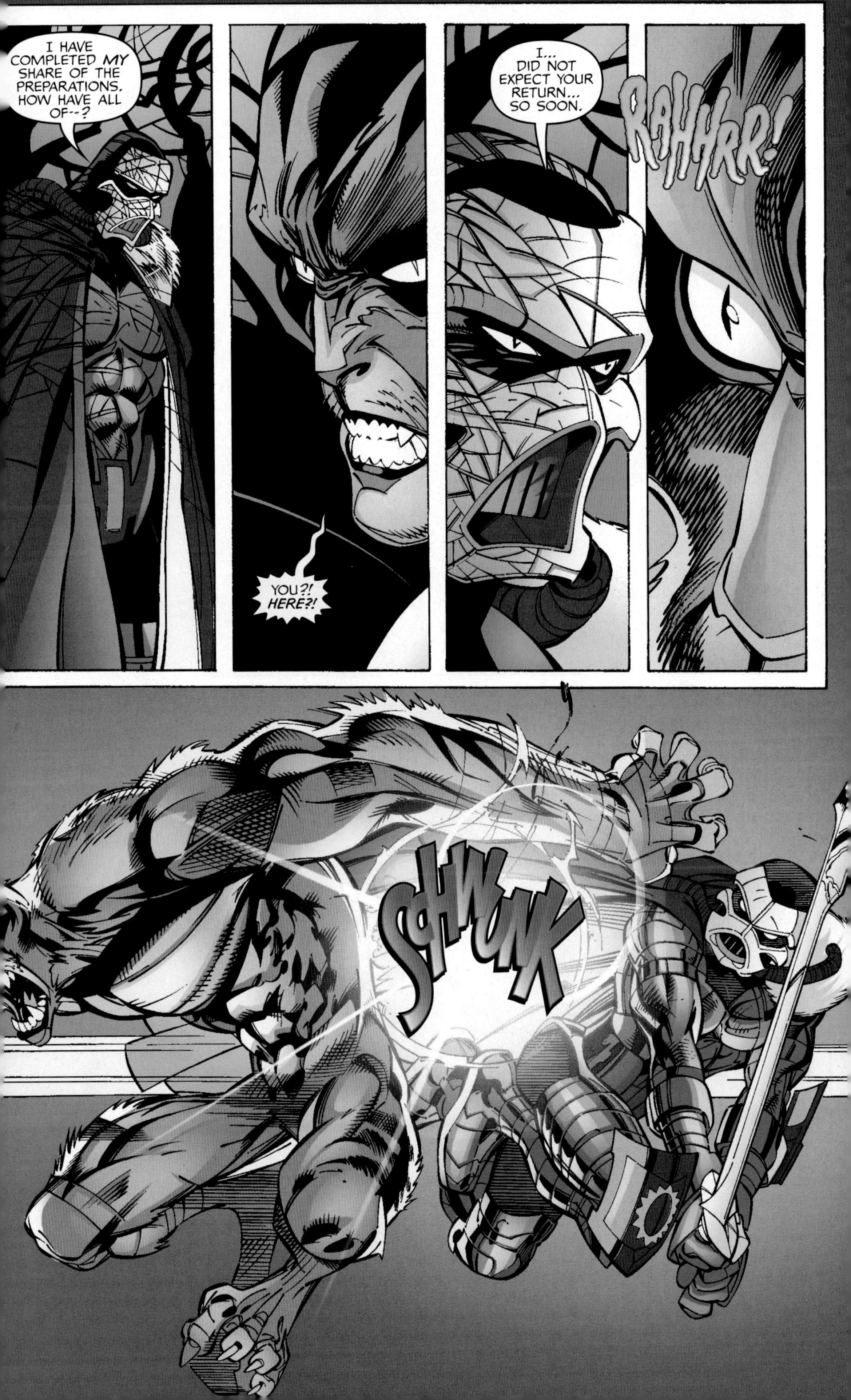
I HAVE COMPLETED MY SHARE OF THE PREPARATIONS. HOW HAVE ALL OF--?
YOU?! HERE?!
I... DID NOT EXPECT YOUR RETURN... SO SOON.
RAHHRR!
SCHWUNK

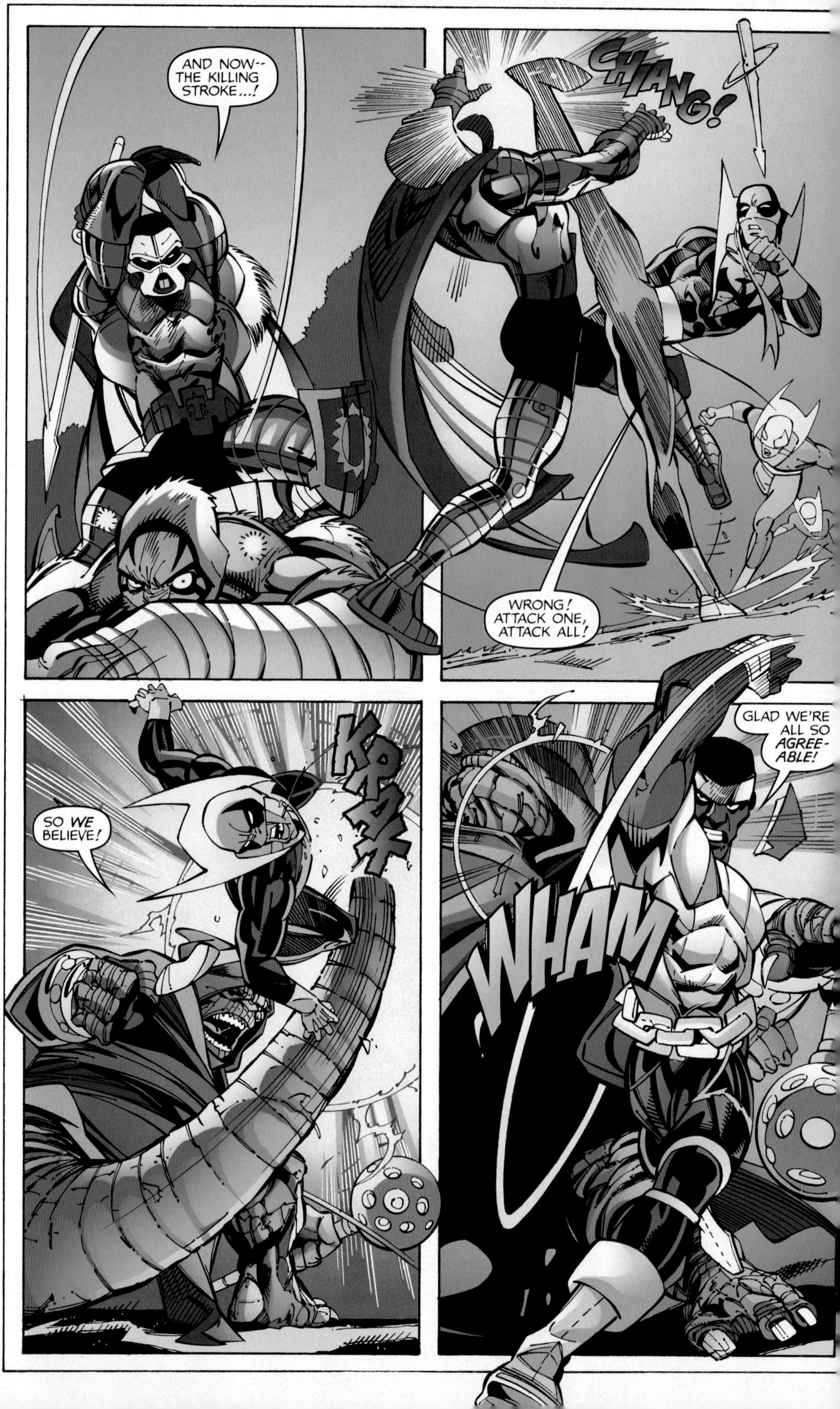
AND NOW--
THE KILLING STROKE...!
CHANG!
WRONG! ATTACK ONE, ATTACK ALL!
SO WE BELIEVE!
KRAK
GLAD WE'RE ALL SO AGREE-ABLE!
WHAM

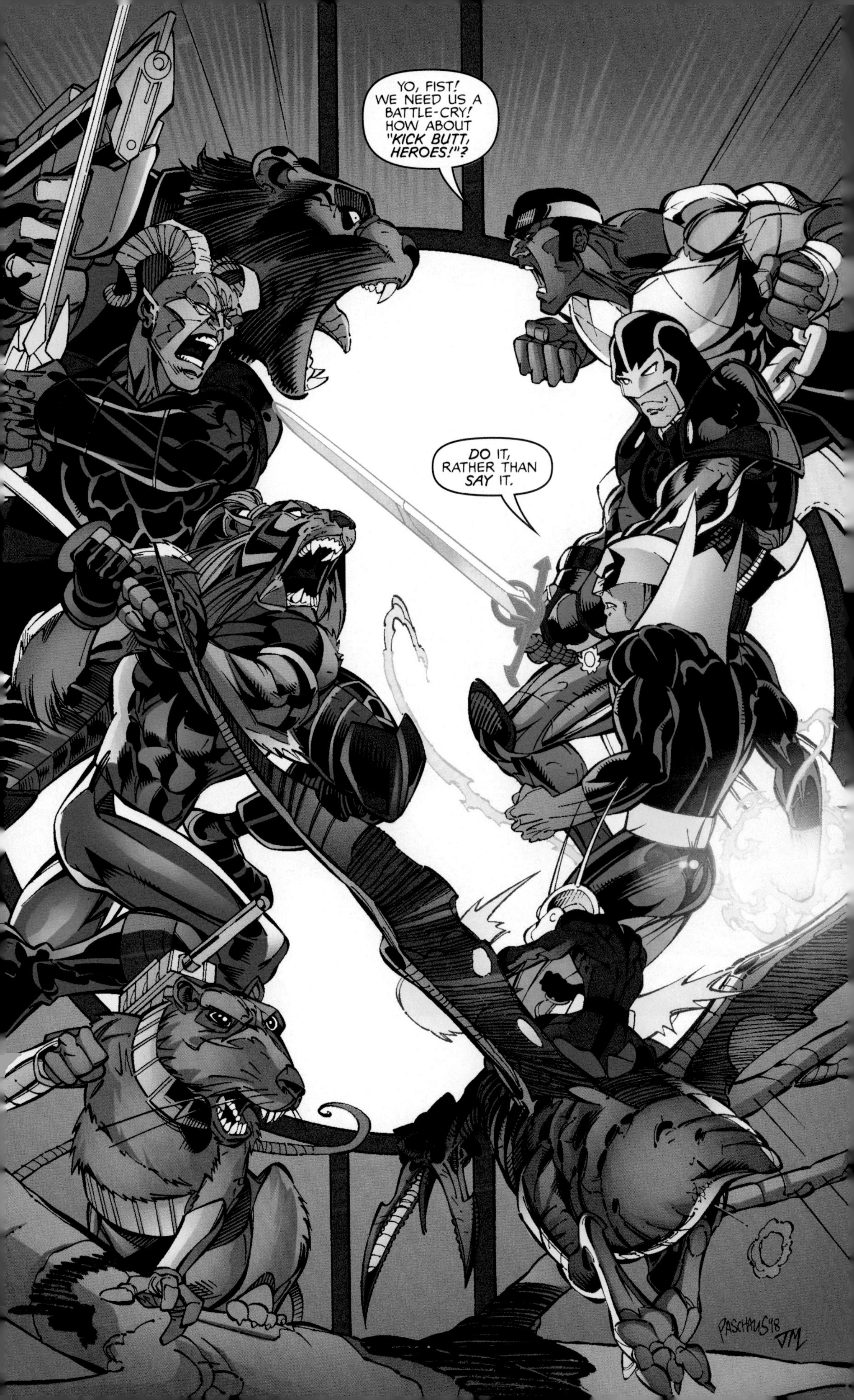
YO, FIST! WE NEED US A BATTLE-CRY! HOW ABOUT "KICK BUTT, HEROES!"?
DO IT, RATHER THAN SAY IT.
PASCHALIS '98 JM

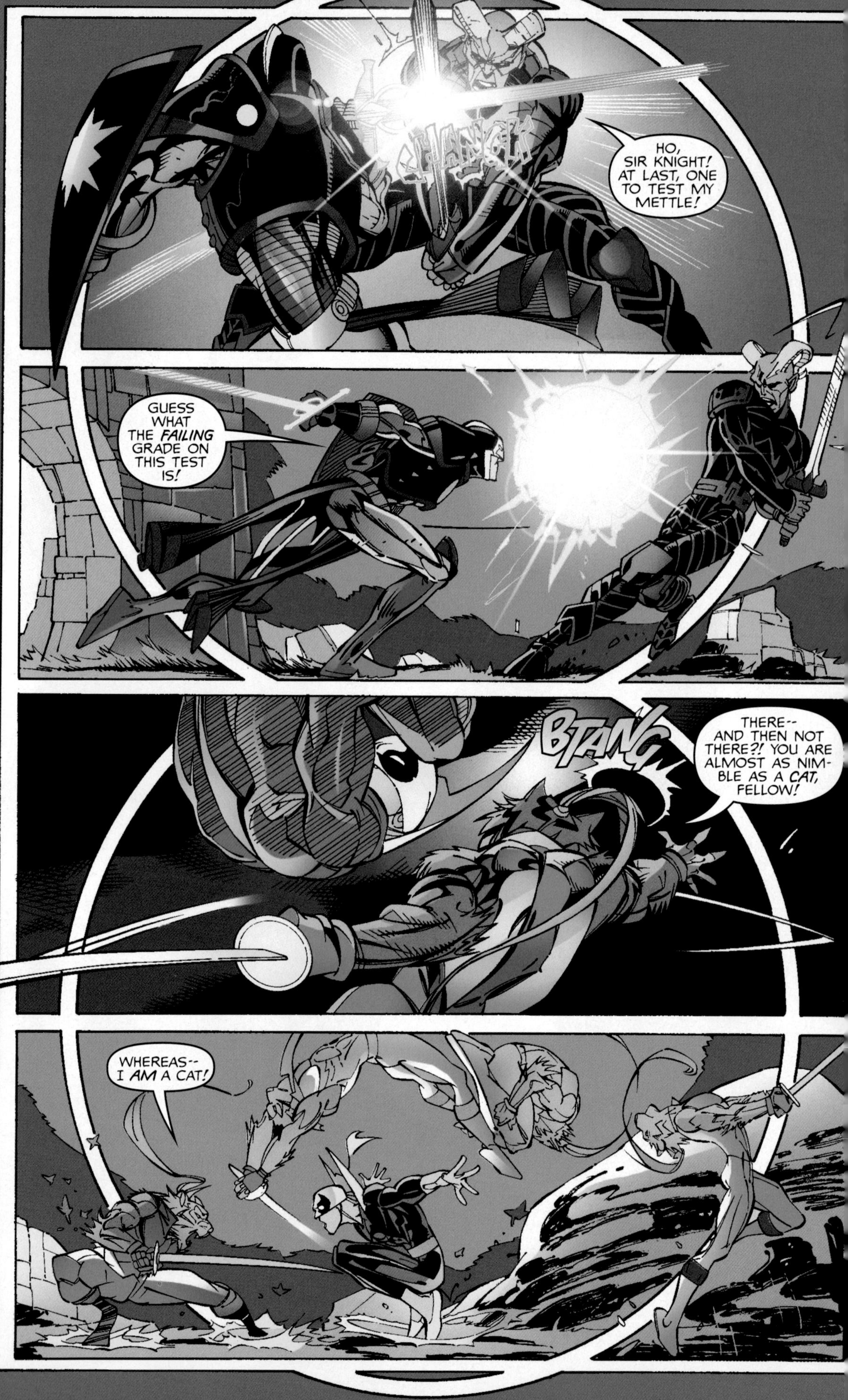
CHANGK
HO, SIR KNIGHT! AT LAST, ONE TO TEST MY METTLE!
GUESS WHAT THE *FAILING* GRADE ON THIS TEST IS!
BTANG
THERE-- AND THEN NOT THERE?! YOU ARE ALMOST AS NIMBLE AS A *CAT,* FELLOW!
WHEREAS-- I *AM* A CAT!

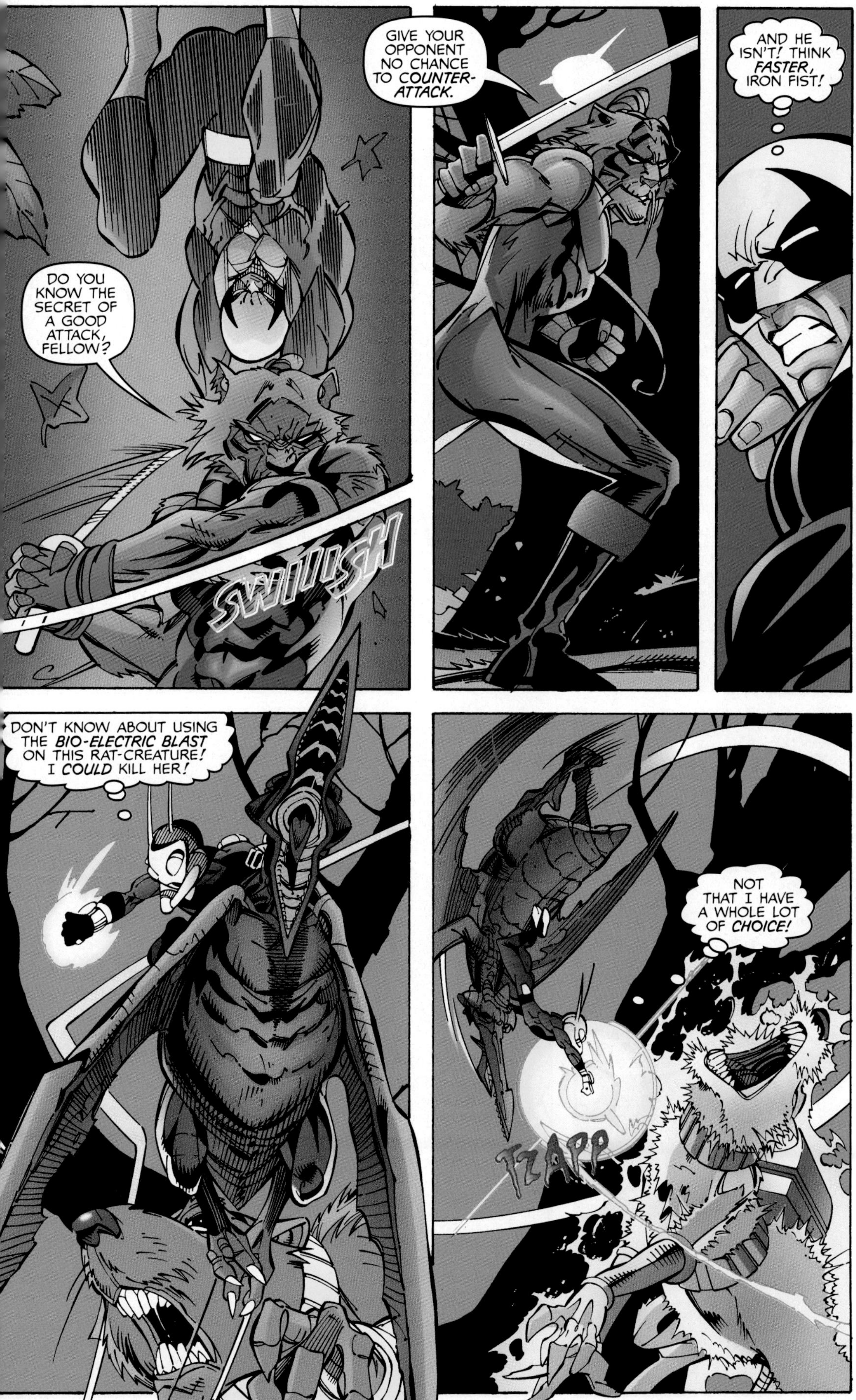
DO YOU KNOW THE SECRET OF A GOOD ATTACK, FELLOW?
SWIIIISH
GIVE YOUR OPPONENT NO CHANCE TO COUNTER-ATTACK.
AND HE ISN'T! THINK FASTER, IRON FIST!
DON'T KNOW ABOUT USING THE BIO-ELECTRIC BLAST ON THIS RAT-CREATURE! I COULD KILL HER!
NOT THAT I HAVE A WHOLE LOT OF CHOICE!
TZAPP

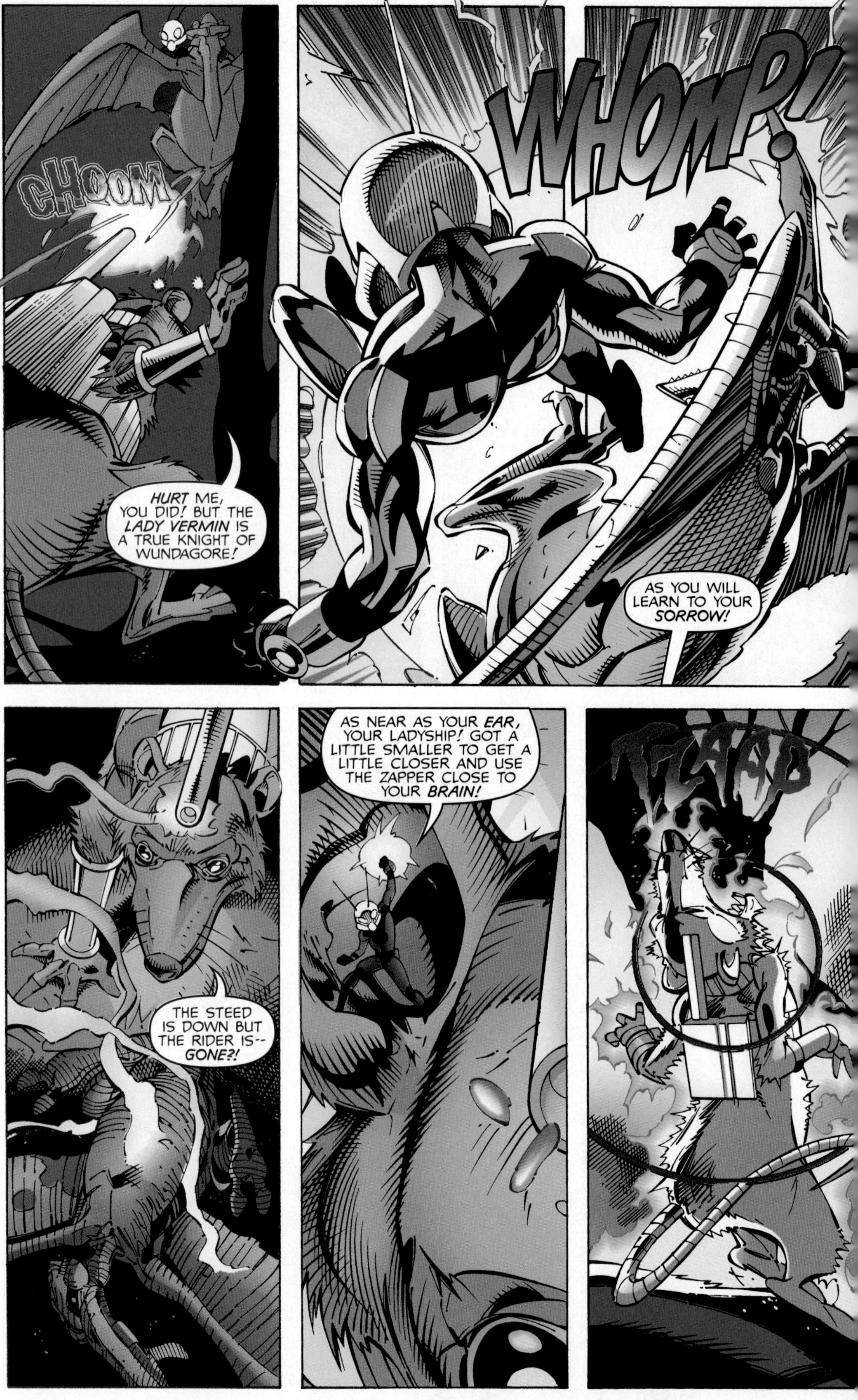
CHOOM
HURT ME, YOU DID! BUT THE LADY VERMIN IS A TRUE KNIGHT OF WUNDAGORE!
WHOMP!
AS YOU WILL LEARN TO YOUR SORROW!
THE STEED IS DOWN BUT THE RIDER IS-- GONE?!
AS NEAR AS YOUR EAR, YOUR LADYSHIP! GOT A LITTLE SMALLER TO GET A LITTLE CLOSER AND USE THE ZAPPER CLOSE TO YOUR BRAIN!
TZZAAB

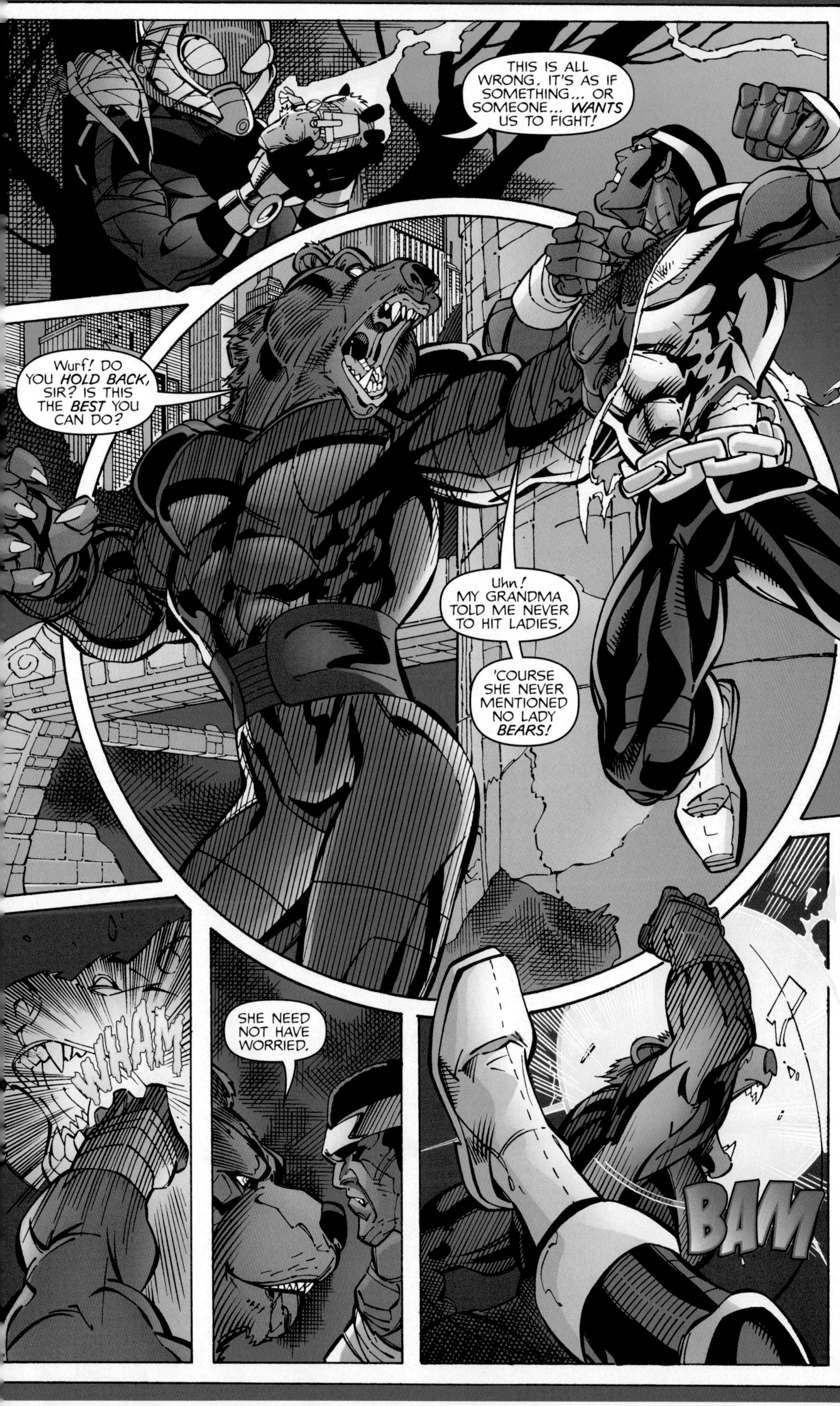
THIS IS ALL WRONG. IT'S AS IF SOMETHING... OR SOMEONE... WANTS US TO FIGHT!
Wurf! DO YOU HOLD BACK, SIR? IS THIS THE BEST YOU CAN DO?
Uhn! MY GRANDMA TOLD ME NEVER TO HIT LADIES.
'COURSE SHE NEVER MENTIONED NO LADY BEARS!
WHAM
SHE NEED NOT HAVE WORRIED.
BAM

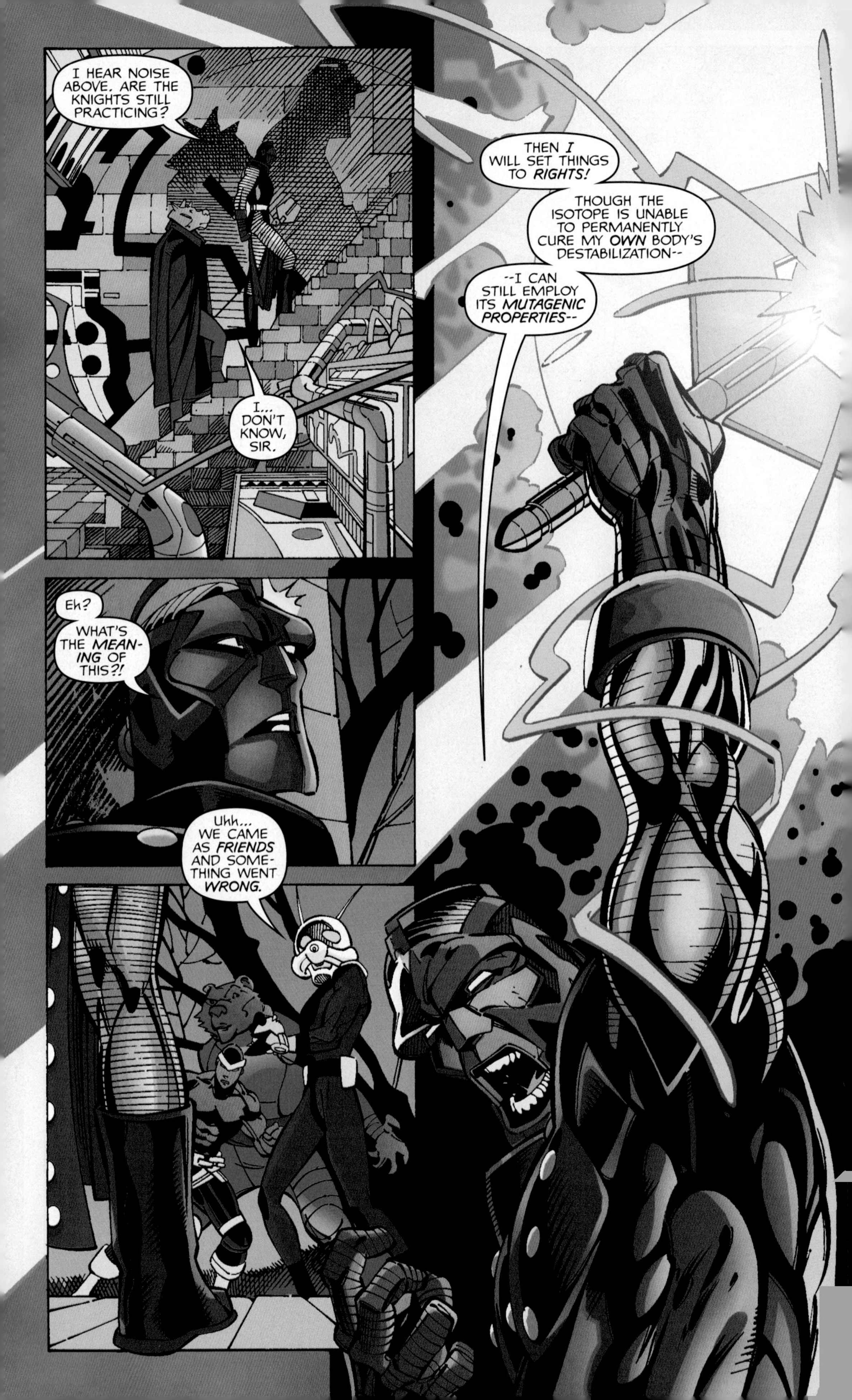
I HEAR NOISE ABOVE. ARE THE KNIGHTS STILL PRACTICING?
I... DON'T KNOW, SIR.
Eh?
WHAT'S THE MEANING OF THIS?!
Uhh... WE CAME AS FRIENDS AND SOMETHING WENT WRONG.
THEN I WILL SET THINGS TO RIGHTS!
THOUGH THE ISOTOPE IS UNABLE TO PERMANENTLY CURE MY OWN BODY'S DESTABILIZATION--
--I CAN STILL EMPLOY ITS MUTAGENIC PROPERTIES--

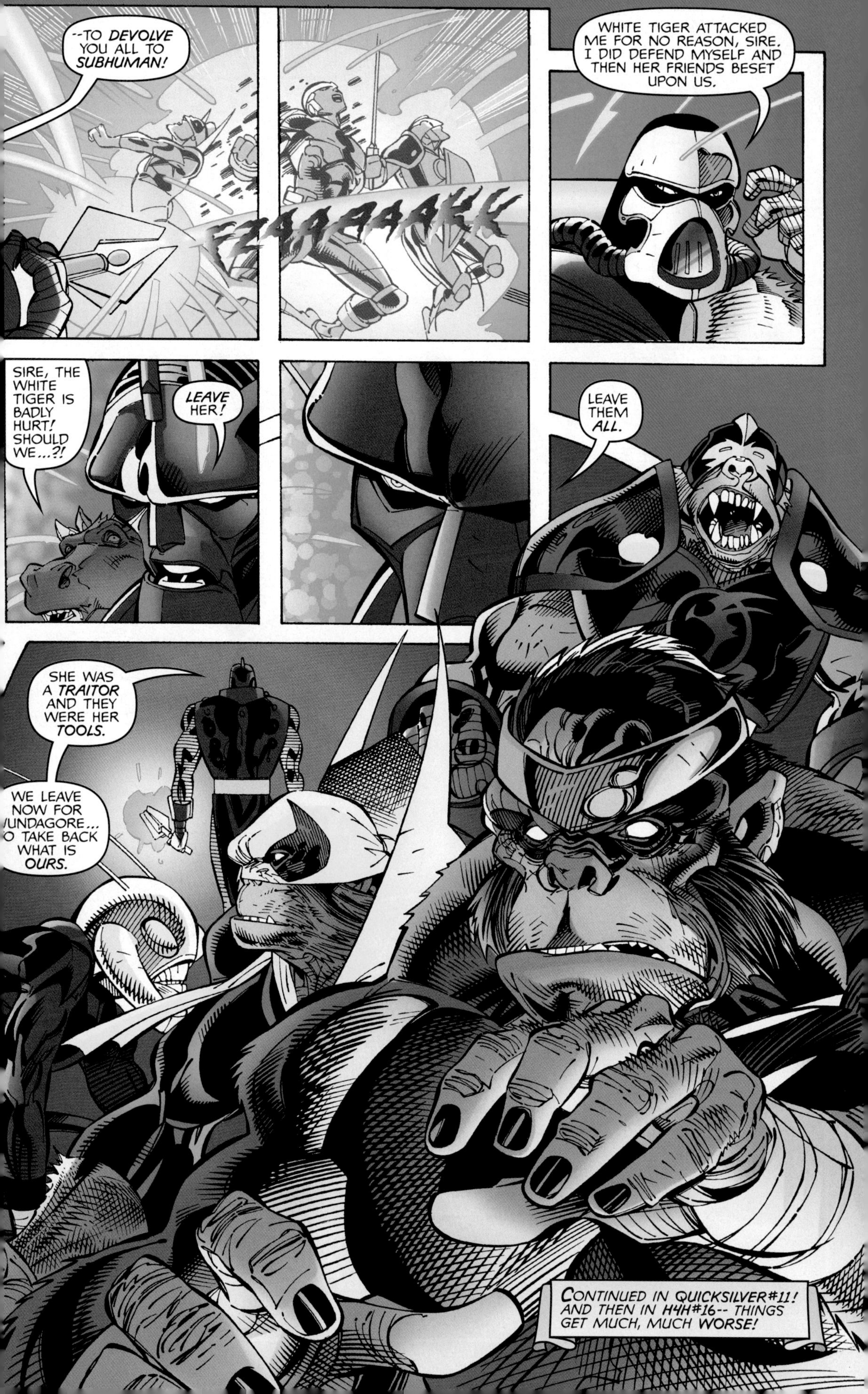
--TO DEVOLVE YOU ALL TO SUBHUMAN!
FZAAAAAAKK
WHITE TIGER ATTACKED ME FOR NO REASON, SIRE. I DID DEFEND MYSELF AND THEN HER FRIENDS BESET UPON US.
SIRE, THE WHITE TIGER IS BADLY HURT! SHOULD WE...?!
LEAVE HER!
LEAVE THEM ALL.
SHE WAS A TRAITOR AND THEY WERE HER TOOLS.
WE LEAVE NOW FOR UNDAGORE... O TAKE BACK WHAT IS OURS.
CONTINUED IN QUICKSILVER #11! AND THEN IN H4H#16-- THINGS GET MUCH, MUCH WORSE!

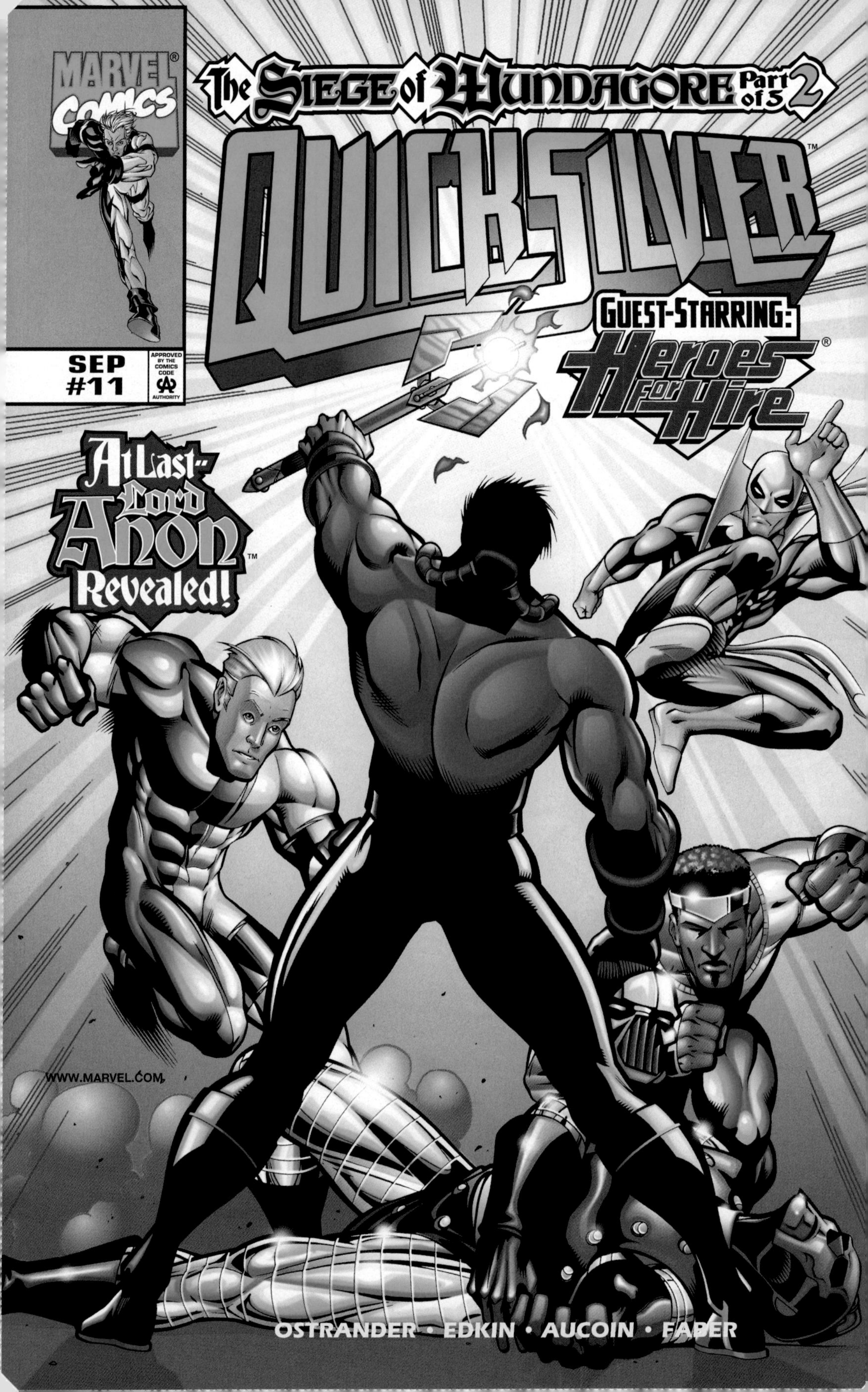

MARVEL COMICS
The Siege of Wundagore Part 2 of 5
QUICKSILVER™
SEP #11
APPROVED BY THE COMICS CODE AUTHORITY
GUEST-STARRING: Heroes For Hire®
At Last- Lord Anon™ Revealed!
WWW.MARVEL.COM
OSTRANDER • EDKIN • AUCOIN • FABER

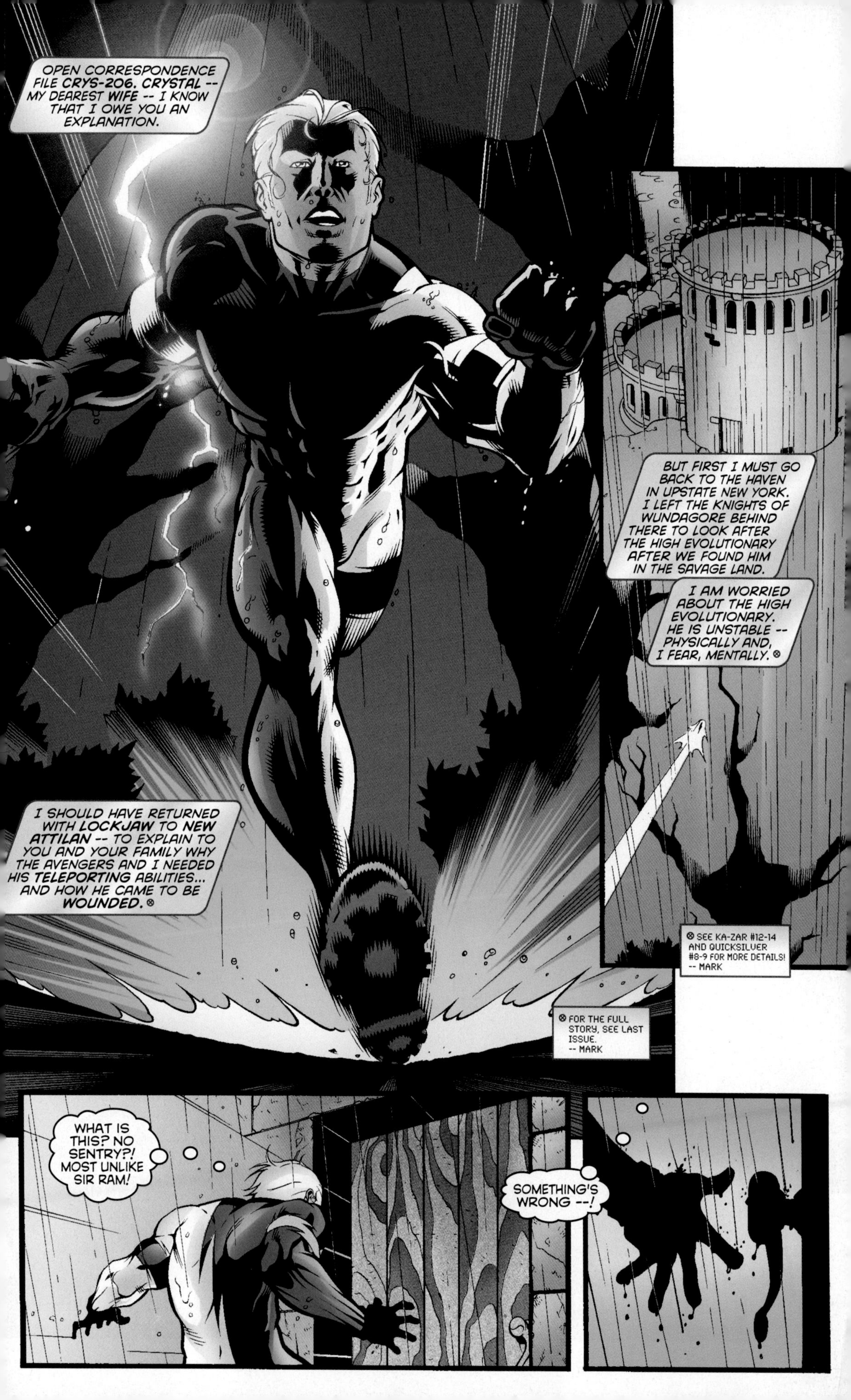

OPEN CORRESPONDENCE FILE CRYS-206. CRYSTAL -- MY DEAREST WIFE -- I KNOW THAT I OWE YOU AN EXPLANATION.
I SHOULD HAVE RETURNED WITH LOCKJAW TO NEW ATTILAN -- TO EXPLAIN TO YOU AND YOUR FAMILY WHY THE AVENGERS AND I NEEDED HIS TELEPORTING ABILITIES... AND HOW HE CAME TO BE WOUNDED. ⊗
⊗ FOR THE FULL STORY, SEE LAST ISSUE. -- MARK
BUT FIRST I MUST GO BACK TO THE HAVEN IN UPSTATE NEW YORK. I LEFT THE KNIGHTS OF WUNDAGORE BEHIND THERE TO LOOK AFTER THE HIGH EVOLUTIONARY AFTER WE FOUND HIM IN THE SAVAGE LAND.
I AM WORRIED ABOUT THE HIGH EVOLUTIONARY. HE IS UNSTABLE -- PHYSICALLY AND, I FEAR, MENTALLY. ⊗
⊗ SEE KA-ZAR #12-14 AND QUICKSILVER #8-9 FOR MORE DETAILS! -- MARK
WHAT IS THIS? NO SENTRY?! MOST UNLIKE SIR RAM!
SOMETHING'S WRONG --!

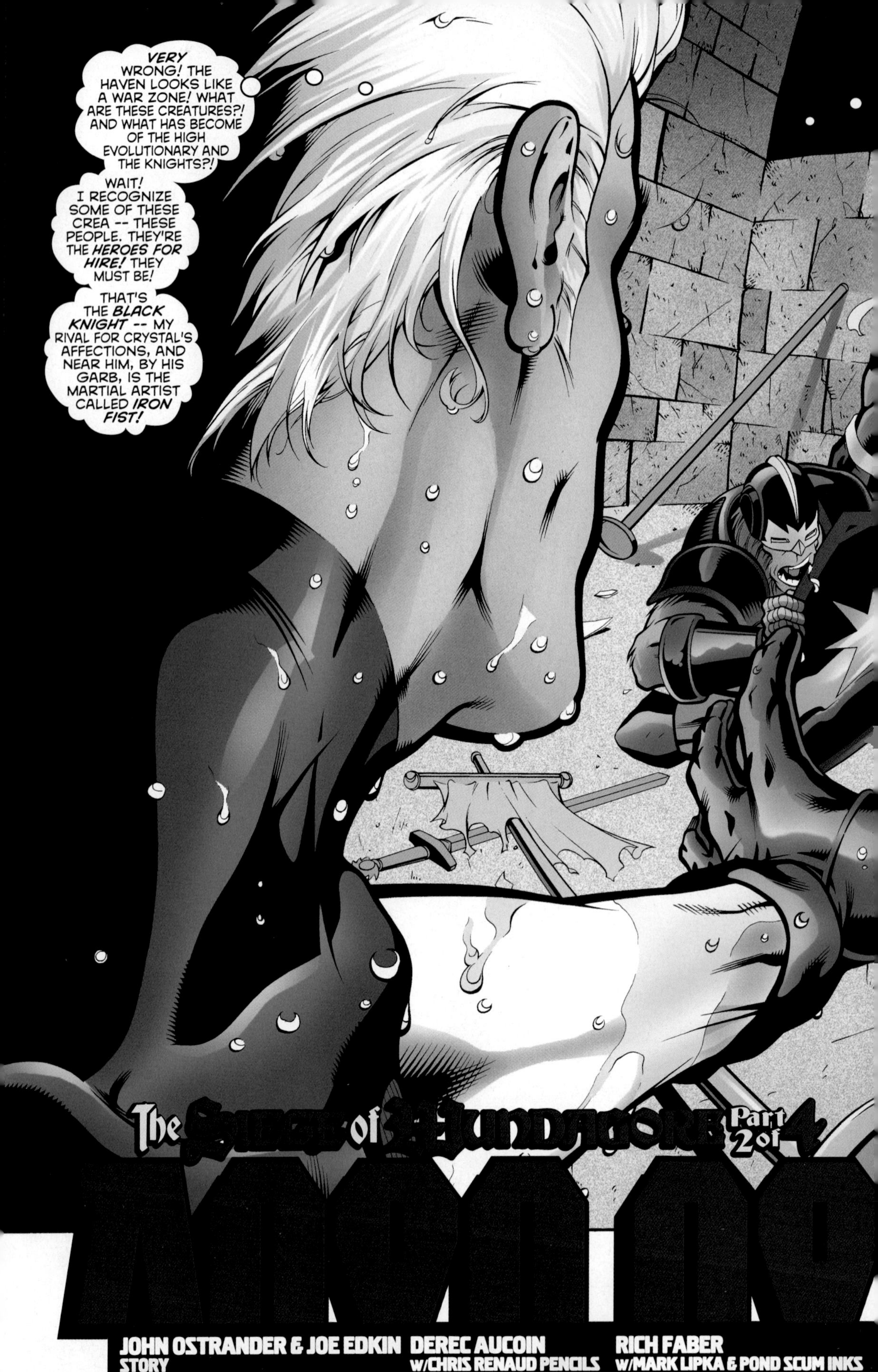
VERY WRONG! THE HAVEN LOOKS LIKE A WAR ZONE! WHAT ARE THESE CREATURES?! AND WHAT HAS BECOME OF THE HIGH EVOLUTIONARY AND THE KNIGHTS?!
WAIT! I RECOGNIZE SOME OF THESE CREA -- THESE PEOPLE. THEY'RE THE HEROES FOR HIRE! THEY MUST BE!
THAT'S THE BLACK KNIGHT -- MY RIVAL FOR CRYSTAL'S AFFECTIONS, AND NEAR HIM, BY HIS GARB, IS THE MARTIAL ARTIST CALLED IRON FIST!
The Siege of Wundagore Part 2 of 4
JOHN OSTRANDER & JOE EDKIN STORY
DEREC AUCOIN w/CHRIS RENAUD PENCILS
RICH FABER w/MARK LIPKA & POND SCUM INKS

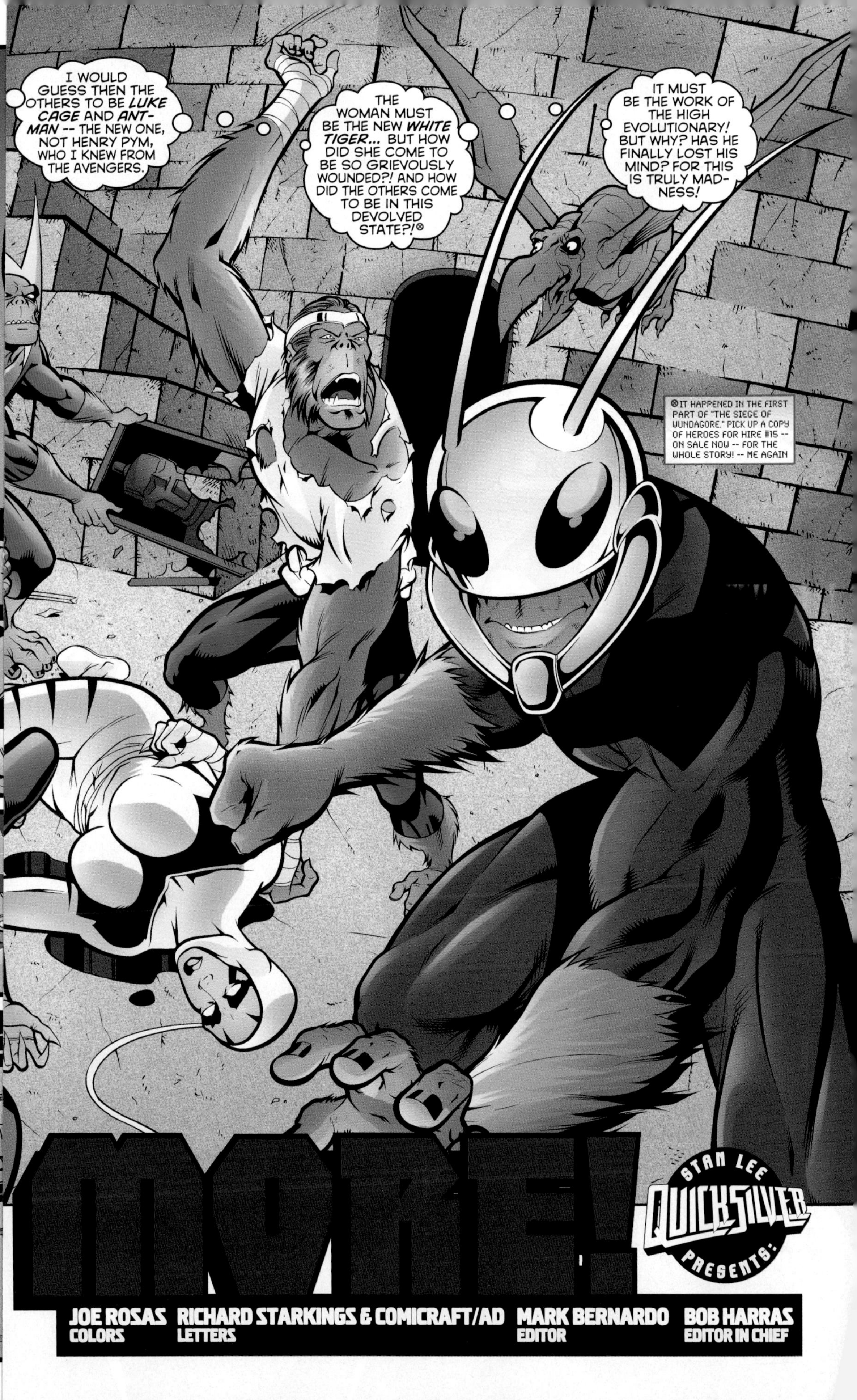
I WOULD GUESS THEN THE OTHERS TO BE *LUKE CAGE* AND *ANT-MAN* -- THE NEW ONE, NOT HENRY PYM, WHO I KNEW FROM THE AVENGERS.
THE WOMAN MUST BE THE NEW *WHITE TIGER...* BUT HOW DID SHE COME TO BE SO GRIEVOUSLY WOUNDED?! AND HOW DID THE OTHERS COME TO BE IN THIS DEVOLVED STATE?!⊗
IT MUST BE THE WORK OF THE HIGH EVOLUTIONARY! BUT WHY? HAS HE FINALLY LOST HIS MIND? FOR THIS IS TRULY MADNESS!
⊗IT HAPPENED IN THE FIRST PART OF "THE SIEGE OF WUNDAGORE." PICK UP A COPY OF HEROES FOR HIRE #15 -- ON SALE NOW -- FOR THE WHOLE STORY! -- ME AGAIN
STAN LEE PRESENTS: QUICKSILVER
JOE ROSAS COLORS
RICHARD STARKINGS & COMICRAFT/AD LETTERS
MARK BERNARDO EDITOR
BOB HARRAS EDITOR IN CHIEF

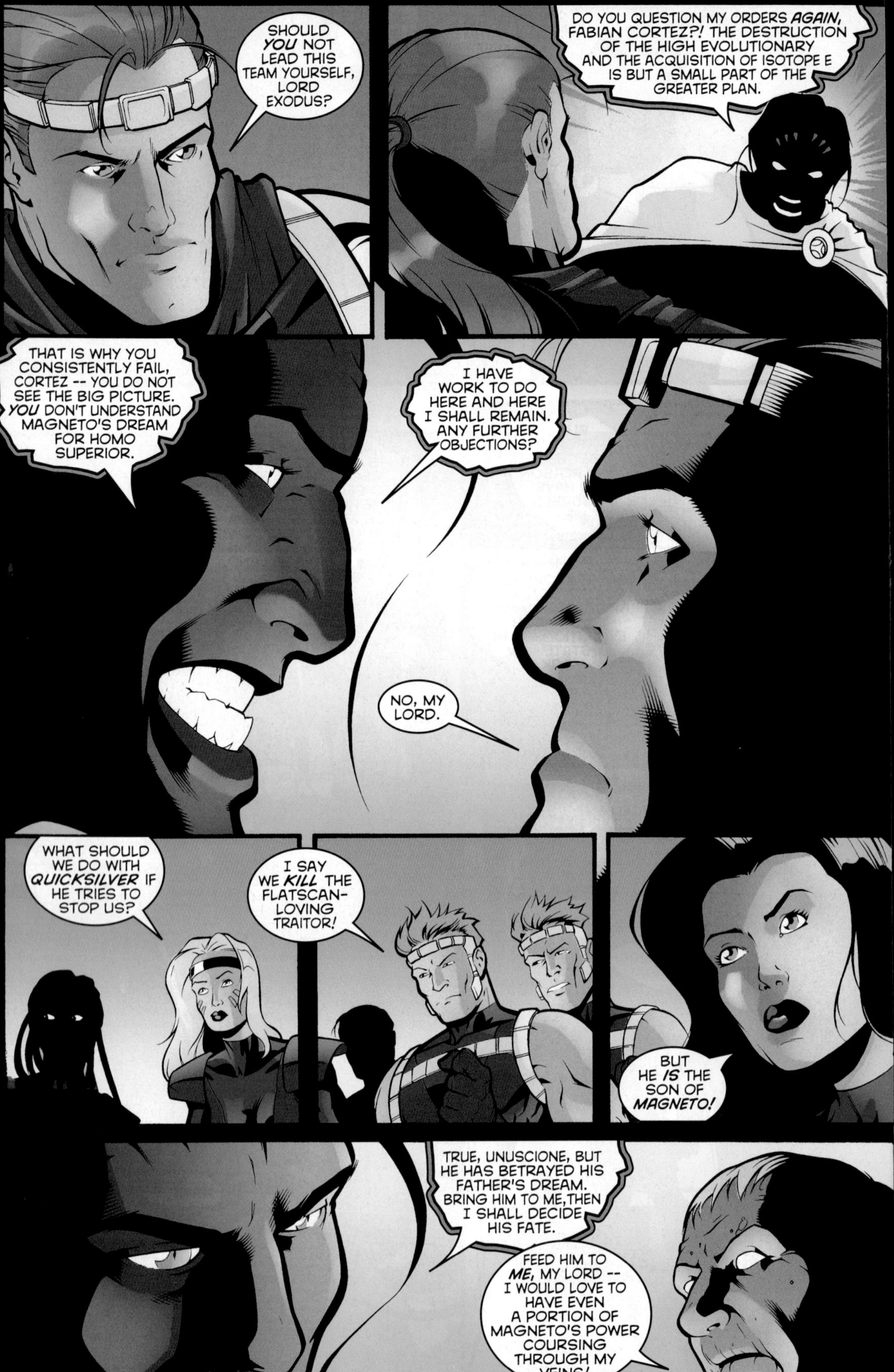
SHOULD YOU NOT LEAD THIS TEAM YOURSELF, LORD EXODUS?
DO YOU QUESTION MY ORDERS AGAIN, FABIAN CORTEZ?! THE DESTRUCTION OF THE HIGH EVOLUTIONARY AND THE ACQUISITION OF ISOTOPE E IS BUT A SMALL PART OF THE GREATER PLAN.
THAT IS WHY YOU CONSISTENTLY FAIL, CORTEZ -- YOU DO NOT SEE THE BIG PICTURE. YOU DON'T UNDERSTAND MAGNETO'S DREAM FOR HOMO SUPERIOR.
I HAVE WORK TO DO HERE AND HERE I SHALL REMAIN. ANY FURTHER OBJECTIONS?
NO, MY LORD.
WHAT SHOULD WE DO WITH QUICKSILVER IF HE TRIES TO STOP US?
I SAY WE KILL THE FLATSCAN-LOVING TRAITOR!
BUT HE IS THE SON OF MAGNETO!
TRUE, UNUSCIONE, BUT HE HAS BETRAYED HIS FATHER'S DREAM. BRING HIM TO ME, THEN I SHALL DECIDE HIS FATE.
FEED HIM TO ME, MY LORD -- I WOULD LOVE TO HAVE EVEN A PORTION OF MAGNETO'S POWER COURSING THROUGH MY VEINS!

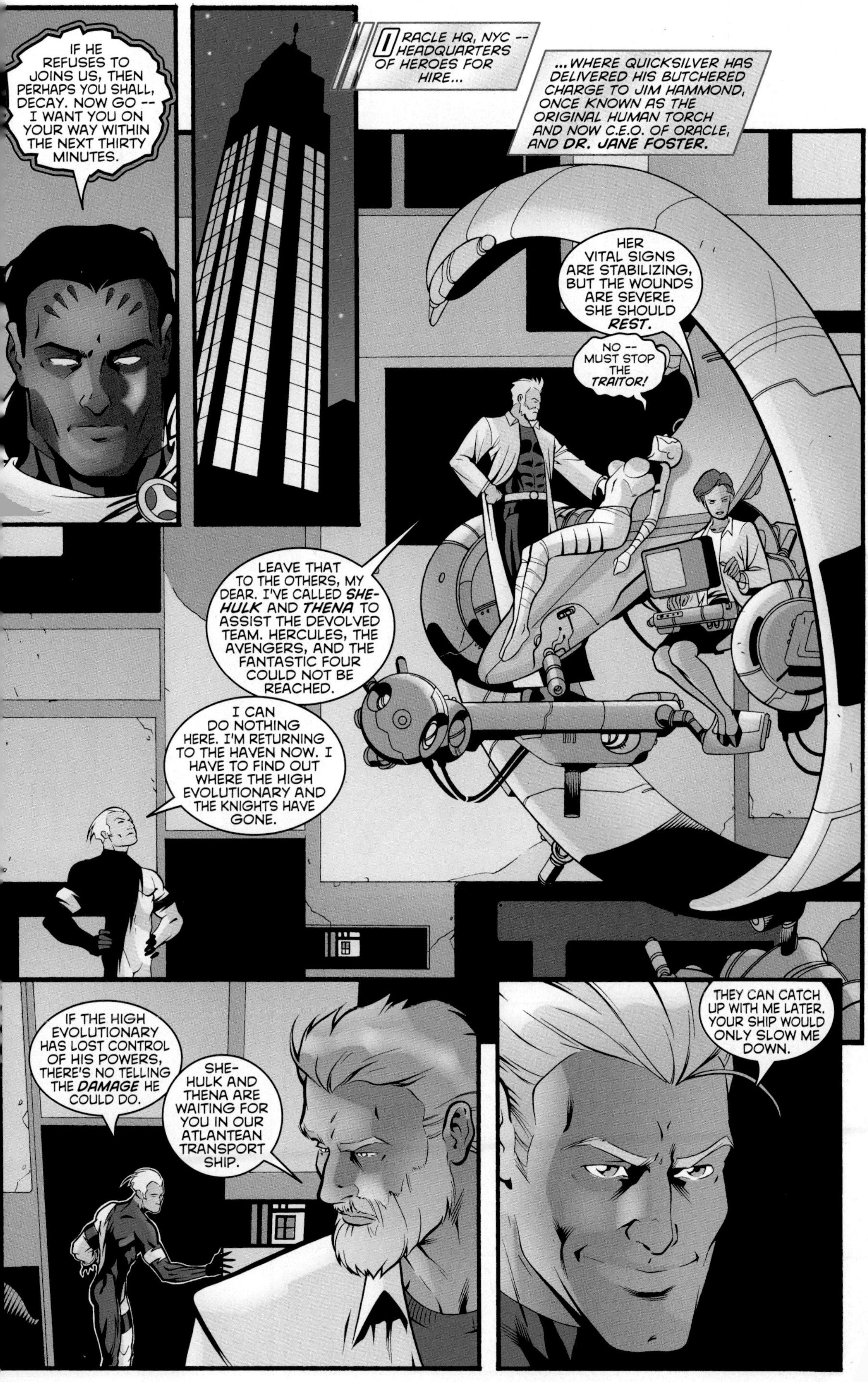
IF HE REFUSES TO JOINS US, THEN PERHAPS YOU SHALL, DECAY. NOW GO -- I WANT YOU ON YOUR WAY WITHIN THE NEXT THIRTY MINUTES.
ORACLE HQ, NYC -- HEADQUARTERS OF HEROES FOR HIRE...
...WHERE QUICKSILVER HAS DELIVERED HIS BUTCHERED CHARGE TO JIM HAMMOND, ONCE KNOWN AS THE ORIGINAL HUMAN TORCH AND NOW C.E.O. OF ORACLE, AND DR. JANE FOSTER.
HER VITAL SIGNS ARE STABILIZING, BUT THE WOUNDS ARE SEVERE. SHE SHOULD REST.
NO -- MUST STOP THE TRAITOR!
LEAVE THAT TO THE OTHERS, MY DEAR. I'VE CALLED SHE-HULK AND THENA TO ASSIST THE DEVOLVED TEAM. HERCULES, THE AVENGERS, AND THE FANTASTIC FOUR COULD NOT BE REACHED.
I CAN DO NOTHING HERE. I'M RETURNING TO THE HAVEN NOW. I HAVE TO FIND OUT WHERE THE HIGH EVOLUTIONARY AND THE KNIGHTS HAVE GONE.
IF THE HIGH EVOLUTIONARY HAS LOST CONTROL OF HIS POWERS, THERE'S NO TELLING THE DAMAGE HE COULD DO.
SHE-HULK AND THENA ARE WAITING FOR YOU IN OUR ATLANTEAN TRANSPORT SHIP.
THEY CAN CATCH UP WITH ME LATER. YOUR SHIP WOULD ONLY SLOW ME DOWN.

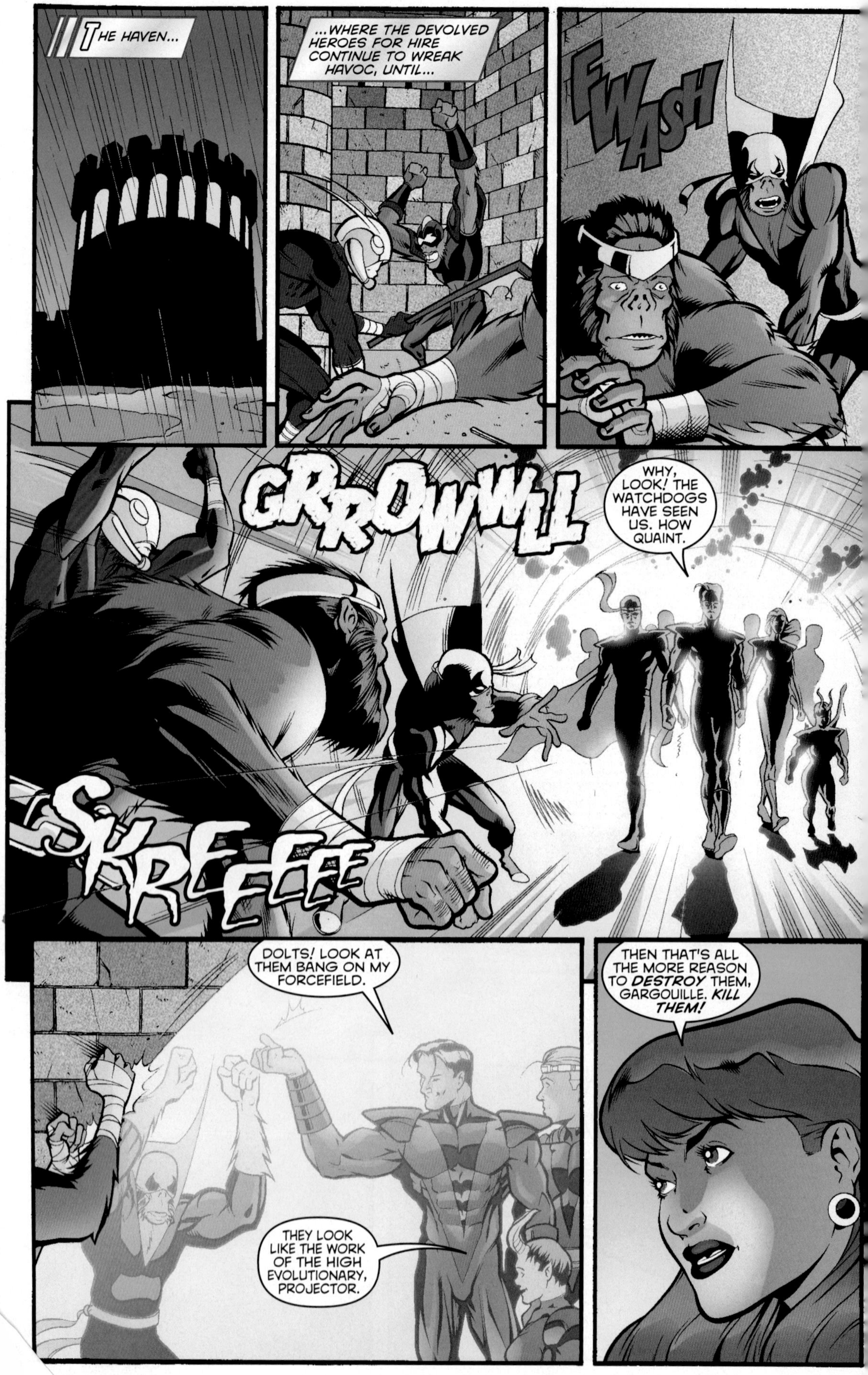
THE HAVEN...
...WHERE THE DEVOLVED HEROES FOR HIRE CONTINUE TO WREAK HAVOC, UNTIL...
FWASH
GRROWWLL
WHY, LOOK! THE WATCHDOGS HAVE SEEN US. HOW QUAINT.
SKREEEEE
DOLTS! LOOK AT THEM BANG ON MY FORCEFIELD.
THEY LOOK LIKE THE WORK OF THE HIGH EVOLUTIONARY, PROJECTOR.
THEN THAT'S ALL THE MORE REASON TO DESTROY THEM, GARGOUILLE. KILL THEM!

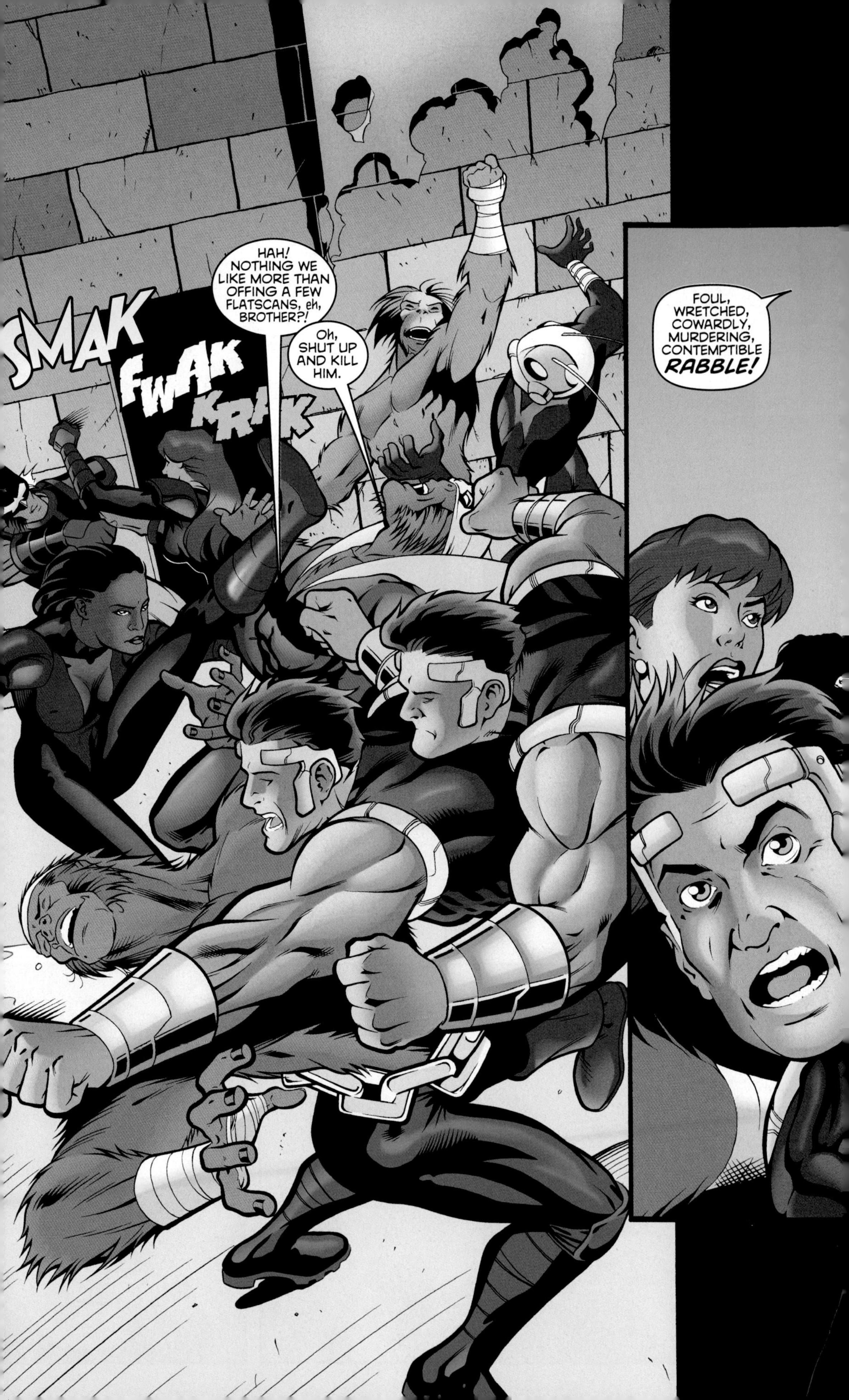
SMAK
FWAK
KRAK
HAH! NOTHING WE LIKE MORE THAN OFFING A FEW FLATSCANS, eh, BROTHER?!
Oh, SHUT UP AND KILL HIM.
FOUL, WRETCHED, COWARDLY, MURDERING, CONTEMPTIBLE RABBLE!

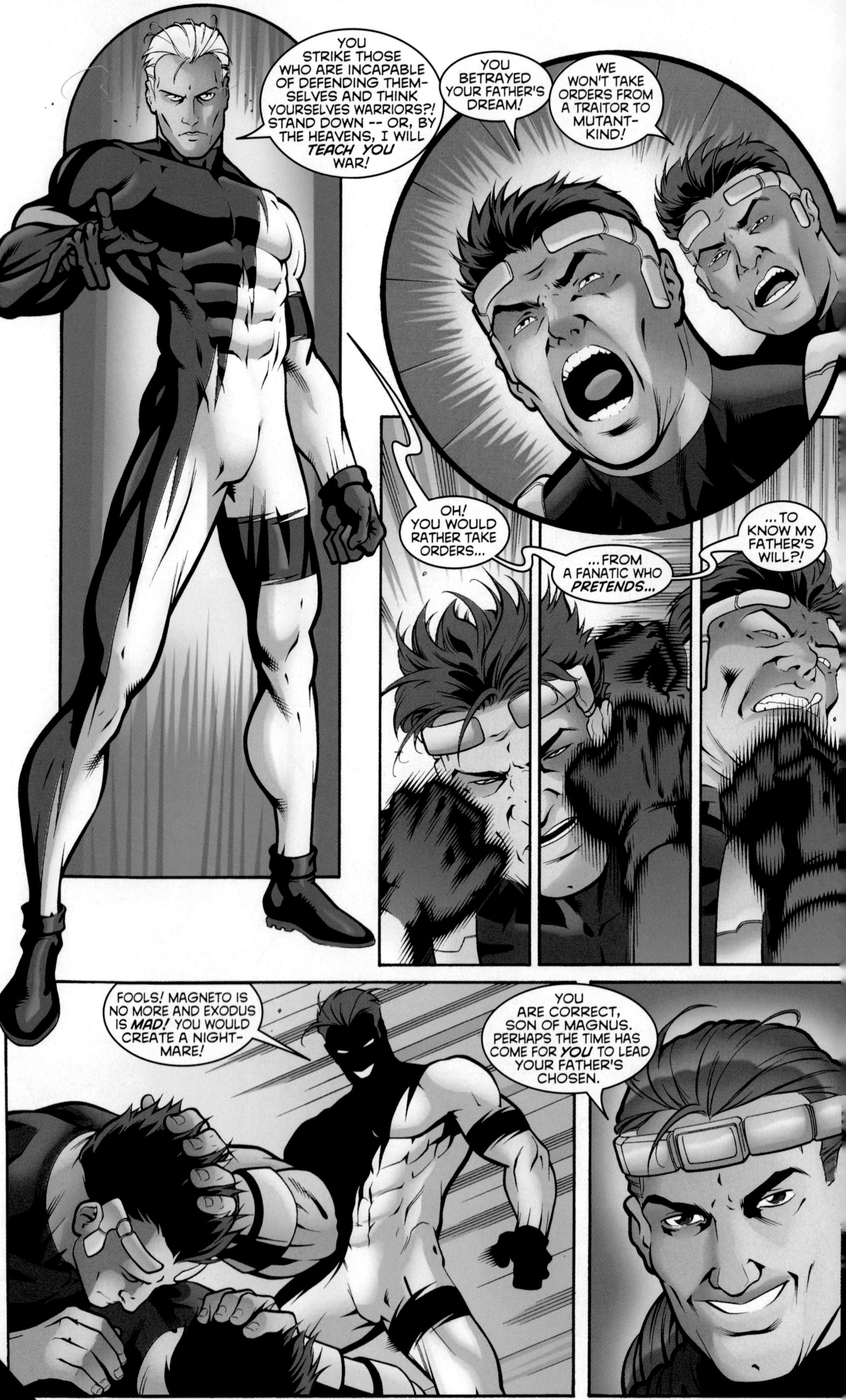
YOU STRIKE THOSE WHO ARE INCAPABLE OF DEFENDING THEMSELVES AND THINK YOURSELVES WARRIORS?! STAND DOWN -- OR, BY THE HEAVENS, I WILL *TEACH YOU* WAR!
YOU BETRAYED YOUR FATHER'S DREAM!
WE WON'T TAKE ORDERS FROM A TRAITOR TO MUTANT-KIND!
OH! YOU WOULD RATHER TAKE ORDERS...
...FROM A FANATIC WHO *PRETENDS*...
...TO KNOW MY FATHER'S WILL?!
FOOLS! MAGNETO IS NO MORE AND EXODUS IS *MAD!* YOU WOULD CREATE A NIGHT-MARE!
YOU ARE CORRECT, SON OF MAGNUS. PERHAPS THE TIME HAS COME FOR *YOU* TO LEAD YOUR FATHER'S CHOSEN.

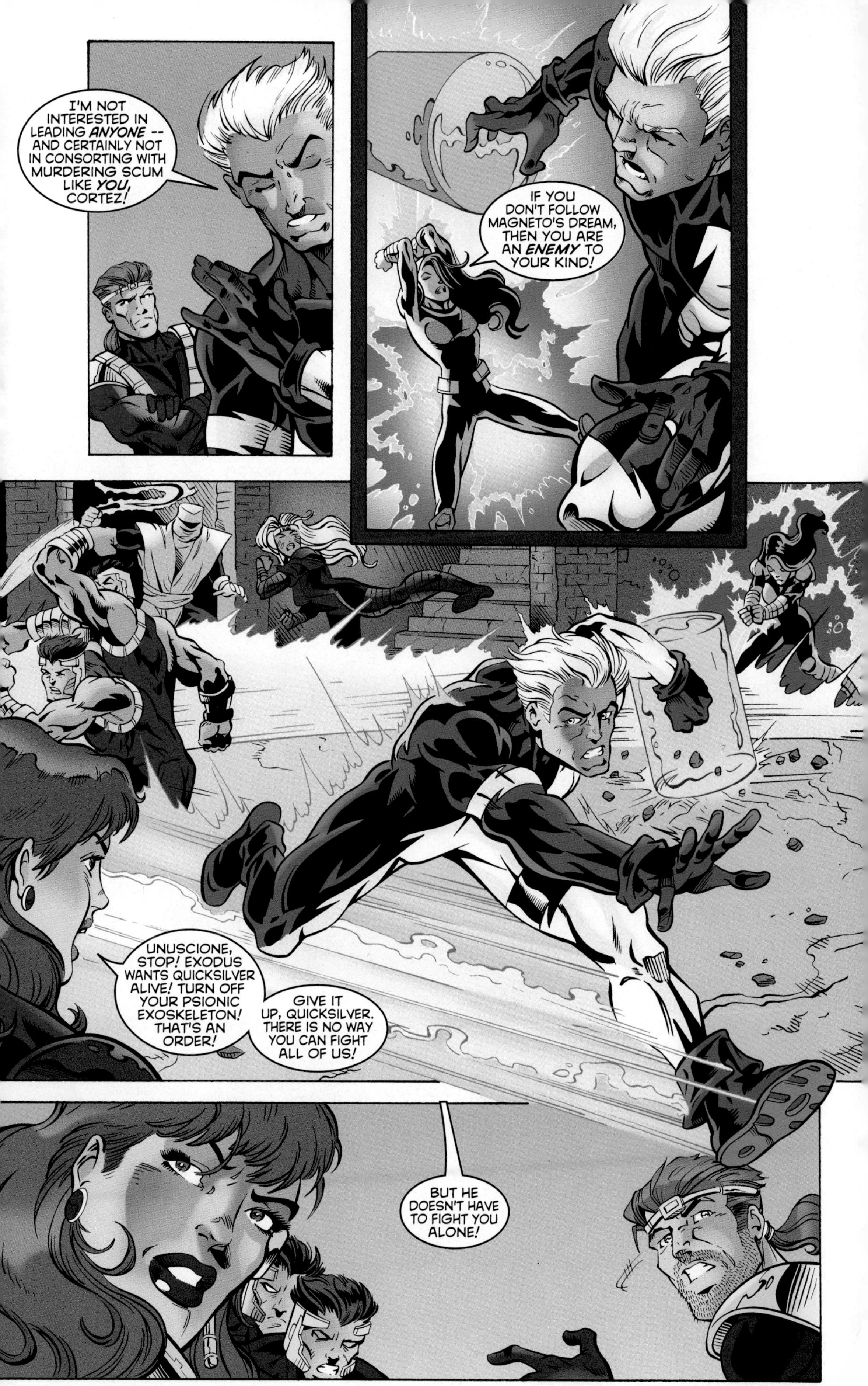

I'M NOT INTERESTED IN LEADING ANYONE -- AND CERTAINLY NOT IN CONSORTING WITH MURDERING SCUM LIKE YOU, CORTEZ!
IF YOU DON'T FOLLOW MAGNETO'S DREAM, THEN YOU ARE AN ENEMY TO YOUR KIND!
UNUSCIONE, STOP! EXODUS WANTS QUICKSILVER ALIVE! TURN OFF YOUR PSIONIC EXOSKELETON! THAT'S AN ORDER!
GIVE IT UP, QUICKSILVER. THERE IS NO WAY YOU CAN FIGHT ALL OF US!
BUT HE DOESN'T HAVE TO FIGHT YOU ALONE!

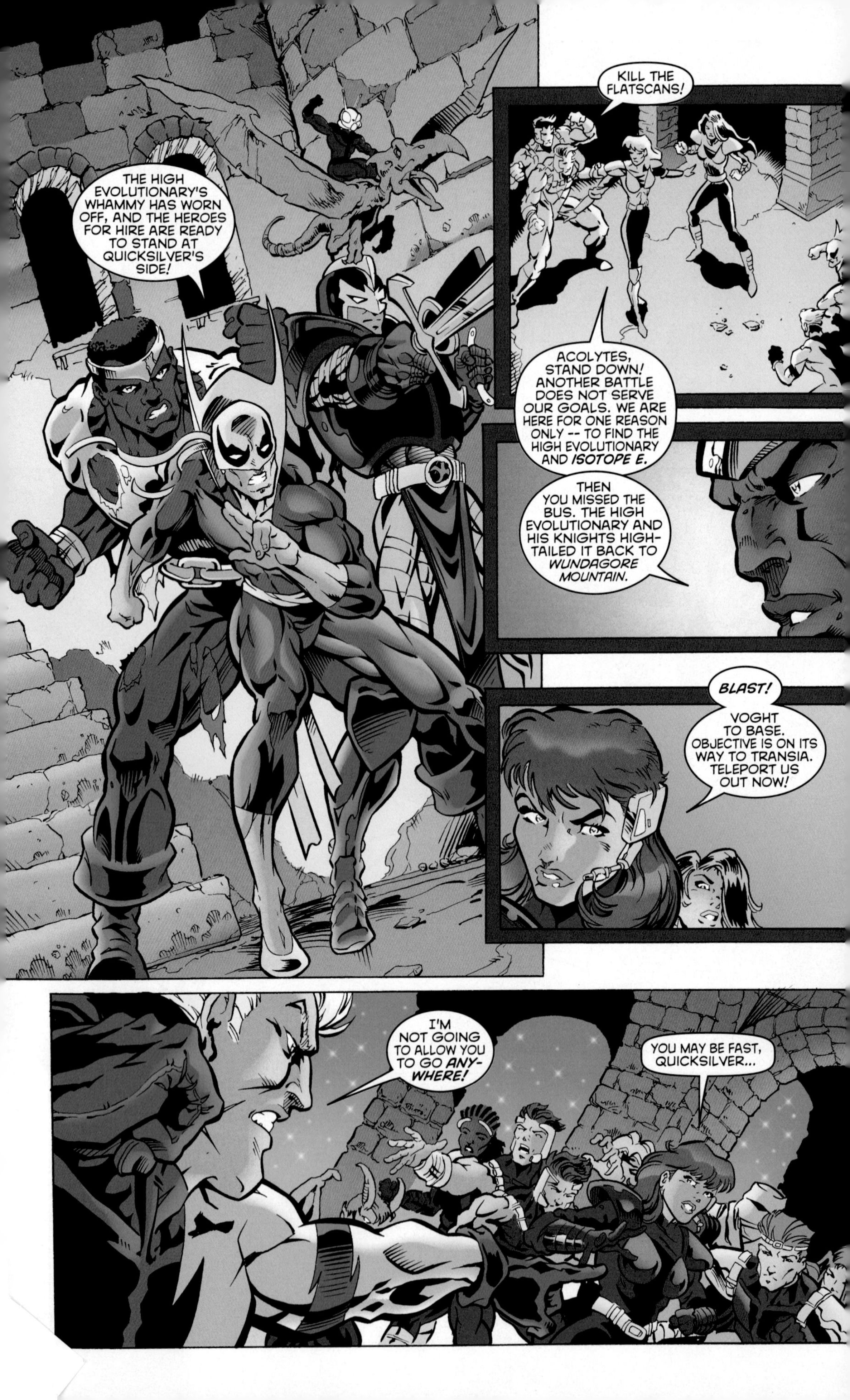
THE HIGH EVOLUTIONARY'S WHAMMY HAS WORN OFF, AND THE HEROES FOR HIRE ARE READY TO STAND AT QUICKSILVER'S SIDE!
KILL THE FLATSCANS!
ACOLYTES, STAND DOWN! ANOTHER BATTLE DOES NOT SERVE OUR GOALS. WE ARE HERE FOR ONE REASON ONLY -- TO FIND THE HIGH EVOLUTIONARY AND ISOTOPE E.
THEN YOU MISSED THE BUS. THE HIGH EVOLUTIONARY AND HIS KNIGHTS HIGH-TAILED IT BACK TO WUNDAGORE MOUNTAIN.
BLAST!
VOGHT TO BASE. OBJECTIVE IS ON ITS WAY TO TRANSIA. TELEPORT US OUT NOW!
I'M NOT GOING TO ALLOW YOU TO GO ANY-WHERE!
YOU MAY BE FAST, QUICKSILVER...

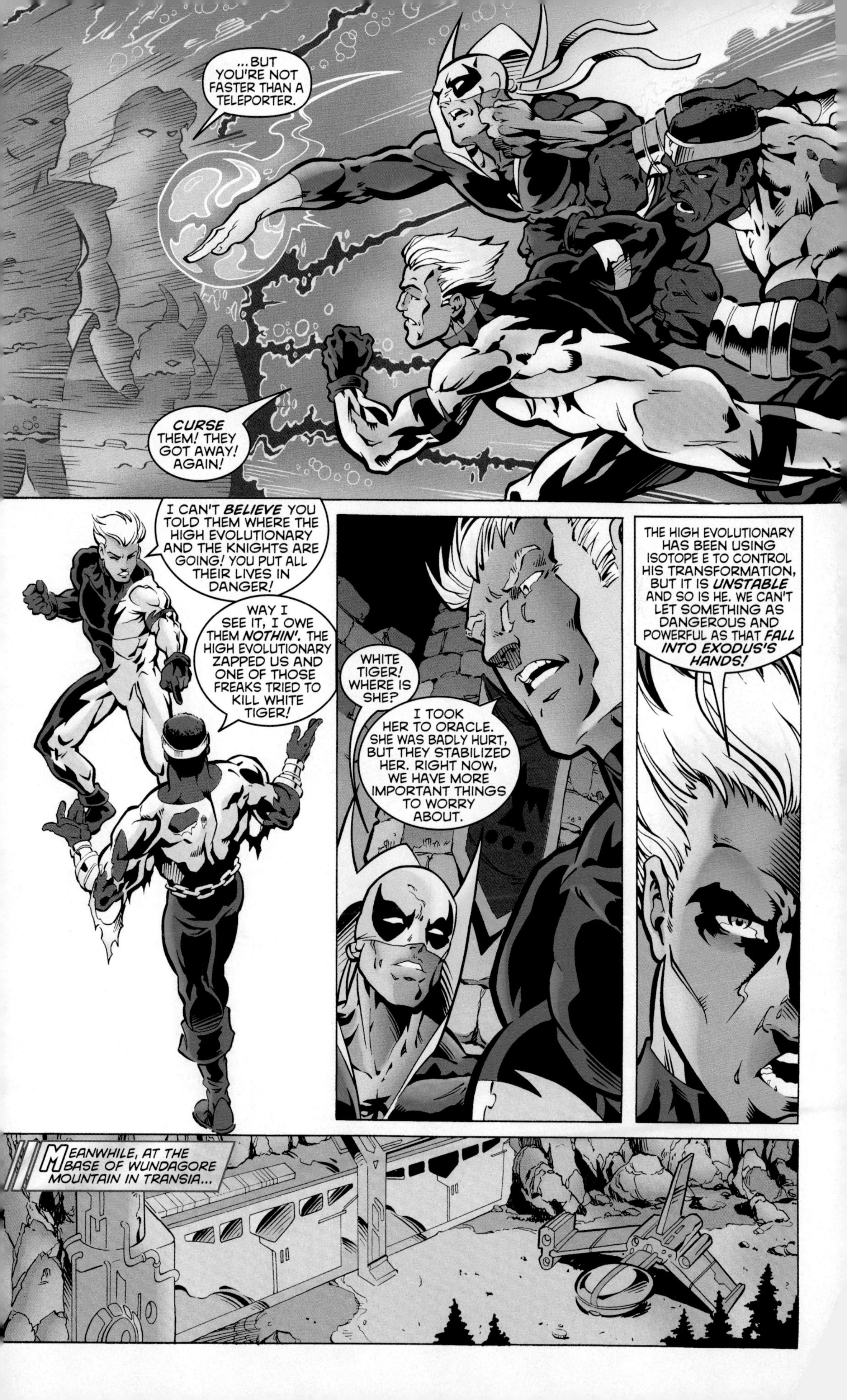
...BUT YOU'RE NOT FASTER THAN A TELEPORTER.
CURSE THEM! THEY GOT AWAY! AGAIN!
I CAN'T BELIEVE YOU TOLD THEM WHERE THE HIGH EVOLUTIONARY AND THE KNIGHTS ARE GOING! YOU PUT ALL THEIR LIVES IN DANGER!
WAY I SEE IT, I OWE THEM NOTHIN'. THE HIGH EVOLUTIONARY ZAPPED US AND ONE OF THOSE FREAKS TRIED TO KILL WHITE TIGER!
WHITE TIGER! WHERE IS SHE?
I TOOK HER TO ORACLE. SHE WAS BADLY HURT, BUT THEY STABILIZED HER. RIGHT NOW, WE HAVE MORE IMPORTANT THINGS TO WORRY ABOUT.
THE HIGH EVOLUTIONARY HAS BEEN USING ISOTOPE E TO CONTROL HIS TRANSFORMATION, BUT IT IS UNSTABLE AND SO IS HE. WE CAN'T LET SOMETHING AS DANGEROUS AND POWERFUL AS THAT FALL INTO EXODUS'S HANDS!
MEANWHILE, AT THE BASE OF WUNDAGORE MOUNTAIN IN TRANSIA...

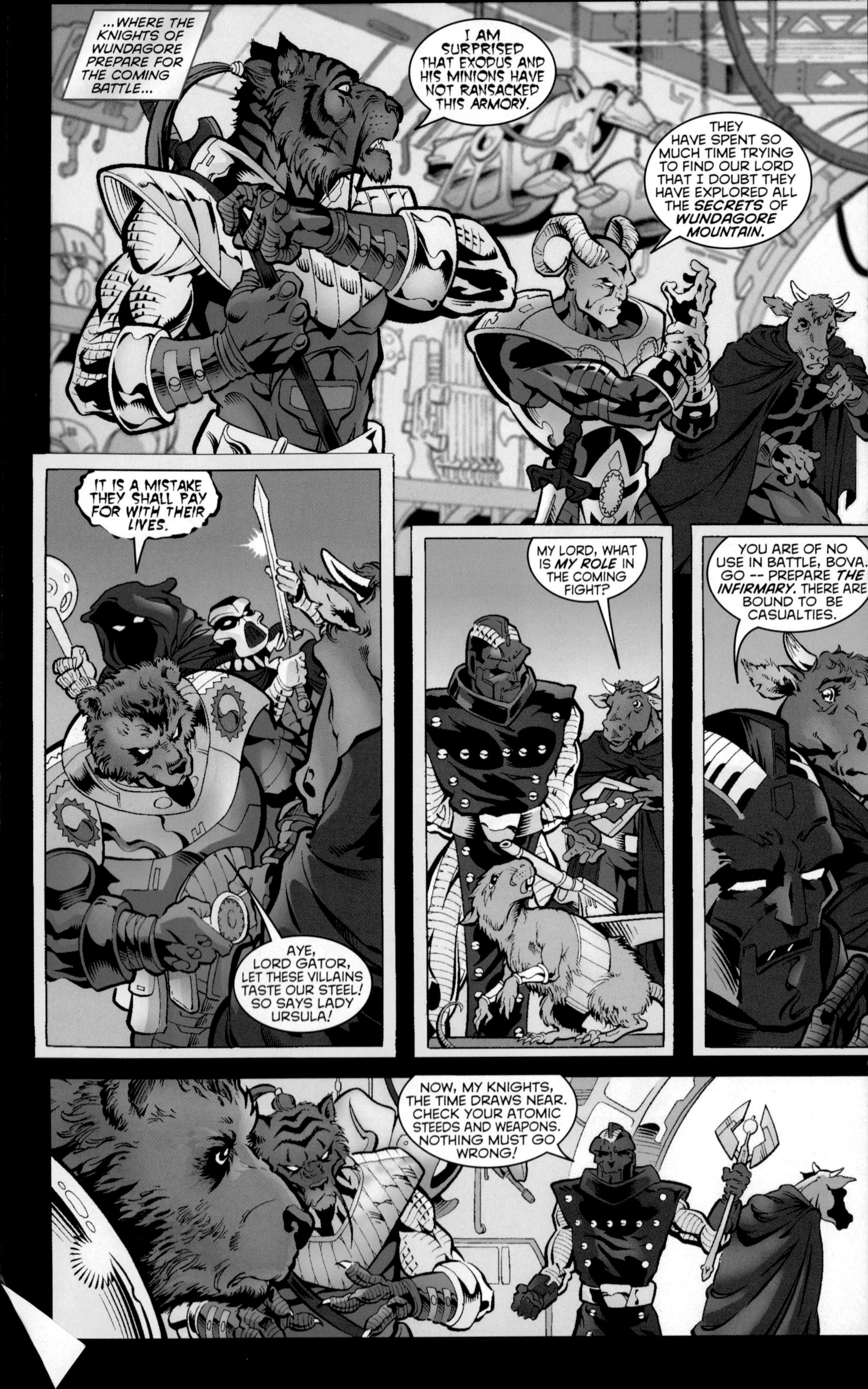
...WHERE THE KNIGHTS OF WUNDAGORE PREPARE FOR THE COMING BATTLE...
I AM SURPRISED THAT EXODUS AND HIS MINIONS HAVE NOT RANSACKED THIS ARMORY.
THEY HAVE SPENT SO MUCH TIME TRYING TO FIND OUR LORD THAT I DOUBT THEY HAVE EXPLORED ALL THE SECRETS OF WUNDAGORE MOUNTAIN.
IT IS A MISTAKE THEY SHALL PAY FOR WITH THEIR LIVES.
AYE, LORD GATOR, LET THESE VILLAINS TASTE OUR STEEL! SO SAYS LADY URSULA!
MY LORD, WHAT IS MY ROLE IN THE COMING FIGHT?
YOU ARE OF NO USE IN BATTLE, BOVA. GO -- PREPARE THE INFIRMARY. THERE ARE BOUND TO BE CASUALTIES.
NOW, MY KNIGHTS, THE TIME DRAWS NEAR. CHECK YOUR ATOMIC STEEDS AND WEAPONS. NOTHING MUST GO WRONG!

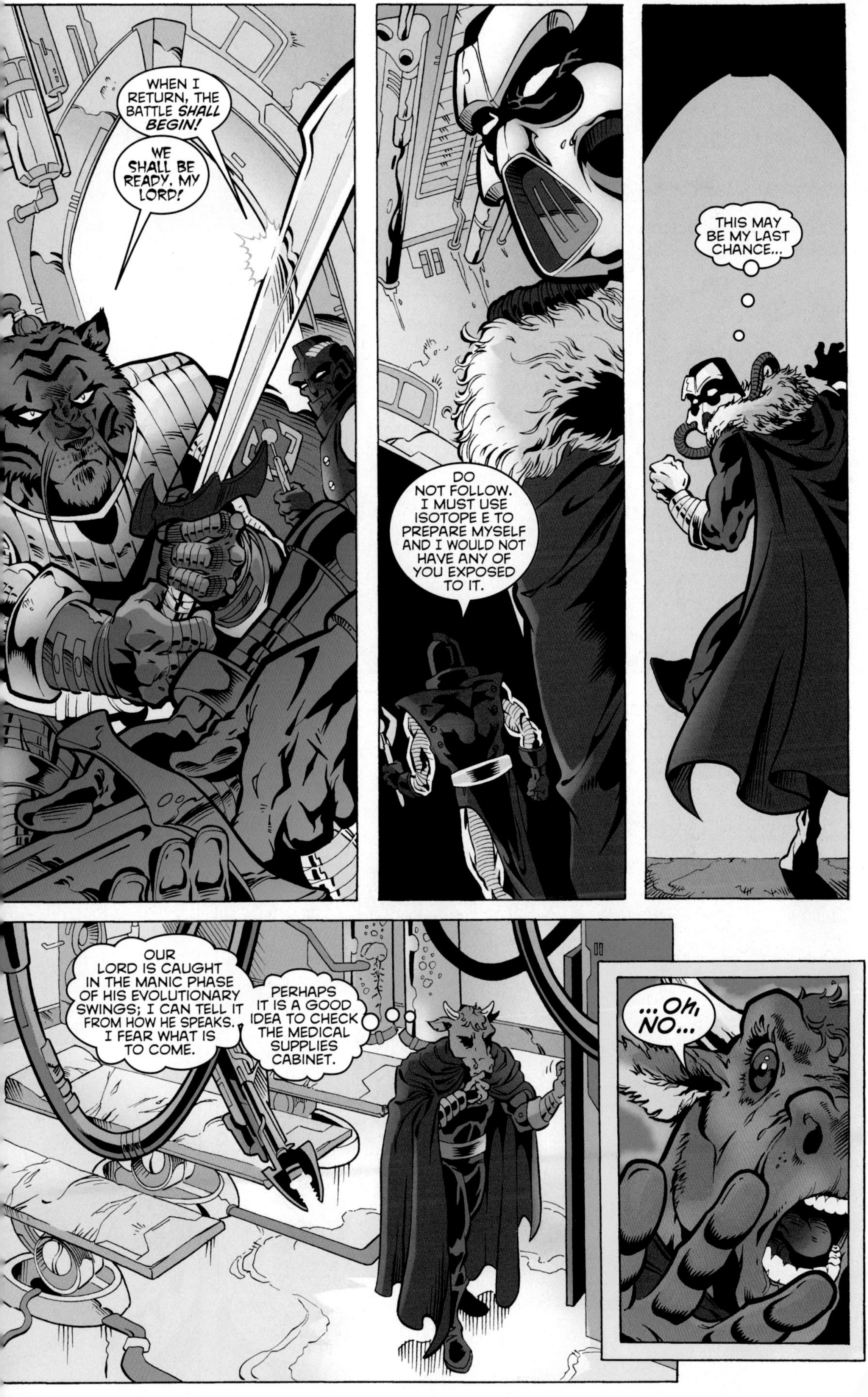
WHEN I RETURN, THE BATTLE SHALL BEGIN!
WE SHALL BE READY, MY LORD!
DO NOT FOLLOW. I MUST USE ISOTOPE E TO PREPARE MYSELF AND I WOULD NOT HAVE ANY OF YOU EXPOSED TO IT.
THIS MAY BE MY LAST CHANCE...
OUR LORD IS CAUGHT IN THE MANIC PHASE OF HIS EVOLUTIONARY SWINGS; I CAN TELL IT FROM HOW HE SPEAKS. I FEAR WHAT IS TO COME.
PERHAPS IT IS A GOOD IDEA TO CHECK THE MEDICAL SUPPLIES CABINET.
...OH, NO...

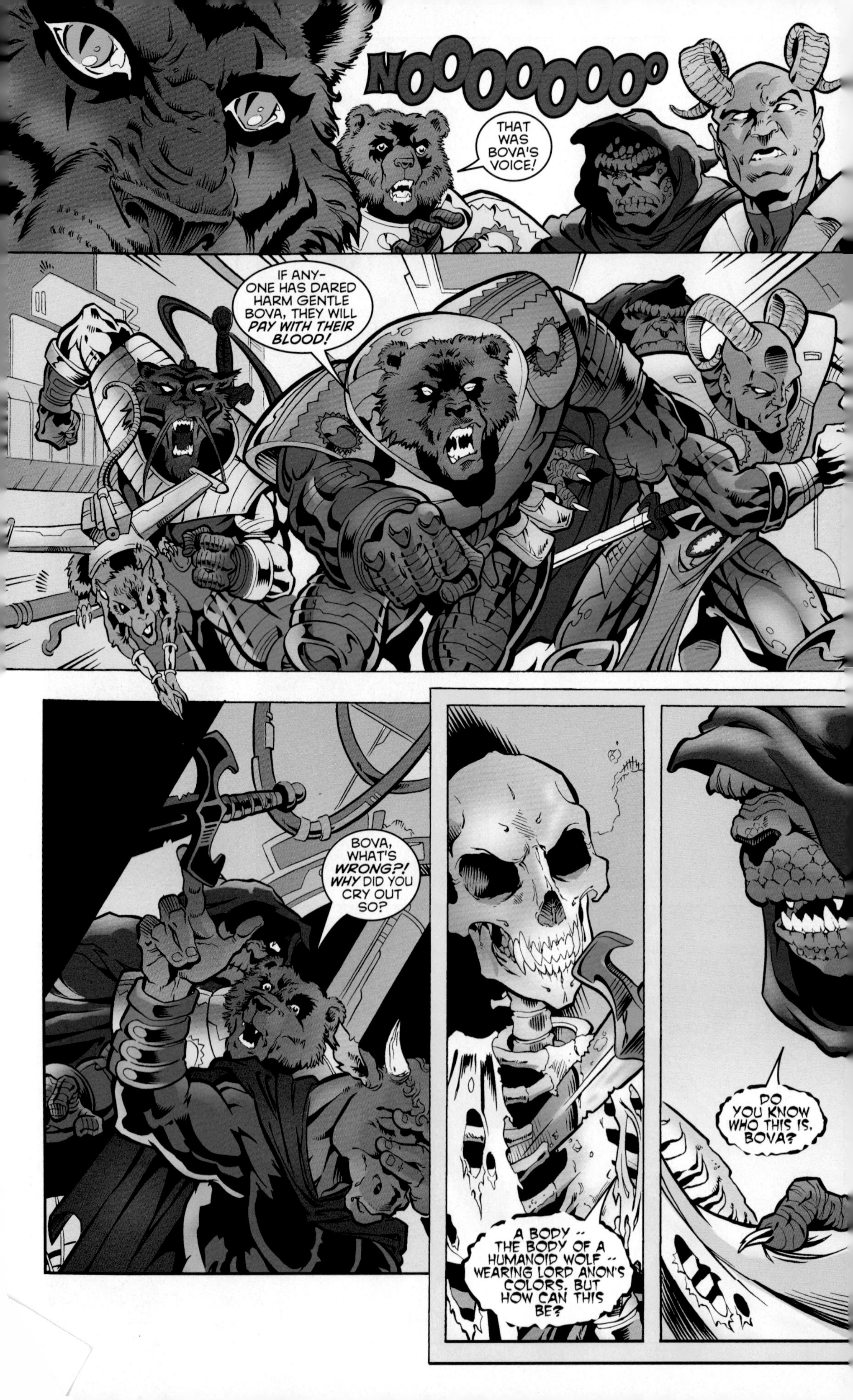
NOOOOOOOOo
THAT WAS BOVA'S VOICE!
IF ANY-ONE HAS DARED HARM GENTLE BOVA, THEY WILL PAY WITH THEIR BLOOD!
BOVA, WHAT'S WRONG?! WHY DID YOU CRY OUT SO?
A BODY -- THE BODY OF A HUMANOID WOLF -- WEARING LORD ANON'S COLORS. BUT HOW CAN THIS BE?
DO YOU KNOW WHO THIS IS, BOVA?

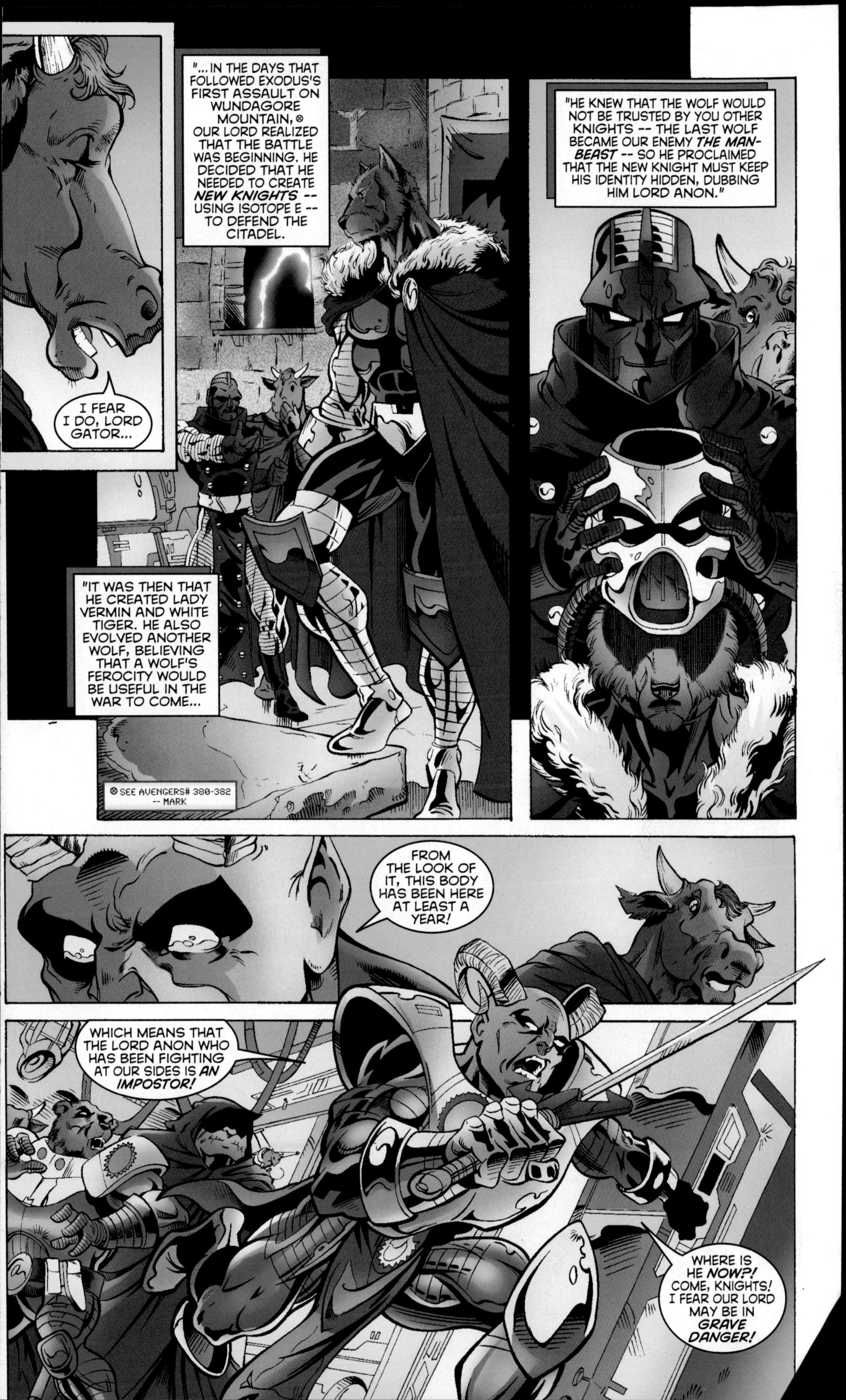
I FEAR I DO, LORD GATOR...
"...IN THE DAYS THAT FOLLOWED EXODUS'S FIRST ASSAULT ON WUNDAGORE MOUNTAIN,⊗ OUR LORD REALIZED THAT THE BATTLE WAS BEGINNING. HE DECIDED THAT HE NEEDED TO CREATE *NEW KNIGHTS* -- USING ISOTOPE E -- TO DEFEND THE CITADEL.
"IT WAS THEN THAT HE CREATED LADY VERMIN AND WHITE TIGER. HE ALSO EVOLVED ANOTHER WOLF, BELIEVING THAT A WOLF'S FEROCITY WOULD BE USEFUL IN THE WAR TO COME...
⊗ SEE AVENGERS# 380-382 -- MARK
"HE KNEW THAT THE WOLF WOULD NOT BE TRUSTED BY YOU OTHER KNIGHTS -- THE LAST WOLF BECAME OUR ENEMY *THE MAN-BEAST* -- SO HE PROCLAIMED THAT THE NEW KNIGHT MUST KEEP HIS IDENTITY HIDDEN, DUBBING HIM LORD ANON."
FROM THE LOOK OF IT, THIS BODY HAS BEEN HERE AT LEAST A YEAR!
WHICH MEANS THAT THE LORD ANON WHO HAS BEEN FIGHTING AT OUR SIDES IS *AN IMPOSTOR!*
WHERE IS HE *NOW?!* COME, KNIGHTS! I FEAR OUR LORD MAY BE IN *GRAVE DANGER!*

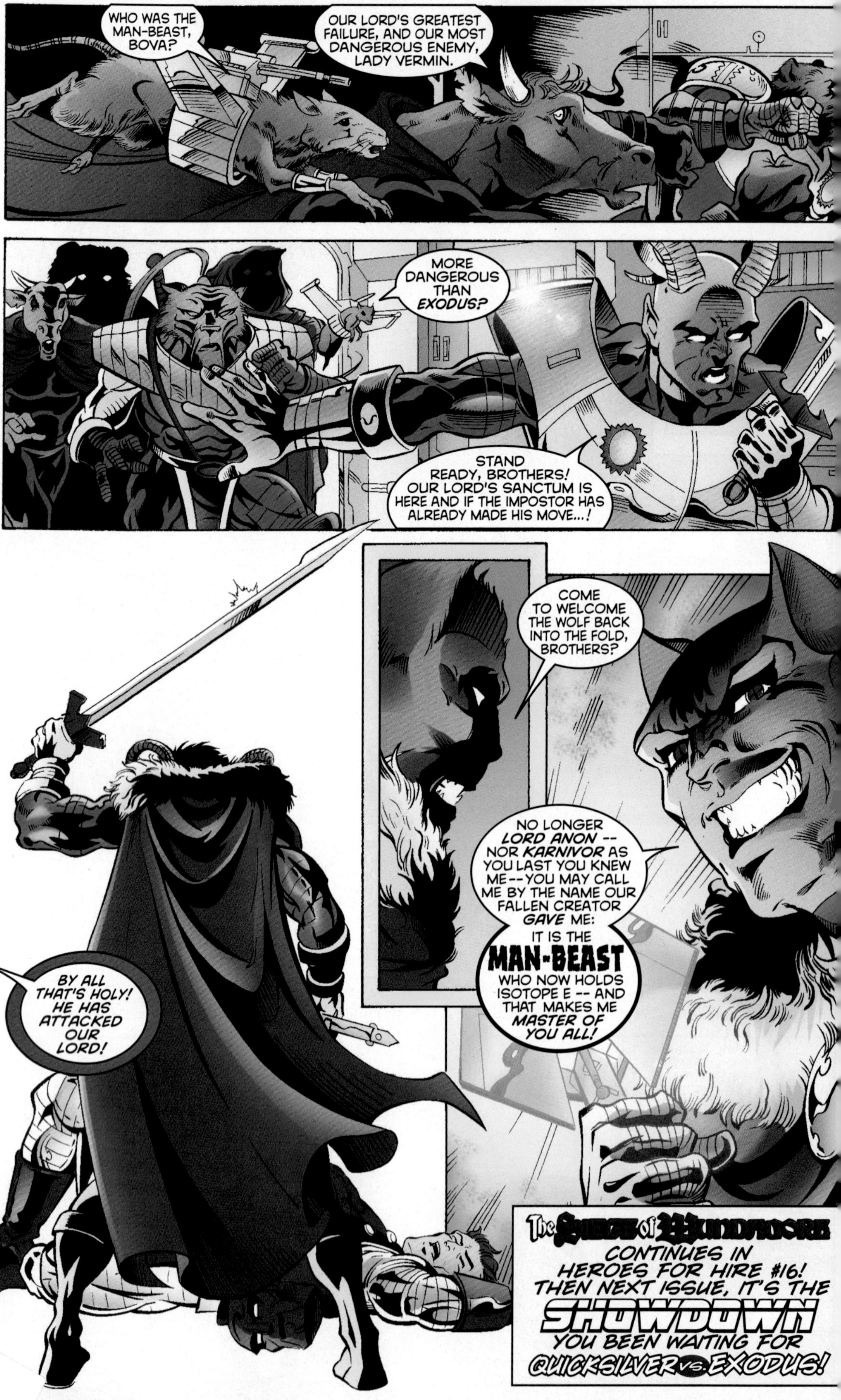

WHO WAS THE MAN-BEAST, BOVA?
OUR LORD'S GREATEST FAILURE, AND OUR MOST DANGEROUS ENEMY, LADY VERMIN.
MORE DANGEROUS THAN EXODUS?
STAND READY, BROTHERS! OUR LORD'S SANCTUM IS HERE AND IF THE IMPOSTOR HAS ALREADY MADE HIS MOVE...!
COME TO WELCOME THE WOLF BACK INTO THE FOLD, BROTHERS?
NO LONGER LORD ANON -- NOR KARNIVOR AS YOU LAST YOU KNEW ME -- YOU MAY CALL ME BY THE NAME OUR FALLEN CREATOR GAVE ME: IT IS THE MAN-BEAST WHO NOW HOLDS ISOTOPE E -- AND THAT MAKES ME MASTER OF YOU ALL!
BY ALL THAT'S HOLY! HE HAS ATTACKED OUR LORD!
The Siege of Wundagore CONTINUES IN HEROES FOR HIRE #16! THEN NEXT ISSUE, IT'S THE SHOWDOWN YOU BEEN WAITING FOR QUICKSILVER vs. EXODUS!

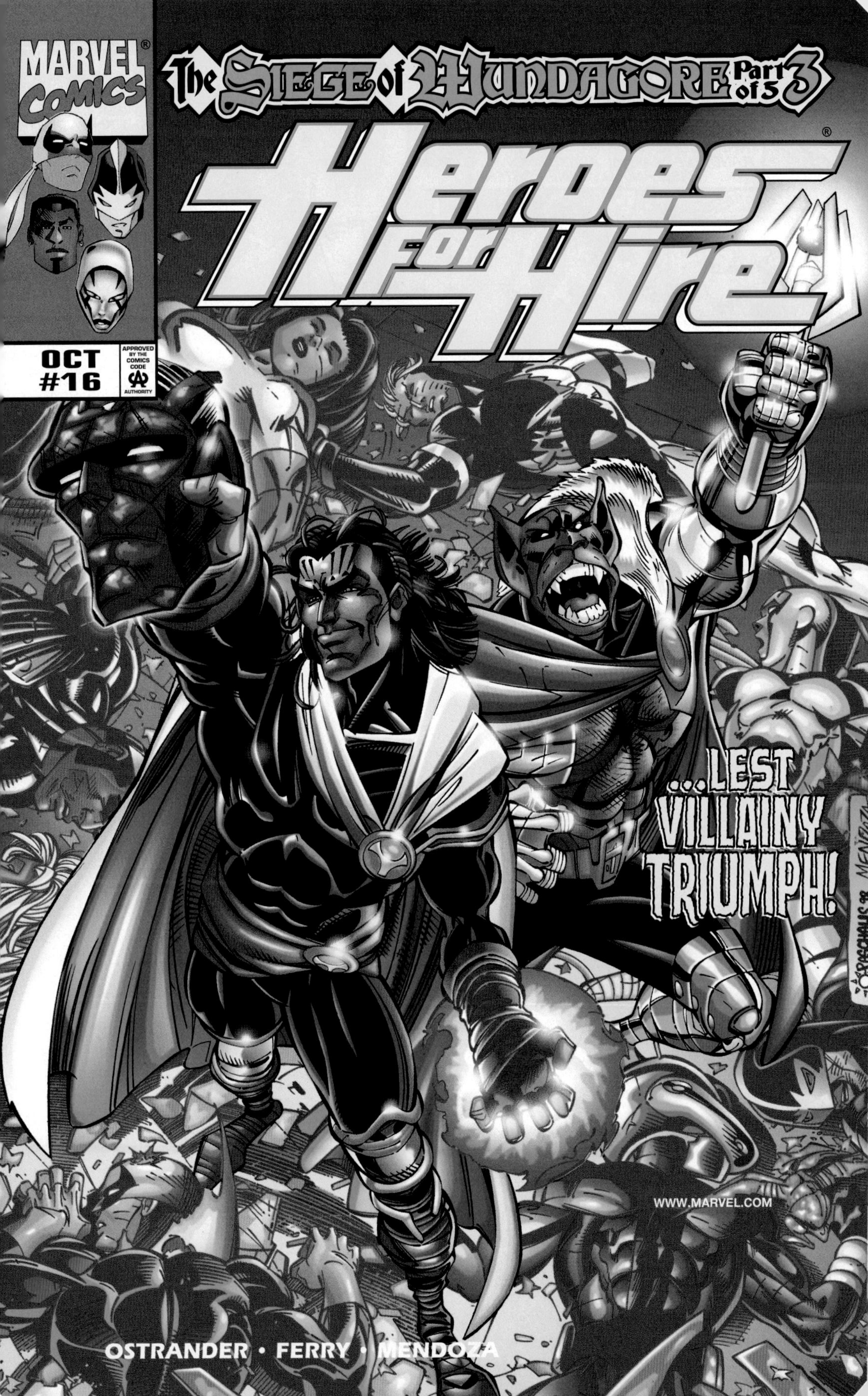

MARVEL COMICS
The SIEGE of WUNDAGORE Part 3 of 5
Heroes For Hire
OCT #16
APPROVED BY THE COMICS CODE AUTHORITY
...LEST VILLAINY TRIUMPH!
WWW.MARVEL.COM
OSTRANDER • FERRY • MENDOZA

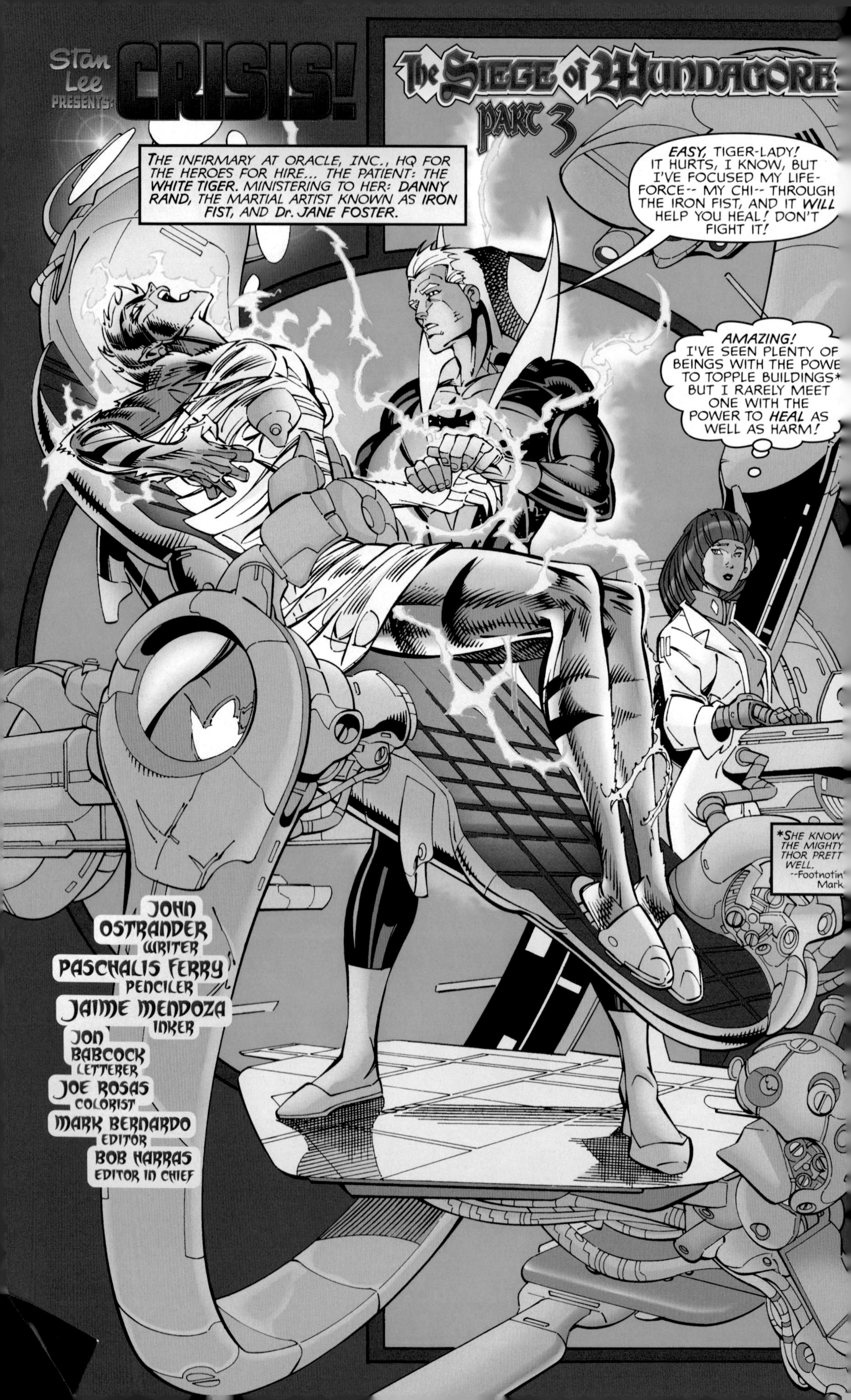
Stan Lee Presents: CRISIS!
The Siege of Wundagore Part 3
THE INFIRMARY AT ORACLE, INC., HQ FOR THE HEROES FOR HIRE... THE PATIENT: THE WHITE TIGER. MINISTERING TO HER: DANNY RAND, THE MARTIAL ARTIST KNOWN AS IRON FIST, AND Dr. JANE FOSTER.
EASY, TIGER-LADY! IT HURTS, I KNOW, BUT I'VE FOCUSED MY LIFE-FORCE-- MY CHI-- THROUGH THE IRON FIST, AND IT WILL HELP YOU HEAL! DON'T FIGHT IT!
AMAZING! I'VE SEEN PLENTY OF BEINGS WITH THE POWE TO TOPPLE BUILDINGS* BUT I RARELY MEET ONE WITH THE POWER TO HEAL AS WELL AS HARM!
*SHE KNOW THE MIGHTY THOR PRETT WELL. --Footnotin' Mark
JOHN OSTRANDER WRITER
PASCHALIS FERRY PENCILER
JAIME MENDOZA INKER
JON BABCOCK LETTERER
JOE ROSAS COLORIST
MARK BERNARDO EDITOR
BOB HARRAS EDITOR IN CHIEF

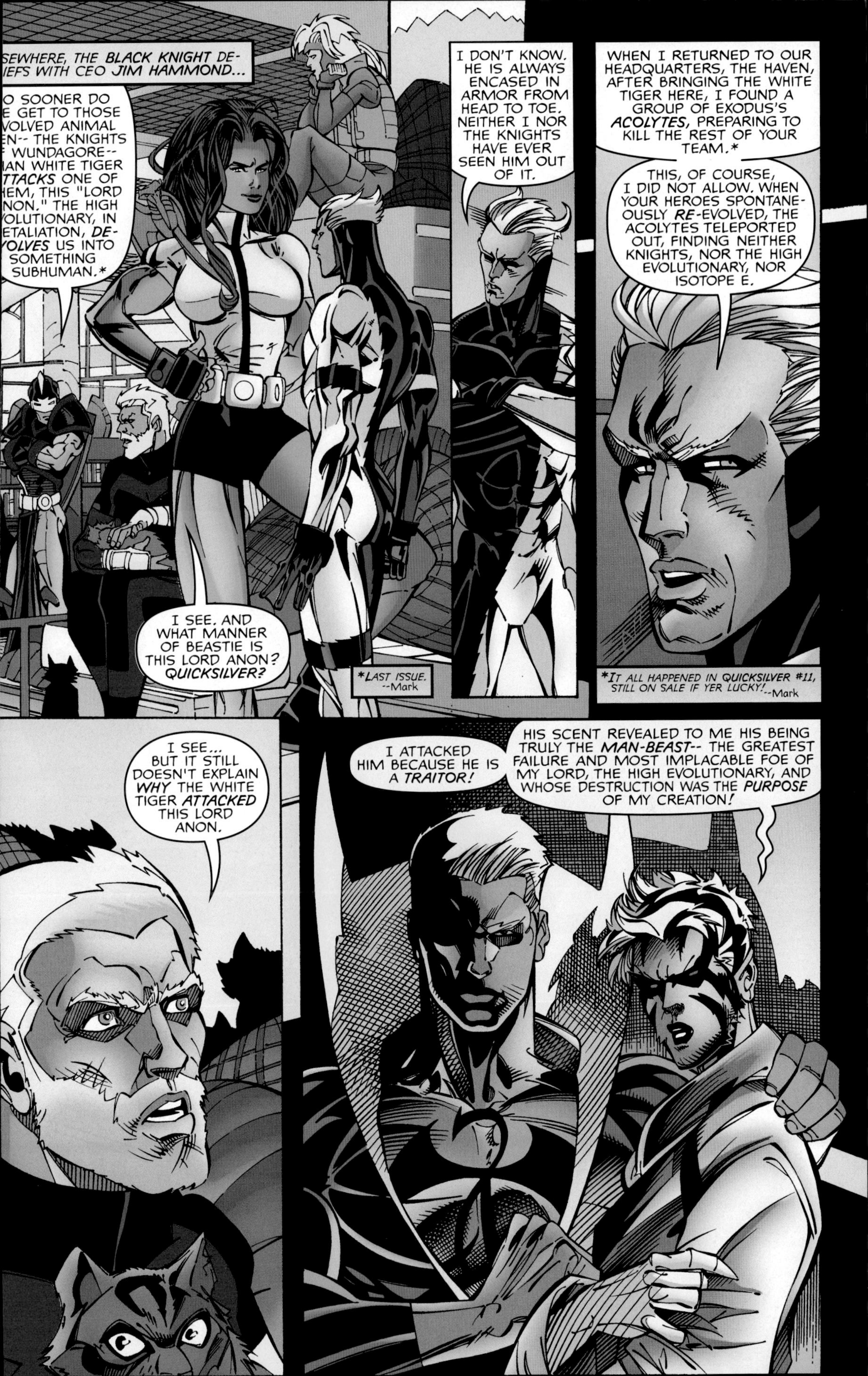
SEWHERE, THE BLACK KNIGHT DE-
IEFS WITH CEO JIM HAMMOND...
O SOONER DO
E GET TO THOSE
VOLVED ANIMAL
EN-- THE KNIGHTS
F WUNDAGORE--
IAN WHITE TIGER
TTACKS ONE OF
HEM, THIS "LORD
NON." THE HIGH
VOLUTIONARY, IN
ETALIATION, DE-
VOLVES US INTO
SOMETHING
SUBHUMAN.*
I SEE. AND WHAT MANNER OF BEASTIE IS THIS LORD ANON? QUICKSILVER?
*LAST ISSUE. --Mark
I DON'T KNOW. HE IS ALWAYS ENCASED IN ARMOR FROM HEAD TO TOE. NEITHER I NOR THE KNIGHTS HAVE EVER SEEN HIM OUT OF IT.
WHEN I RETURNED TO OUR HEADQUARTERS, THE HAVEN, AFTER BRINGING THE WHITE TIGER HERE, I FOUND A GROUP OF EXODUS'S ACOLYTES, PREPARING TO KILL THE REST OF YOUR TEAM.*
THIS, OF COURSE, I DID NOT ALLOW. WHEN YOUR HEROES SPONTANEOUSLY RE-EVOLVED, THE ACOLYTES TELEPORTED OUT, FINDING NEITHER KNIGHTS, NOR THE HIGH EVOLUTIONARY, NOR ISOTOPE E.
*IT ALL HAPPENED IN QUICKSILVER #11, STILL ON SALE IF YER LUCKY! --Mark
I SEE... BUT IT STILL DOESN'T EXPLAIN WHY THE WHITE TIGER ATTACKED THIS LORD ANON.
I ATTACKED HIM BECAUSE HE IS A TRAITOR!
HIS SCENT REVEALED TO ME HIS BEING TRULY THE MAN-BEAST-- THE GREATEST FAILURE AND MOST IMPLACABLE FOE OF MY LORD, THE HIGH EVOLUTIONARY, AND WHOSE DESTRUCTION WAS THE PURPOSE OF MY CREATION!

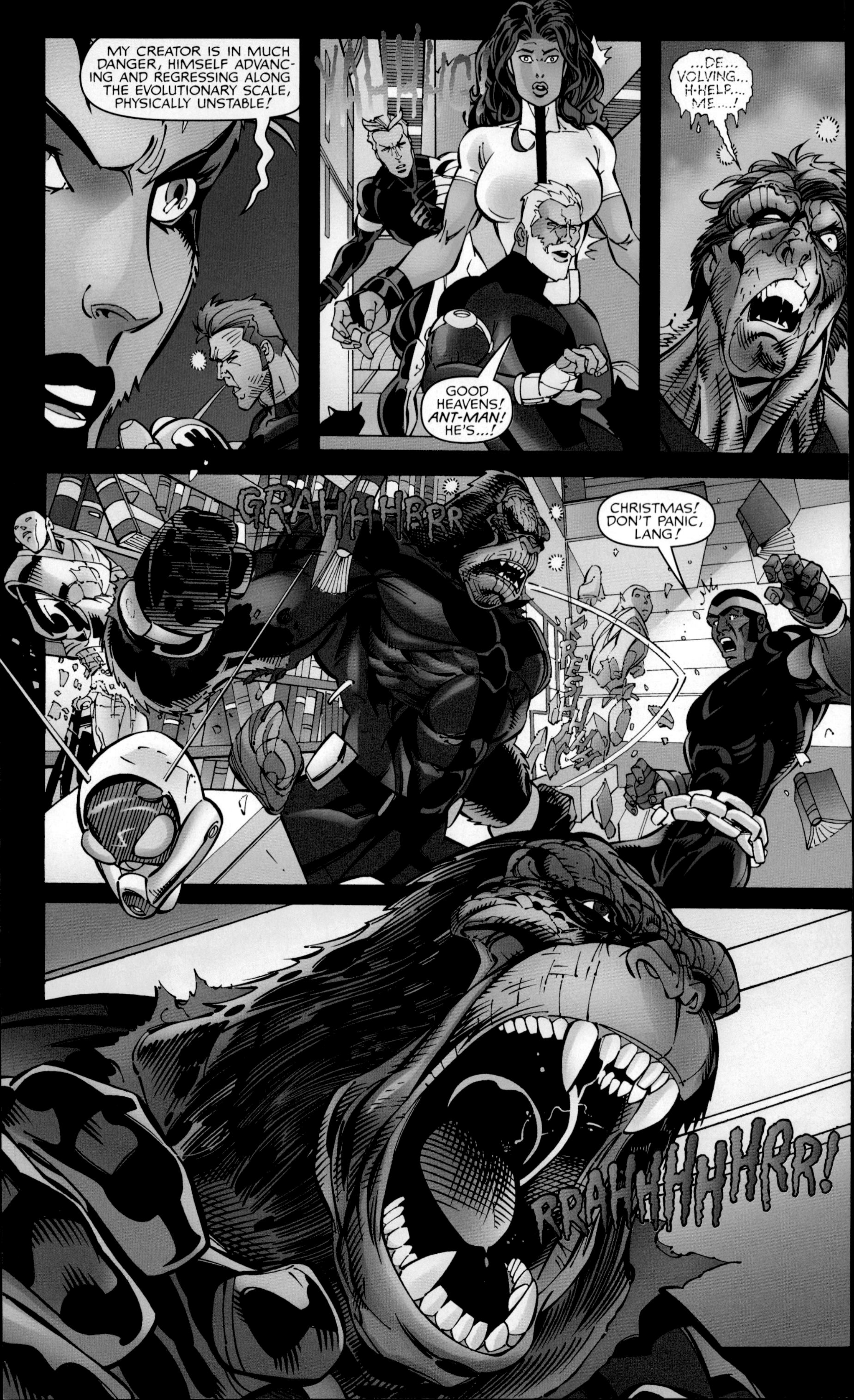
MY CREATOR IS IN MUCH DANGER, HIMSELF ADVANCING AND REGRESSING ALONG THE EVOLUTIONARY SCALE, PHYSICALLY UNSTABLE!
GOOD HEAVENS! ANT-MAN! HE'S...!
...DE... VOLVING... H-HELP... ME....!
GRAHHHHRRR
CHRISTMAS! DON'T PANIC, LANG!
RRAHHHHHRR!

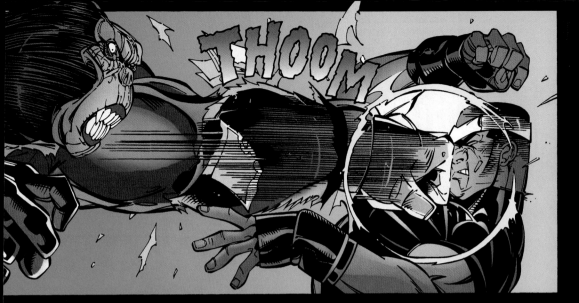

THOOM

Whoa! THAT SMARTS EVEN THROUGH *STEEL-HARD* SKIN!

'KAY, IF YOU AIN'T GONNA CALM YOUR *OWN* BAD SELF DOWN...

WHOMP!

...I'LL JUST HAVE'TA LEND YOU A *HAND!*

S'OKAY, GANG.

LANG'S COMIN' *BACK* TO HIMSELF.

WE'RE ALL EVOLUTION-ARILY *UNSTABLE*-- AND OUR ONLY PRAYER OF GETTING RIGHT IS WITH THE HIGH EVOLUTIONARY AND ISOTOPE E--

--AND THEY'RE AT *WUNDAGORE* MOUNTAIN.

THEN THAT'S WHERE YOU'RE ALL GOING.

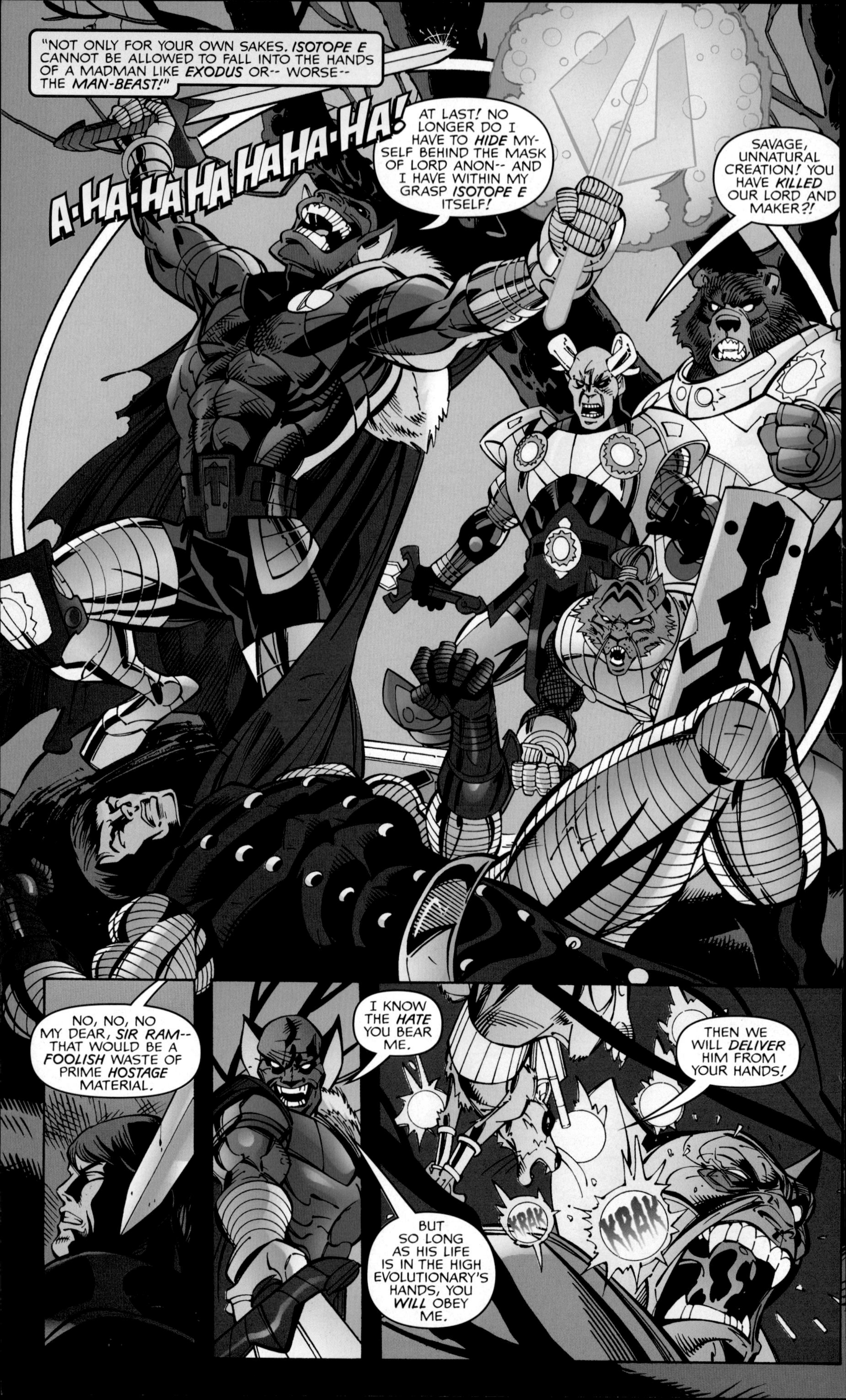
"NOT ONLY FOR YOUR OWN SAKES. ISOTOPE E CANNOT BE ALLOWED TO FALL INTO THE HANDS OF A MADMAN LIKE EXODUS OR-- WORSE-- THE MAN-BEAST!"
A-HA-HA HA HAHA-HA!
AT LAST! NO LONGER DO I HAVE TO HIDE MYSELF BEHIND THE MASK OF LORD ANON-- AND I HAVE WITHIN MY GRASP ISOTOPE E ITSELF!
SAVAGE, UNNATURAL CREATION! YOU HAVE KILLED OUR LORD AND MAKER?!
NO, NO, NO MY DEAR, SIR RAM-- THAT WOULD BE A FOOLISH WASTE OF PRIME HOSTAGE MATERIAL.
I KNOW THE HATE YOU BEAR ME.
BUT SO LONG AS HIS LIFE IS IN THE HIGH EVOLUTIONARY'S HANDS, YOU WILL OBEY ME.
THEN WE WILL DELIVER HIM FROM YOUR HANDS!
KRAK
KRAK

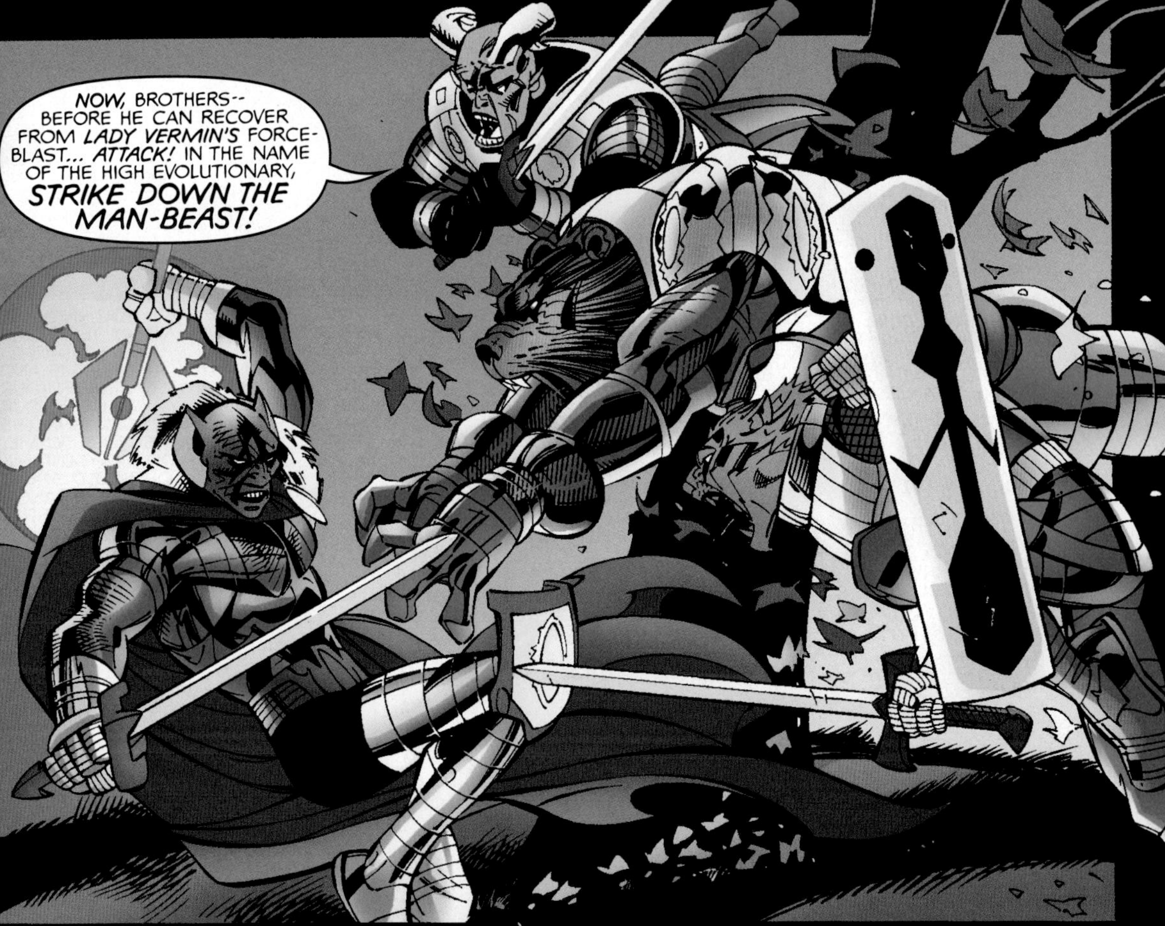
NOW, BROTHERS-- BEFORE HE CAN RECOVER FROM LADY VERMIN'S FORCE-BLAST... ATTACK! IN THE NAME OF THE HIGH EVOLUTIONARY, STRIKE DOWN THE MAN-BEAST!

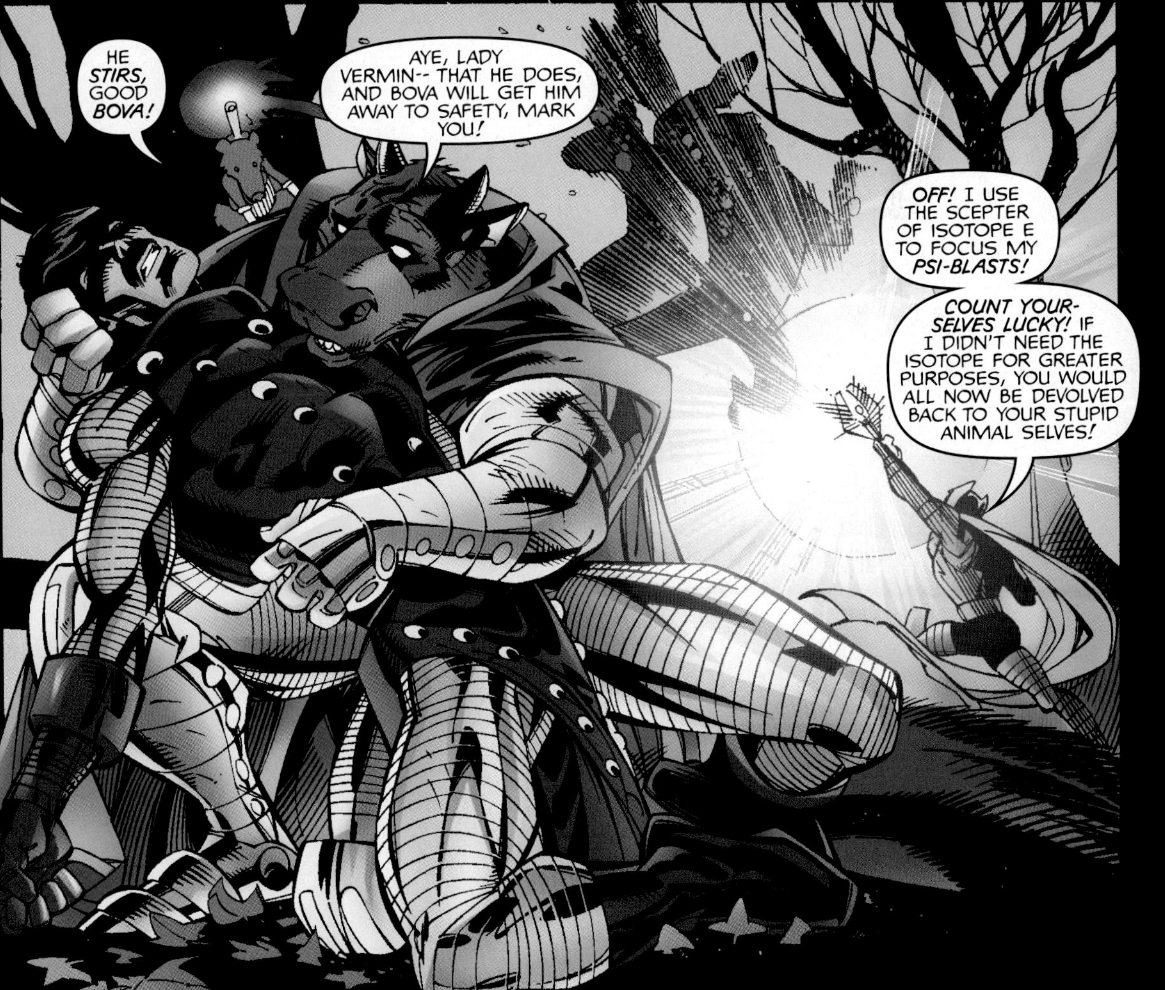
HE STIRS, GOOD BOVA!
AYE, LADY VERMIN-- THAT HE DOES, AND BOVA WILL GET HIM AWAY TO SAFETY, MARK YOU!
OFF! I USE THE SCEPTER OF ISOTOPE E TO FOCUS MY PSI-BLASTS!
COUNT YOURSELVES LUCKY! IF I DIDN'T NEED THE ISOTOPE FOR GREATER PURPOSES, YOU WOULD ALL NOW BE DEVOLVED BACK TO YOUR STUPID ANIMAL SELVES!

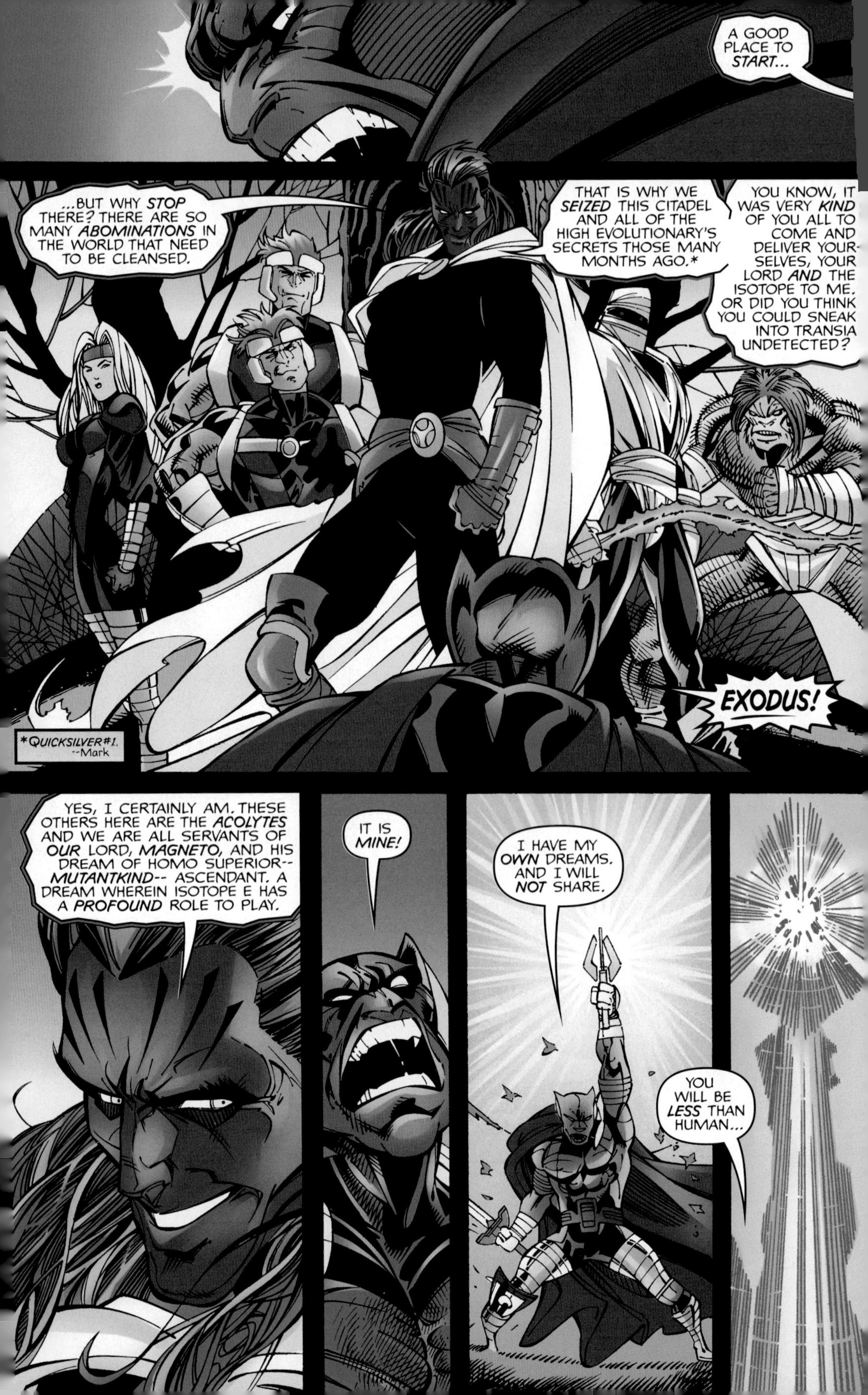
A GOOD PLACE TO *START*...
...BUT WHY *STOP* THERE? THERE ARE SO MANY *ABOMINATIONS* IN THE WORLD THAT NEED TO BE CLEANSED.
THAT IS WHY WE *SEIZED* THIS CITADEL AND ALL OF THE HIGH EVOLUTIONARY'S SECRETS THOSE MANY MONTHS AGO.*
YOU KNOW, IT WAS VERY *KIND* OF YOU ALL TO COME AND DELIVER YOURSELVES, YOUR LORD *AND* THE ISOTOPE TO ME. OR DID YOU THINK YOU COULD SNEAK INTO TRANSIA UNDETECTED?
EXODUS!
*QUICKSILVER #1. --Mark
YES, I CERTAINLY AM. THESE OTHERS HERE ARE THE *ACOLYTES* AND WE ARE ALL SERVANTS OF *OUR* LORD, *MAGNETO,* AND HIS DREAM OF HOMO SUPERIOR-- *MUTANTKIND*-- ASCENDANT. A DREAM WHEREIN ISOTOPE E HAS A *PROFOUND* ROLE TO PLAY.
IT IS *MINE!*
I HAVE MY *OWN* DREAMS. AND I WILL *NOT* SHARE.
YOU WILL BE *LESS* THAN HUMAN...

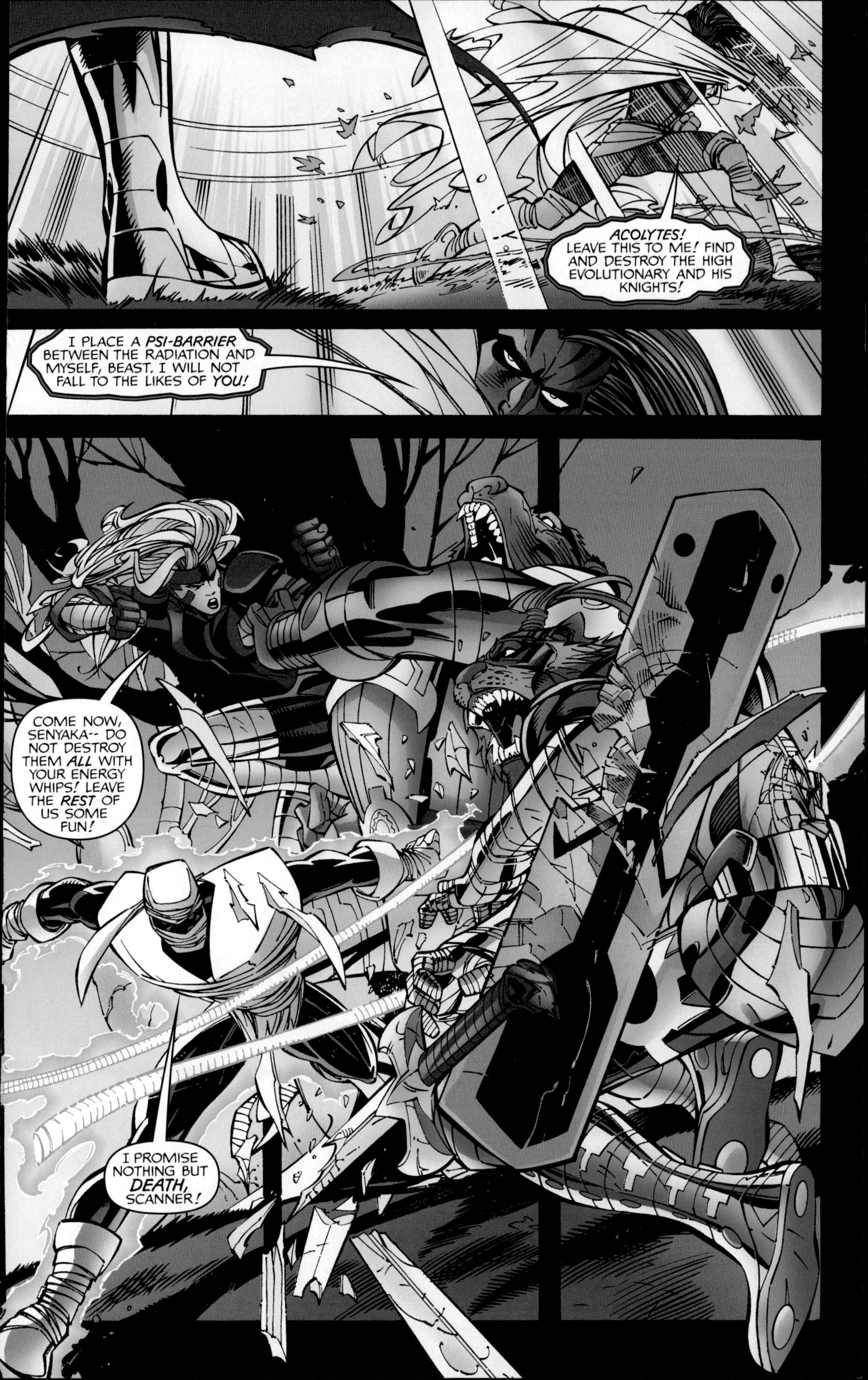
ACOLYTES! LEAVE THIS TO ME! FIND AND DESTROY THE HIGH EVOLUTIONARY AND HIS KNIGHTS!
I PLACE A PSI-BARRIER BETWEEN THE RADIATION AND MYSELF, BEAST. I WILL NOT FALL TO THE LIKES OF YOU!
COME NOW, SENYAKA-- DO NOT DESTROY THEM ALL WITH YOUR ENERGY WHIPS! LEAVE THE REST OF US SOME FUN!
I PROMISE NOTHING BUT DEATH, SCANNER!

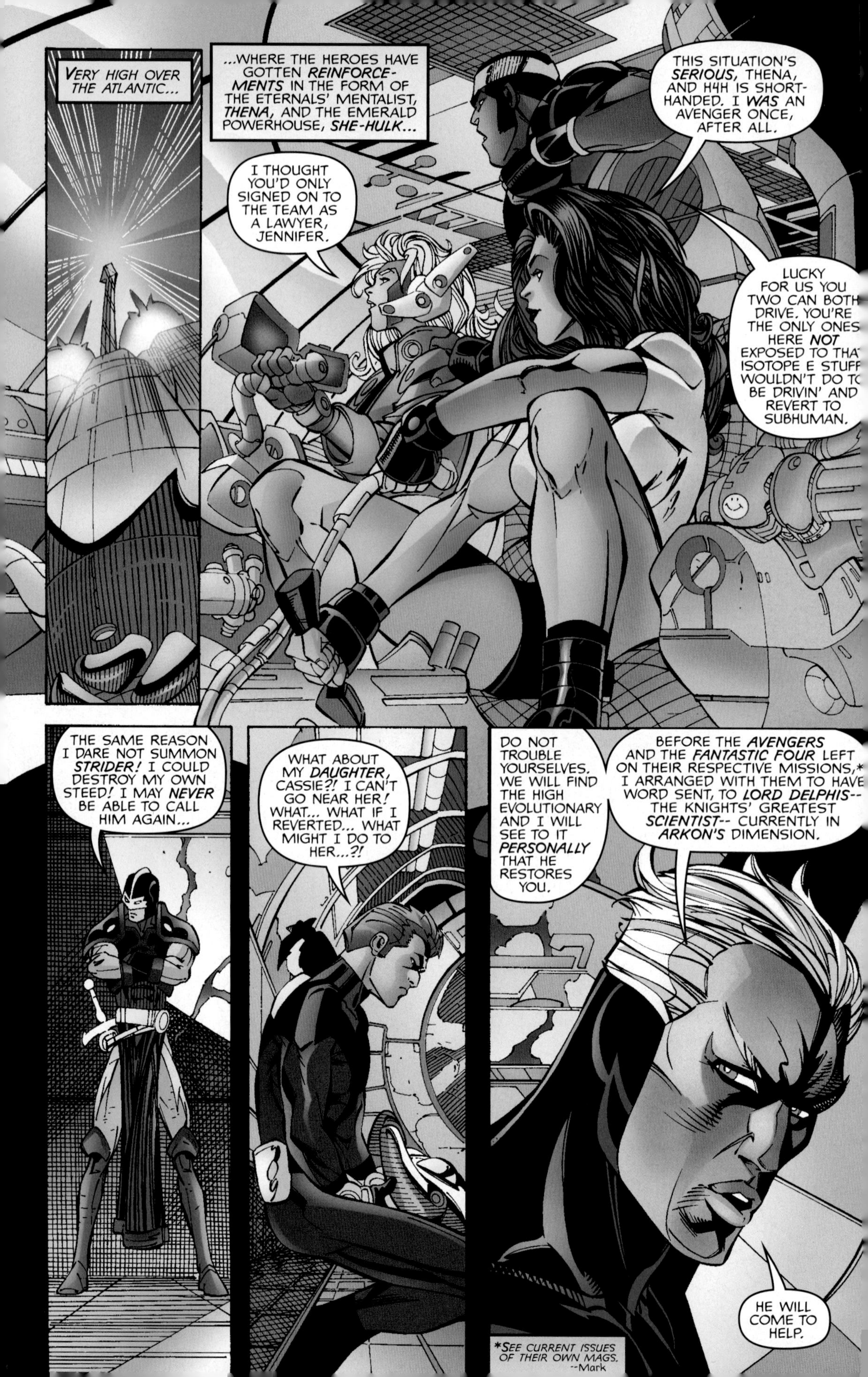

VERY HIGH OVER THE ATLANTIC...
...WHERE THE HEROES HAVE GOTTEN REINFORCE-MENTS IN THE FORM OF THE ETERNALS' MENTALIST, THENA, AND THE EMERALD POWERHOUSE, SHE-HULK...
THIS SITUATION'S SERIOUS, THENA, AND H4H IS SHORT-HANDED. I WAS AN AVENGER ONCE, AFTER ALL.
I THOUGHT YOU'D ONLY SIGNED ON TO THE TEAM AS A LAWYER, JENNIFER.
LUCKY FOR US YOU TWO CAN BOTH DRIVE. YOU'RE THE ONLY ONES HERE NOT EXPOSED TO THAT ISOTOPE E STUFF. WOULDN'T DO TO BE DRIVIN' AND REVERT TO SUBHUMAN.
THE SAME REASON I DARE NOT SUMMON STRIDER! I COULD DESTROY MY OWN STEED! I MAY NEVER BE ABLE TO CALL HIM AGAIN...
WHAT ABOUT MY DAUGHTER, CASSIE?! I CAN'T GO NEAR HER! WHAT... WHAT IF I REVERTED... WHAT MIGHT I DO TO HER...?!
DO NOT TROUBLE YOURSELVES. WE WILL FIND THE HIGH EVOLUTIONARY AND I WILL SEE TO IT PERSONALLY THAT HE RESTORES YOU.
BEFORE THE AVENGERS AND THE FANTASTIC FOUR LEFT ON THEIR RESPECTIVE MISSIONS,* I ARRANGED WITH THEM TO HAVE WORD SENT, TO LORD DELPHIS-- THE KNIGHTS' GREATEST SCIENTIST-- CURRENTLY IN ARKON'S DIMENSION.
HE WILL COME TO HELP.
*SEE CURRENT ISSUES OF THEIR OWN MAGS. --Mark

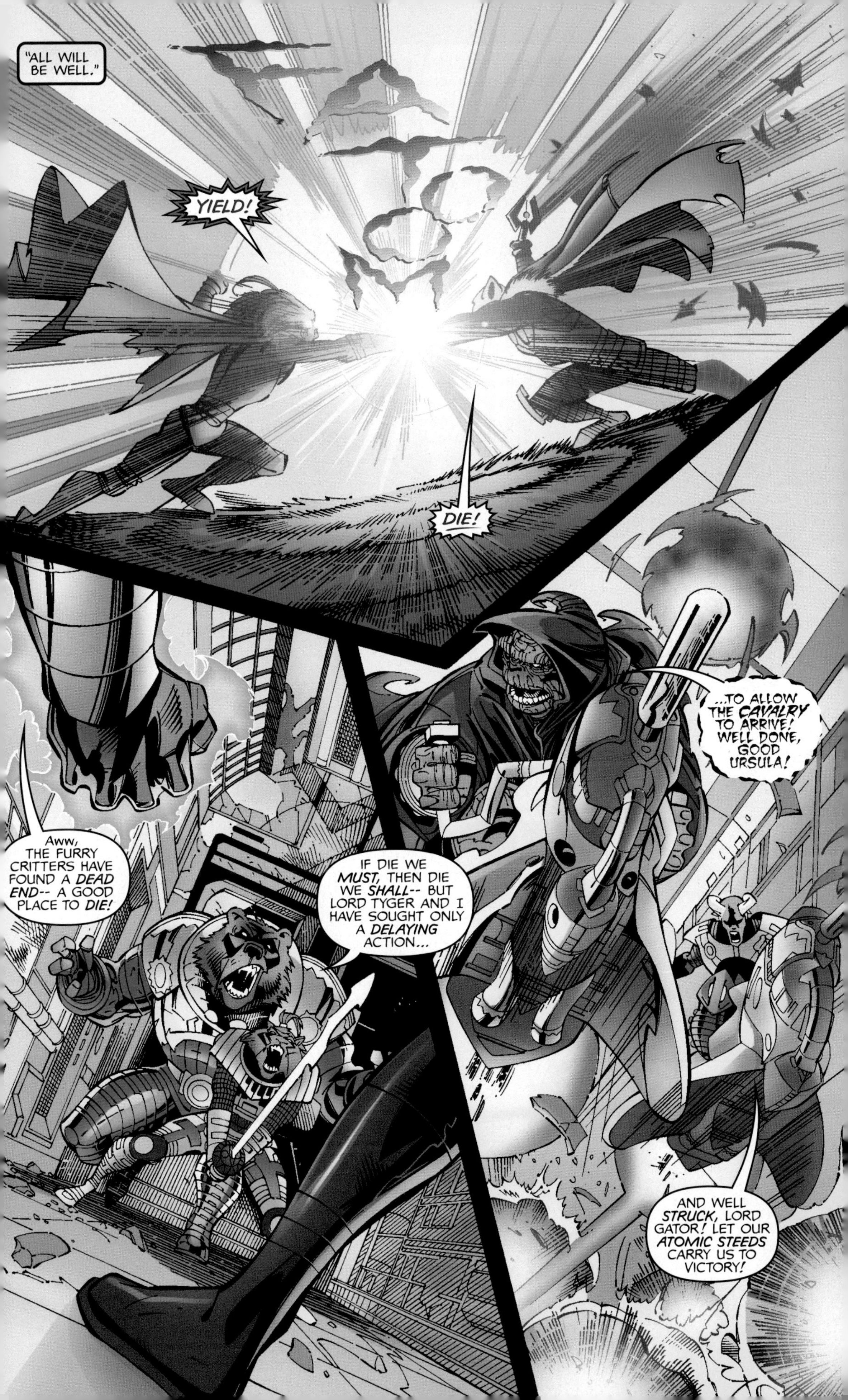
"ALL WILL BE WELL."
YIELD!
DIE!
...TO ALLOW THE CAVALRY TO ARRIVE! WELL DONE, GOOD URSULA!
Aww, THE FURRY CRITTERS HAVE FOUND A DEAD END-- A GOOD PLACE TO DIE!
IF DIE WE MUST, THEN DIE WE SHALL-- BUT LORD TYGER AND I HAVE SOUGHT ONLY A DELAYING ACTION...
AND WELL STRUCK, LORD GATOR! LET OUR ATOMIC STEEDS CARRY US TO VICTORY!

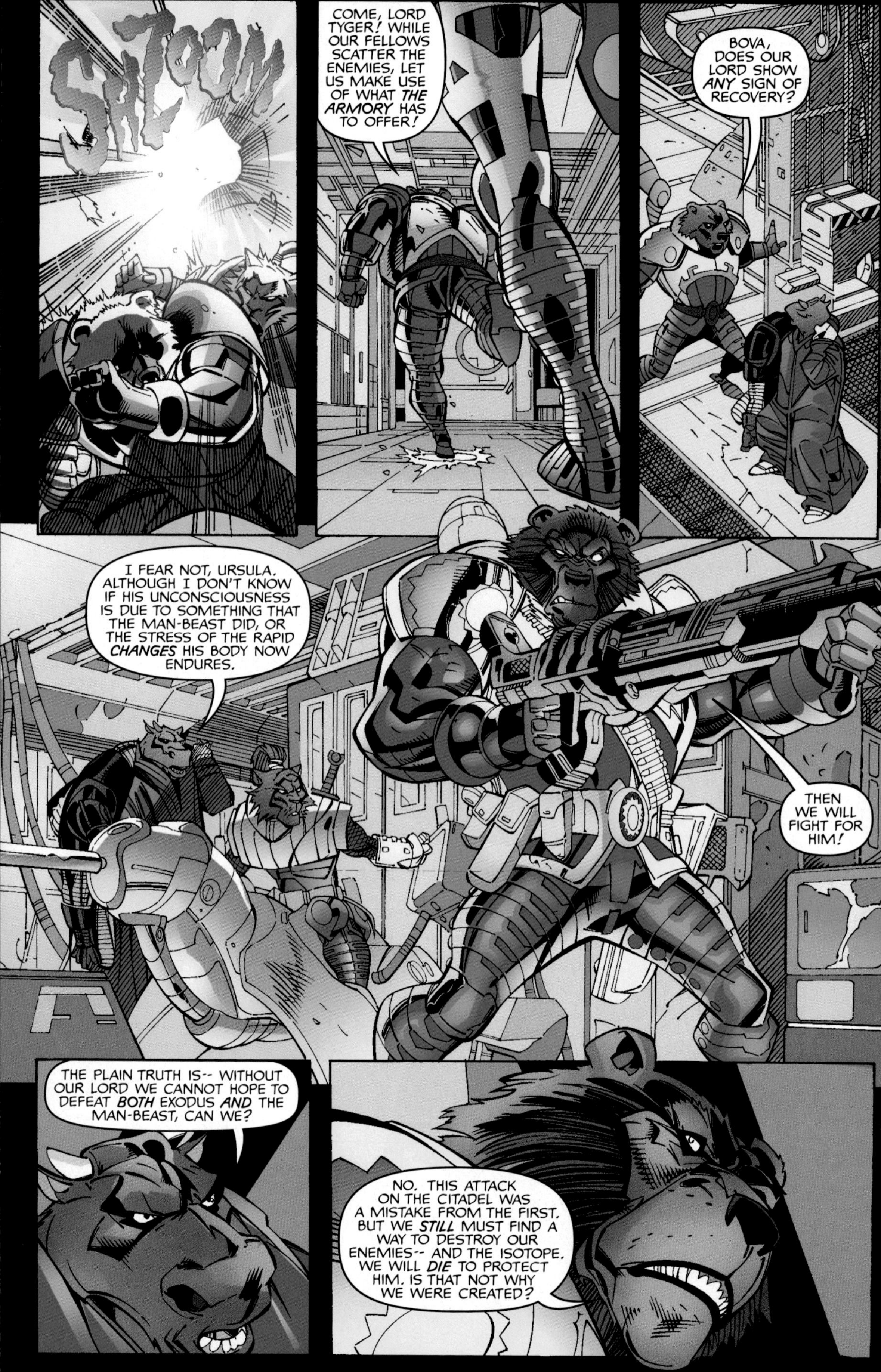
SHZOOM
COME, LORD TYGER! WHILE OUR FELLOWS SCATTER THE ENEMIES, LET US MAKE USE OF WHAT THE ARMORY HAS TO OFFER!
BOVA, DOES OUR LORD SHOW ANY SIGN OF RECOVERY?
I FEAR NOT, URSULA. ALTHOUGH I DON'T KNOW IF HIS UNCONSCIOUSNESS IS DUE TO SOMETHING THAT THE MAN-BEAST DID, OR THE STRESS OF THE RAPID CHANGES HIS BODY NOW ENDURES.
THEN WE WILL FIGHT FOR HIM!
THE PLAIN TRUTH IS-- WITHOUT OUR LORD WE CANNOT HOPE TO DEFEAT BOTH EXODUS AND THE MAN-BEAST, CAN WE?
NO. THIS ATTACK ON THE CITADEL WAS A MISTAKE FROM THE FIRST. BUT WE STILL MUST FIND A WAY TO DESTROY OUR ENEMIES-- AND THE ISOTOPE. WE WILL DIE TO PROTECT HIM. IS THAT NOT WHY WE WERE CREATED?

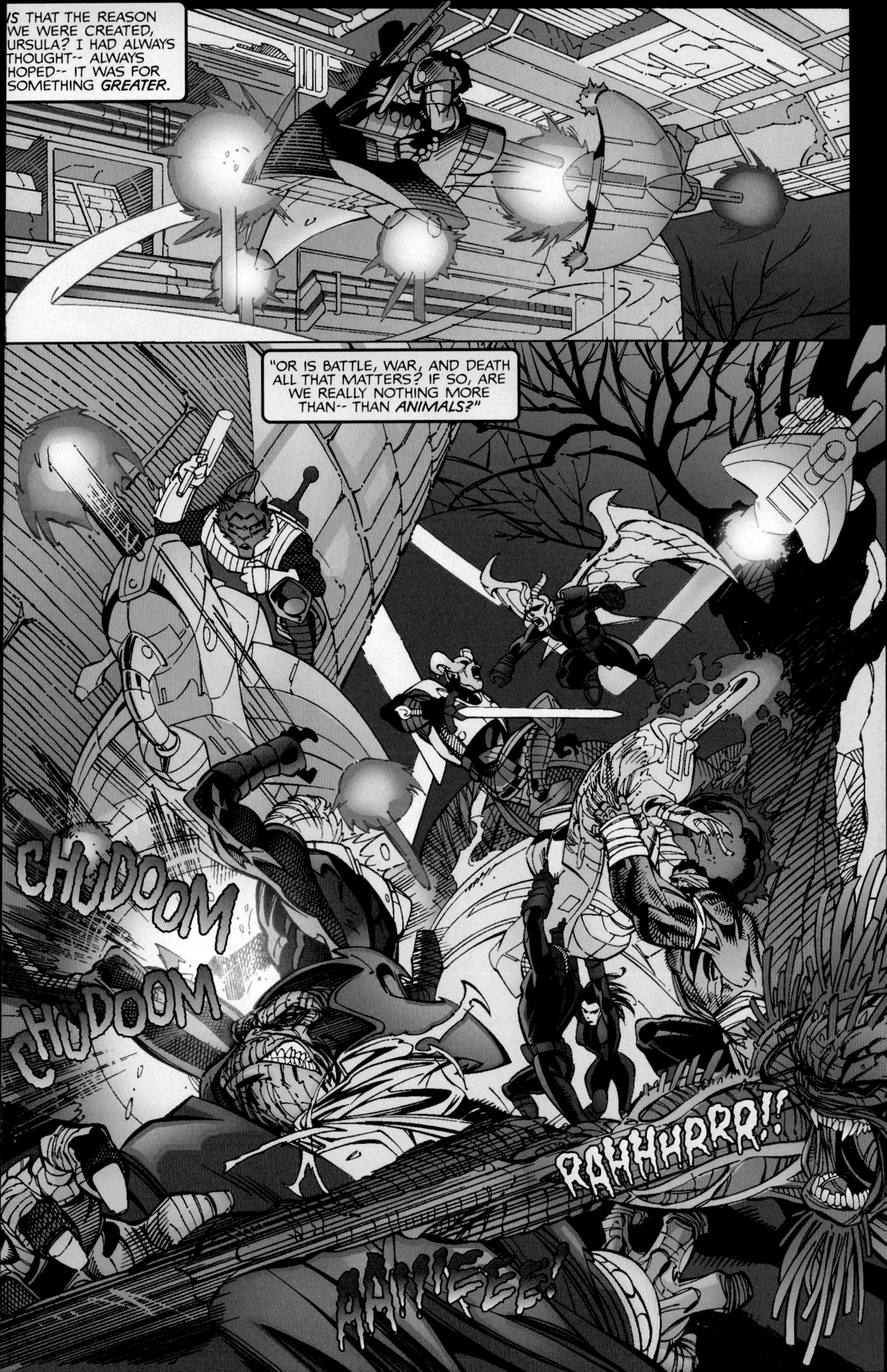
IS THAT THE REASON WE WERE CREATED, URSULA? I HAD ALWAYS THOUGHT-- ALWAYS HOPED-- IT WAS FOR SOMETHING *GREATER*.
"OR IS BATTLE, WAR, AND DEATH ALL THAT MATTERS? IF SO, ARE WE REALLY NOTHING MORE THAN-- THAN *ANIMALS?*"
CHUDOOM
CHUDOOM
RAHHHRRR!!
AAIIEEE!

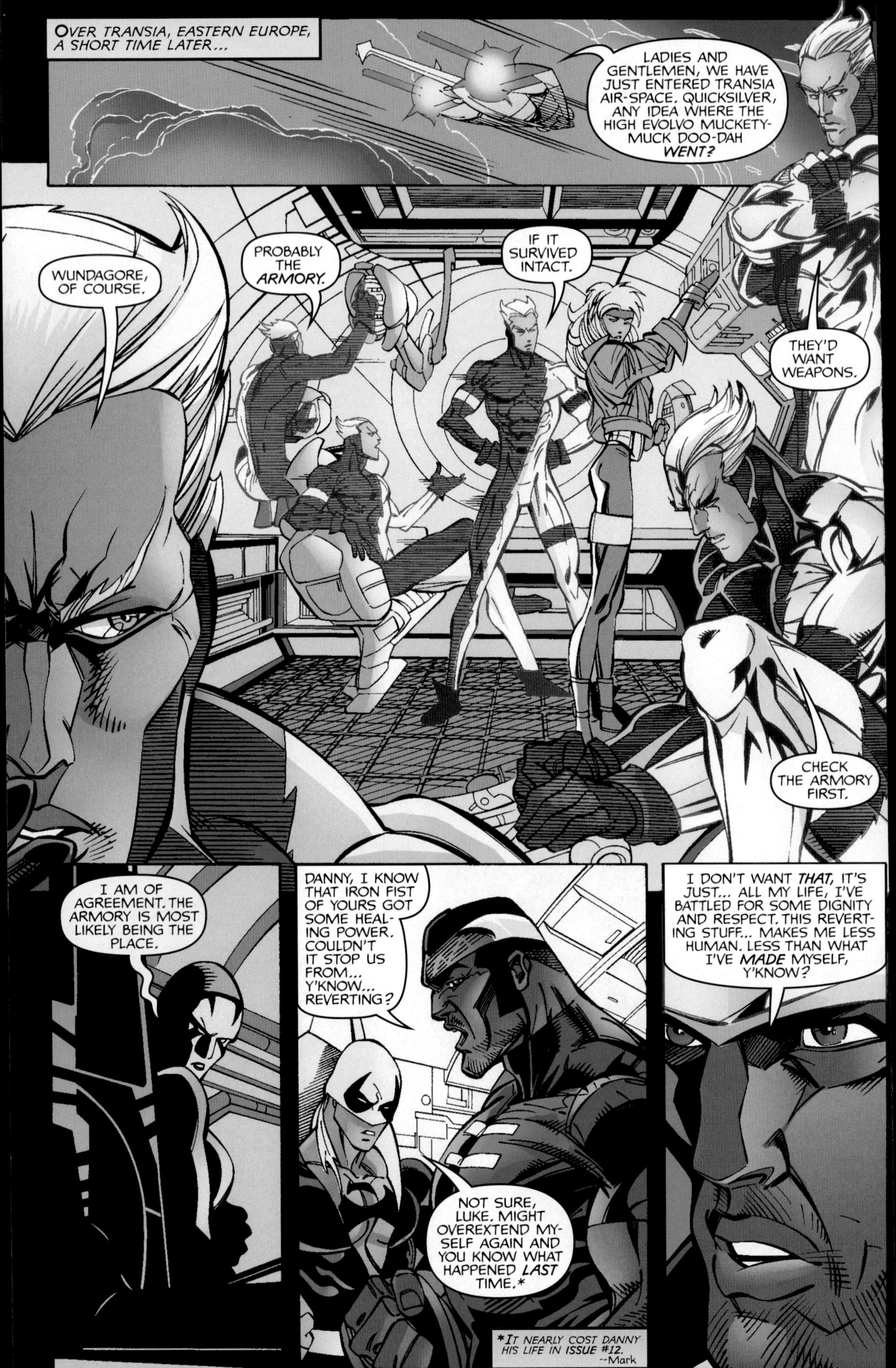
OVER TRANSIA, EASTERN EUROPE, A SHORT TIME LATER...
LADIES AND GENTLEMEN, WE HAVE JUST ENTERED TRANSIA AIR-SPACE. QUICKSILVER, ANY IDEA WHERE THE HIGH EVOLVO MUCKETY-MUCK DOO-DAH WENT?
WUNDAGORE, OF COURSE.
PROBABLY THE ARMORY.
IF IT SURVIVED INTACT.
THEY'D WANT WEAPONS.
CHECK THE ARMORY FIRST.
I AM OF AGREEMENT. THE ARMORY IS MOST LIKELY BEING THE PLACE.
DANNY, I KNOW THAT IRON FIST OF YOURS GOT SOME HEALING POWER. COULDN'T IT STOP US FROM... Y'KNOW... REVERTING?
NOT SURE, LUKE. MIGHT OVEREXTEND MYSELF AGAIN AND YOU KNOW WHAT HAPPENED LAST TIME.*
I DON'T WANT THAT, IT'S JUST... ALL MY LIFE, I'VE BATTLED FOR SOME DIGNITY AND RESPECT. THIS REVERTING STUFF... MAKES ME LESS HUMAN. LESS THAN WHAT I'VE MADE MYSELF, Y'KNOW?
*IT NEARLY COST DANNY HIS LIFE IN ISSUE #12. --Mark

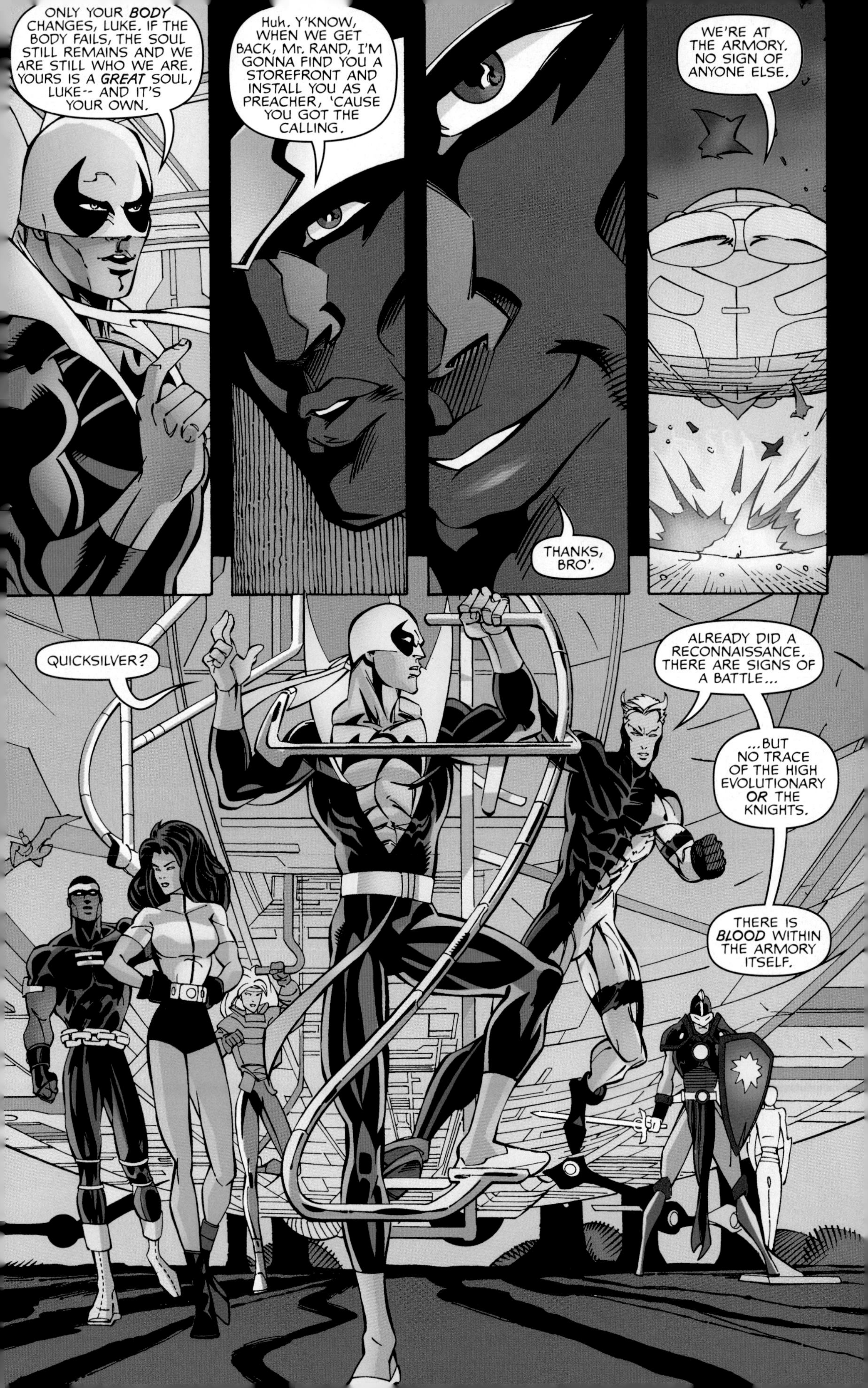
ONLY YOUR BODY CHANGES, LUKE. IF THE BODY FAILS, THE SOUL STILL REMAINS AND WE ARE STILL WHO WE ARE. YOURS IS A GREAT SOUL, LUKE-- AND IT'S YOUR OWN.
Huh. Y'KNOW, WHEN WE GET BACK, Mr. RAND, I'M GONNA FIND YOU A STOREFRONT AND INSTALL YOU AS A PREACHER, 'CAUSE YOU GOT THE CALLING.
THANKS, BRO'.
WE'RE AT THE ARMORY. NO SIGN OF ANYONE ELSE.
QUICKSILVER?
ALREADY DID A RECONNAISSANCE. THERE ARE SIGNS OF A BATTLE...
...BUT NO TRACE OF THE HIGH EVOLUTIONARY OR THE KNIGHTS.
THERE IS BLOOD WITHIN THE ARMORY ITSELF.

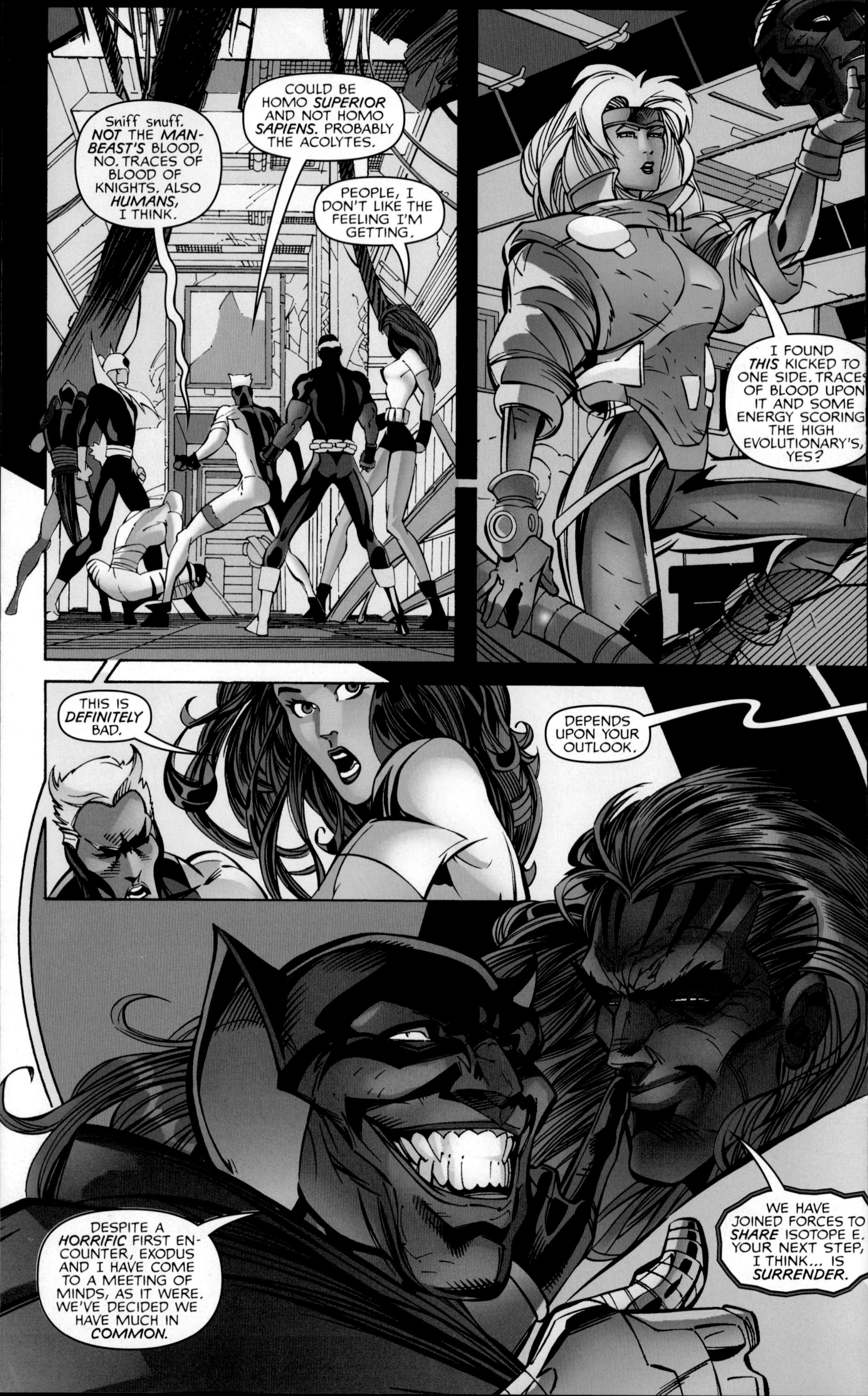
Sniff snuff. NOT THE MAN-BEAST'S BLOOD, NO. TRACES OF BLOOD OF KNIGHTS. ALSO HUMANS, I THINK.
COULD BE HOMO SUPERIOR AND NOT HOMO SAPIENS. PROBABLY THE ACOLYTES.
PEOPLE, I DON'T LIKE THE FEELING I'M GETTING.
I FOUND THIS KICKED TO ONE SIDE. TRACES OF BLOOD UPON IT AND SOME ENERGY SCORING. THE HIGH EVOLUTIONARY'S, YES?
THIS IS DEFINITELY BAD.
DEPENDS UPON YOUR OUTLOOK.
DESPITE A HORRIFIC FIRST ENCOUNTER, EXODUS AND I HAVE COME TO A MEETING OF MINDS, AS IT WERE. WE'VE DECIDED WE HAVE MUCH IN COMMON.
WE HAVE JOINED FORCES TO SHARE ISOTOPE E. YOUR NEXT STEP, I THINK... IS SURRENDER.

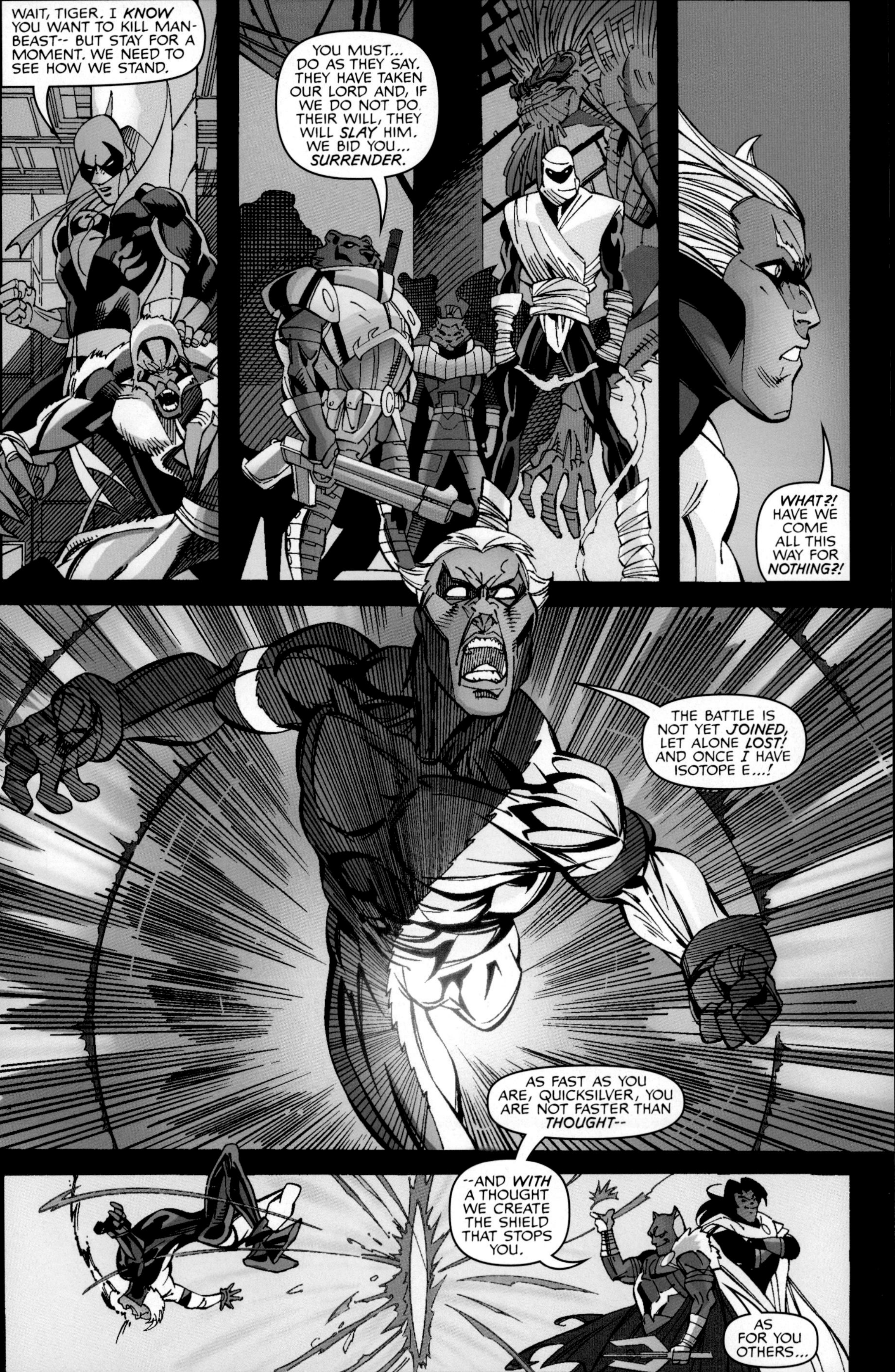
WAIT, TIGER. I KNOW YOU WANT TO KILL MAN-BEAST-- BUT STAY FOR A MOMENT. WE NEED TO SEE HOW WE STAND.
YOU MUST... DO AS THEY SAY. THEY HAVE TAKEN OUR LORD AND, IF WE DO NOT DO THEIR WILL, THEY WILL SLAY HIM. WE BID YOU... SURRENDER.
WHAT?! HAVE WE COME ALL THIS WAY FOR NOTHING?!
THE BATTLE IS NOT YET JOINED, LET ALONE LOST! AND ONCE I HAVE ISOTOPE E...!
AS FAST AS YOU ARE, QUICKSILVER, YOU ARE NOT FASTER THAN THOUGHT--
--AND WITH A THOUGHT WE CREATE THE SHIELD THAT STOPS YOU.
AS FOR YOU OTHERS...

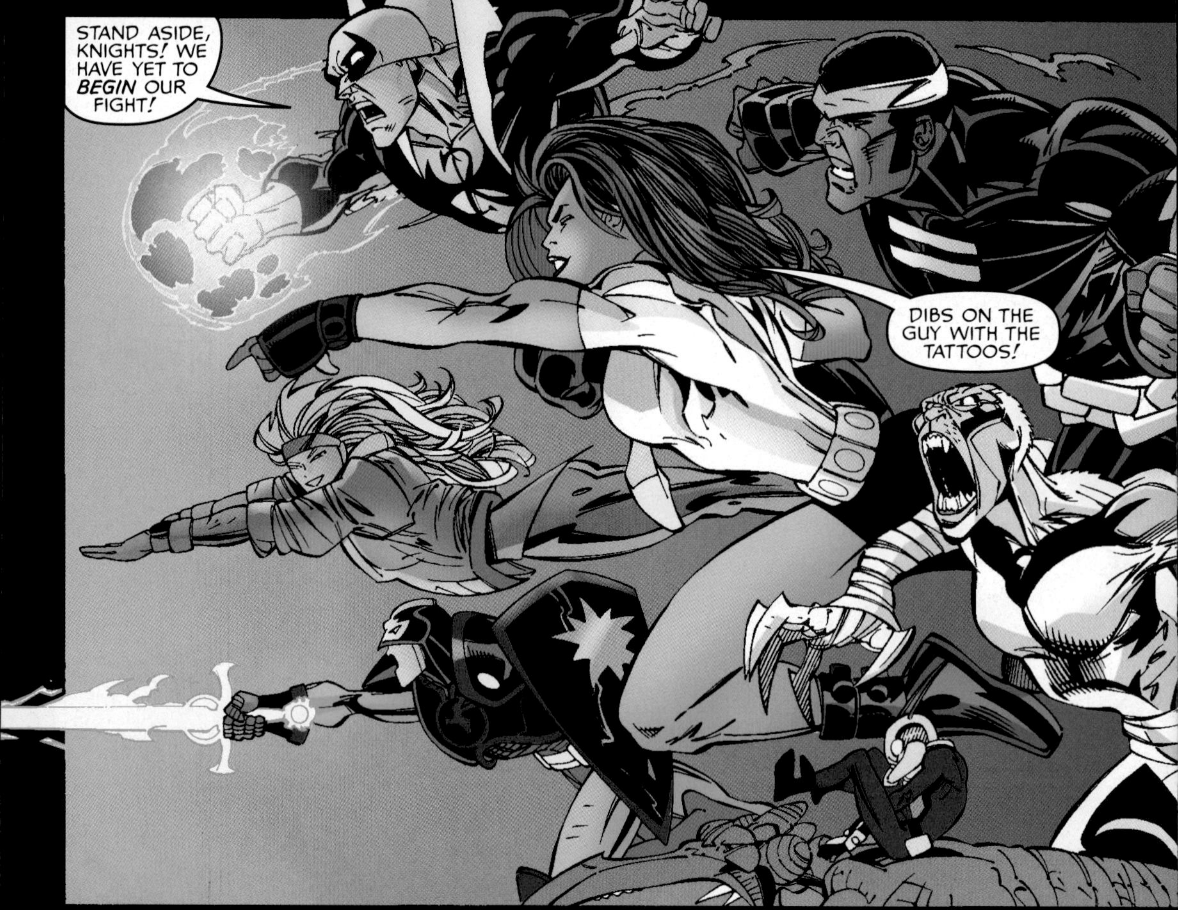
STAND ASIDE, KNIGHTS! WE HAVE YET TO *BEGIN* OUR FIGHT!
DIBS ON THE GUY WITH THE TATTOOS!

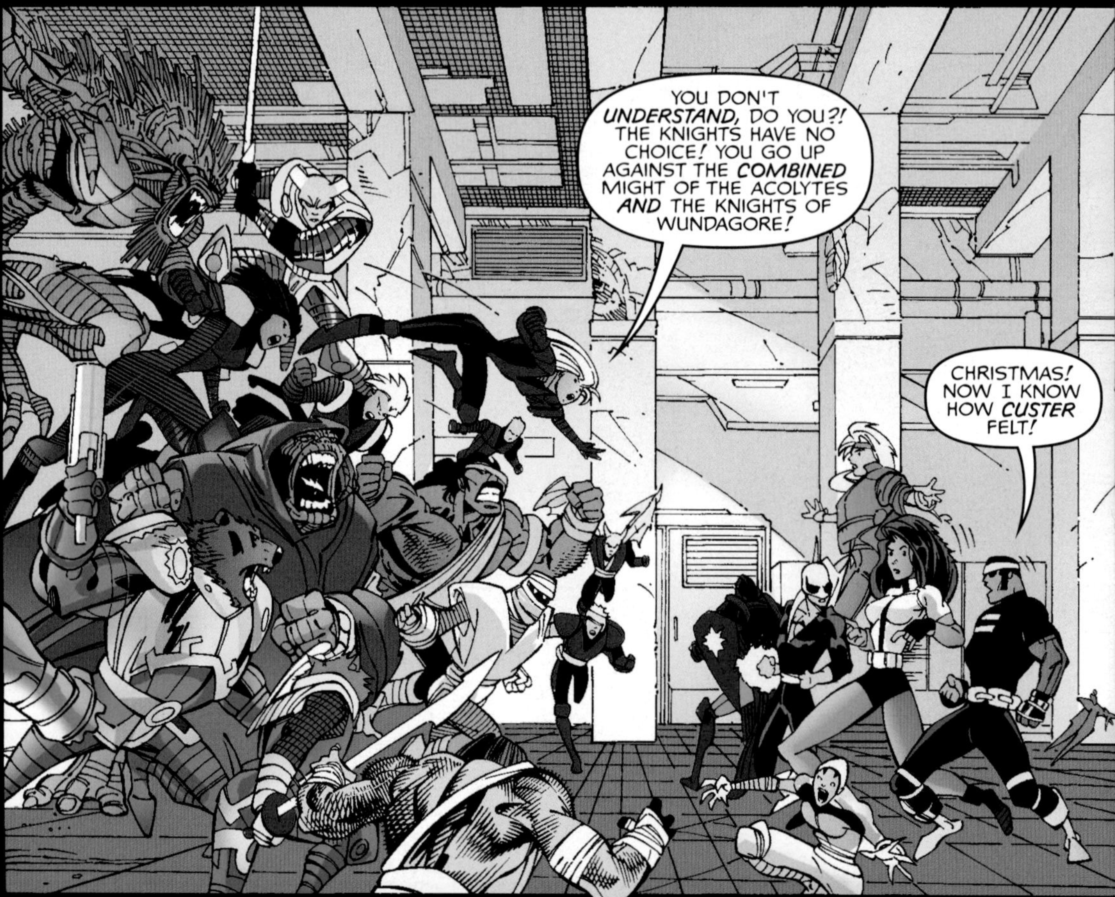
YOU DON'T *UNDERSTAND*, DO YOU?! THE KNIGHTS HAVE NO CHOICE! YOU GO UP AGAINST THE *COMBINED* MIGHT OF THE ACOLYTES *AND* THE KNIGHTS OF WUNDAGORE!
CHRISTMAS! NOW I KNOW HOW *CUSTER* FELT!

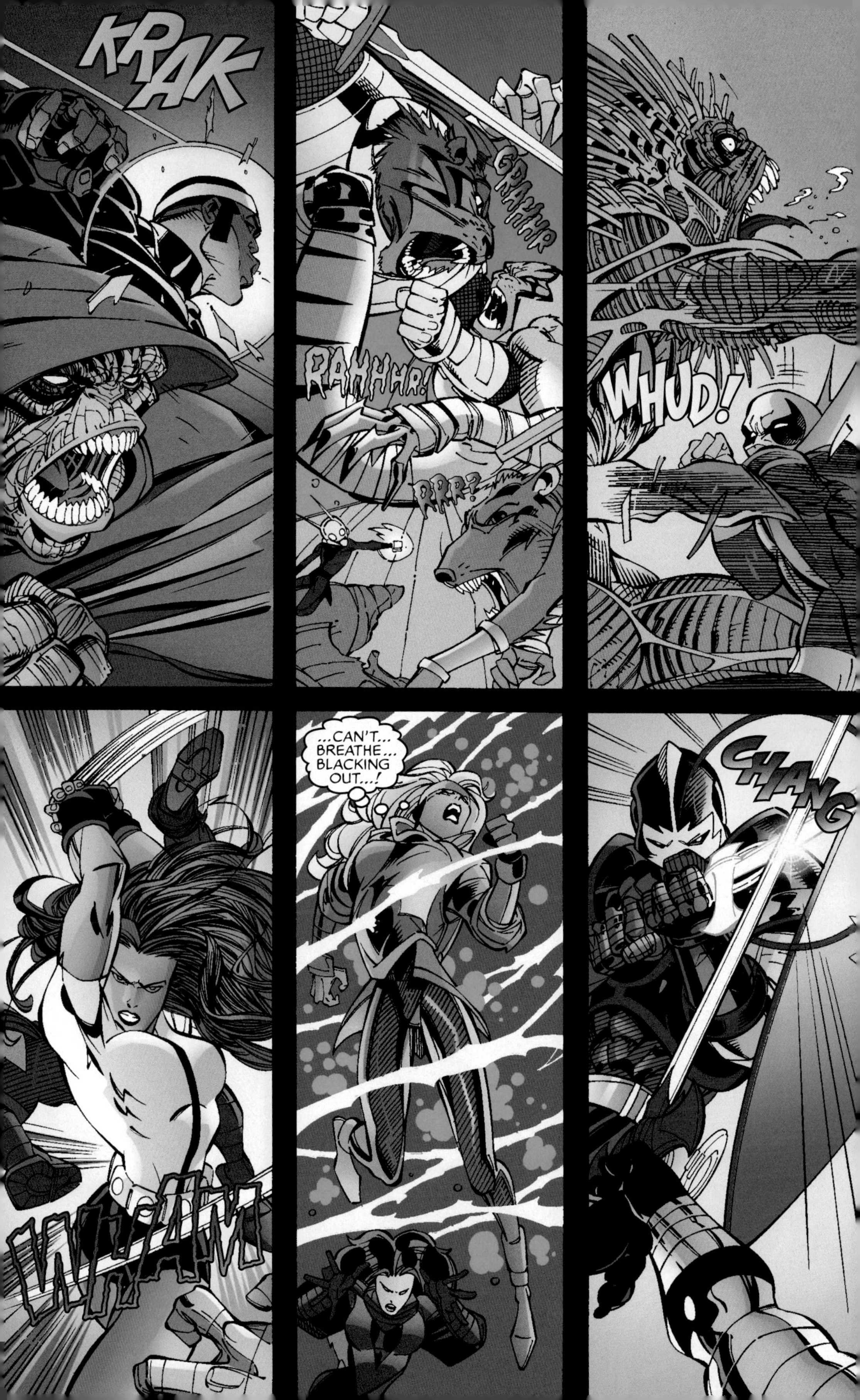
KRAK
GRAHHHR
RAHHHR!
WHUD!
...CAN'T... BREATHE... BLACKING OUT...!
CHANG

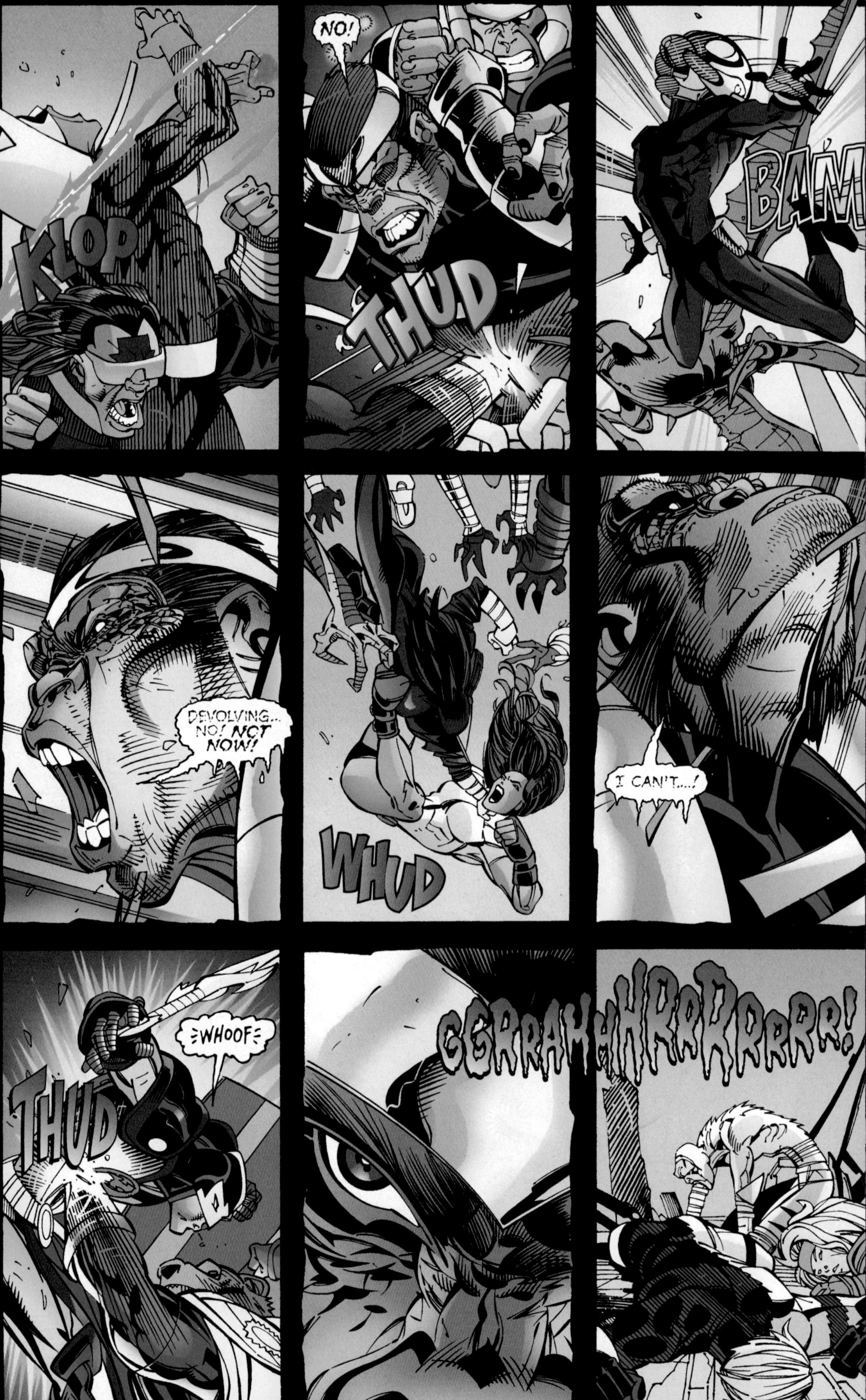
KLOP
NO!
THUD
BAM
DEVOLVING... NO! NOT NOW!
WHUD
I CAN'T....!
THUD
WHOOF
GGRRAHHHRRRRrrrr!

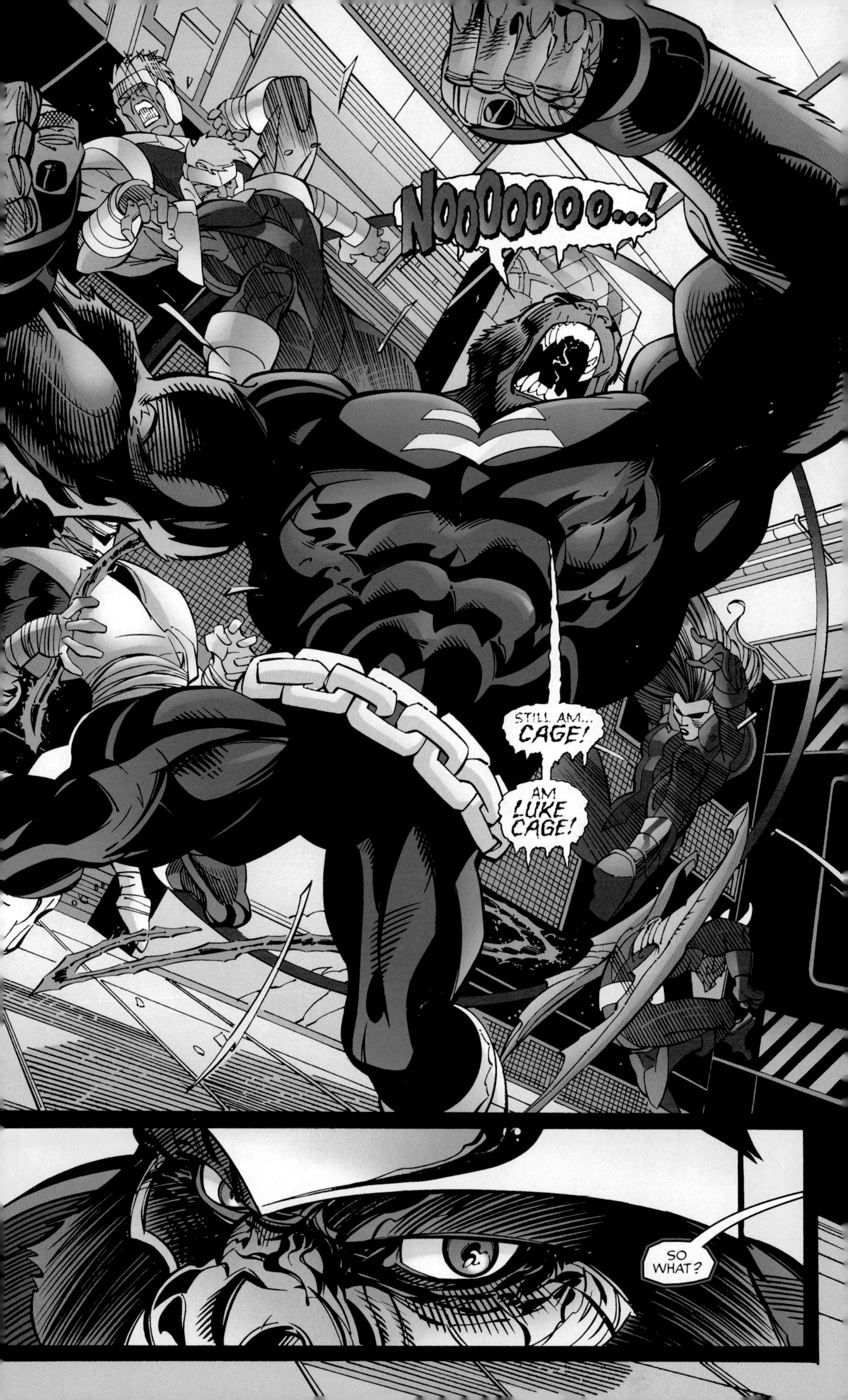
NOOOOOOO...!
STILL AM... CAGE!
AM LUKE CAGE!
SO WHAT?

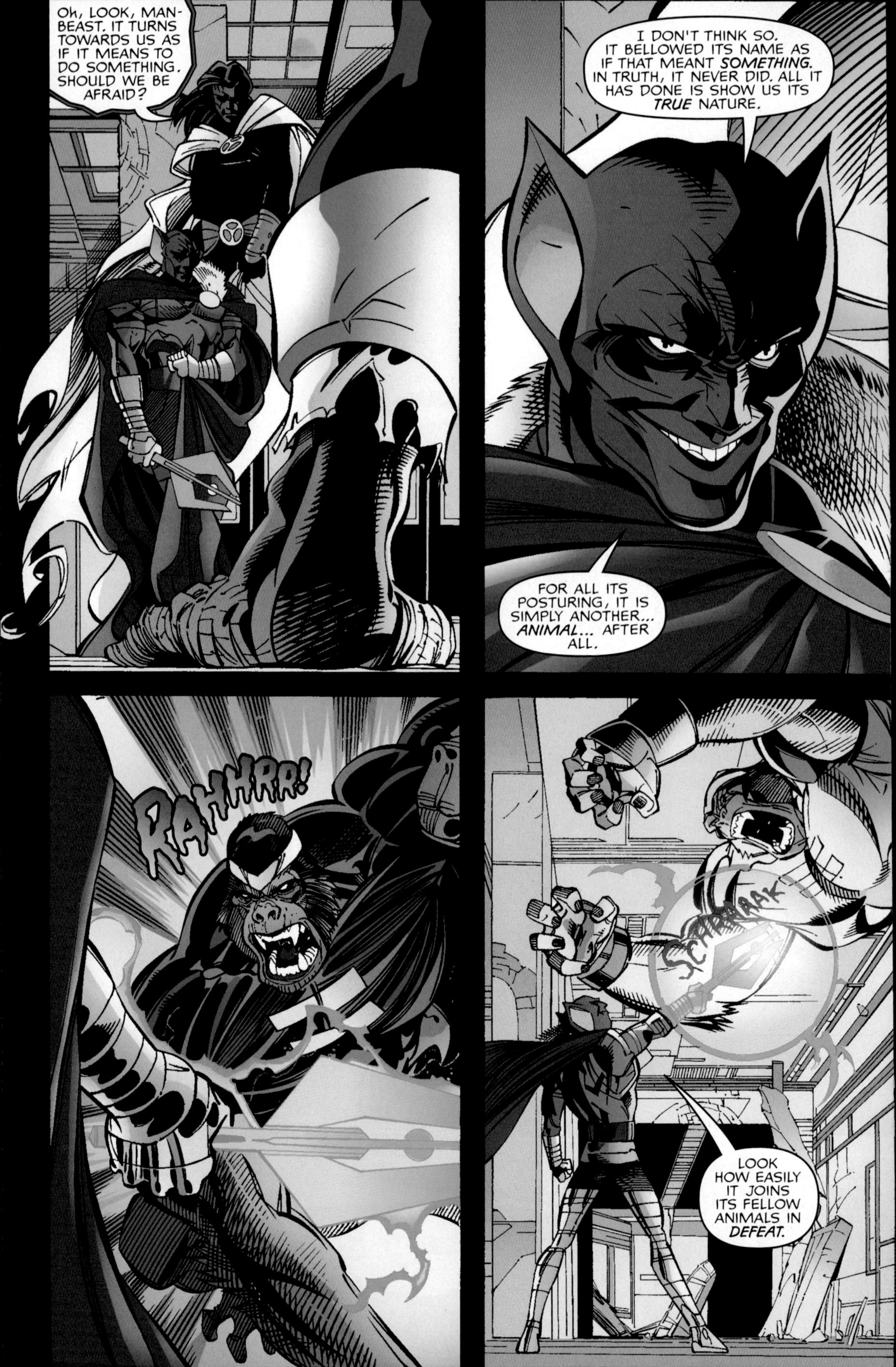

Oh, LOOK, MAN-BEAST. IT TURNS TOWARDS US AS IF IT MEANS TO DO SOMETHING. SHOULD WE BE AFRAID?
I DON'T THINK SO. IT BELLOWED ITS NAME AS IF THAT MEANT *SOMETHING*. IN TRUTH, IT NEVER DID. ALL IT HAS DONE IS SHOW US ITS *TRUE* NATURE.
FOR ALL ITS POSTURING, IT IS SIMPLY ANOTHER... *ANIMAL*... AFTER ALL.
RAHHRRR!
SCHRRAAK
LOOK HOW EASILY IT JOINS ITS FELLOW ANIMALS IN *DEFEAT*.

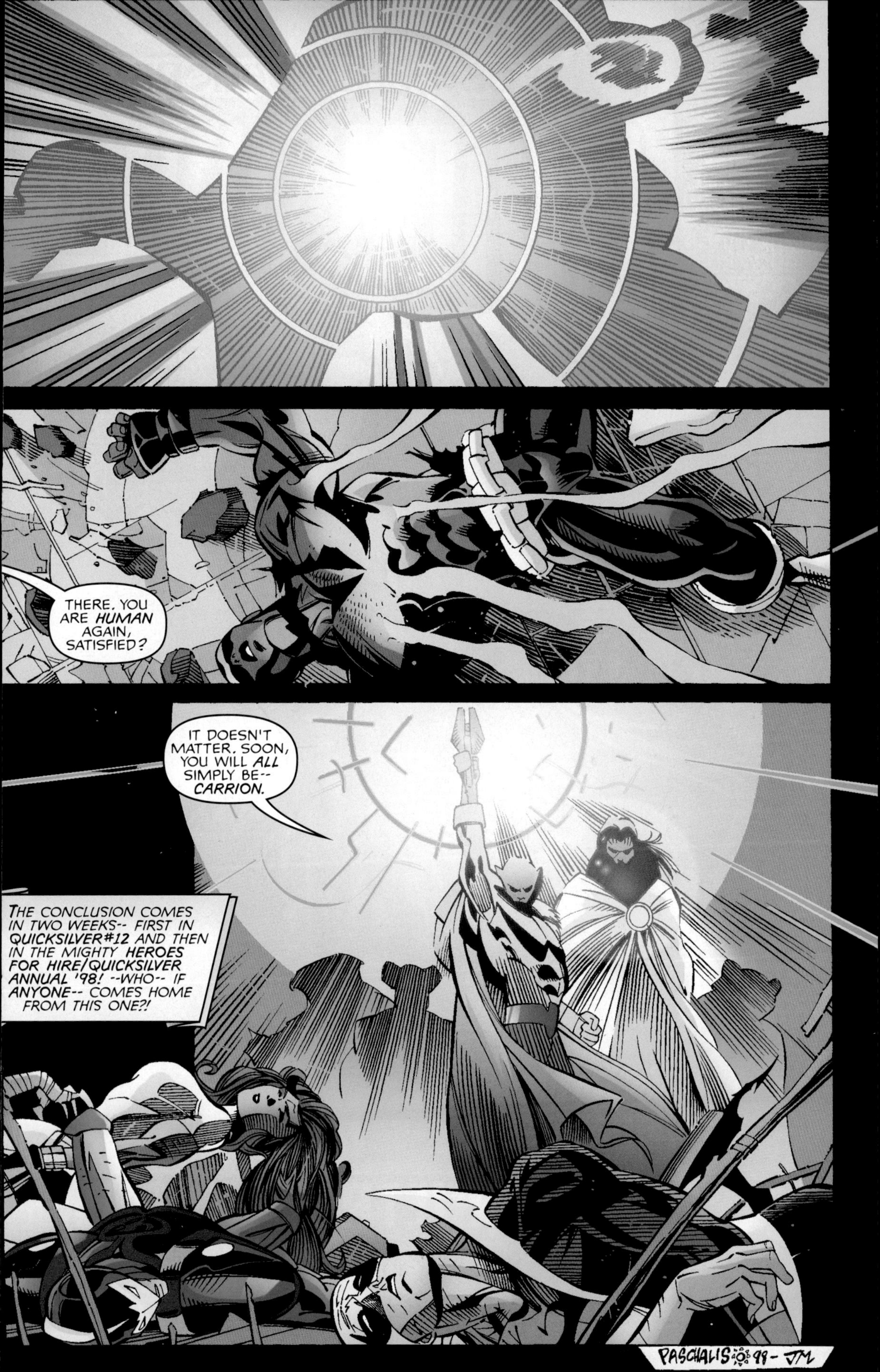
THERE. YOU ARE HUMAN AGAIN, SATISFIED?
IT DOESN'T MATTER. SOON, YOU WILL ALL SIMPLY BE-- CARRION.
THE CONCLUSION COMES IN TWO WEEKS-- FIRST IN QUICKSILVER #12 AND THEN IN THE MIGHTY HEROES FOR HIRE/QUICKSILVER ANNUAL '98! --WHO-- IF ANYONE-- COMES HOME FROM THIS ONE?!
PASCHALIS 98 - JM

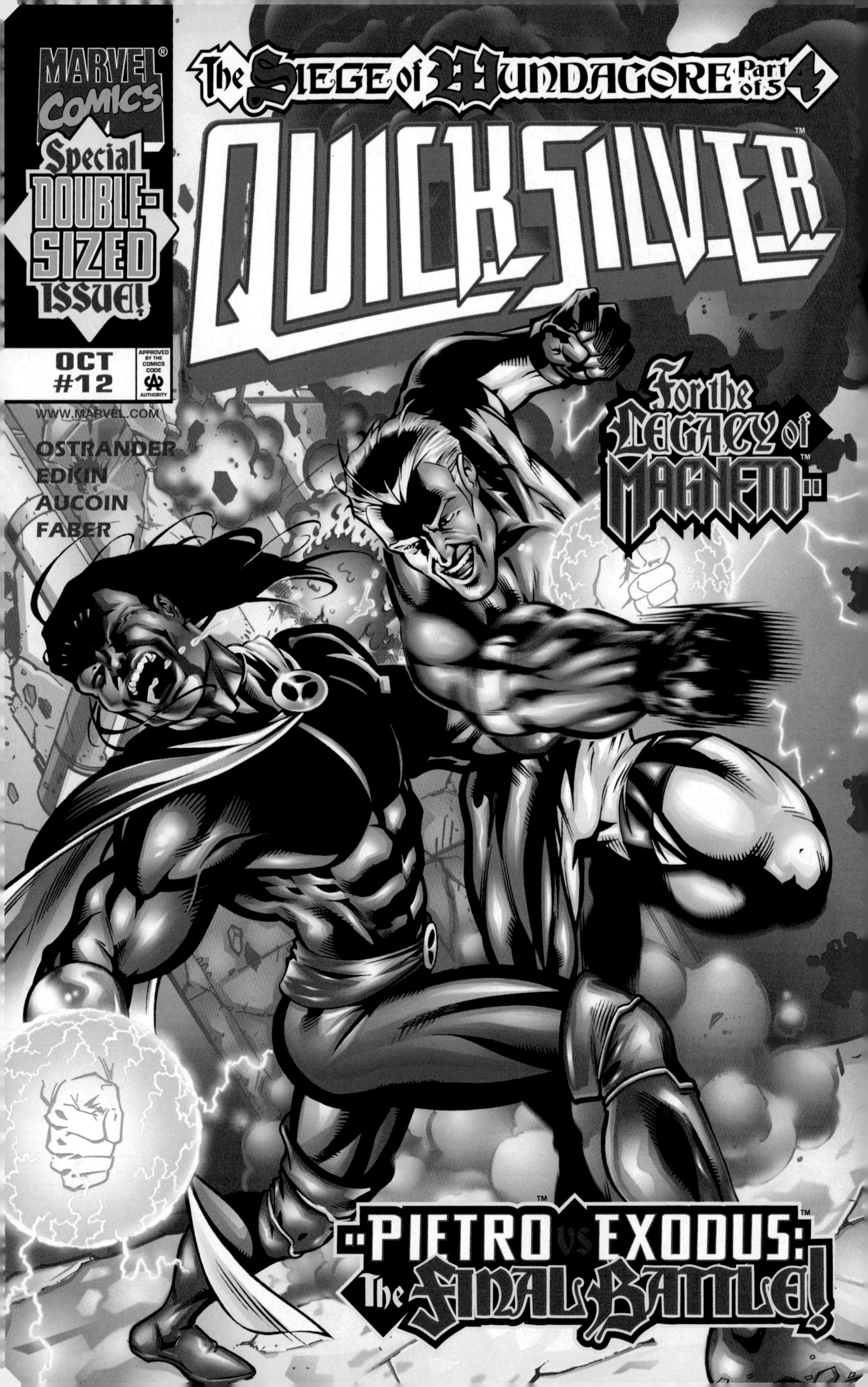

MARVEL® COMICS
Special DOUBLE-SIZED ISSUE!
OCT #12
APPROVED BY THE COMICS CODE AUTHORITY
WWW.MARVEL.COM
OSTRANDER
EDKIN
AUCOIN
FABER
The Siege of Wundagore Part 4 of 5
QUICKSILVER™
For the Legacy of MAGNETO™..
..PIETRO™ vs EXODUS™:
The FINAL BATTLE!

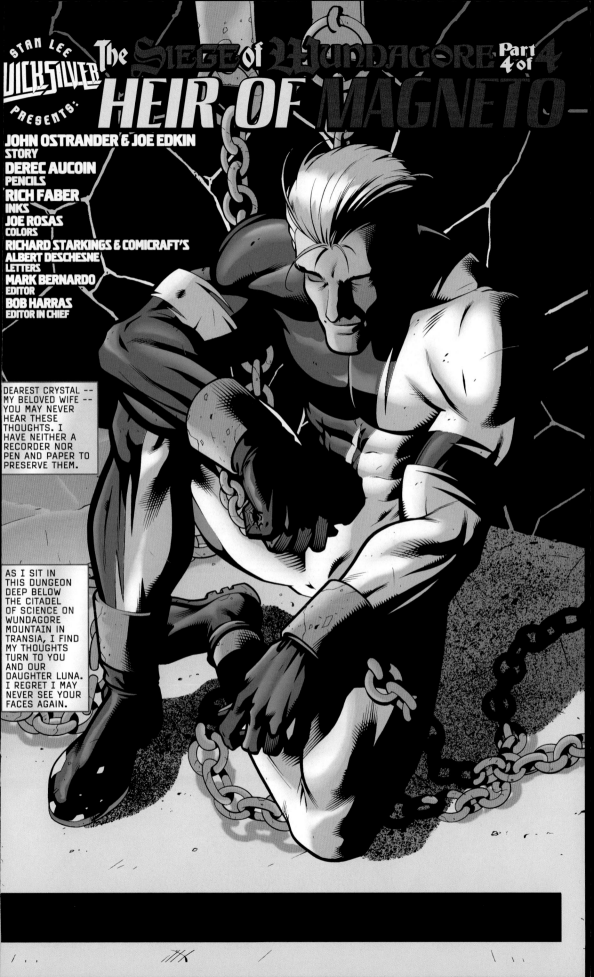

STAN LEE
QUICKSILVER
PRESENTS:

The SIEGE of WUNDAGORE Part 4 of 4
HEIR OF MAGNETO—

JOHN OSTRANDER & JOE EDKIN
STORY

DEREC AUCOIN
PENCILS

RICH FABER
INKS

JOE ROSAS
COLORS

RICHARD STARKINGS & COMICRAFT'S
ALBERT DESCHESNE
LETTERS

MARK BERNARDO
EDITOR

BOB HARRAS
EDITOR IN CHIEF

DEAREST CRYSTAL -- MY BELOVED WIFE -- YOU MAY NEVER HEAR THESE THOUGHTS. I HAVE NEITHER A RECORDER NOR PEN AND PAPER TO PRESERVE THEM.

AS I SIT IN THIS DUNGEON DEEP BELOW THE CITADEL OF SCIENCE ON WUNDAGORE MOUNTAIN IN TRANSIA, I FIND MY THOUGHTS TURN TO YOU AND OUR DAUGHTER LUNA. I REGRET I MAY NEVER SEE YOUR FACES AGAIN.

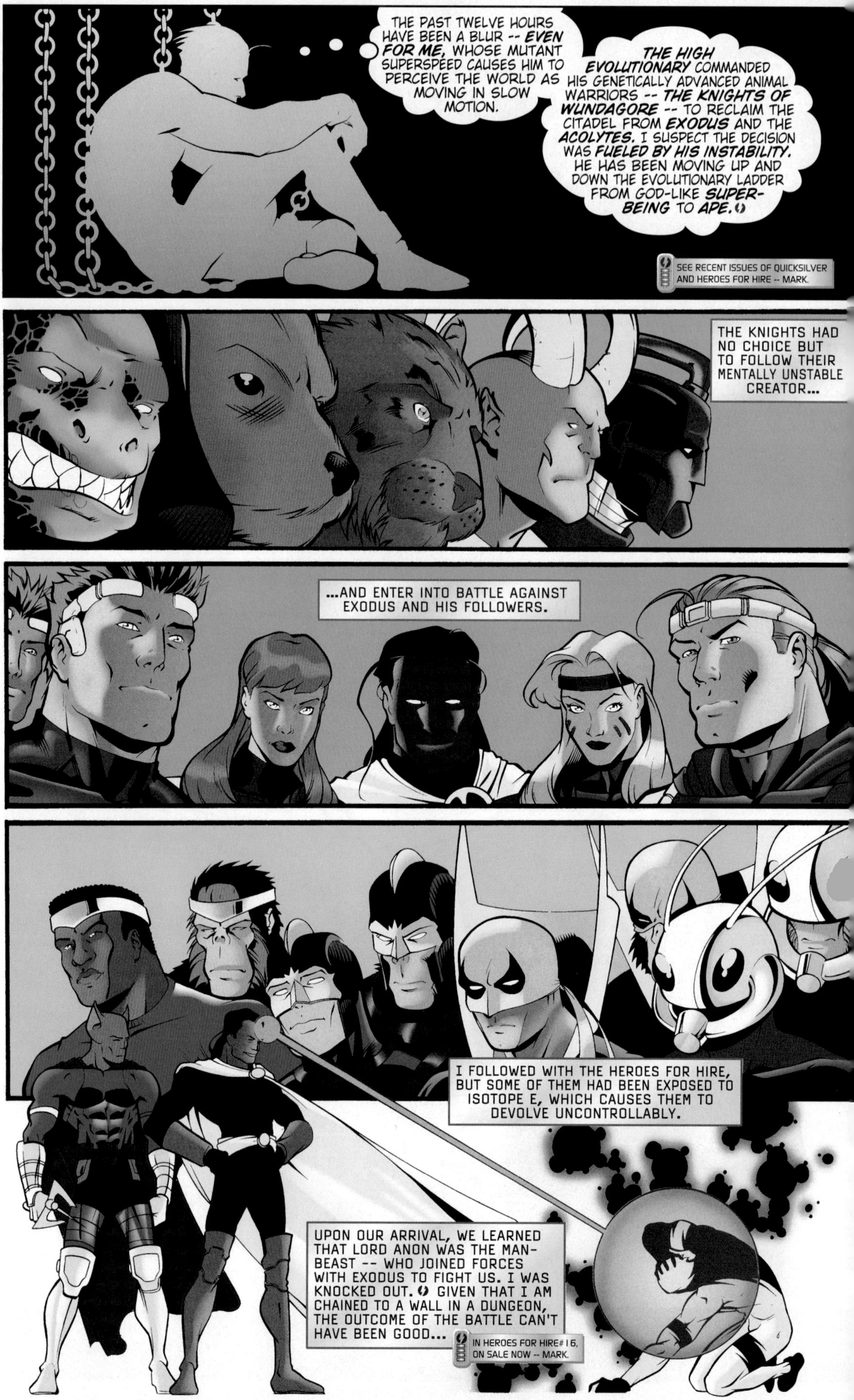
THE PAST TWELVE HOURS HAVE BEEN A BLUR -- EVEN FOR ME, WHOSE MUTANT SUPERSPEED CAUSES HIM TO PERCEIVE THE WORLD AS MOVING IN SLOW MOTION.
THE HIGH EVOLUTIONARY COMMANDED HIS GENETICALLY ADVANCED ANIMAL WARRIORS -- THE KNIGHTS OF WUNDAGORE -- TO RECLAIM THE CITADEL FROM EXODUS AND THE ACOLYTES. I SUSPECT THE DECISION WAS FUELED BY HIS INSTABILITY. HE HAS BEEN MOVING UP AND DOWN THE EVOLUTIONARY LADDER FROM GOD-LIKE SUPER-BEING TO APE.
SEE RECENT ISSUES OF QUICKSILVER AND HEROES FOR HIRE -- MARK.
THE KNIGHTS HAD NO CHOICE BUT TO FOLLOW THEIR MENTALLY UNSTABLE CREATOR...
...AND ENTER INTO BATTLE AGAINST EXODUS AND HIS FOLLOWERS.
I FOLLOWED WITH THE HEROES FOR HIRE, BUT SOME OF THEM HAD BEEN EXPOSED TO ISOTOPE E, WHICH CAUSES THEM TO DEVOLVE UNCONTROLLABLY.
UPON OUR ARRIVAL, WE LEARNED THAT LORD ANON WAS THE MAN-BEAST -- WHO JOINED FORCES WITH EXODUS TO FIGHT US. I WAS KNOCKED OUT. GIVEN THAT I AM CHAINED TO A WALL IN A DUNGEON, THE OUTCOME OF THE BATTLE CAN'T HAVE BEEN GOOD...
IN HEROES FOR HIRE#16, ON SALE NOW -- MARK.

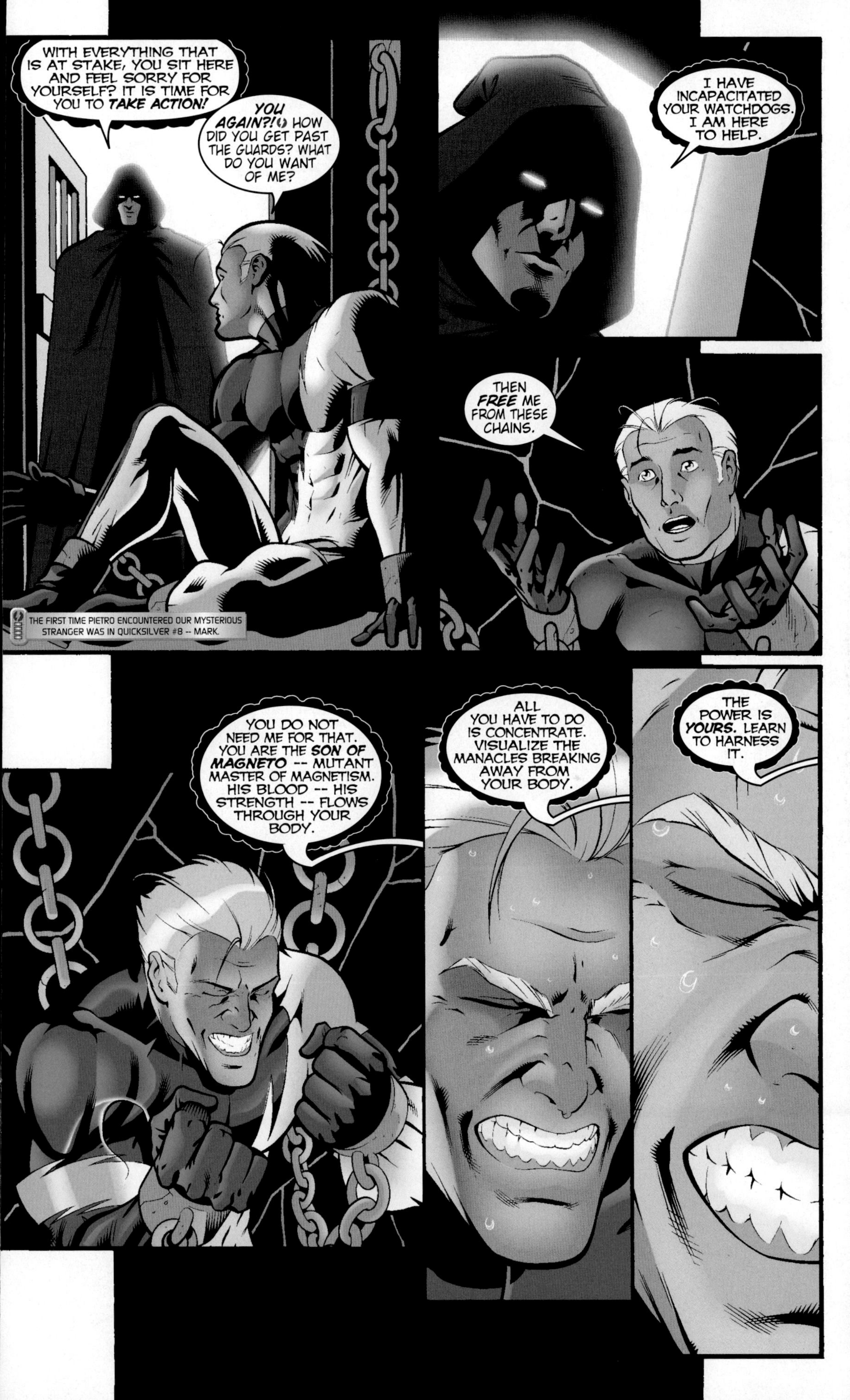
WITH EVERYTHING THAT IS AT STAKE, YOU SIT HERE AND FEEL SORRY FOR YOURSELF? IT IS TIME FOR YOU TO TAKE ACTION!
YOU AGAIN?! HOW DID YOU GET PAST THE GUARDS? WHAT DO YOU WANT OF ME?
THE FIRST TIME PIETRO ENCOUNTERED OUR MYSTERIOUS STRANGER WAS IN QUICKSILVER #8 -- MARK.
I HAVE INCAPACITATED YOUR WATCHDOGS. I AM HERE TO HELP.
THEN FREE ME FROM THESE CHAINS.
YOU DO NOT NEED ME FOR THAT. YOU ARE THE SON OF MAGNETO -- MUTANT MASTER OF MAGNETISM. HIS BLOOD -- HIS STRENGTH -- FLOWS THROUGH YOUR BODY.
ALL YOU HAVE TO DO IS CONCENTRATE. VISUALIZE THE MANACLES BREAKING AWAY FROM YOUR BODY.
THE POWER IS YOURS. LEARN TO HARNESS IT.

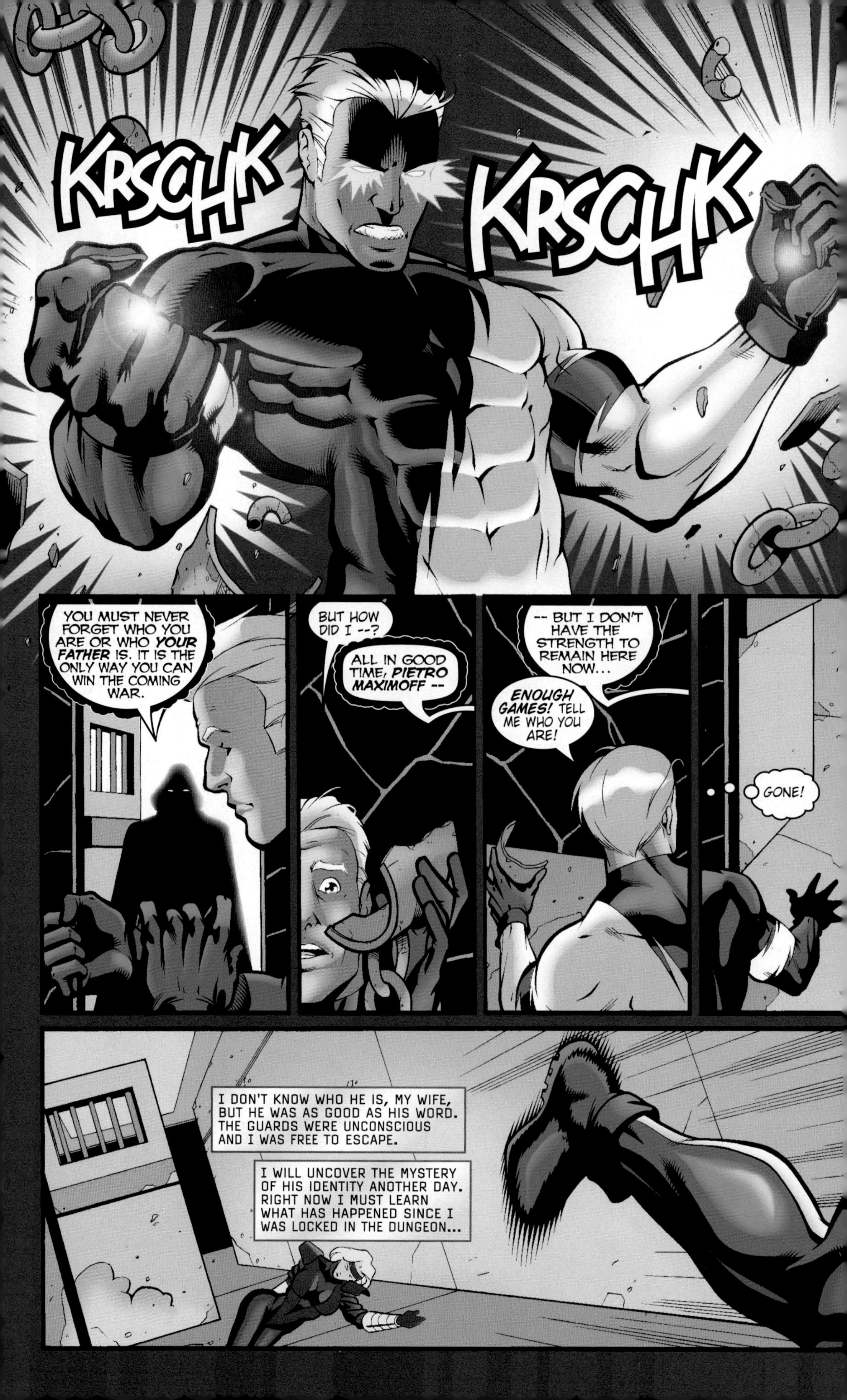
KRSCHK
KRSCHK
YOU MUST NEVER FORGET WHO YOU ARE OR WHO YOUR FATHER IS. IT IS THE ONLY WAY YOU CAN WIN THE COMING WAR.
BUT HOW DID I --?
ALL IN GOOD TIME, PIETRO MAXIMOFF --
-- BUT I DON'T HAVE THE STRENGTH TO REMAIN HERE NOW...
ENOUGH GAMES! TELL ME WHO YOU ARE!
GONE!
I DON'T KNOW WHO HE IS, MY WIFE, BUT HE WAS AS GOOD AS HIS WORD. THE GUARDS WERE UNCONSCIOUS AND I WAS FREE TO ESCAPE.
I WILL UNCOVER THE MYSTERY OF HIS IDENTITY ANOTHER DAY. RIGHT NOW I MUST LEARN WHAT HAS HAPPENED SINCE I WAS LOCKED IN THE DUNGEON...

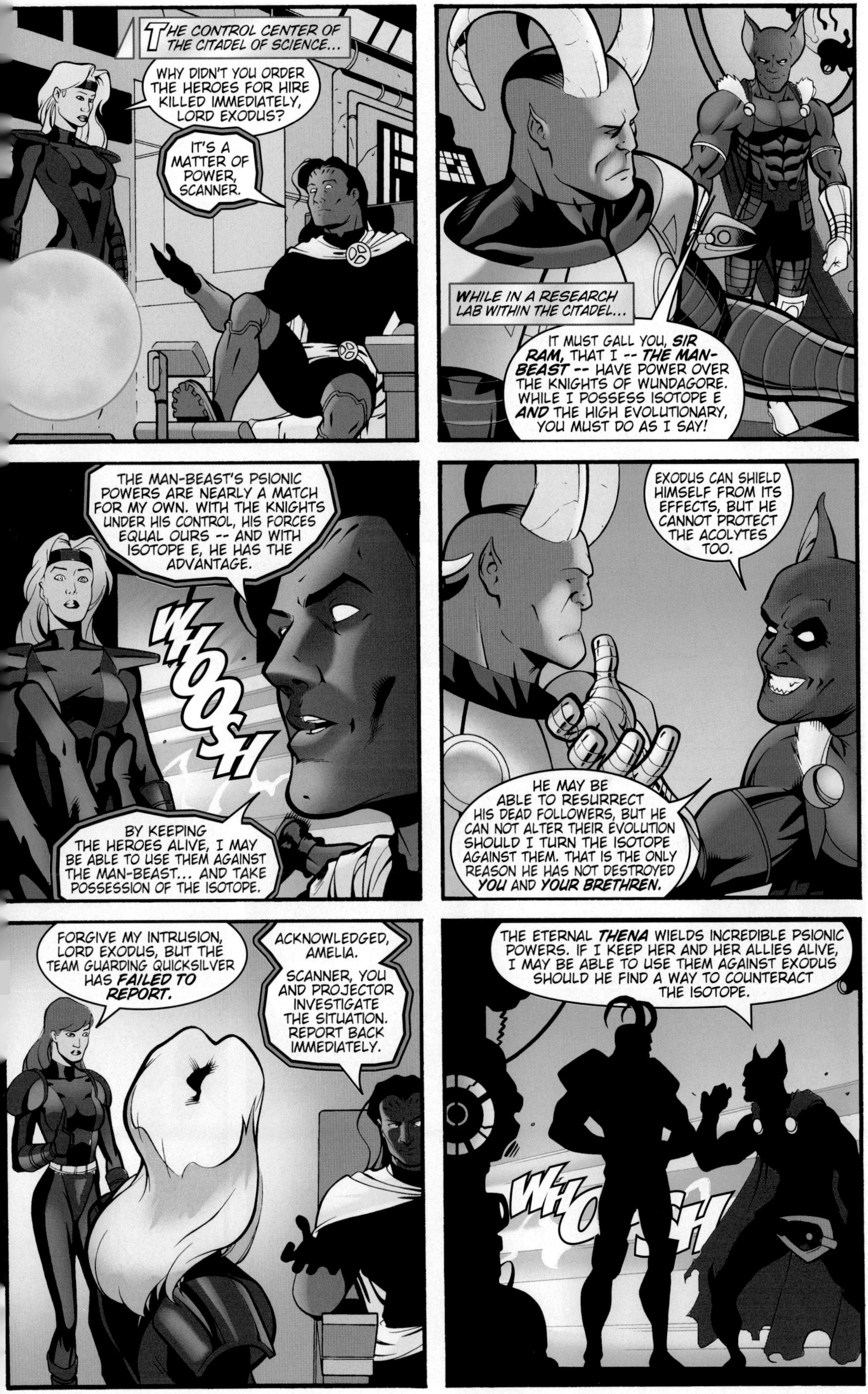
THE CONTROL CENTER OF THE CITADEL OF SCIENCE...
WHY DIDN'T YOU ORDER THE HEROES FOR HIRE KILLED IMMEDIATELY, LORD EXODUS?
IT'S A MATTER OF POWER, SCANNER.
WHILE IN A RESEARCH LAB WITHIN THE CITADEL...
IT MUST GALL YOU, SIR RAM, THAT I -- THE MAN-BEAST -- HAVE POWER OVER THE KNIGHTS OF WUNDAGORE. WHILE I POSSESS ISOTOPE E AND THE HIGH EVOLUTIONARY, YOU MUST DO AS I SAY!
THE MAN-BEAST'S PSIONIC POWERS ARE NEARLY A MATCH FOR MY OWN. WITH THE KNIGHTS UNDER HIS CONTROL, HIS FORCES EQUAL OURS -- AND WITH ISOTOPE E, HE HAS THE ADVANTAGE.
WHOOSH
BY KEEPING THE HEROES ALIVE, I MAY BE ABLE TO USE THEM AGAINST THE MAN-BEAST... AND TAKE POSSESSION OF THE ISOTOPE.
EXODUS CAN SHIELD HIMSELF FROM ITS EFFECTS, BUT HE CANNOT PROTECT THE ACOLYTES TOO.
HE MAY BE ABLE TO RESURRECT HIS DEAD FOLLOWERS, BUT HE CAN NOT ALTER THEIR EVOLUTION SHOULD I TURN THE ISOTOPE AGAINST THEM. THAT IS THE ONLY REASON HE HAS NOT DESTROYED YOU AND YOUR BRETHREN.
FORGIVE MY INTRUSION, LORD EXODUS, BUT THE TEAM GUARDING QUICKSILVER HAS FAILED TO REPORT.
ACKNOWLEDGED, AMELIA.
SCANNER, YOU AND PROJECTOR INVESTIGATE THE SITUATION. REPORT BACK IMMEDIATELY.
THE ETERNAL THENA WIELDS INCREDIBLE PSIONIC POWERS. IF I KEEP HER AND HER ALLIES ALIVE, I MAY BE ABLE TO USE THEM AGAINST EXODUS SHOULD HE FIND A WAY TO COUNTERACT THE ISOTOPE.

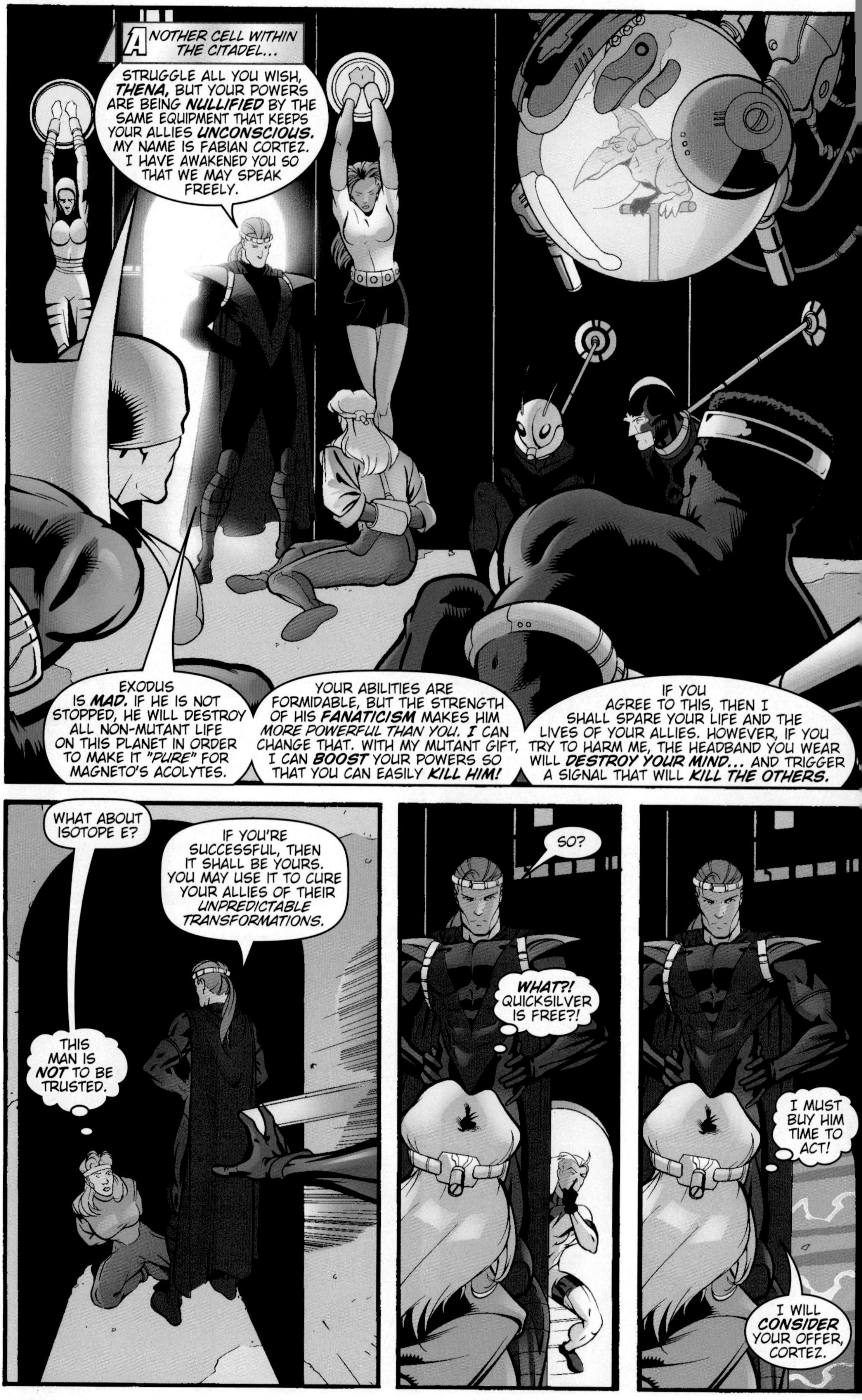
ANOTHER CELL WITHIN THE CITADEL...
STRUGGLE ALL YOU WISH, THENA, BUT YOUR POWERS ARE BEING NULLIFIED BY THE SAME EQUIPMENT THAT KEEPS YOUR ALLIES UNCONSCIOUS. MY NAME IS FABIAN CORTEZ. I HAVE AWAKENED YOU SO THAT WE MAY SPEAK FREELY.
EXODUS IS MAD. IF HE IS NOT STOPPED, HE WILL DESTROY ALL NON-MUTANT LIFE ON THIS PLANET IN ORDER TO MAKE IT "PURE" FOR MAGNETO'S ACOLYTES.
YOUR ABILITIES ARE FORMIDABLE, BUT THE STRENGTH OF HIS FANATICISM MAKES HIM MORE POWERFUL THAN YOU. I CAN CHANGE THAT. WITH MY MUTANT GIFT, I CAN BOOST YOUR POWERS SO THAT YOU CAN EASILY KILL HIM!
IF YOU AGREE TO THIS, THEN I SHALL SPARE YOUR LIFE AND THE LIVES OF YOUR ALLIES. HOWEVER, IF YOU TRY TO HARM ME, THE HEADBAND YOU WEAR WILL DESTROY YOUR MIND... AND TRIGGER A SIGNAL THAT WILL KILL THE OTHERS.
WHAT ABOUT ISOTOPE E?
IF YOU'RE SUCCESSFUL, THEN IT SHALL BE YOURS. YOU MAY USE IT TO CURE YOUR ALLIES OF THEIR UNPREDICTABLE TRANSFORMATIONS.
THIS MAN IS NOT TO BE TRUSTED.
SO?
WHAT?! QUICKSILVER IS FREE?!
I MUST BUY HIM TIME TO ACT!
I WILL CONSIDER YOUR OFFER, CORTEZ.

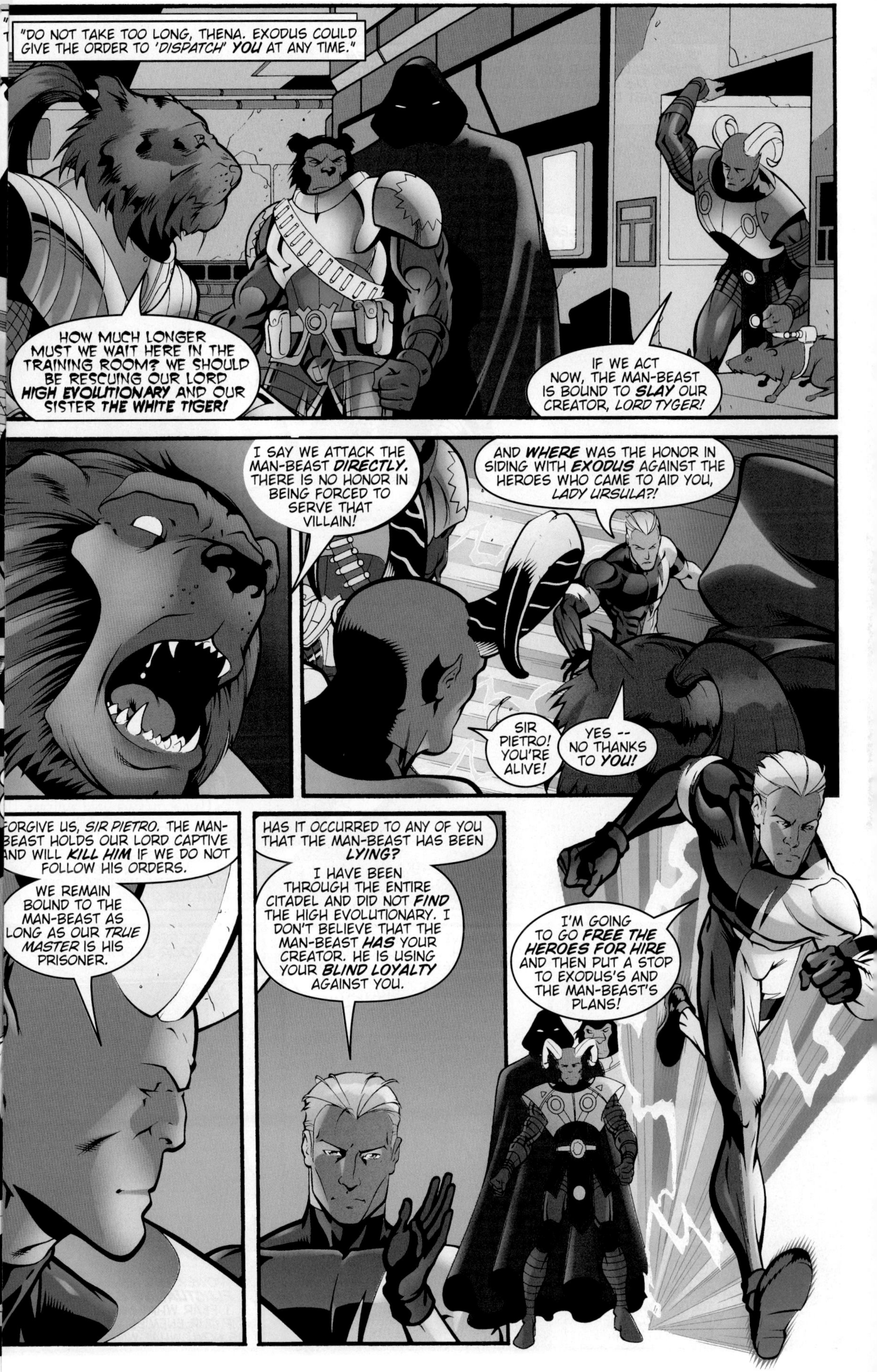
"DO NOT TAKE TOO LONG, THENA. EXODUS COULD GIVE THE ORDER TO 'DISPATCH' YOU AT ANY TIME."
HOW MUCH LONGER MUST WE WAIT HERE IN THE TRAINING ROOM? WE SHOULD BE RESCUING OUR LORD HIGH EVOLUTIONARY AND OUR SISTER THE WHITE TIGER!
IF WE ACT NOW, THE MAN-BEAST IS BOUND TO SLAY OUR CREATOR, LORD TYGER!
I SAY WE ATTACK THE MAN-BEAST DIRECTLY. THERE IS NO HONOR IN BEING FORCED TO SERVE THAT VILLAIN!
AND WHERE WAS THE HONOR IN SIDING WITH EXODUS AGAINST THE HEROES WHO CAME TO AID YOU, LADY URSULA?!
SIR PIETRO! YOU'RE ALIVE!
YES -- NO THANKS TO YOU!
FORGIVE US, SIR PIETRO. THE MAN-BEAST HOLDS OUR LORD CAPTIVE AND WILL KILL HIM IF WE DO NOT FOLLOW HIS ORDERS.
WE REMAIN BOUND TO THE MAN-BEAST AS LONG AS OUR TRUE MASTER IS HIS PRISONER.
HAS IT OCCURRED TO ANY OF YOU THAT THE MAN-BEAST HAS BEEN LYING?
I HAVE BEEN THROUGH THE ENTIRE CITADEL AND DID NOT FIND THE HIGH EVOLUTIONARY. I DON'T BELIEVE THAT THE MAN-BEAST HAS YOUR CREATOR. HE IS USING YOUR BLIND LOYALTY AGAINST YOU.
I'M GOING TO GO FREE THE HEROES FOR HIRE AND THEN PUT A STOP TO EXODUS'S AND THE MAN-BEAST'S PLANS!

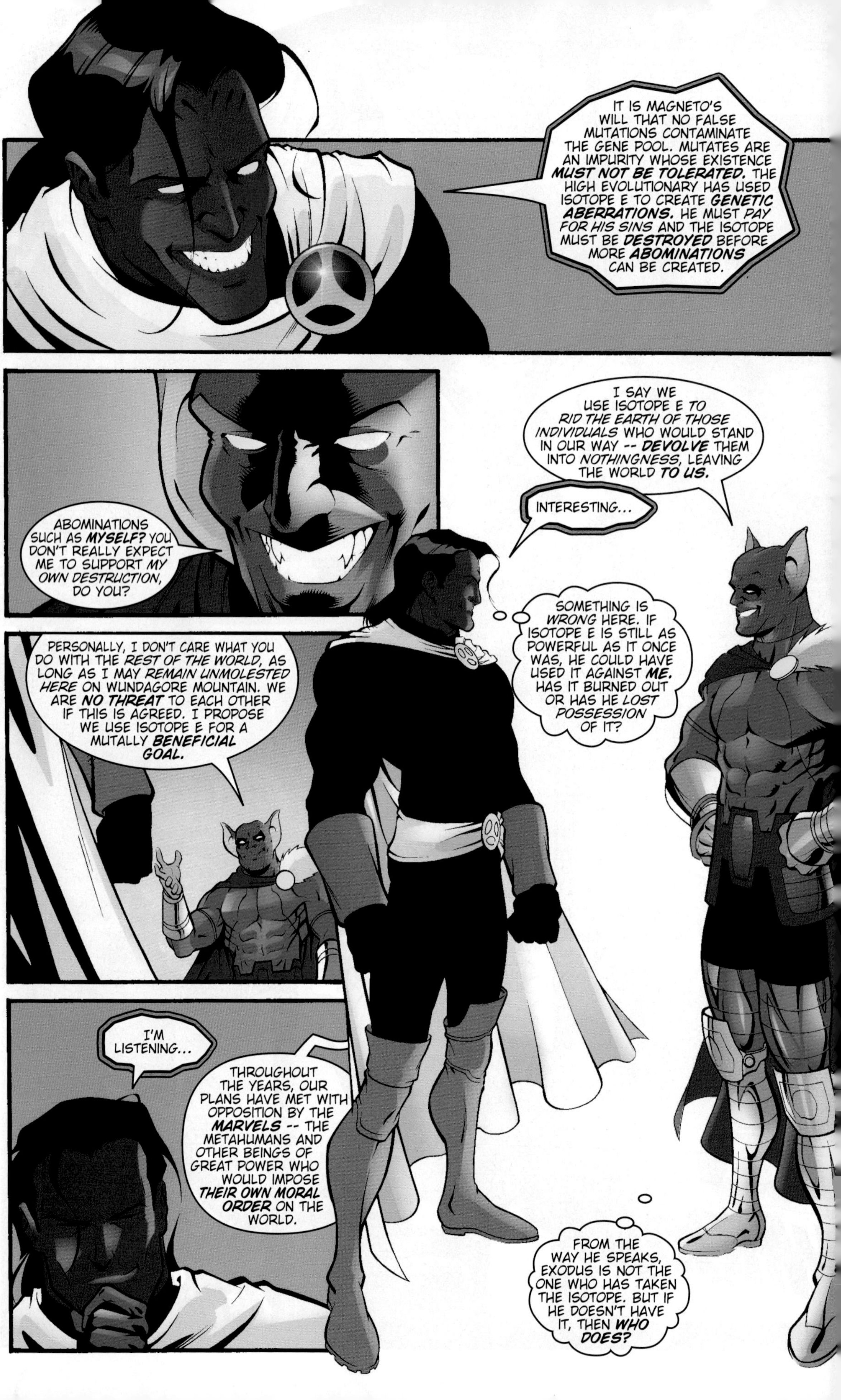
IT IS MAGNETO'S WILL THAT NO FALSE MUTATIONS CONTAMINATE THE GENE POOL. MUTATES ARE AN IMPURITY WHOSE EXISTENCE MUST NOT BE TOLERATED. THE HIGH EVOLUTIONARY HAS USED ISOTOPE E TO CREATE GENETIC ABERRATIONS. HE MUST PAY FOR HIS SINS AND THE ISOTOPE MUST BE DESTROYED BEFORE MORE ABOMINATIONS CAN BE CREATED.
ABOMINATIONS SUCH AS MYSELF? YOU DON'T REALLY EXPECT ME TO SUPPORT MY OWN DESTRUCTION, DO YOU?
PERSONALLY, I DON'T CARE WHAT YOU DO WITH THE REST OF THE WORLD, AS LONG AS I MAY REMAIN UNMOLESTED HERE ON WUNDAGORE MOUNTAIN. WE ARE NO THREAT TO EACH OTHER IF THIS IS AGREED. I PROPOSE WE USE ISOTOPE E FOR A MUTALLY BENEFICIAL GOAL.
I'M LISTENING...
THROUGHOUT THE YEARS, OUR PLANS HAVE MET WITH OPPOSITION BY THE MARVELS -- THE METAHUMANS AND OTHER BEINGS OF GREAT POWER WHO WOULD IMPOSE THEIR OWN MORAL ORDER ON THE WORLD.
I SAY WE USE ISOTOPE E TO RID THE EARTH OF THOSE INDIVIDUALS WHO WOULD STAND IN OUR WAY -- DEVOLVE THEM INTO NOTHINGNESS, LEAVING THE WORLD TO US.
INTERESTING...
SOMETHING IS WRONG HERE. IF ISOTOPE E IS STILL AS POWERFUL AS IT ONCE WAS, HE COULD HAVE USED IT AGAINST ME. HAS IT BURNED OUT OR HAS HE LOST POSSESSION OF IT?
FROM THE WAY HE SPEAKS, EXODUS IS NOT THE ONE WHO HAS TAKEN THE ISOTOPE. BUT IF HE DOESN'T HAVE IT, THEN WHO DOES?

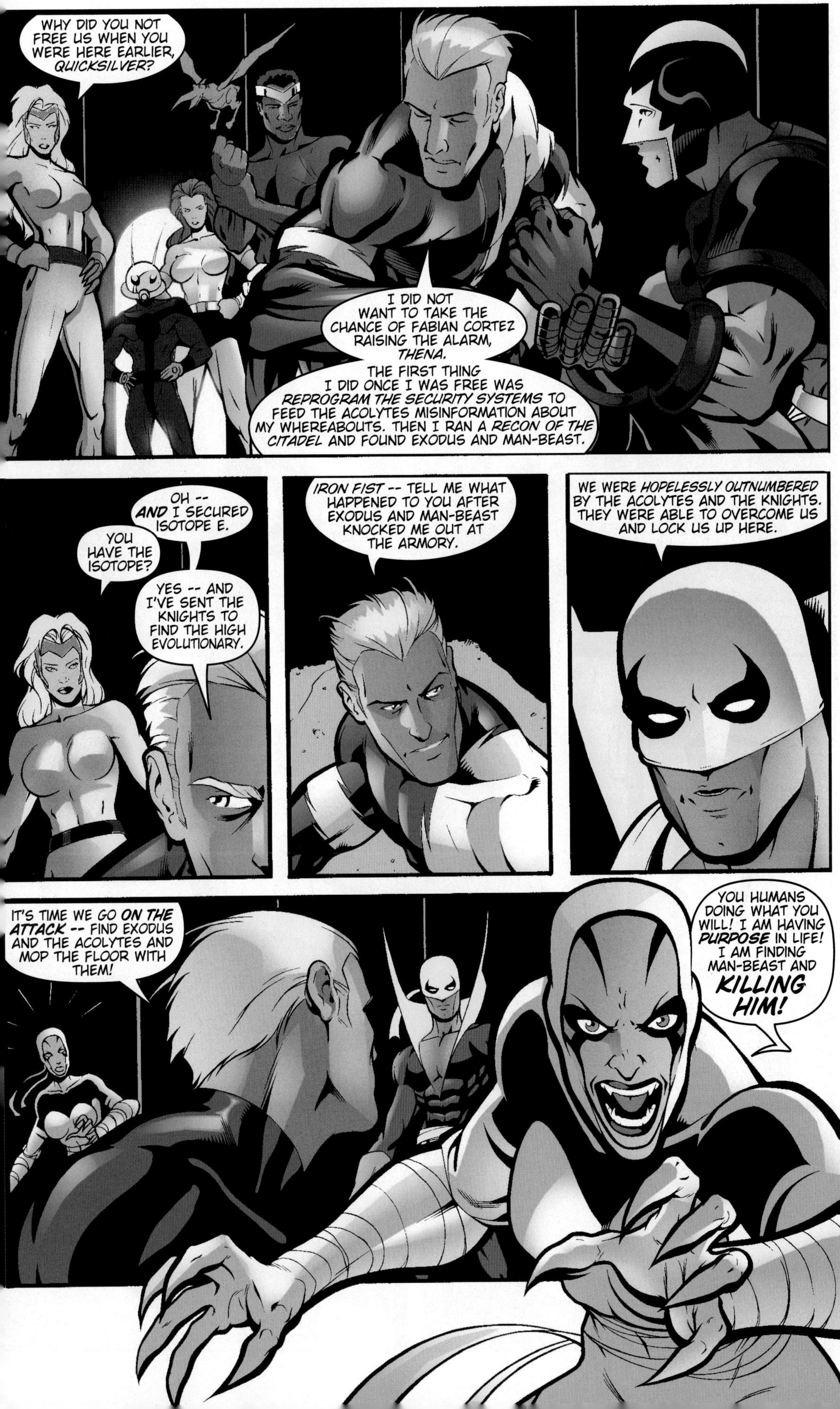
WHY DID YOU NOT FREE US WHEN YOU WERE HERE EARLIER, *QUICKSILVER?*
I DID NOT WANT TO TAKE THE CHANCE OF FABIAN CORTEZ RAISING THE ALARM, *THENA.*
THE FIRST THING I DID ONCE I WAS FREE WAS *REPROGRAM THE SECURITY SYSTEMS* TO FEED THE ACOLYTES MISINFORMATION ABOUT MY WHEREABOUTS. THEN I RAN A *RECON OF THE CITADEL* AND FOUND EXODUS AND MAN-BEAST.
OH -- ***AND*** I SECURED ISOTOPE E.
YOU HAVE THE ISOTOPE?
YES -- AND I'VE SENT THE KNIGHTS TO FIND THE HIGH EVOLUTIONARY.
IRON FIST -- TELL ME WHAT HAPPENED TO YOU AFTER EXODUS AND MAN-BEAST KNOCKED ME OUT AT THE ARMORY.
WE WERE *HOPELESSLY OUTNUMBERED* BY THE ACOLYTES AND THE KNIGHTS. THEY WERE ABLE TO OVERCOME US AND LOCK US UP HERE.
IT'S TIME WE GO **ON THE ATTACK** -- FIND EXODUS AND THE ACOLYTES AND MOP THE FLOOR WITH THEM!
YOU HUMANS DOING WHAT YOU WILL! I AM HAVING ***PURPOSE*** IN LIFE! I AM FINDING MAN-BEAST AND ***KILLING HIM!***

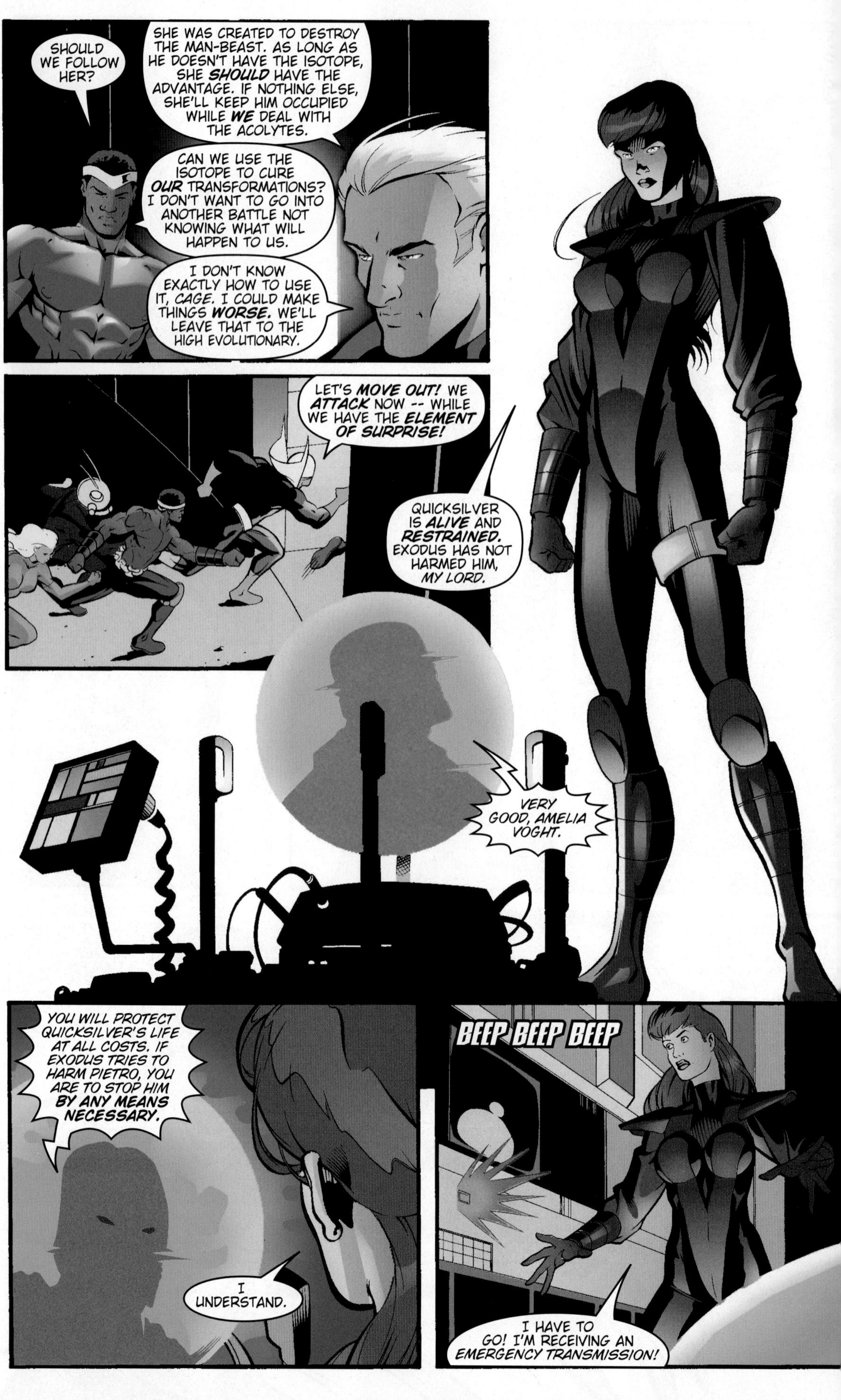
SHOULD WE FOLLOW HER?
SHE WAS CREATED TO DESTROY THE MAN-BEAST. AS LONG AS HE DOESN'T HAVE THE ISOTOPE, SHE SHOULD HAVE THE ADVANTAGE. IF NOTHING ELSE, SHE'LL KEEP HIM OCCUPIED WHILE WE DEAL WITH THE ACOLYTES.
CAN WE USE THE ISOTOPE TO CURE OUR TRANSFORMATIONS? I DON'T WANT TO GO INTO ANOTHER BATTLE NOT KNOWING WHAT WILL HAPPEN TO US.
I DON'T KNOW EXACTLY HOW TO USE IT, CAGE. I COULD MAKE THINGS WORSE. WE'LL LEAVE THAT TO THE HIGH EVOLUTIONARY.
LET'S MOVE OUT! WE ATTACK NOW -- WHILE WE HAVE THE ELEMENT OF SURPRISE!
QUICKSILVER IS ALIVE AND RESTRAINED. EXODUS HAS NOT HARMED HIM, MY LORD.
VERY GOOD, AMELIA VOGHT.
YOU WILL PROTECT QUICKSILVER'S LIFE AT ALL COSTS. IF EXODUS TRIES TO HARM PIETRO, YOU ARE TO STOP HIM BY ANY MEANS NECESSARY.
I UNDERSTAND.
BEEP BEEP BEEP
I HAVE TO GO! I'M RECEIVING AN EMERGENCY TRANSMISSION!

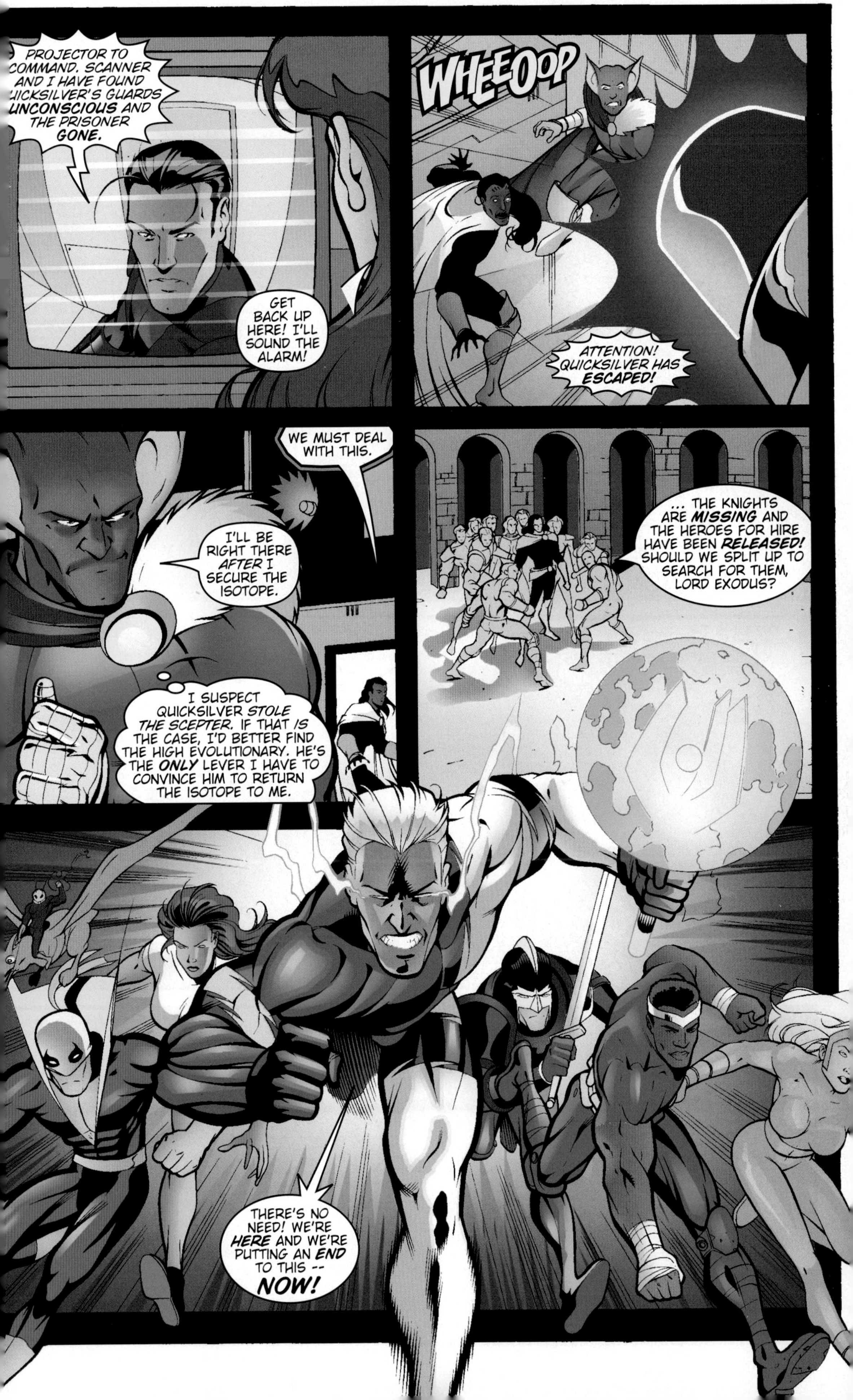
PROJECTOR TO COMMAND. SCANNER AND I HAVE FOUND QUICKSILVER'S GUARDS UNCONSCIOUS AND THE PRISONER GONE.
GET BACK UP HERE! I'LL SOUND THE ALARM!
WHEEOOP
ATTENTION! QUICKSILVER HAS ESCAPED!
WE MUST DEAL WITH THIS.
I'LL BE RIGHT THERE AFTER I SECURE THE ISOTOPE.
I SUSPECT QUICKSILVER STOLE THE SCEPTER. IF THAT IS THE CASE, I'D BETTER FIND THE HIGH EVOLUTIONARY. HE'S THE ONLY LEVER I HAVE TO CONVINCE HIM TO RETURN THE ISOTOPE TO ME.
... THE KNIGHTS ARE MISSING AND THE HEROES FOR HIRE HAVE BEEN RELEASED! SHOULD WE SPLIT UP TO SEARCH FOR THEM, LORD EXODUS?
THERE'S NO NEED! WE'RE HERE AND WE'RE PUTTING AN END TO THIS -- NOW!

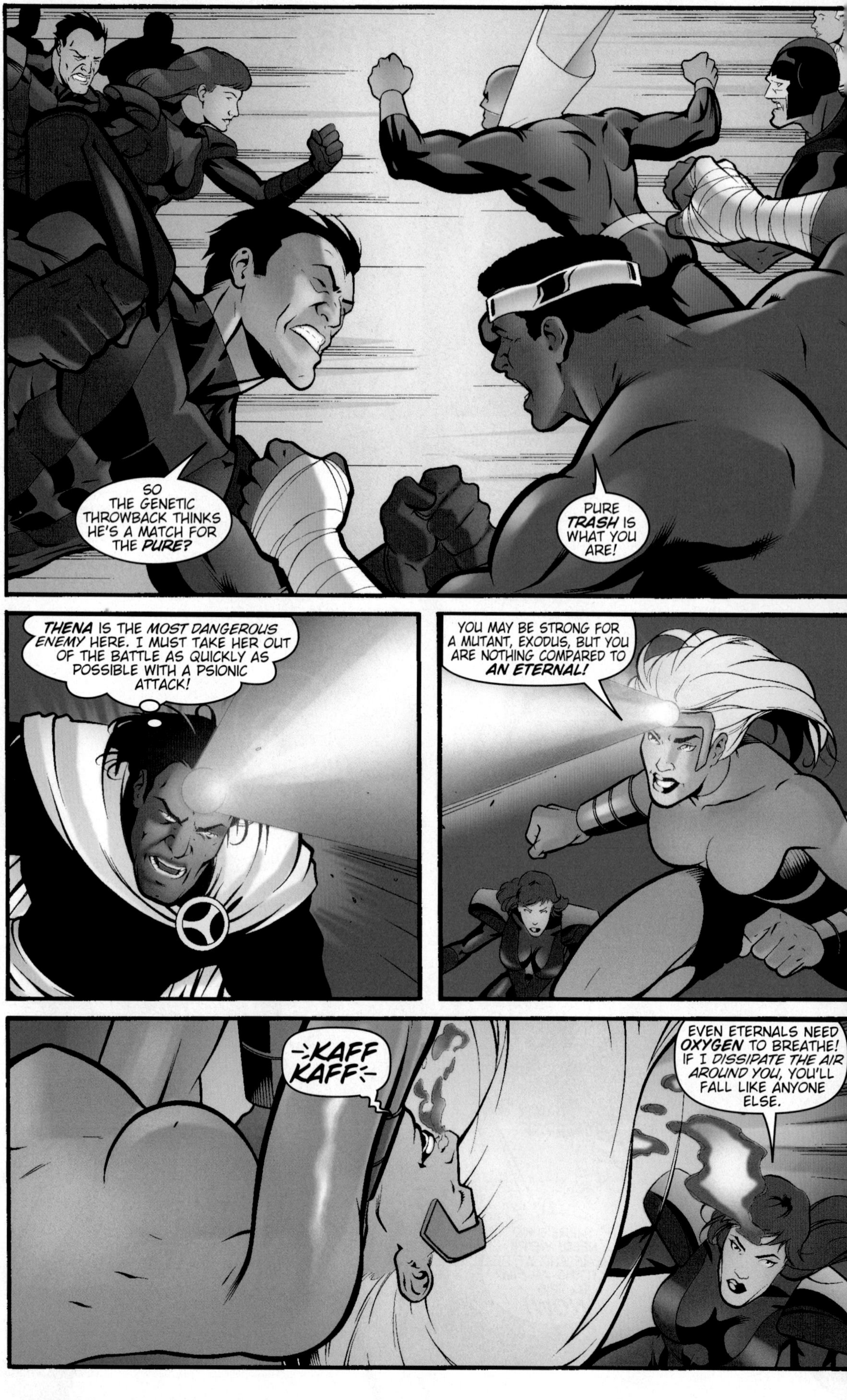
SO THE GENETIC THROWBACK THINKS HE'S A MATCH FOR THE *PURE?*
PURE *TRASH* IS WHAT YOU ARE!
THENA IS THE *MOST DANGEROUS ENEMY* HERE. I MUST TAKE HER OUT OF THE BATTLE AS QUICKLY AS POSSIBLE WITH A PSIONIC ATTACK!
YOU MAY BE STRONG FOR A MUTANT, EXODUS, BUT YOU ARE NOTHING COMPARED TO *AN ETERNAL!*
KAFF KAFF
EVEN ETERNALS NEED *OXYGEN* TO BREATHE! IF I *DISSIPATE THE AIR AROUND YOU*, YOU'LL FALL LIKE ANYONE ELSE.

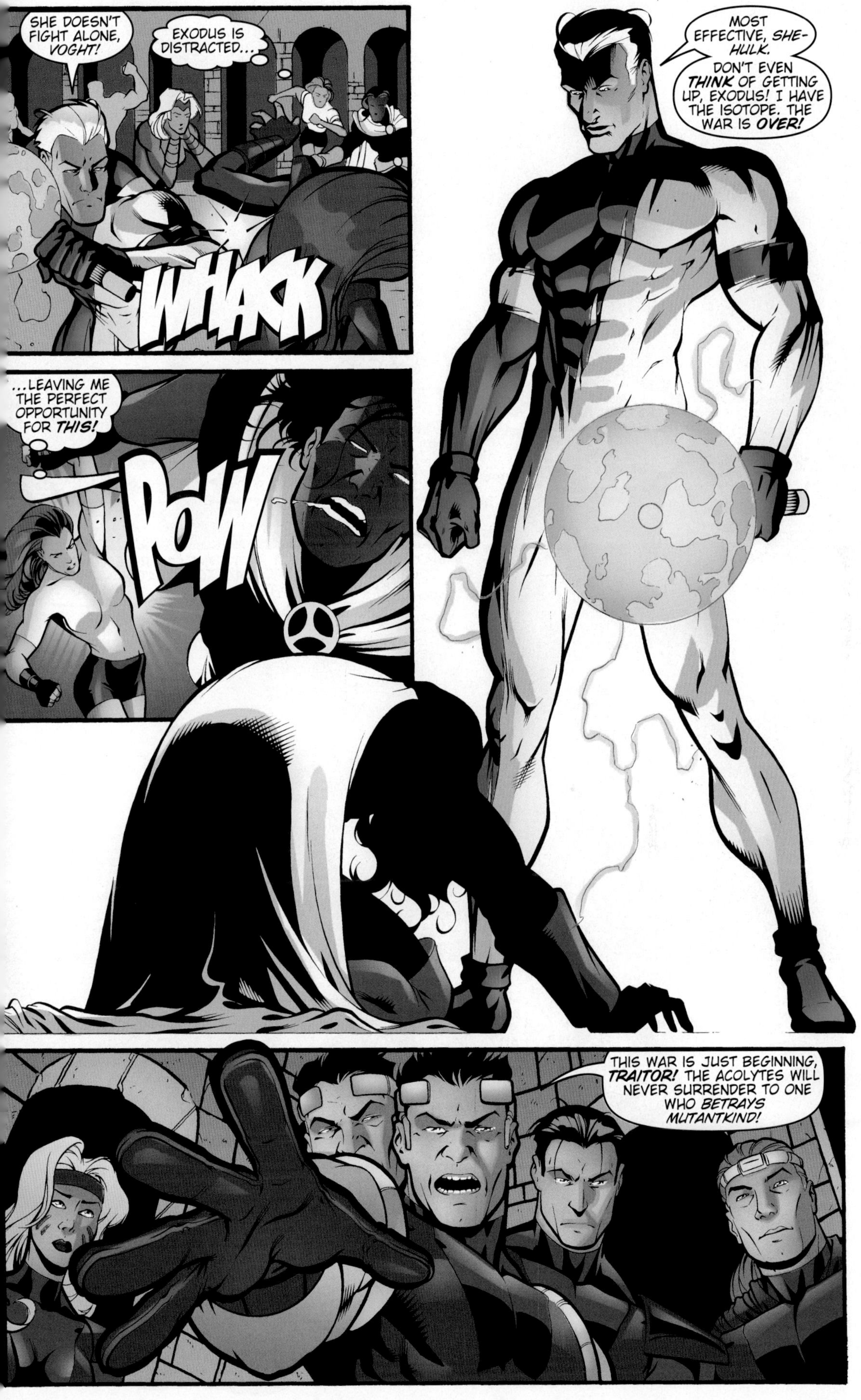

SHE DOESN'T FIGHT ALONE, VOGHT!
EXODUS IS DISTRACTED...
WHACK
...LEAVING ME THE PERFECT OPPORTUNITY FOR THIS!
POW
MOST EFFECTIVE, SHE-HULK.
DON'T EVEN THINK OF GETTING UP, EXODUS! I HAVE THE ISOTOPE. THE WAR IS OVER!
THIS WAR IS JUST BEGINNING, TRAITOR! THE ACOLYTES WILL NEVER SURRENDER TO ONE WHO BETRAYS MUTANTKIND!

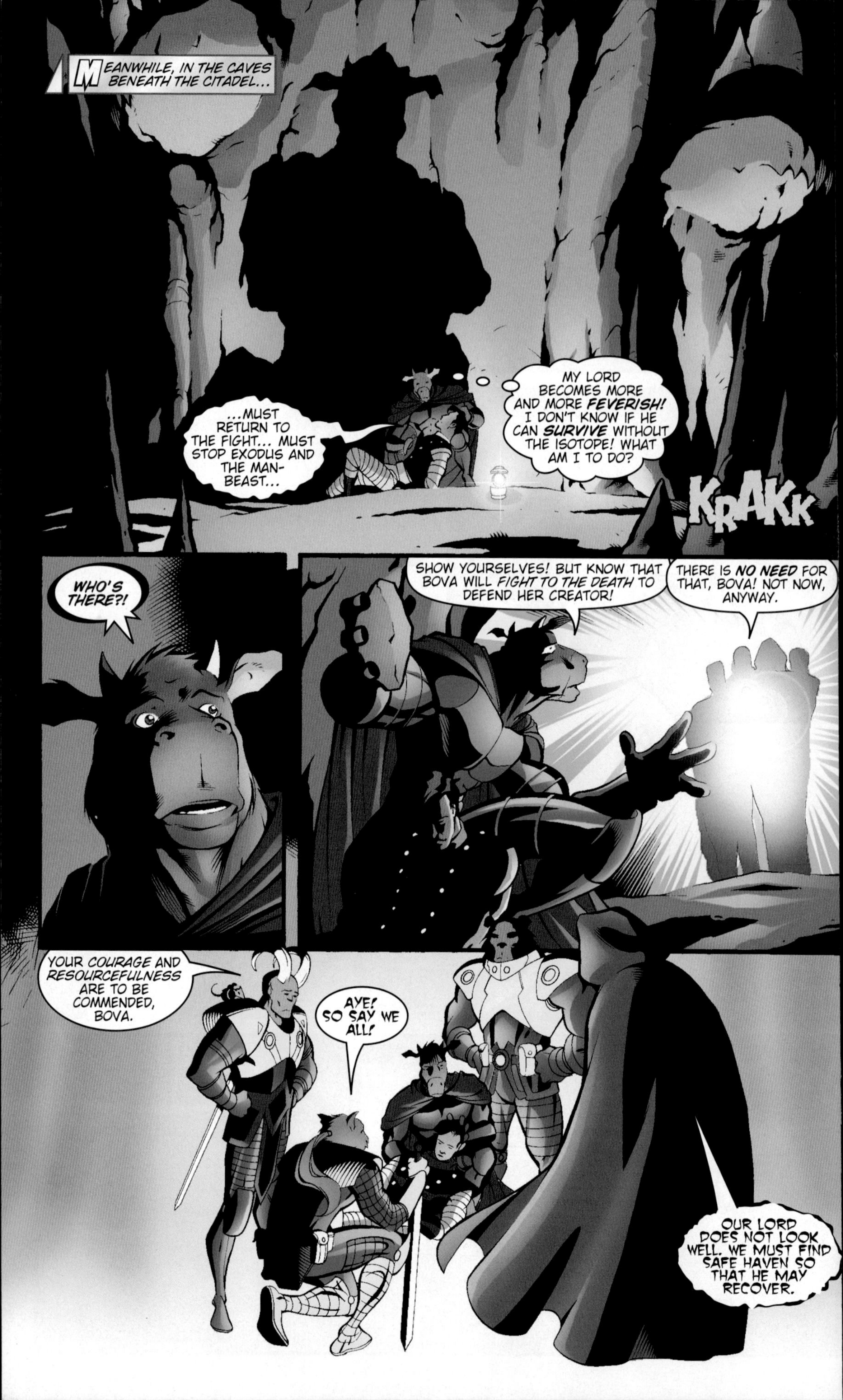
MEANWHILE, IN THE CAVES BENEATH THE CITADEL...
...MUST RETURN TO THE FIGHT... MUST STOP EXODUS AND THE MAN-BEAST...
MY LORD BECOMES MORE AND MORE FEVERISH! I DON'T KNOW IF HE CAN SURVIVE WITHOUT THE ISOTOPE! WHAT AM I TO DO?
KRAKK
WHO'S THERE?!
SHOW YOURSELVES! BUT KNOW THAT BOVA WILL FIGHT TO THE DEATH TO DEFEND HER CREATOR!
THERE IS NO NEED FOR THAT, BOVA! NOT NOW, ANYWAY.
YOUR COURAGE AND RESOURCEFULNESS ARE TO BE COMMENDED, BOVA.
AYE! SO SAY WE ALL!
OUR LORD DOES NOT LOOK WELL. WE MUST FIND SAFE HAVEN SO THAT HE MAY RECOVER.

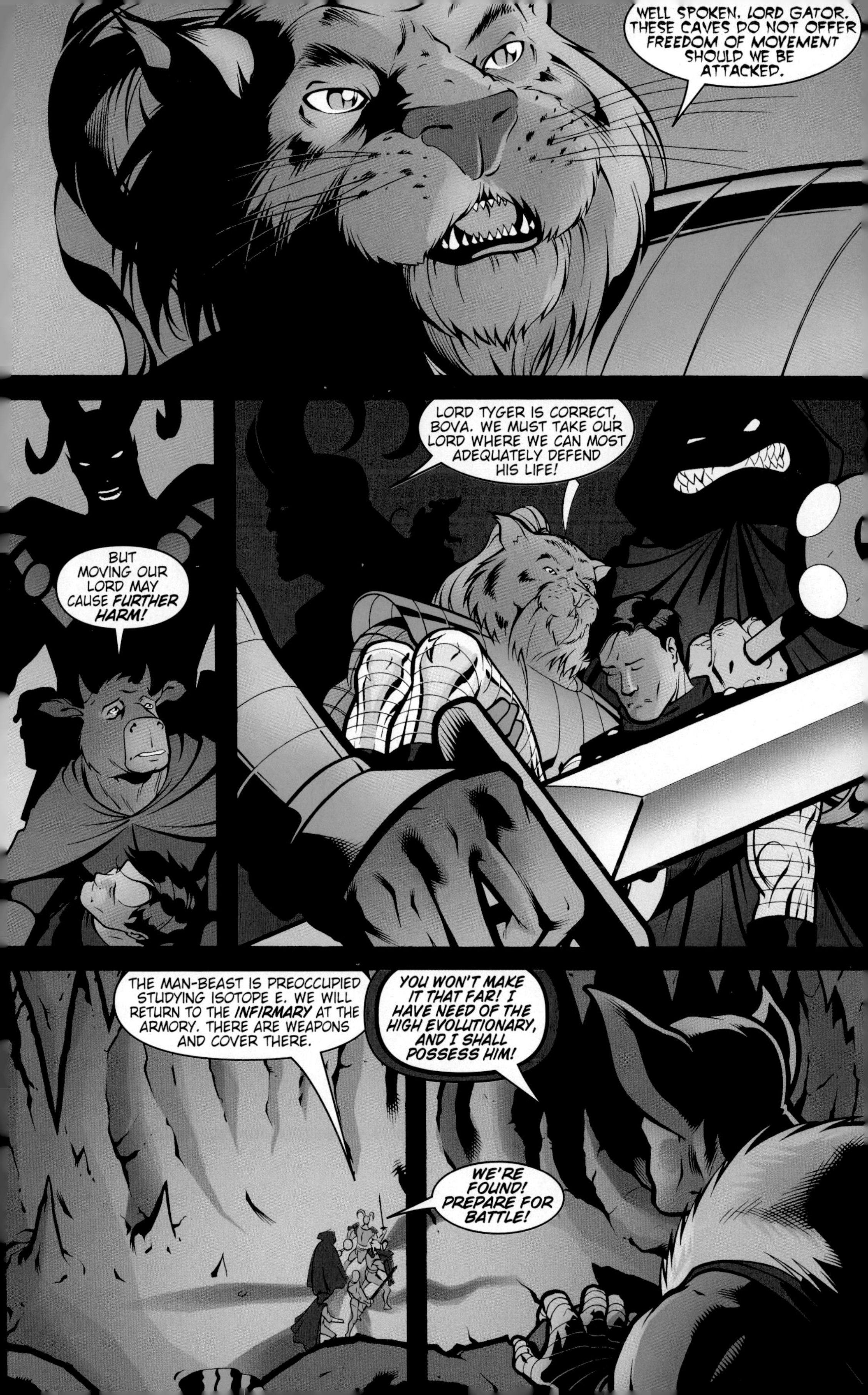
WELL SPOKEN, LORD GATOR. THESE CAVES DO NOT OFFER FREEDOM OF MOVEMENT SHOULD WE BE ATTACKED.
BUT MOVING OUR LORD MAY CAUSE FURTHER HARM!
LORD TYGER IS CORRECT, BOVA. WE MUST TAKE OUR LORD WHERE WE CAN MOST ADEQUATELY DEFEND HIS LIFE!
THE MAN-BEAST IS PREOCCUPIED STUDYING ISOTOPE E. WE WILL RETURN TO THE INFIRMARY AT THE ARMORY. THERE ARE WEAPONS AND COVER THERE.
YOU WON'T MAKE IT THAT FAR! I HAVE NEED OF THE HIGH EVOLUTIONARY, AND I SHALL POSSESS HIM!
WE'RE FOUND! PREPARE FOR BATTLE!

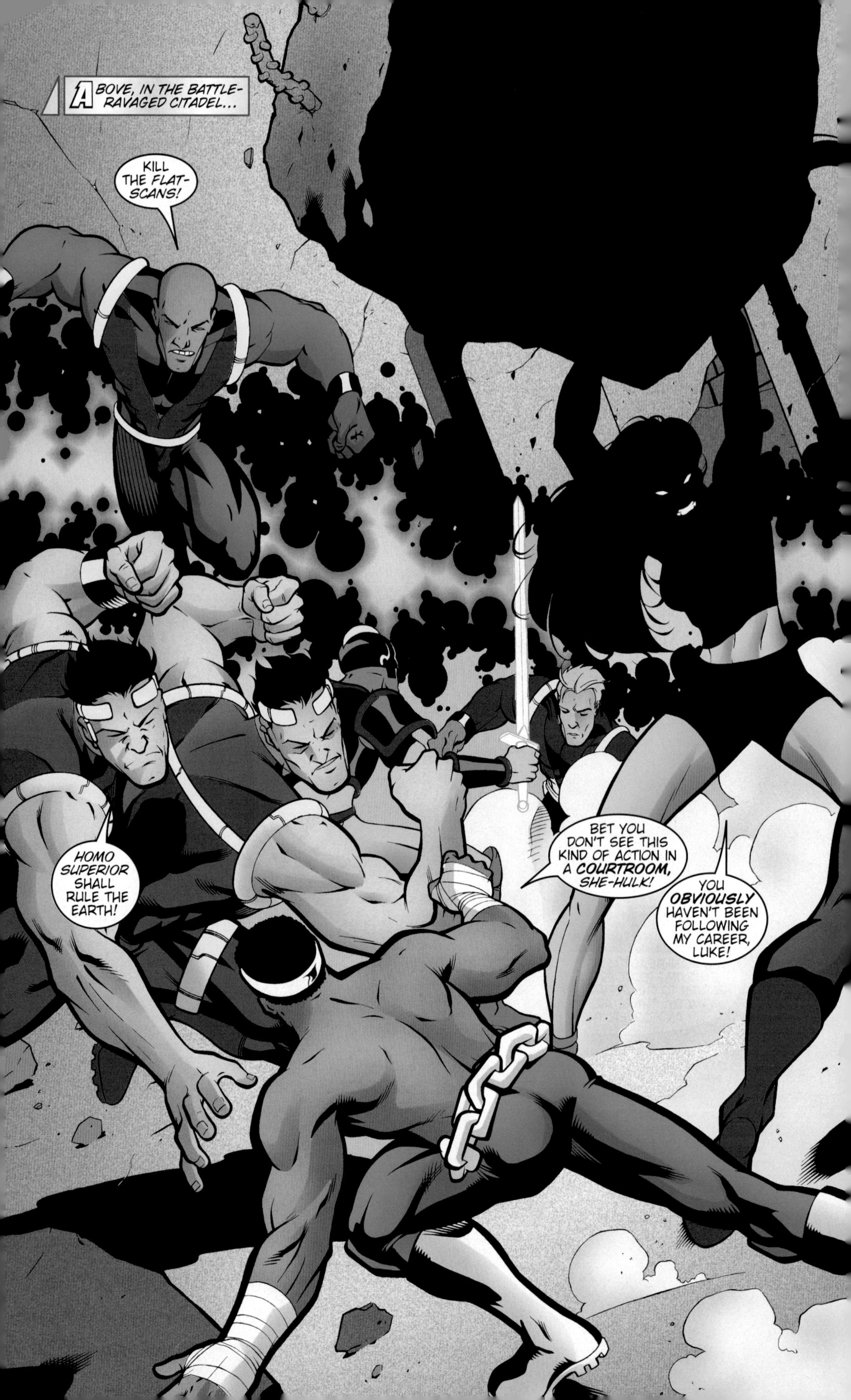
ABOVE, IN THE BATTLE-RAVAGED CITADEL...
KILL THE FLAT-SCANS!
HOMO SUPERIOR SHALL RULE THE EARTH!
BET YOU DON'T SEE THIS KIND OF ACTION IN A COURTROOM, SHE-HULK!
YOU OBVIOUSLY HAVEN'T BEEN FOLLOWING MY CAREER, LUKE!

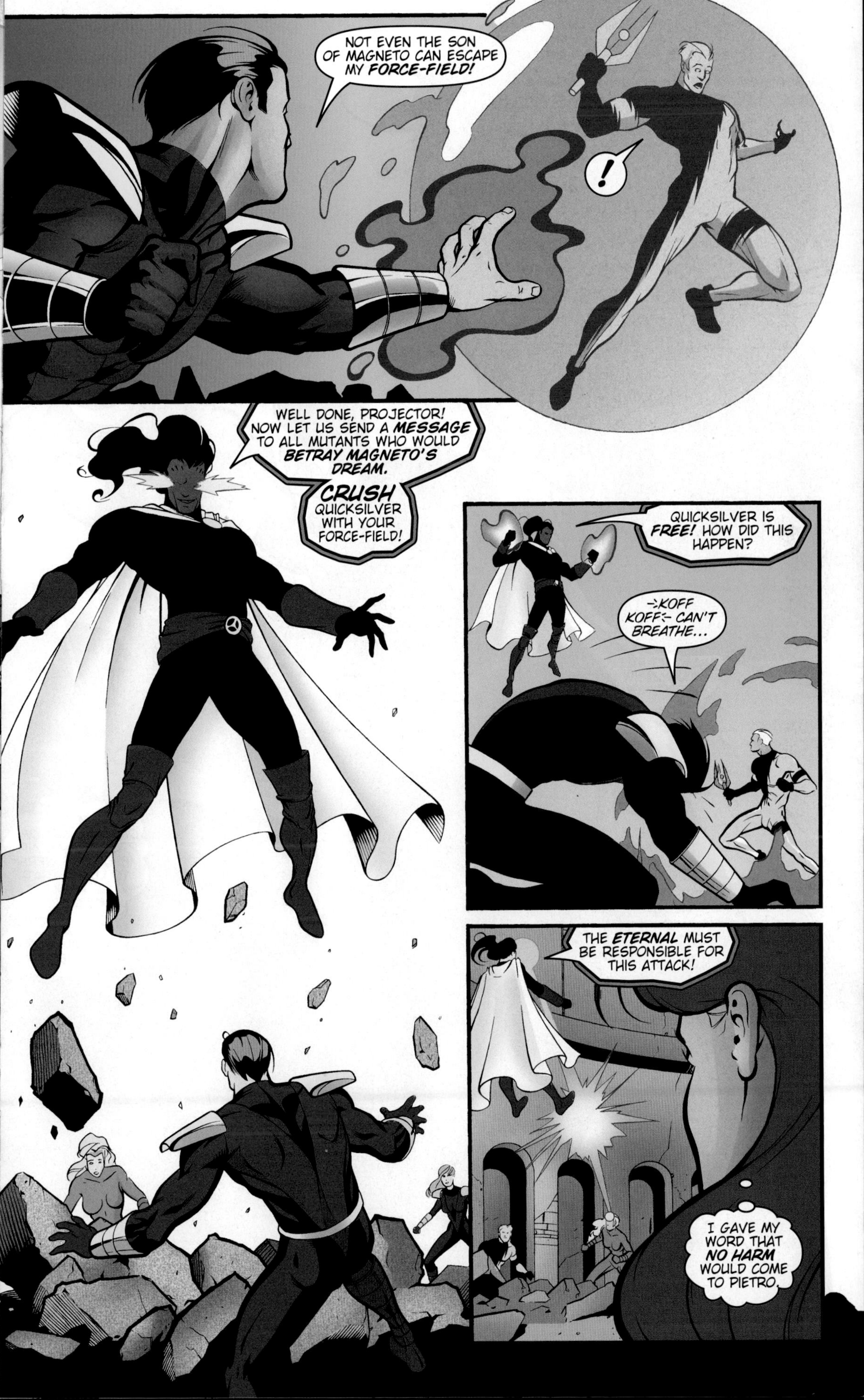
NOT EVEN THE SON OF MAGNETO CAN ESCAPE MY FORCE-FIELD!
!
WELL DONE, PROJECTOR! NOW LET US SEND A MESSAGE TO ALL MUTANTS WHO WOULD BETRAY MAGNETO'S DREAM.
CRUSH QUICKSILVER WITH YOUR FORCE-FIELD!
QUICKSILVER IS FREE! HOW DID THIS HAPPEN?
-KOFF KOFF- CAN'T BREATHE...
THE ETERNAL MUST BE RESPONSIBLE FOR THIS ATTACK!
I GAVE MY WORD THAT NO HARM WOULD COME TO PIETRO.

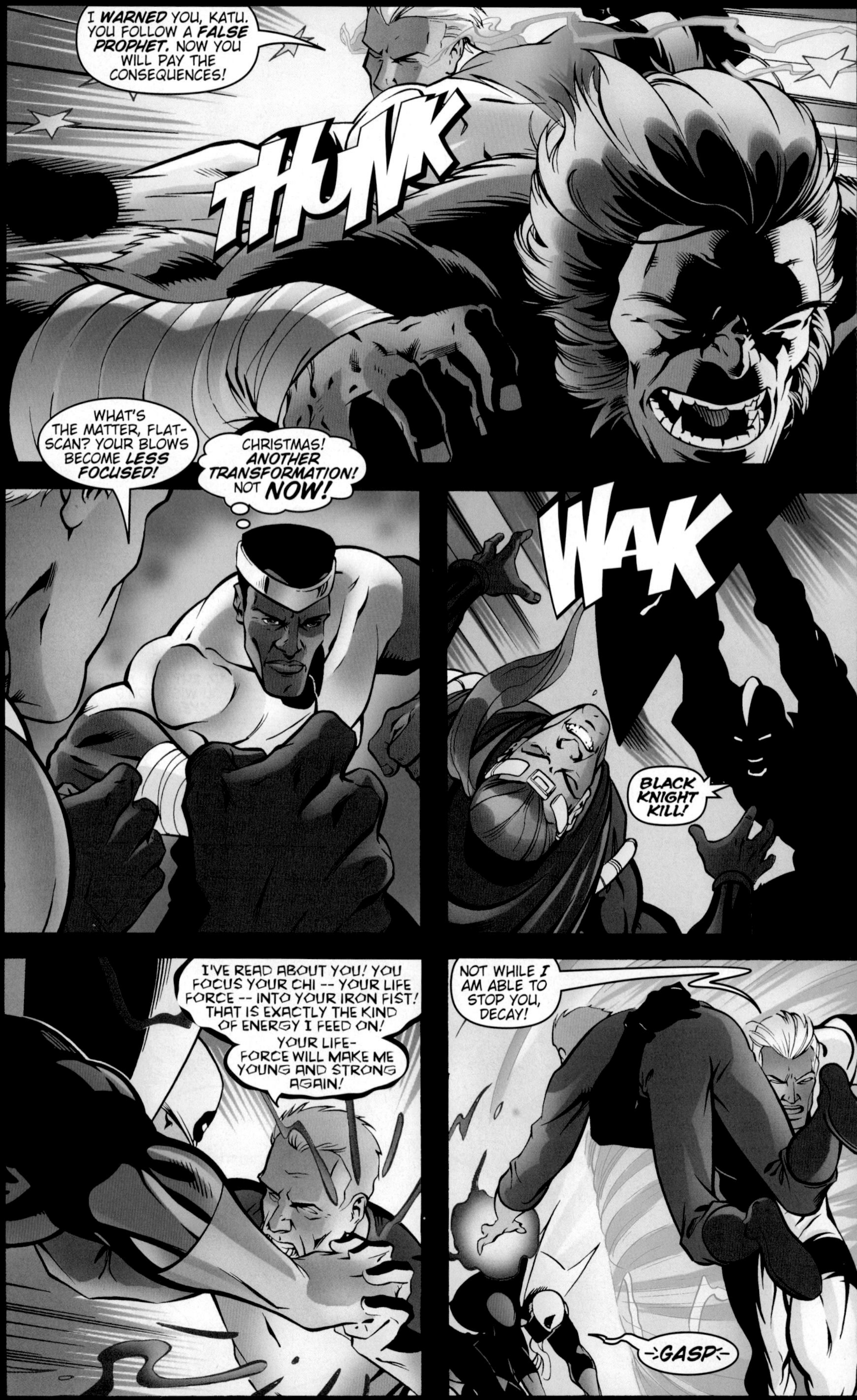
I WARNED YOU, KATU. YOU FOLLOW A FALSE PROPHET. NOW YOU WILL PAY THE CONSEQUENCES!
THUNK
WHAT'S THE MATTER, FLAT-SCAN? YOUR BLOWS BECOME LESS FOCUSED!
CHRISTMAS! ANOTHER TRANSFORMATION! NOT NOW!
WAK
BLACK KNIGHT KILL!
I'VE READ ABOUT YOU! YOU FOCUS YOUR CHI -- YOUR LIFE FORCE -- INTO YOUR IRON FIST! THAT IS EXACTLY THE KIND OF ENERGY I FEED ON!
YOUR LIFE-FORCE WILL MAKE ME YOUNG AND STRONG AGAIN!
NOT WHILE I AM ABLE TO STOP YOU, DECAY!
GASP

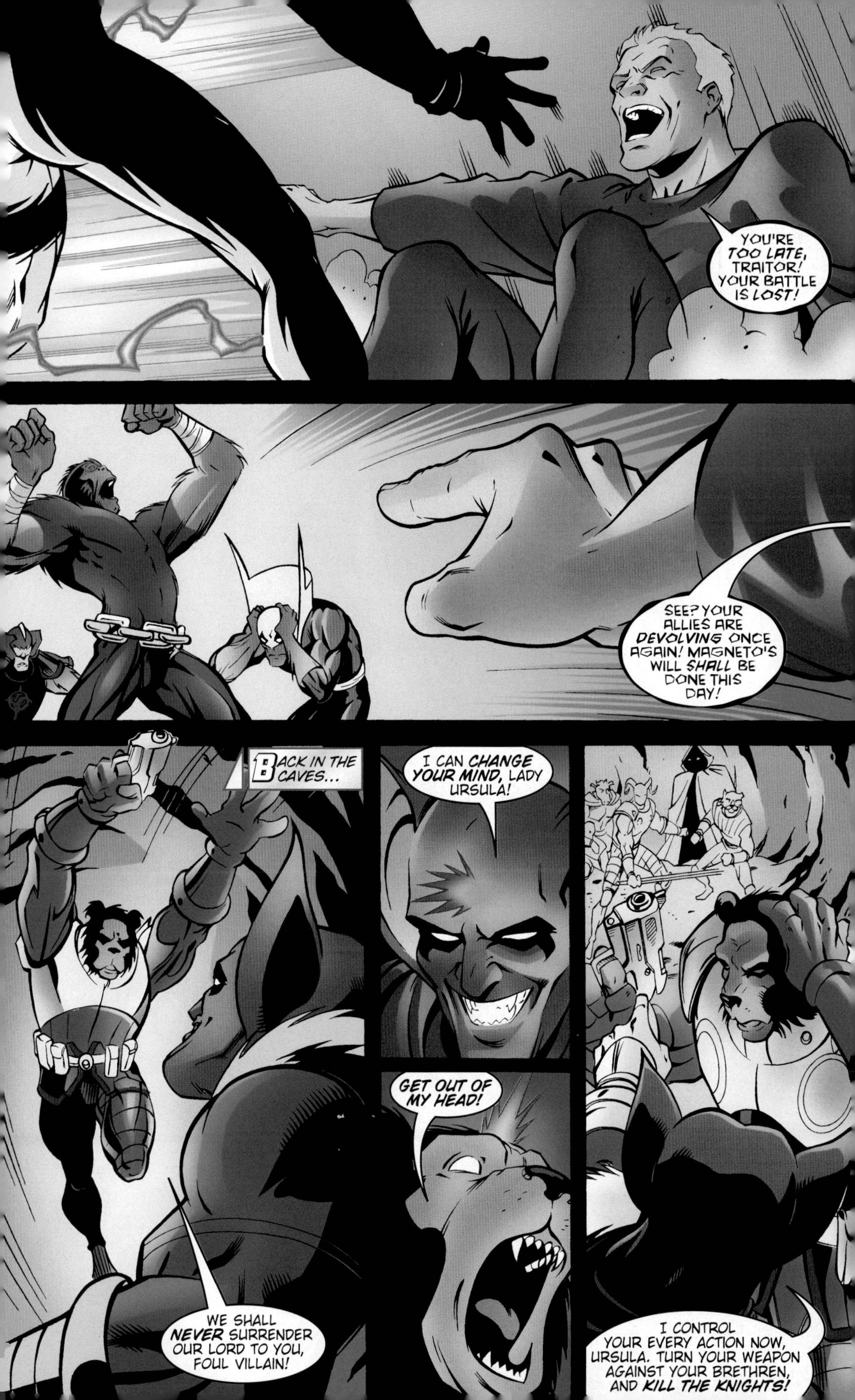
YOU'RE TOO LATE, TRAITOR! YOUR BATTLE IS LOST!
SEE? YOUR ALLIES ARE DEVOLVING ONCE AGAIN! MAGNETO'S WILL SHALL BE DONE THIS DAY!
BACK IN THE CAVES...
WE SHALL NEVER SURRENDER OUR LORD TO YOU, FOUL VILLAIN!
I CAN CHANGE YOUR MIND, LADY URSULA!
GET OUT OF MY HEAD!
I CONTROL YOUR EVERY ACTION NOW, URSULA. TURN YOUR WEAPON AGAINST YOUR BRETHREN, AND KILL THE KNIGHTS!

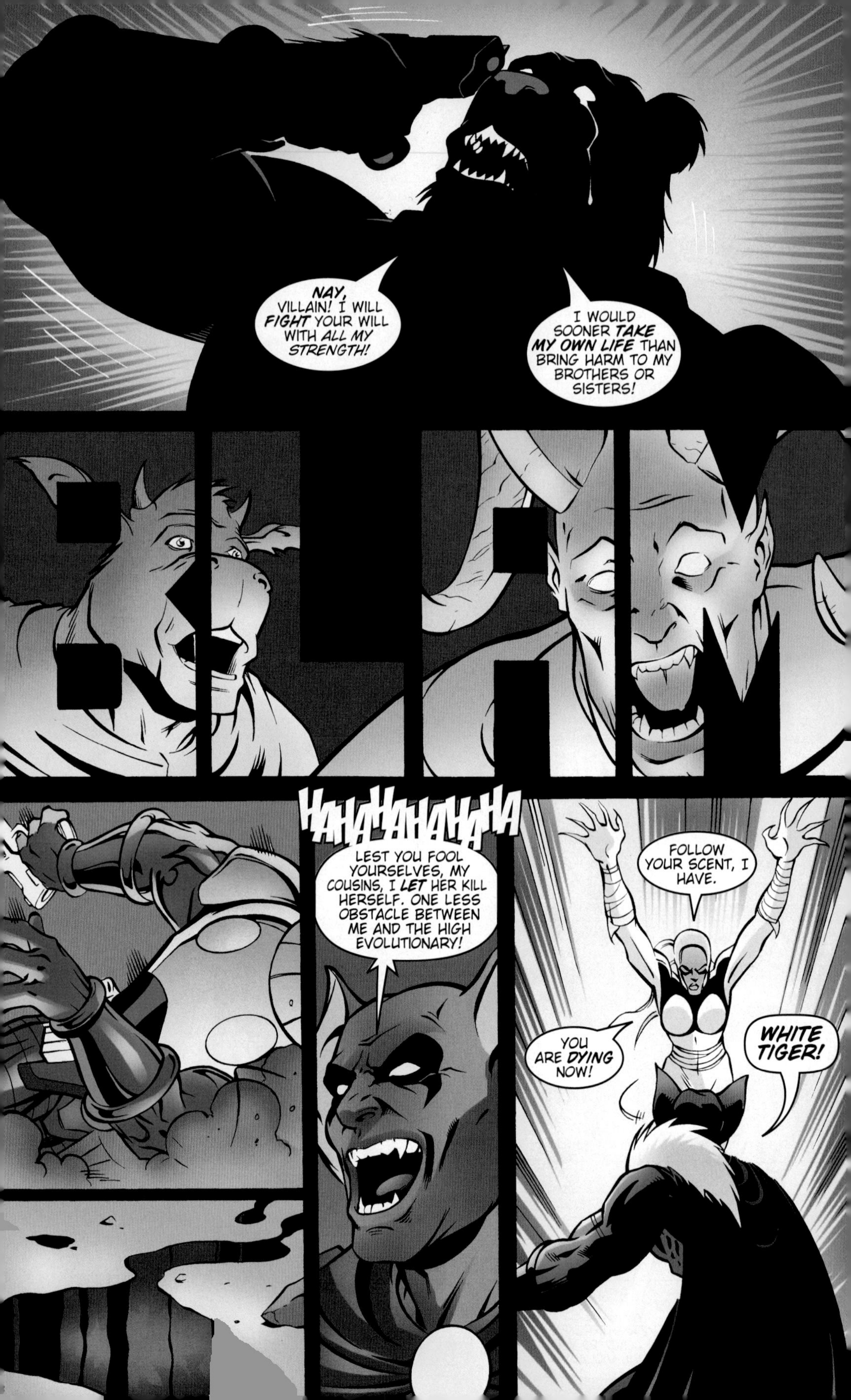
NAY, VILLAIN! I WILL FIGHT YOUR WILL WITH ALL MY STRENGTH!
I WOULD SOONER TAKE MY OWN LIFE THAN BRING HARM TO MY BROTHERS OR SISTERS!
HAHAHAHAHAHAHA
LEST YOU FOOL YOURSELVES, MY COUSINS, I LET HER KILL HERSELF. ONE LESS OBSTACLE BETWEEN ME AND THE HIGH EVOLUTIONARY!
FOLLOW YOUR SCENT, I HAVE.
YOU ARE DYING NOW!
WHITE TIGER!

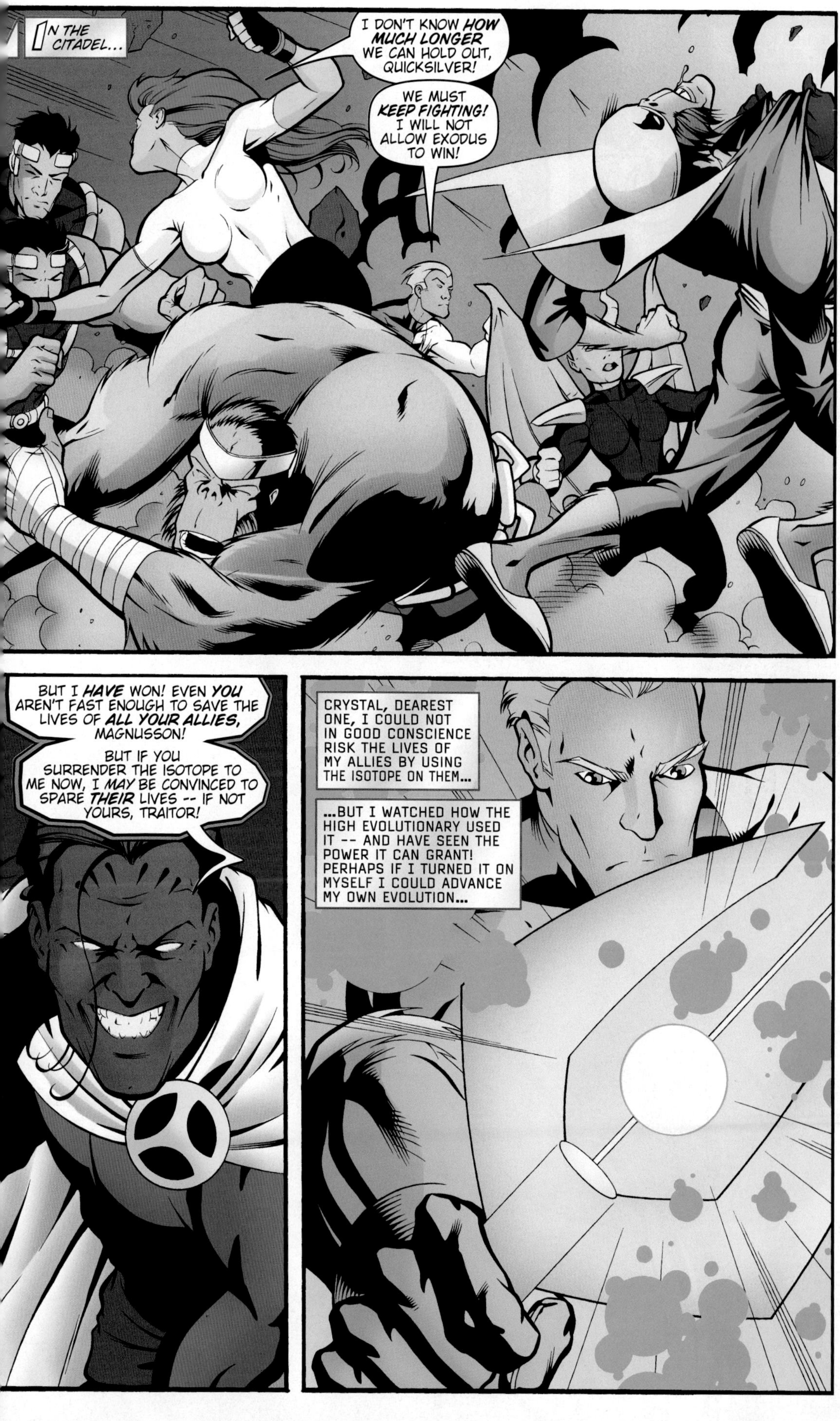
IN THE CITADEL...
I DON'T KNOW HOW MUCH LONGER WE CAN HOLD OUT, QUICKSILVER!
WE MUST KEEP FIGHTING! I WILL NOT ALLOW EXODUS TO WIN!
BUT I HAVE WON! EVEN YOU AREN'T FAST ENOUGH TO SAVE THE LIVES OF ALL YOUR ALLIES, MAGNUSSON!
BUT IF YOU SURRENDER THE ISOTOPE TO ME NOW, I MAY BE CONVINCED TO SPARE THEIR LIVES -- IF NOT YOURS, TRAITOR!
CRYSTAL, DEAREST ONE, I COULD NOT IN GOOD CONSCIENCE RISK THE LIVES OF MY ALLIES BY USING THE ISOTOPE ON THEM...
...BUT I WATCHED HOW THE HIGH EVOLUTIONARY USED IT -- AND HAVE SEEN THE POWER IT CAN GRANT! PERHAPS IF I TURNED IT ON MYSELF I COULD ADVANCE MY OWN EVOLUTION...

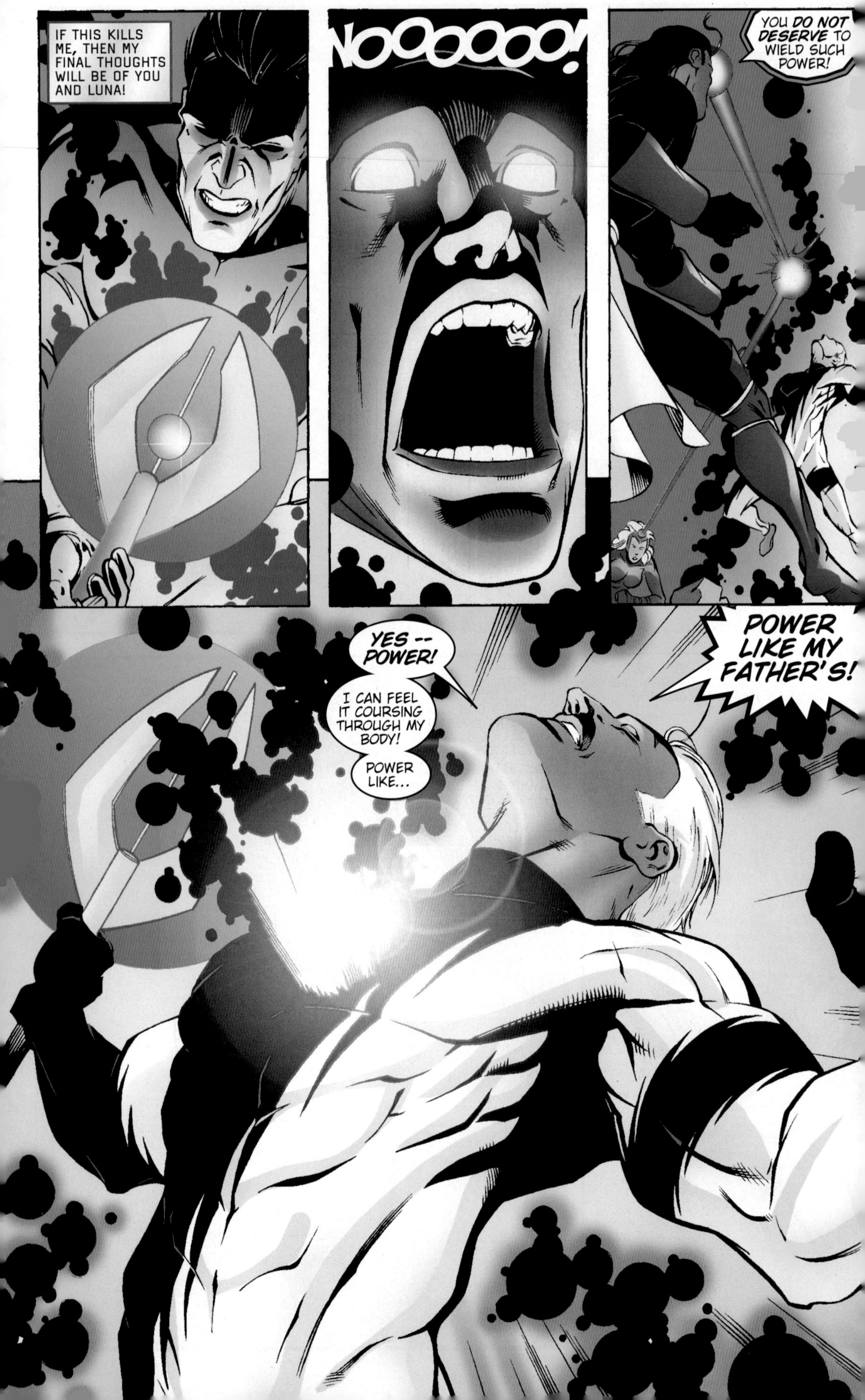

IF THIS KILLS ME, THEN MY FINAL THOUGHTS WILL BE OF YOU AND LUNA!
NOOOOOO!
YOU DO NOT DESERVE TO WIELD SUCH POWER!
YES -- POWER!
I CAN FEEL IT COURSING THROUGH MY BODY!
POWER LIKE...
POWER LIKE MY FATHER'S!

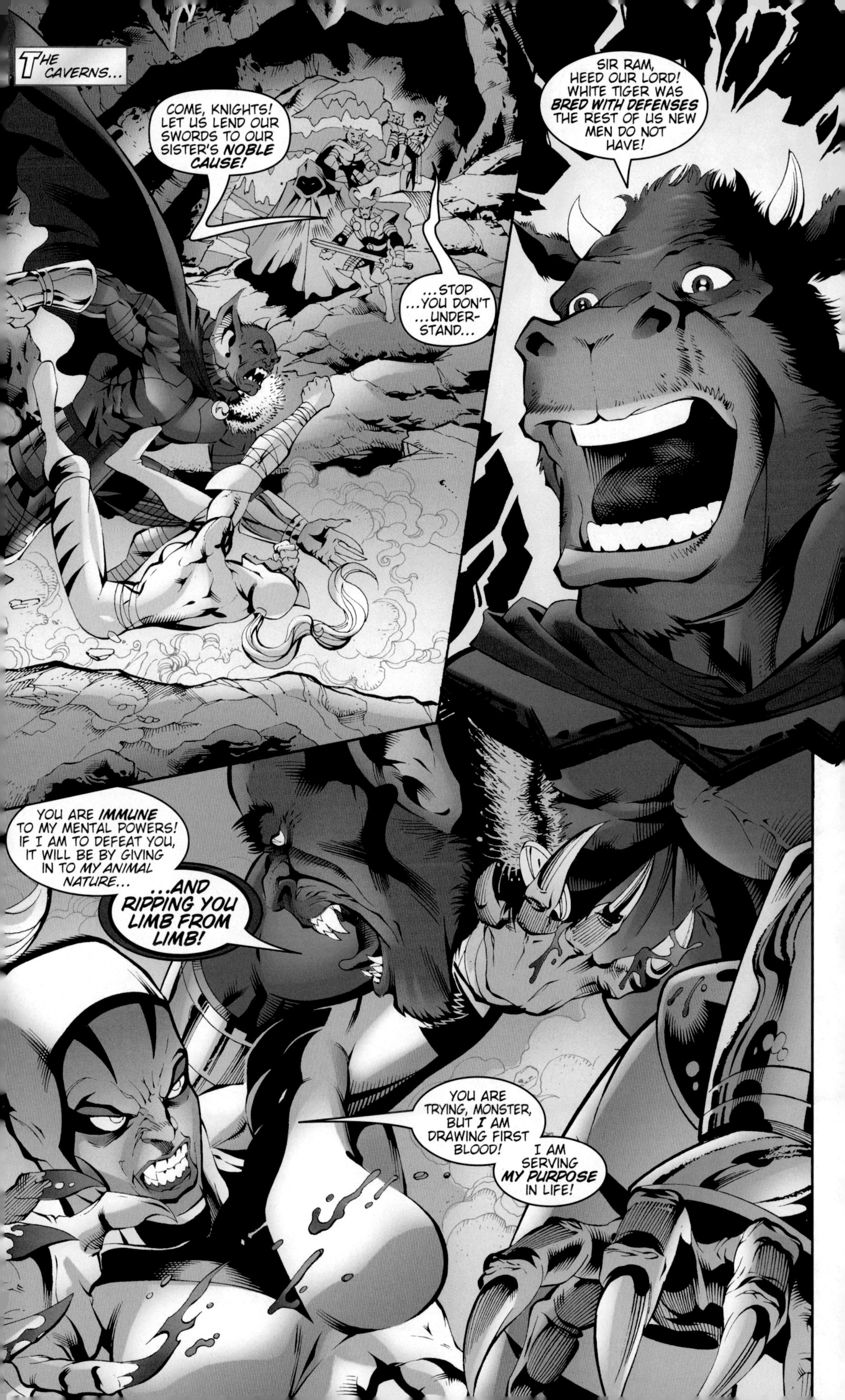
THE CAVERNS...
COME, KNIGHTS! LET US LEND OUR SWORDS TO OUR SISTER'S NOBLE CAUSE!
...STOP ...YOU DON'T ...UNDER-STAND...
SIR RAM, HEED OUR LORD! WHITE TIGER WAS BRED WITH DEFENSES THE REST OF US NEW MEN DO NOT HAVE!
YOU ARE IMMUNE TO MY MENTAL POWERS! IF I AM TO DEFEAT YOU, IT WILL BE BY GIVING IN TO MY ANIMAL NATURE...
...AND RIPPING YOU LIMB FROM LIMB!
YOU ARE TRYING, MONSTER, BUT I AM DRAWING FIRST BLOOD!
I AM SERVING MY PURPOSE IN LIFE!

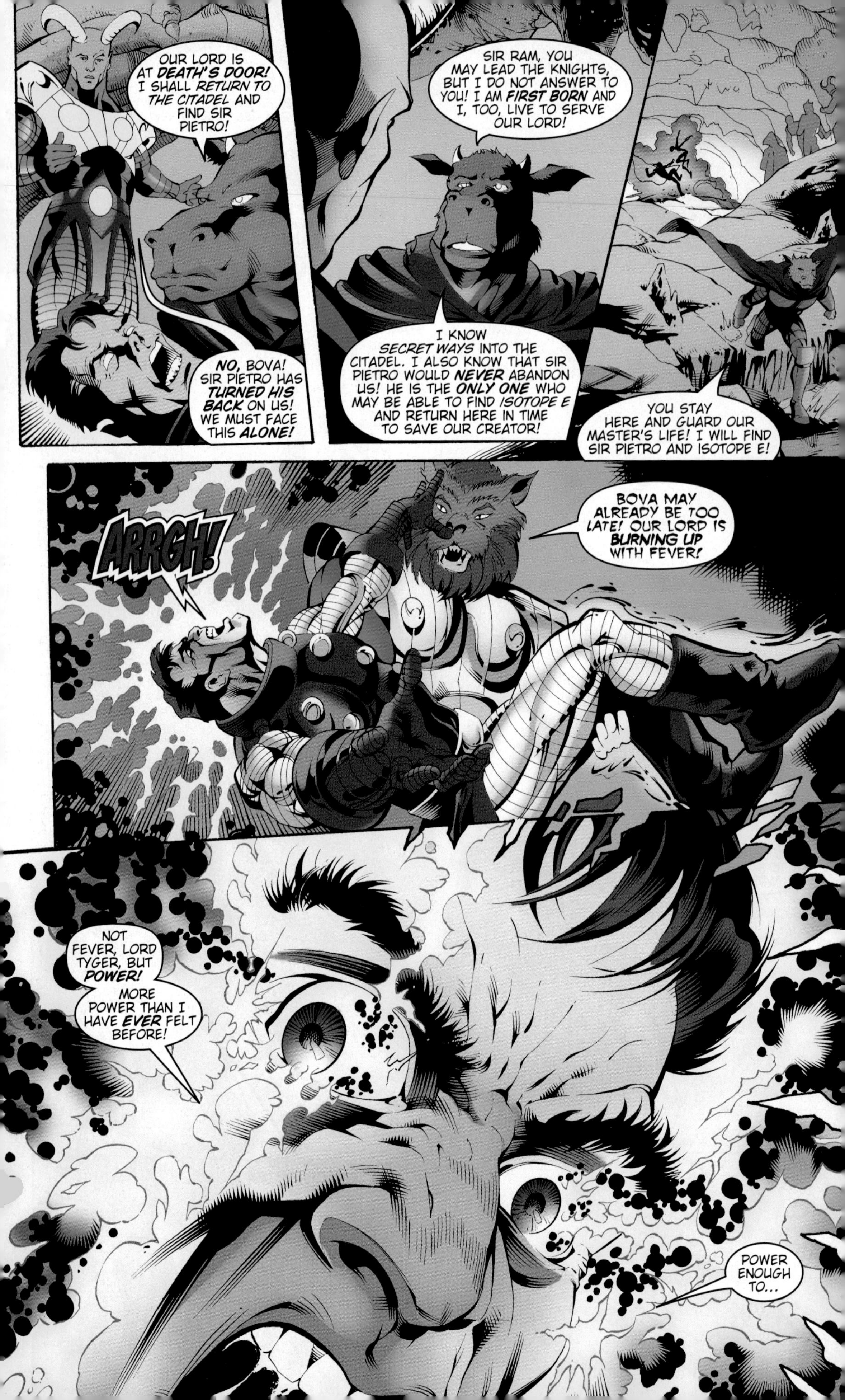
OUR LORD IS AT DEATH'S DOOR! I SHALL RETURN TO THE CITADEL AND FIND SIR PIETRO!
NO, BOVA! SIR PIETRO HAS TURNED HIS BACK ON US! WE MUST FACE THIS ALONE!
SIR RAM, YOU MAY LEAD THE KNIGHTS, BUT I DO NOT ANSWER TO YOU! I AM FIRST BORN AND I, TOO, LIVE TO SERVE OUR LORD!
I KNOW SECRET WAYS INTO THE CITADEL. I ALSO KNOW THAT SIR PIETRO WOULD NEVER ABANDON US! HE IS THE ONLY ONE WHO MAY BE ABLE TO FIND ISOTOPE E AND RETURN HERE IN TIME TO SAVE OUR CREATOR!
YOU STAY HERE AND GUARD OUR MASTER'S LIFE! I WILL FIND SIR PIETRO AND ISOTOPE E!
ARRGH!
BOVA MAY ALREADY BE TOO LATE! OUR LORD IS BURNING UP WITH FEVER!
NOT FEVER, LORD TYGER, BUT POWER!
MORE POWER THAN I HAVE EVER FELT BEFORE!
POWER ENOUGH TO...

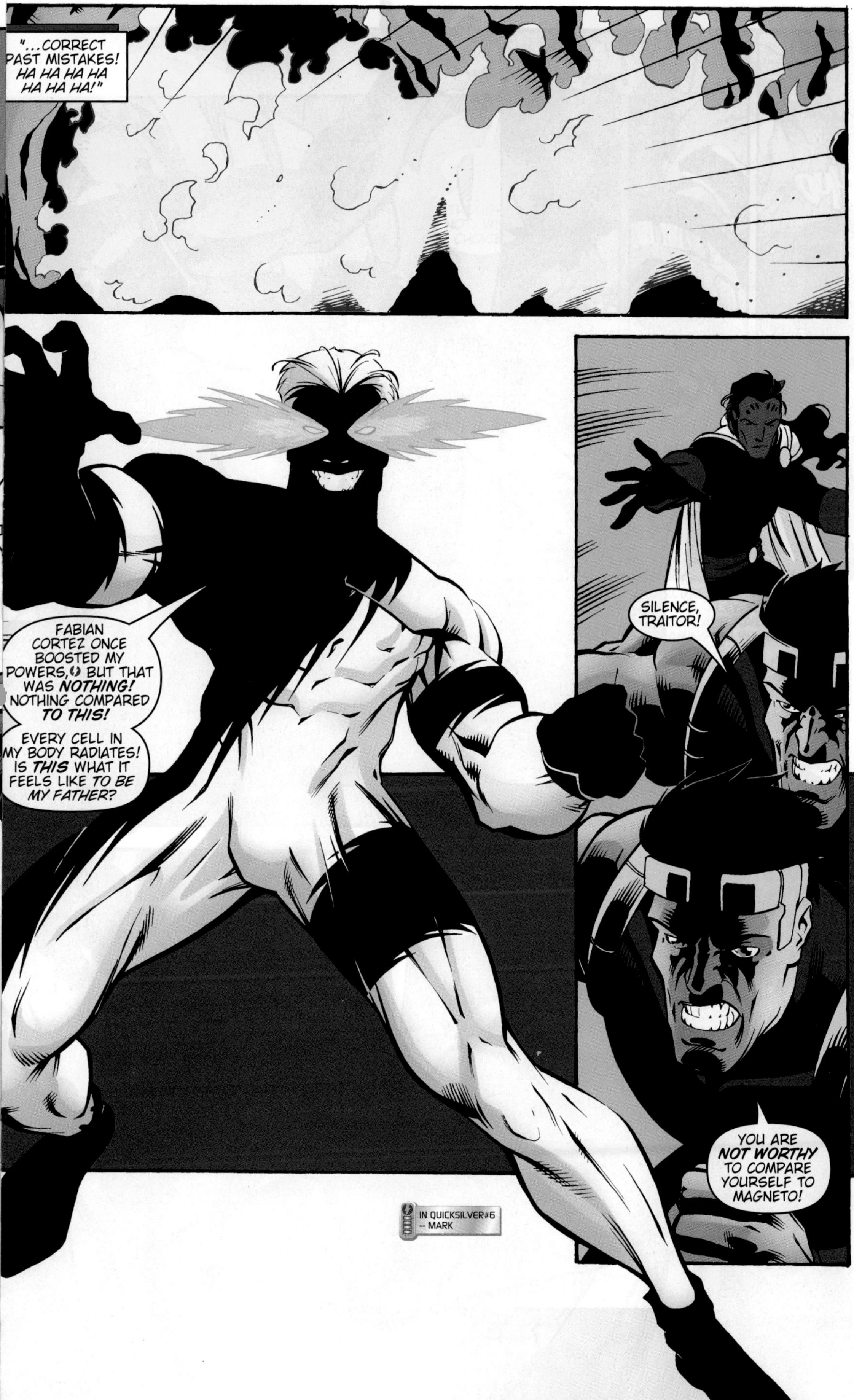
"...CORRECT PAST MISTAKES! HA HA HA HA HA HA HA!"
FABIAN CORTEZ ONCE BOOSTED MY POWERS, BUT THAT WAS NOTHING! NOTHING COMPARED TO THIS!
EVERY CELL IN MY BODY RADIATES! IS THIS WHAT IT FEELS LIKE TO BE MY FATHER?
SILENCE, TRAITOR!
YOU ARE NOT WORTHY TO COMPARE YOURSELF TO MAGNETO!
IN QUICKSILVER#6 -- MARK

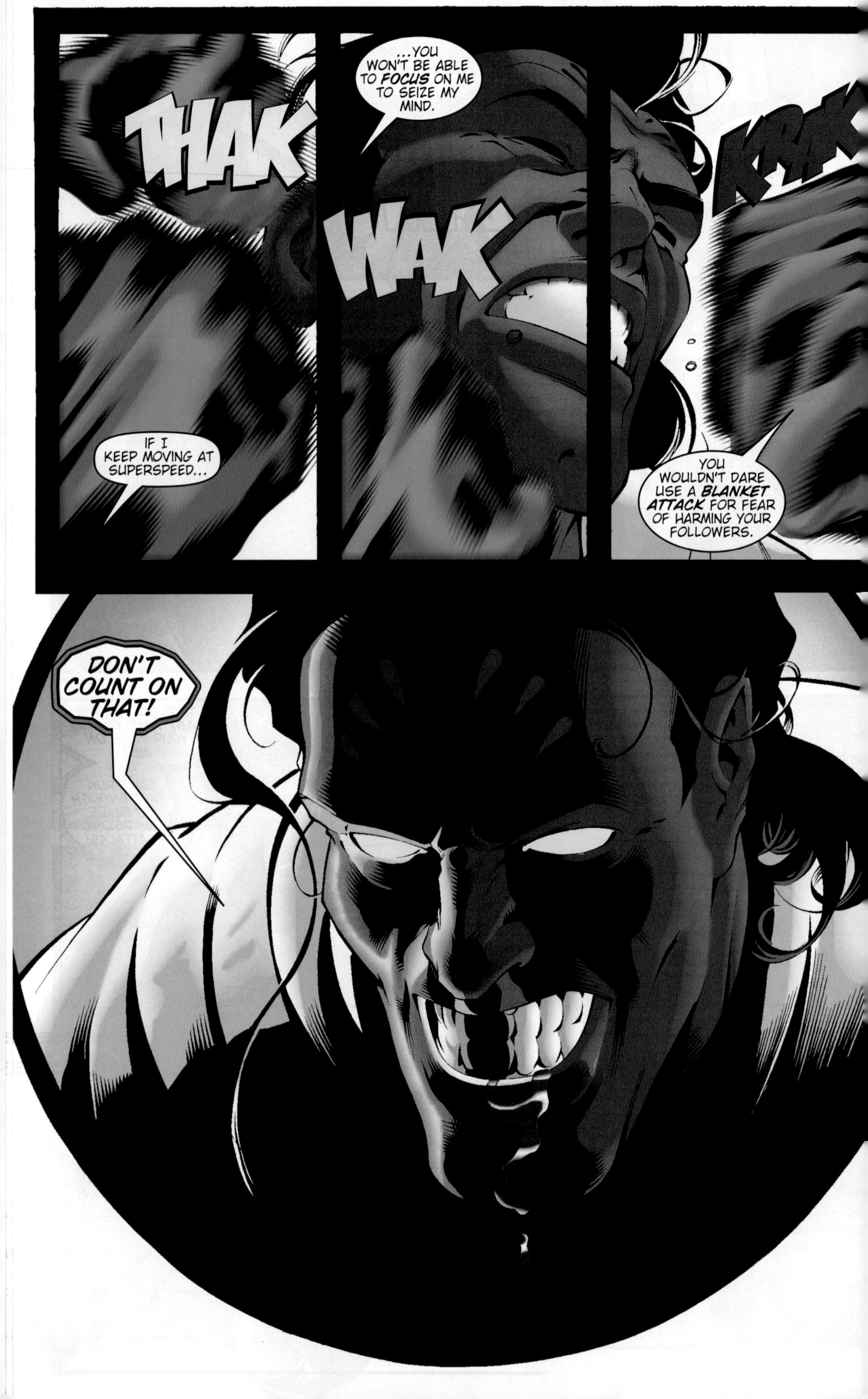
THAK
IF I KEEP MOVING AT SUPERSPEED...
...YOU WON'T BE ABLE TO FOCUS ON ME TO SEIZE MY MIND.
WAK
KRAK
YOU WOULDN'T DARE USE A BLANKET ATTACK FOR FEAR OF HARMING YOUR FOLLOWERS.
DON'T COUNT ON THAT!

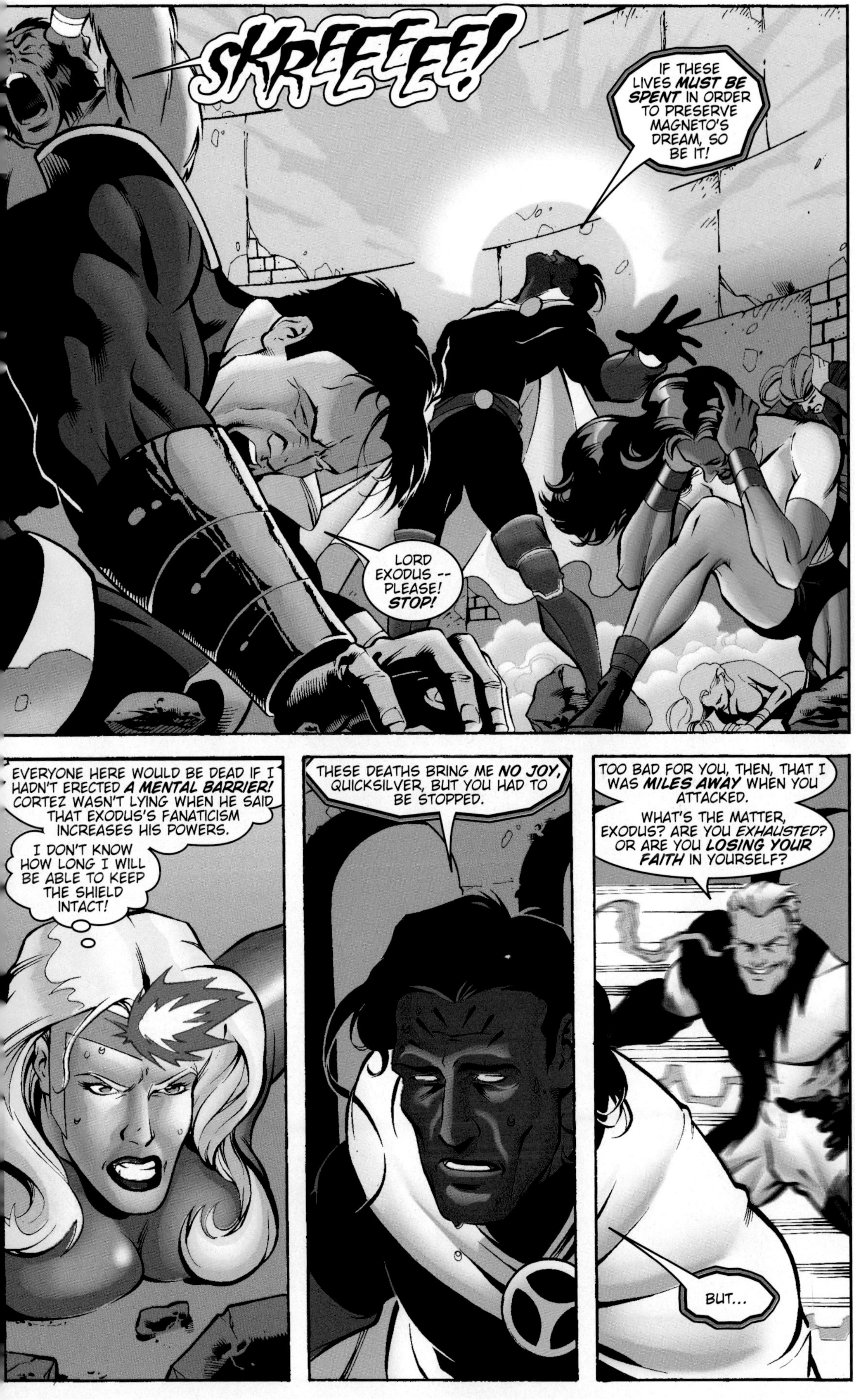
SKREEEEE!
IF THESE LIVES MUST BE SPENT IN ORDER TO PRESERVE MAGNETO'S DREAM, SO BE IT!
LORD EXODUS -- PLEASE! STOP!
EVERYONE HERE WOULD BE DEAD IF I HADN'T ERECTED A MENTAL BARRIER! CORTEZ WASN'T LYING WHEN HE SAID THAT EXODUS'S FANATICISM INCREASES HIS POWERS.
I DON'T KNOW HOW LONG I WILL BE ABLE TO KEEP THE SHIELD INTACT!
THESE DEATHS BRING ME NO JOY, QUICKSILVER, BUT YOU HAD TO BE STOPPED.
TOO BAD FOR YOU, THEN, THAT I WAS MILES AWAY WHEN YOU ATTACKED.
WHAT'S THE MATTER, EXODUS? ARE YOU EXHAUSTED? OR ARE YOU LOSING YOUR FAITH IN YOURSELF?
BUT...

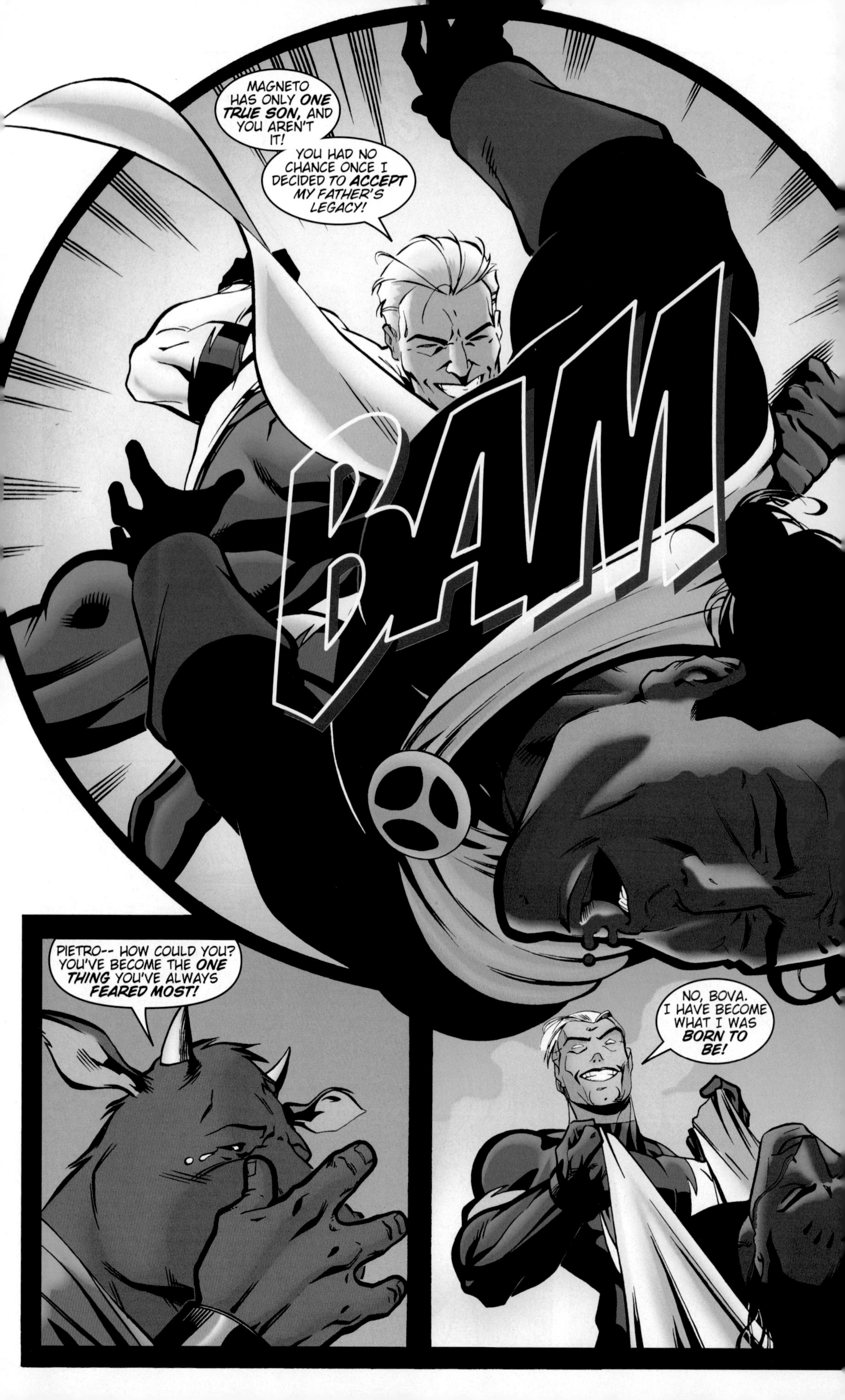
MAGNETO HAS ONLY ONE TRUE SON, AND YOU AREN'T IT!
YOU HAD NO CHANCE ONCE I DECIDED TO ACCEPT MY FATHER'S LEGACY!
BAM
PIETRO-- HOW COULD YOU? YOU'VE BECOME THE ONE THING YOU'VE ALWAYS FEARED MOST!
NO, BOVA. I HAVE BECOME WHAT I WAS BORN TO BE!

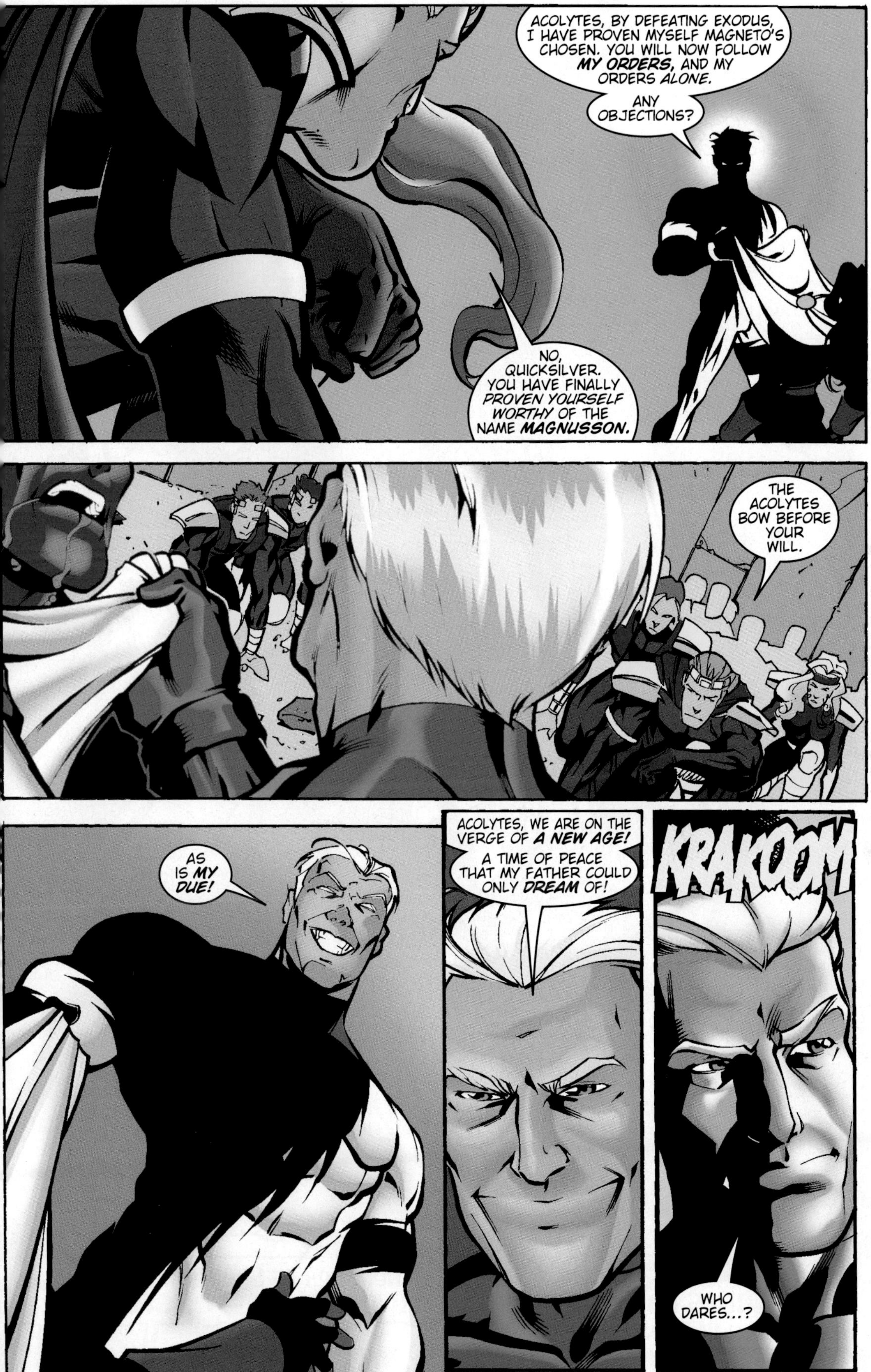

ACOLYTES, BY DEFEATING EXODUS, I HAVE PROVEN MYSELF MAGNETO'S CHOSEN. YOU WILL NOW FOLLOW **MY ORDERS,** AND MY ORDERS *ALONE.*
ANY OBJECTIONS?
NO, QUICKSILVER. YOU HAVE FINALLY *PROVEN YOURSELF WORTHY* OF THE NAME **MAGNUSSON.**
THE ACOLYTES BOW BEFORE YOUR WILL.
AS IS **MY DUE!**
ACOLYTES, WE ARE ON THE VERGE OF ***A NEW AGE!***
A TIME OF PEACE THAT MY FATHER COULD ONLY ***DREAM*** OF!
KRAKOOM
WHO DARES...?

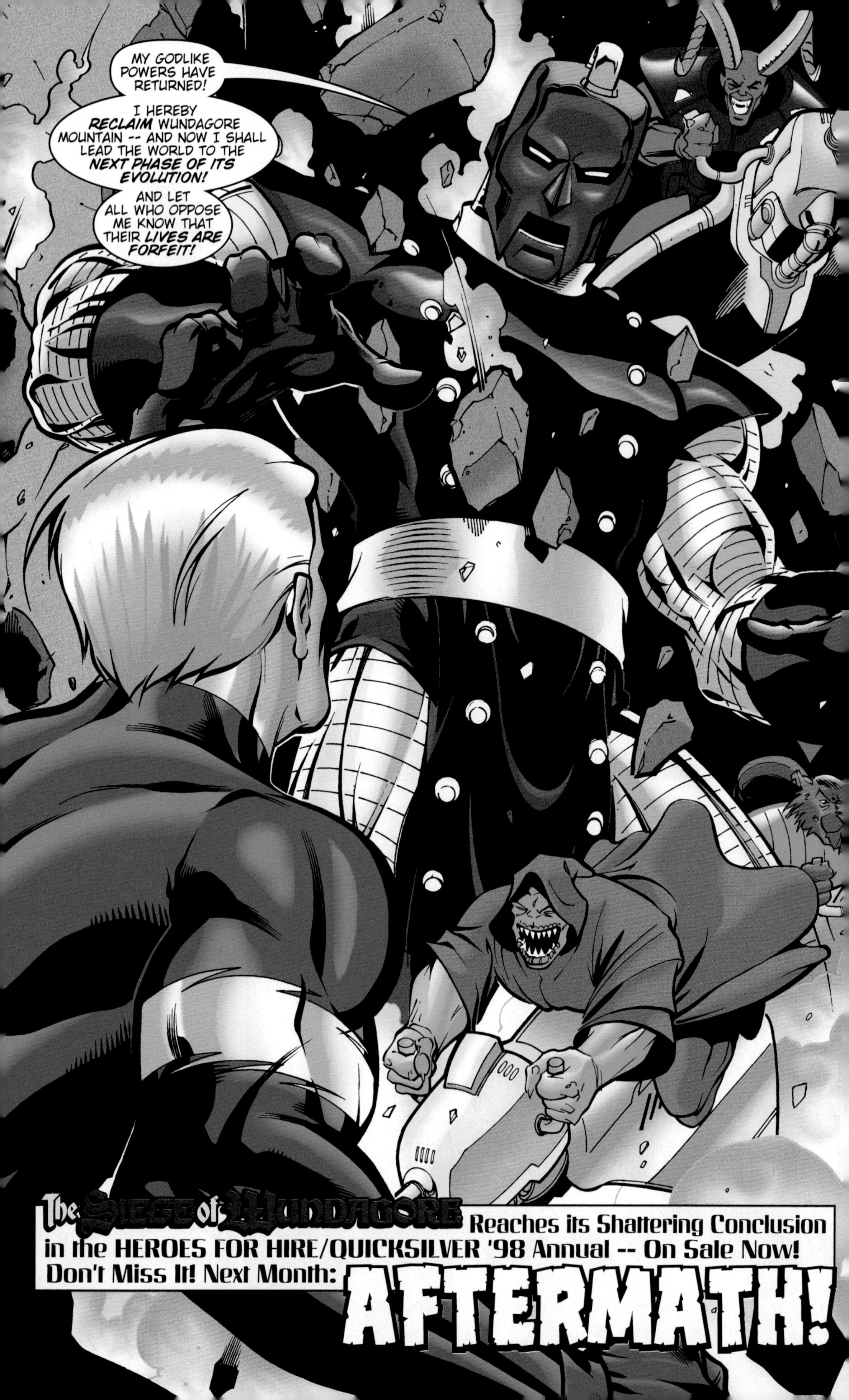
MY GODLIKE POWERS HAVE RETURNED!
I HEREBY RECLAIM WUNDAGORE MOUNTAIN -- AND NOW I SHALL LEAD THE WORLD TO THE NEXT PHASE OF ITS EVOLUTION!
AND LET ALL WHO OPPOSE ME KNOW THAT THEIR LIVES ARE FORFEIT!
The Siege of Wundagore Reaches its Shattering Conclusion in the HEROES FOR HIRE/QUICKSILVER '98 Annual -- On Sale Now! Don't Miss It! Next Month:
AFTERMATH!

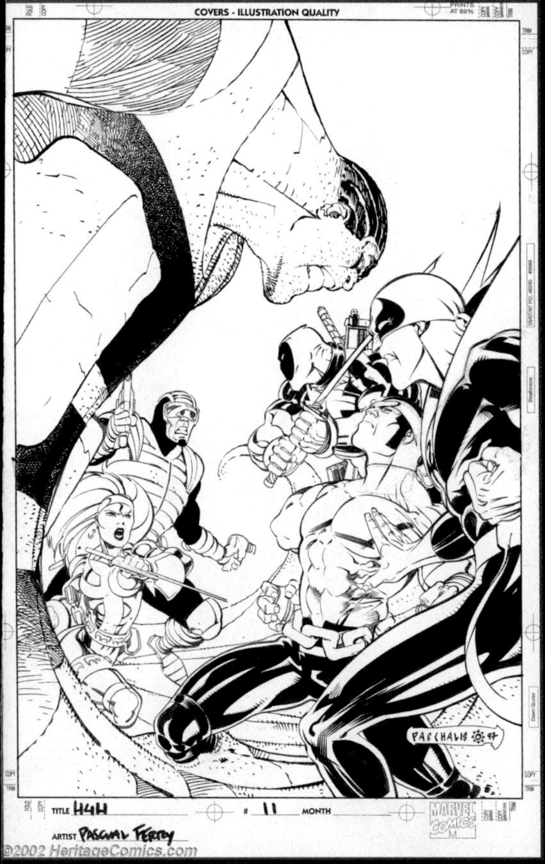

COVERS - ILLUSTRATION QUALITY
PRINTS AT 69%
PASCHALIS 97
TITLE H4H # 11 MONTH
ARTIST PASQUAL FERRY
©2002 HeritageComics.com

Heroes For Hire #11, cover art by **PASQUAL FERRY**

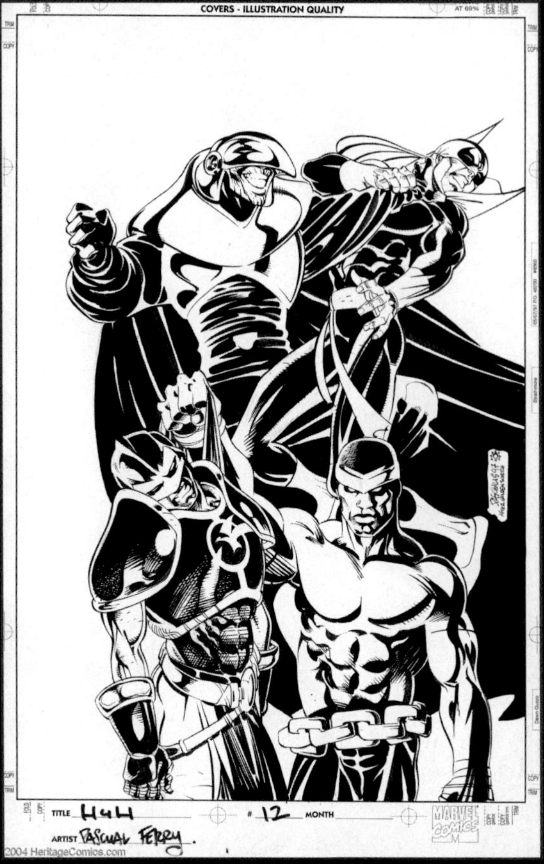

COVERS - ILLUSTRATION QUALITY
AT 69%
TITLE H4H # 12 MONTH
ARTIST PASQUAL FERRY.
2004 HeritageComics.com

Heroes For Hire #12, cover art by **PASQUAL FERRY**

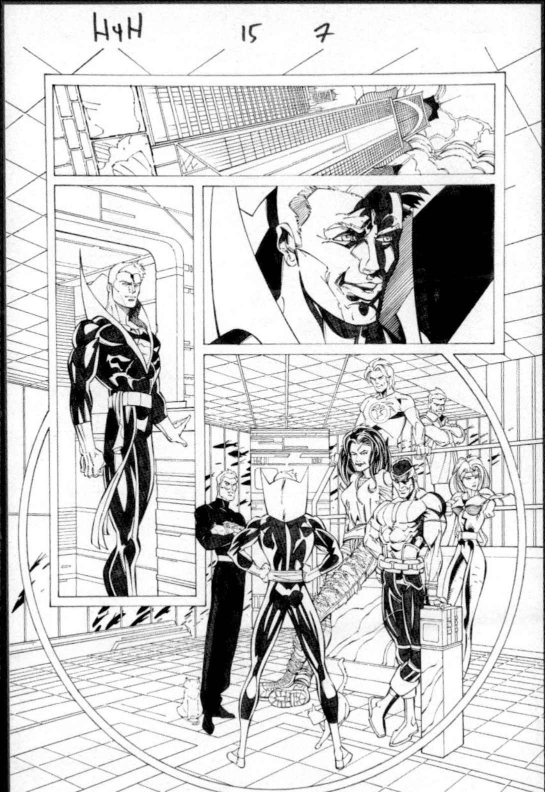

H4H 15 7

Heroes For Hire #15, page 7 art by
PASQUAL FERRY & **JAIME MENDOZA**

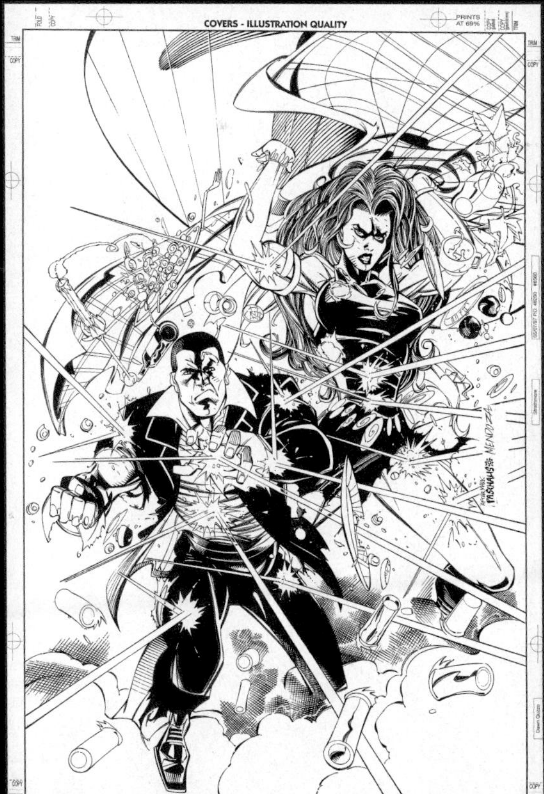

COVERS - ILLUSTRATION QUALITY
PRINTS AT 69%
TITLE H4H # 17 MONTH
ARTIST PASQUAL FERRY - JAIME MENDOZA

Heroes For Hire #17, cover art by
PASQUAL FERRY & **JAIME MENDOZA**

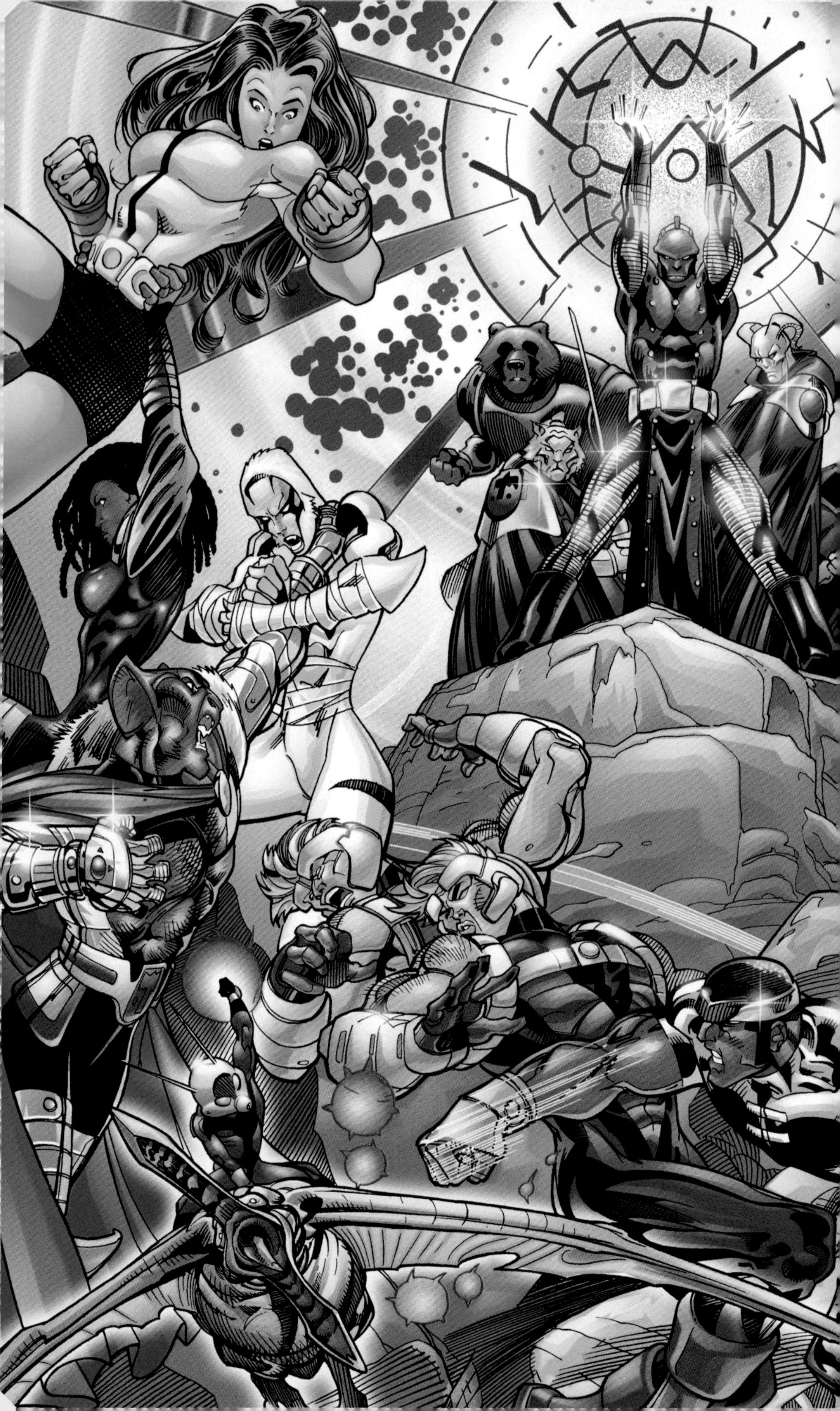

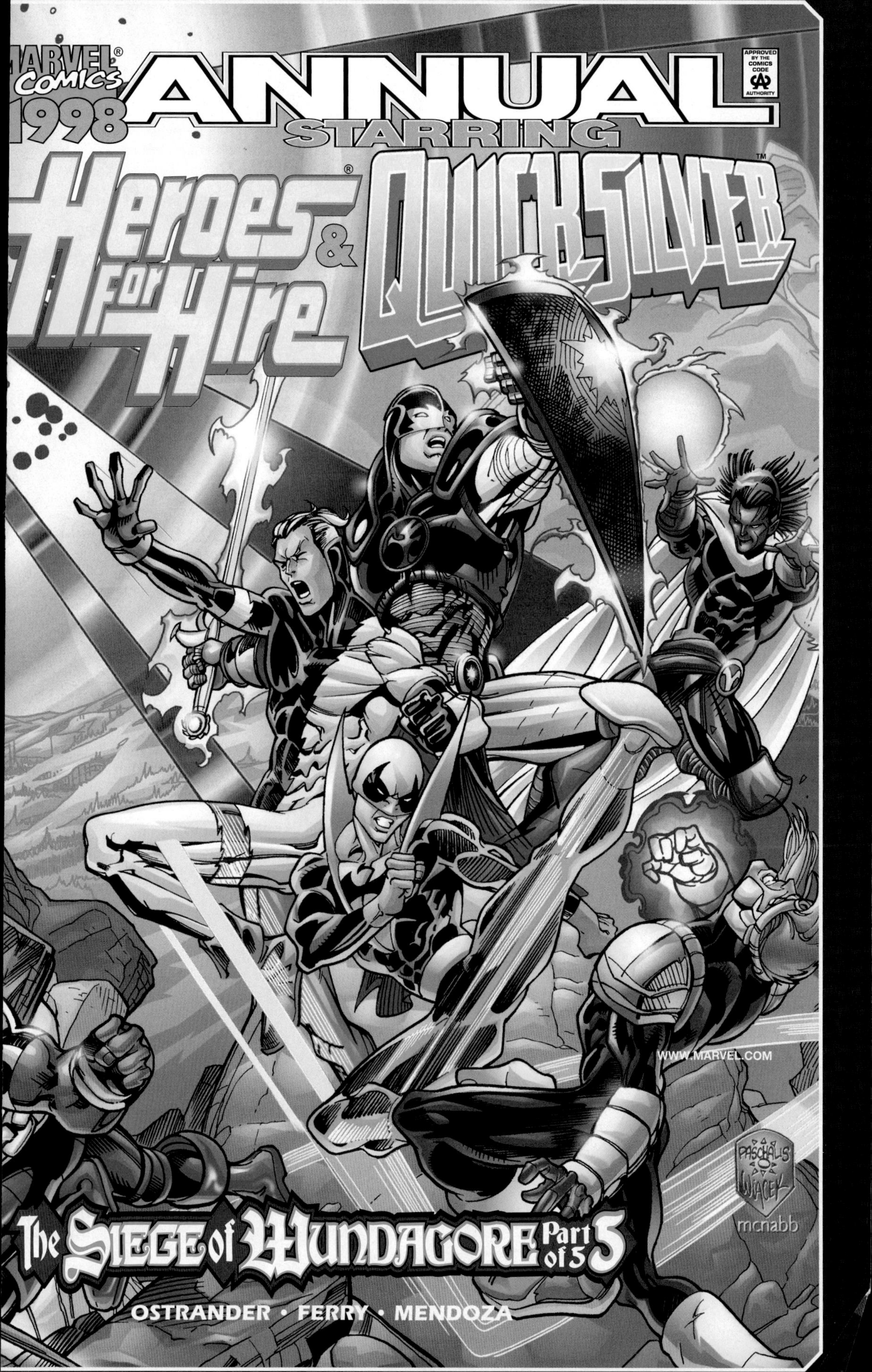

MARVEL COMICS
1998
ANNUAL
STARRING
APPROVED BY THE COMICS CODE AUTHORITY
Heroes for Hire & QUICKSILVER
WWW.MARVEL.COM
PASCHALIS WIACEK
mcnabb
The Siege of Wundagore Part 5 of 5
OSTRANDER • FERRY • MENDOZA

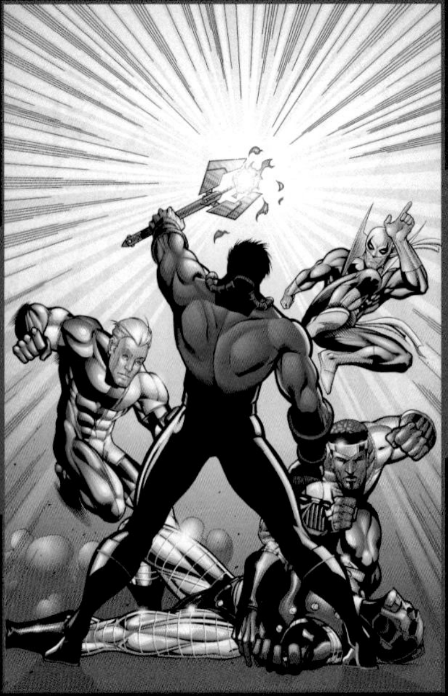

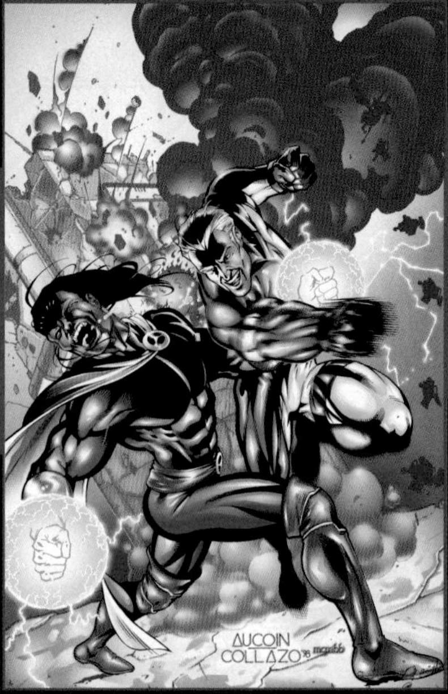
AUCOIN
COLLAZO

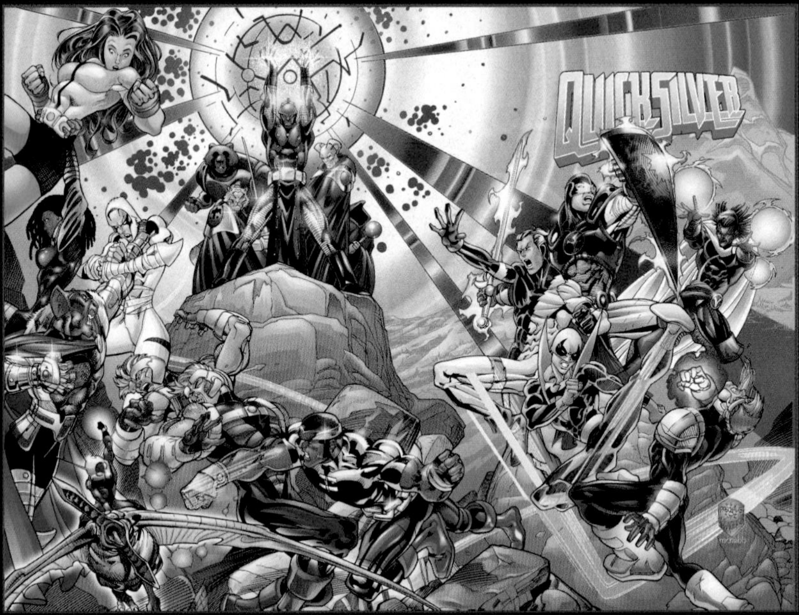
QUICKSILVER

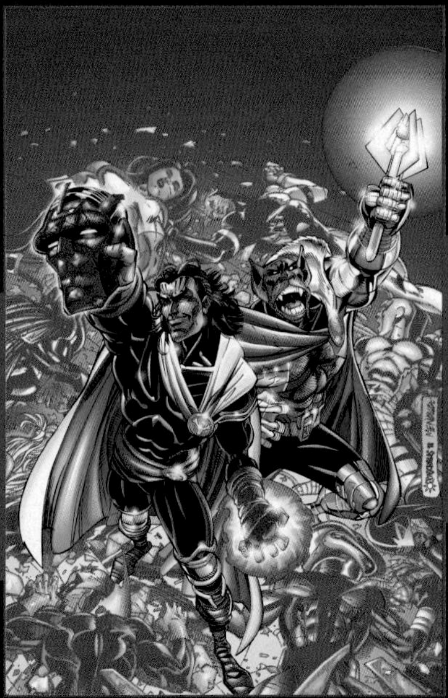

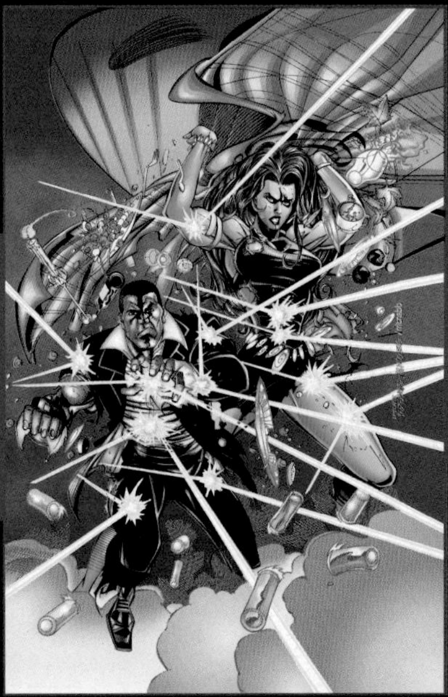

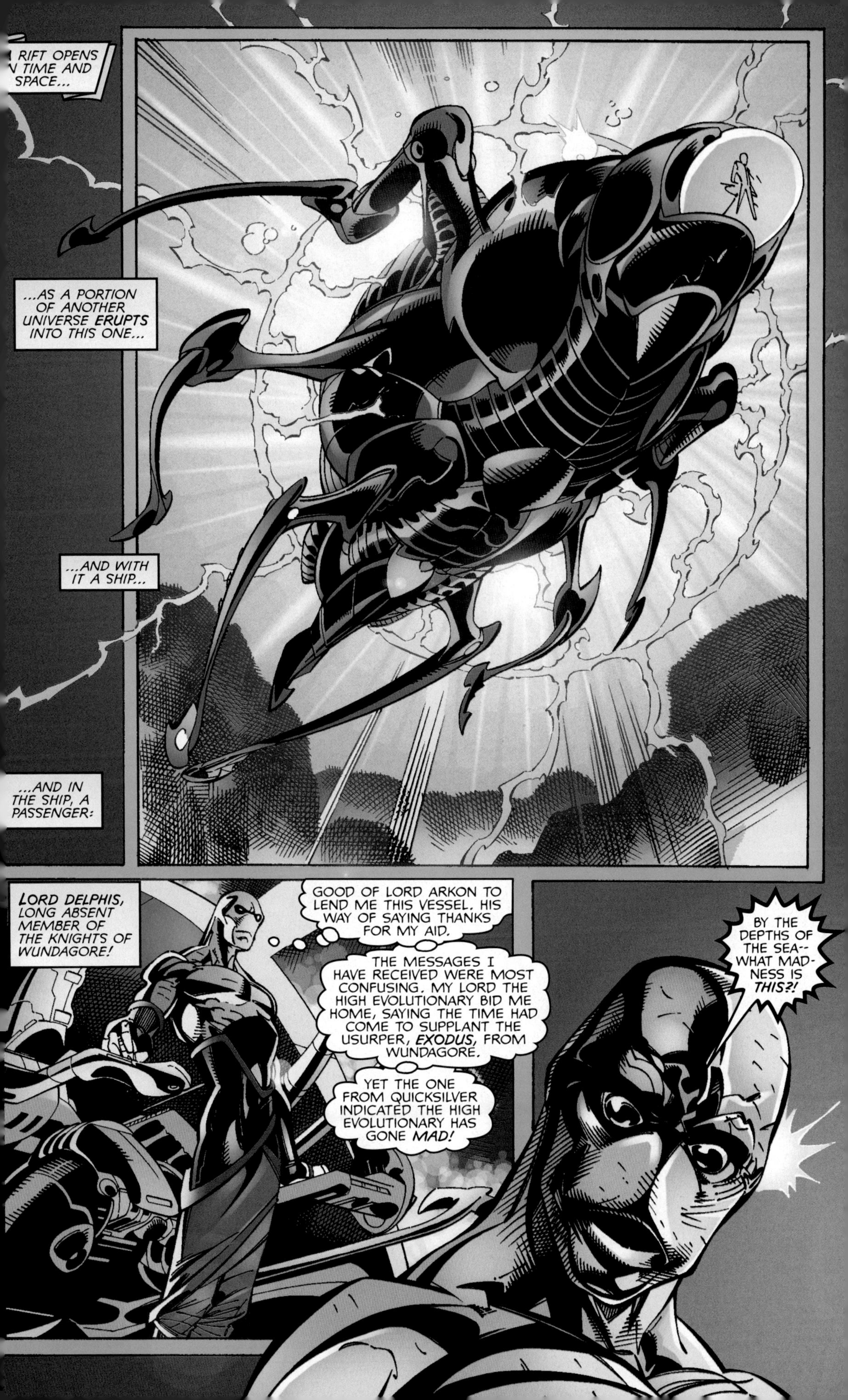

RIFT OPENS
N TIME AND
SPACE...
...AS A PORTION OF ANOTHER UNIVERSE ERUPTS INTO THIS ONE...
...AND WITH IT A SHIP...
...AND IN THE SHIP, A PASSENGER:
LORD DELPHIS, LONG ABSENT MEMBER OF THE KNIGHTS OF WUNDAGORE!
GOOD OF LORD ARKON TO LEND ME THIS VESSEL. HIS WAY OF SAYING THANKS FOR MY AID.
THE MESSAGES I HAVE RECEIVED WERE MOST CONFUSING. MY LORD THE HIGH EVOLUTIONARY BID ME HOME, SAYING THE TIME HAD COME TO SUPPLANT THE USURPER, EXODUS, FROM WUNDAGORE.
YET THE ONE FROM QUICKSILVER INDICATED THE HIGH EVOLUTIONARY HAS GONE MAD!
BY THE DEPTHS OF THE SEA--WHAT MADNESS IS THIS?!

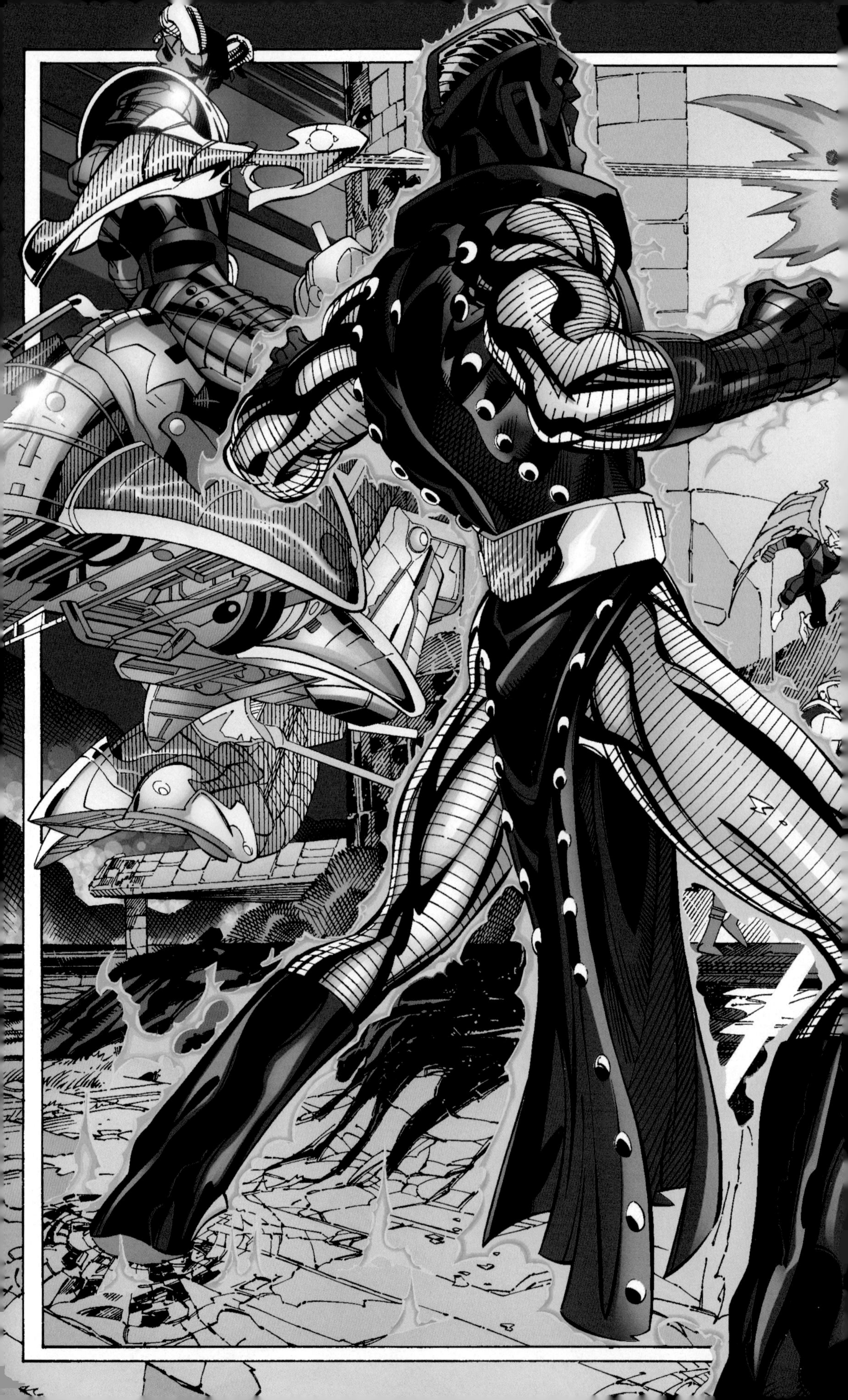

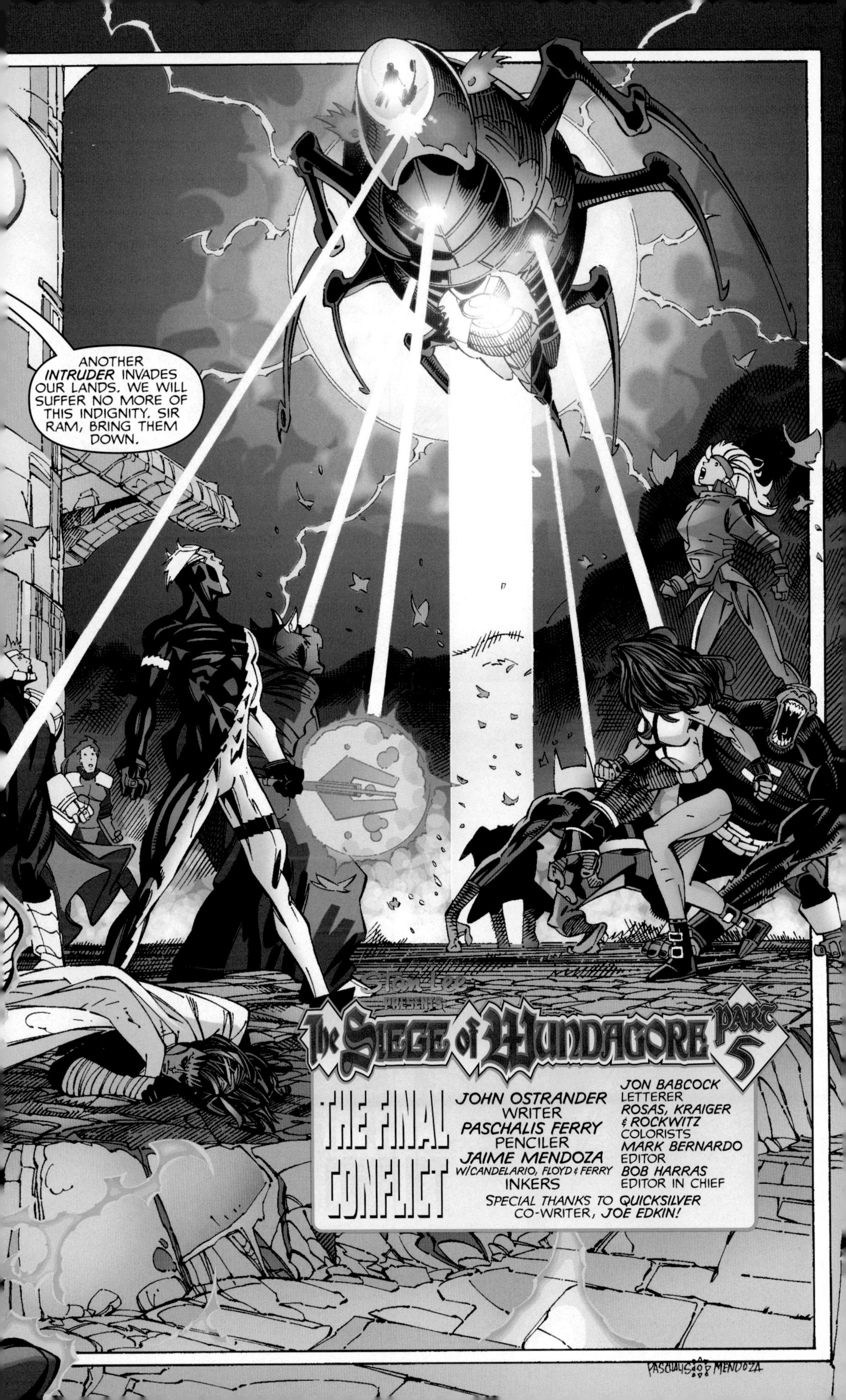

ANOTHER INTRUDER INVADES OUR LANDS. WE WILL SUFFER NO MORE OF THIS INDIGNITY. SIR RAM, BRING THEM DOWN.
Stan Lee PRESENTS:
The Siege of Wundagore PART 5
THE FINAL CONFLICT
JOHN OSTRANDER WRITER
PASCHALIS FERRY PENCILER
JAIME MENDOZA W/CANDELARIO, FLOYD & FERRY INKERS
JON BABCOCK LETTERER
ROSAS, KRAIGER & ROCKWITZ COLORISTS
MARK BERNARDO EDITOR
BOB HARRAS EDITOR IN CHIEF
SPECIAL THANKS TO QUICKSILVER CO-WRITER, JOE EDKIN!
PASCHALIS MENDOZA

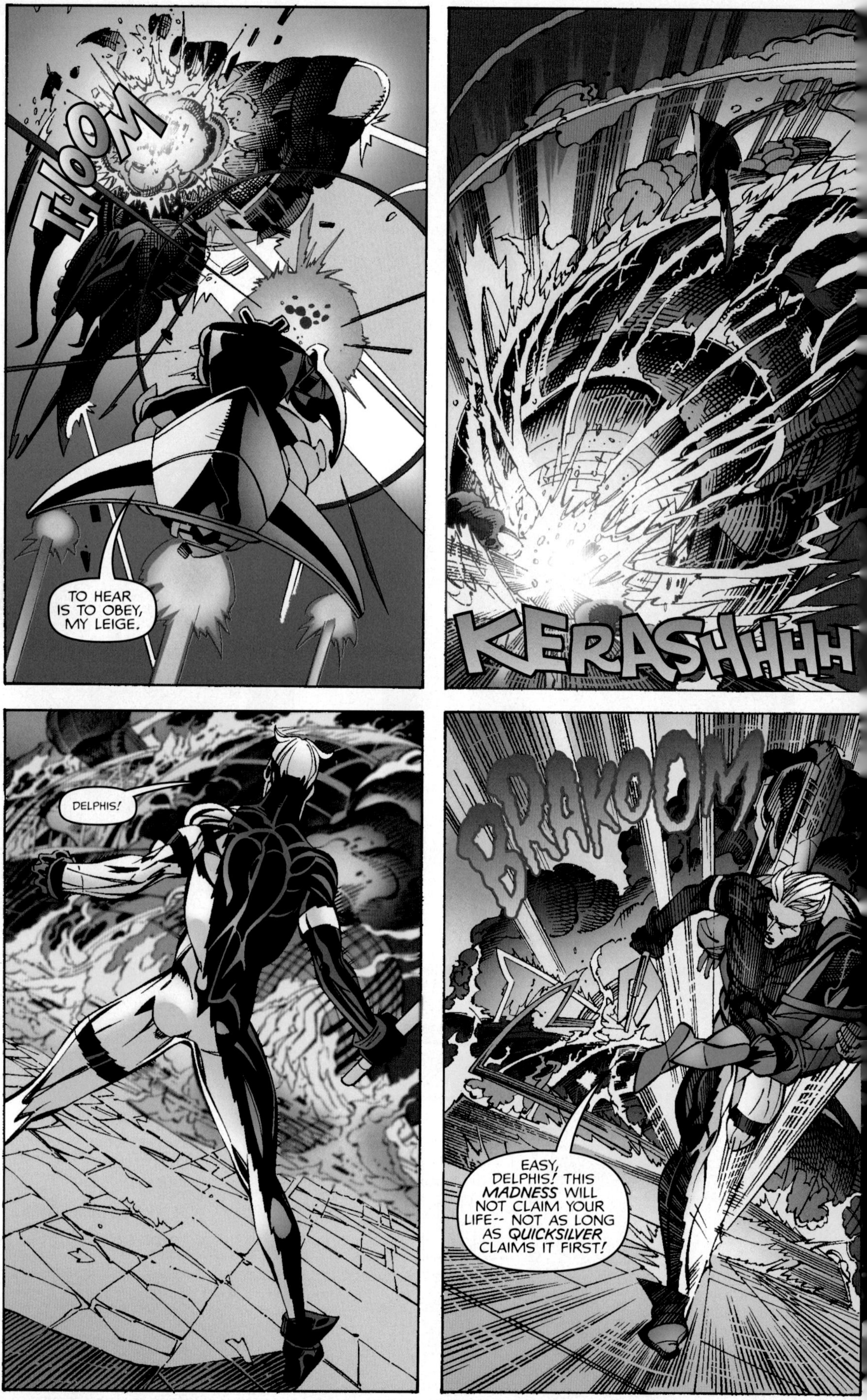
THOOM
TO HEAR IS TO OBEY, MY LEIGE.
KERASHHHH
DELPHIS!
BRAKOOM
EASY, DELPHIS! THIS *MADNESS* WILL NOT CLAIM YOUR LIFE-- NOT AS LONG AS *QUICKSILVER* CLAIMS IT FIRST!

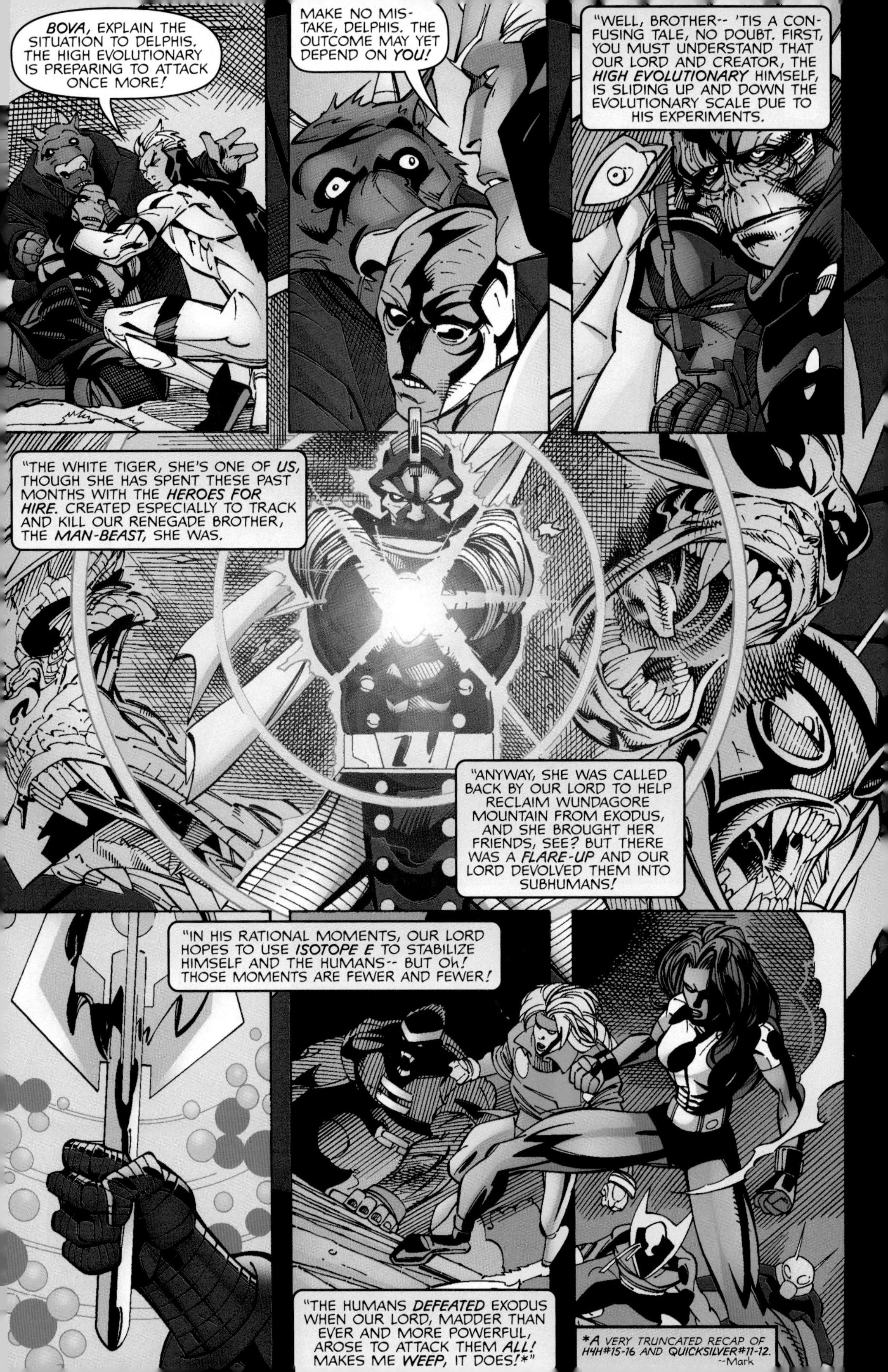
BOVA, EXPLAIN THE SITUATION TO DELPHIS. THE HIGH EVOLUTIONARY IS PREPARING TO ATTACK ONCE MORE!
MAKE NO MISTAKE, DELPHIS. THE OUTCOME MAY YET DEPEND ON YOU!
"WELL, BROTHER-- 'TIS A CONFUSING TALE, NO DOUBT. FIRST, YOU MUST UNDERSTAND THAT OUR LORD AND CREATOR, THE HIGH EVOLUTIONARY HIMSELF, IS SLIDING UP AND DOWN THE EVOLUTIONARY SCALE DUE TO HIS EXPERIMENTS.
"THE WHITE TIGER, SHE'S ONE OF US, THOUGH SHE HAS SPENT THESE PAST MONTHS WITH THE HEROES FOR HIRE. CREATED ESPECIALLY TO TRACK AND KILL OUR RENEGADE BROTHER, THE MAN-BEAST, SHE WAS.
"ANYWAY, SHE WAS CALLED BACK BY OUR LORD TO HELP RECLAIM WUNDAGORE MOUNTAIN FROM EXODUS, AND SHE BROUGHT HER FRIENDS, SEE? BUT THERE WAS A FLARE-UP AND OUR LORD DEVOLVED THEM INTO SUBHUMANS!
"IN HIS RATIONAL MOMENTS, OUR LORD HOPES TO USE ISOTOPE E TO STABILIZE HIMSELF AND THE HUMANS-- BUT Oh! THOSE MOMENTS ARE FEWER AND FEWER!
"THE HUMANS DEFEATED EXODUS WHEN OUR LORD, MADDER THAN EVER AND MORE POWERFUL, AROSE TO ATTACK THEM ALL! MAKES ME WEEP, IT DOES!"*
*A VERY TRUNCATED RECAP OF H4H#15-16 AND QUICKSILVER#11-12. --Mark

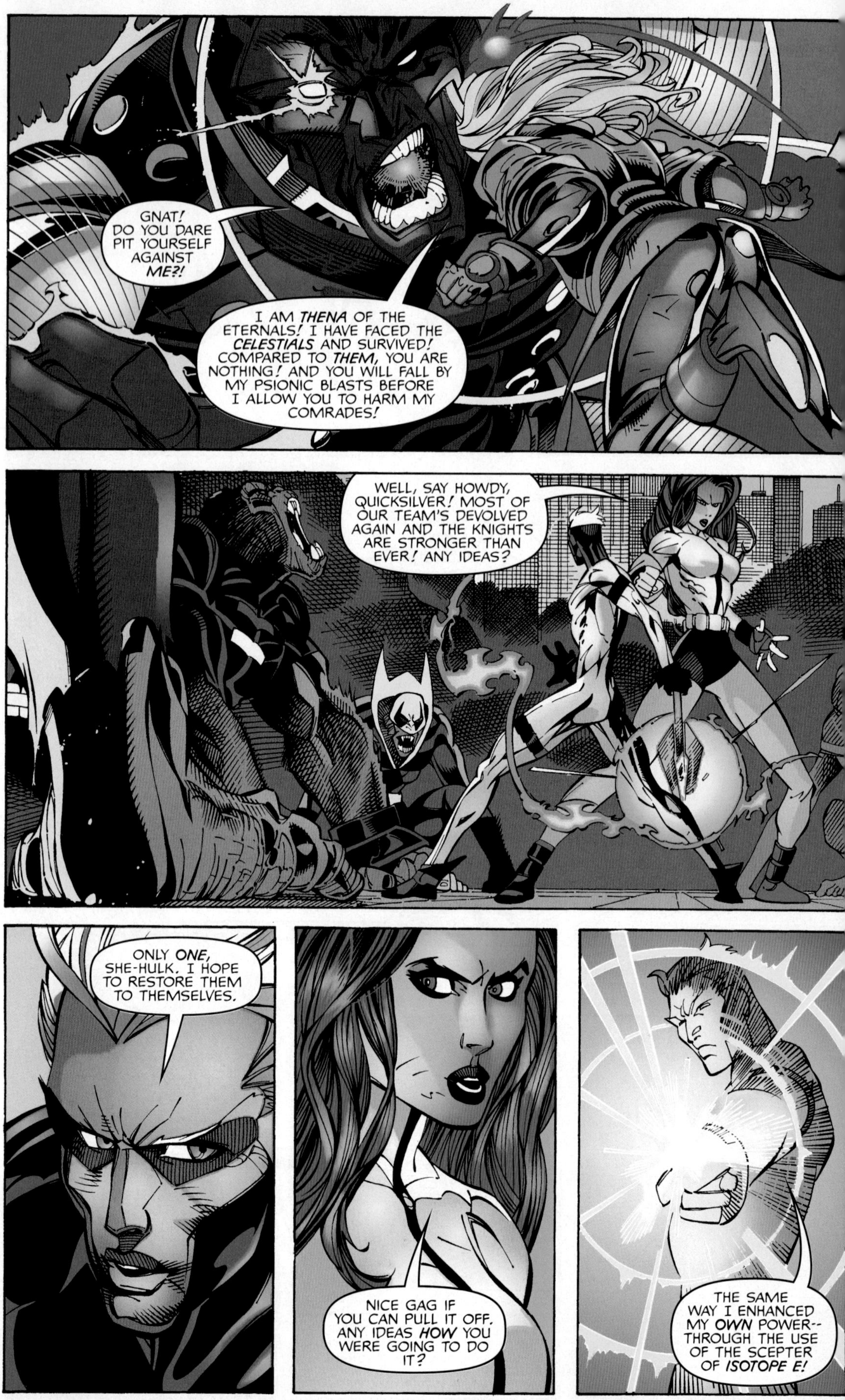
GNAT! DO YOU DARE PIT YOURSELF AGAINST *ME?!*
I AM *THENA* OF THE ETERNALS! I HAVE FACED THE *CELESTIALS* AND SURVIVED! COMPARED TO *THEM,* YOU ARE NOTHING! AND YOU WILL FALL BY MY PSIONIC BLASTS BEFORE I ALLOW YOU TO HARM MY COMRADES!
WELL, SAY HOWDY, QUICKSILVER! MOST OF OUR TEAM'S DEVOLVED AGAIN AND THE KNIGHTS ARE STRONGER THAN EVER! ANY IDEAS?
ONLY *ONE,* SHE-HULK. I HOPE TO RESTORE THEM TO THEMSELVES.
NICE GAG IF YOU CAN PULL IT OFF. ANY IDEAS *HOW* YOU WERE GOING TO DO IT?
THE SAME WAY I ENHANCED MY *OWN* POWER-- THROUGH THE USE OF THE SCEPTER OF *ISOTOPE E!*

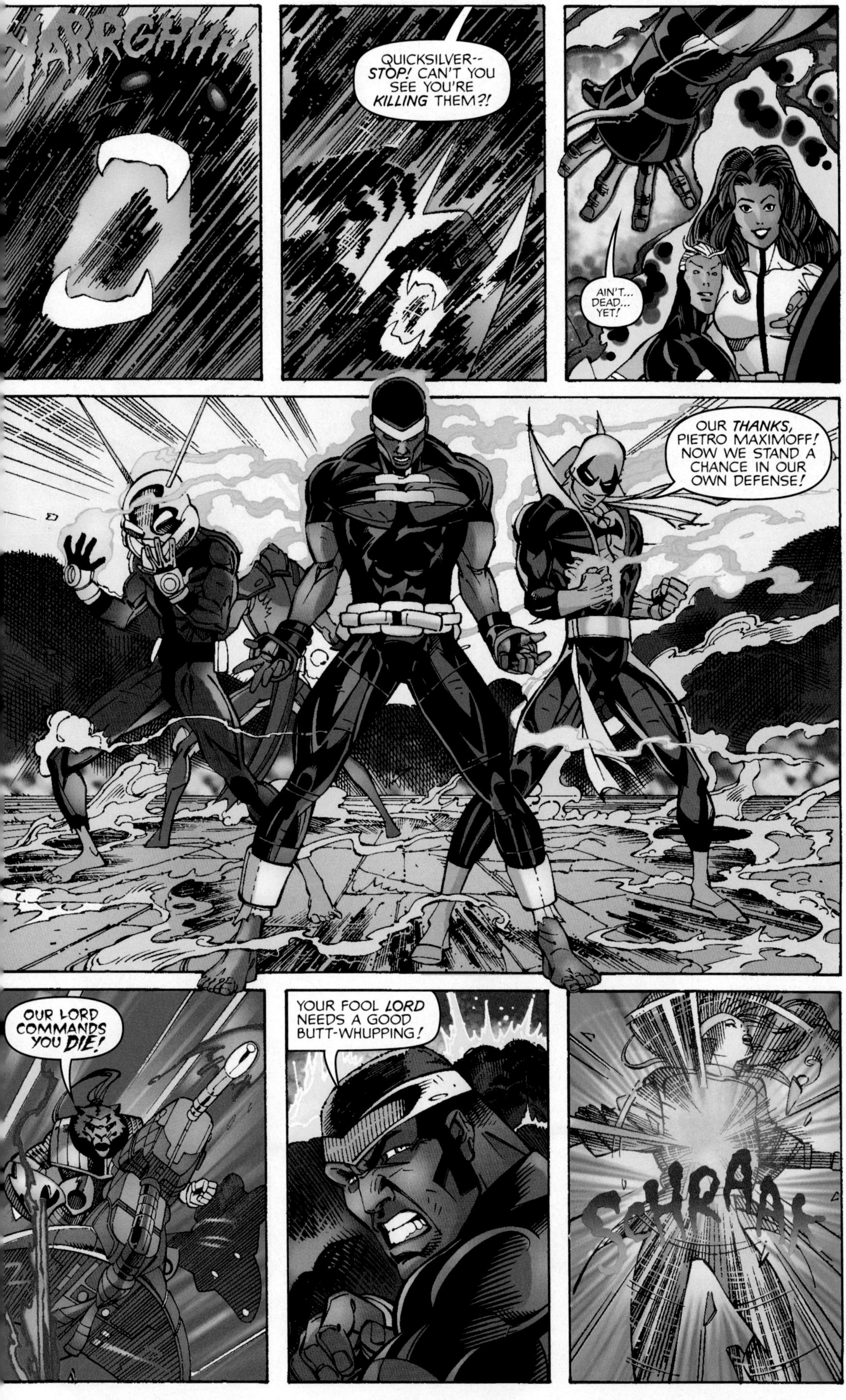
YARRGHHH
QUICKSILVER-- STOP! CAN'T YOU SEE YOU'RE KILLING THEM?!
AIN'T... DEAD... YET!
OUR THANKS, PIETRO MAXIMOFF! NOW WE STAND A CHANCE IN OUR OWN DEFENSE!
OUR LORD COMMANDS YOU DIE!
YOUR FOOL LORD NEEDS A GOOD BUTT-WHUPPING!
SCHRAAK

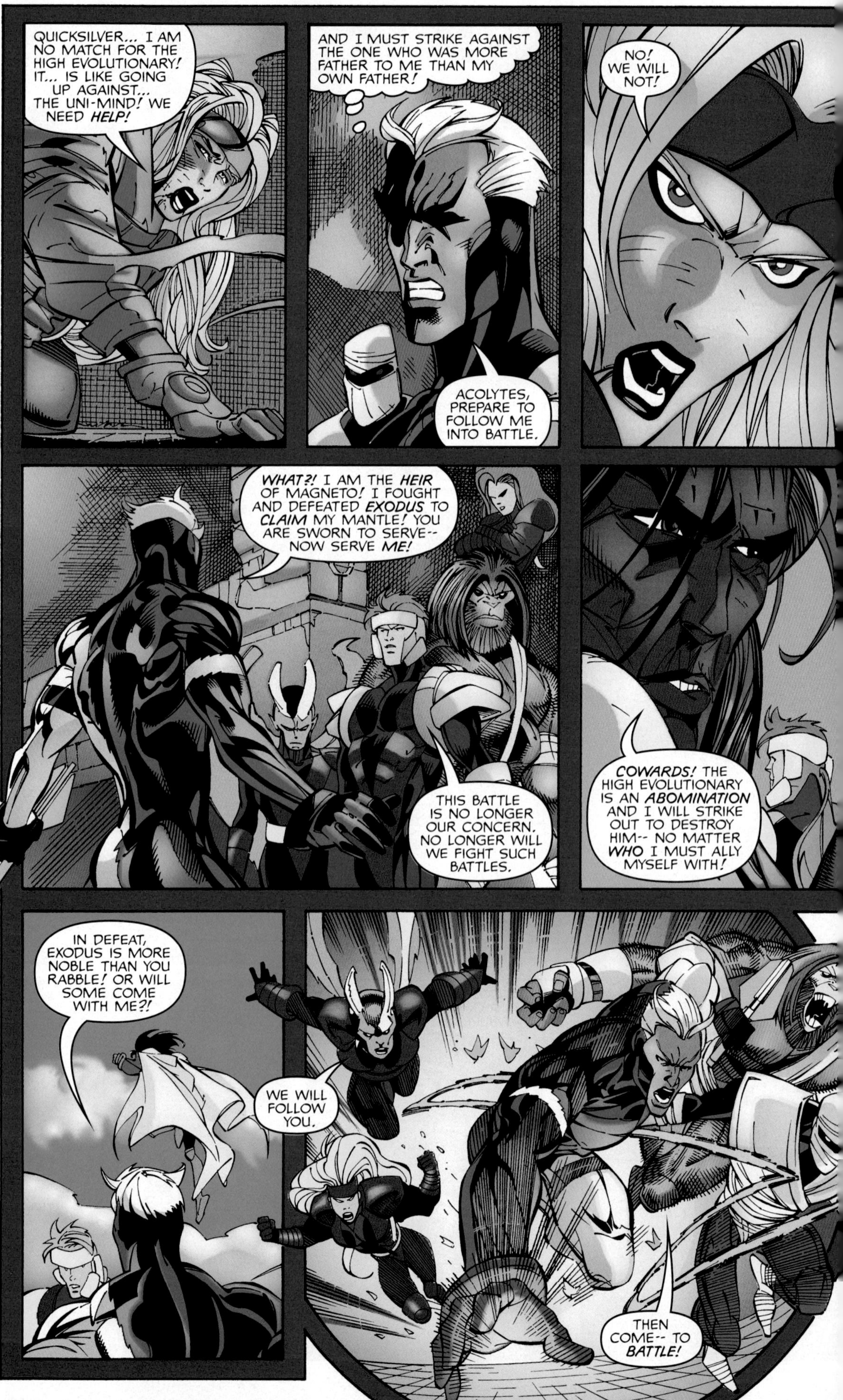
QUICKSILVER... I AM NO MATCH FOR THE HIGH EVOLUTIONARY! IT... IS LIKE GOING UP AGAINST... THE UNI-MIND! WE NEED HELP!
AND I MUST STRIKE AGAINST THE ONE WHO WAS MORE FATHER TO ME THAN MY OWN FATHER!
ACOLYTES, PREPARE TO FOLLOW ME INTO BATTLE.
NO! WE WILL NOT!
WHAT?! I AM THE HEIR OF MAGNETO! I FOUGHT AND DEFEATED EXODUS TO CLAIM MY MANTLE! YOU ARE SWORN TO SERVE-- NOW SERVE ME!
THIS BATTLE IS NO LONGER OUR CONCERN. NO LONGER WILL WE FIGHT SUCH BATTLES.
COWARDS! THE HIGH EVOLUTIONARY IS AN ABOMINATION AND I WILL STRIKE OUT TO DESTROY HIM-- NO MATTER WHO I MUST ALLY MYSELF WITH!
IN DEFEAT, EXODUS IS MORE NOBLE THAN YOU RABBLE! OR WILL SOME COME WITH ME?!
WE WILL FOLLOW YOU.
THEN COME-- TO BATTLE!

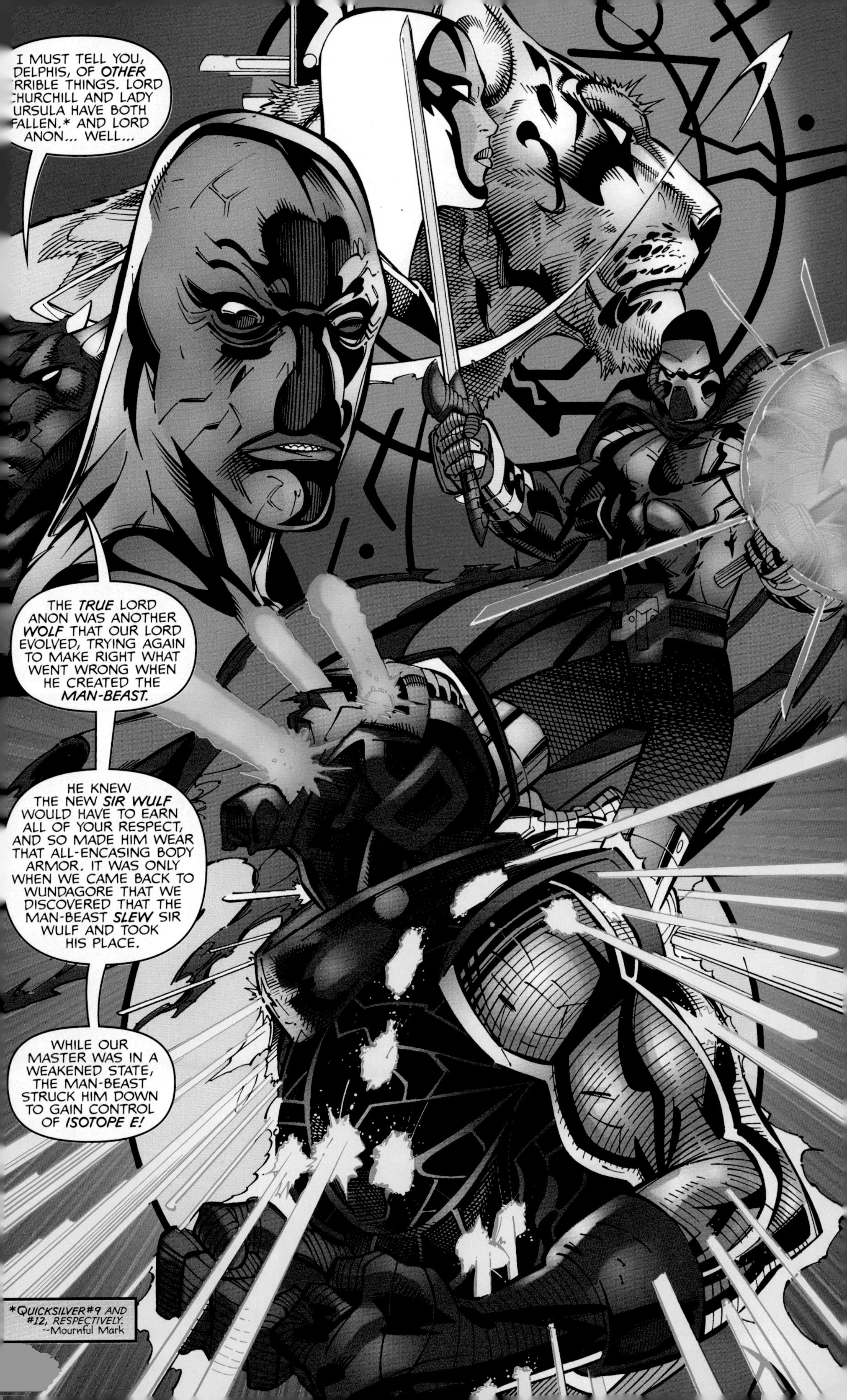
I MUST TELL YOU, DELPHIS, OF OTHER TERRIBLE THINGS. LORD CHURCHILL AND LADY URSULA HAVE BOTH FALLEN.* AND LORD ANON... WELL...
THE TRUE LORD ANON WAS ANOTHER WOLF THAT OUR LORD EVOLVED, TRYING AGAIN TO MAKE RIGHT WHAT WENT WRONG WHEN HE CREATED THE MAN-BEAST.
HE KNEW THE NEW SIR WULF WOULD HAVE TO EARN ALL OF YOUR RESPECT, AND SO MADE HIM WEAR THAT ALL-ENCASING BODY ARMOR. IT WAS ONLY WHEN WE CAME BACK TO WUNDAGORE THAT WE DISCOVERED THAT THE MAN-BEAST SLEW SIR WULF AND TOOK HIS PLACE.
WHILE OUR MASTER WAS IN A WEAKENED STATE, THE MAN-BEAST STRUCK HIM DOWN TO GAIN CONTROL OF ISOTOPE E!
*QUICKSILVER #9 AND #12, RESPECTIVELY. --Mournful Mark

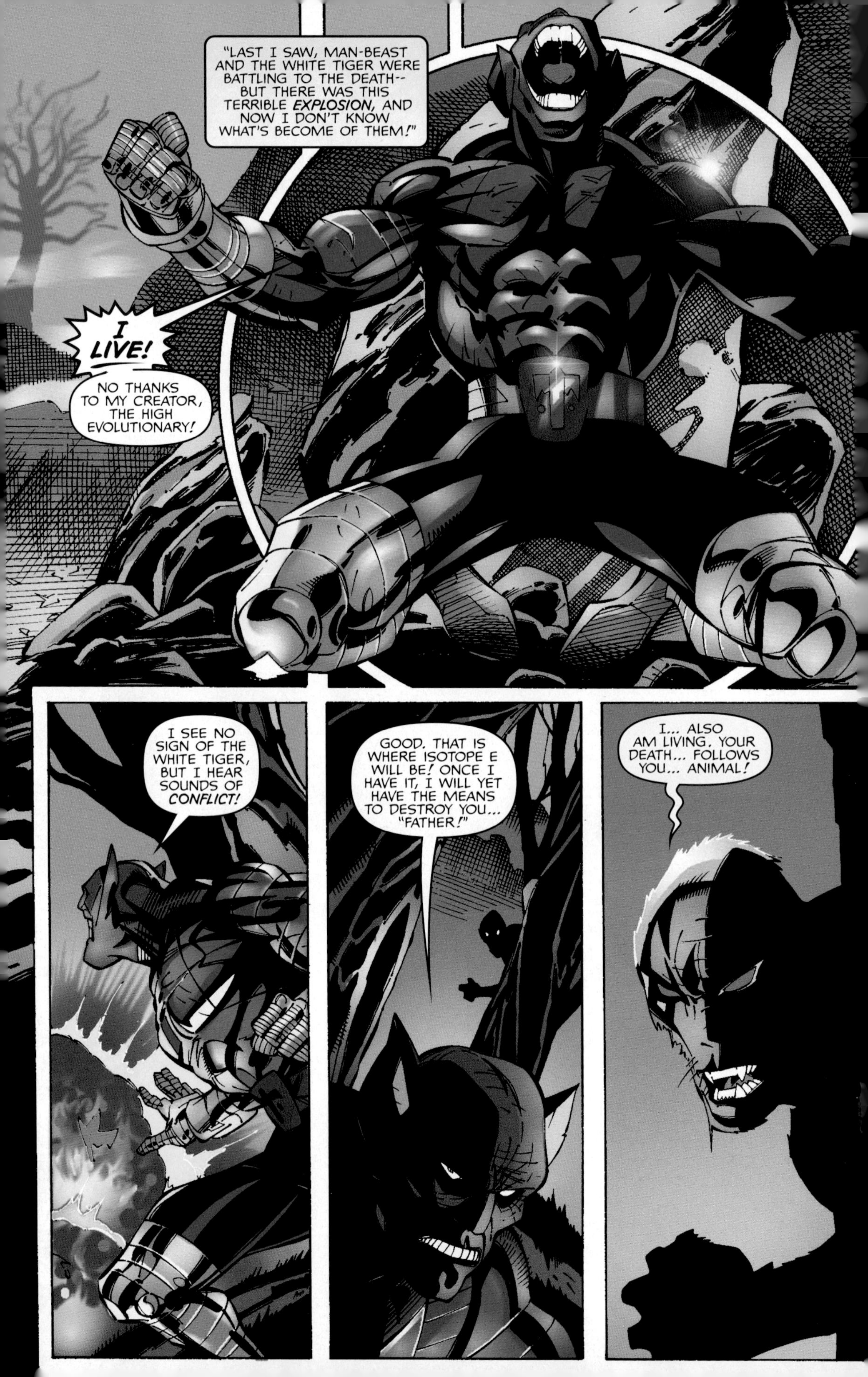

"LAST I SAW, MAN-BEAST AND THE WHITE TIGER WERE BATTLING TO THE DEATH-- BUT THERE WAS THIS TERRIBLE *EXPLOSION*, AND NOW I DON'T KNOW WHAT'S BECOME OF THEM!"
I LIVE!
NO THANKS TO MY CREATOR, THE HIGH EVOLUTIONARY!
I SEE NO SIGN OF THE WHITE TIGER, BUT I HEAR SOUNDS OF *CONFLICT!*
GOOD. THAT IS WHERE ISOTOPE E WILL BE! ONCE I HAVE IT, I WILL YET HAVE THE MEANS TO DESTROY YOU... "FATHER!"
I... ALSO AM LIVING. YOUR DEATH... FOLLOWS YOU... ANIMAL!

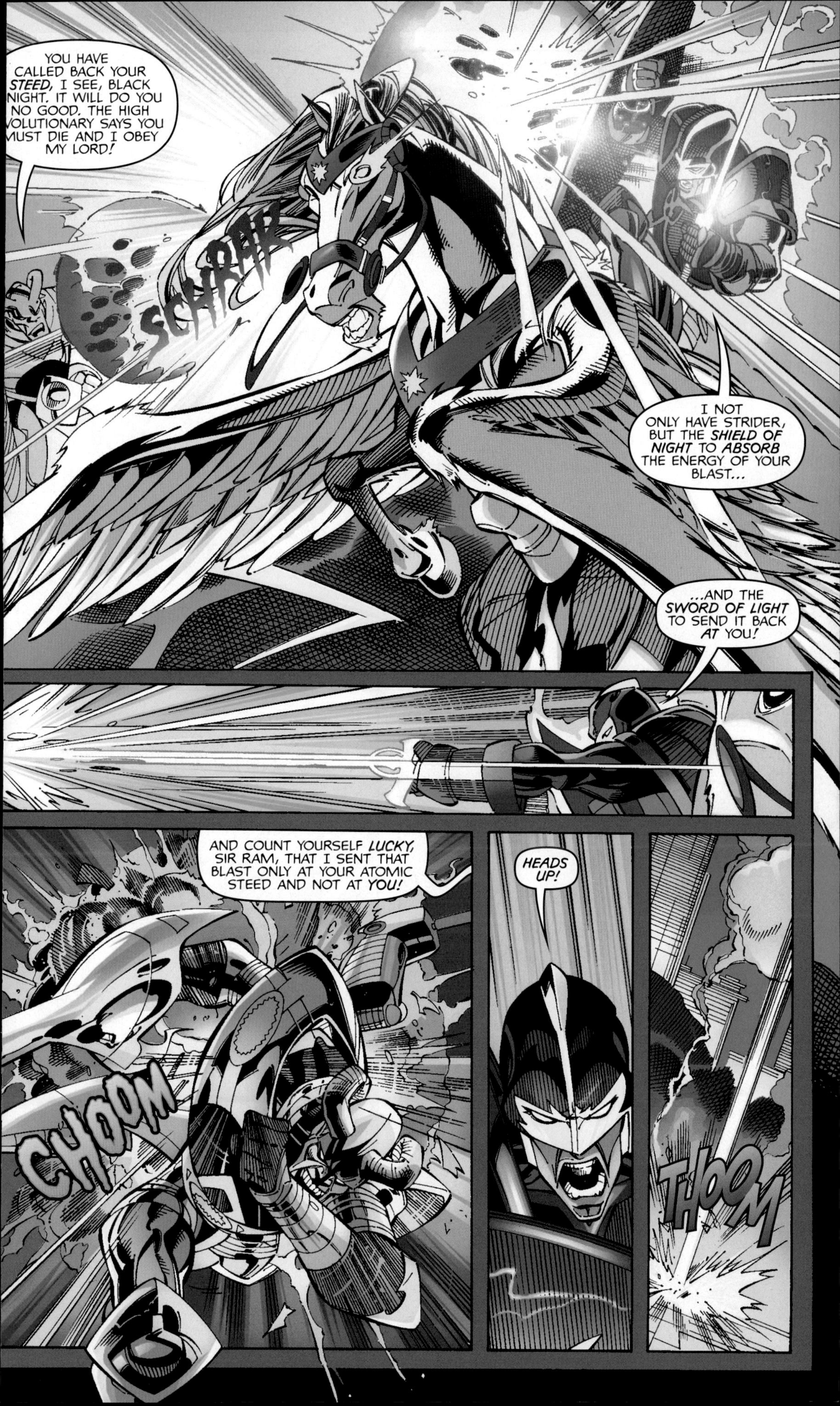

YOU HAVE CALLED BACK YOUR STEED, I SEE, BLACK KNIGHT. IT WILL DO YOU NO GOOD. THE HIGH EVOLUTIONARY SAYS YOU MUST DIE AND I OBEY MY LORD!
SCHRAK
I NOT ONLY HAVE STRIDER, BUT THE SHIELD OF NIGHT TO ABSORB THE ENERGY OF YOUR BLAST...
...AND THE SWORD OF LIGHT TO SEND IT BACK AT YOU!
AND COUNT YOURSELF LUCKY, SIR RAM, THAT I SENT THAT BLAST ONLY AT YOUR ATOMIC STEED AND NOT AT YOU!
CHOOM
HEADS UP!
THOOM

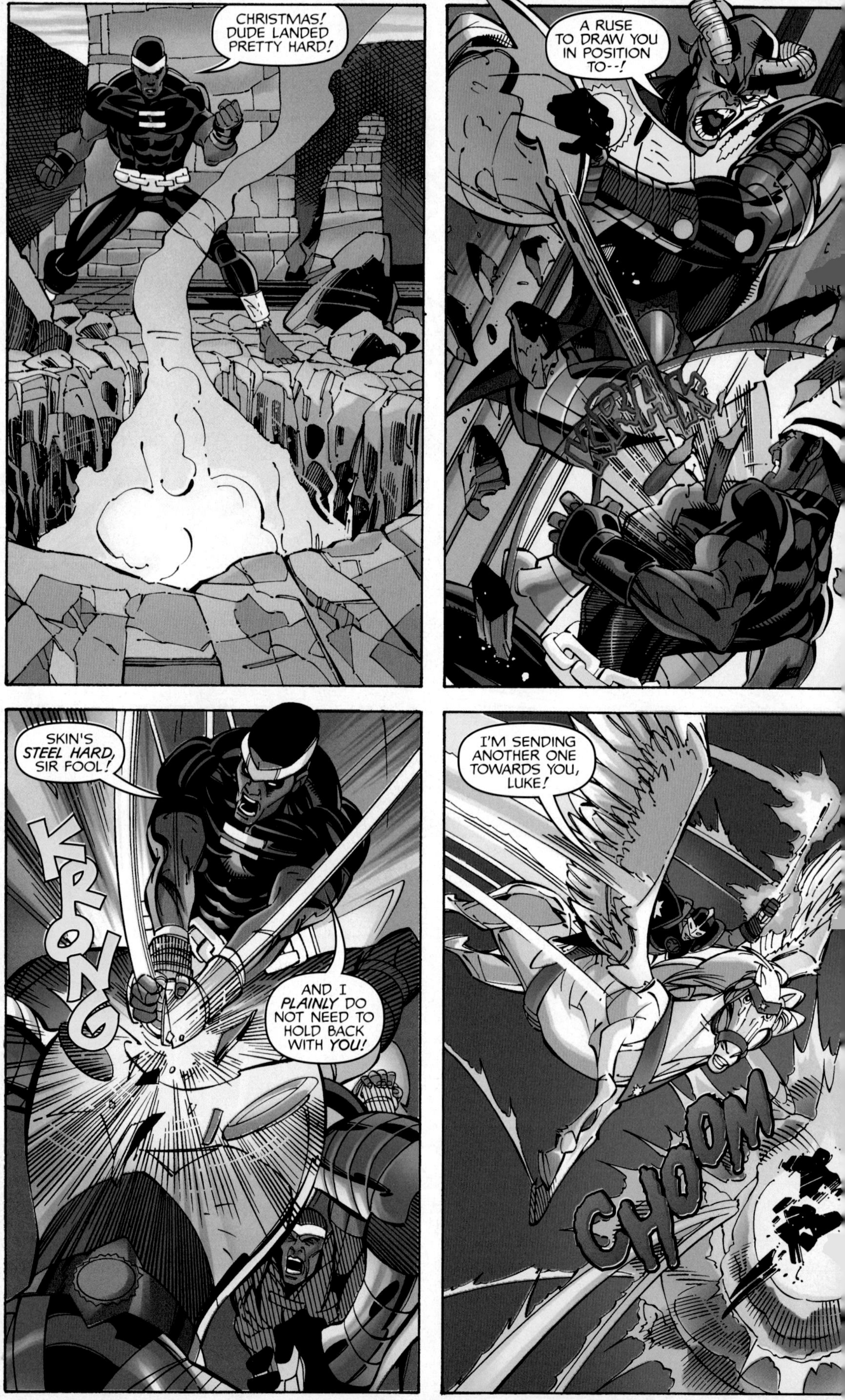
CHRISTMAS! DUDE LANDED PRETTY HARD!
A RUSE TO DRAW YOU IN POSITION TO--!
SKIN'S *STEEL HARD,* SIR FOOL!
KRONG
AND I *PLAINLY* DO NOT NEED TO HOLD BACK WITH *YOU!*
I'M SENDING ANOTHER ONE TOWARDS YOU, LUKE!
CHOOM

LORD DELPHIS-- WHOSE SIDE WILL YOU FIGHT WITH NOW?

I FIGHT FOR MY CREATOR, THE HIGH EVOLUTIONARY! TO HIM I OWE MY VERY EXISTENCE!

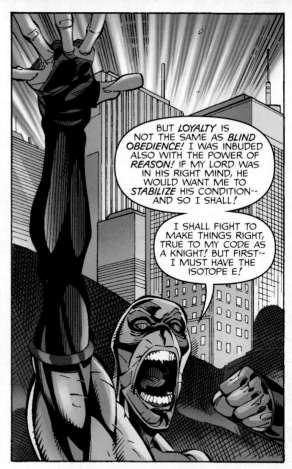

BUT *LOYALTY* IS NOT THE SAME AS *BLIND OBEDIENCE!* I WAS INBUDED ALSO WITH THE POWER OF *REASON!* IF MY LORD WAS IN HIS RIGHT MIND, HE WOULD WANT ME TO *STABILIZE* HIS CONDITION-- AND SO I SHALL!

I SHALL FIGHT TO MAKE THINGS RIGHT, TRUE TO MY CODE AS A KNIGHT! BUT FIRST-- I MUST HAVE THE ISOTOPE E!

NO GOOD! EXODUS'S PSI-POWER IS HAVING NO MORE EFFECT ON THE EVOLUTIONARY THAN *MINE!*

HE IGNORES ME, THINKING ME NOTHING! BUT I AM *DECAY!* AS I SIPHON HIS POWER, MY ENEMY DIES WHILE I GROW STRONG!

NO! NOOO! THE POWER'S TOO *GREAT....!*

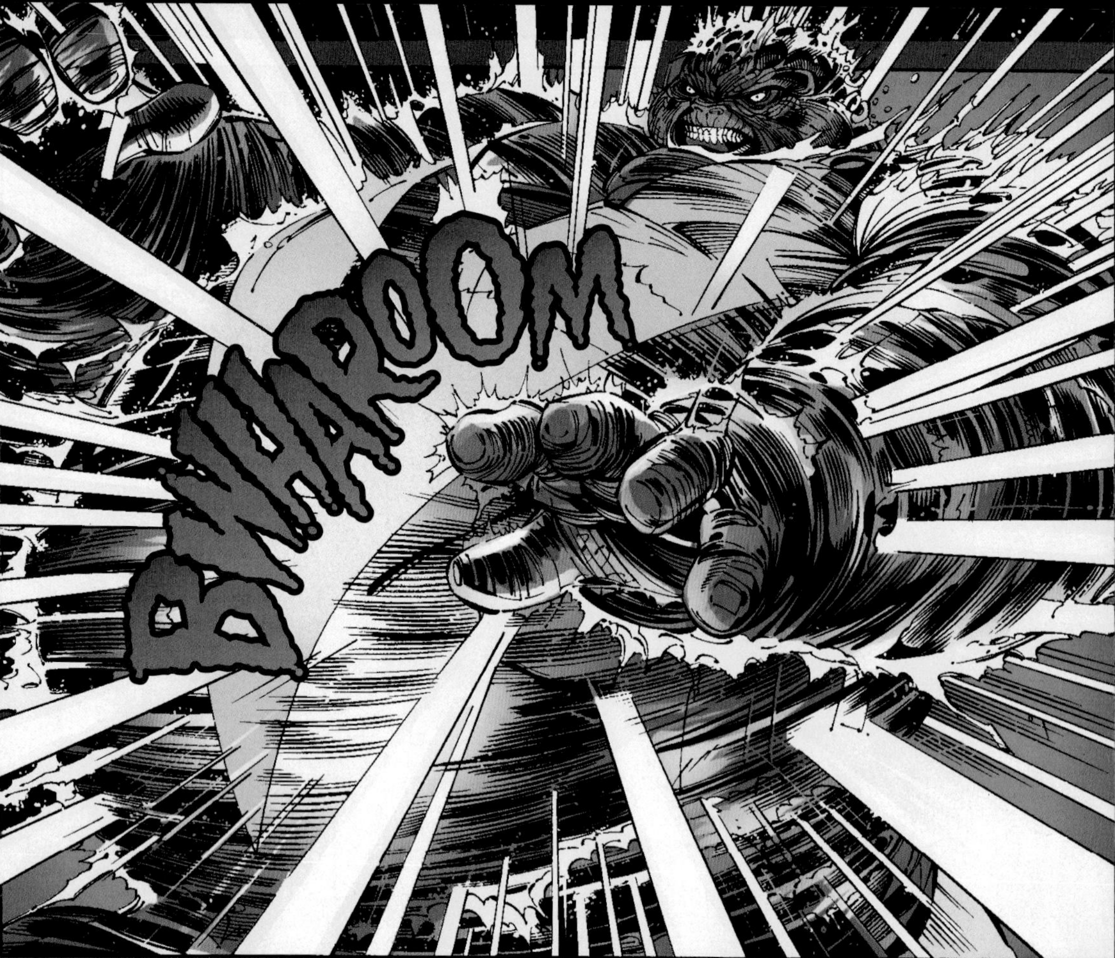
BWHOOM

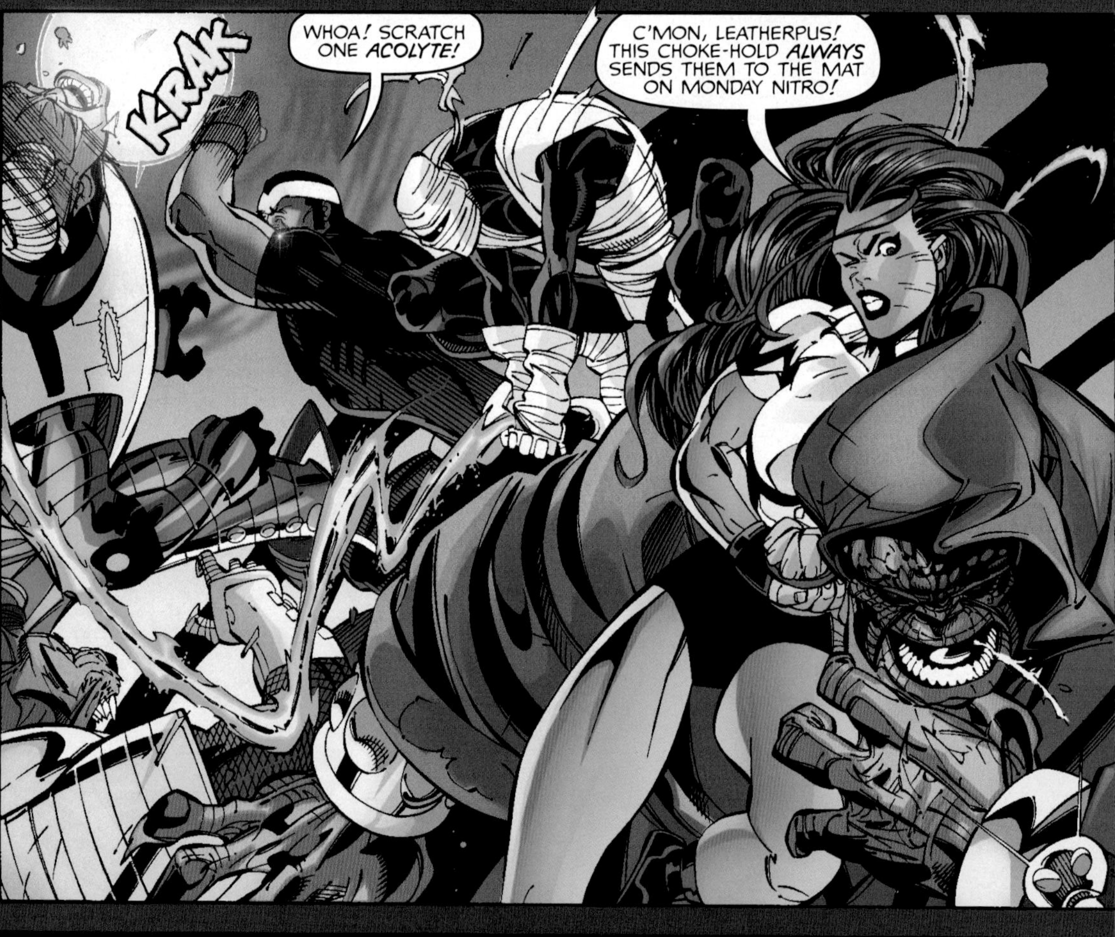
KRAK
WHOA! SCRATCH ONE *ACOLYTE!*
C'MON, LEATHERPUS! THIS CHOKE-HOLD *ALWAYS* SENDS THEM TO THE MAT ON MONDAY NITRO!

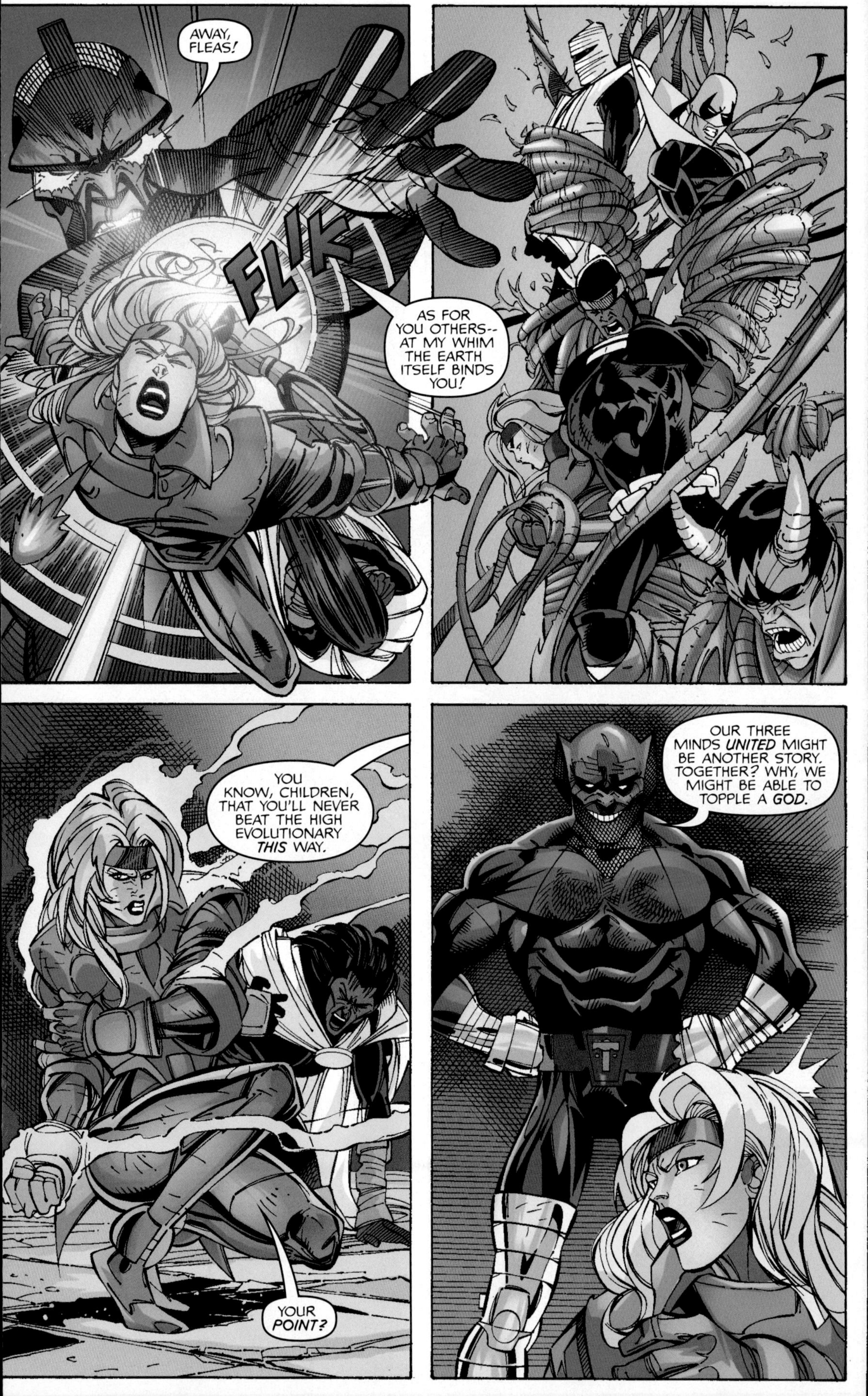

AWAY, FLEAS!
FLIK
AS FOR YOU OTHERS--AT MY WHIM THE EARTH ITSELF BINDS YOU!
YOU KNOW, CHILDREN, THAT YOU'LL NEVER BEAT THE HIGH EVOLUTIONARY THIS WAY.
YOUR POINT?
OUR THREE MINDS UNITED MIGHT BE ANOTHER STORY. TOGETHER? WHY, WE MIGHT BE ABLE TO TOPPLE A GOD.

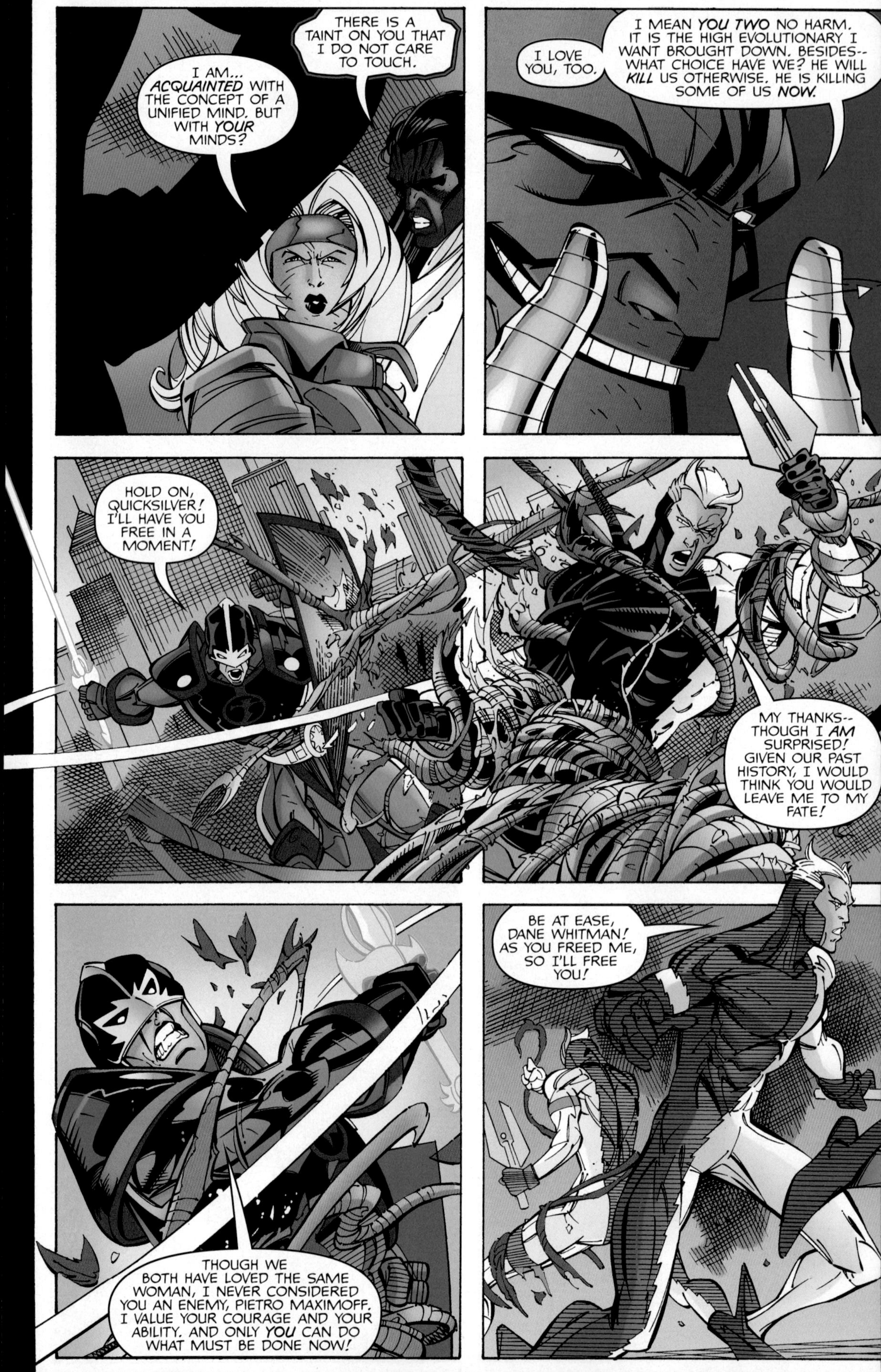
I AM... ACQUAINTED WITH THE CONCEPT OF A UNIFIED MIND. BUT WITH YOUR MINDS?
THERE IS A TAINT ON YOU THAT I DO NOT CARE TO TOUCH.
I LOVE YOU, TOO.
I MEAN YOU TWO NO HARM. IT IS THE HIGH EVOLUTIONARY I WANT BROUGHT DOWN. BESIDES-- WHAT CHOICE HAVE WE? HE WILL KILL US OTHERWISE. HE IS KILLING SOME OF US NOW.
HOLD ON, QUICKSILVER! I'LL HAVE YOU FREE IN A MOMENT!
MY THANKS-- THOUGH I AM SURPRISED! GIVEN OUR PAST HISTORY, I WOULD THINK YOU WOULD LEAVE ME TO MY FATE!
THOUGH WE BOTH HAVE LOVED THE SAME WOMAN, I NEVER CONSIDERED YOU AN ENEMY, PIETRO MAXIMOFF. I VALUE YOUR COURAGE AND YOUR ABILITY. AND ONLY YOU CAN DO WHAT MUST BE DONE NOW!
BE AT EASE, DANE WHITMAN! AS YOU FREED ME, SO I'LL FREE YOU!

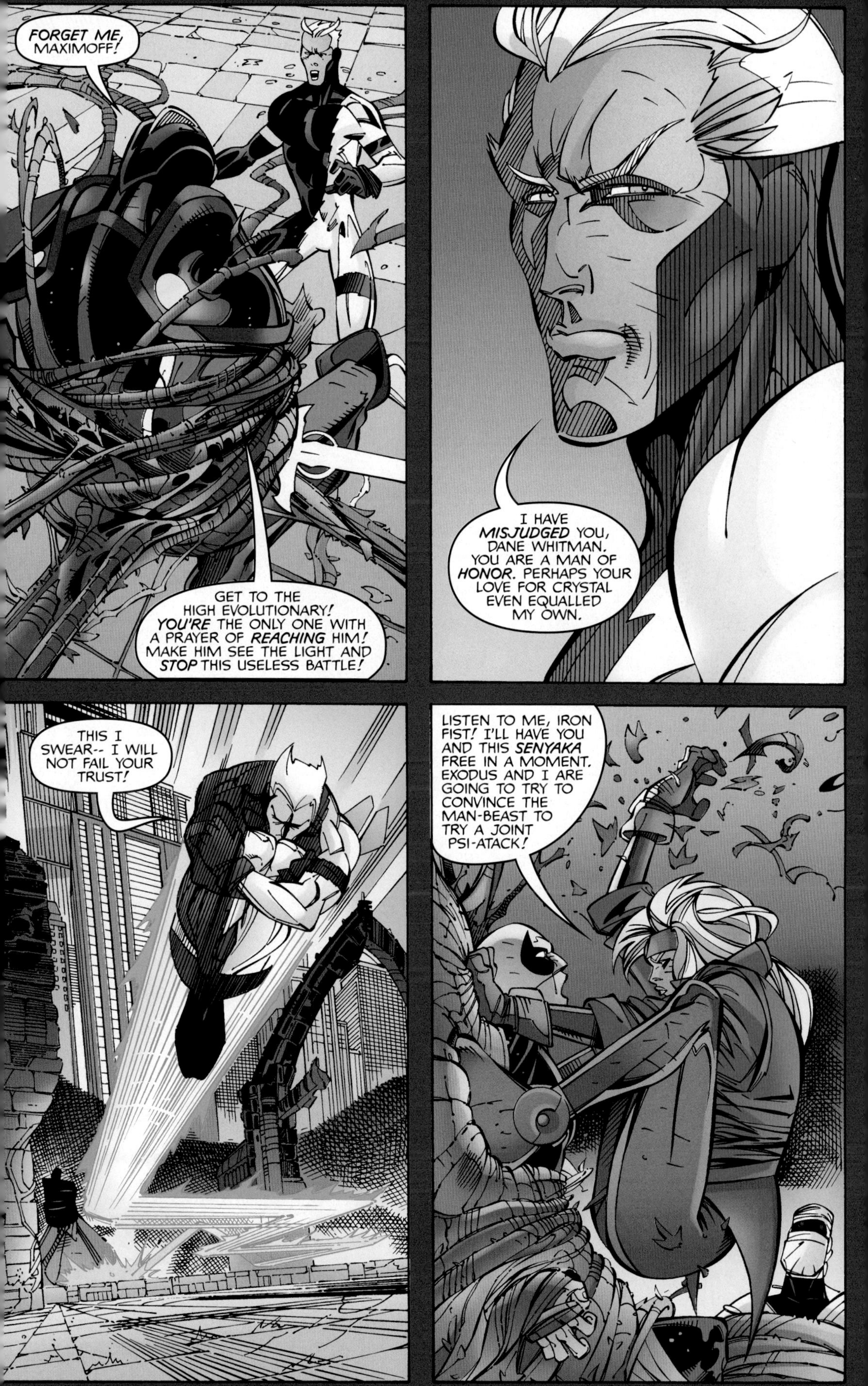
FORGET ME, MAXIMOFF!
GET TO THE HIGH EVOLUTIONARY! YOU'RE THE ONLY ONE WITH A PRAYER OF REACHING HIM! MAKE HIM SEE THE LIGHT AND STOP THIS USELESS BATTLE!
I HAVE MISJUDGED YOU, DANE WHITMAN. YOU ARE A MAN OF HONOR. PERHAPS YOUR LOVE FOR CRYSTAL EVEN EQUALLED MY OWN.
THIS I SWEAR-- I WILL NOT FAIL YOUR TRUST!
LISTEN TO ME, IRON FIST! I'LL HAVE YOU AND THIS SENYAKA FREE IN A MOMENT. EXODUS AND I ARE GOING TO TRY TO CONVINCE THE MAN-BEAST TO TRY A JOINT PSI-ATACK!

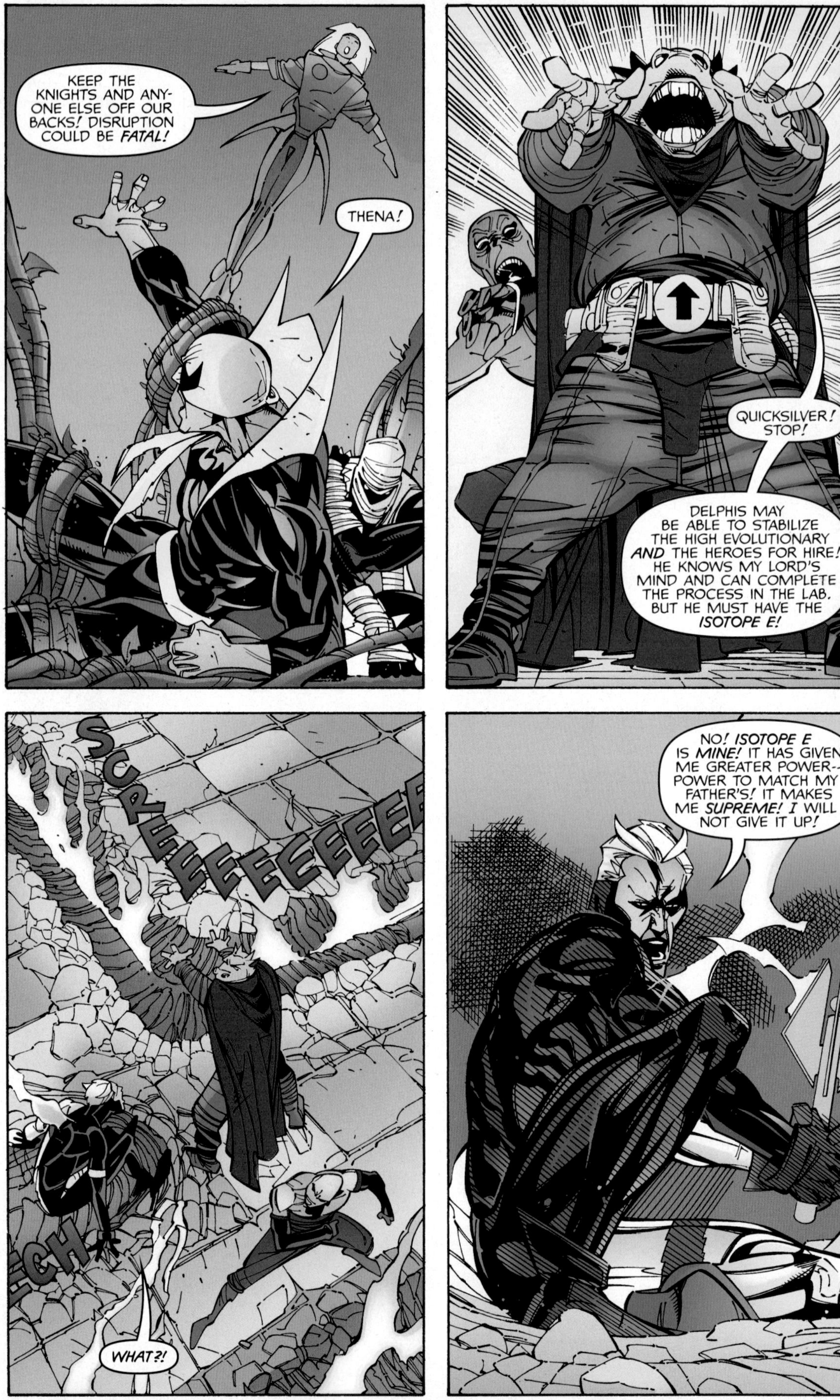
KEEP THE KNIGHTS AND ANYONE ELSE OFF OUR BACKS! DISRUPTION COULD BE FATAL!
THENA!
QUICKSILVER! STOP!
DELPHIS MAY BE ABLE TO STABILIZE THE HIGH EVOLUTIONARY AND THE HEROES FOR HIRE! HE KNOWS MY LORD'S MIND AND CAN COMPLETE THE PROCESS IN THE LAB. BUT HE MUST HAVE THE ISOTOPE E!
SCREEEEEEEEEE
WHAT?!
NO! ISOTOPE E IS MINE! IT HAS GIVEN ME GREATER POWER--POWER TO MATCH MY FATHER'S! IT MAKES ME SUPREME! I WILL NOT GIVE IT UP!

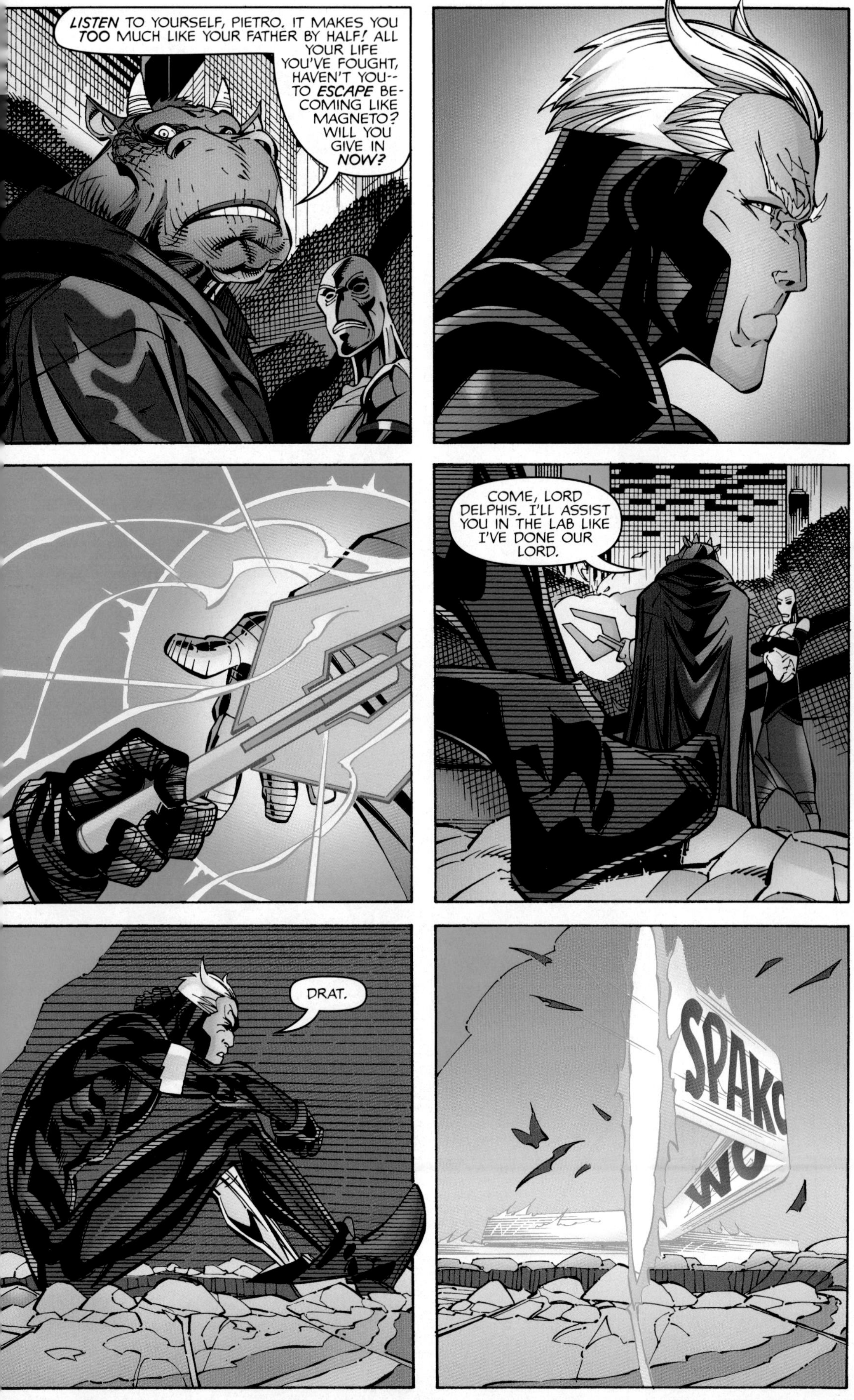
LISTEN TO YOURSELF, PIETRO. IT MAKES YOU TOO MUCH LIKE YOUR FATHER BY HALF! ALL YOUR LIFE YOU'VE FOUGHT, HAVEN'T YOU-- TO ESCAPE BE-COMING LIKE MAGNETO? WILL YOU GIVE IN NOW?
COME, LORD DELPHIS. I'LL ASSIST YOU IN THE LAB LIKE I'VE DONE OUR LORD.
DRAT.
SPAKO

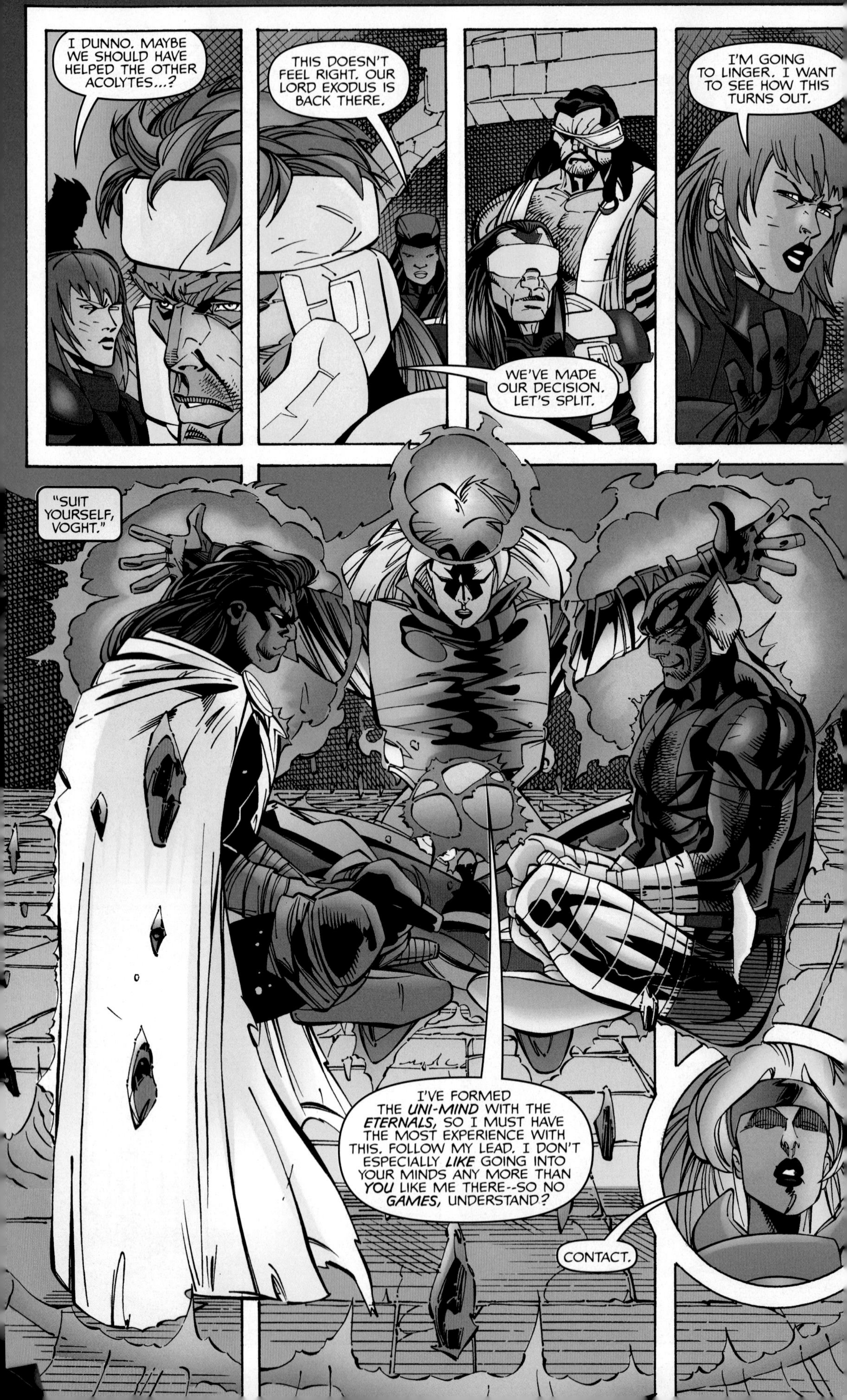
I DUNNO. MAYBE WE SHOULD HAVE HELPED THE OTHER ACOLYTES...?
THIS DOESN'T FEEL RIGHT. OUR LORD EXODUS IS BACK THERE.
WE'VE MADE OUR DECISION. LET'S SPLIT.
I'M GOING TO LINGER. I WANT TO SEE HOW THIS TURNS OUT.
"SUIT YOURSELF, VOGHT."
I'VE FORMED THE UNI-MIND WITH THE ETERNALS, SO I MUST HAVE THE MOST EXPERIENCE WITH THIS. FOLLOW MY LEAD. I DON'T ESPECIALLY LIKE GOING INTO YOUR MINDS ANY MORE THAN YOU LIKE ME THERE--SO NO GAMES, UNDERSTAND?
CONTACT.

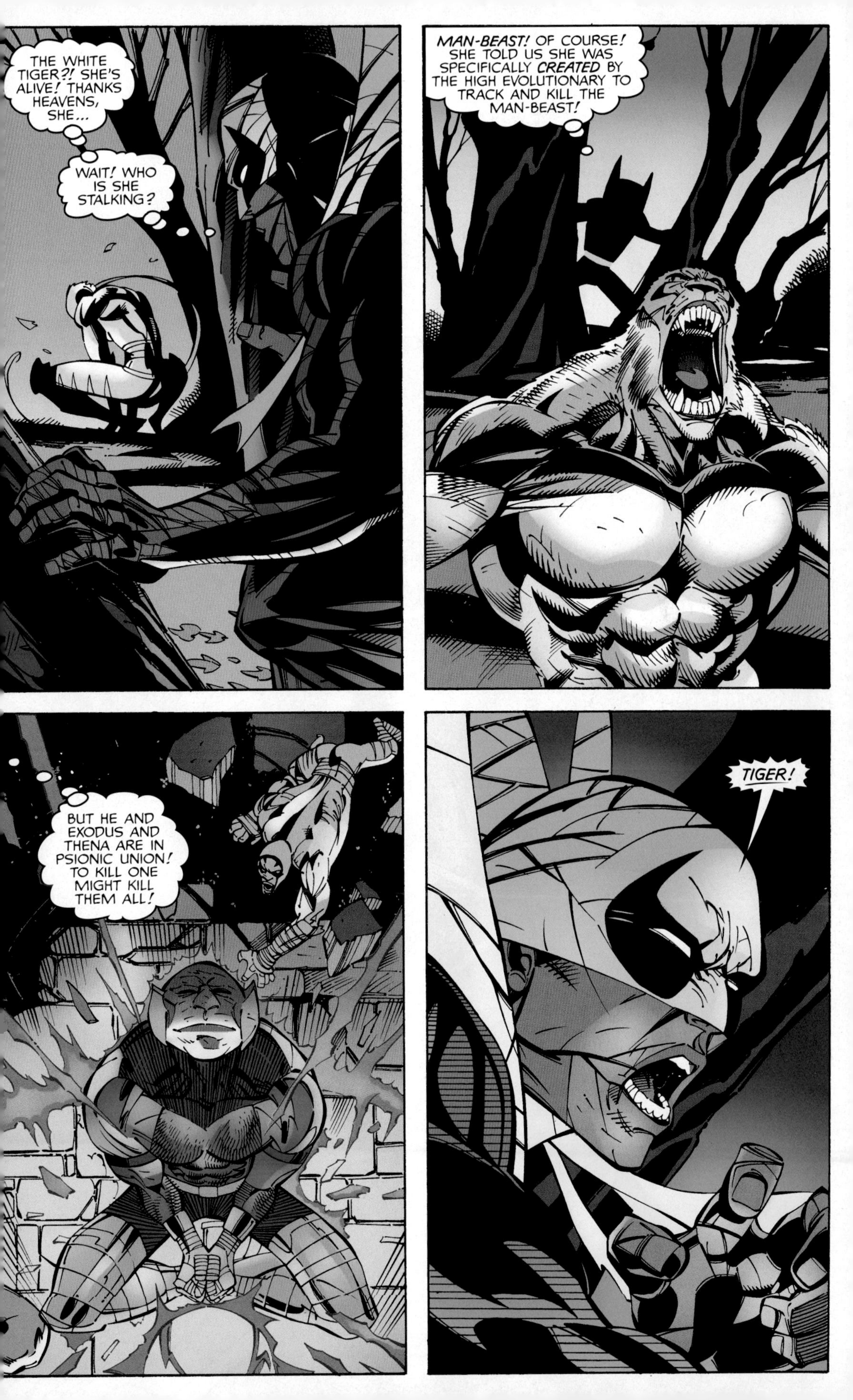

THE WHITE TIGER?! SHE'S ALIVE! THANKS HEAVENS, SHE...
WAIT! WHO IS SHE STALKING?
MAN-BEAST! OF COURSE! SHE TOLD US SHE WAS SPECIFICALLY CREATED BY THE HIGH EVOLUTIONARY TO TRACK AND KILL THE MAN-BEAST!
BUT HE AND EXODUS AND THENA ARE IN PSIONIC UNION! TO KILL ONE MIGHT KILL THEM ALL!
TIGER!

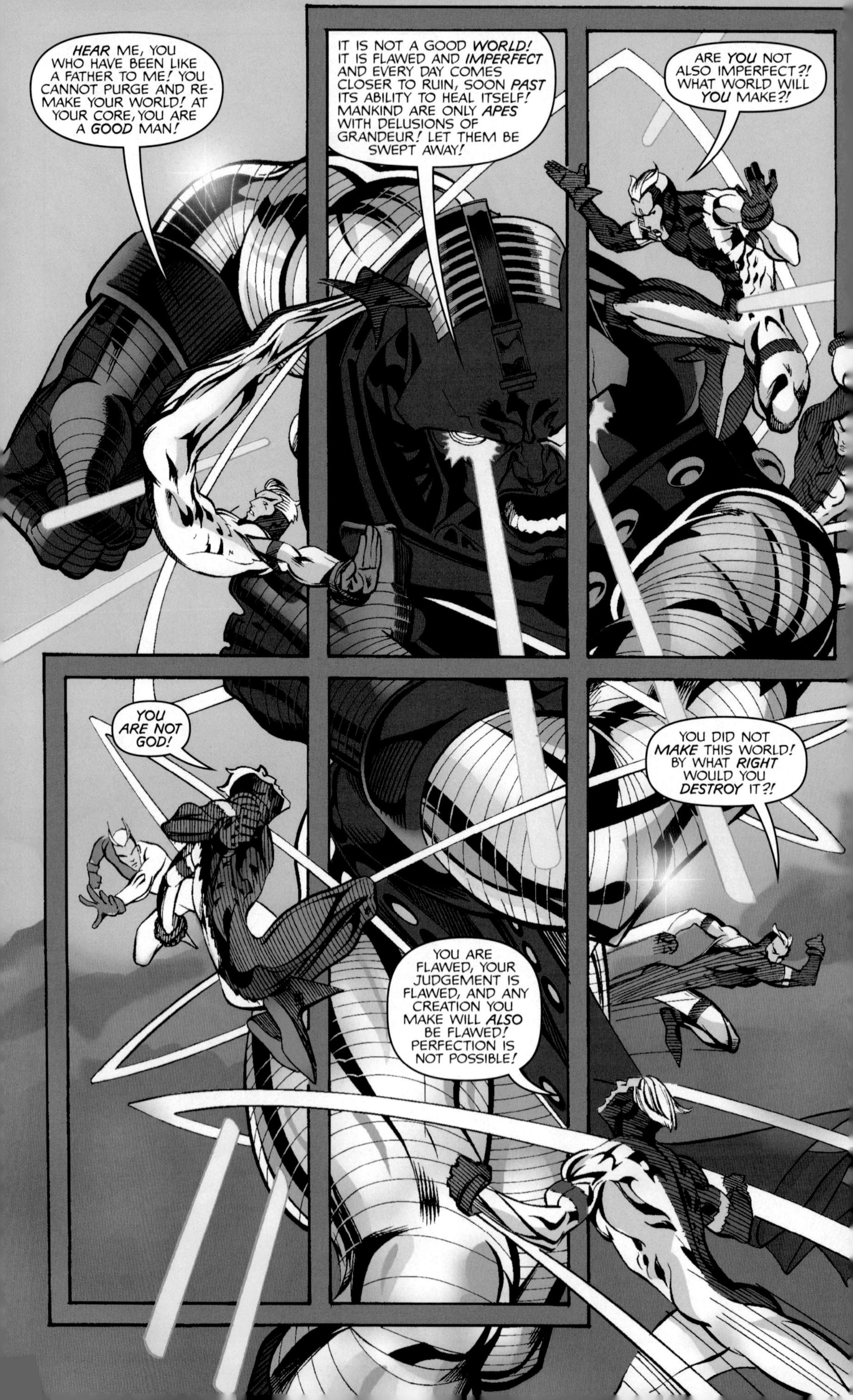
HEAR ME, YOU WHO HAVE BEEN LIKE A FATHER TO ME! YOU CANNOT PURGE AND RE-MAKE YOUR WORLD! AT YOUR CORE, YOU ARE A GOOD MAN!
IT IS NOT A GOOD WORLD! IT IS FLAWED AND IMPERFECT AND EVERY DAY COMES CLOSER TO RUIN, SOON PAST ITS ABILITY TO HEAL ITSELF! MANKIND ARE ONLY APES WITH DELUSIONS OF GRANDEUR! LET THEM BE SWEPT AWAY!
ARE YOU NOT ALSO IMPERFECT?! WHAT WORLD WILL YOU MAKE?!
YOU ARE NOT GOD!
YOU DID NOT MAKE THIS WORLD! BY WHAT RIGHT WOULD YOU DESTROY IT?!
YOU ARE FLAWED, YOUR JUDGEMENT IS FLAWED, AND ANY CREATION YOU MAKE WILL ALSO BE FLAWED! PERFECTION IS NOT POSSIBLE!

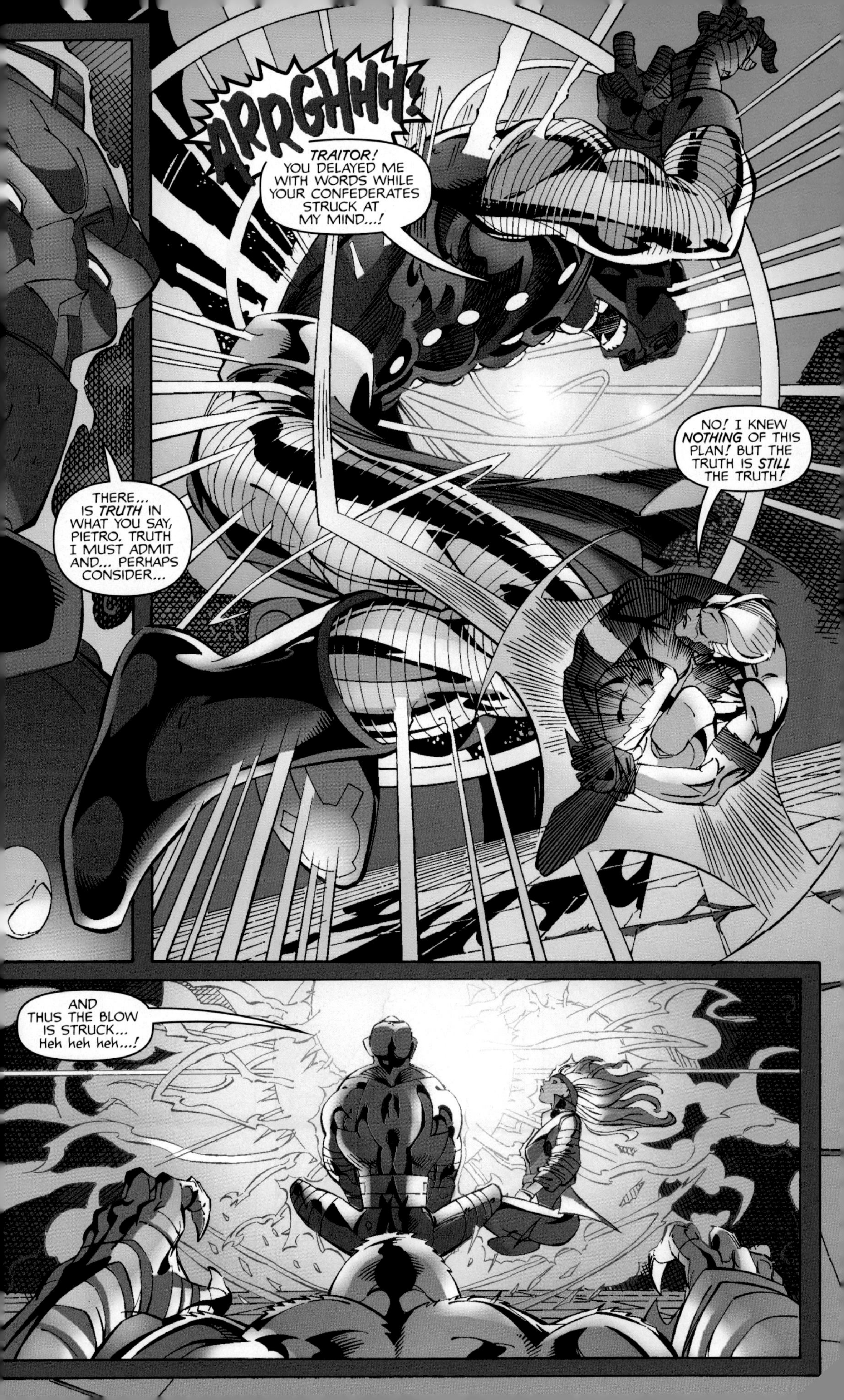
ARRGHHH!
TRAITOR! YOU DELAYED ME WITH WORDS WHILE YOUR CONFEDERATES STRUCK AT MY MIND...!
NO! I KNEW NOTHING OF THIS PLAN! BUT THE TRUTH IS STILL THE TRUTH!
THERE... IS TRUTH IN WHAT YOU SAY, PIETRO. TRUTH I MUST ADMIT AND... PERHAPS CONSIDER...
AND THUS THE BLOW IS STRUCK... Heh heh heh...!

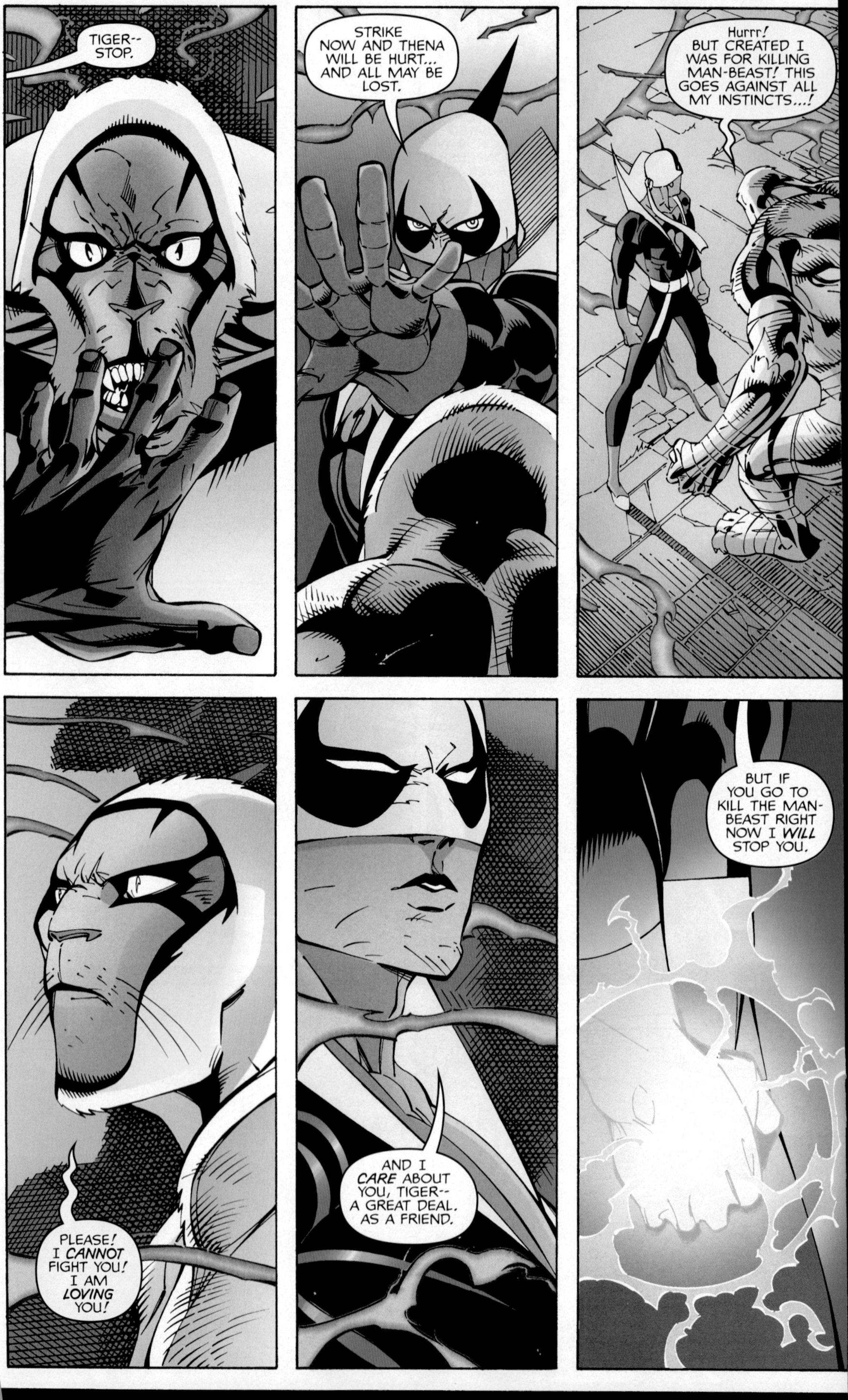
TIGER--
STOP.
STRIKE NOW AND THENA WILL BE HURT... AND ALL MAY BE LOST.
Hurrr! BUT CREATED I WAS FOR KILLING MAN-BEAST! THIS GOES AGAINST ALL MY INSTINCTS...!
PLEASE! I CANNOT FIGHT YOU! I AM LOVING YOU!
AND I CARE ABOUT YOU, TIGER-- A GREAT DEAL. AS A FRIEND.
BUT IF YOU GO TO KILL THE MAN-BEAST RIGHT NOW I WILL STOP YOU.

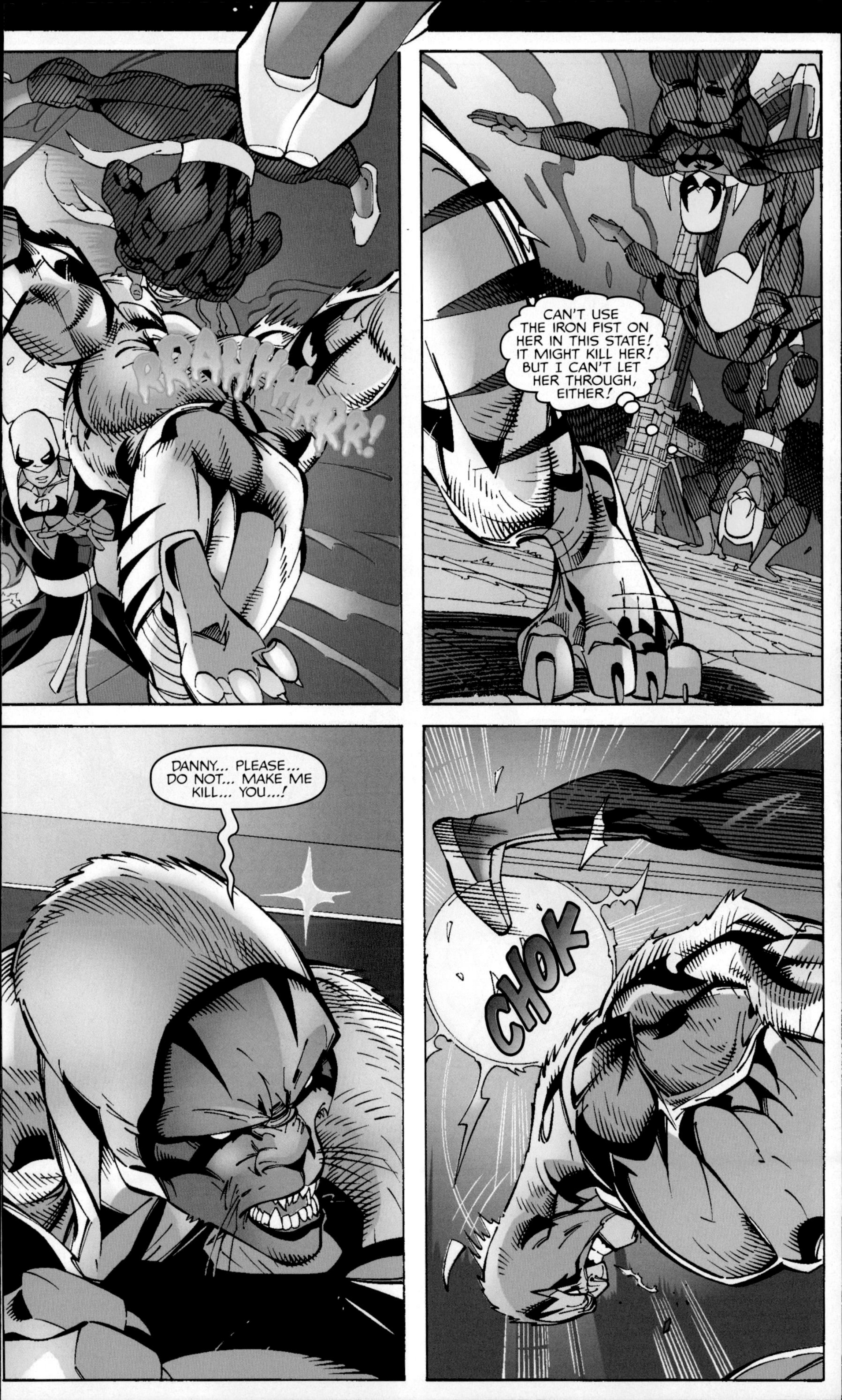
RRAHHHRRRR!
CAN'T USE THE IRON FIST ON HER IN THIS STATE! IT MIGHT KILL HER! BUT I CAN'T LET HER THROUGH, EITHER!
DANNY... PLEASE... DO NOT... MAKE ME KILL... YOU...!
CHOK

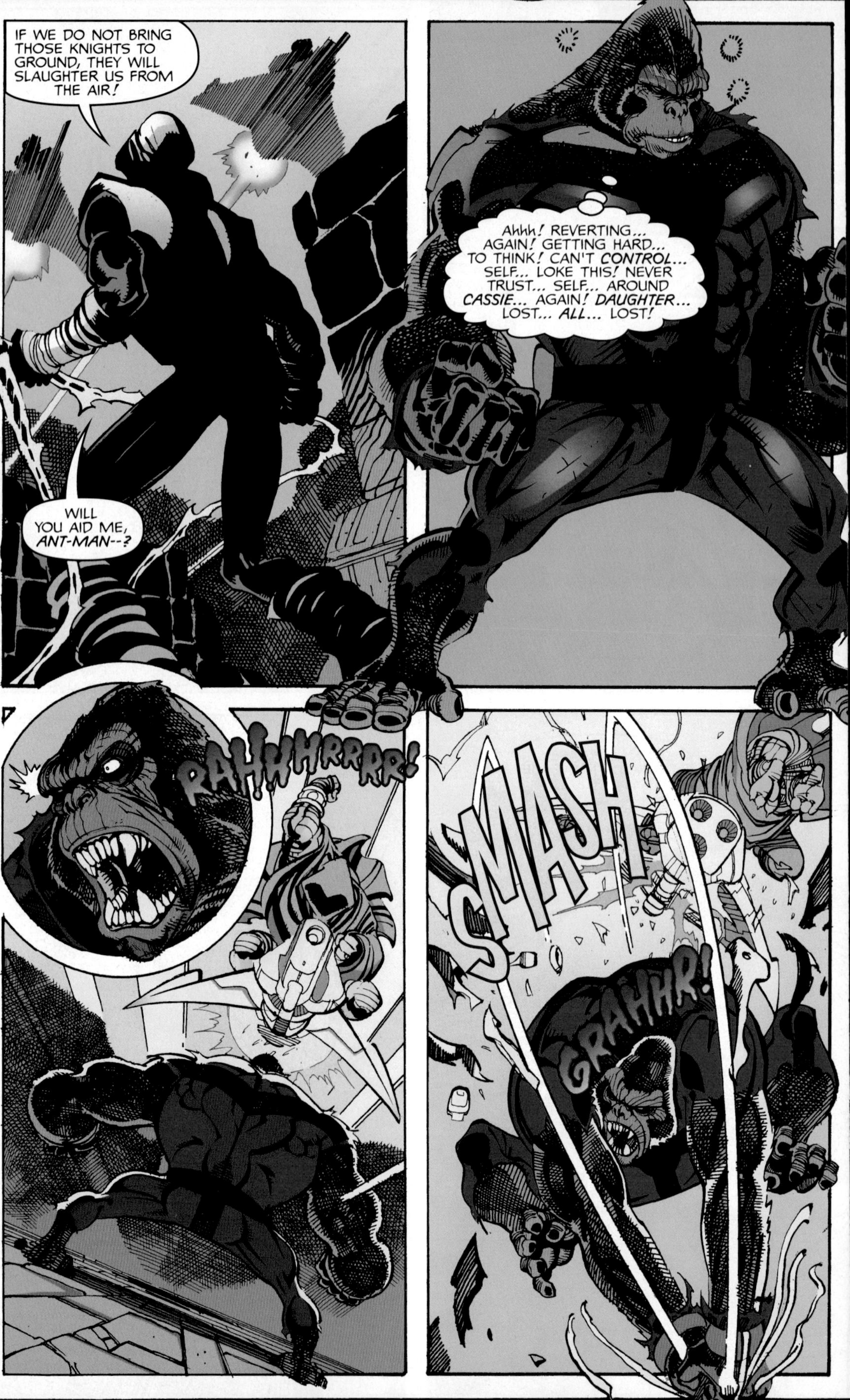
IF WE DO NOT BRING THOSE KNIGHTS TO GROUND, THEY WILL SLAUGHTER US FROM THE AIR!
WILL YOU AID ME, ANT-MAN--?
Ahhh! REVERTING... AGAIN! GETTING HARD... TO THINK! CAN'T CONTROL... SELF... LOKE THIS! NEVER TRUST... SELF... AROUND CASSIE... AGAIN! DAUGHTER... LOST... ALL... LOST!
RAHHHRRRRR!
SMASH
GRAHHR!

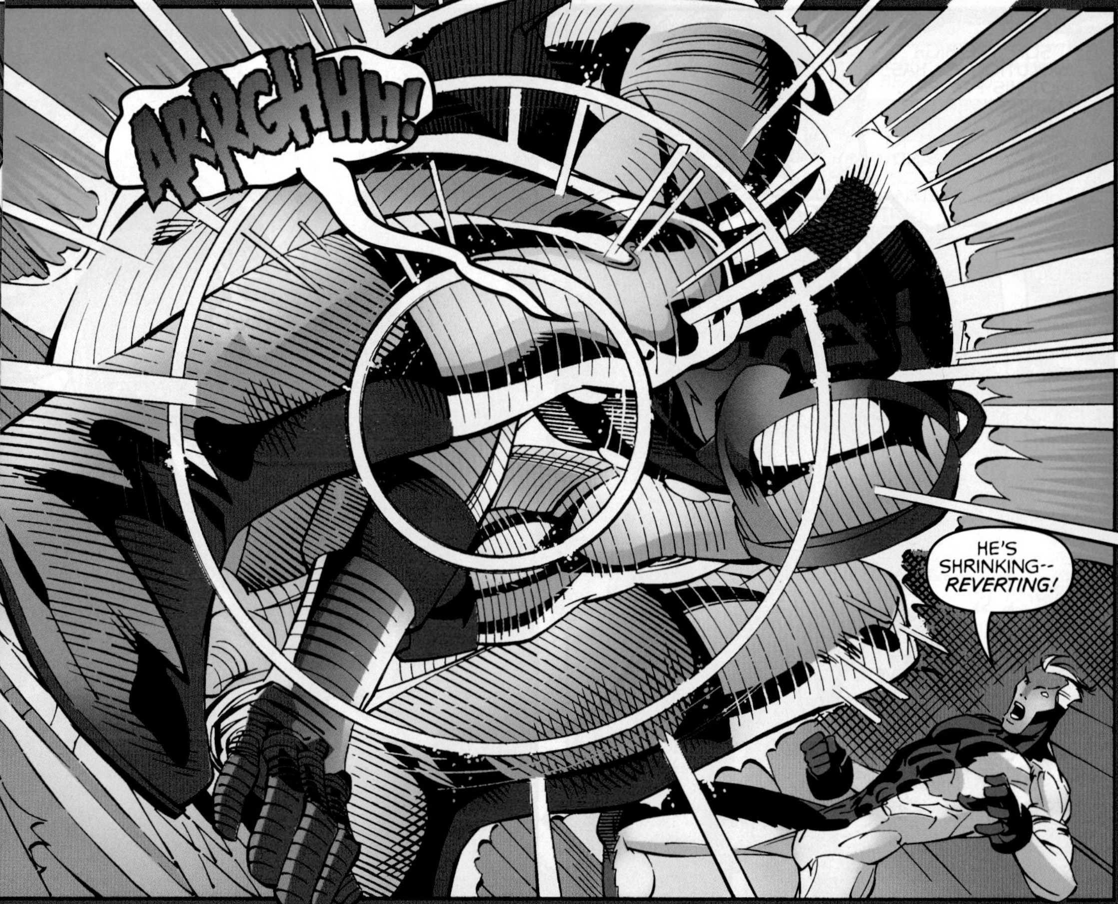
ARRGHHH!
HE'S SHRINKING-- REVERTING!
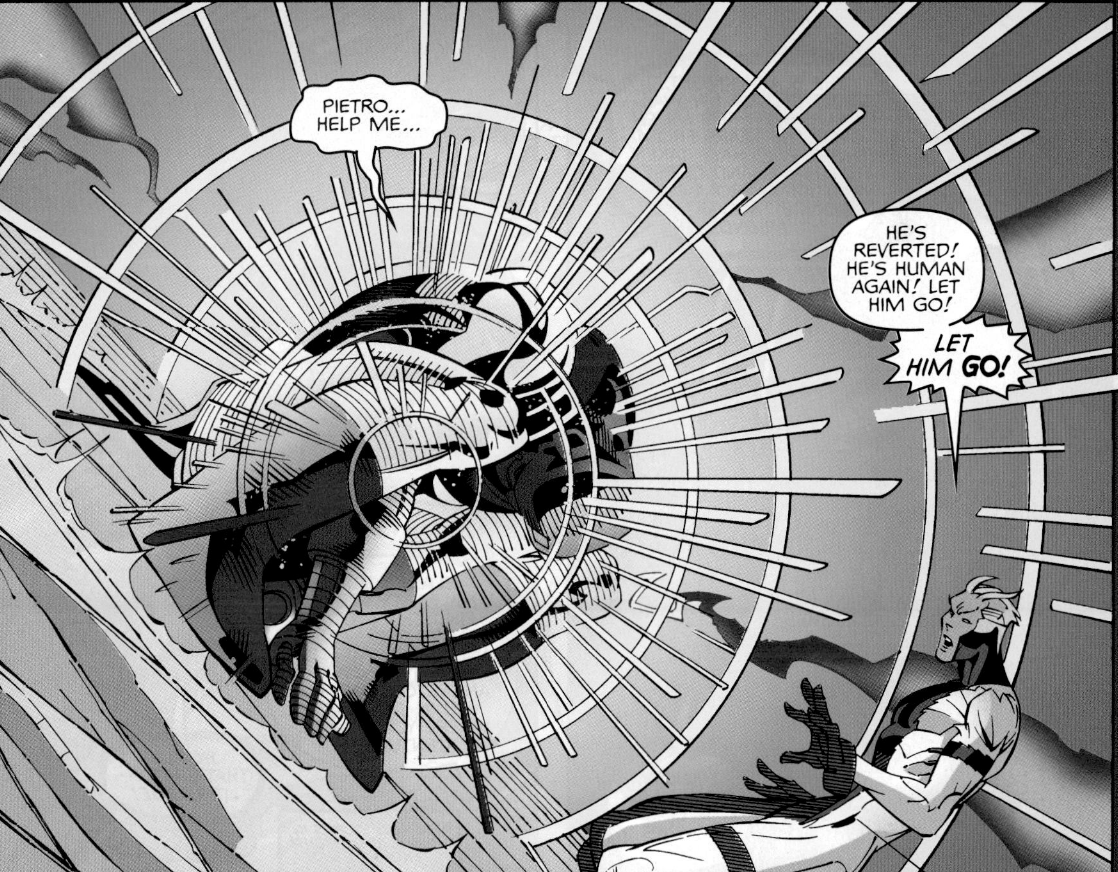
PIETRO... HELP ME...
HE'S REVERTED! HE'S HUMAN AGAIN! LET HIM GO!
LET HIM GO!

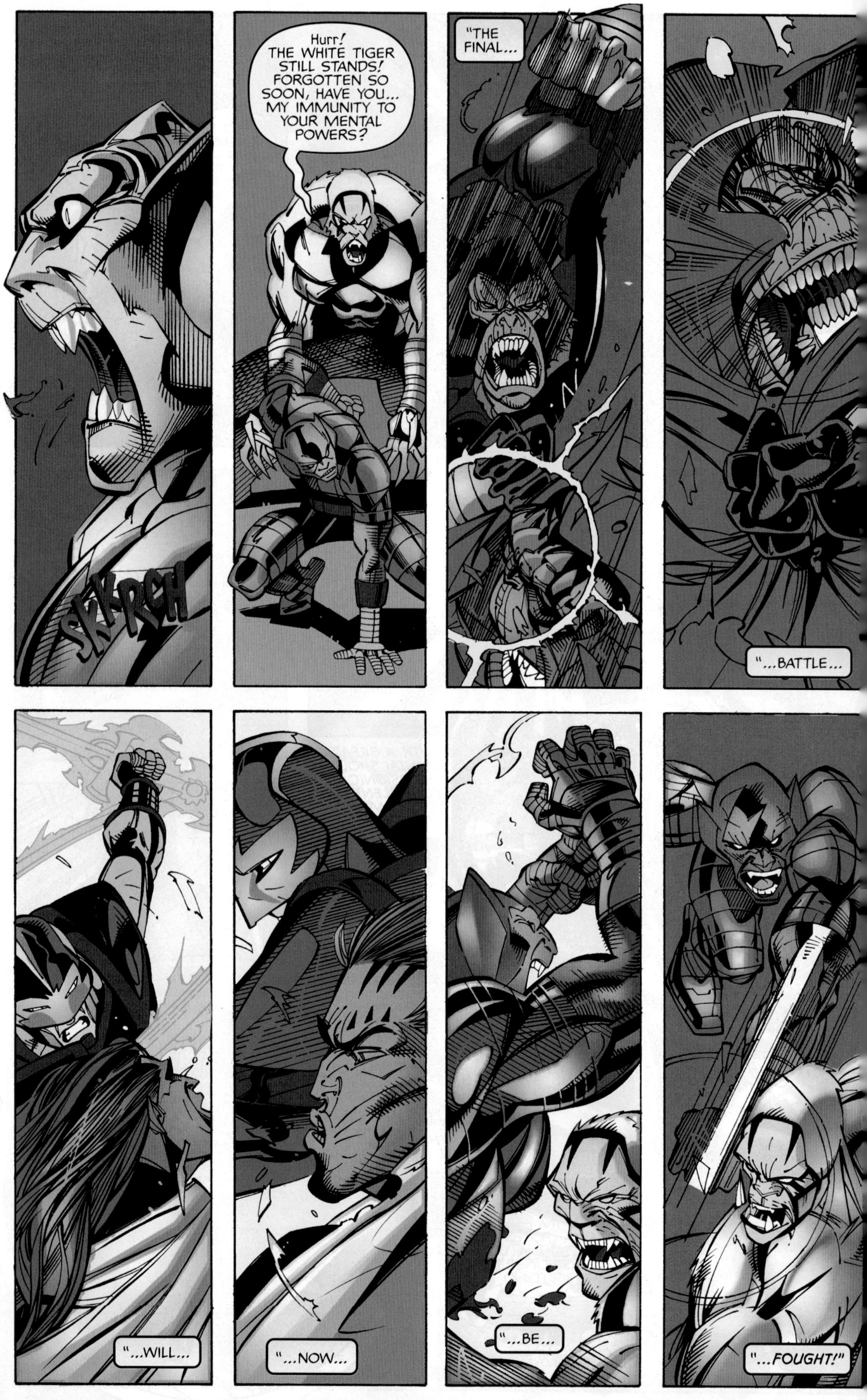
SKKRCH
Hurr! THE WHITE TIGER STILL STANDS! FORGOTTEN SO SOON, HAVE YOU... MY IMMUNITY TO YOUR MENTAL POWERS?
"THE FINAL...
"...BATTLE...
"...WILL...
"...NOW...
"...BE...
"...FOUGHT!"

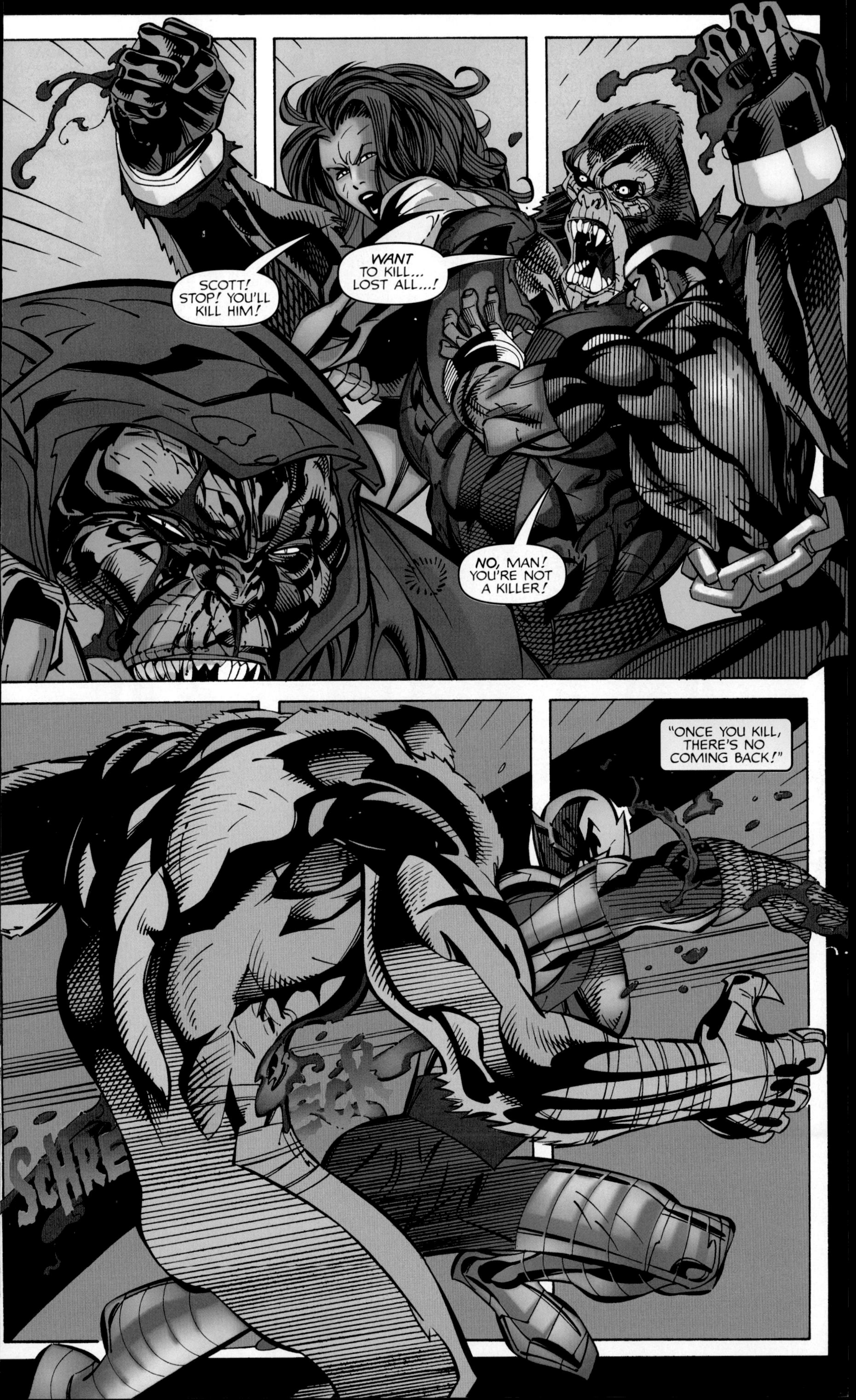
SCOTT! STOP! YOU'LL KILL HIM!
WANT TO KILL... LOST ALL...!
NO, MAN! YOU'RE NOT A KILLER!
"ONCE YOU KILL, THERE'S NO COMING BACK!"
SCHRE
ECK

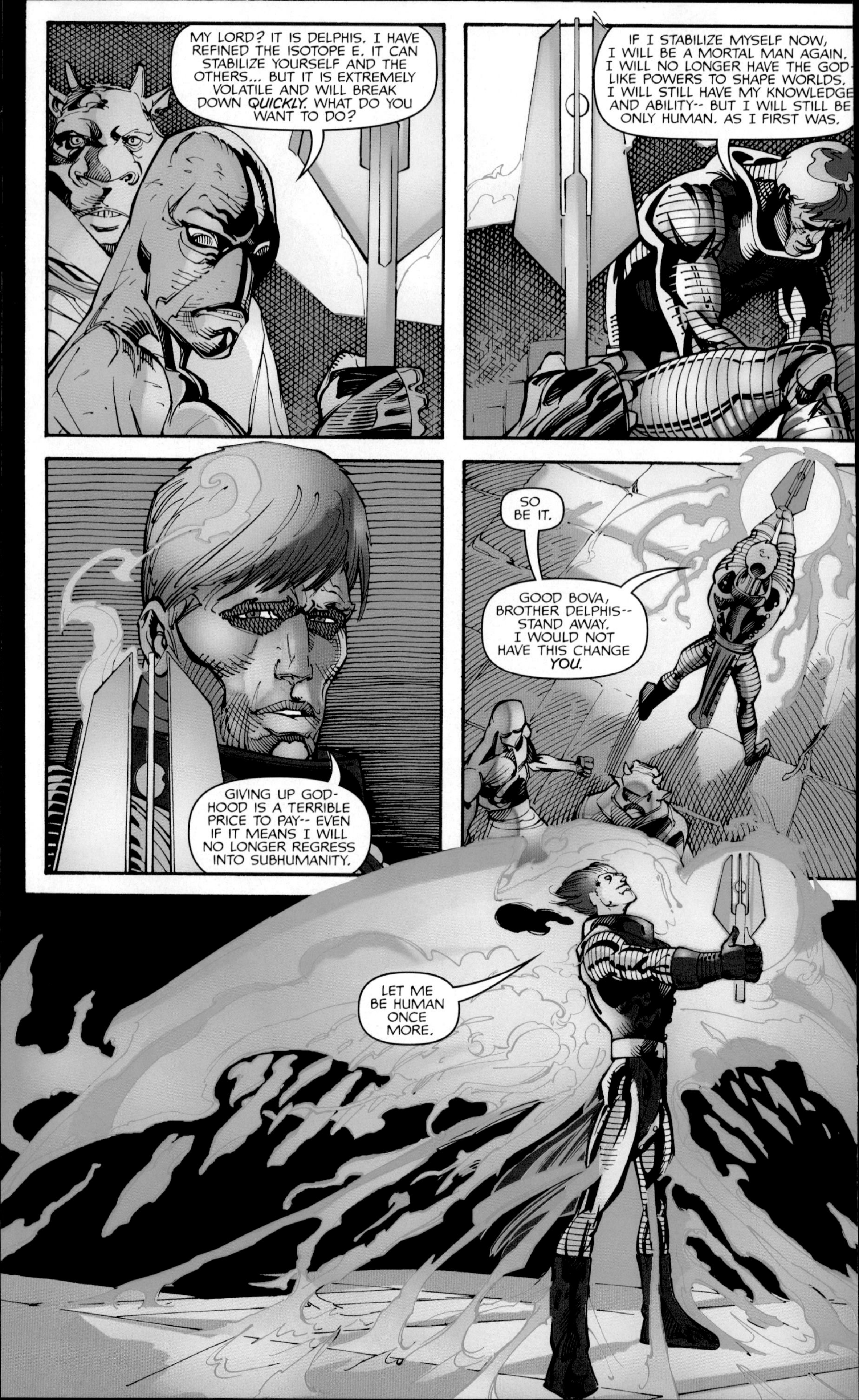
MY LORD? IT IS DELPHIS. I HAVE REFINED THE ISOTOPE E. IT CAN STABILIZE YOURSELF AND THE OTHERS... BUT IT IS EXTREMELY VOLATILE AND WILL BREAK DOWN QUICKLY. WHAT DO YOU WANT TO DO?
IF I STABILIZE MYSELF NOW, I WILL BE A MORTAL MAN AGAIN. I WILL NO LONGER HAVE THE GOD-LIKE POWERS TO SHAPE WORLDS. I WILL STILL HAVE MY KNOWLEDGE AND ABILITY-- BUT I WILL STILL BE ONLY HUMAN. AS I FIRST WAS.
GIVING UP GOD-HOOD IS A TERRIBLE PRICE TO PAY-- EVEN IF IT MEANS I WILL NO LONGER REGRESS INTO SUBHUMANITY.
SO BE IT.
GOOD BOVA, BROTHER DELPHIS-- STAND AWAY. I WOULD NOT HAVE THIS CHANGE YOU.
LET ME BE HUMAN ONCE MORE.

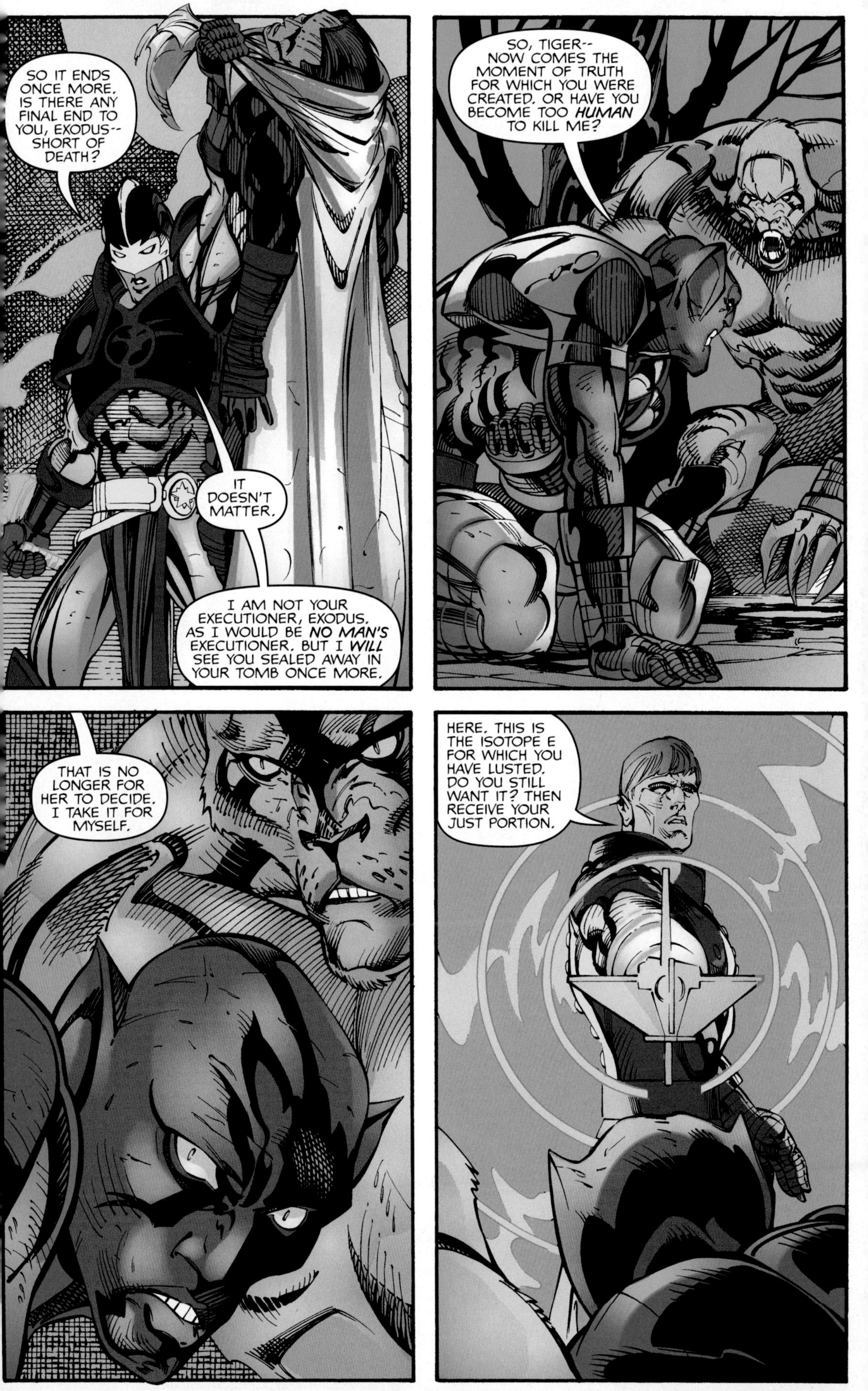
SO IT ENDS ONCE MORE. IS THERE ANY FINAL END TO YOU, EXODUS-- SHORT OF DEATH?
IT DOESN'T MATTER.
I AM NOT YOUR EXECUTIONER, EXODUS. AS I WOULD BE NO MAN'S EXECUTIONER. BUT I WILL SEE YOU SEALED AWAY IN YOUR TOMB ONCE MORE.
SO, TIGER-- NOW COMES THE MOMENT OF TRUTH FOR WHICH YOU WERE CREATED. OR HAVE YOU BECOME TOO HUMAN TO KILL ME?
THAT IS NO LONGER FOR HER TO DECIDE. I TAKE IT FOR MYSELF.
HERE. THIS IS THE ISOTOPE E FOR WHICH YOU HAVE LUSTED. DO YOU STILL WANT IT? THEN RECEIVE YOUR JUST PORTION.

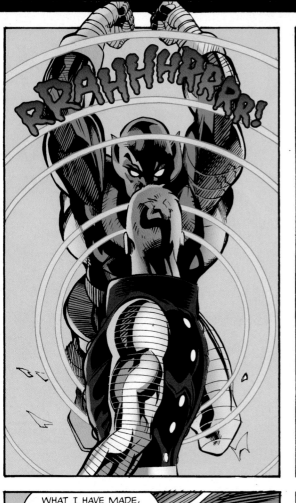

RRAHHHRRRr!

FASSHHH

WHAT I HAVE MADE, I HAVE UNMADE. WOLF YOU WERE AND WOLF YOU ARE, REMEMBERING NOTHING OF WHAT YOU WERE. GO, WOLF.

AND NOW I WILL MAKE RIGHT WHAT I DID WRONGFULLY.

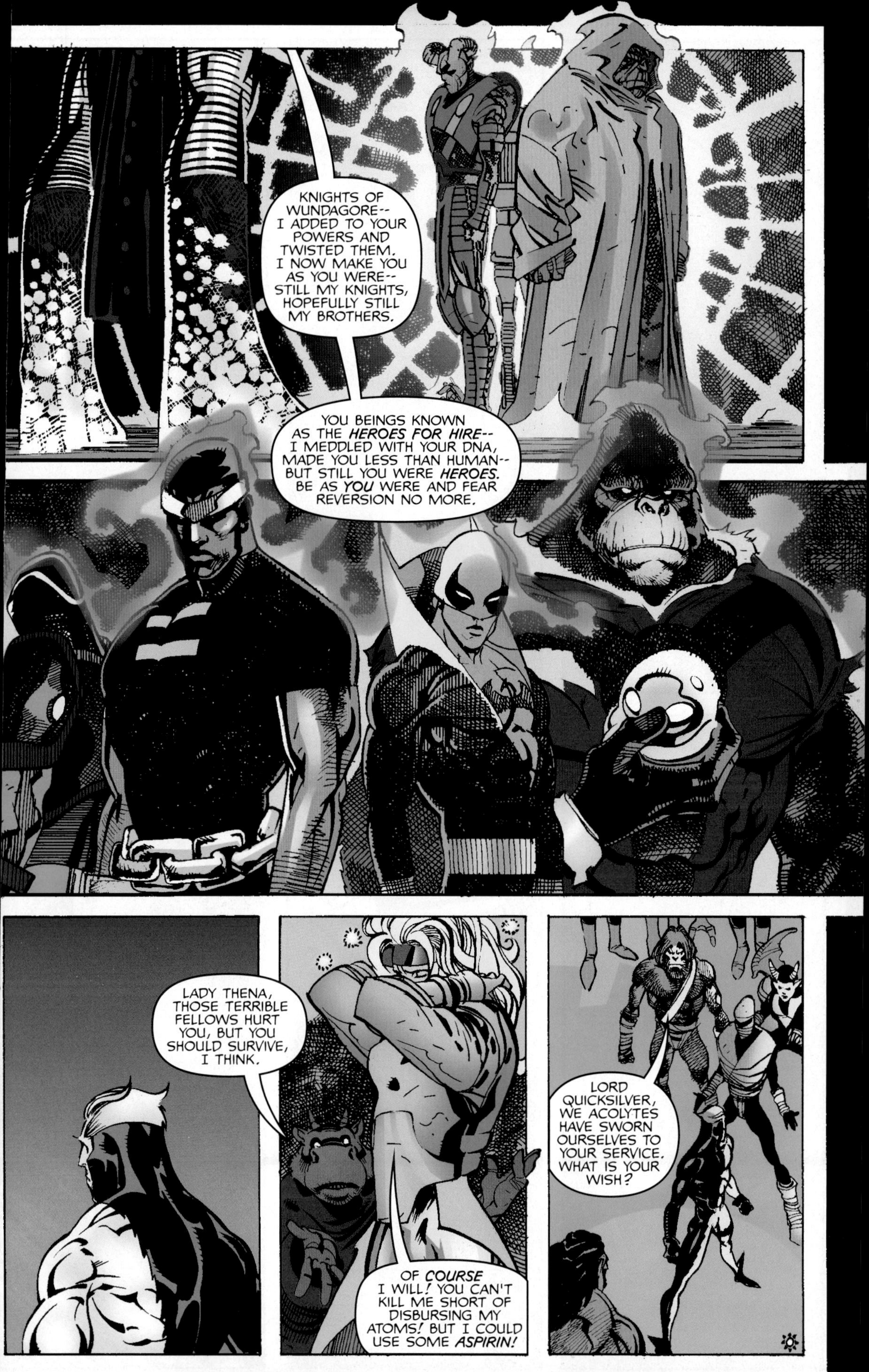
KNIGHTS OF WUNDAGORE-- I ADDED TO YOUR POWERS AND TWISTED THEM. I NOW MAKE YOU AS YOU WERE-- STILL MY KNIGHTS, HOPEFULLY STILL MY BROTHERS.
YOU BEINGS KNOWN AS THE HEROES FOR HIRE-- I MEDDLED WITH YOUR DNA, MADE YOU LESS THAN HUMAN-- BUT STILL YOU WERE HEROES. BE AS YOU WERE AND FEAR REVERSION NO MORE.
LADY THENA, THOSE TERRIBLE FELLOWS HURT YOU, BUT YOU SHOULD SURVIVE, I THINK.
OF COURSE I WILL! YOU CAN'T KILL ME SHORT OF DISBURSING MY ATOMS! BUT I COULD USE SOME ASPIRIN!
LORD QUICKSILVER, WE ACOLYTES HAVE SWORN OURSELVES TO YOUR SERVICE. WHAT IS YOUR WISH?

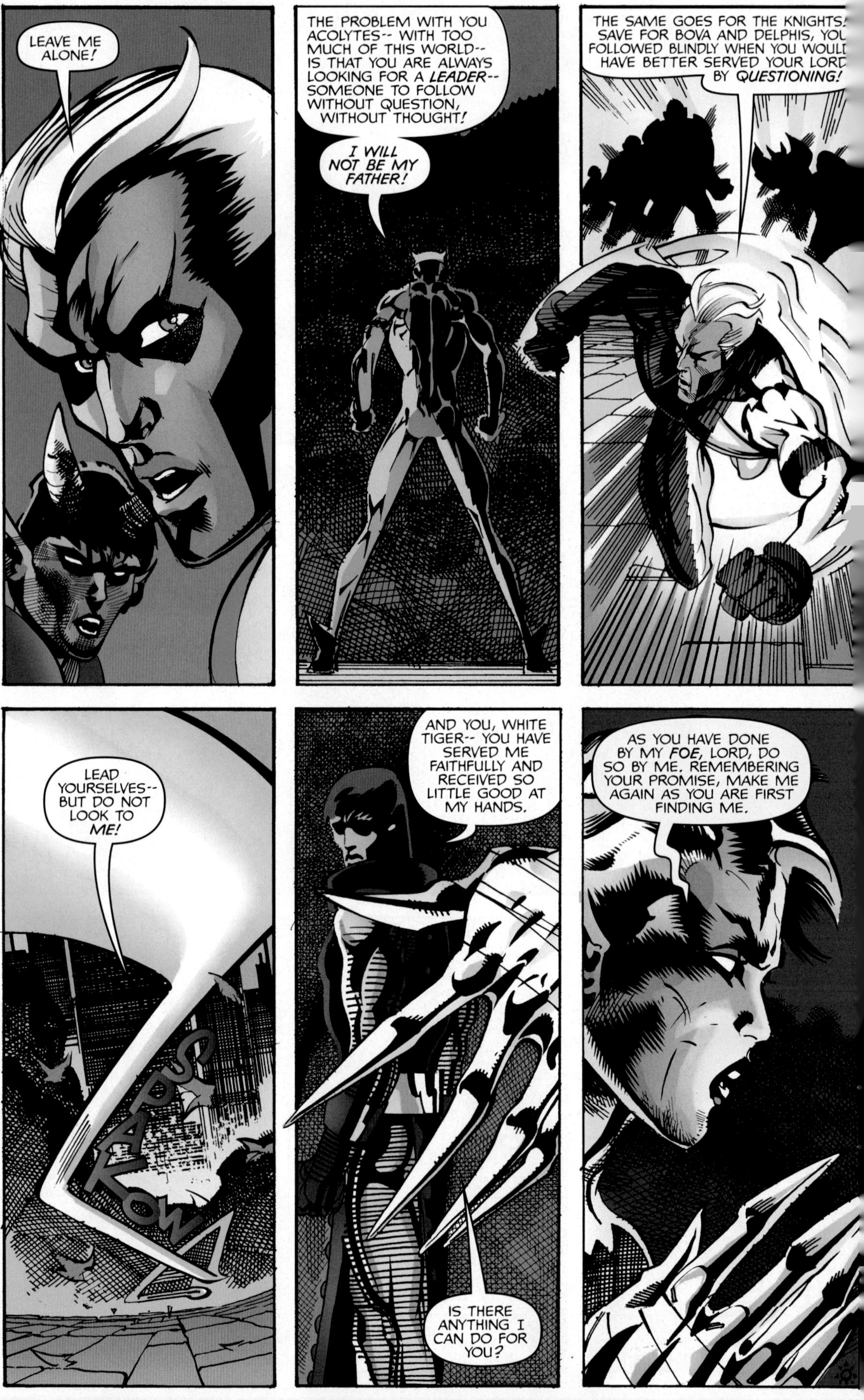
LEAVE ME ALONE!
THE PROBLEM WITH YOU ACOLYTES-- WITH TOO MUCH OF THIS WORLD-- IS THAT YOU ARE ALWAYS LOOKING FOR A *LEADER*-- SOMEONE TO FOLLOW WITHOUT QUESTION, WITHOUT THOUGHT!
I WILL NOT BE MY FATHER!
THE SAME GOES FOR THE KNIGHTS! SAVE FOR BOVA AND DELPHIS, YOU FOLLOWED BLINDLY WHEN YOU WOULD HAVE BETTER SERVED YOUR LORD BY *QUESTIONING!*
LEAD YOURSELVES-- BUT DO NOT LOOK TO *ME!*
SPAKOW
AND YOU, WHITE TIGER-- YOU HAVE SERVED ME FAITHFULLY AND RECEIVED SO LITTLE GOOD AT MY HANDS.
IS THERE ANYTHING I CAN DO FOR YOU?
AS YOU HAVE DONE BY MY *FOE,* LORD, DO SO BY ME. REMEMBERING YOUR PROMISE, MAKE ME AGAIN AS YOU ARE FIRST FINDING ME.

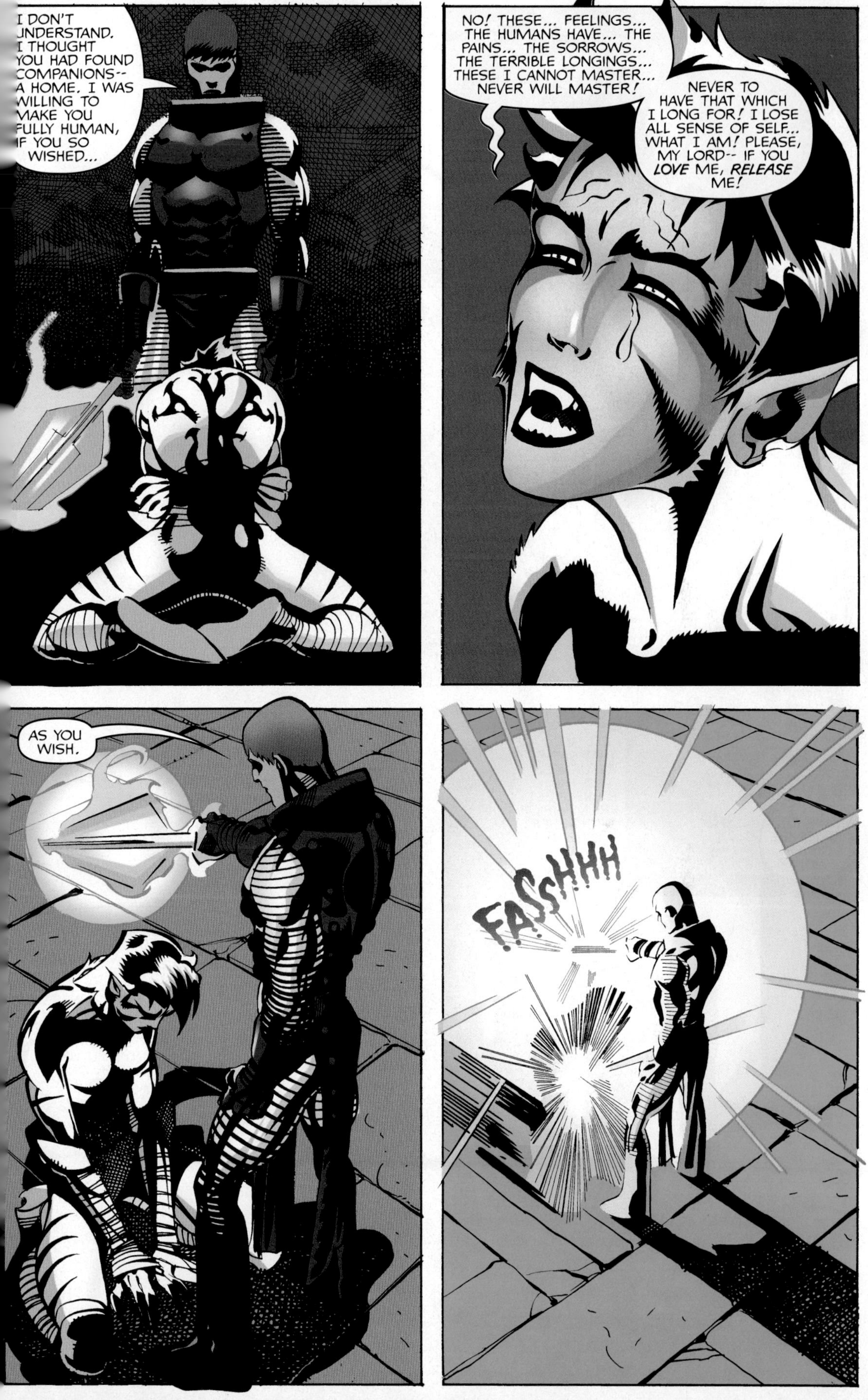
I DON'T UNDERSTAND. I THOUGHT YOU HAD FOUND COMPANIONS-- A HOME. I WAS WILLING TO MAKE YOU FULLY HUMAN, IF YOU SO WISHED...
NO! THESE... FEELINGS... THE HUMANS HAVE... THE PAINS... THE SORROWS... THE TERRIBLE LONGINGS... THESE I CANNOT MASTER... NEVER WILL MASTER!
NEVER TO HAVE THAT WHICH I LONG FOR! I LOSE ALL SENSE OF SELF... WHAT I AM! PLEASE, MY LORD-- IF YOU LOVE ME, RELEASE ME!
AS YOU WISH.
FASSHHH

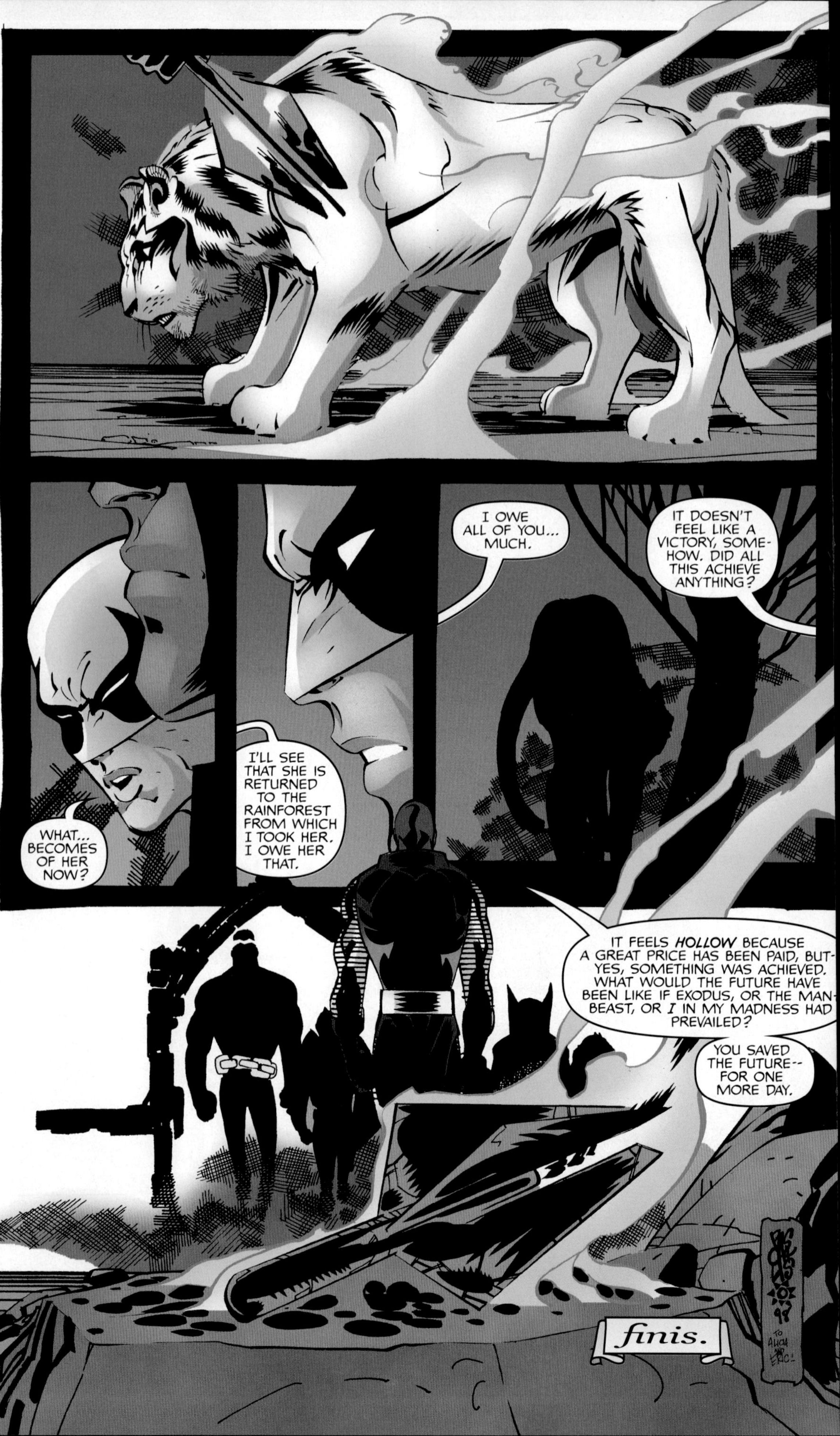

WHAT... BECOMES OF HER NOW?
I'LL SEE THAT SHE IS RETURNED TO THE RAINFOREST FROM WHICH I TOOK HER. I OWE HER THAT.
I OWE ALL OF YOU... MUCH.
IT DOESN'T FEEL LIKE A VICTORY, SOMEHOW. DID ALL THIS ACHIEVE ANYTHING?
IT FEELS HOLLOW BECAUSE A GREAT PRICE HAS BEEN PAID, BUT-YES, SOMETHING WAS ACHIEVED. WHAT WOULD THE FUTURE HAVE BEEN LIKE IF EXODUS, OR THE MAN-BEAST, OR I IN MY MADNESS HAD PREVAILED?
YOU SAVED THE FUTURE--FOR ONE MORE DAY.
finis.

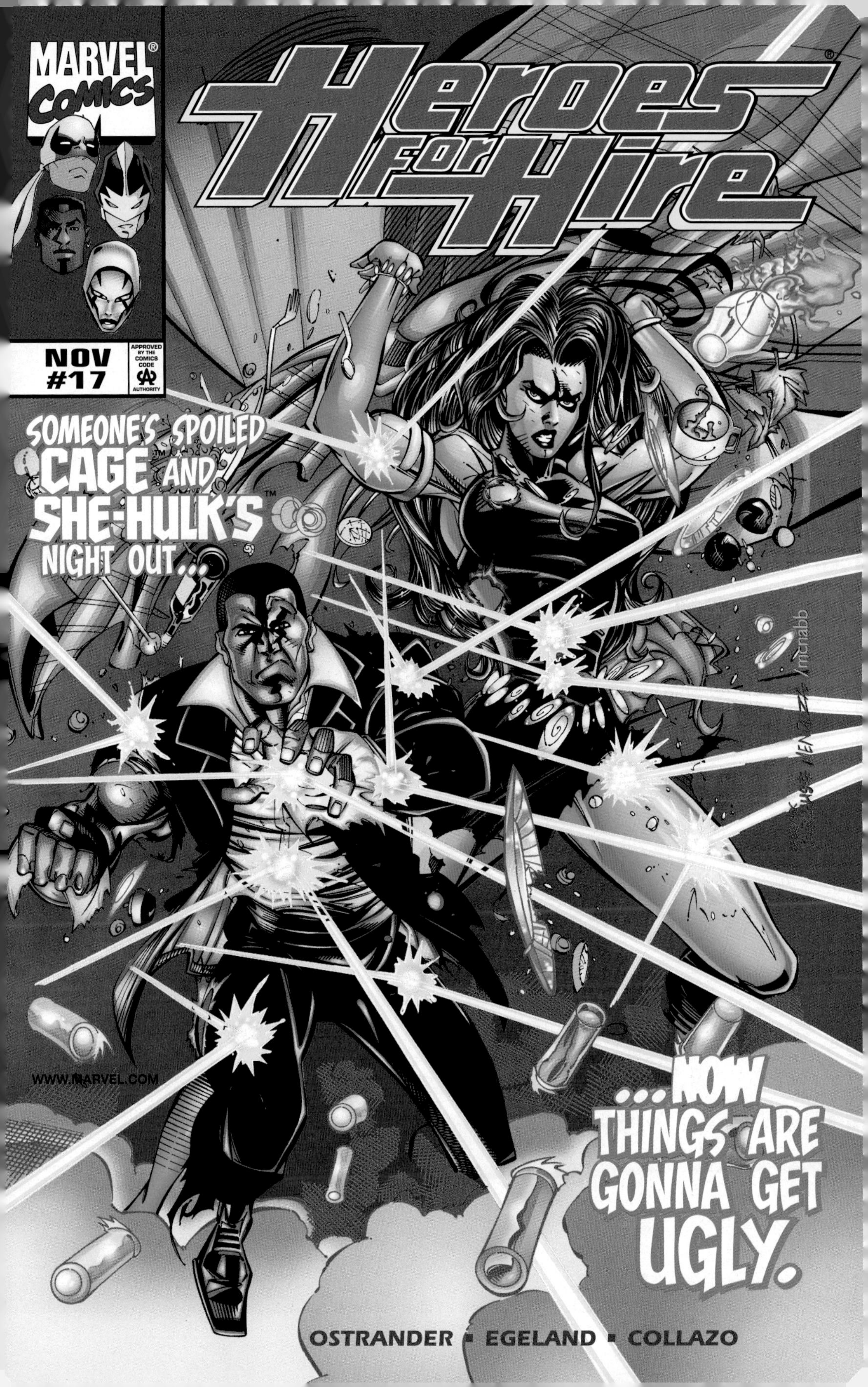
MARVEL COMICS
Heroes for Hire
NOV #17
APPROVED BY THE COMICS CODE AUTHORITY
SOMEONE'S SPOILED CAGE AND SHE-HULK'S NIGHT OUT...
WWW.MARVEL.COM
...NOW THINGS ARE GONNA GET UGLY.
OSTRANDER • EGELAND • COLLAZO

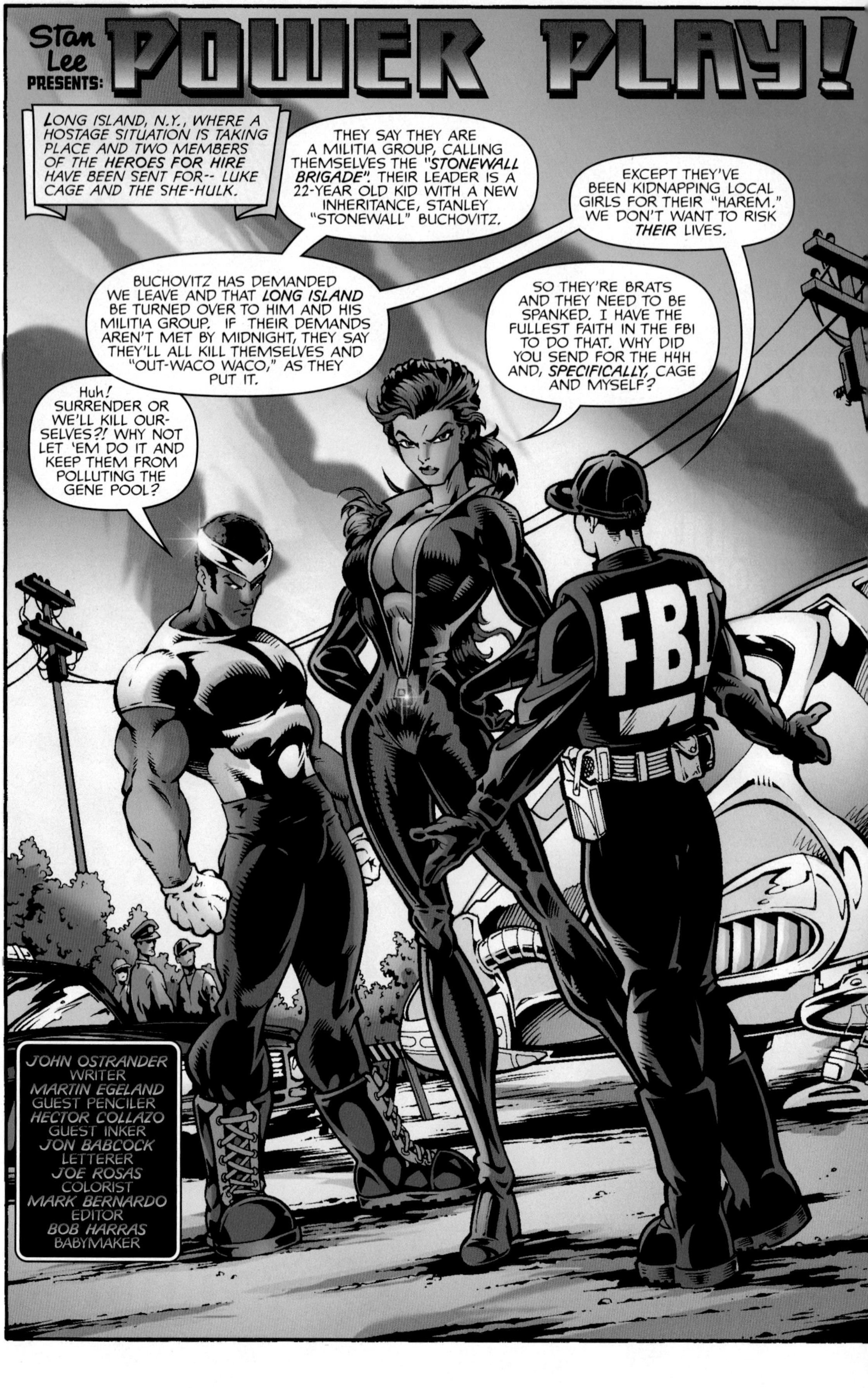
Stan Lee PRESENTS: POWER PLAY!
LONG ISLAND, N.Y., WHERE A HOSTAGE SITUATION IS TAKING PLACE AND TWO MEMBERS OF THE HEROES FOR HIRE HAVE BEEN SENT FOR-- LUKE CAGE AND THE SHE-HULK.
THEY SAY THEY ARE A MILITIA GROUP, CALLING THEMSELVES THE "STONEWALL BRIGADE". THEIR LEADER IS A 22-YEAR OLD KID WITH A NEW INHERITANCE, STANLEY "STONEWALL" BUCHOVITZ.
EXCEPT THEY'VE BEEN KIDNAPPING LOCAL GIRLS FOR THEIR "HAREM." WE DON'T WANT TO RISK THEIR LIVES.
BUCHOVITZ HAS DEMANDED WE LEAVE AND THAT LONG ISLAND BE TURNED OVER TO HIM AND HIS MILITIA GROUP. IF THEIR DEMANDS AREN'T MET BY MIDNIGHT, THEY SAY THEY'LL ALL KILL THEMSELVES AND "OUT-WACO WACO," AS THEY PUT IT.
SO THEY'RE BRATS AND THEY NEED TO BE SPANKED. I HAVE THE FULLEST FAITH IN THE FBI TO DO THAT. WHY DID YOU SEND FOR THE H4H AND, SPECIFICALLY, CAGE AND MYSELF?
Huh! SURRENDER OR WE'LL KILL OURSELVES?! WHY NOT LET 'EM DO IT AND KEEP THEM FROM POLLUTING THE GENE POOL?
FBI
JOHN OSTRANDER WRITER
MARTIN EGELAND GUEST PENCILER
HECTOR COLLAZO GUEST INKER
JON BABCOCK LETTERER
JOE ROSAS COLORIST
MARK BERNARDO EDITOR
BOB HARRAS BABYMAKER

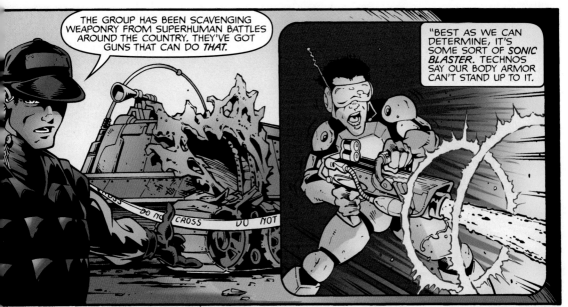

THE GROUP HAS BEEN SCAVENGING WEAPONRY FROM SUPERHUMAN BATTLES AROUND THE COUNTRY. THEY'VE GOT GUNS THAT CAN DO *THAT*.

"BEST AS WE CAN DETERMINE, IT'S SOME SORT OF *SONIC BLASTER*. TECHNOS SAY OUR BODY ARMOR CAN'T STAND UP TO IT.

THESE KIDS ARE LOOPY BUT THAT DOESN'T MEAN THEY AREN'T DANGEROUS. WE'RE HOPING YOU TWO HAVE SUFFICIENT BODY MASS TO STAND UP TO THE WEAPONS.

SOUNDS REASONABLE. WAY I FIGURE, WE TAKE THEIR COMMAND POST AND THE GAME'S OVER. I SUGGEST THAT WE GO IN FROM OPPOSITE SIDES WHILE YOU GUYS OUT FRONT GIVE US SOME COVER.

WHO DIED AND LEFT *YOU* IN CHARGE, CAGE?

YOU GOT A *BETTER* PLAN?

ACTUALLY, THAT *WAS* MY PLAN. YOU JUST BEAT ME TO IT.

LET'S GO.

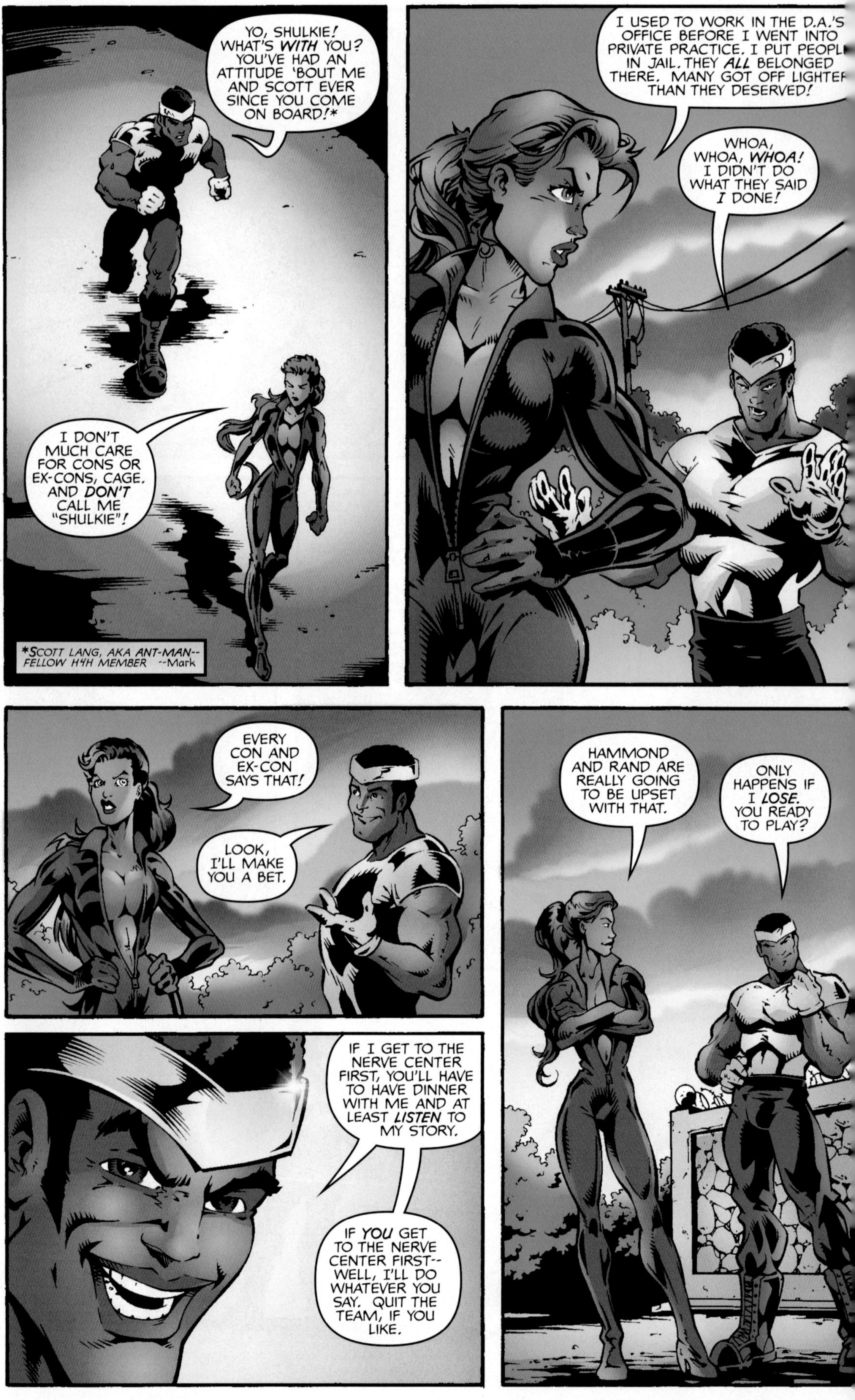
YO, SHULKIE! WHAT'S WITH YOU? YOU'VE HAD AN ATTITUDE 'BOUT ME AND SCOTT EVER SINCE YOU COME ON BOARD!*
I DON'T MUCH CARE FOR CONS OR EX-CONS, CAGE. AND DON'T CALL ME "SHULKIE"!
*SCOTT LANG, AKA ANT-MAN-- FELLOW H4H MEMBER --Mark
I USED TO WORK IN THE D.A.'S OFFICE BEFORE I WENT INTO PRIVATE PRACTICE. I PUT PEOPL IN JAIL. THEY ALL BELONGED THERE. MANY GOT OFF LIGHTE THAN THEY DESERVED!
WHOA, WHOA, WHOA! I DIDN'T DO WHAT THEY SAID I DONE!
EVERY CON AND EX-CON SAYS THAT!
LOOK, I'LL MAKE YOU A BET.
IF I GET TO THE NERVE CENTER FIRST, YOU'LL HAVE TO HAVE DINNER WITH ME AND AT LEAST LISTEN TO MY STORY.
IF YOU GET TO THE NERVE CENTER FIRST-- WELL, I'LL DO WHATEVER YOU SAY. QUIT THE TEAM, IF YOU LIKE.
HAMMOND AND RAND ARE REALLY GOING TO BE UPSET WITH THAT.
ONLY HAPPENS IF I LOSE. YOU READY TO PLAY?

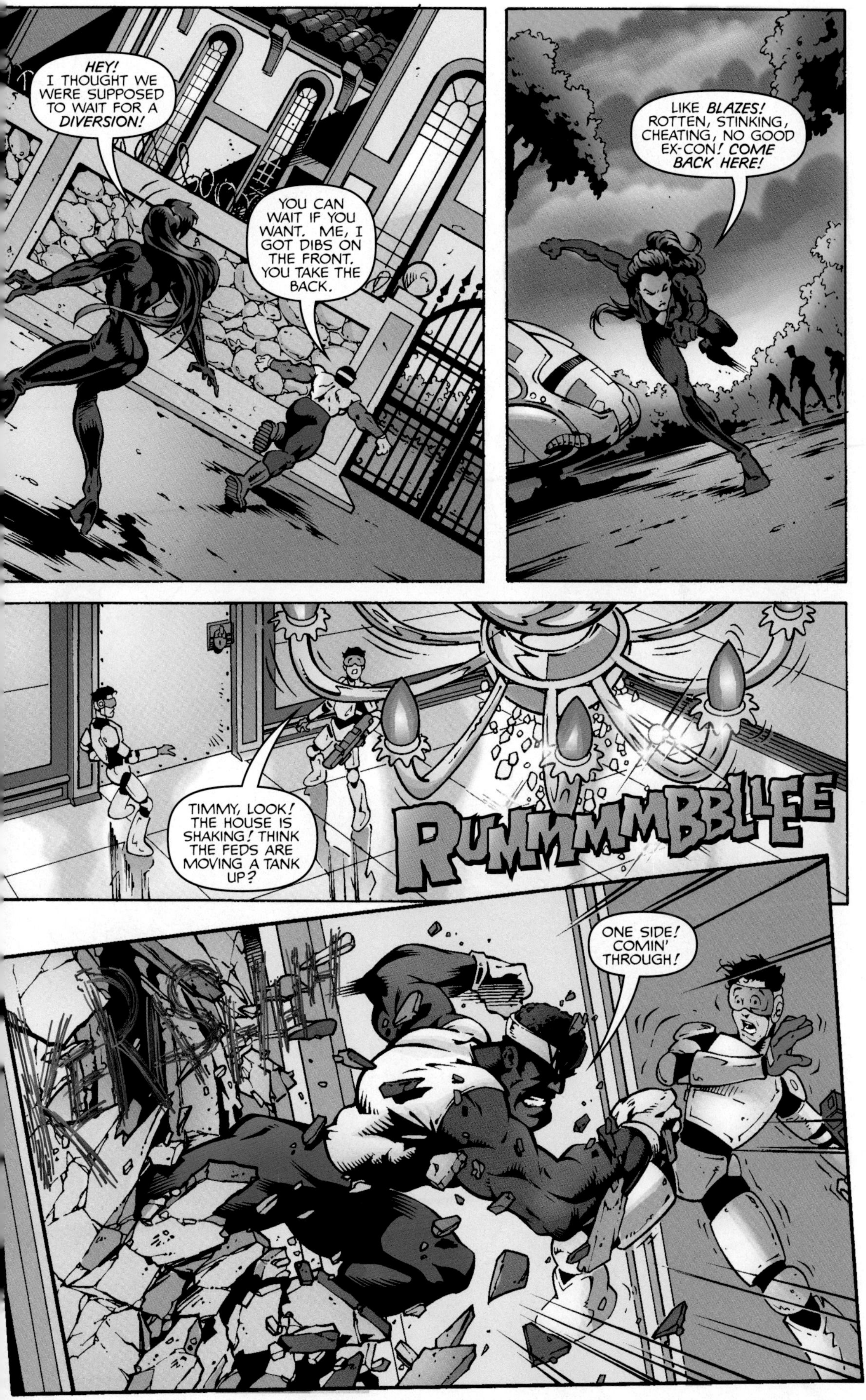
HEY! I THOUGHT WE WERE SUPPOSED TO WAIT FOR A DIVERSION!
YOU CAN WAIT IF YOU WANT. ME, I GOT DIBS ON THE FRONT. YOU TAKE THE BACK.
LIKE BLAZES! ROTTEN, STINKING, CHEATING, NO GOOD EX-CON! COME BACK HERE!
TIMMY, LOOK! THE HOUSE IS SHAKING! THINK THE FEDS ARE MOVING A TANK UP?
RUMMMMBBLLEE
ONE SIDE! COMIN' THROUGH!

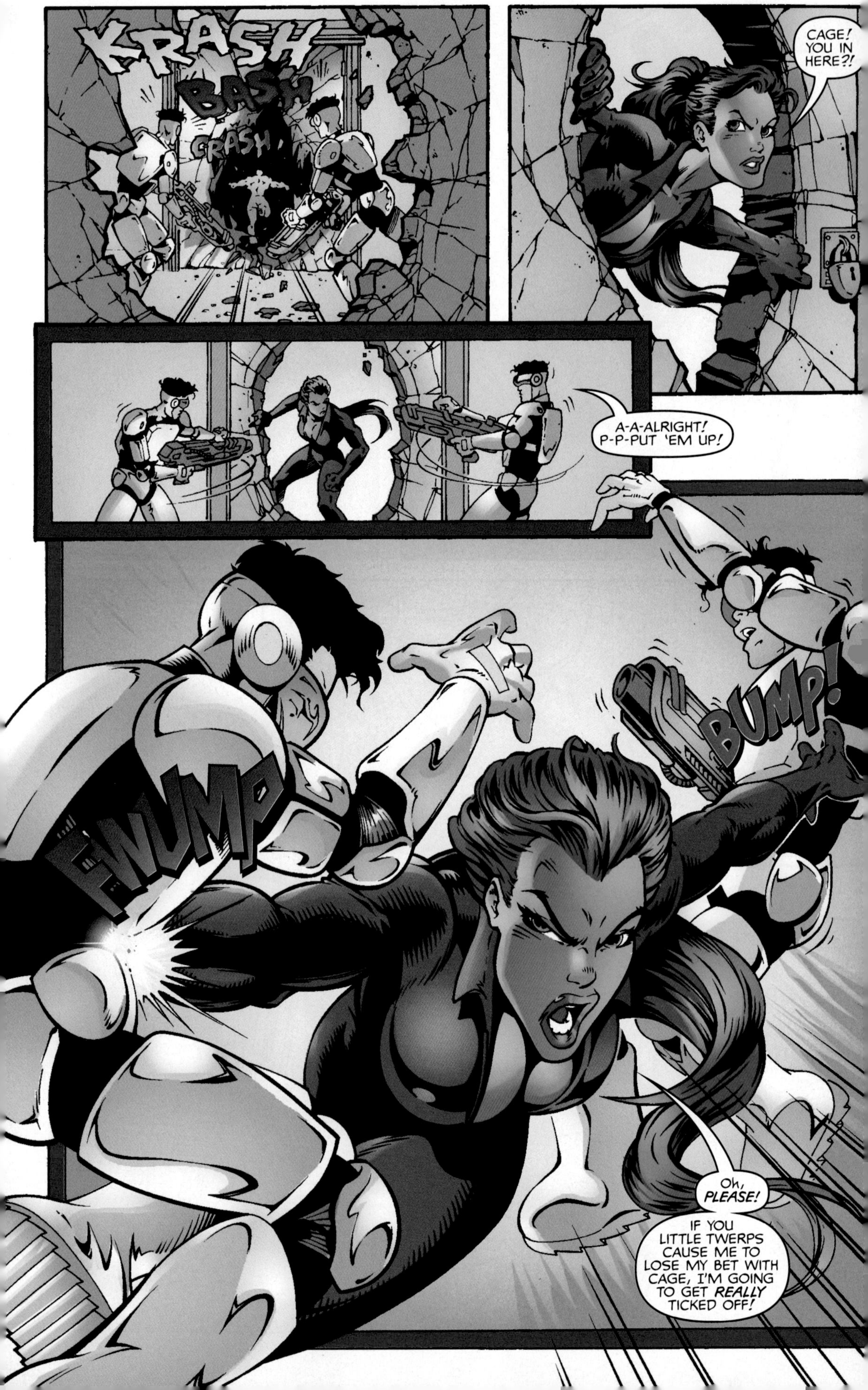
KRASH
BASH
CRASH
CAGE! YOU IN HERE?!
A-A-ALRIGHT! P-P-PUT 'EM UP!
BUMP!
FWUMP
Oh, PLEASE!
IF YOU LITTLE TWERPS CAUSE ME TO LOSE MY BET WITH CAGE, I'M GOING TO GET REALLY TICKED OFF!

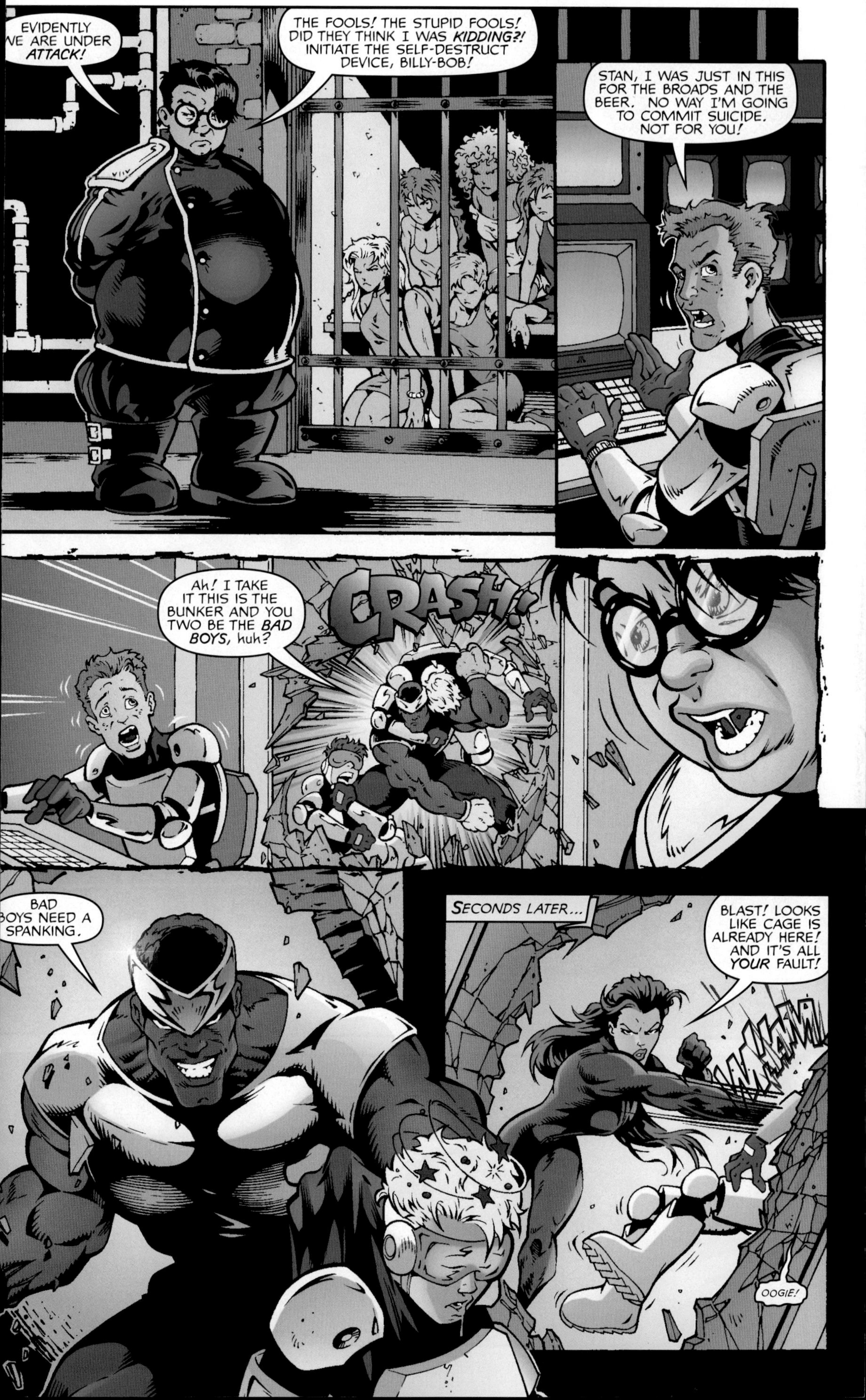
EVIDENTLY WE ARE UNDER *ATTACK!*
THE FOOLS! THE STUPID FOOLS! DID THEY THINK I WAS *KIDDING?!* INITIATE THE SELF-DESTRUCT DEVICE, BILLY-BOB!
STAN, I WAS JUST IN THIS FOR THE BROADS AND THE BEER. NO WAY I'M GOING TO COMMIT SUICIDE. NOT FOR YOU!
Ah! I TAKE IT THIS IS THE BUNKER AND YOU TWO BE THE *BAD BOYS,* huh?
CRASH!
BAD BOYS NEED A SPANKING.
SECONDS LATER...
BLAST! LOOKS LIKE CAGE IS ALREADY HERE! AND IT'S ALL *YOUR* FAULT!
OOGIE!

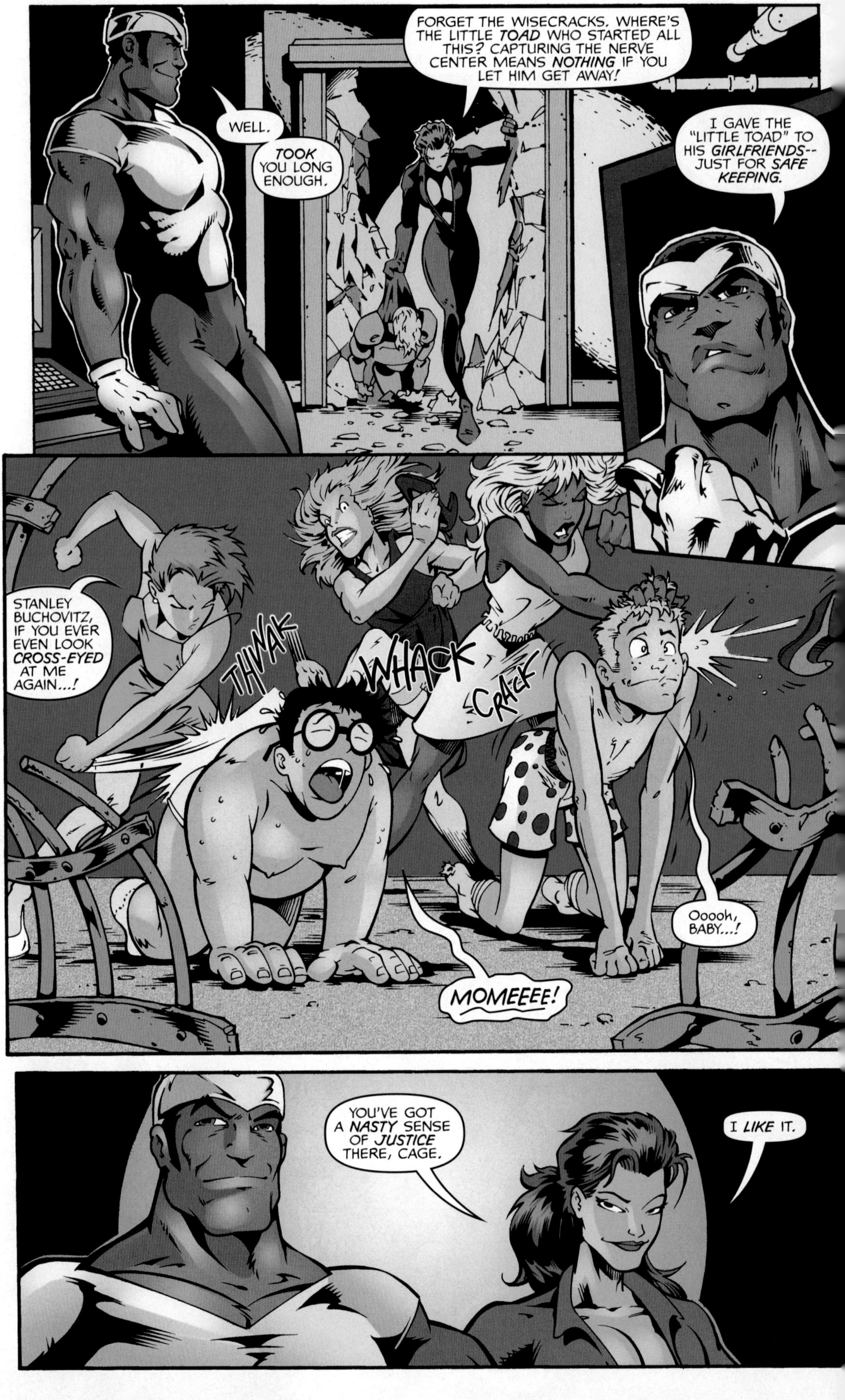
FORGET THE WISECRACKS. WHERE'S THE LITTLE TOAD WHO STARTED ALL THIS? CAPTURING THE NERVE CENTER MEANS NOTHING IF YOU LET HIM GET AWAY!
WELL.
TOOK YOU LONG ENOUGH.
I GAVE THE "LITTLE TOAD" TO HIS GIRLFRIENDS-- JUST FOR SAFE KEEPING.
STANLEY BUCHOVITZ, IF YOU EVER EVEN LOOK CROSS-EYED AT ME AGAIN...!
THWAK
WHACK
CRACK
Ooooh, BABY...!
MOMEEEE!
YOU'VE GOT A NASTY SENSE OF JUSTICE THERE, CAGE.
I LIKE IT.

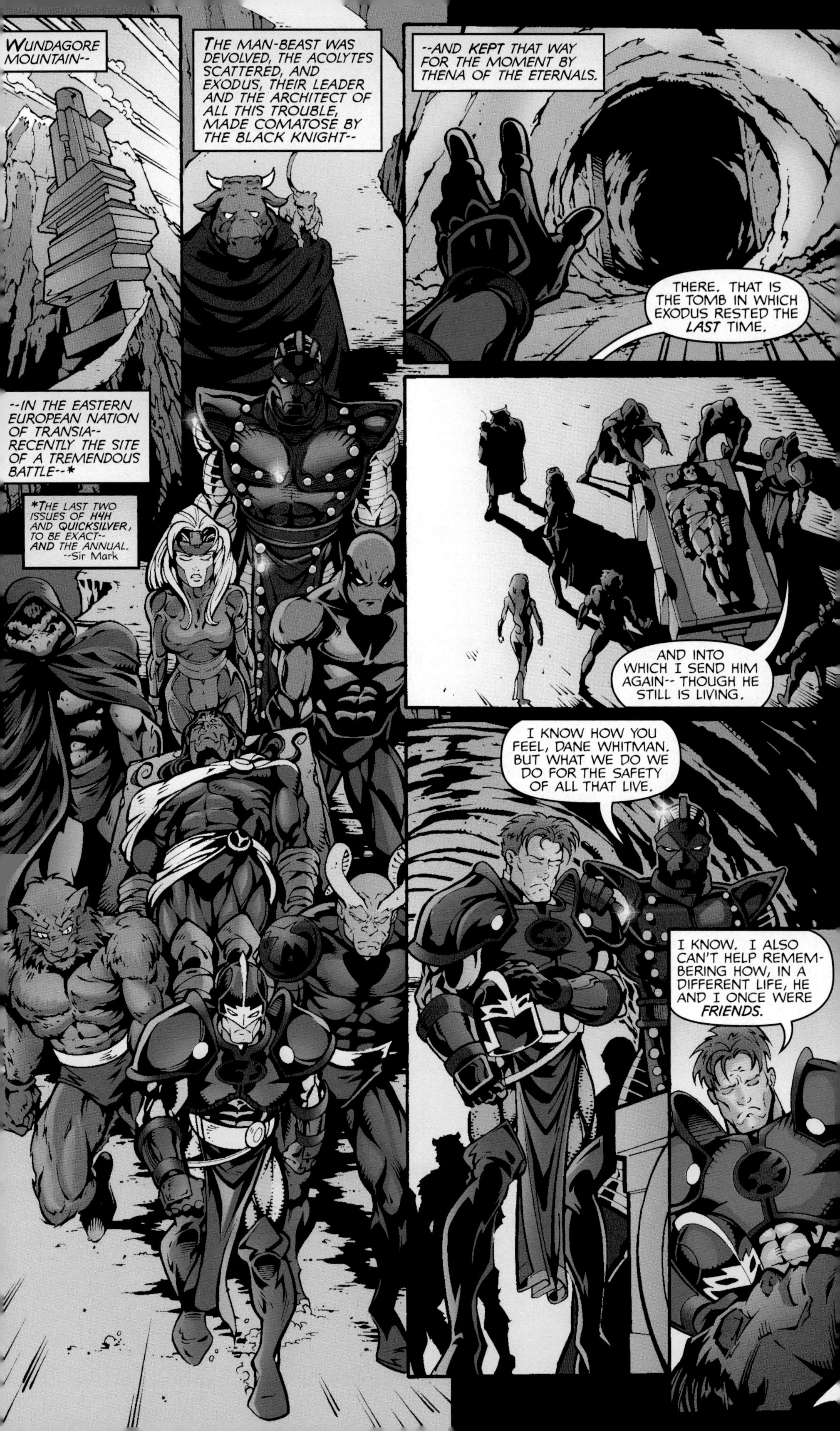
WUNDAGORE MOUNTAIN--
--IN THE EASTERN EUROPEAN NATION OF TRANSIA--RECENTLY THE SITE OF A TREMENDOUS BATTLE--*
*THE LAST TWO ISSUES OF H4H AND QUICKSILVER, TO BE EXACT--AND THE ANNUAL. --Sir Mark
THE MAN-BEAST WAS DEVOLVED, THE ACOLYTES SCATTERED, AND EXODUS, THEIR LEADER AND THE ARCHITECT OF ALL THIS TROUBLE, MADE COMATOSE BY THE BLACK KNIGHT--
--AND KEPT THAT WAY FOR THE MOMENT BY THENA OF THE ETERNALS.
THERE. THAT IS THE TOMB IN WHICH EXODUS RESTED THE LAST TIME.
AND INTO WHICH I SEND HIM AGAIN-- THOUGH HE STILL IS LIVING.
I KNOW HOW YOU FEEL, DANE WHITMAN. BUT WHAT WE DO WE DO FOR THE SAFETY OF ALL THAT LIVE.
I KNOW. I ALSO CAN'T HELP REMEMBERING HOW, IN A DIFFERENT LIFE, HE AND I ONCE WERE FRIENDS.

NOW THE TOMB MUST BE SEALED, AT MY WORD, THENA, IF YOU AND THE HIGH EVOLUTIONARY WOULD CHANNEL YOUR POWER INTO THE SHIELD OF KNIGHT--

--NOW!--

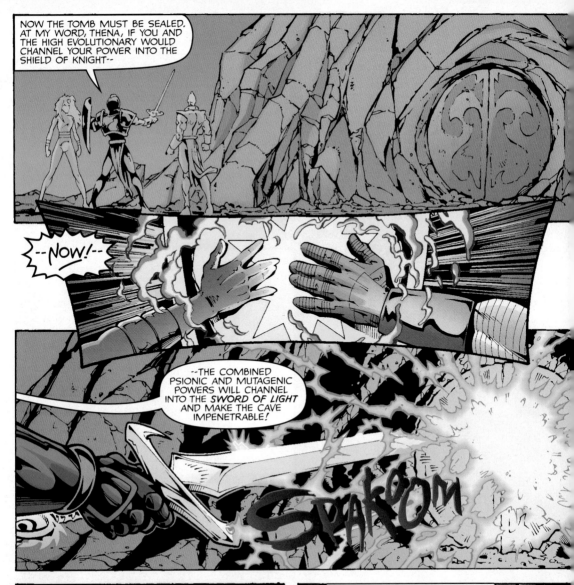

--THE COMBINED PSIONIC AND MUTAGENIC POWERS WILL CHANNEL INTO THE SWORD OF LIGHT AND MAKE THE CAVE IMPENETRABLE!

SPAKOOM

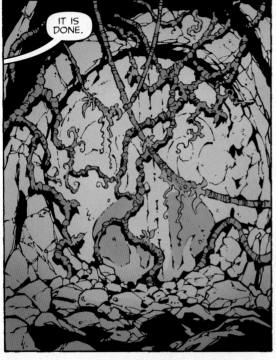

IT IS DONE.

WE SHOULD BE GETTING BACK TO THE HEROES FOR HIRE. WE STAYED JUST LONG ENOUGH TO TIDY UP AFTER THE BATTLE.

TARRY A MOMENT LONGER.

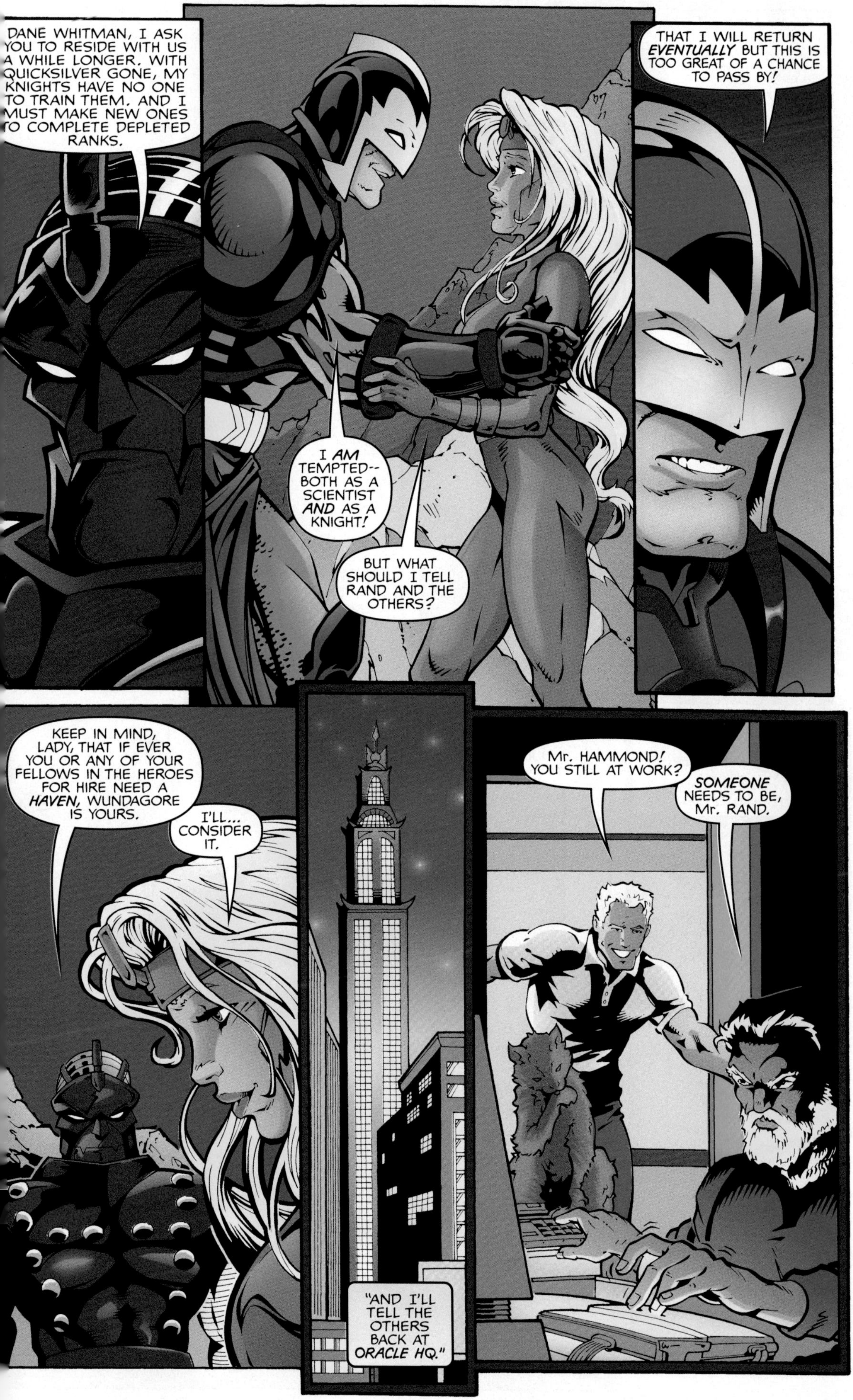
DANE WHITMAN, I ASK YOU TO RESIDE WITH US A WHILE LONGER. WITH QUICKSILVER GONE, MY KNIGHTS HAVE NO ONE TO TRAIN THEM. AND I MUST MAKE NEW ONES TO COMPLETE DEPLETED RANKS.
I *AM* TEMPTED--BOTH AS A SCIENTIST *AND* AS A KNIGHT!
BUT WHAT SHOULD I TELL RAND AND THE OTHERS?
THAT I WILL RETURN *EVENTUALLY* BUT THIS IS TOO GREAT OF A CHANCE TO PASS BY!
KEEP IN MIND, LADY, THAT IF EVER YOU OR ANY OF YOUR FELLOWS IN THE HEROES FOR HIRE NEED A *HAVEN,* WUNDAGORE IS YOURS.
I'LL... CONSIDER IT.
"AND I'LL TELL THE OTHERS BACK AT *ORACLE HQ.*"
Mr. HAMMOND! YOU STILL AT WORK?
SOMEONE NEEDS TO BE, Mr. RAND.

BESIDES, I'M JUST A MACHINE. I DON'T *NEED* TO REST.

"JUST A MACHINE." RIGHT. JIM, AS IRON FIST, I'VE FOUGHT FLESH AND BLOOD PEOPLE *LESS HUMAN* THAN YOU.

DANIEL, IS THERE SOMETHING THAT YOU *WANT?* BESIDES JUST ANNOYING ME?

I WAS LOOKING FOR LUKE. MISTY IS BUSY TONIGHT SO I THOUGHT LUKE AND I COULD DO SOMETHING.

HE AND THE SHE-HULK WENT OFF TO DINNER TOGETHER.

WOW! LUKE AND JENNIFER ARE OUT ON A *DATE?!*

HE CALLED IT A DATE; *SHE* CALLED IT A PAYOFF.

GUESS I'[L] JUST SIT H[ERE] AND BOTH[ER] *YOU,* THE[N]

AND, HIGH ATOP ONE OF MANHATTAN'S TALLEST BUILDINGS IS ONE OF THE SWANKEST NEW EATERIES-- *HEAVEN'S GRILL*-- CATERING TO THE TASTES OF THE ELITE AND CELEBRITIES.

OKAY. I'M IMPRESSED, CAGE. MAYBE I SHOULD LOSE BETS MORE OFTEN.

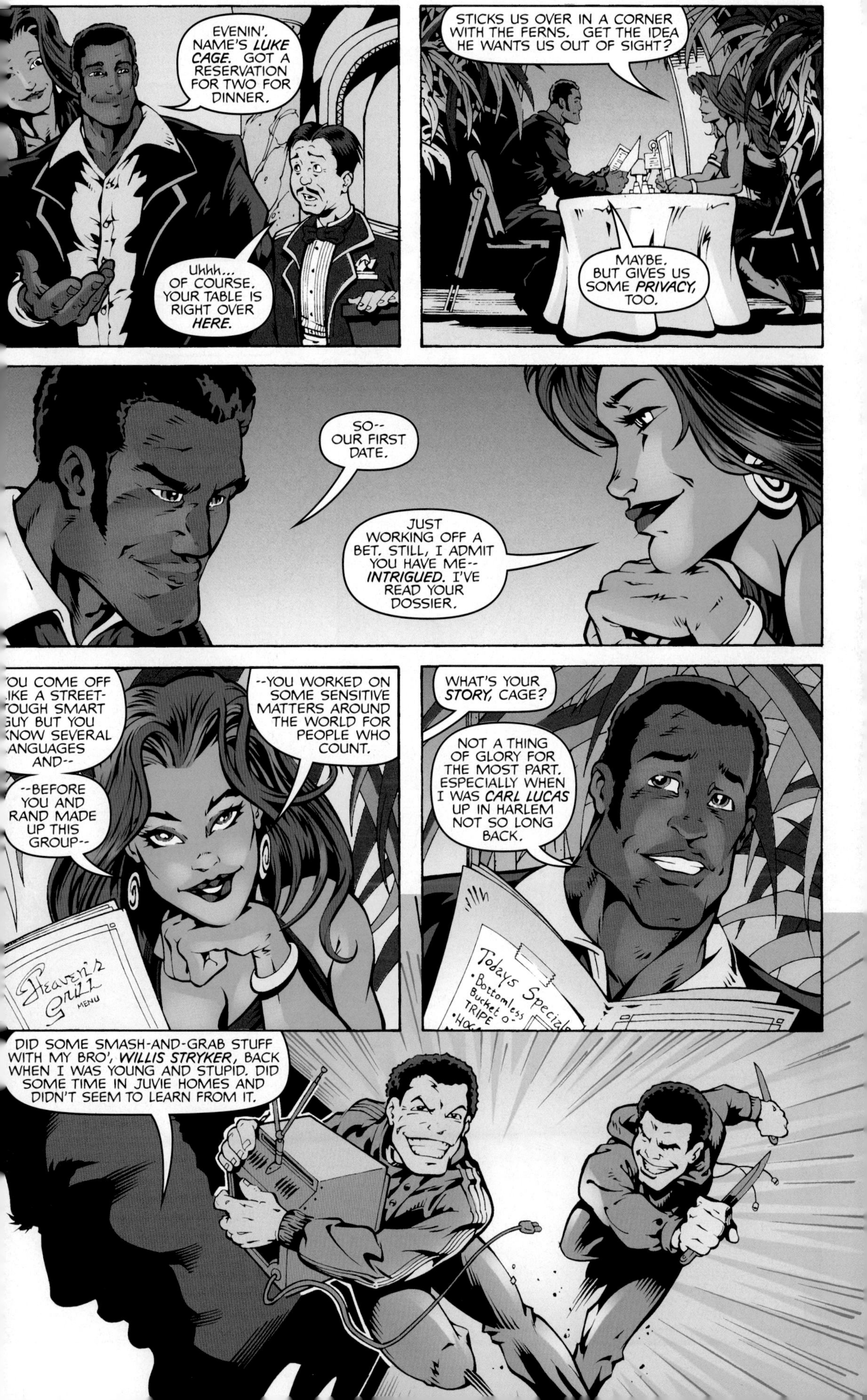

EVENIN', NAME'S LUKE CAGE. GOT A RESERVATION FOR TWO FOR DINNER.
Uhhh... OF COURSE. YOUR TABLE IS RIGHT OVER HERE.
STICKS US OVER IN A CORNER WITH THE FERNS. GET THE IDEA HE WANTS US OUT OF SIGHT?
MAYBE. BUT GIVES US SOME PRIVACY, TOO.
SO-- OUR FIRST DATE.
JUST WORKING OFF A BET. STILL, I ADMIT YOU HAVE ME-- INTRIGUED. I'VE READ YOUR DOSSIER.
YOU COME OFF LIKE A STREET-TOUGH SMART GUY BUT YOU KNOW SEVERAL LANGUAGES AND--
--BEFORE YOU AND RAND MADE UP THIS GROUP--
--YOU WORKED ON SOME SENSITIVE MATTERS AROUND THE WORLD FOR PEOPLE WHO COUNT.
Heaven's Grill MENU
WHAT'S YOUR STORY, CAGE?
NOT A THING OF GLORY FOR THE MOST PART. ESPECIALLY WHEN I WAS CARL LUCAS UP IN HARLEM NOT SO LONG BACK.
Todays Specials
•Bottomless Bucket o' TRIPE
DID SOME SMASH-AND-GRAB STUFF WITH MY BRO', WILLIS STRYKER, BACK WHEN I WAS YOUNG AND STUPID. DID SOME TIME IN JUVIE HOMES AND DIDN'T SEEM TO LEARN FROM IT.

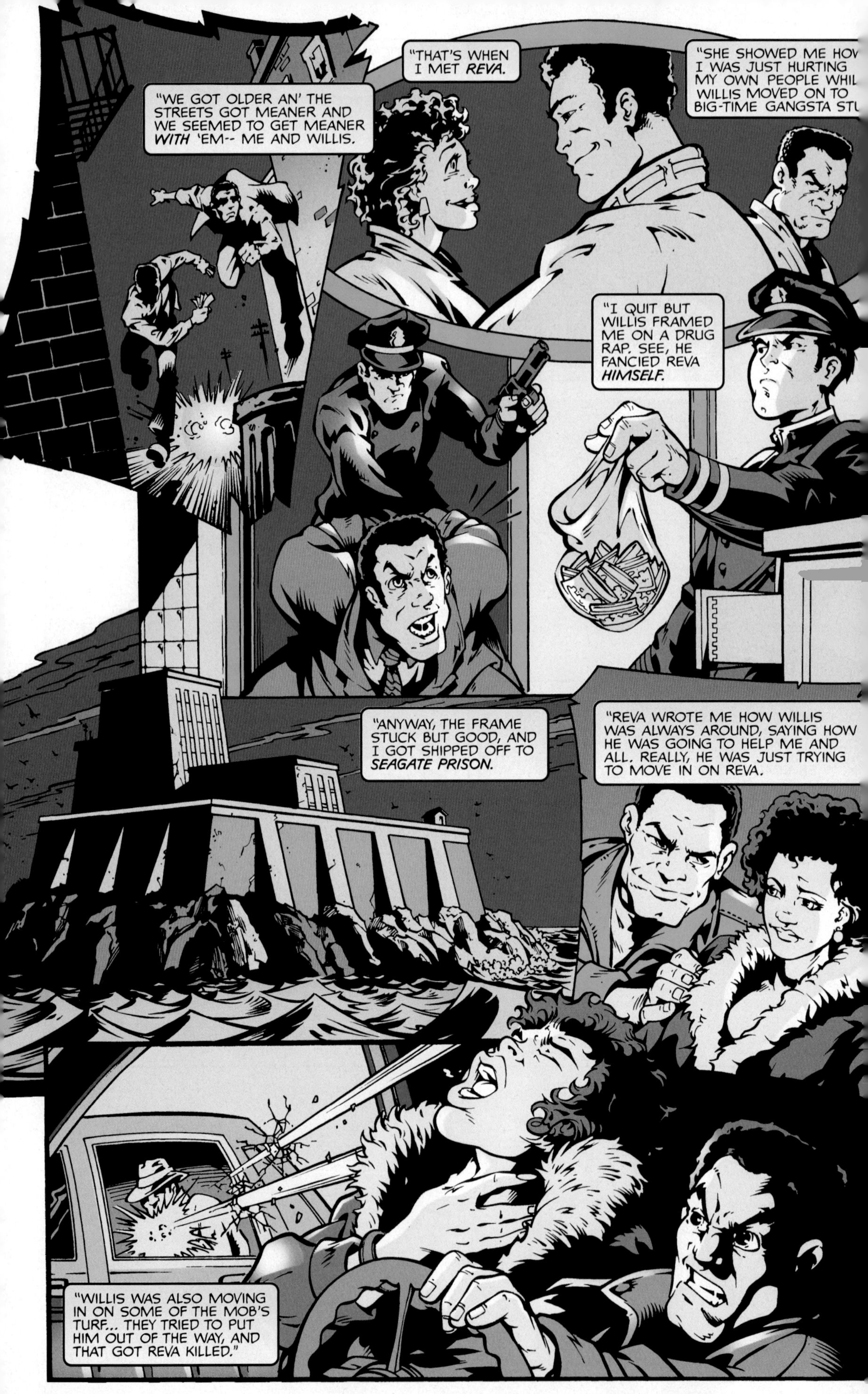
"WE GOT OLDER AN' THE STREETS GOT MEANER AND WE SEEMED TO GET MEANER WITH 'EM-- ME AND WILLIS.
"THAT'S WHEN I MET REVA.
"SHE SHOWED ME HOW I WAS JUST HURTING MY OWN PEOPLE WHIL WILLIS MOVED ON TO BIG-TIME GANGSTA STU
"I QUIT BUT WILLIS FRAMED ME ON A DRUG RAP. SEE, HE FANCIED REVA HIMSELF.
"ANYWAY, THE FRAME STUCK BUT GOOD, AND I GOT SHIPPED OFF TO SEAGATE PRISON.
"REVA WROTE ME HOW WILLIS WAS ALWAYS AROUND, SAYING HOW HE WAS GOING TO HELP ME AND ALL. REALLY, HE WAS JUST TRYING TO MOVE IN ON REVA.
"WILLIS WAS ALSO MOVING IN ON SOME OF THE MOB'S TURF... THEY TRIED TO PUT HIM OUT OF THE WAY, AND THAT GOT REVA KILLED."

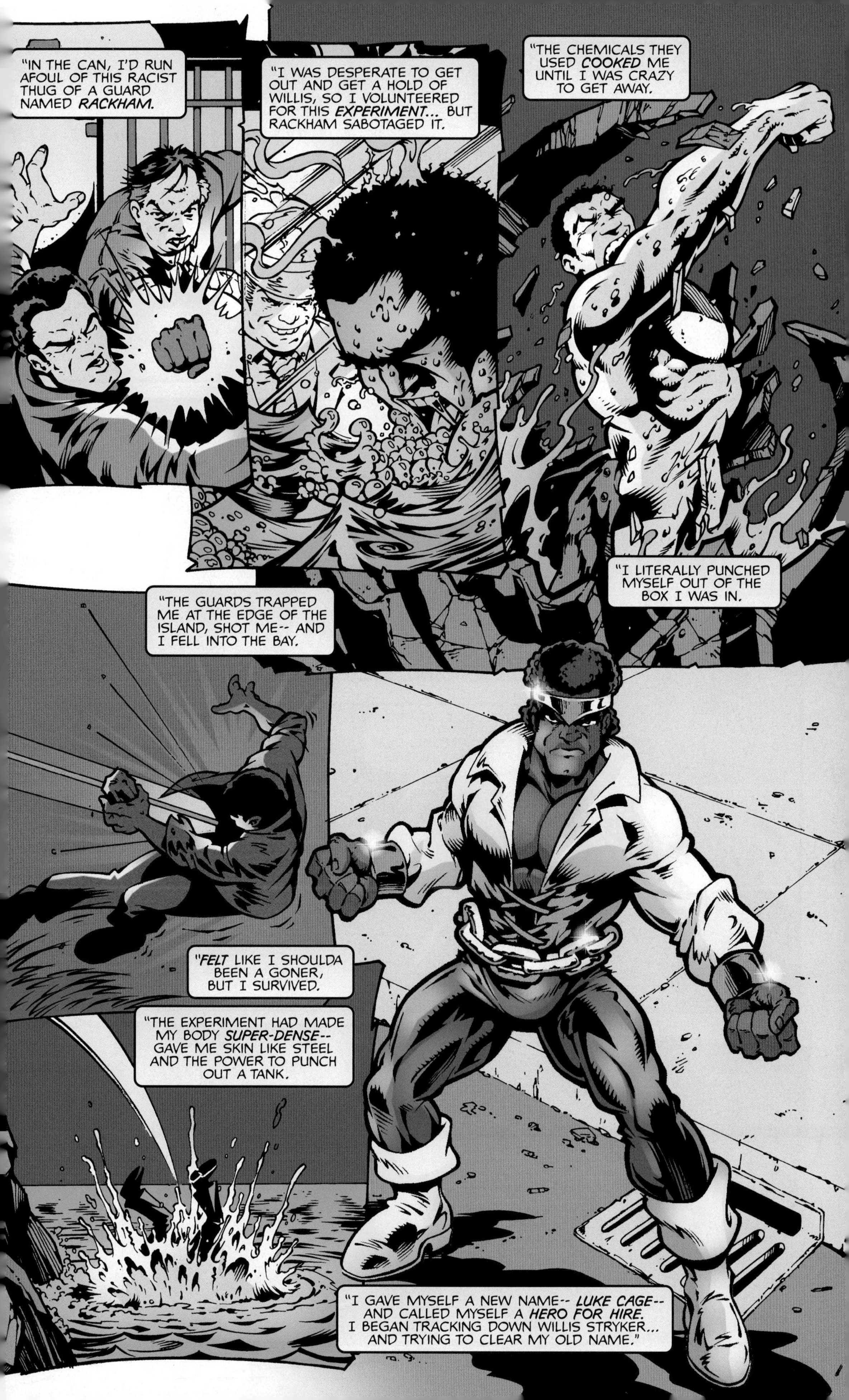
"IN THE CAN, I'D RUN AFOUL OF THIS RACIST THUG OF A GUARD NAMED RACKHAM.
"I WAS DESPERATE TO GET OUT AND GET A HOLD OF WILLIS, SO I VOLUNTEERED FOR THIS EXPERIMENT... BUT RACKHAM SABOTAGED IT.
"THE CHEMICALS THEY USED COOKED ME UNTIL I WAS CRAZY TO GET AWAY.
"I LITERALLY PUNCHED MYSELF OUT OF THE BOX I WAS IN.
"THE GUARDS TRAPPED ME AT THE EDGE OF THE ISLAND, SHOT ME-- AND I FELL INTO THE BAY.
"FELT LIKE I SHOULDA BEEN A GONER, BUT I SURVIVED.
"THE EXPERIMENT HAD MADE MY BODY SUPER-DENSE-- GAVE ME SKIN LIKE STEEL AND THE POWER TO PUNCH OUT A TANK.
"I GAVE MYSELF A NEW NAME-- LUKE CAGE-- AND CALLED MYSELF A HERO FOR HIRE. I BEGAN TRACKING DOWN WILLIS STRYKER... AND TRYING TO CLEAR MY OLD NAME."

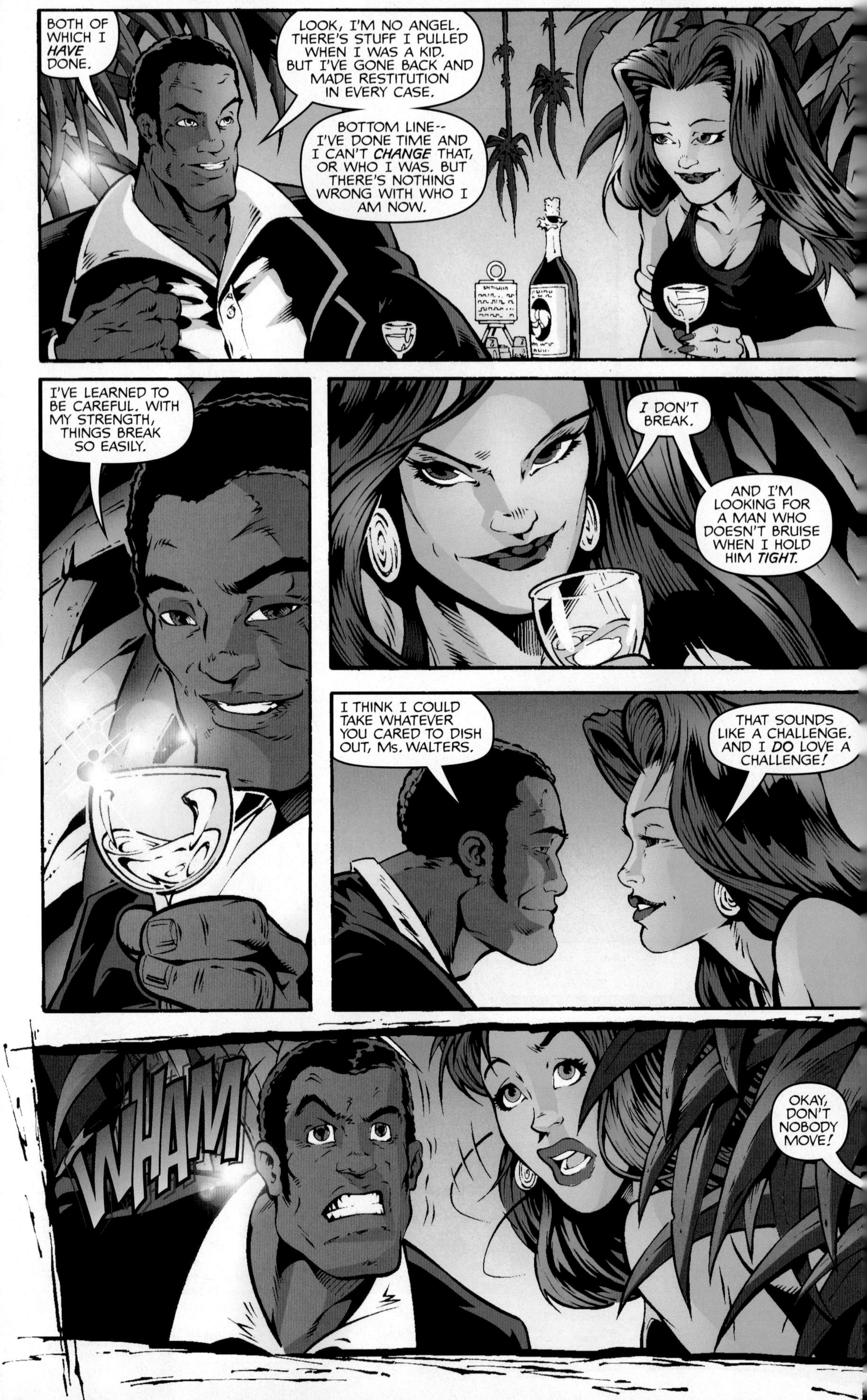
BOTH OF WHICH I *HAVE* DONE.
LOOK, I'M NO ANGEL. THERE'S STUFF I PULLED WHEN I WAS A KID. BUT I'VE GONE BACK AND MADE RESTITUTION IN EVERY CASE.
BOTTOM LINE-- I'VE DONE TIME AND I CAN'T ***CHANGE*** THAT, OR WHO I WAS. BUT THERE'S NOTHING WRONG WITH WHO I AM NOW.
I'VE LEARNED TO BE CAREFUL. WITH MY STRENGTH, THINGS BREAK SO EASILY.
I DON'T BREAK.
AND I'M LOOKING FOR A MAN WHO DOESN'T BRUISE WHEN I HOLD HIM ***TIGHT.***
I THINK I COULD TAKE WHATEVER YOU CARED TO DISH OUT, Ms. WALTERS.
THAT SOUNDS LIKE A CHALLENGE. AND I ***DO*** LOVE A CHALLENGE!
WHAM
OKAY, DON'T NOBODY MOVE!

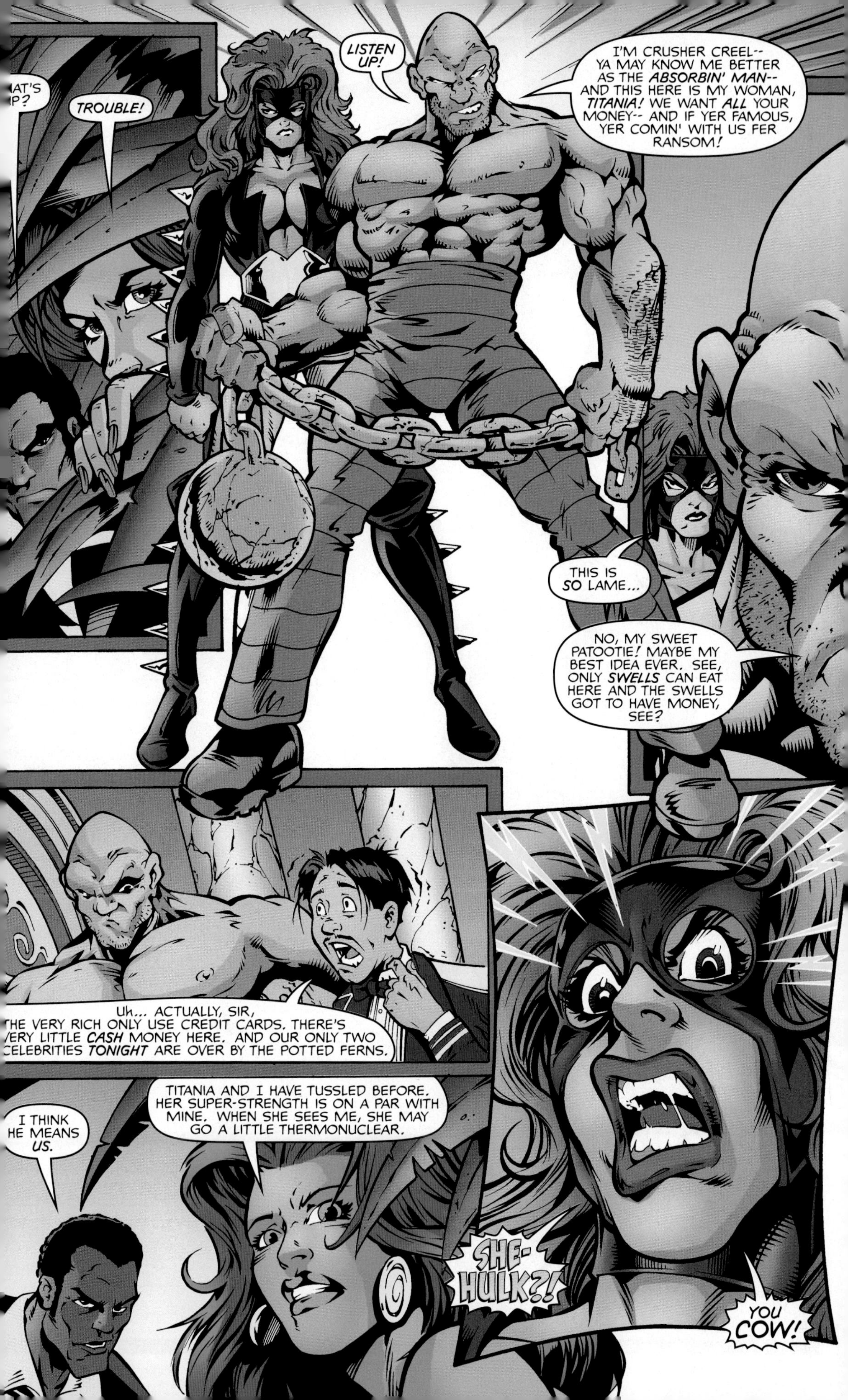

...AT'S
...P?
TROUBLE!
LISTEN UP!
I'M CRUSHER CREEL-- YA MAY KNOW ME BETTER AS THE ABSORBIN' MAN-- AND THIS HERE IS MY WOMAN, TITANIA! WE WANT ALL YOUR MONEY-- AND IF YER FAMOUS, YER COMIN' WITH US FER RANSOM!
THIS IS SO LAME...
NO, MY SWEET PATOOTIE! MAYBE MY BEST IDEA EVER. SEE, ONLY SWELLS CAN EAT HERE AND THE SWELLS GOT TO HAVE MONEY, SEE?
Uh... ACTUALLY, SIR, THE VERY RICH ONLY USE CREDIT CARDS. THERE'S VERY LITTLE CASH MONEY HERE. AND OUR ONLY TWO CELEBRITIES TONIGHT ARE OVER BY THE POTTED FERNS.
I THINK HE MEANS US.
TITANIA AND I HAVE TUSSLED BEFORE. HER SUPER-STRENGTH IS ON A PAR WITH MINE. WHEN SHE SEES ME, SHE MAY GO A LITTLE THERMONUCLEAR.
SHE-HULK?!
YOU COW!

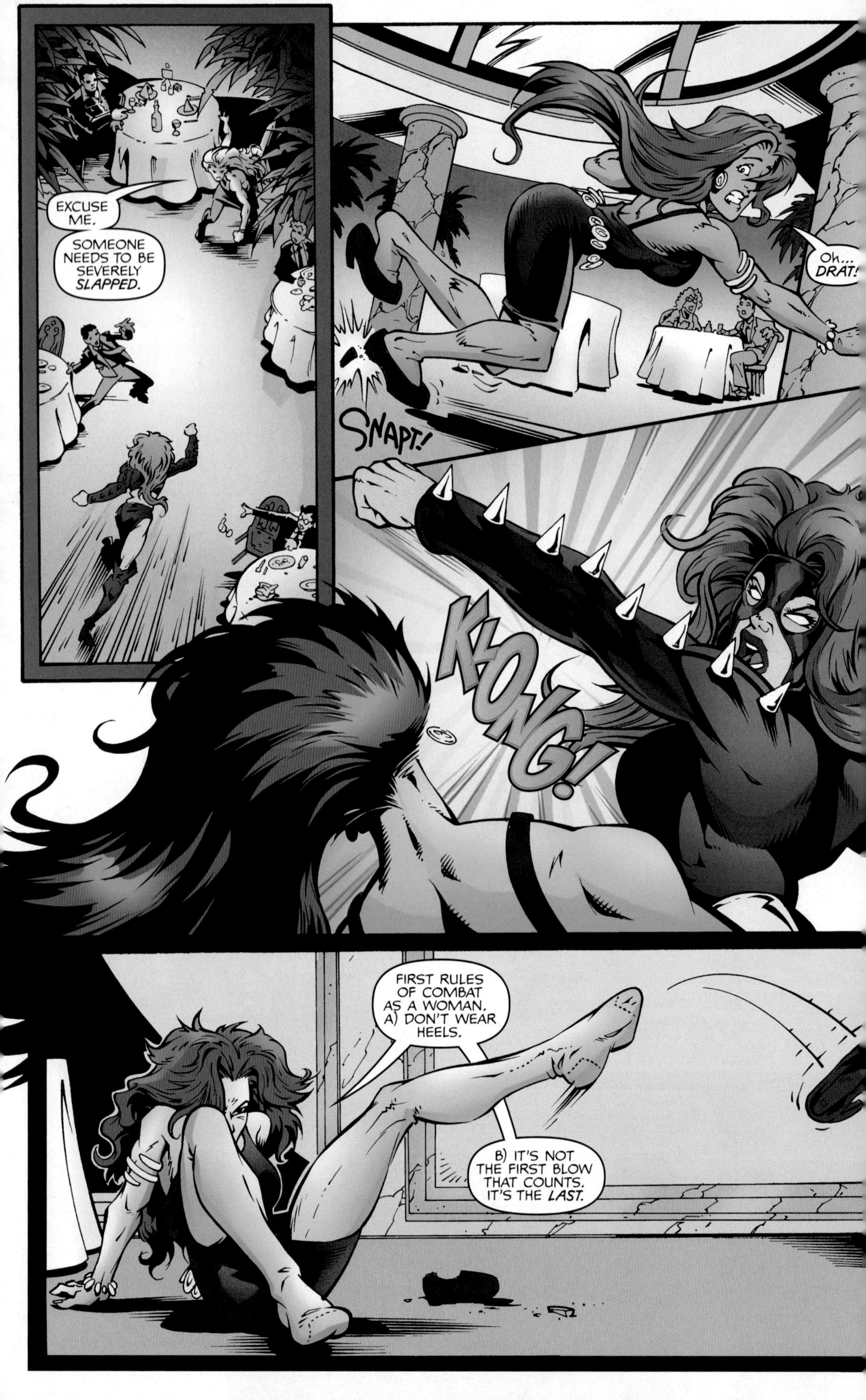
EXCUSE ME.
SOMEONE NEEDS TO BE SEVERELY *SLAPPED*.
Oh... *DRAT!*
SNAPT!
KLONG!
FIRST RULES OF COMBAT AS A WOMAN. A) DON'T WEAR HEELS.
B) IT'S NOT THE FIRST BLOW THAT COUNTS. IT'S THE *LAST*.

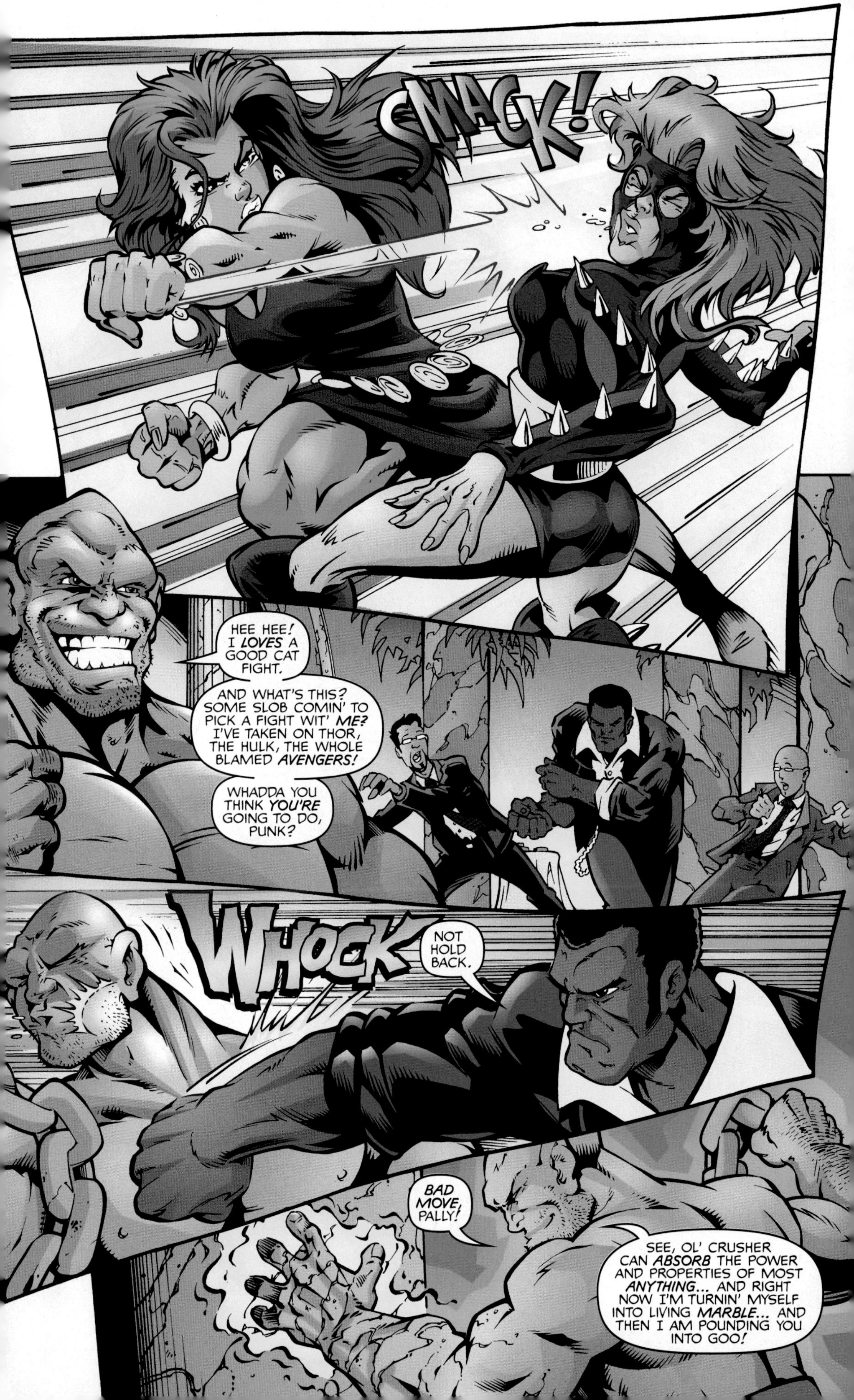
SMACK!
HEE HEE! I LOVES A GOOD CAT FIGHT.
AND WHAT'S THIS? SOME SLOB COMIN' TO PICK A FIGHT WIT' ME? I'VE TAKEN ON THOR, THE HULK, THE WHOLE BLAMED AVENGERS!
WHADDA YOU THINK YOU'RE GOING TO DO, PUNK?
WHOCK
NOT HOLD BACK.
BAD MOVE, PALLY!
SEE, OL' CRUSHER CAN ABSORB THE POWER AND PROPERTIES OF MOST ANYTHING... AND RIGHT NOW I'M TURNIN' MYSELF INTO LIVING MARBLE... AND THEN I AM POUNDING YOU INTO GOO!

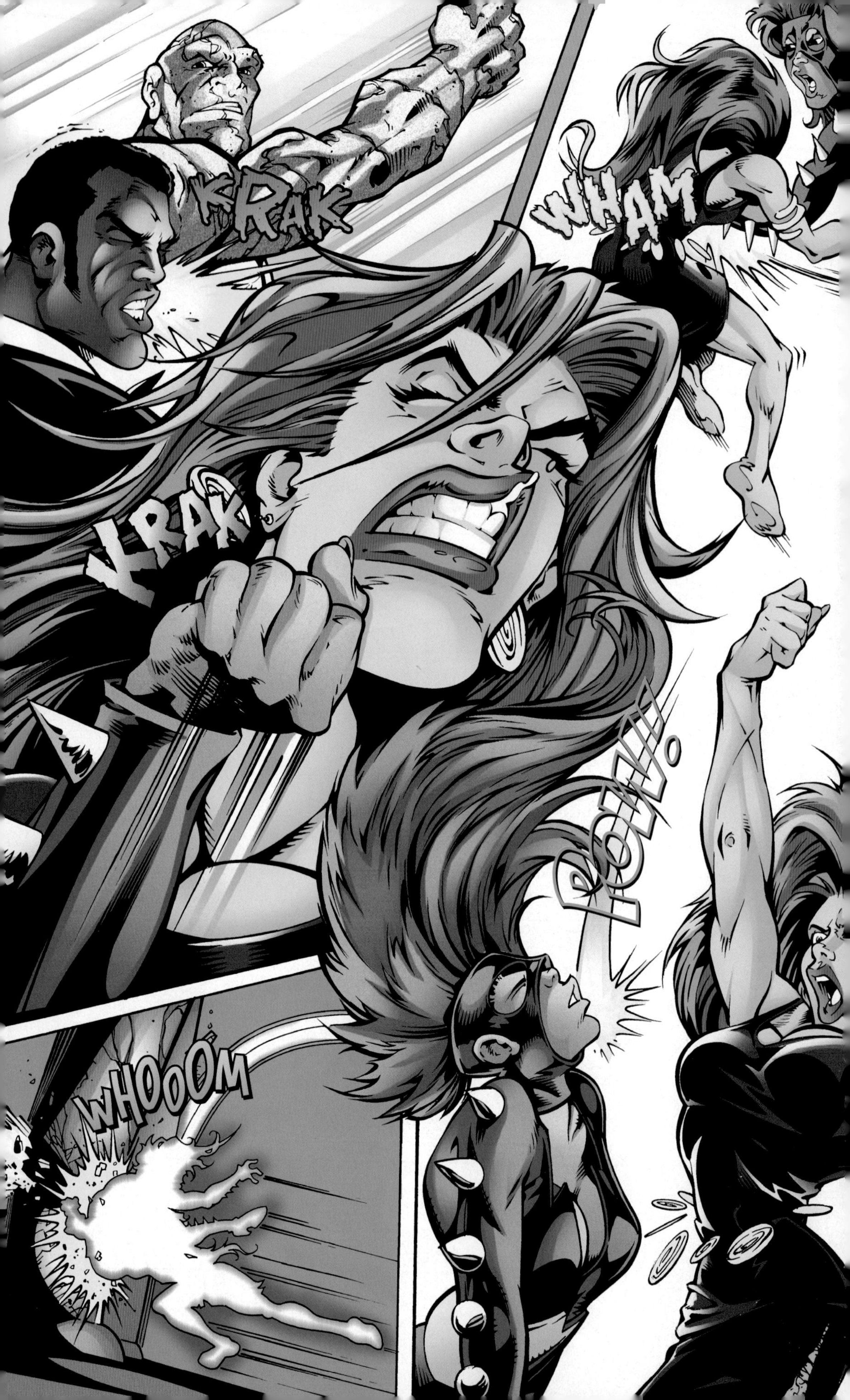

KRAK
WHAM
KRAK
POW!!
WHOOOM

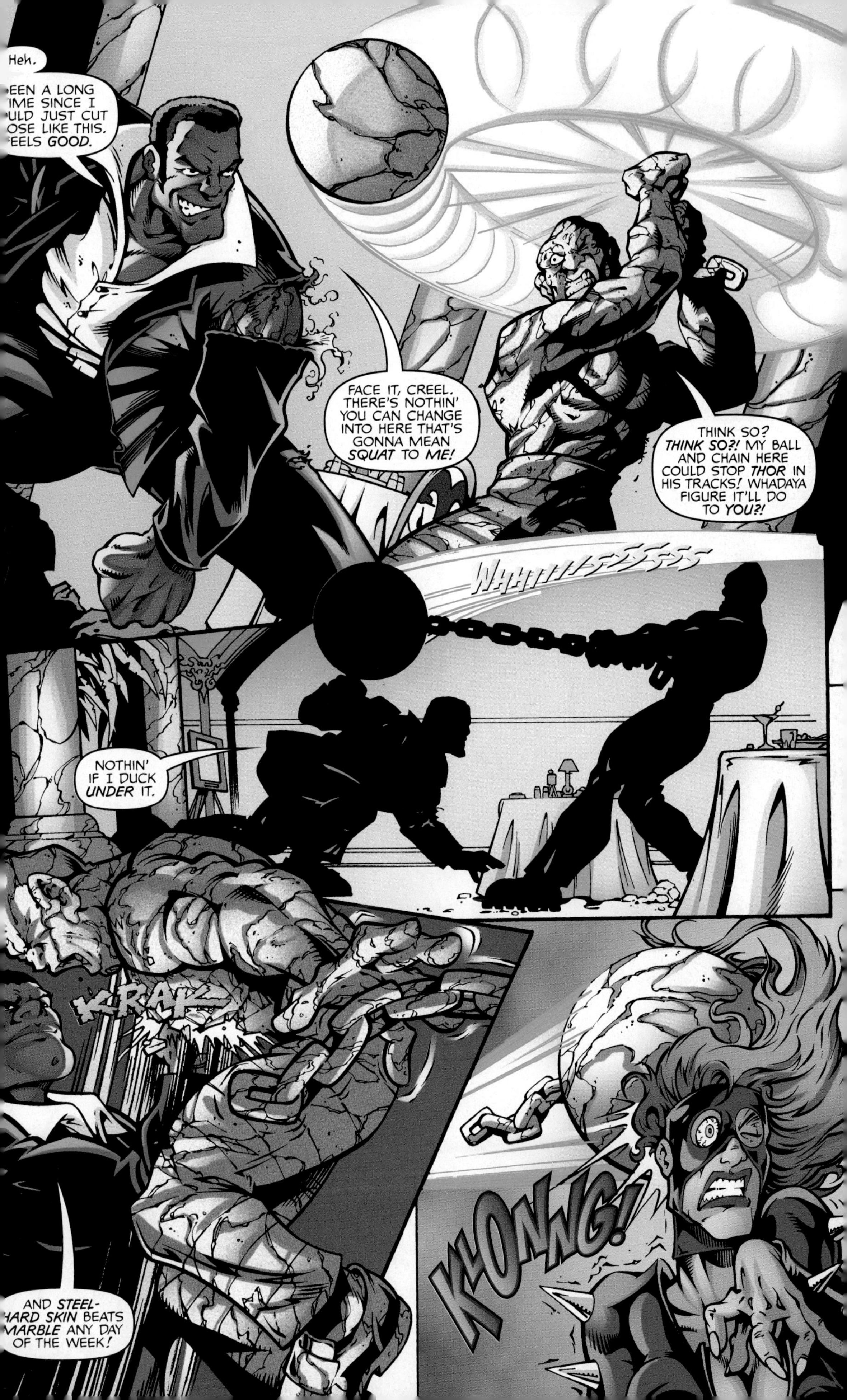
Heh.
EEN A LONG IME SINCE I ULD JUST CUT OSE LIKE THIS. EELS GOOD.
FACE IT, CREEL. THERE'S NOTHIN' YOU CAN CHANGE INTO HERE THAT'S GONNA MEAN SQUAT TO ME!
THINK SO? THINK SO?! MY BALL AND CHAIN HERE COULD STOP THOR IN HIS TRACKS! WHADAYA FIGURE IT'LL DO TO YOU?!
WHHHHSSSSS
NOTHIN' IF I DUCK UNDER IT.
KRAK
AND STEEL-HARD SKIN BEATS MARBLE ANY DAY OF THE WEEK!
KLONNG!

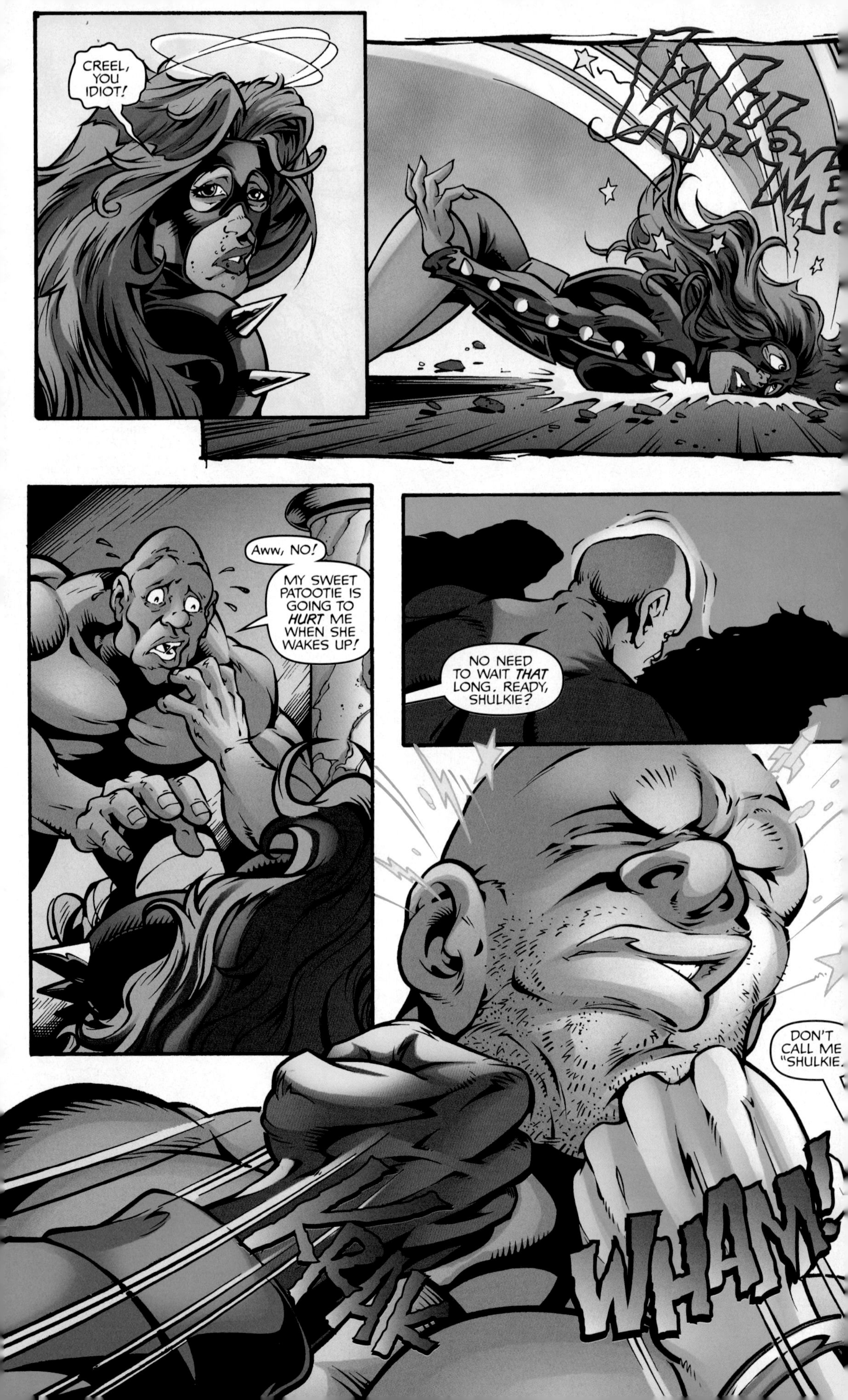
CREEL, YOU IDIOT!
AWW, NO!
MY SWEET PATOOTIE IS GOING TO *HURT* ME WHEN SHE WAKES UP!
NO NEED TO WAIT *THAT* LONG. READY, SHULKIE?
DON'T CALL ME "SHULKIE."
WHAM!

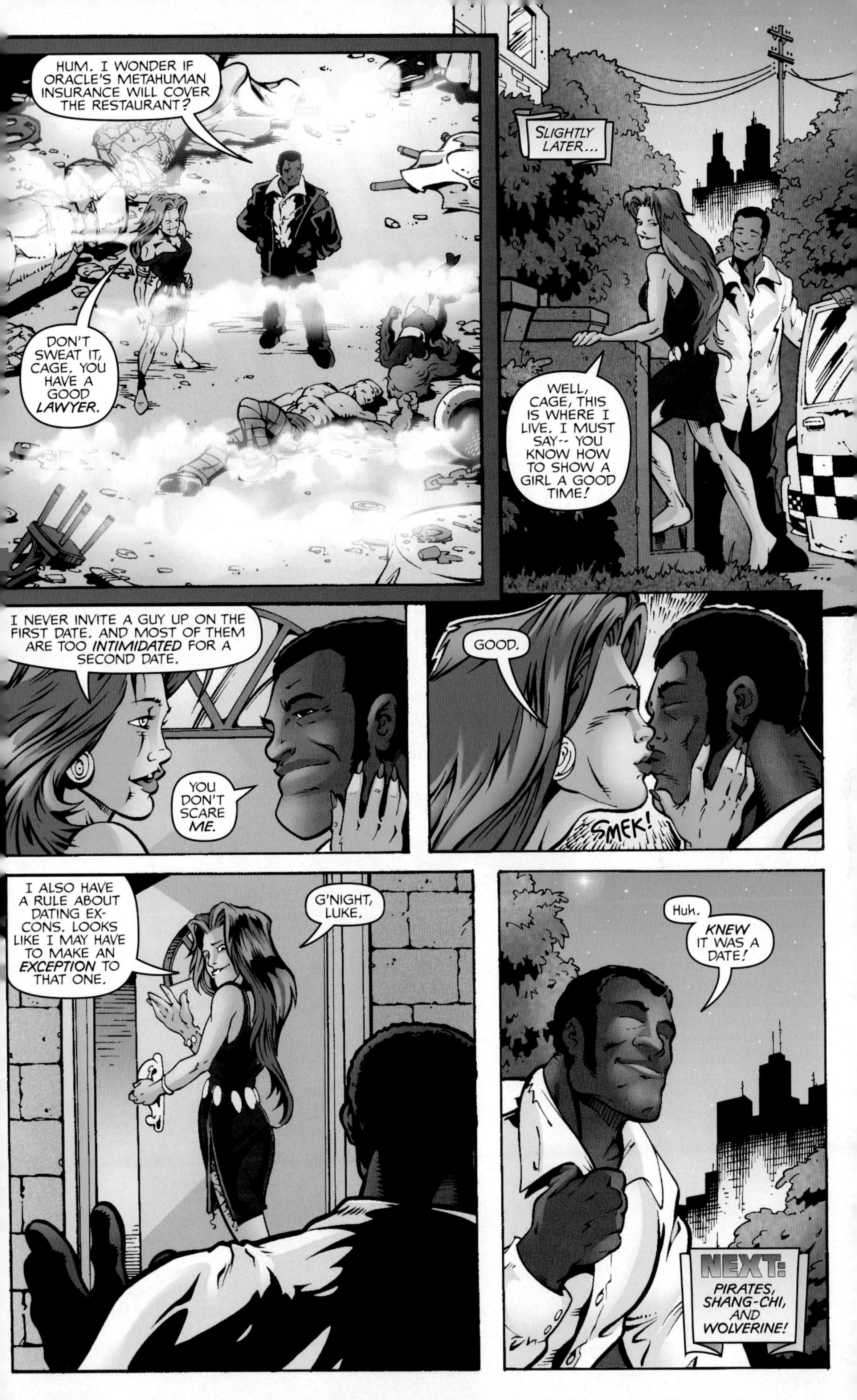
HUM. I WONDER IF ORACLE'S METAHUMAN INSURANCE WILL COVER THE RESTAURANT?
DON'T SWEAT IT, CAGE. YOU HAVE A GOOD *LAWYER*.
SLIGHTLY LATER...
WELL, CAGE, THIS IS WHERE I LIVE. I MUST SAY-- YOU KNOW HOW TO SHOW A GIRL A GOOD TIME!
I NEVER INVITE A GUY UP ON THE FIRST DATE, AND MOST OF THEM ARE TOO *INTIMIDATED* FOR A SECOND DATE.
YOU DON'T SCARE *ME*.
GOOD.
SMEK!
I ALSO HAVE A RULE ABOUT DATING EX-CONS. LOOKS LIKE I MAY HAVE TO MAKE AN *EXCEPTION* TO THAT ONE.
G'NIGHT, LUKE.
Huh. *KNEW* IT WAS A DATE!
NEXT:
PIRATES, SHANG-CHI, AND WOLVERINE!

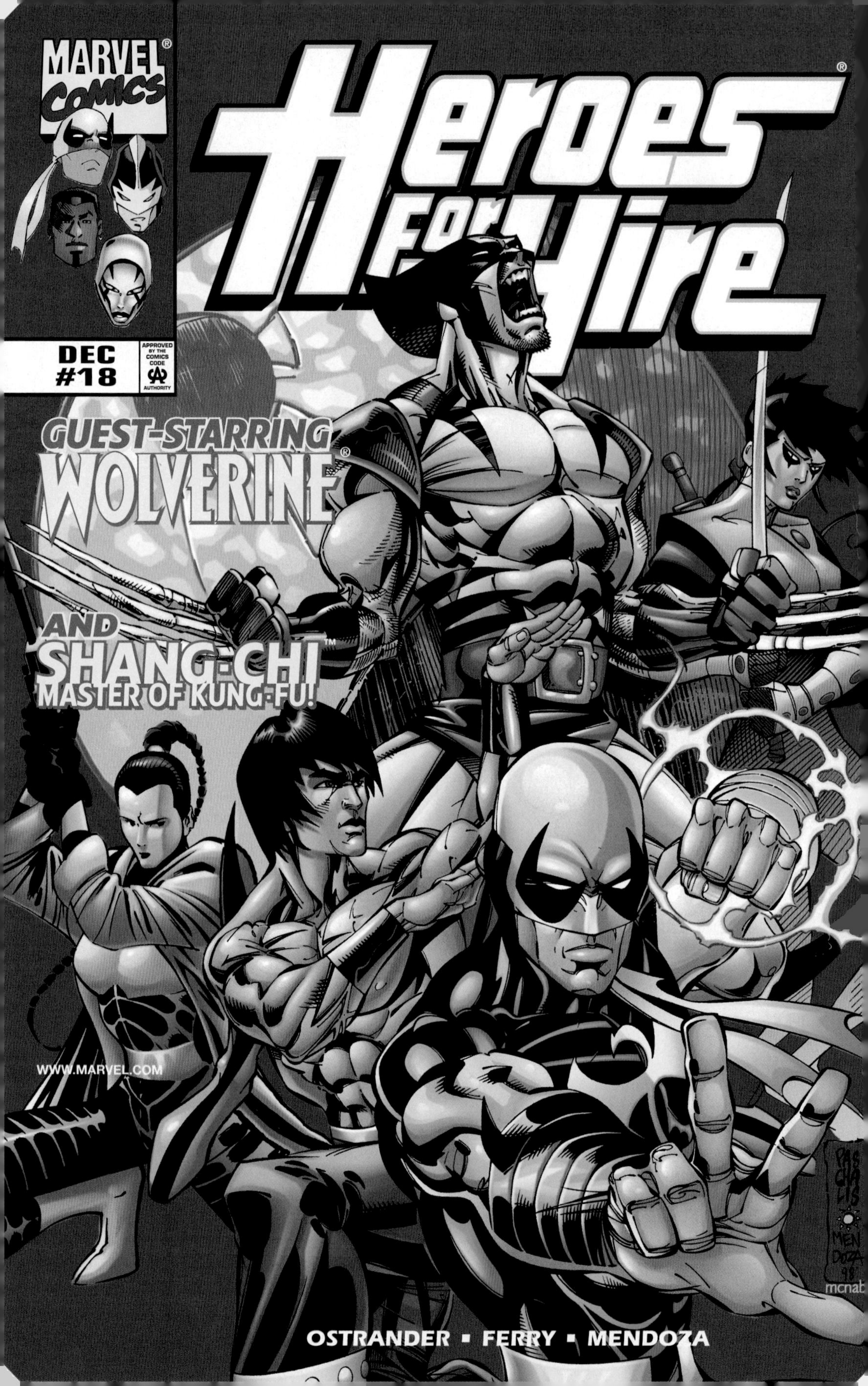

MARVEL COMICS
Heroes For Hire
DEC #18
APPROVED BY THE COMICS CODE AUTHORITY
GUEST-STARRING WOLVERINE
AND SHANG-CHI MASTER OF KUNG-FU!
WWW.MARVEL.COM
PASCHALIS MENDOZA '98
mcnat
OSTRANDER • FERRY • MENDOZA

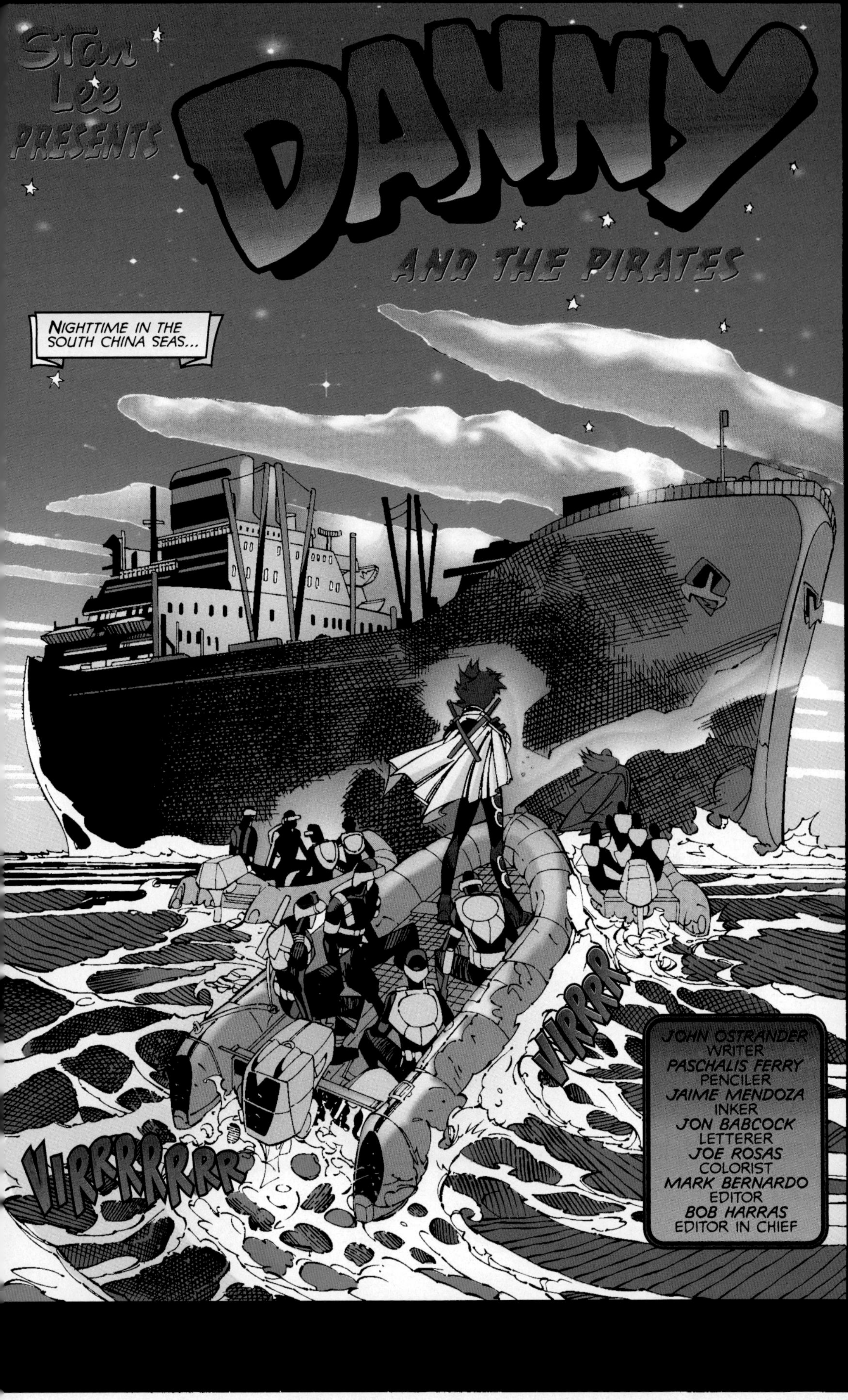
Stan Lee PRESENTS
DANNY
AND THE PIRATES
NIGHTTIME IN THE SOUTH CHINA SEAS...
VIRRRR
VIRRRRRRR
JOHN OSTRANDER
WRITER
PASCHALIS FERRY
PENCILER
JAIME MENDOZA
INKER
JON BABCOCK
LETTERER
JOE ROSAS
COLORIST
MARK BERNARDO
EDITOR
BOB HARRAS
EDITOR IN CHIEF

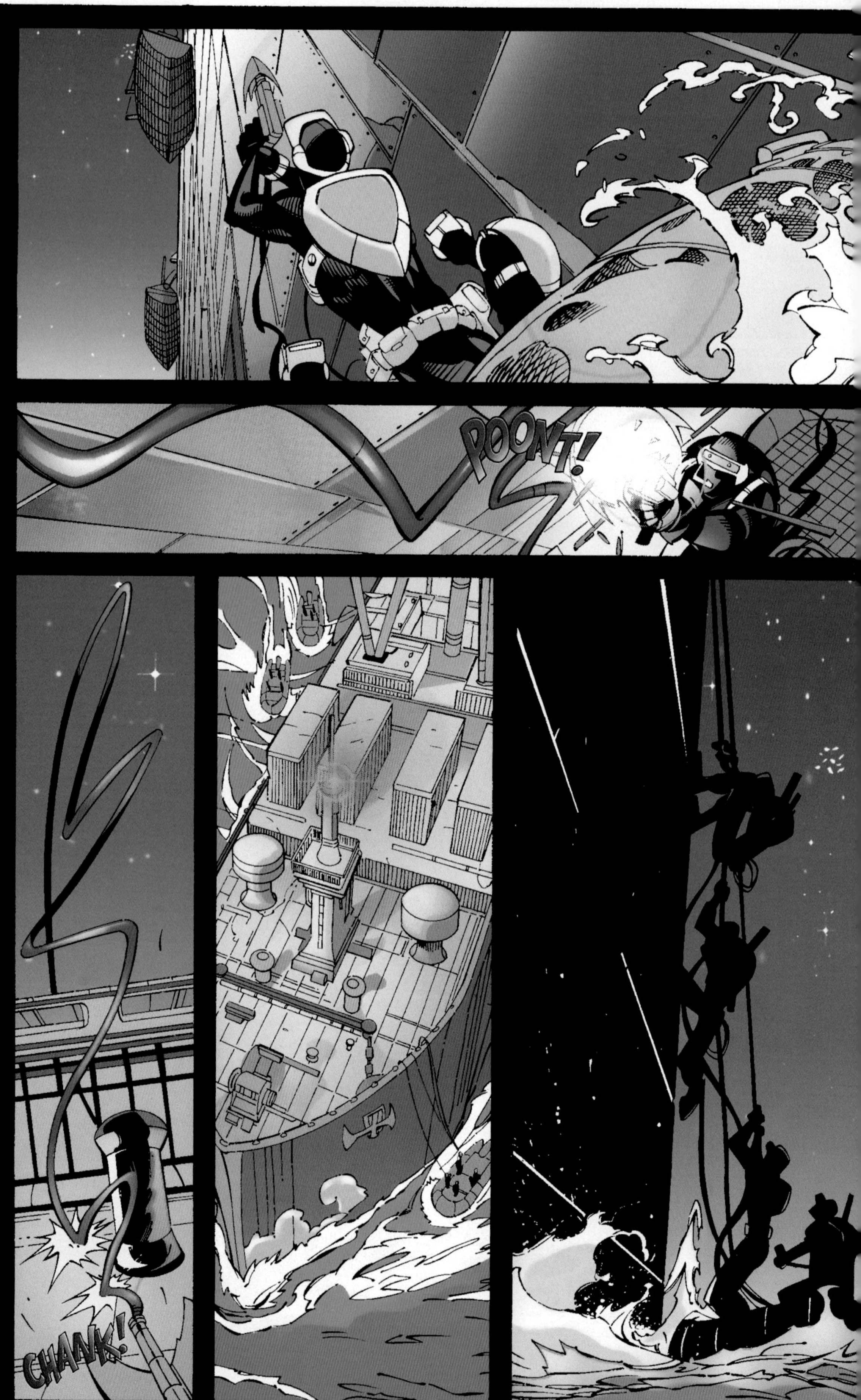
POONT!
CHANK!

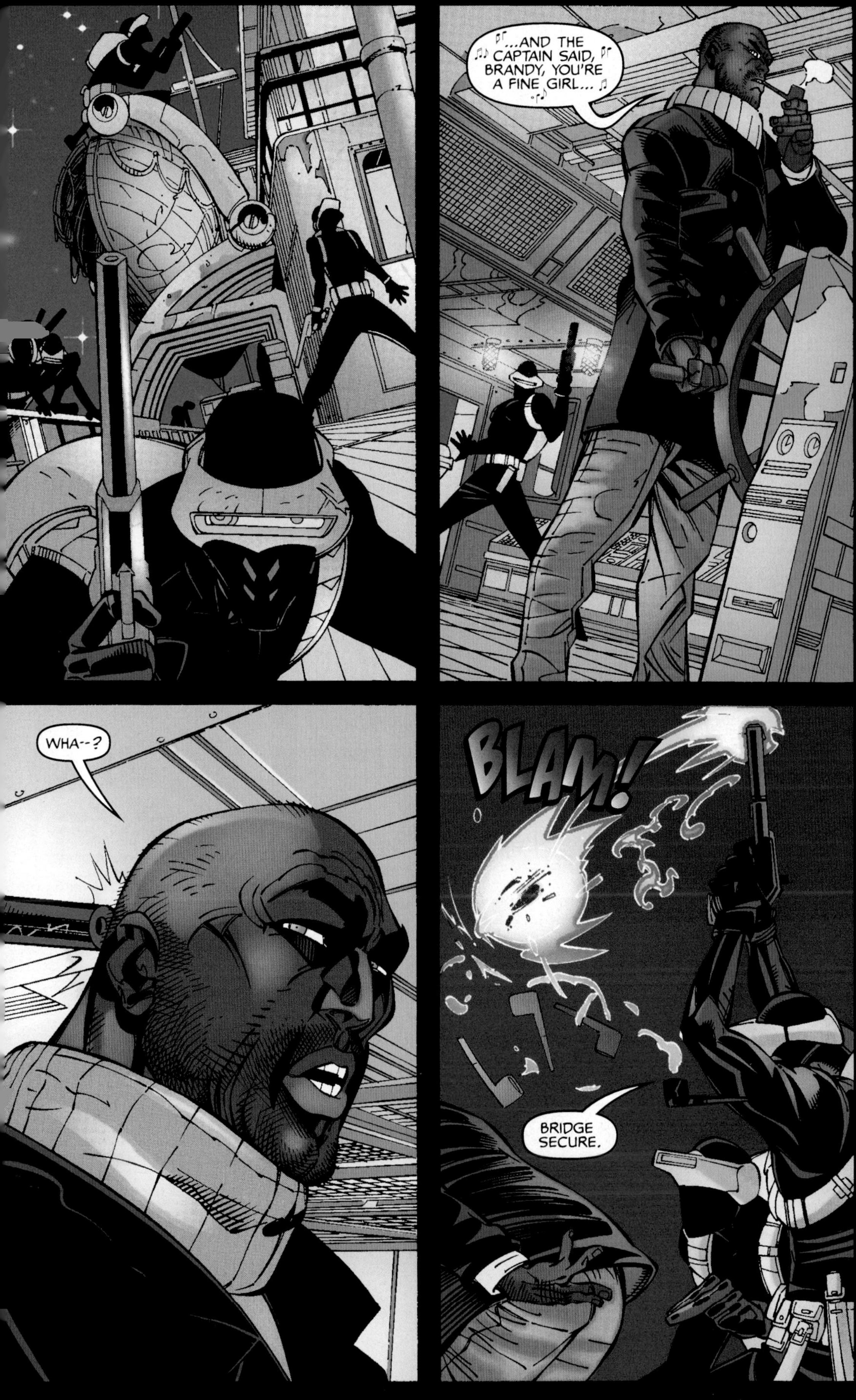
...AND THE CAPTAIN SAID, BRANDY, YOU'RE A FINE GIRL...
WHA--?
BLAM!
BRIDGE SECURE.

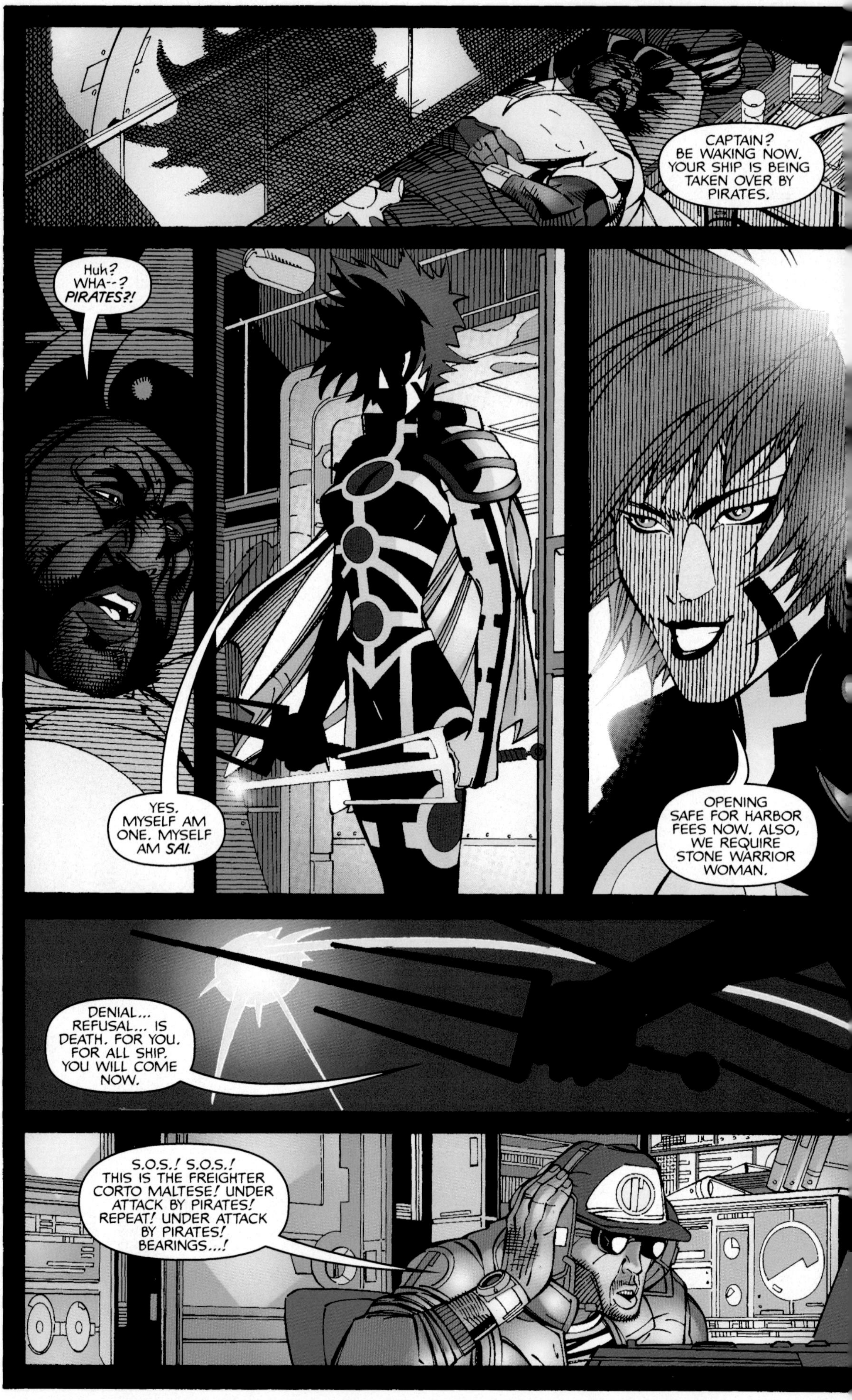
CAPTAIN? BE WAKING NOW. YOUR SHIP IS BEING TAKEN OVER BY PIRATES.
Huh? WHA--? *PIRATES?!*
YES. MYSELF AM ONE. MYSELF AM *SAI.*
OPENING SAFE FOR HARBOR FEES NOW. ALSO, WE REQUIRE STONE WARRIOR WOMAN.
DENIAL... REFUSAL... IS DEATH. FOR YOU. FOR ALL SHIP. YOU WILL COME NOW.
S.O.S.! S.O.S.! THIS IS THE FREIGHTER CORTO MALTESE! UNDER ATTACK BY PIRATES! REPEAT! UNDER ATTACK BY PIRATES! BEARINGS...!

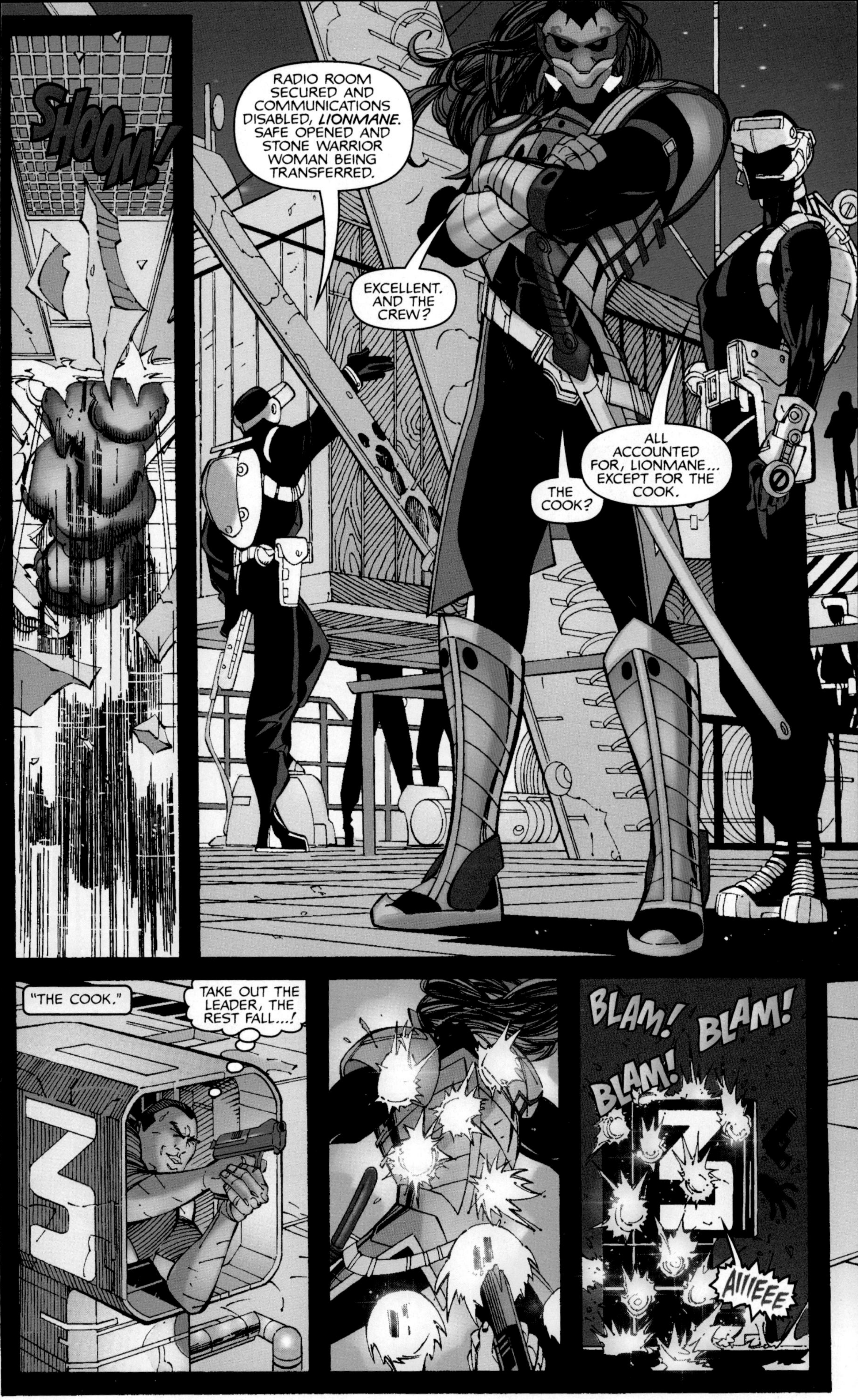
SHOOM!
RADIO ROOM SECURED AND COMMUNICATIONS DISABLED, *LIONMANE.* SAFE OPENED AND STONE WARRIOR WOMAN BEING TRANSFERRED.
EXCELLENT. AND THE CREW?
ALL ACCOUNTED FOR, LIONMANE... EXCEPT FOR THE COOK.
THE COOK?
"THE COOK."
TAKE OUT THE LEADER, THE REST FALL...!
BLAM!
BLAM!
BLAM!
AIIIEEE

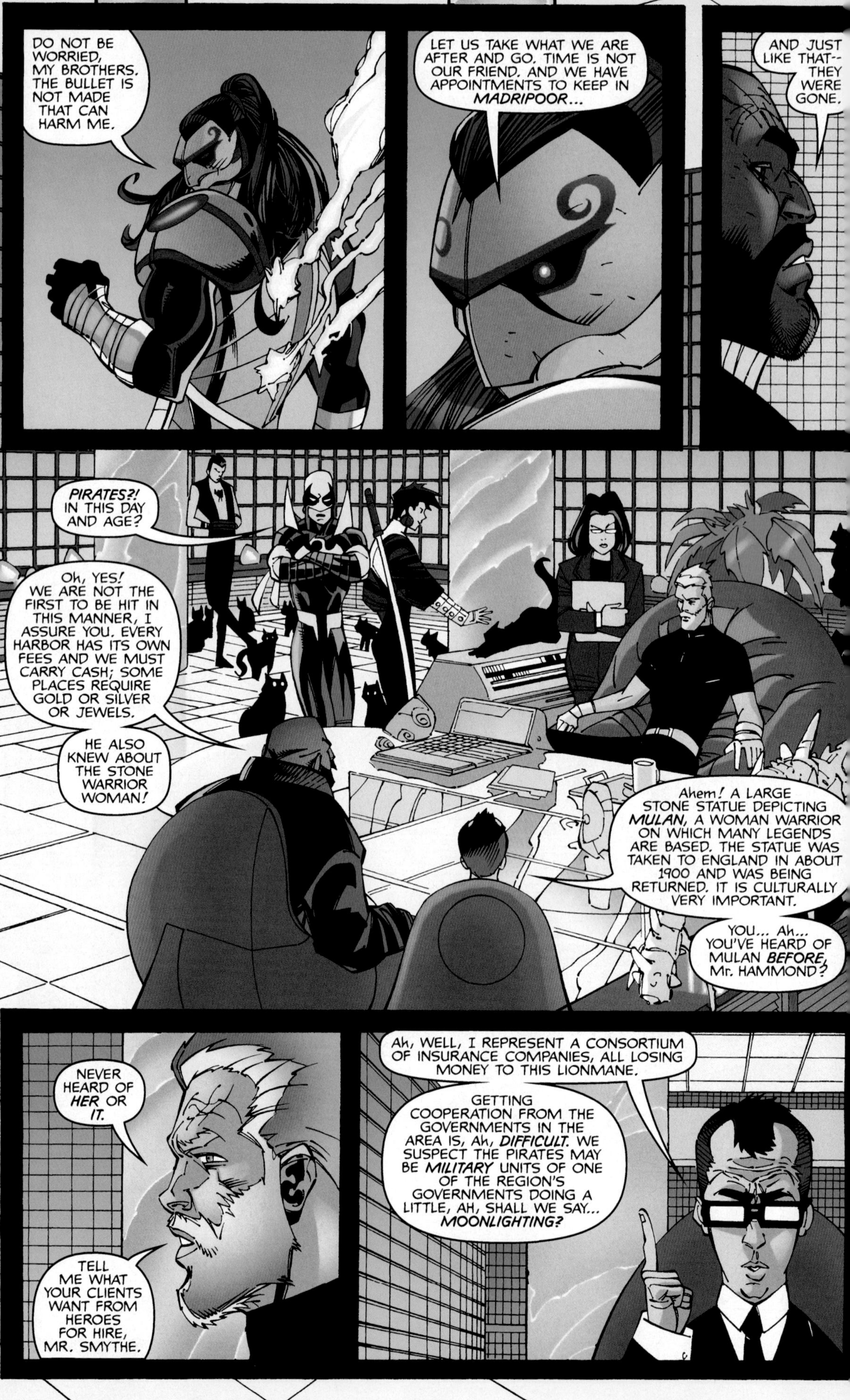

DO NOT BE WORRIED, MY BROTHERS. THE BULLET IS NOT MADE THAT CAN HARM ME.
LET US TAKE WHAT WE ARE AFTER AND GO. TIME IS NOT OUR FRIEND, AND WE HAVE APPOINTMENTS TO KEEP IN MADRIPOOR...
AND JUST LIKE THAT--THEY WERE GONE.
PIRATES?! IN THIS DAY AND AGE?
Oh, YES! WE ARE NOT THE FIRST TO BE HIT IN THIS MANNER, I ASSURE YOU. EVERY HARBOR HAS ITS OWN FEES AND WE MUST CARRY CASH; SOME PLACES REQUIRE GOLD OR SILVER OR JEWELS.
HE ALSO KNEW ABOUT THE STONE WARRIOR WOMAN!
Ahem! A LARGE STONE STATUE DEPICTING MULAN, A WOMAN WARRIOR ON WHICH MANY LEGENDS ARE BASED. THE STATUE WAS TAKEN TO ENGLAND IN ABOUT 1900 AND WAS BEING RETURNED. IT IS CULTURALLY VERY IMPORTANT.
YOU... Ah... YOU'VE HEARD OF MULAN BEFORE, Mr. HAMMOND?
NEVER HEARD OF HER OR IT.
TELL ME WHAT YOUR CLIENTS WANT FROM HEROES FOR HIRE, MR. SMYTHE.
Ah, WELL, I REPRESENT A CONSORTIUM OF INSURANCE COMPANIES, ALL LOSING MONEY TO THIS LIONMANE.
GETTING COOPERATION FROM THE GOVERNMENTS IN THE AREA IS, Ah, DIFFICULT. WE SUSPECT THE PIRATES MAY BE MILITARY UNITS OF ONE OF THE REGION'S GOVERNMENTS DOING A LITTLE, AH, SHALL WE SAY... MOONLIGHTING?

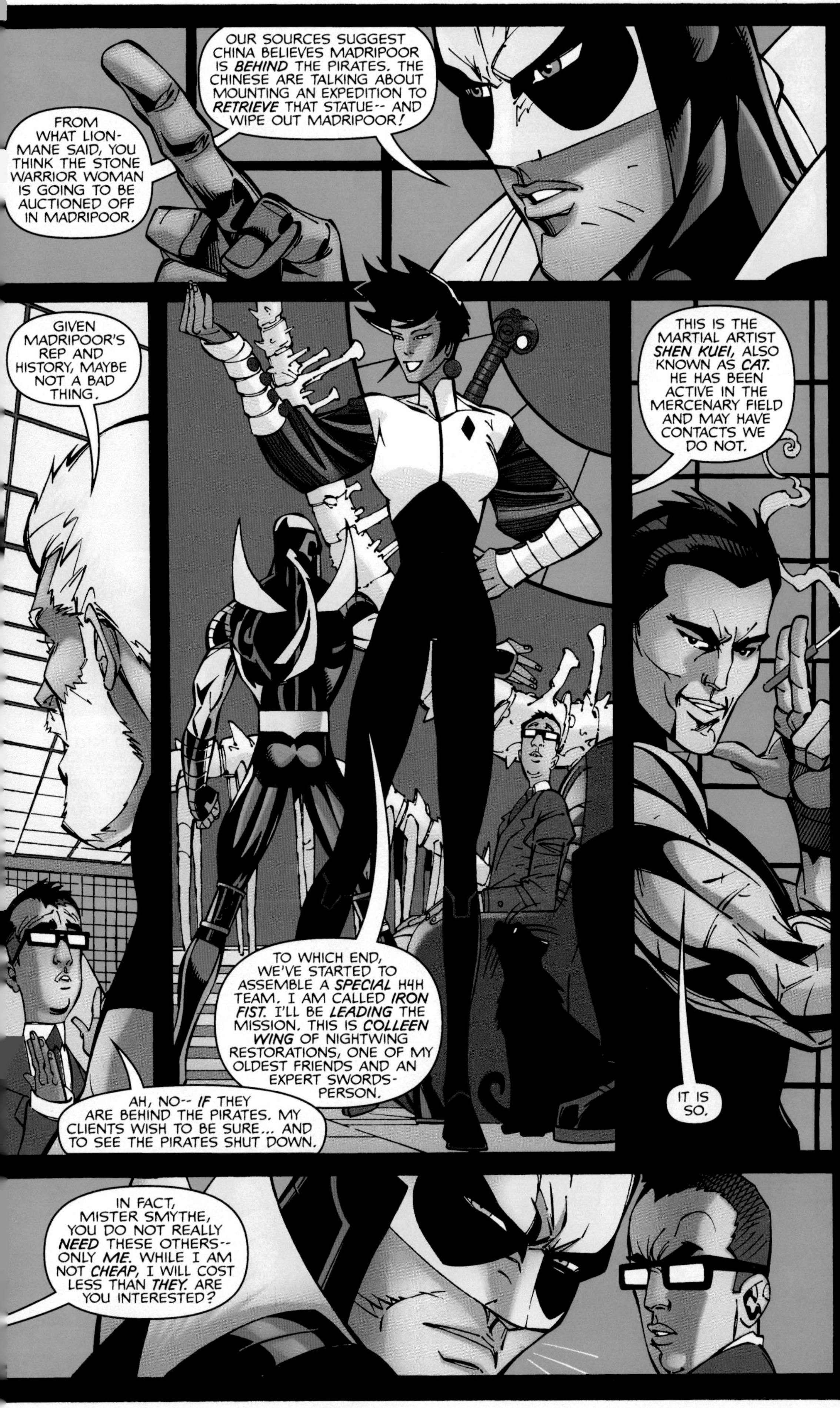
FROM WHAT LION-MANE SAID, YOU THINK THE STONE WARRIOR WOMAN IS GOING TO BE AUCTIONED OFF IN MADRIPOOR.
OUR SOURCES SUGGEST CHINA BELIEVES MADRIPOOR IS BEHIND THE PIRATES. THE CHINESE ARE TALKING ABOUT MOUNTING AN EXPEDITION TO RETRIEVE THAT STATUE-- AND WIPE OUT MADRIPOOR!
GIVEN MADRIPOOR'S REP AND HISTORY, MAYBE NOT A BAD THING.
AH, NO-- IF THEY ARE BEHIND THE PIRATES. MY CLIENTS WISH TO BE SURE... AND TO SEE THE PIRATES SHUT DOWN.
TO WHICH END, WE'VE STARTED TO ASSEMBLE A SPECIAL H4H TEAM. I AM CALLED IRON FIST. I'LL BE LEADING THE MISSION. THIS IS COLLEEN WING OF NIGHTWING RESTORATIONS, ONE OF MY OLDEST FRIENDS AND AN EXPERT SWORDS-PERSON.
THIS IS THE MARTIAL ARTIST SHEN KUEI, ALSO KNOWN AS CAT. HE HAS BEEN ACTIVE IN THE MERCENARY FIELD AND MAY HAVE CONTACTS WE DO NOT.
IT IS SO.
IN FACT, MISTER SMYTHE, YOU DO NOT REALLY NEED THESE OTHERS-- ONLY ME. WHILE I AM NOT CHEAP, I WILL COST LESS THAN THEY. ARE YOU INTERESTED?

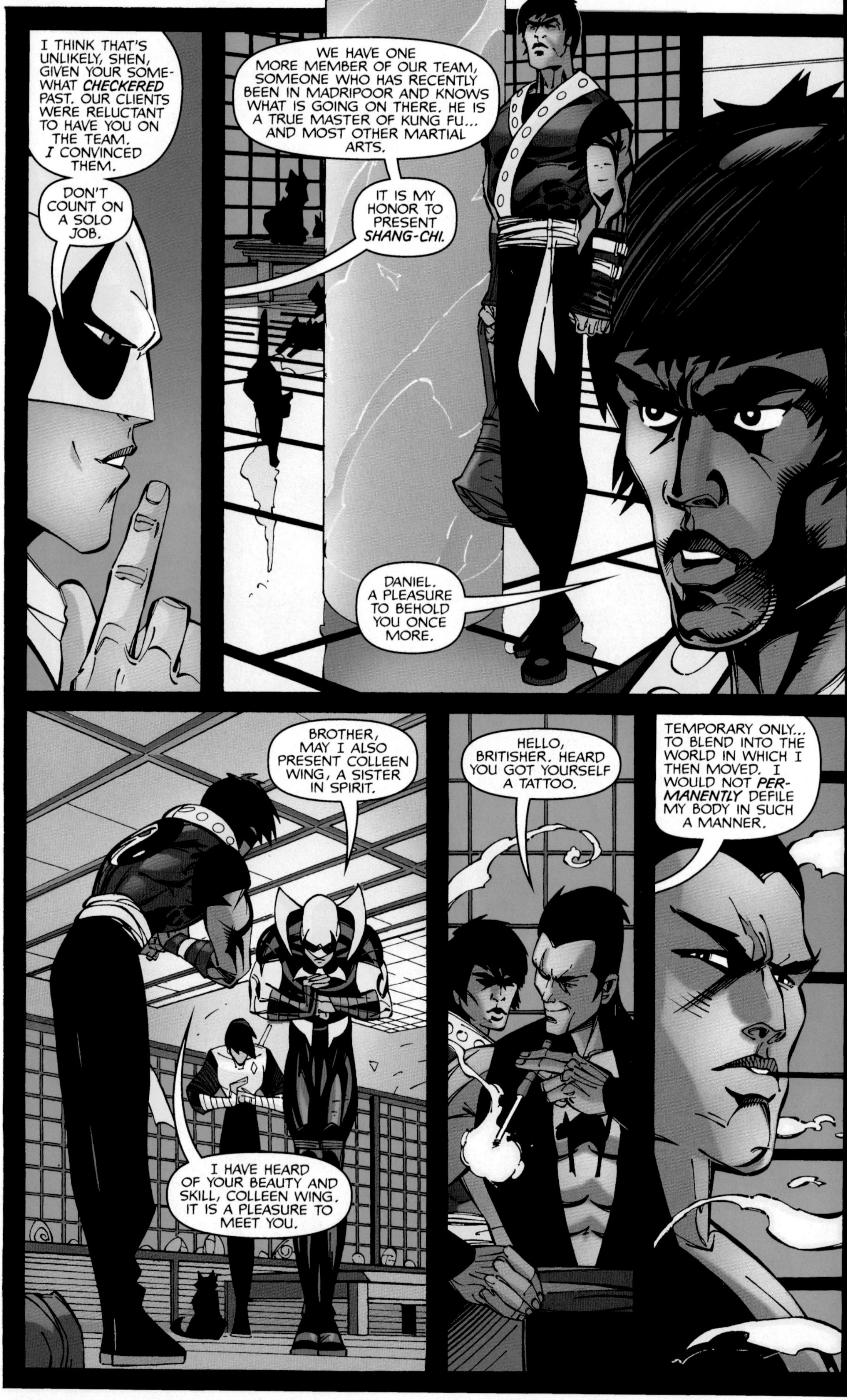
I THINK THAT'S UNLIKELY, SHEN, GIVEN YOUR SOME-WHAT CHECKERED PAST. OUR CLIENTS WERE RELUCTANT TO HAVE YOU ON THE TEAM. I CONVINCED THEM.
DON'T COUNT ON A SOLO JOB.
WE HAVE ONE MORE MEMBER OF OUR TEAM, SOMEONE WHO HAS RECENTLY BEEN IN MADRIPOOR AND KNOWS WHAT IS GOING ON THERE. HE IS A TRUE MASTER OF KUNG FU... AND MOST OTHER MARTIAL ARTS.
IT IS MY HONOR TO PRESENT SHANG-CHI.
DANIEL. A PLEASURE TO BEHOLD YOU ONCE MORE.
BROTHER, MAY I ALSO PRESENT COLLEEN WING, A SISTER IN SPIRIT.
I HAVE HEARD OF YOUR BEAUTY AND SKILL, COLLEEN WING. IT IS A PLEASURE TO MEET YOU.
HELLO, BRITISHER. HEARD YOU GOT YOURSELF A TATTOO.
TEMPORARY ONLY... TO BLEND INTO THE WORLD IN WHICH I THEN MOVED. I WOULD NOT PER-MANENTLY DEFILE MY BODY IN SUCH A MANNER.

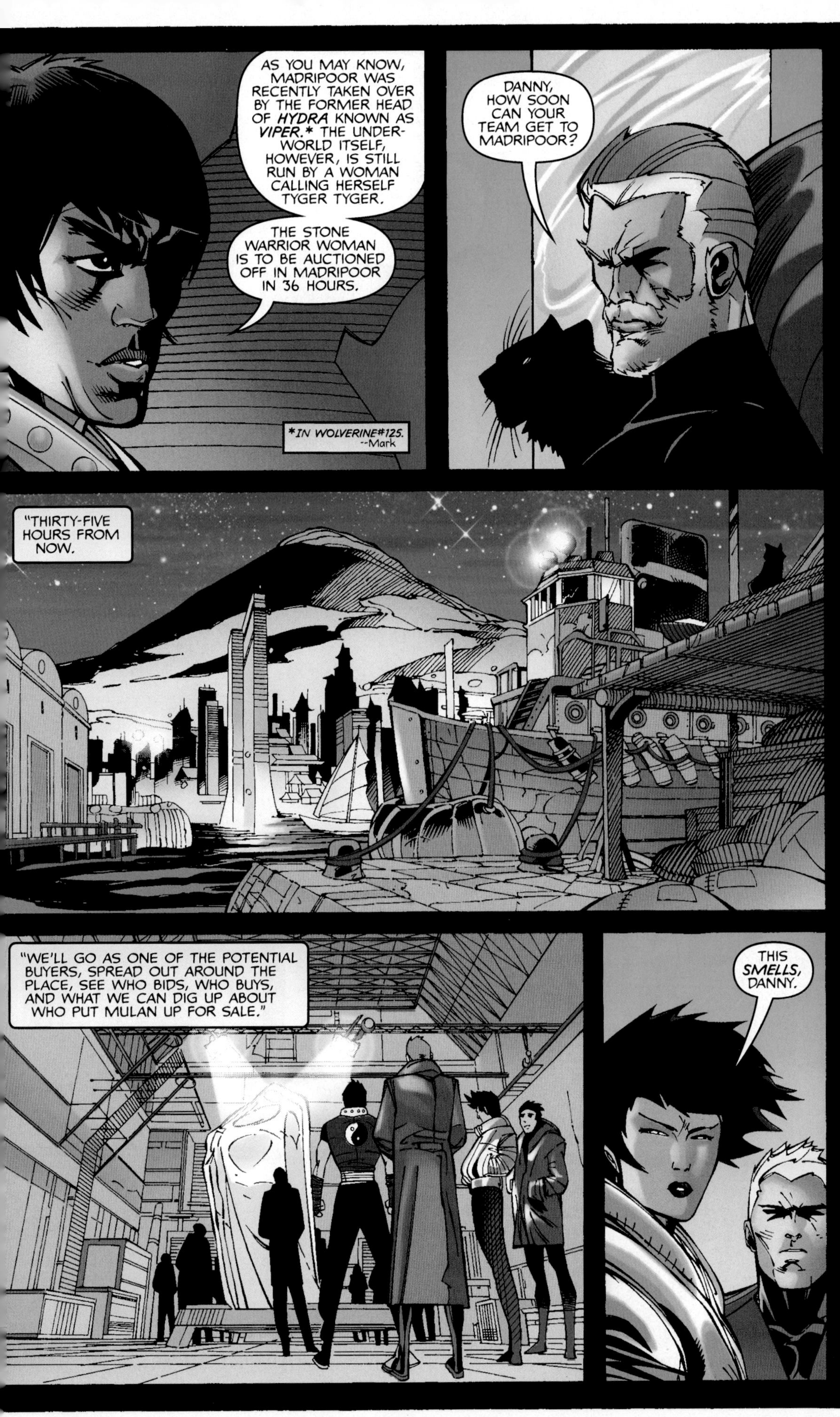
AS YOU MAY KNOW, MADRIPOOR WAS RECENTLY TAKEN OVER BY THE FORMER HEAD OF *HYDRA* KNOWN AS *VIPER.** THE UNDER-WORLD ITSELF, HOWEVER, IS STILL RUN BY A WOMAN CALLING HERSELF TYGER TYGER.
THE STONE WARRIOR WOMAN IS TO BE AUCTIONED OFF IN MADRIPOOR IN 36 HOURS.
**IN WOLVERINE #125.* --Mark
DANNY, HOW SOON CAN YOUR TEAM GET TO MADRIPOOR?
"THIRTY-FIVE HOURS FROM NOW.
"WE'LL GO AS ONE OF THE POTENTIAL BUYERS, SPREAD OUT AROUND THE PLACE, SEE WHO BIDS, WHO BUYS, AND WHAT WE CAN DIG UP ABOUT WHO PUT MULAN UP FOR SALE."
THIS *SMELLS,* DANNY.

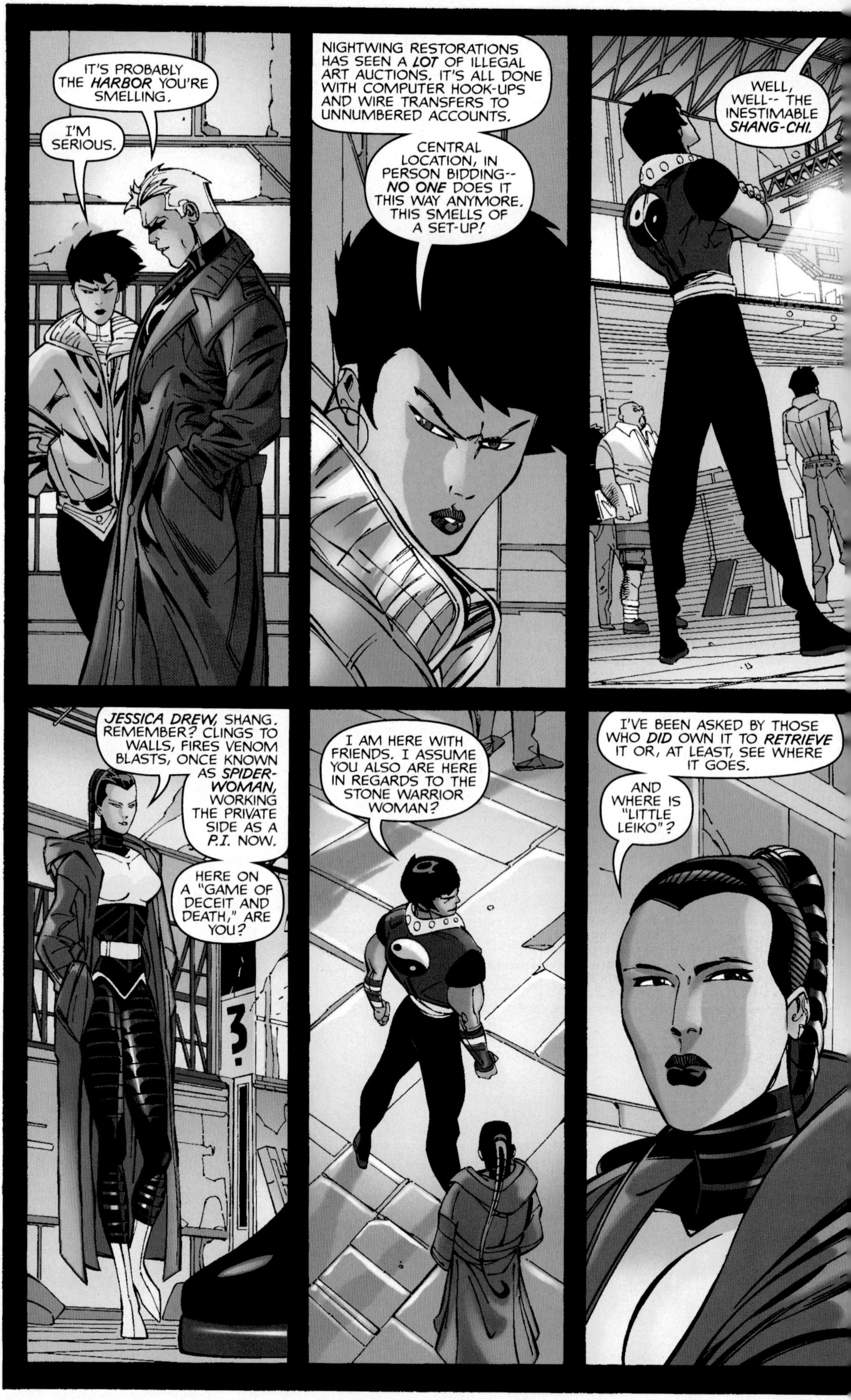
IT'S PROBABLY THE HARBOR YOU'RE SMELLING.
I'M SERIOUS.
NIGHTWING RESTORATIONS HAS SEEN A LOT OF ILLEGAL ART AUCTIONS. IT'S ALL DONE WITH COMPUTER HOOK-UPS AND WIRE TRANSFERS TO UNNUMBERED ACCOUNTS.
CENTRAL LOCATION, IN PERSON BIDDING-- NO ONE DOES IT THIS WAY ANYMORE. THIS SMELLS OF A SET-UP!
WELL, WELL-- THE INESTIMABLE SHANG-CHI.
JESSICA DREW, SHANG. REMEMBER? CLINGS TO WALLS, FIRES VENOM BLASTS, ONCE KNOWN AS SPIDER-WOMAN, WORKING THE PRIVATE SIDE AS A P.I. NOW.
HERE ON A "GAME OF DECEIT AND DEATH," ARE YOU?
I AM HERE WITH FRIENDS. I ASSUME YOU ALSO ARE HERE IN REGARDS TO THE STONE WARRIOR WOMAN?
I'VE BEEN ASKED BY THOSE WHO DID OWN IT TO RETRIEVE IT OR, AT LEAST, SEE WHERE IT GOES.
AND WHERE IS "LITTLE LEIKO"?
3

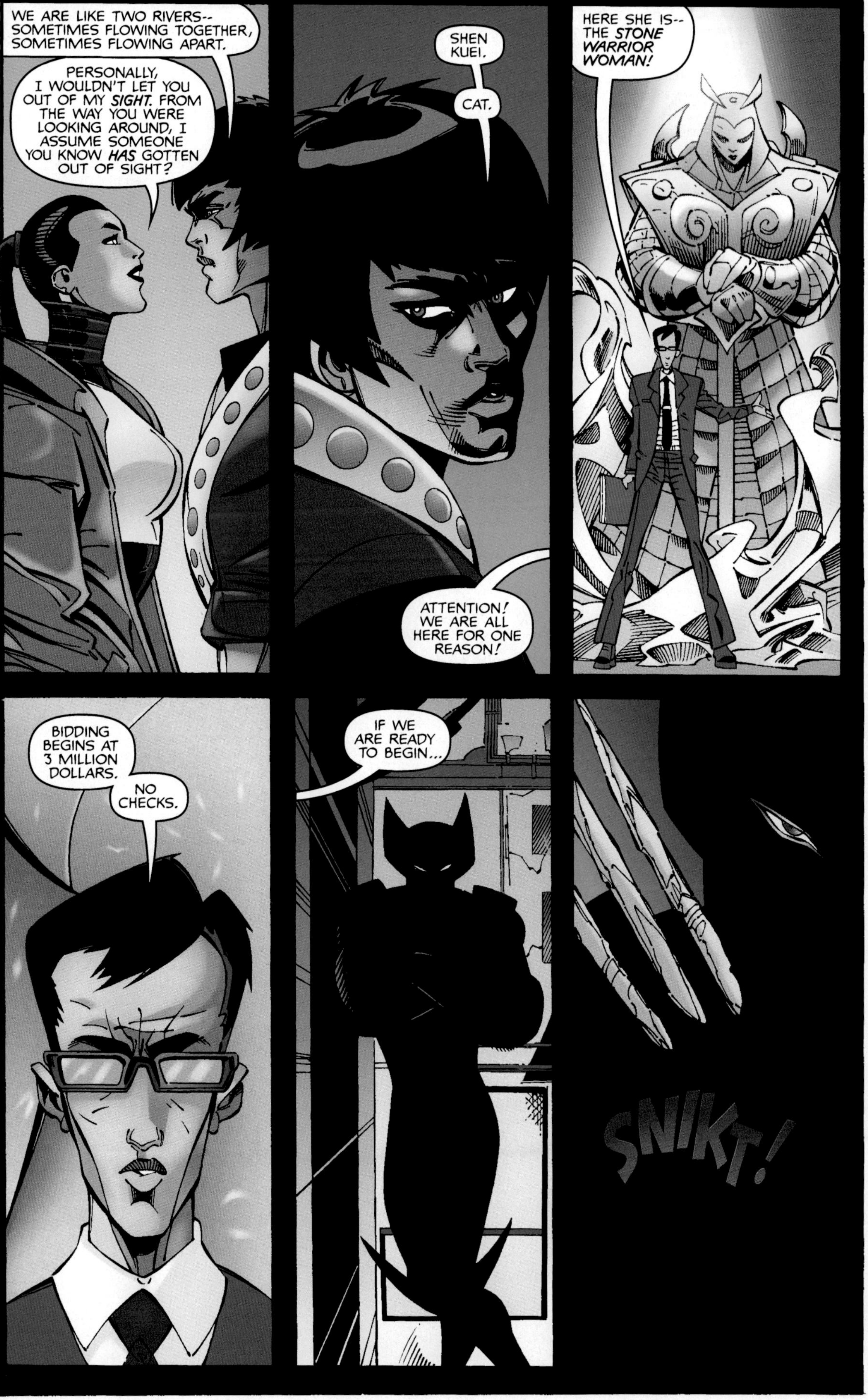
WE ARE LIKE TWO RIVERS-- SOMETIMES FLOWING TOGETHER, SOMETIMES FLOWING APART.
PERSONALLY, I WOULDN'T LET YOU OUT OF MY *SIGHT.* FROM THE WAY YOU WERE LOOKING AROUND, I ASSUME SOMEONE YOU KNOW *HAS* GOTTEN OUT OF SIGHT?
SHEN KUEI.
CAT.
ATTENTION! WE ARE ALL HERE FOR ONE REASON!
HERE SHE IS-- THE *STONE WARRIOR WOMAN!*
BIDDING BEGINS AT 3 MILLION DOLLARS.
NO CHECKS.
IF WE ARE READY TO BEGIN...
SNIKT!

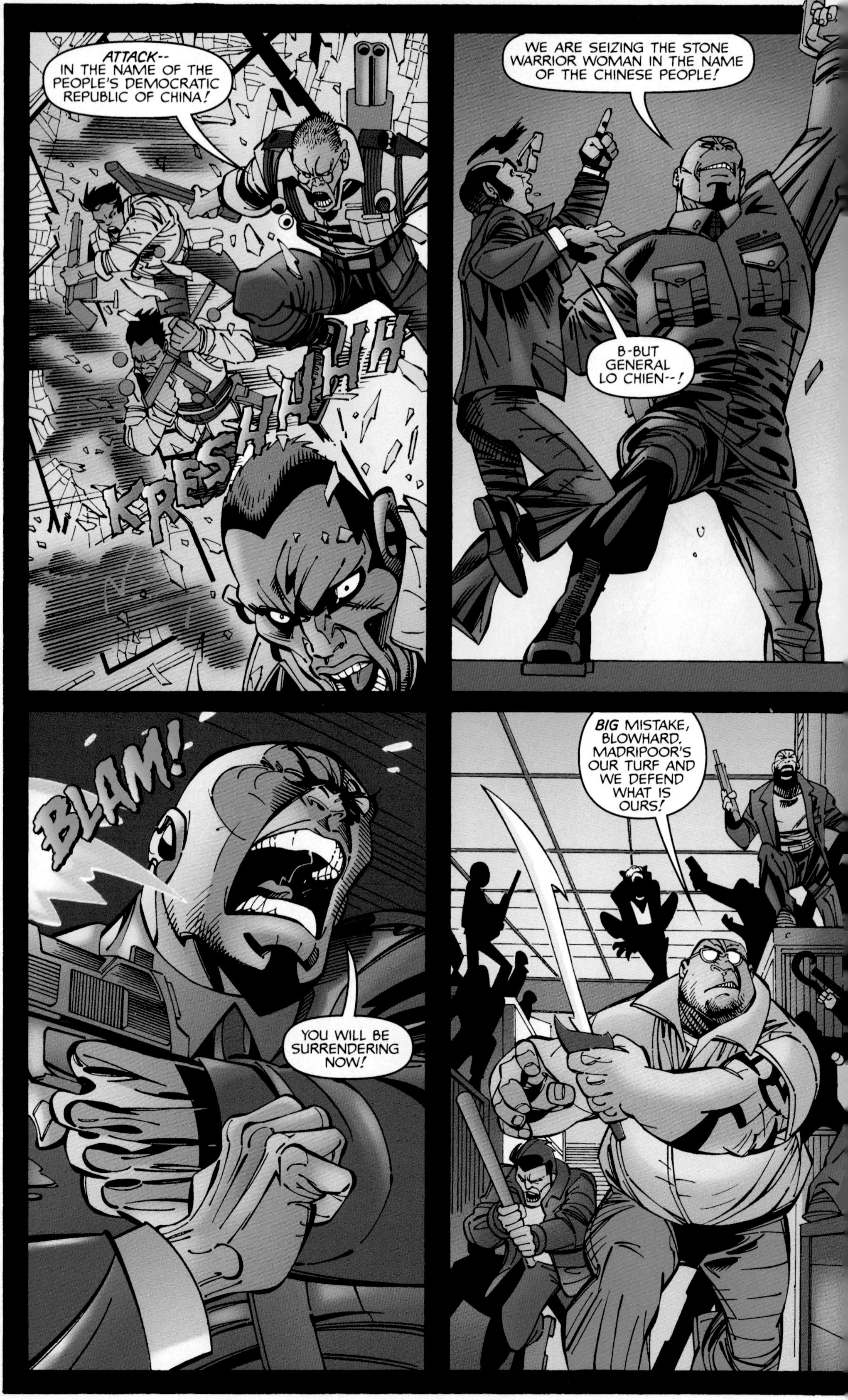
ATTACK-- IN THE NAME OF THE PEOPLE'S DEMOCRATIC REPUBLIC OF CHINA!
KRESHHHHH
WE ARE SEIZING THE STONE WARRIOR WOMAN IN THE NAME OF THE CHINESE PEOPLE!
B-BUT GENERAL LO CHIEN--!
BLAM!
YOU WILL BE SURRENDERING NOW!
BIG MISTAKE, BLOWHARD. MADRIPOOR'S OUR TURF AND WE DEFEND WHAT IS OURS!

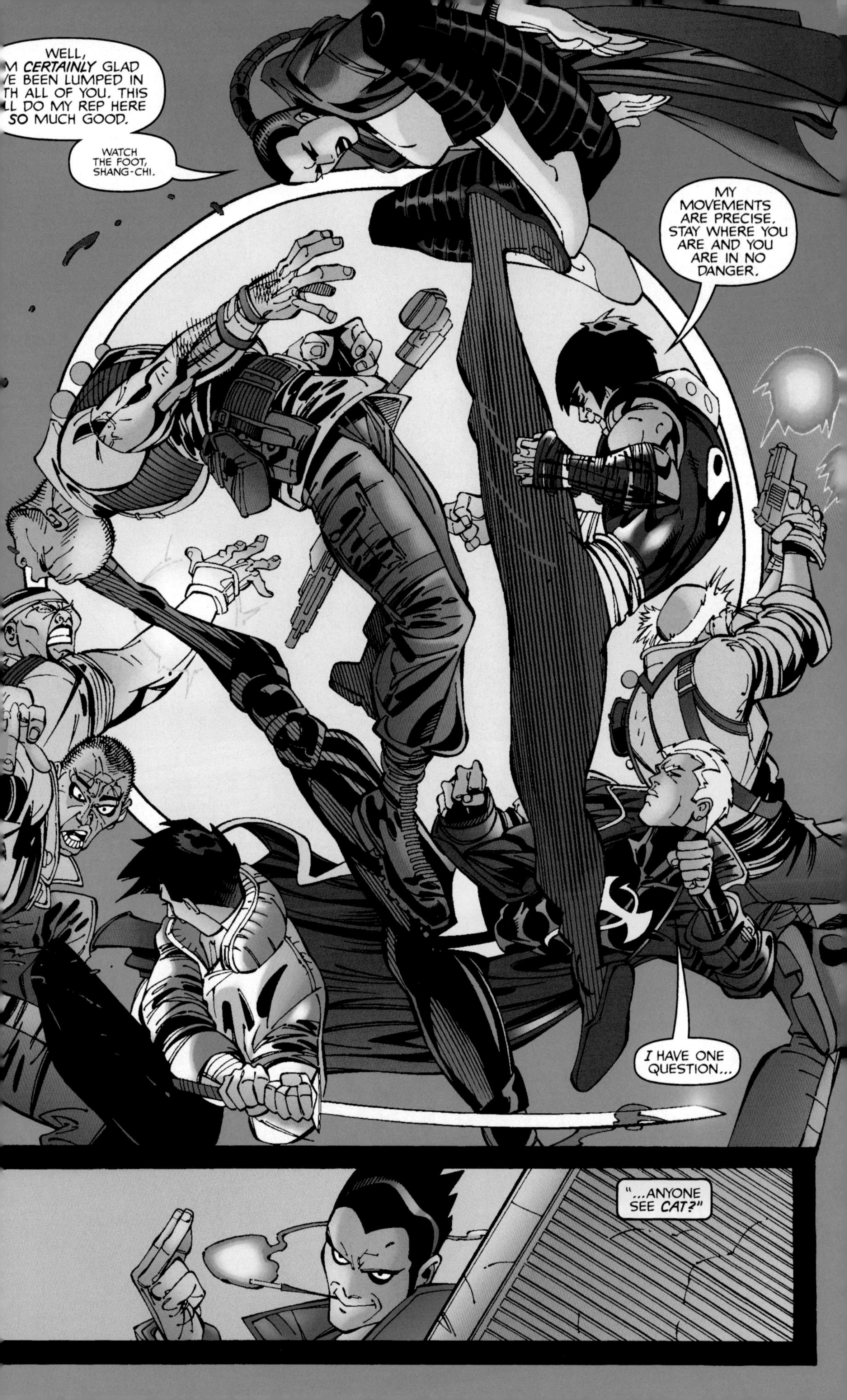

WELL,
M *CERTAINLY* GLAD
VE BEEN LUMPED IN
TH ALL OF YOU. THIS
LL DO MY REP HERE
SO MUCH GOOD.
WATCH THE FOOT, SHANG-CHI.
MY MOVEMENTS ARE PRECISE. STAY WHERE YOU ARE AND YOU ARE IN NO DANGER.
I HAVE ONE QUESTION...
"...ANYONE SEE *CAT?*"

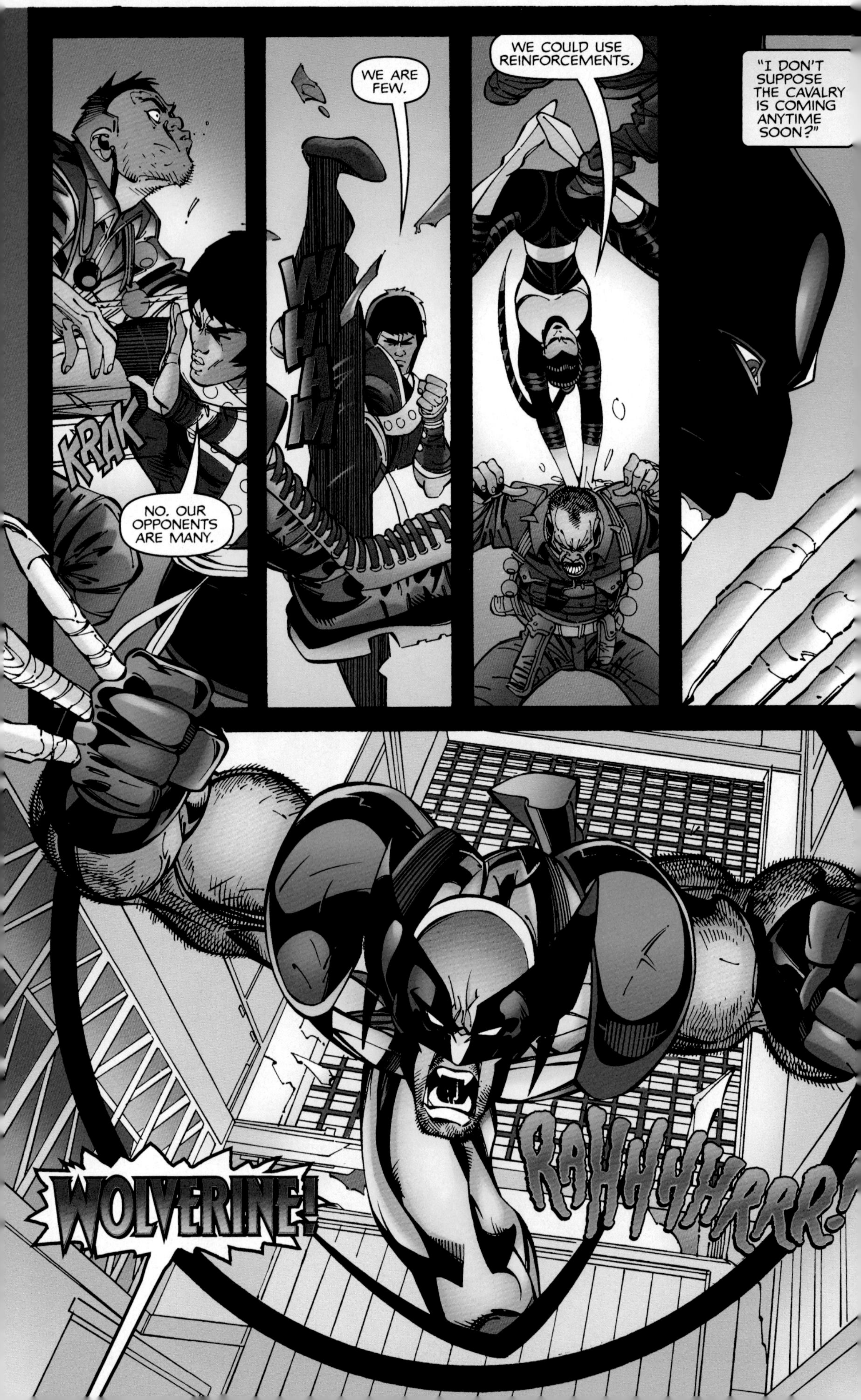
KRAK
NO. OUR OPPONENTS ARE MANY.
WE ARE FEW.
WHAM
WE COULD USE REINFORCEMENTS.
"I DON'T SUPPOSE THE CAVALRY IS COMING ANYTIME SOON?"
WOLVERINE!
RAHHHHRRR!

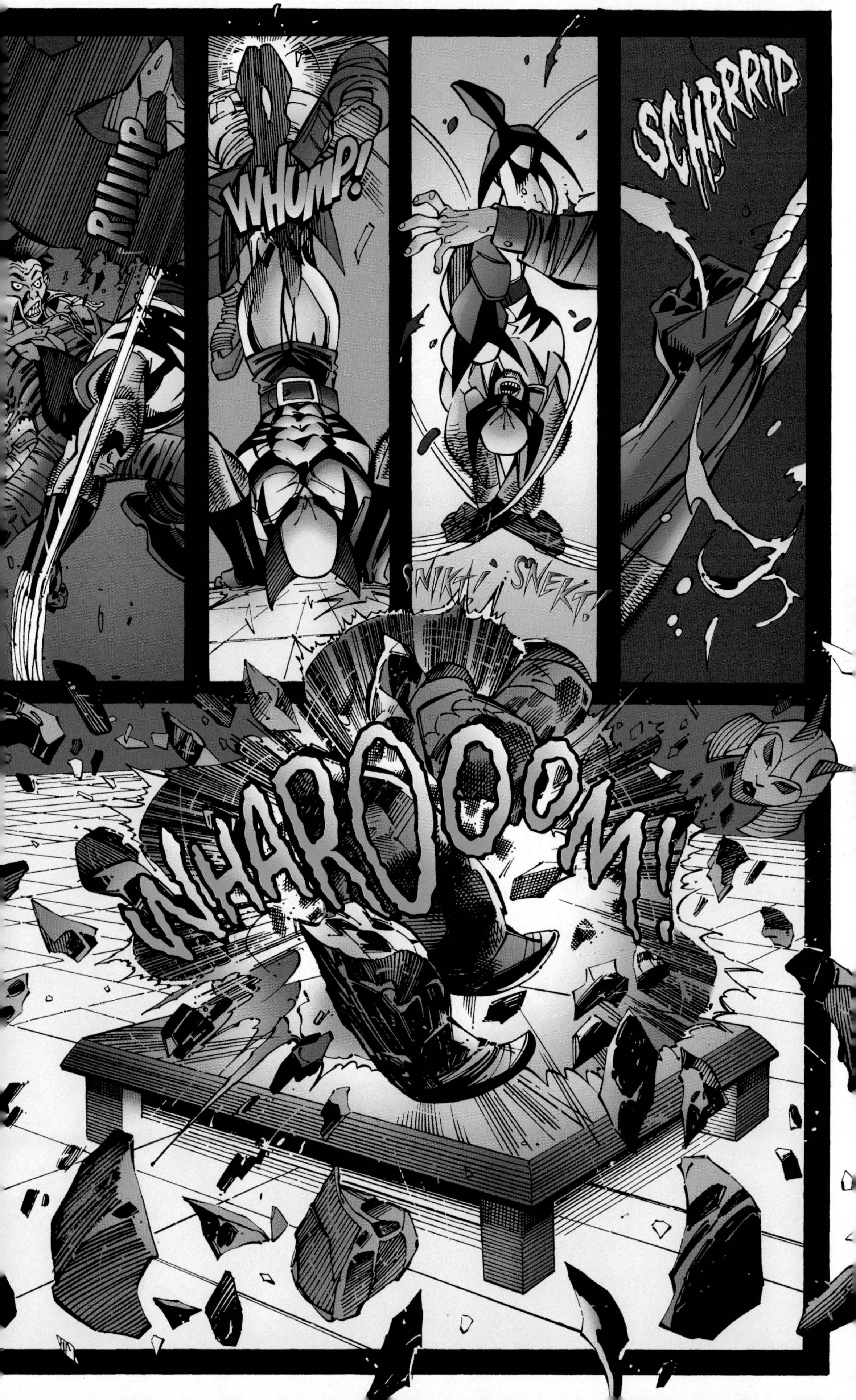
RIIIIP
WHUMP!
SCHRRRIP
SNIKT! SNEKT!
WHAROOOOM!

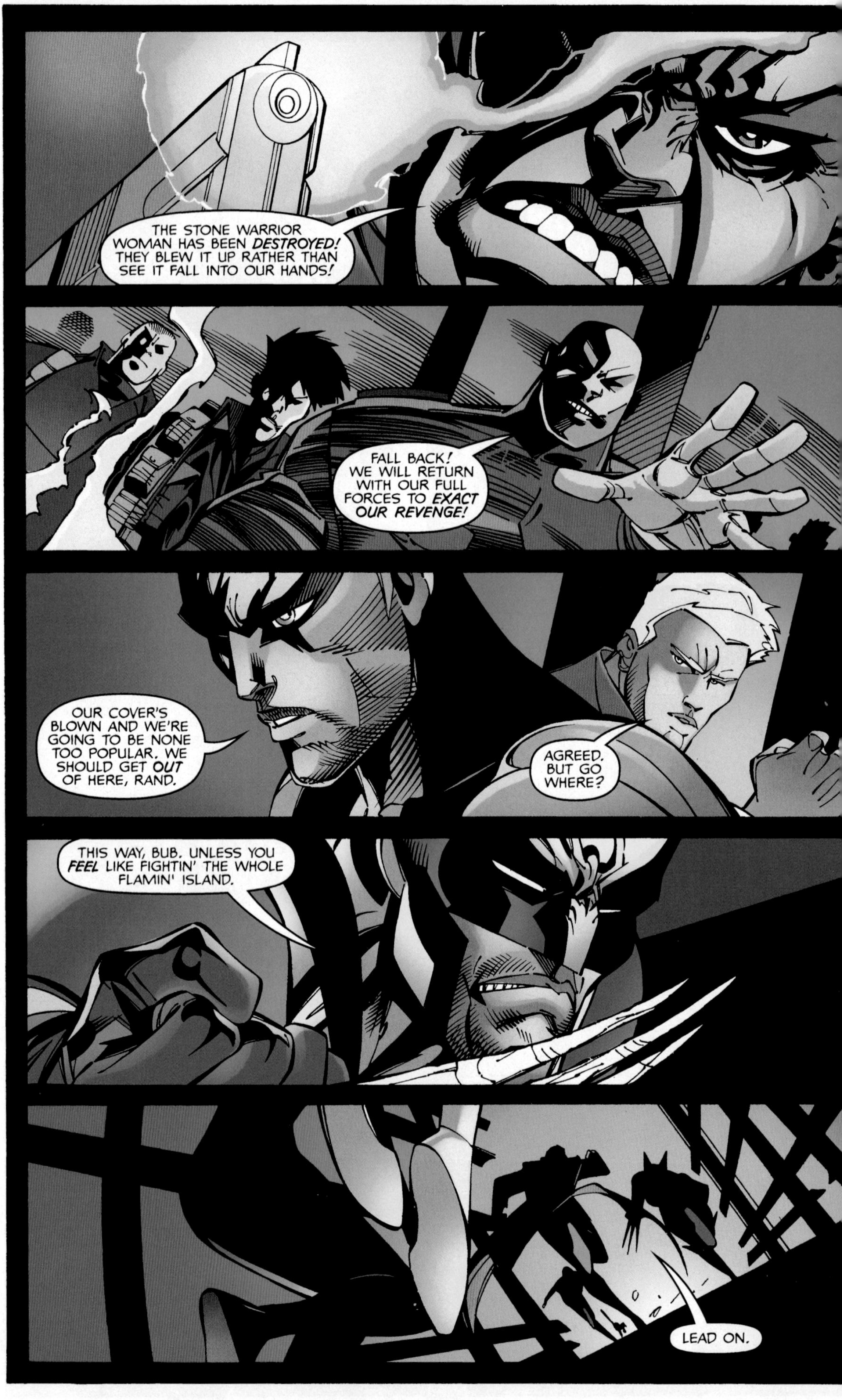
THE STONE WARRIOR WOMAN HAS BEEN *DESTROYED!* THEY BLEW IT UP RATHER THAN SEE IT FALL INTO OUR HANDS!
FALL BACK! WE WILL RETURN WITH OUR FULL FORCES TO *EXACT OUR REVENGE!*
OUR COVER'S BLOWN AND WE'RE GOING TO BE NONE TOO POPULAR. WE SHOULD GET *OUT* OF HERE, RAND.
AGREED. BUT GO WHERE?
THIS WAY, BUB. UNLESS YOU *FEEL* LIKE FIGHTIN' THE WHOLE FLAMIN' ISLAND.
LEAD ON.

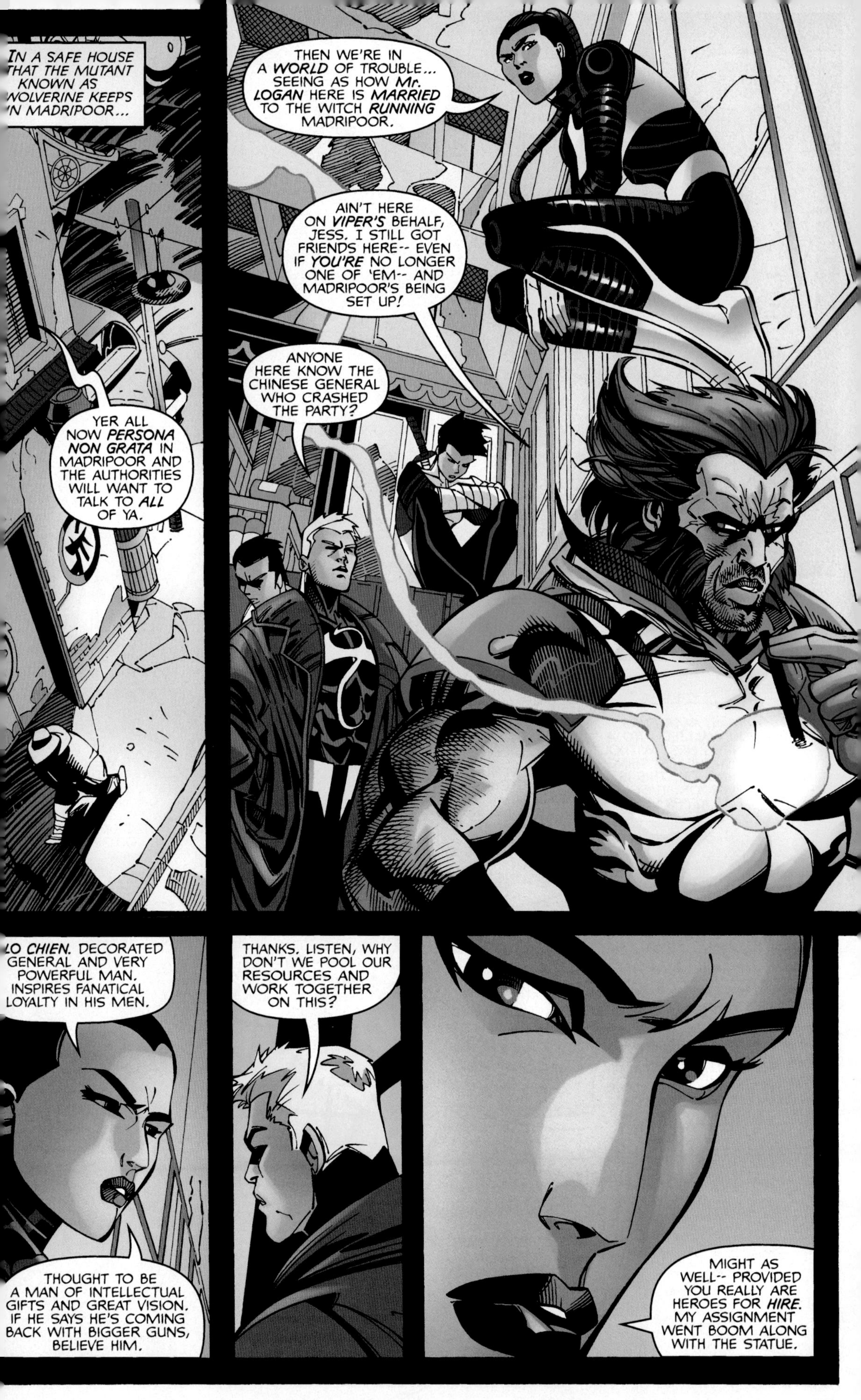
IN A SAFE HOUSE THAT THE MUTANT KNOWN AS WOLVERINE KEEPS IN MADRIPOOR...
THEN WE'RE IN A WORLD OF TROUBLE... SEEING AS HOW Mr. LOGAN HERE IS MARRIED TO THE WITCH RUNNING MADRIPOOR.
AIN'T HERE ON VIPER'S BEHALF, JESS. I STILL GOT FRIENDS HERE-- EVEN IF YOU'RE NO LONGER ONE OF 'EM-- AND MADRIPOOR'S BEING SET UP!
ANYONE HERE KNOW THE CHINESE GENERAL WHO CRASHED THE PARTY?
YER ALL NOW PERSONA NON GRATA IN MADRIPOOR AND THE AUTHORITIES WILL WANT TO TALK TO ALL OF YA.
LO CHIEN. DECORATED GENERAL AND VERY POWERFUL MAN. INSPIRES FANATICAL LOYALTY IN HIS MEN.
THOUGHT TO BE A MAN OF INTELLECTUAL GIFTS AND GREAT VISION. IF HE SAYS HE'S COMING BACK WITH BIGGER GUNS, BELIEVE HIM.
THANKS. LISTEN, WHY DON'T WE POOL OUR RESOURCES AND WORK TOGETHER ON THIS?
MIGHT AS WELL-- PROVIDED YOU REALLY ARE HEROES FOR HIRE. MY ASSIGNMENT WENT BOOM ALONG WITH THE STATUE.

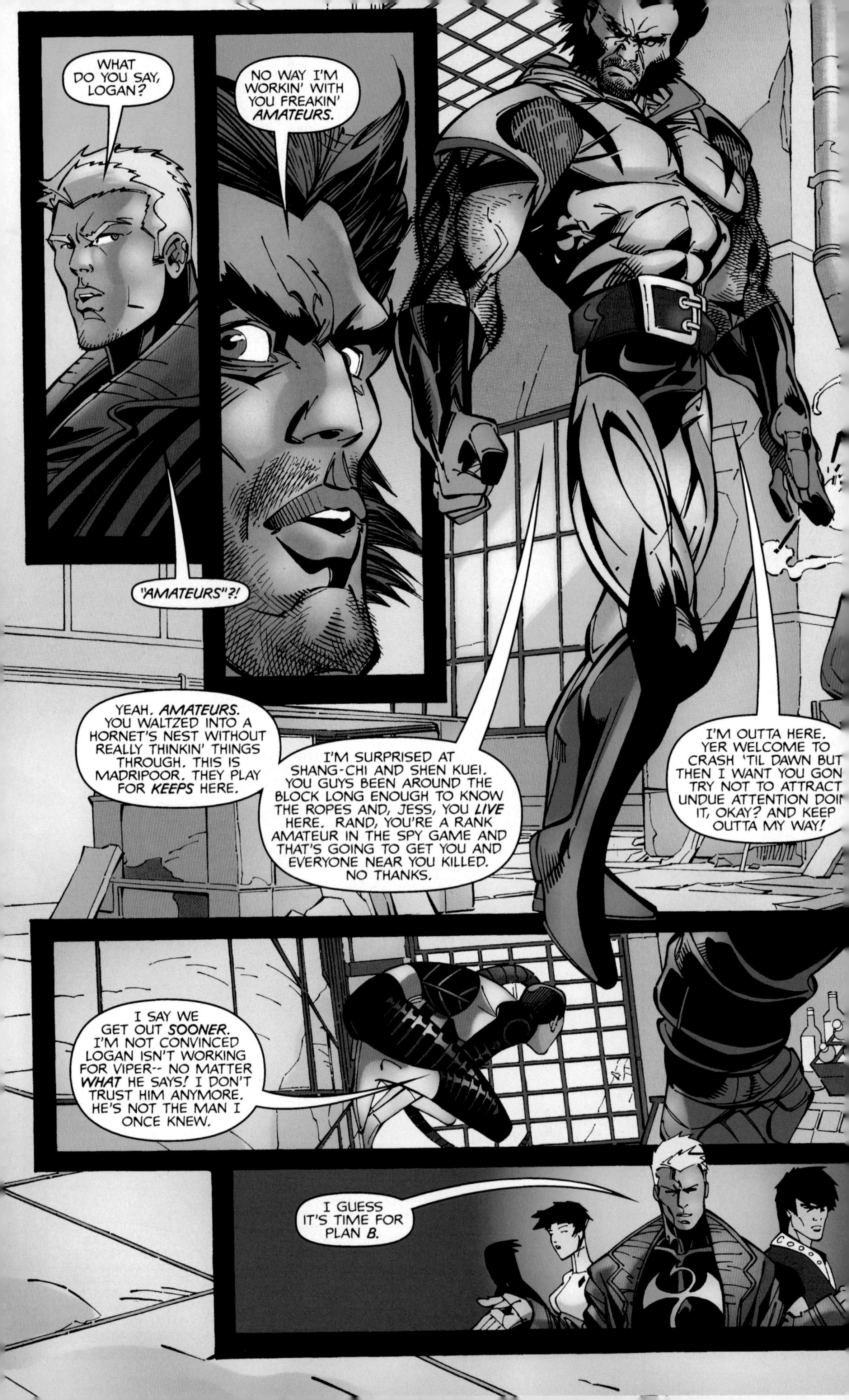
WHAT DO YOU SAY, LOGAN?
NO WAY I'M WORKIN' WITH YOU FREAKIN' *AMATEURS.*
"AMATEURS"?!
YEAH. *AMATEURS.* YOU WALTZED INTO A HORNET'S NEST WITHOUT REALLY THINKIN' THINGS THROUGH. THIS IS MADRIPOOR. THEY PLAY FOR *KEEPS* HERE.
I'M SURPRISED AT SHANG-CHI AND SHEN KUEI. YOU GUYS BEEN AROUND THE BLOCK LONG ENOUGH TO KNOW THE ROPES AND, JESS, YOU *LIVE* HERE. RAND, YOU'RE A RANK AMATEUR IN THE SPY GAME AND THAT'S GOING TO GET YOU AND EVERYONE NEAR YOU KILLED. NO THANKS.
I'M OUTTA HERE. YER WELCOME TO CRASH 'TIL DAWN BUT THEN I WANT YOU GON TRY NOT TO ATTRACT UNDUE ATTENTION DOI IT, OKAY? AND KEEP OUTTA MY WAY!
I SAY WE GET OUT *SOONER.* I'M NOT CONVINCED LOGAN ISN'T WORKING FOR VIPER-- NO MATTER *WHAT* HE SAYS! I DON'T TRUST HIM ANYMORE. HE'S NOT THE MAN I ONCE KNEW.
I GUESS IT'S TIME FOR PLAN *B.*

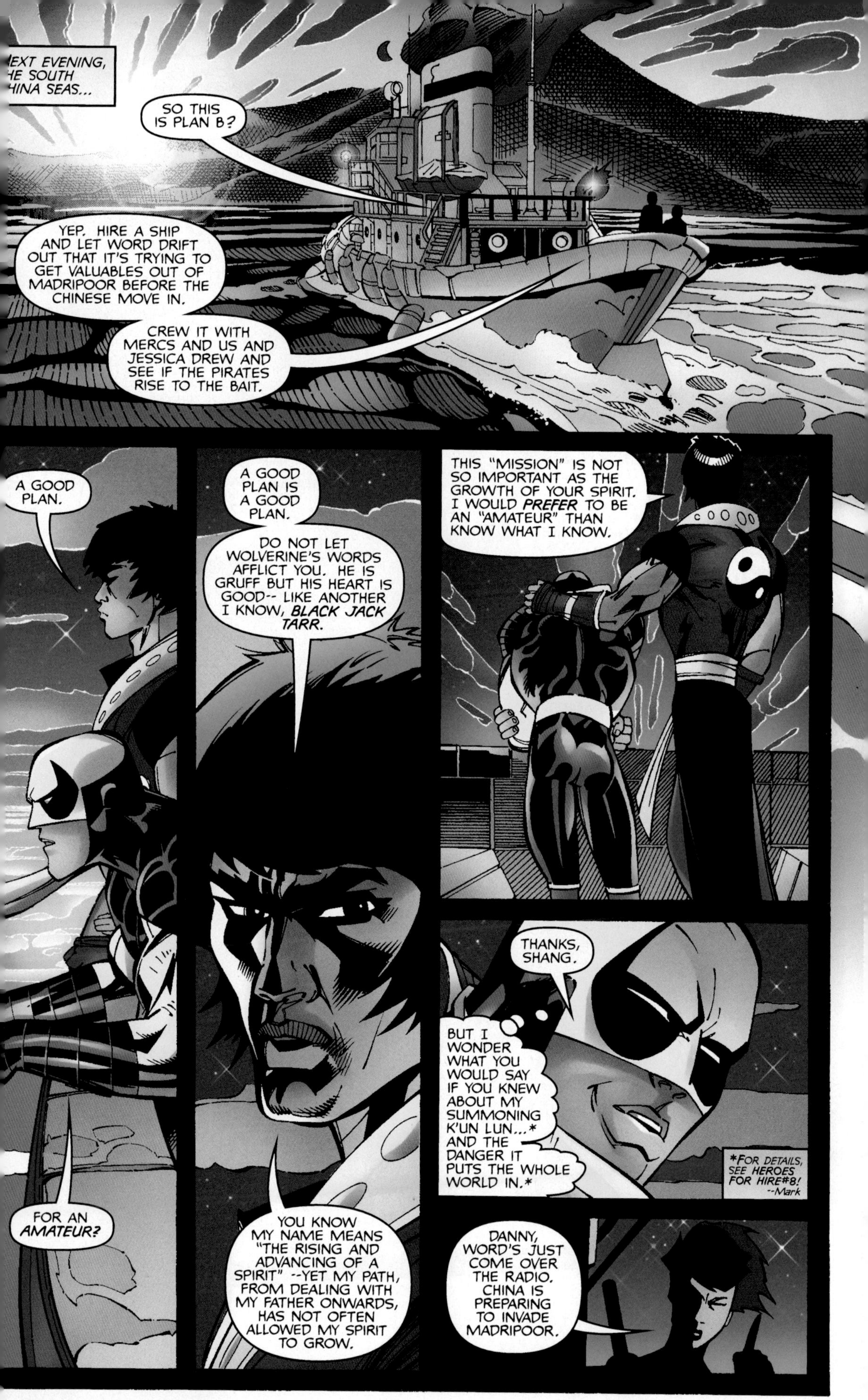

NEXT EVENING, THE SOUTH CHINA SEAS...
SO THIS IS PLAN B?
YEP. HIRE A SHIP AND LET WORD DRIFT OUT THAT IT'S TRYING TO GET VALUABLES OUT OF MADRIPOOR BEFORE THE CHINESE MOVE IN.
CREW IT WITH MERCS AND US AND JESSICA DREW AND SEE IF THE PIRATES RISE TO THE BAIT.
A GOOD PLAN.
FOR AN *AMATEUR?*
A GOOD PLAN IS A GOOD PLAN.
DO NOT LET WOLVERINE'S WORDS AFFLICT YOU. HE IS GRUFF BUT HIS HEART IS GOOD-- LIKE ANOTHER I KNOW, ***BLACK JACK TARR.***
YOU KNOW MY NAME MEANS "THE RISING AND ADVANCING OF A SPIRIT" --YET MY PATH, FROM DEALING WITH MY FATHER ONWARDS, HAS NOT OFTEN ALLOWED MY SPIRIT TO GROW.
THIS "MISSION" IS NOT SO IMPORTANT AS THE GROWTH OF YOUR SPIRIT. I WOULD ***PREFER*** TO BE AN "AMATEUR" THAN KNOW WHAT I KNOW.
THANKS, SHANG.
BUT I WONDER WHAT YOU WOULD SAY IF YOU KNEW ABOUT MY SUMMONING K'UN LUN...* AND THE DANGER IT PUTS THE WHOLE WORLD IN.*
*FOR DETAILS, SEE *HEROES FOR HIRE* #8! --Mark
DANNY, WORD'S JUST COME OVER THE RADIO. CHINA IS PREPARING TO INVADE MADRIPOOR.

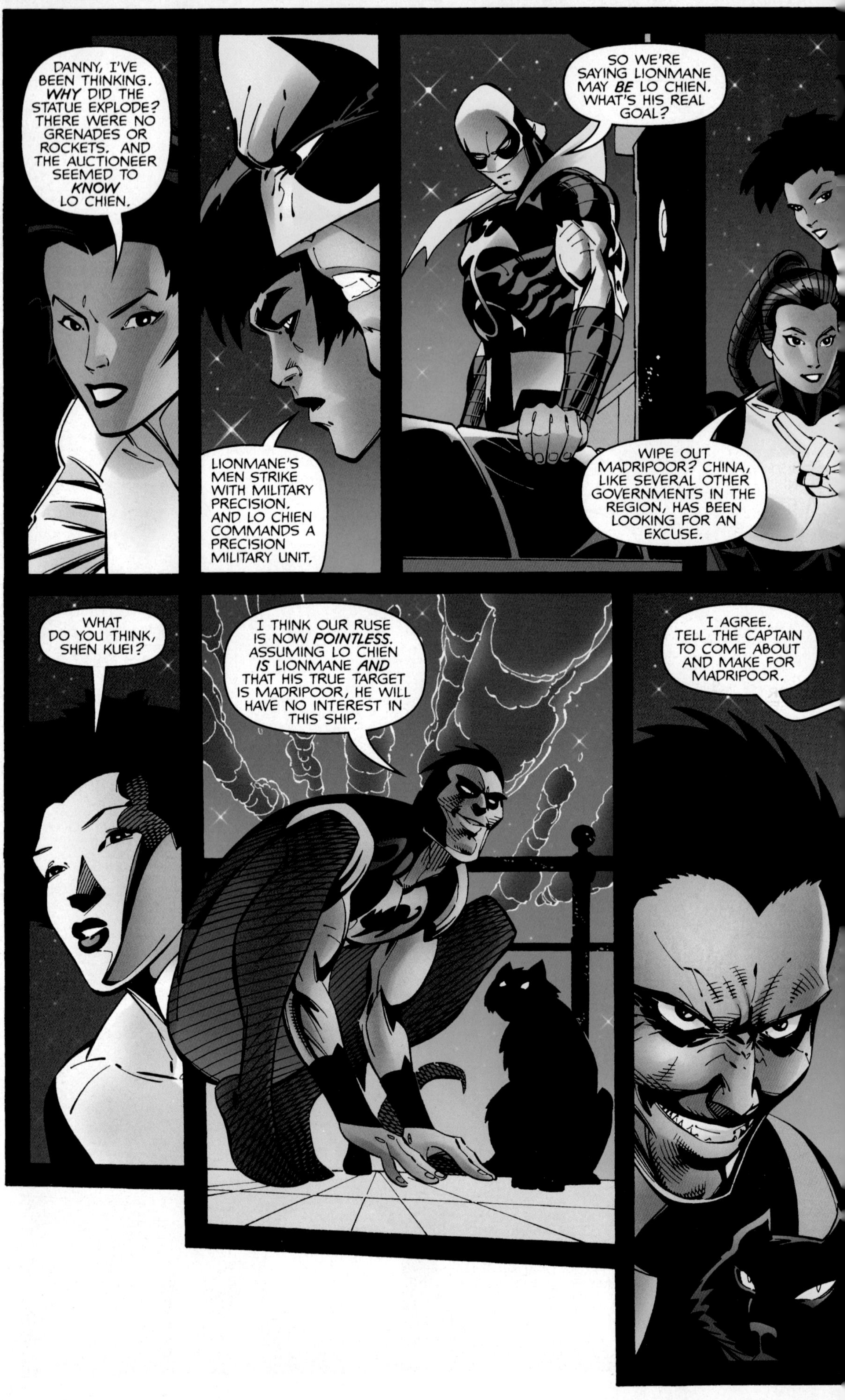
DANNY, I'VE BEEN THINKING. WHY DID THE STATUE EXPLODE? THERE WERE NO GRENADES OR ROCKETS. AND THE AUCTIONEER SEEMED TO KNOW LO CHIEN.
LIONMANE'S MEN STRIKE WITH MILITARY PRECISION. AND LO CHIEN COMMANDS A PRECISION MILITARY UNIT.
SO WE'RE SAYING LIONMANE MAY BE LO CHIEN. WHAT'S HIS REAL GOAL?
WIPE OUT MADRIPOOR? CHINA, LIKE SEVERAL OTHER GOVERNMENTS IN THE REGION, HAS BEEN LOOKING FOR AN EXCUSE.
WHAT DO YOU THINK, SHEN KUEI?
I THINK OUR RUSE IS NOW POINTLESS. ASSUMING LO CHIEN IS LIONMANE AND THAT HIS TRUE TARGET IS MADRIPOOR, HE WILL HAVE NO INTEREST IN THIS SHIP.
I AGREE. TELL THE CAPTAIN TO COME ABOUT AND MAKE FOR MADRIPOOR.

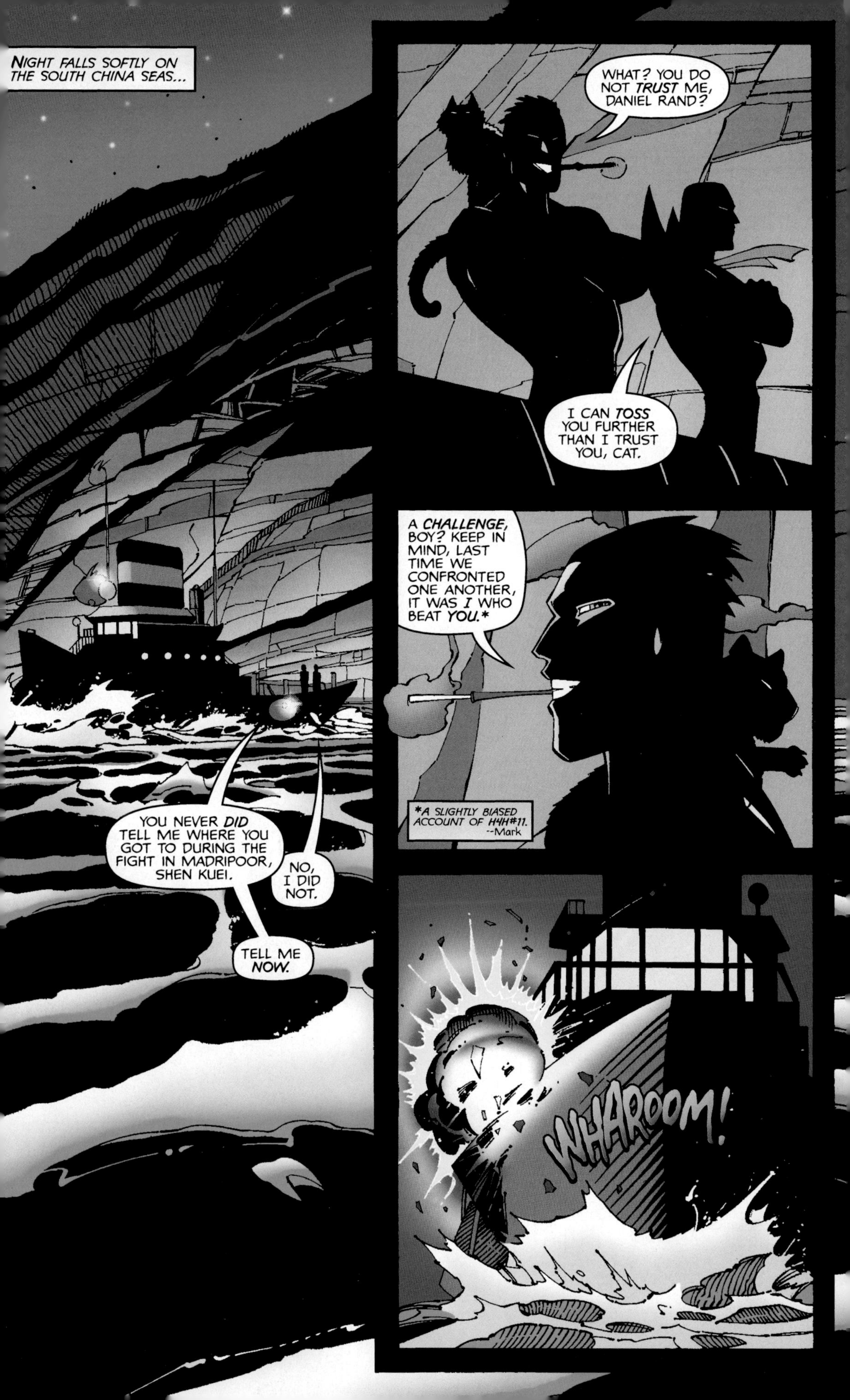
NIGHT FALLS SOFTLY ON THE SOUTH CHINA SEAS...
YOU NEVER DID TELL ME WHERE YOU GOT TO DURING THE FIGHT IN MADRIPOOR, SHEN KUEI.
NO, I DID NOT.
TELL ME NOW.
WHAT? YOU DO NOT TRUST ME, DANIEL RAND?
I CAN TOSS YOU FURTHER THAN I TRUST YOU, CAT.
A CHALLENGE, BOY? KEEP IN MIND, LAST TIME WE CONFRONTED ONE ANOTHER, IT WAS I WHO BEAT YOU.*
*A SLIGHTLY BIASED ACCOUNT OF H4H#11. --Mark
WHAROOM!

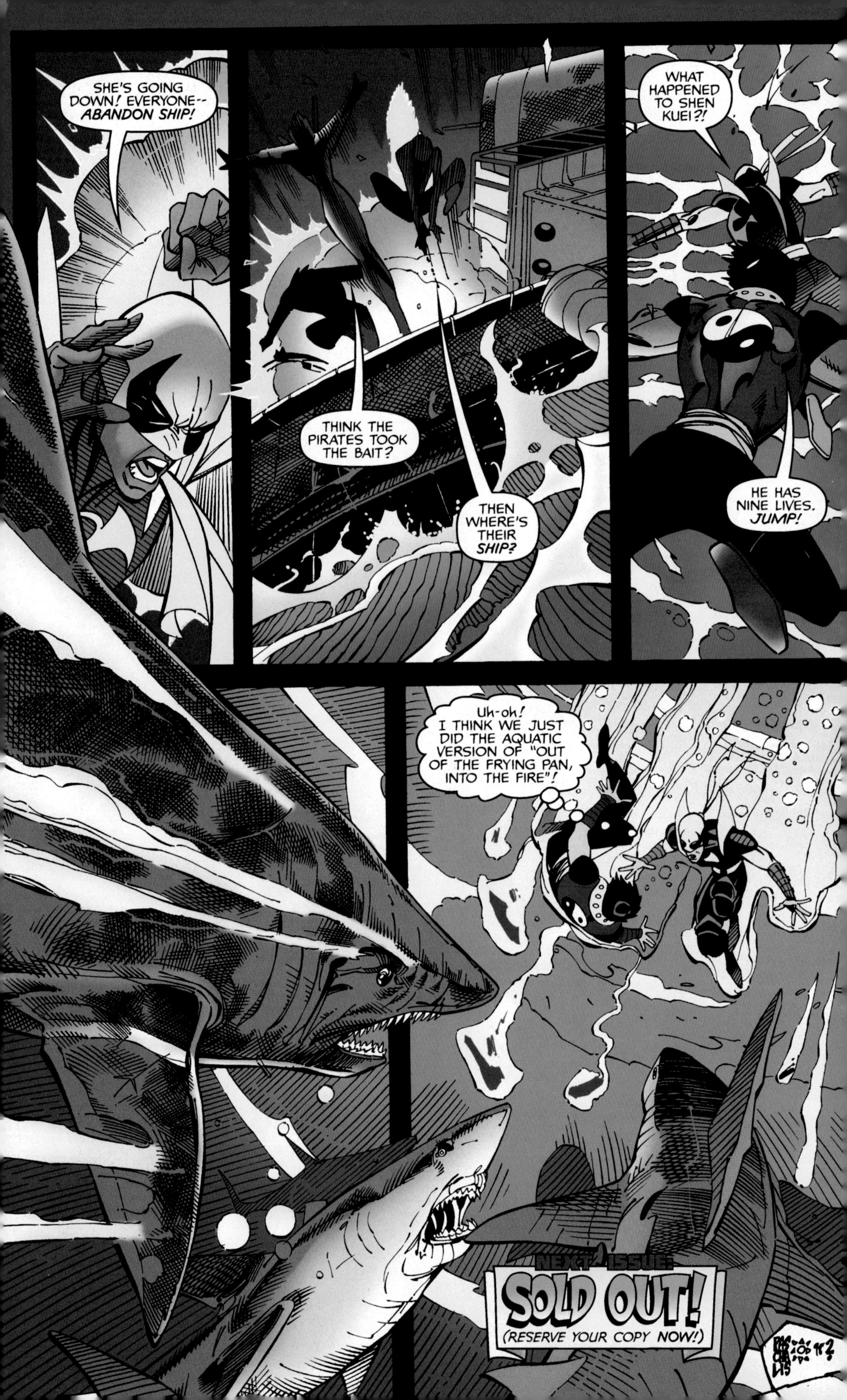
SHE'S GOING DOWN! EVERYONE-- ABANDON SHIP!
THINK THE PIRATES TOOK THE BAIT?
THEN WHERE'S THEIR SHIP?
WHAT HAPPENED TO SHEN KUEI?!
HE HAS NINE LIVES. JUMP!
Uh-oh! I THINK WE JUST DID THE AQUATIC VERSION OF "OUT OF THE FRYING PAN, INTO THE FIRE"!
NEXT ISSUE:
SOLD OUT!
(RESERVE YOUR COPY NOW!)

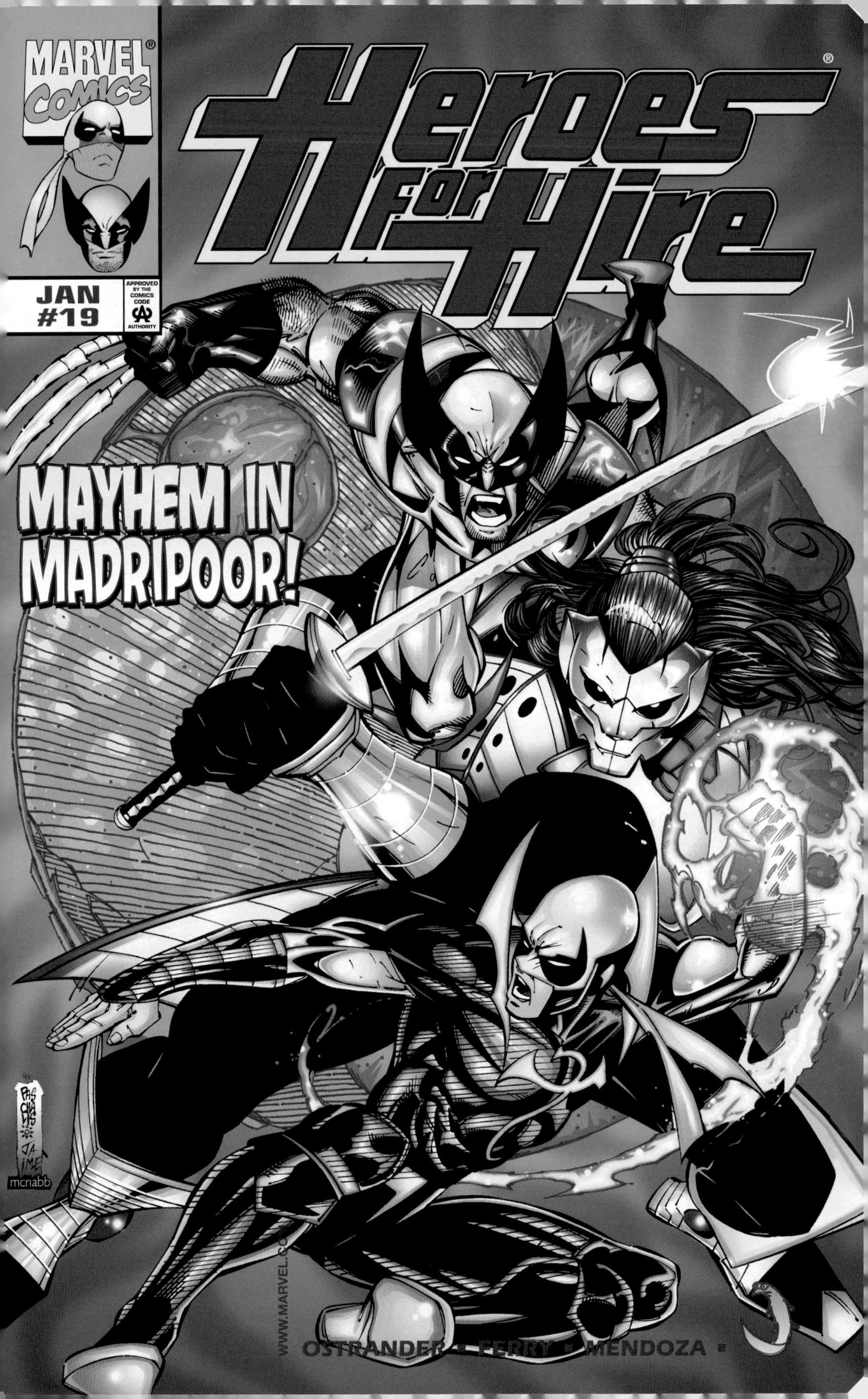
MARVEL COMICS
Heroes for Hire
JAN
#19
APPROVED BY THE COMICS CODE AUTHORITY
MAYHEM IN MADRIPOOR!
WWW.MARVEL.COM
OSTRANDER • FERRY • MENDOZA
mcnabb

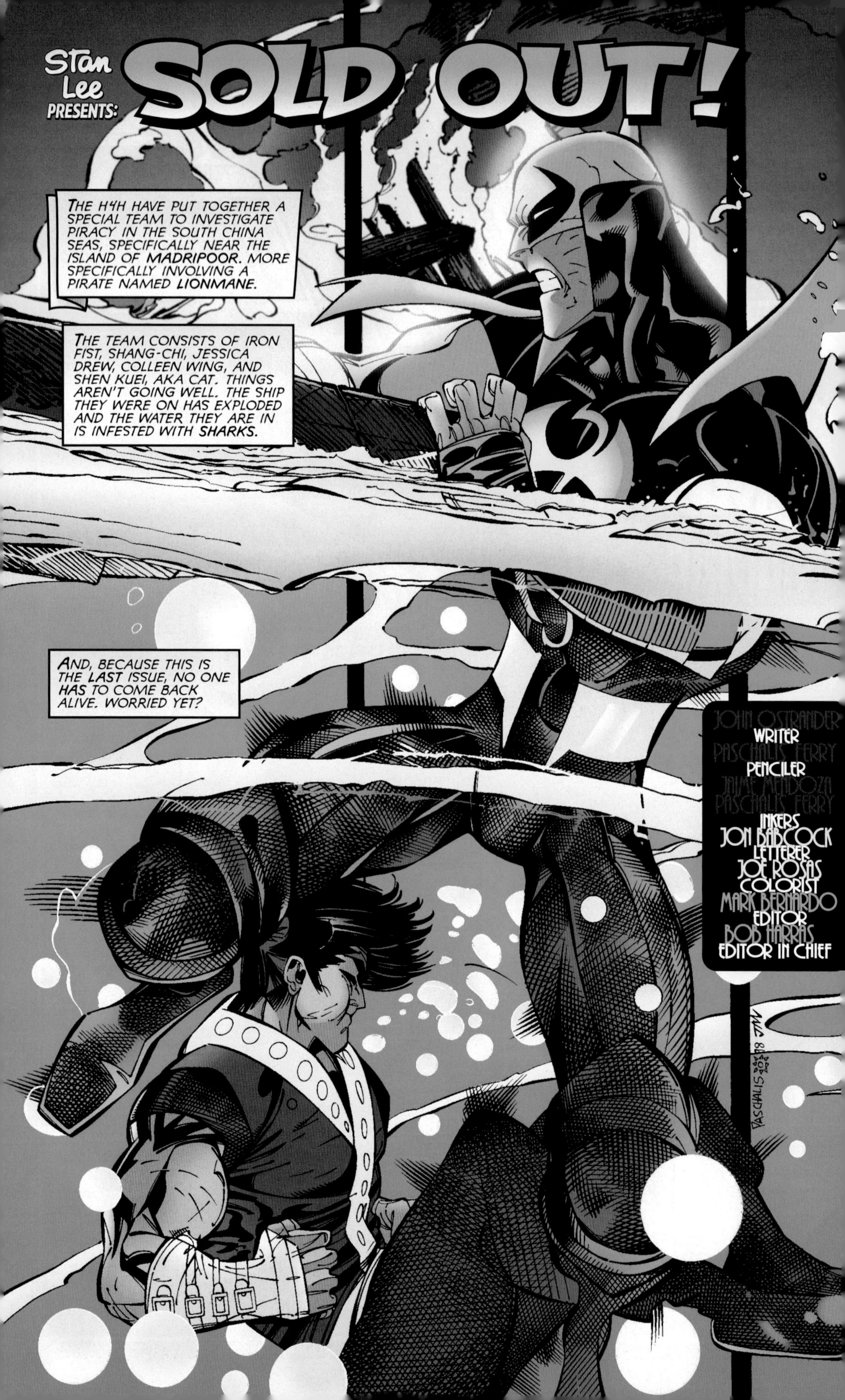
Stan Lee PRESENTS:
SOLD OUT!
THE H4H HAVE PUT TOGETHER A SPECIAL TEAM TO INVESTIGATE PIRACY IN THE SOUTH CHINA SEAS, SPECIFICALLY NEAR THE ISLAND OF MADRIPOOR. MORE SPECIFICALLY INVOLVING A PIRATE NAMED LIONMANE.
THE TEAM CONSISTS OF IRON FIST, SHANG-CHI, JESSICA DREW, COLLEEN WING, AND SHEN KUEI, AKA CAT. THINGS AREN'T GOING WELL. THE SHIP THEY WERE ON HAS EXPLODED AND THE WATER THEY ARE IN IS INFESTED WITH SHARKS.
AND, BECAUSE THIS IS THE LAST ISSUE, NO ONE HAS TO COME BACK ALIVE. WORRIED YET?
JOHN OSTRANDER WRITER
PASCHALIS FERRY PENCILER
JAIME MENDOZA
PASCHALIS FERRY INKERS
JON BABCOCK LETTERER
JOE ROSAS COLORIST
MARK BERNARDO EDITOR
BOB HARRAS EDITOR IN CHIEF

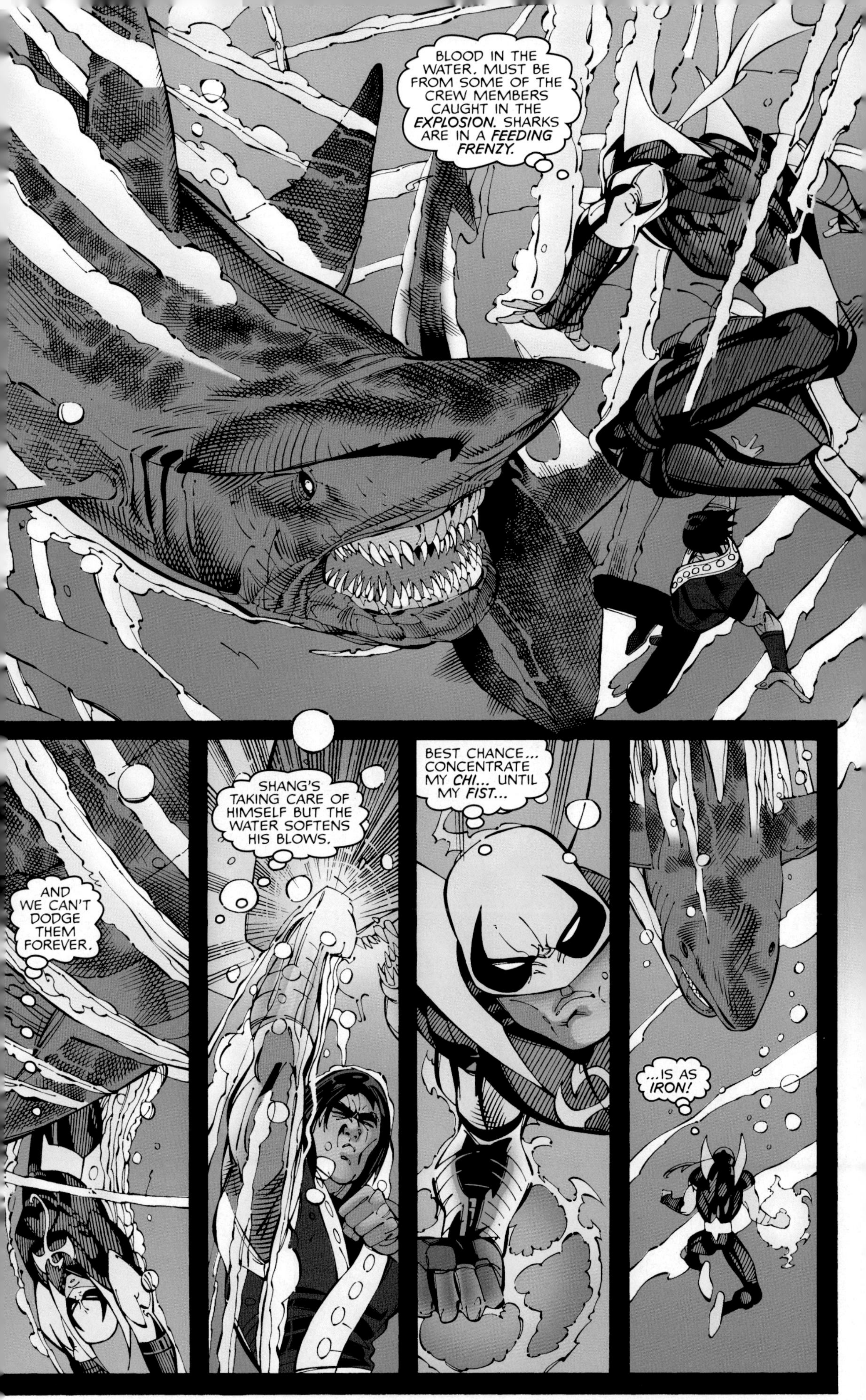
BLOOD IN THE WATER. MUST BE FROM SOME OF THE CREW MEMBERS CAUGHT IN THE *EXPLOSION.* SHARKS ARE IN A *FEEDING FRENZY.*
AND WE CAN'T DODGE THEM FOREVER.
SHANG'S TAKING CARE OF HIMSELF BUT THE WATER SOFTENS HIS BLOWS.
BEST CHANCE... CONCENTRATE MY *CHI*... UNTIL MY *FIST*...
...IS AS *IRON!*

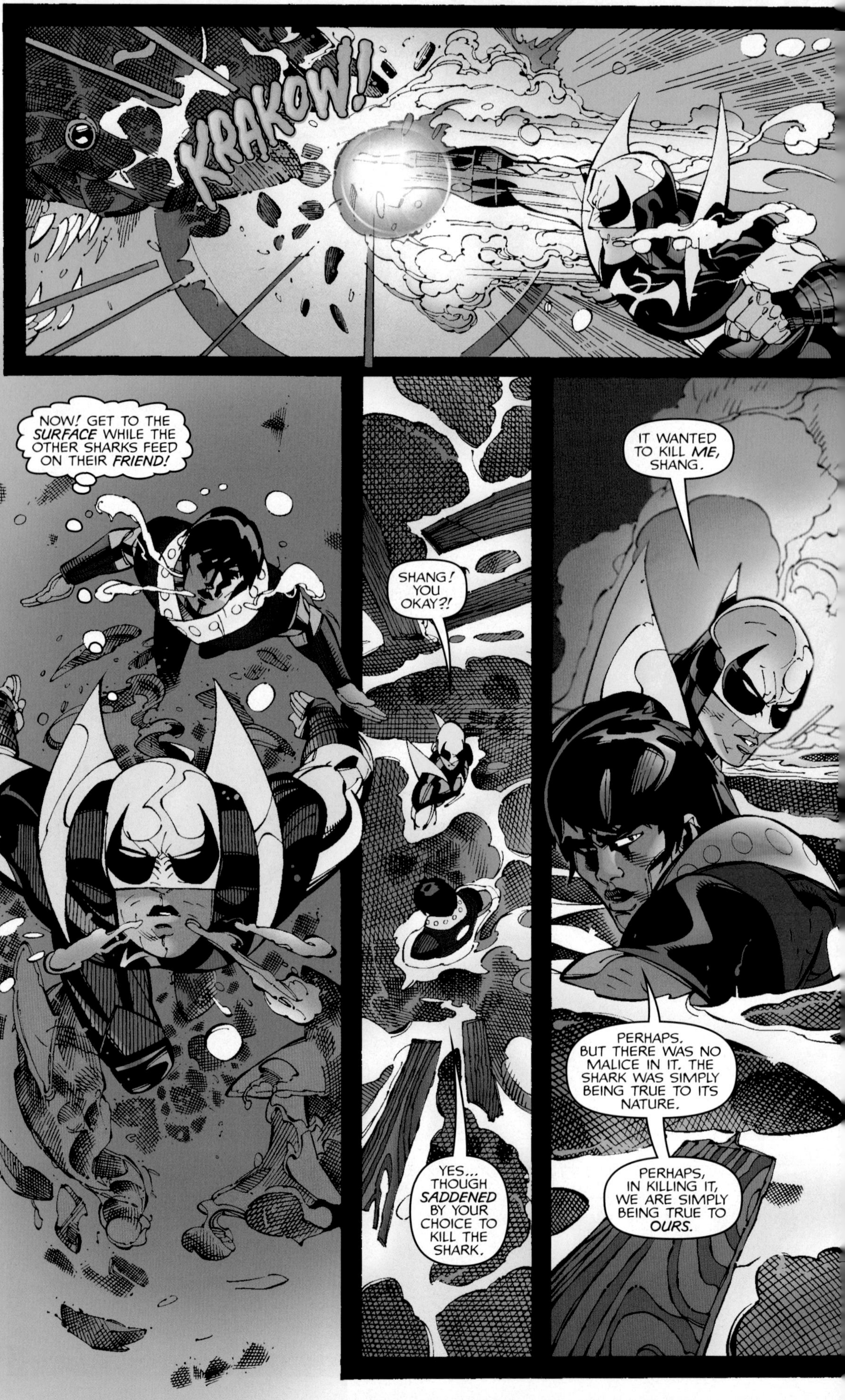

KRAKOW!!
NOW! GET TO THE SURFACE WHILE THE OTHER SHARKS FEED ON THEIR FRIEND!
SHANG! YOU OKAY?!
YES... THOUGH SADDENED BY YOUR CHOICE TO KILL THE SHARK.
IT WANTED TO KILL ME, SHANG.
PERHAPS. BUT THERE WAS NO MALICE IN IT. THE SHARK WAS SIMPLY BEING TRUE TO ITS NATURE.
PERHAPS, IN KILLING IT, WE ARE SIMPLY BEING TRUE TO OURS.

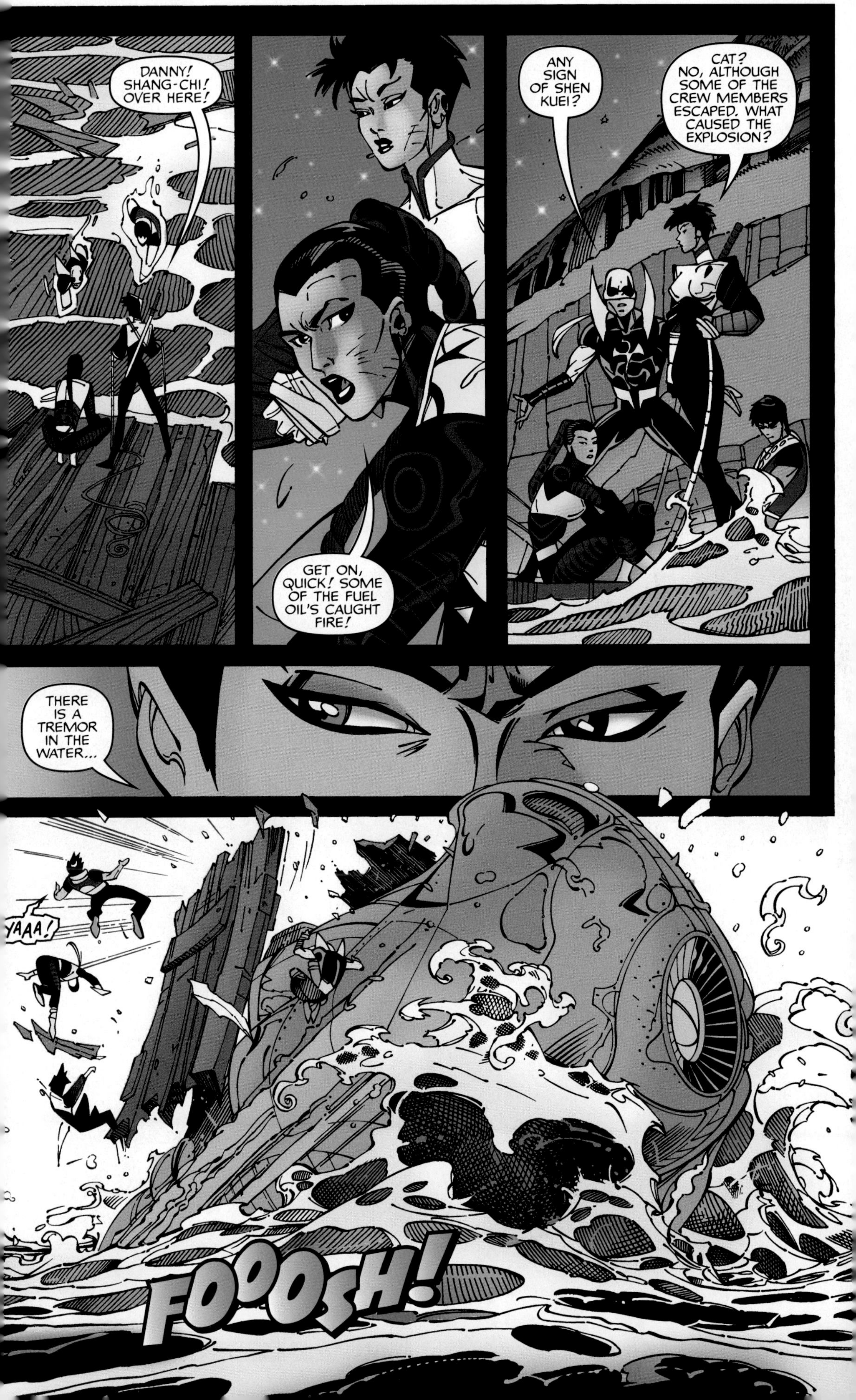
DANNY! SHANG-CHI! OVER HERE!
GET ON, QUICK! SOME OF THE FUEL OIL'S CAUGHT FIRE!
ANY SIGN OF SHEN KUEI?
CAT? NO, ALTHOUGH SOME OF THE CREW MEMBERS ESCAPED. WHAT CAUSED THE EXPLOSION?
THERE IS A TREMOR IN THE WATER...
YAAA!
FOOOSH!

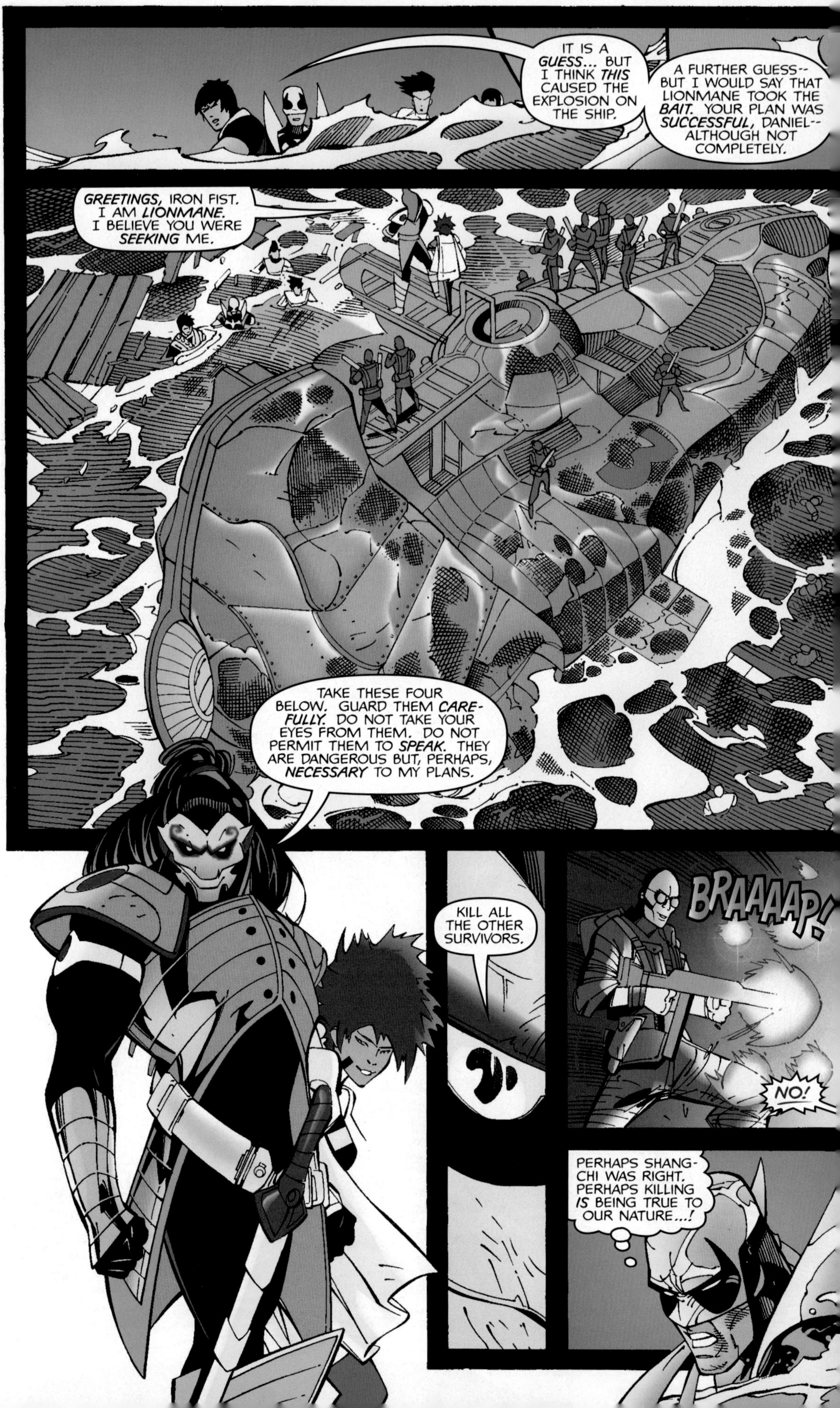
IT IS A GUESS... BUT I THINK THIS CAUSED THE EXPLOSION ON THE SHIP.
A FURTHER GUESS--BUT I WOULD SAY THAT LIONMANE TOOK THE BAIT. YOUR PLAN WAS SUCCESSFUL, DANIEL--ALTHOUGH NOT COMPLETELY.
GREETINGS, IRON FIST. I AM LIONMANE. I BELIEVE YOU WERE SEEKING ME.
TAKE THESE FOUR BELOW. GUARD THEM CAREFULLY. DO NOT TAKE YOUR EYES FROM THEM. DO NOT PERMIT THEM TO SPEAK. THEY ARE DANGEROUS BUT, PERHAPS, NECESSARY TO MY PLANS.
KILL ALL THE OTHER SURVIVORS.
BRAAAAP!
NO!
PERHAPS SHANG-CHI WAS RIGHT. PERHAPS KILLING IS BEING TRUE TO OUR NATURE...!

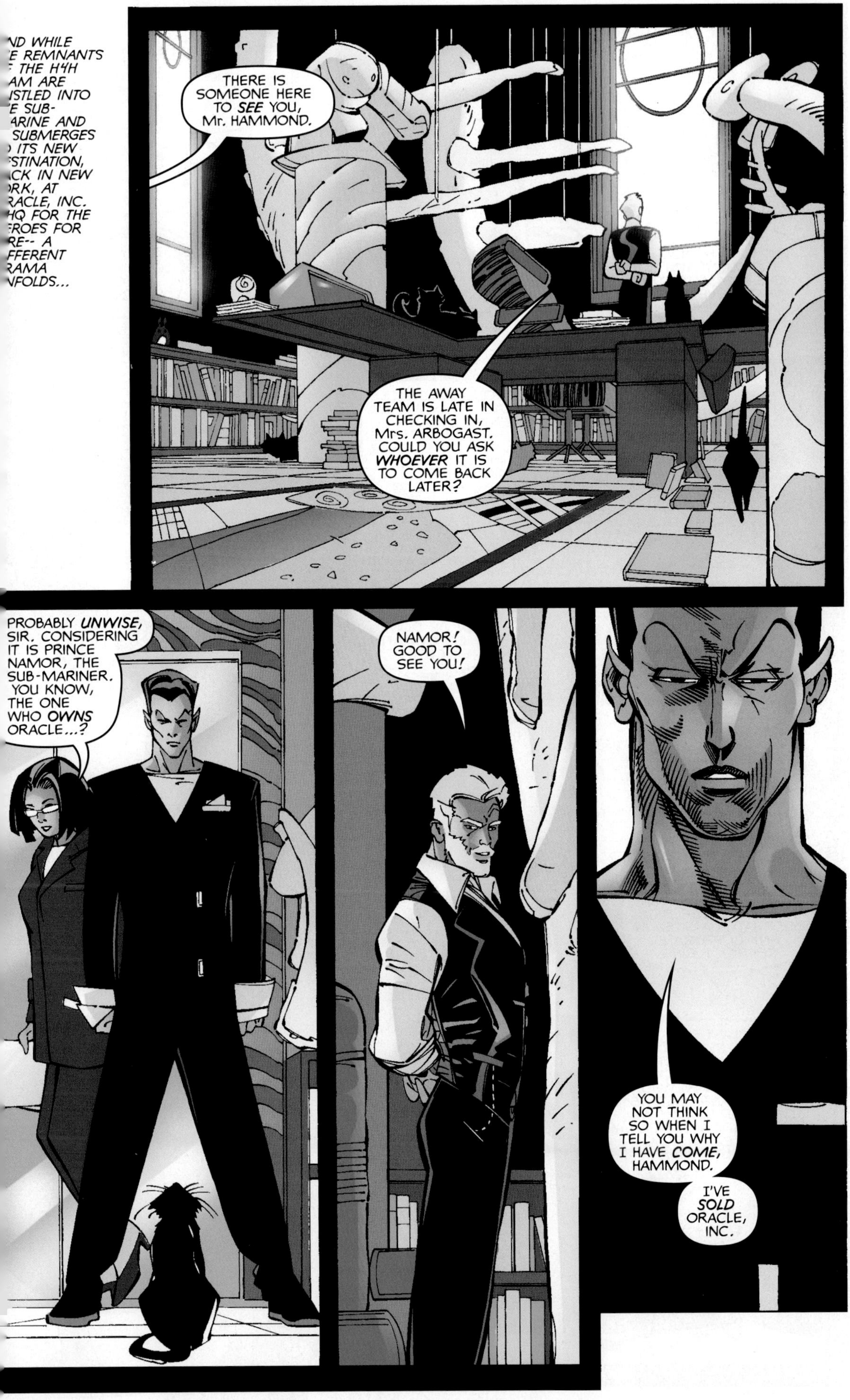
ND WHILE E REMNANTS F THE H4H AM ARE ISTLED INTO E SUB- ARINE AND SUBMERGES ITS NEW ESTINATION, ACK IN NEW ORK, AT RACLE, INC. HQ FOR THE EROES FOR RE-- A FFERENT RAMA NFOLDS...
THERE IS SOMEONE HERE TO SEE YOU, Mr. HAMMOND.
THE AWAY TEAM IS LATE IN CHECKING IN, Mrs. ARBOGAST. COULD YOU ASK WHOEVER IT IS TO COME BACK LATER?
PROBABLY UNWISE, SIR. CONSIDERING IT IS PRINCE NAMOR, THE SUB-MARINER. YOU KNOW, THE ONE WHO OWNS ORACLE...?
NAMOR! GOOD TO SEE YOU!
YOU MAY NOT THINK SO WHEN I TELL YOU WHY I HAVE COME, HAMMOND.
I'VE SOLD ORACLE, INC.

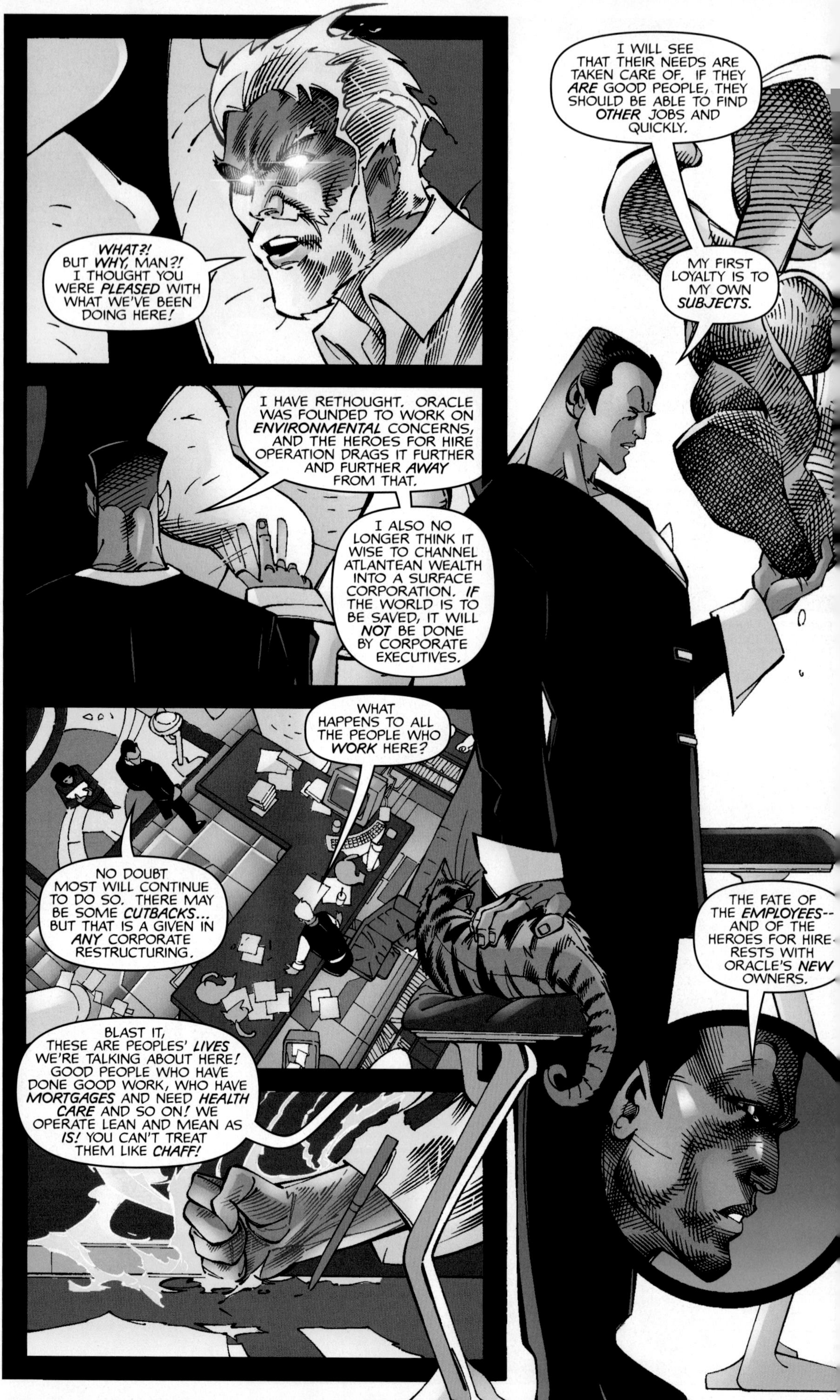
WHAT?! BUT WHY, MAN?! I THOUGHT YOU WERE PLEASED WITH WHAT WE'VE BEEN DOING HERE!
I WILL SEE THAT THEIR NEEDS ARE TAKEN CARE OF. IF THEY ARE GOOD PEOPLE, THEY SHOULD BE ABLE TO FIND OTHER JOBS AND QUICKLY.
MY FIRST LOYALTY IS TO MY OWN SUBJECTS.
I HAVE RETHOUGHT. ORACLE WAS FOUNDED TO WORK ON ENVIRONMENTAL CONCERNS, AND THE HEROES FOR HIRE OPERATION DRAGS IT FURTHER AND FURTHER AWAY FROM THAT.
I ALSO NO LONGER THINK IT WISE TO CHANNEL ATLANTEAN WEALTH INTO A SURFACE CORPORATION. IF THE WORLD IS TO BE SAVED, IT WILL NOT BE DONE BY CORPORATE EXECUTIVES.
WHAT HAPPENS TO ALL THE PEOPLE WHO WORK HERE?
NO DOUBT MOST WILL CONTINUE TO DO SO. THERE MAY BE SOME CUTBACKS... BUT THAT IS A GIVEN IN ANY CORPORATE RESTRUCTURING.
BLAST IT, THESE ARE PEOPLES' LIVES WE'RE TALKING ABOUT HERE! GOOD PEOPLE WHO HAVE DONE GOOD WORK, WHO HAVE MORTGAGES AND NEED HEALTH CARE AND SO ON! WE OPERATE LEAN AND MEAN AS IS! YOU CAN'T TREAT THEM LIKE CHAFF!
THE FATE OF THE EMPLOYEES-- AND OF THE HEROES FOR HIRE-- RESTS WITH ORACLE'S NEW OWNERS.

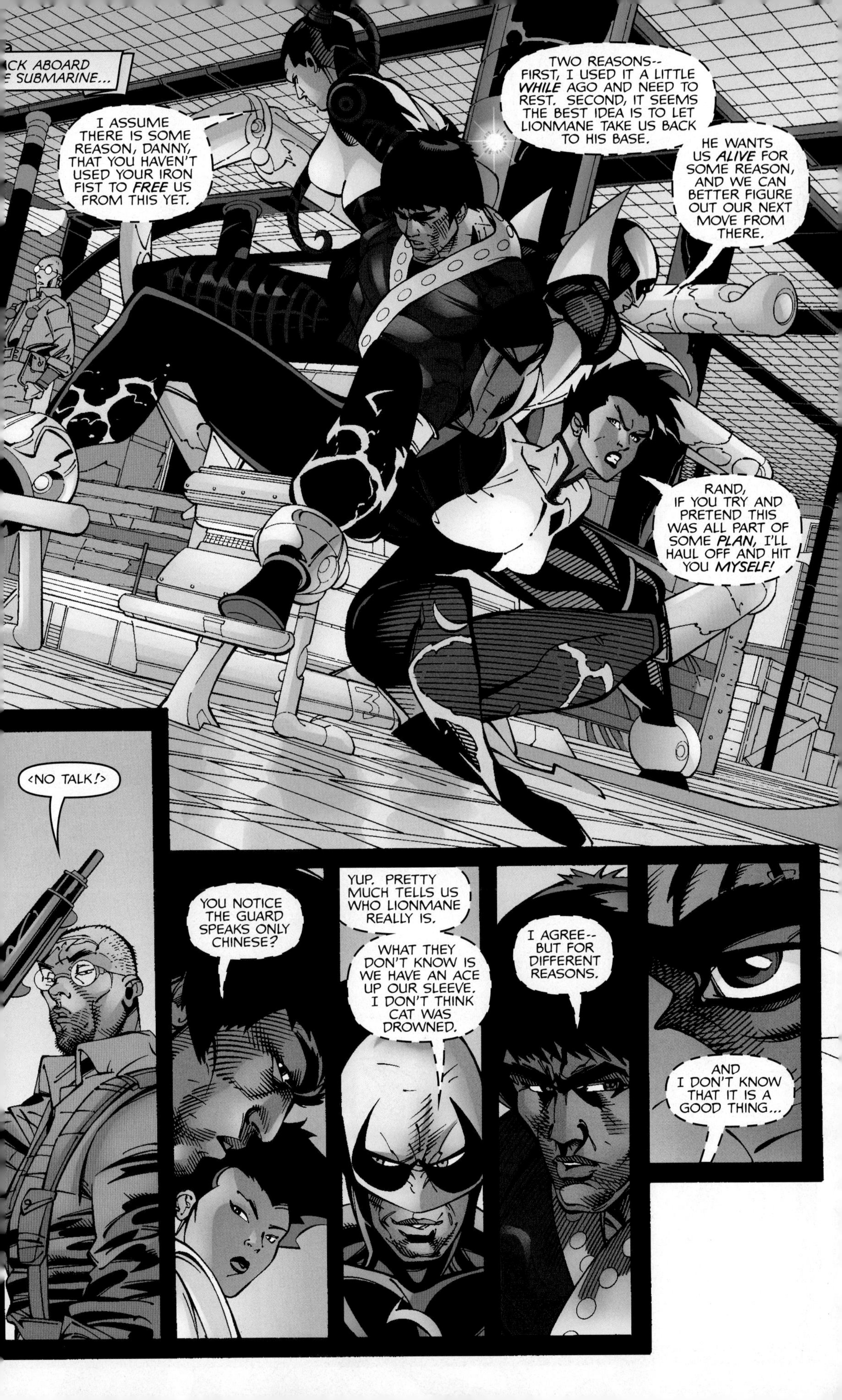
...CK ABOARD
...E SUBMARINE...
I ASSUME THERE IS SOME REASON, DANNY, THAT YOU HAVEN'T USED YOUR IRON FIST TO *FREE* US FROM THIS YET.
TWO REASONS-- FIRST, I USED IT A LITTLE *WHILE* AGO AND NEED TO REST. SECOND, IT SEEMS THE BEST IDEA IS TO LET LIONMANE TAKE US BACK TO HIS BASE.
HE WANTS US *ALIVE* FOR SOME REASON, AND WE CAN BETTER FIGURE OUT OUR NEXT MOVE FROM THERE.
RAND, IF YOU TRY AND PRETEND THIS WAS ALL PART OF SOME *PLAN*, I'LL HAUL OFF AND HIT YOU *MYSELF!*
<NO TALK!>
YOU NOTICE THE GUARD SPEAKS ONLY CHINESE?
YUP. PRETTY MUCH TELLS US WHO LIONMANE REALLY IS.
WHAT THEY DON'T KNOW IS WE HAVE AN ACE UP OUR SLEEVE. I DON'T THINK CAT WAS DROWNED.
I AGREE-- BUT FOR DIFFERENT REASONS.
AND I DON'T KNOW THAT IT IS A GOOD THING...

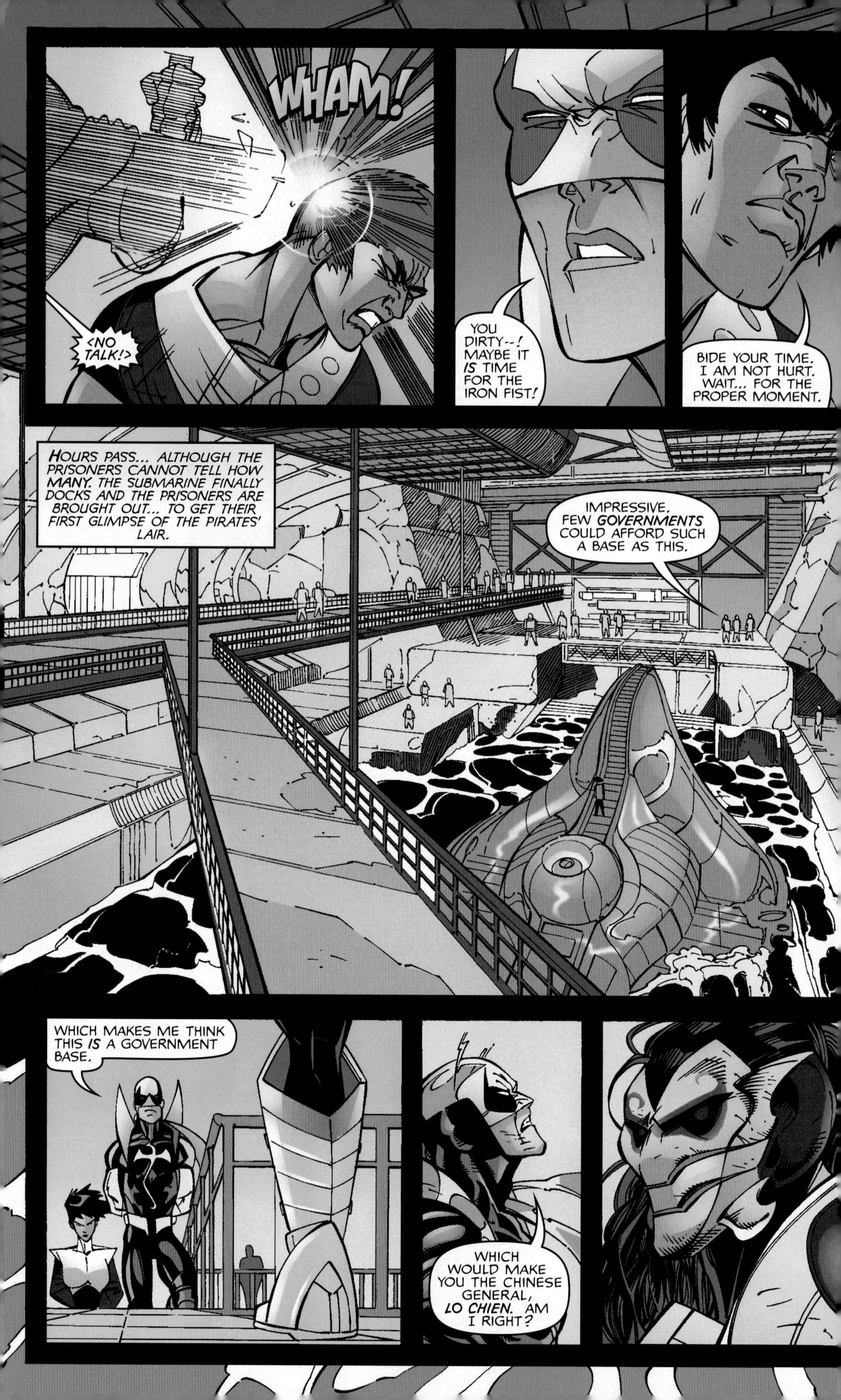
WHAM!
<NO TALK!>
YOU DIRTY--! MAYBE IT *IS* TIME FOR THE IRON FIST!
BIDE YOUR TIME. I AM NOT HURT. WAIT... FOR THE PROPER MOMENT.
HOURS PASS... ALTHOUGH THE PRISONERS CANNOT TELL HOW *MANY*. THE SUBMARINE FINALLY DOCKS AND THE PRISONERS ARE BROUGHT OUT... TO GET THEIR FIRST GLIMPSE OF THE PIRATES' LAIR.
IMPRESSIVE. FEW *GOVERNMENTS* COULD AFFORD SUCH A BASE AS THIS.
WHICH MAKES ME THINK THIS *IS* A GOVERNMENT BASE.
WHICH WOULD MAKE YOU THE CHINESE GENERAL, *LO CHIEN*. AM I RIGHT?

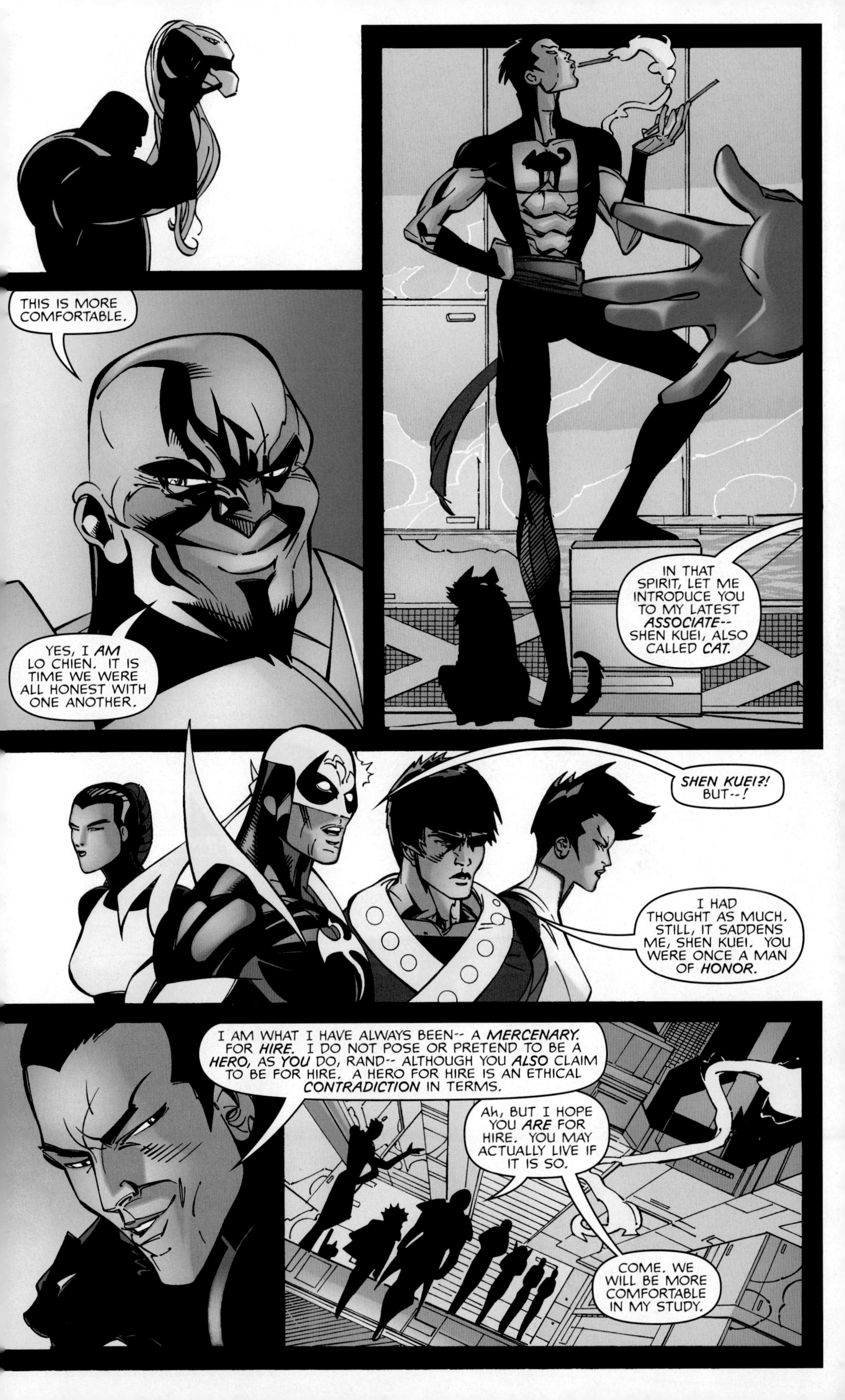
THIS IS MORE COMFORTABLE.
YES, I AM LO CHIEN. IT IS TIME WE WERE ALL HONEST WITH ONE ANOTHER.
IN THAT SPIRIT, LET ME INTRODUCE YOU TO MY LATEST ASSOCIATE-- SHEN KUEI, ALSO CALLED CAT.
SHEN KUEI?! BUT--!
I HAD THOUGHT AS MUCH. STILL, IT SADDENS ME, SHEN KUEI. YOU WERE ONCE A MAN OF HONOR.
I AM WHAT I HAVE ALWAYS BEEN-- A MERCENARY. FOR HIRE. I DO NOT POSE OR PRETEND TO BE A HERO, AS YOU DO, RAND-- ALTHOUGH YOU ALSO CLAIM TO BE FOR HIRE. A HERO FOR HIRE IS AN ETHICAL CONTRADICTION IN TERMS.
Ah, BUT I HOPE YOU ARE FOR HIRE. YOU MAY ACTUALLY LIVE IF IT IS SO.
COME. WE WILL BE MORE COMFORTABLE IN MY STUDY.

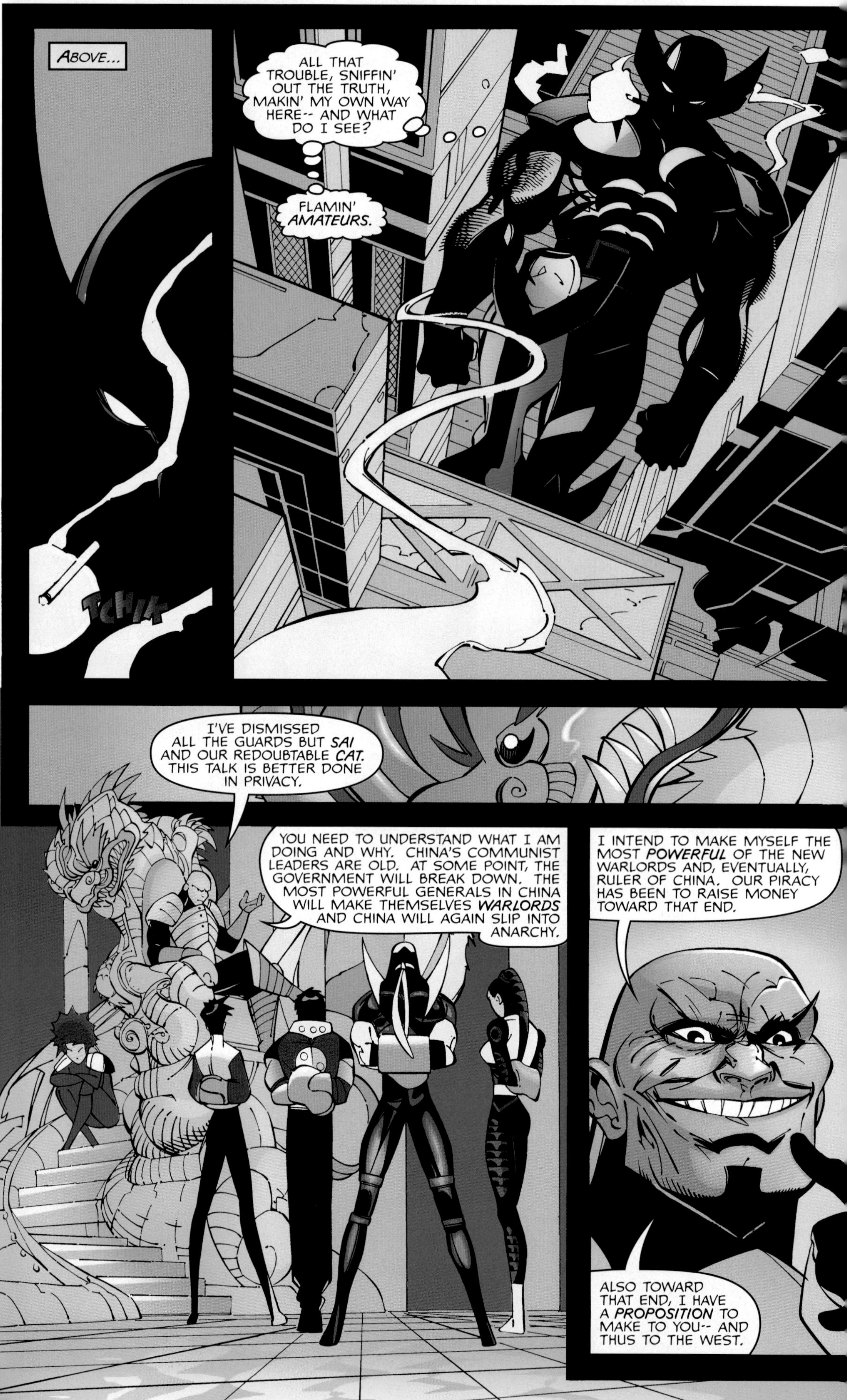
ABOVE...
ALL THAT TROUBLE, SNIFFIN' OUT THE TRUTH, MAKIN' MY OWN WAY HERE-- AND WHAT DO I SEE?
FLAMIN' AMATEURS.
TCHIK
I'VE DISMISSED ALL THE GUARDS BUT SAI AND OUR REDOUBTABLE CAT. THIS TALK IS BETTER DONE IN PRIVACY.
YOU NEED TO UNDERSTAND WHAT I AM DOING AND WHY. CHINA'S COMMUNIST LEADERS ARE OLD. AT SOME POINT, THE GOVERNMENT WILL BREAK DOWN. THE MOST POWERFUL GENERALS IN CHINA WILL MAKE THEMSELVES WARLORDS AND CHINA WILL AGAIN SLIP INTO ANARCHY.
I INTEND TO MAKE MYSELF THE MOST POWERFUL OF THE NEW WARLORDS AND, EVENTUALLY, RULER OF CHINA. OUR PIRACY HAS BEEN TO RAISE MONEY TOWARD THAT END.
ALSO TOWARD THAT END, I HAVE A PROPOSITION TO MAKE TO YOU-- AND THUS TO THE WEST.

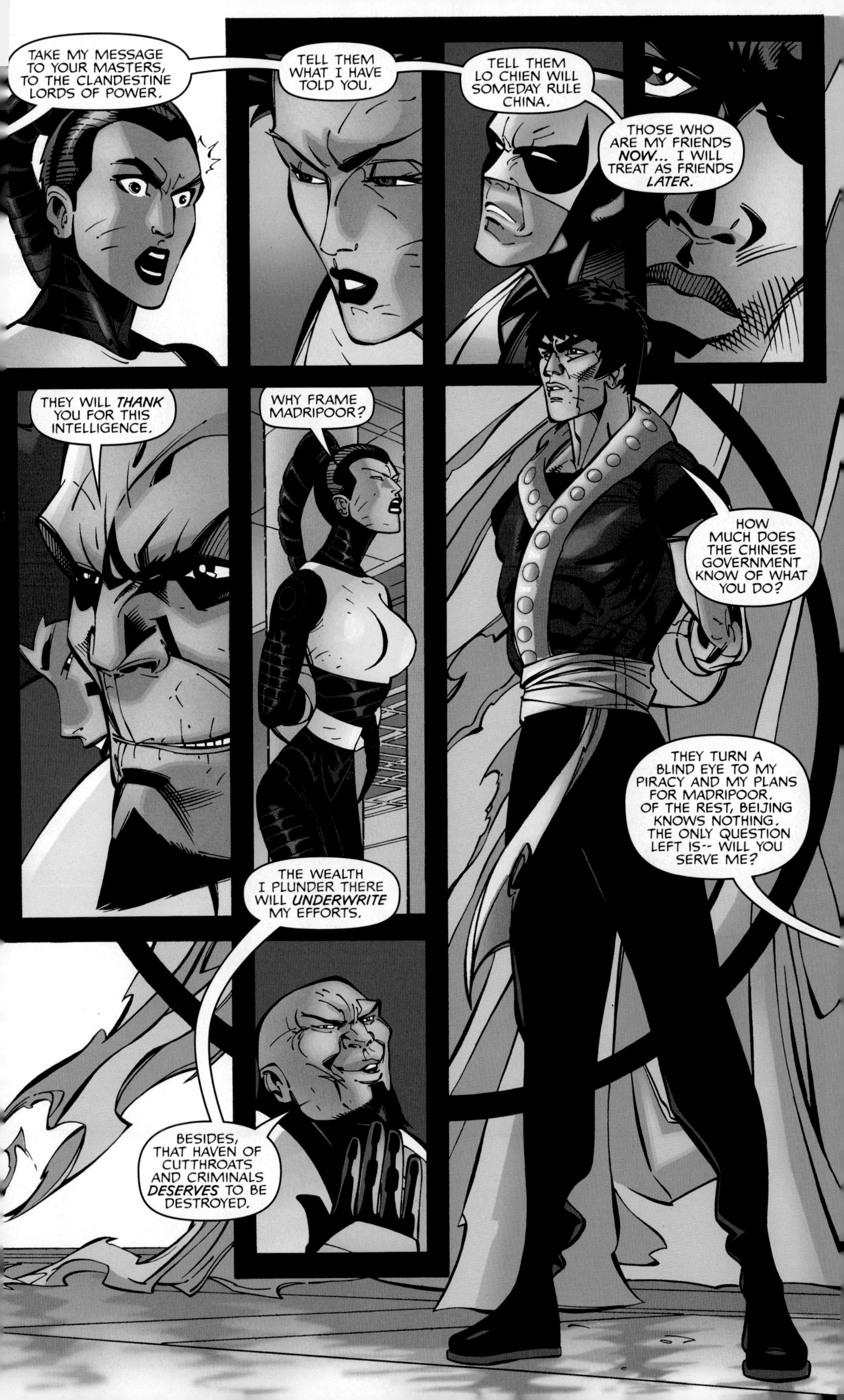
TAKE MY MESSAGE TO YOUR MASTERS, TO THE CLANDESTINE LORDS OF POWER.
TELL THEM WHAT I HAVE TOLD YOU.
TELL THEM LO CHIEN WILL SOMEDAY RULE CHINA.
THOSE WHO ARE MY FRIENDS *NOW*... I WILL TREAT AS FRIENDS *LATER*.
THEY WILL *THANK* YOU FOR THIS INTELLIGENCE.
WHY FRAME MADRIPOOR?
THE WEALTH I PLUNDER THERE WILL *UNDERWRITE* MY EFFORTS.
BESIDES, THAT HAVEN OF CUTTHROATS AND CRIMINALS *DESERVES* TO BE DESTROYED.
HOW MUCH DOES THE CHINESE GOVERNMENT KNOW OF WHAT YOU DO?
THEY TURN A BLIND EYE TO MY PIRACY AND MY PLANS FOR MADRIPOOR. OF THE REST, BEIJING KNOWS NOTHING. THE ONLY QUESTION LEFT IS-- WILL YOU SERVE ME?

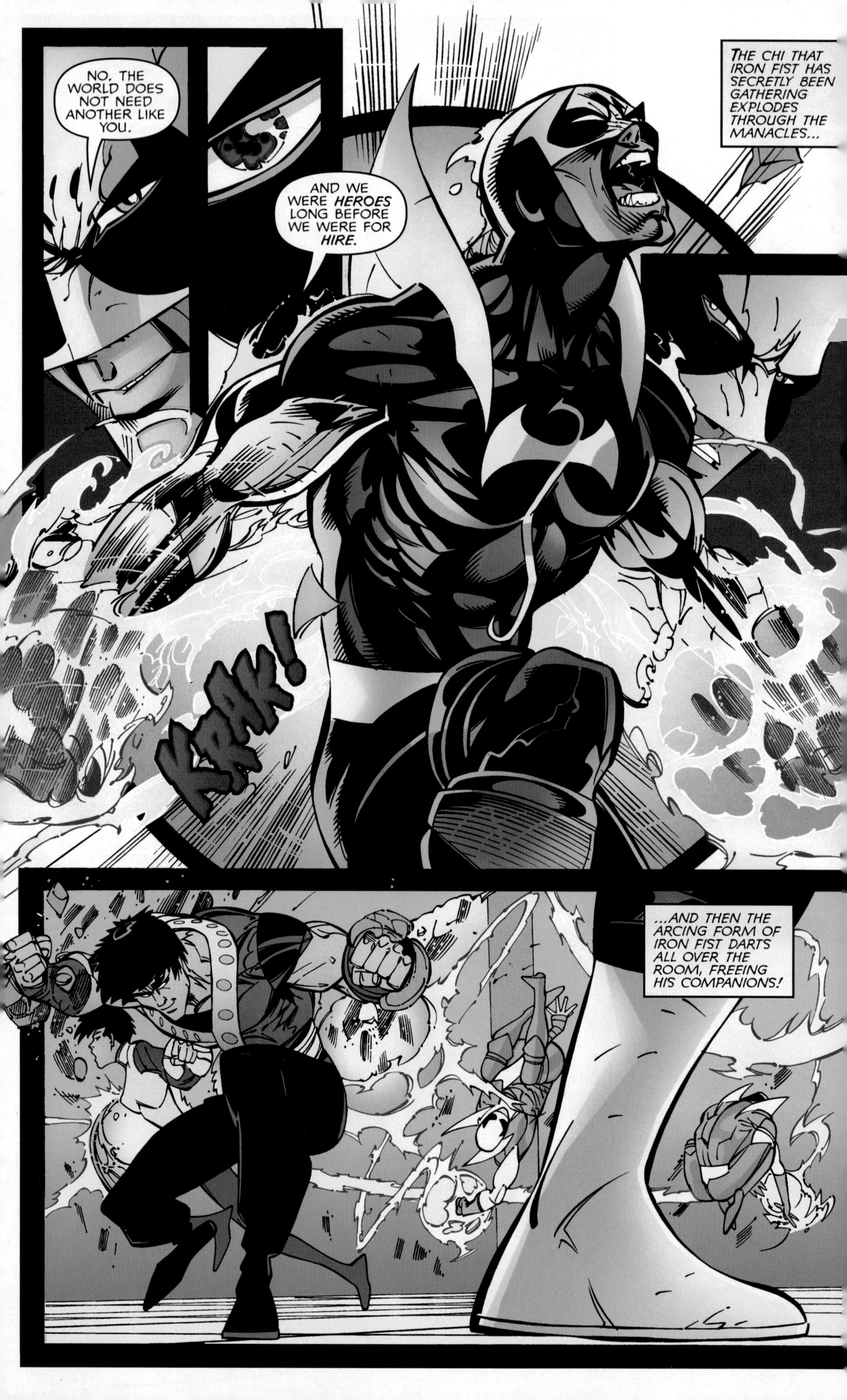
NO. THE WORLD DOES NOT NEED ANOTHER LIKE YOU.
AND WE WERE HEROES LONG BEFORE WE WERE FOR HIRE.
THE CHI THAT IRON FIST HAS SECRETLY BEEN GATHERING EXPLODES THROUGH THE MANACLES...
KRAK!
...AND THEN THE ARCING FORM OF IRON FIST DARTS ALL OVER THE ROOM, FREEING HIS COMPANIONS!

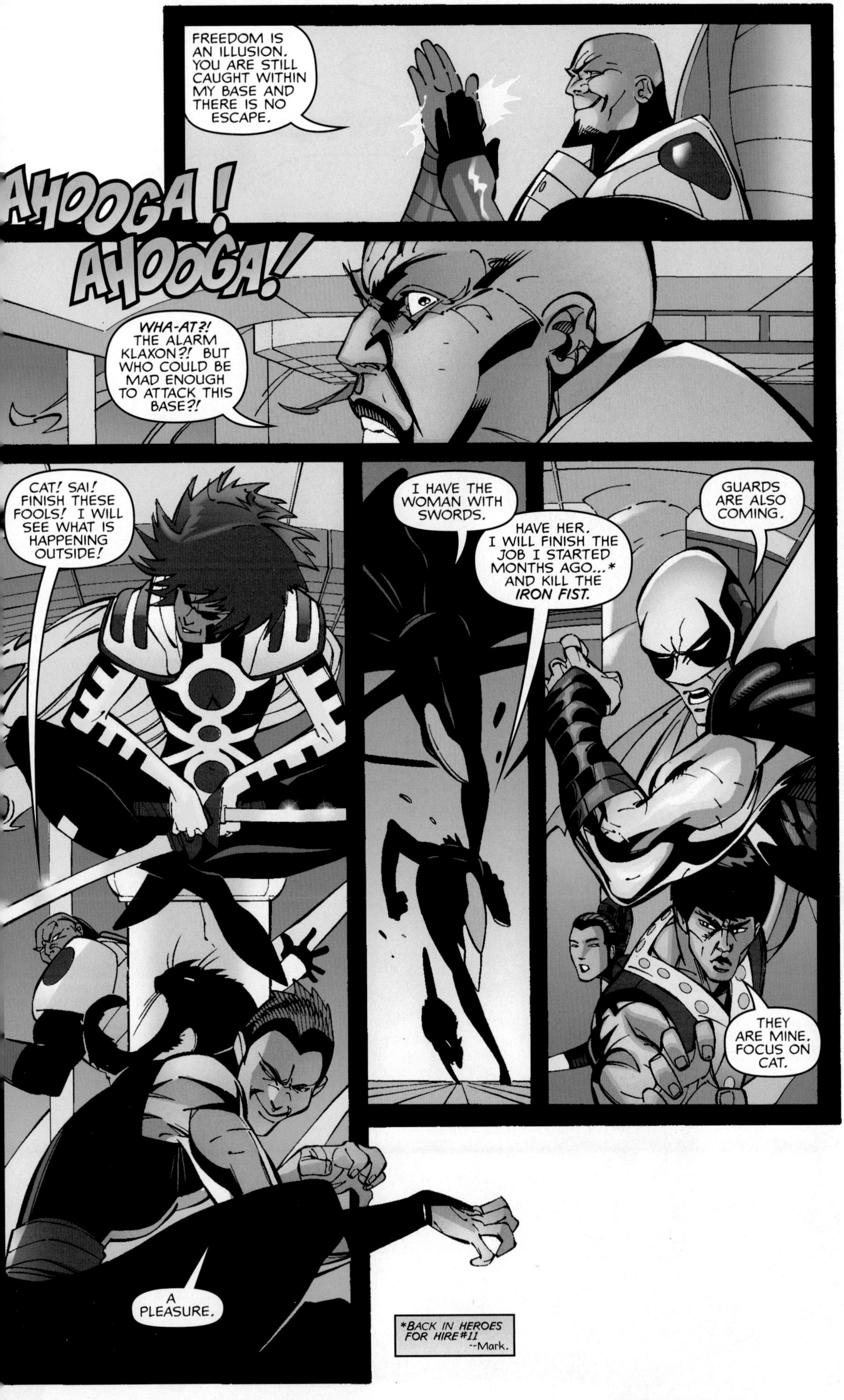

FREEDOM IS AN ILLUSION. YOU ARE STILL CAUGHT WITHIN MY BASE AND THERE IS NO ESCAPE.
AHOOGA! AHOOGA!
WHA-AT?! THE ALARM KLAXON?! BUT WHO COULD BE MAD ENOUGH TO ATTACK THIS BASE?!
CAT! SAI! FINISH THESE FOOLS! I WILL SEE WHAT IS HAPPENING OUTSIDE!
I HAVE THE WOMAN WITH SWORDS.
HAVE HER. I WILL FINISH THE JOB I STARTED MONTHS AGO...* AND KILL THE IRON FIST.
GUARDS ARE ALSO COMING.
THEY ARE MINE. FOCUS ON CAT.
A PLEASURE.
*BACK IN HEROES FOR HIRE #11 --Mark.

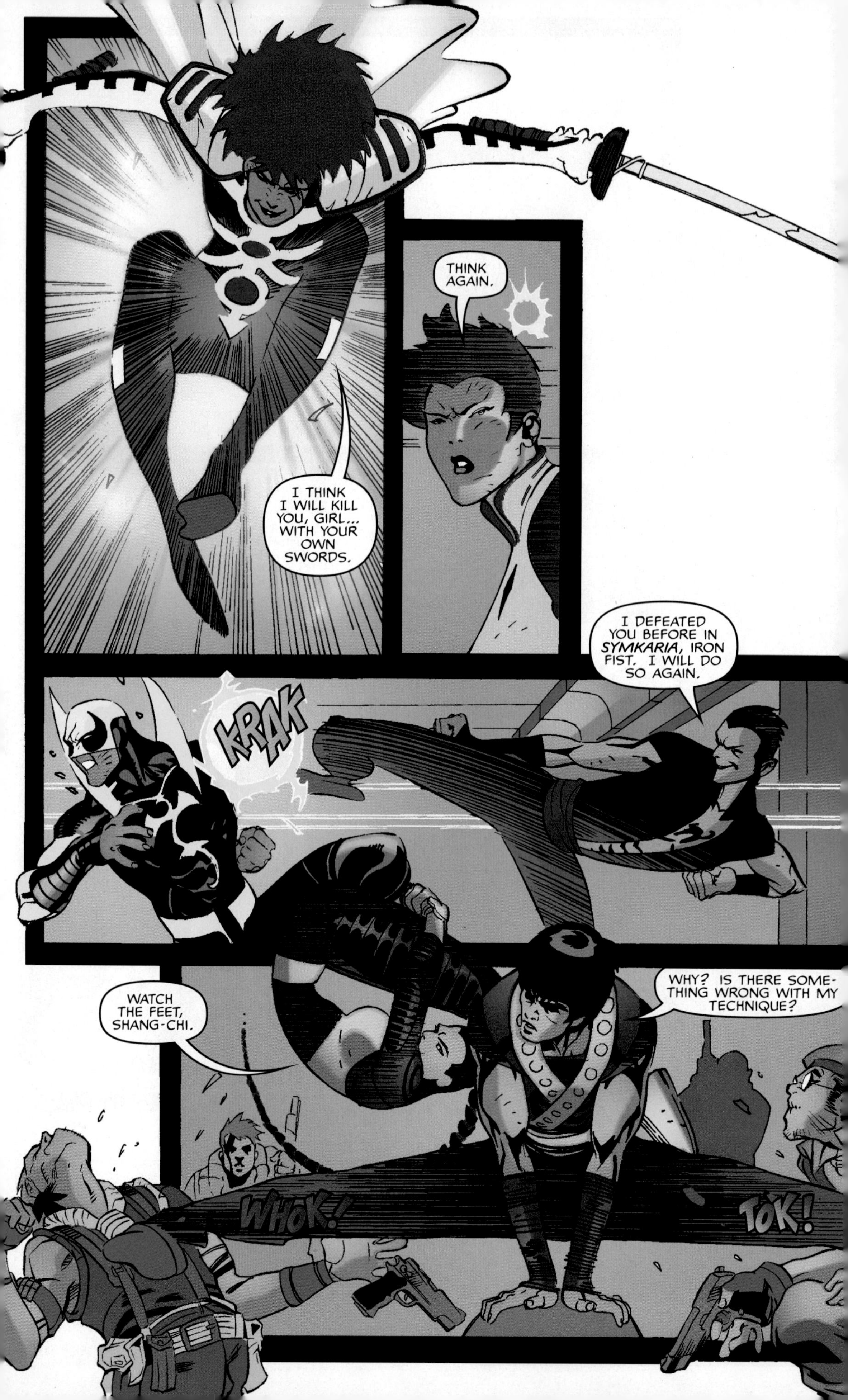
I THINK I WILL KILL YOU, GIRL... WITH YOUR OWN SWORDS.
THINK AGAIN.
I DEFEATED YOU BEFORE IN SYMKARIA, IRON FIST. I WILL DO SO AGAIN.
KRAK
WATCH THE FEET, SHANG-CHI.
WHY? IS THERE SOME-THING WRONG WITH MY TECHNIQUE?
WHOK!
TOK!

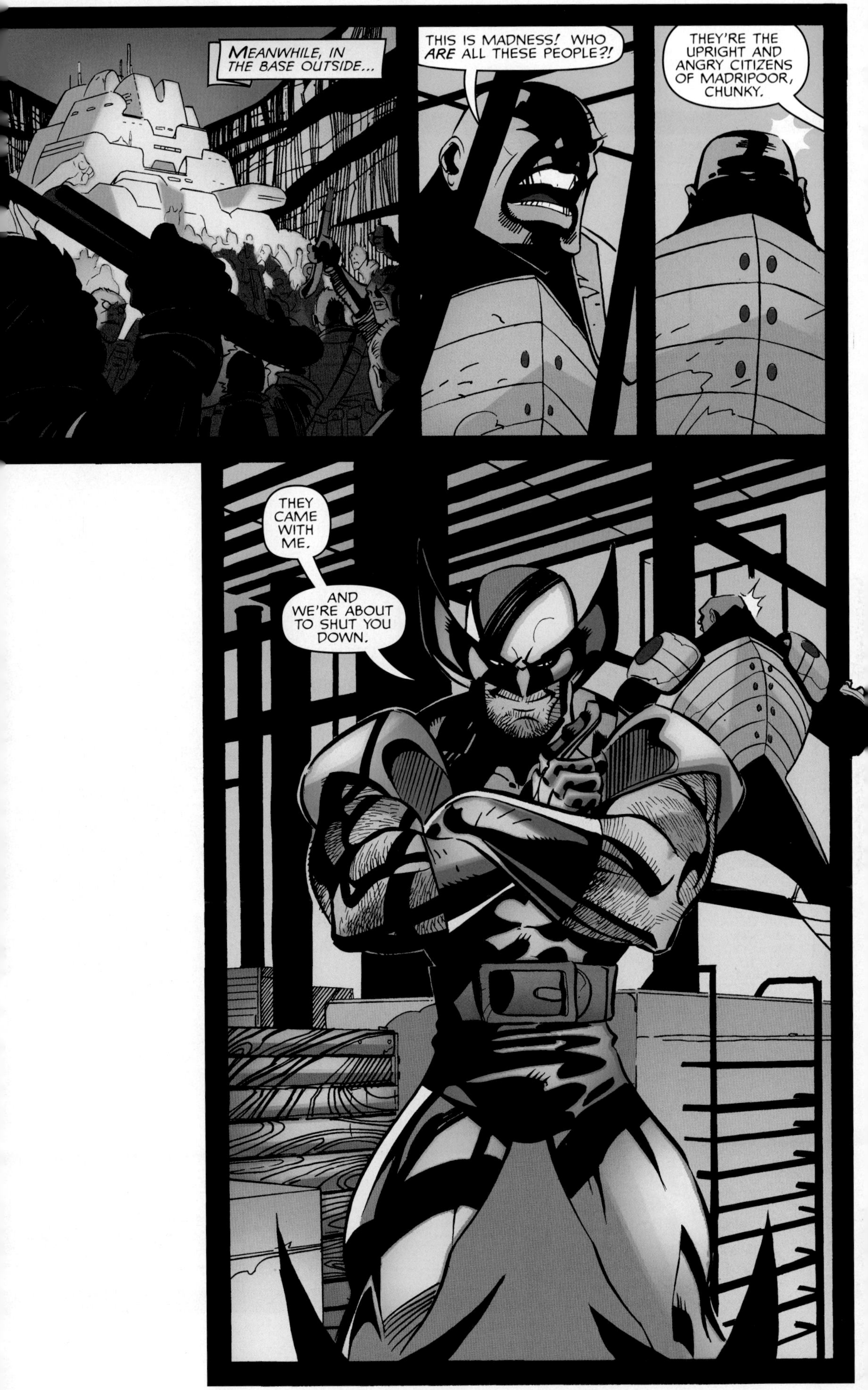
MEANWHILE, IN THE BASE OUTSIDE...
THIS IS MADNESS! WHO ARE ALL THESE PEOPLE?!
THEY'RE THE UPRIGHT AND ANGRY CITIZENS OF MADRIPOOR, CHUNKY.
THEY CAME WITH ME.
AND WE'RE ABOUT TO SHUT YOU DOWN.

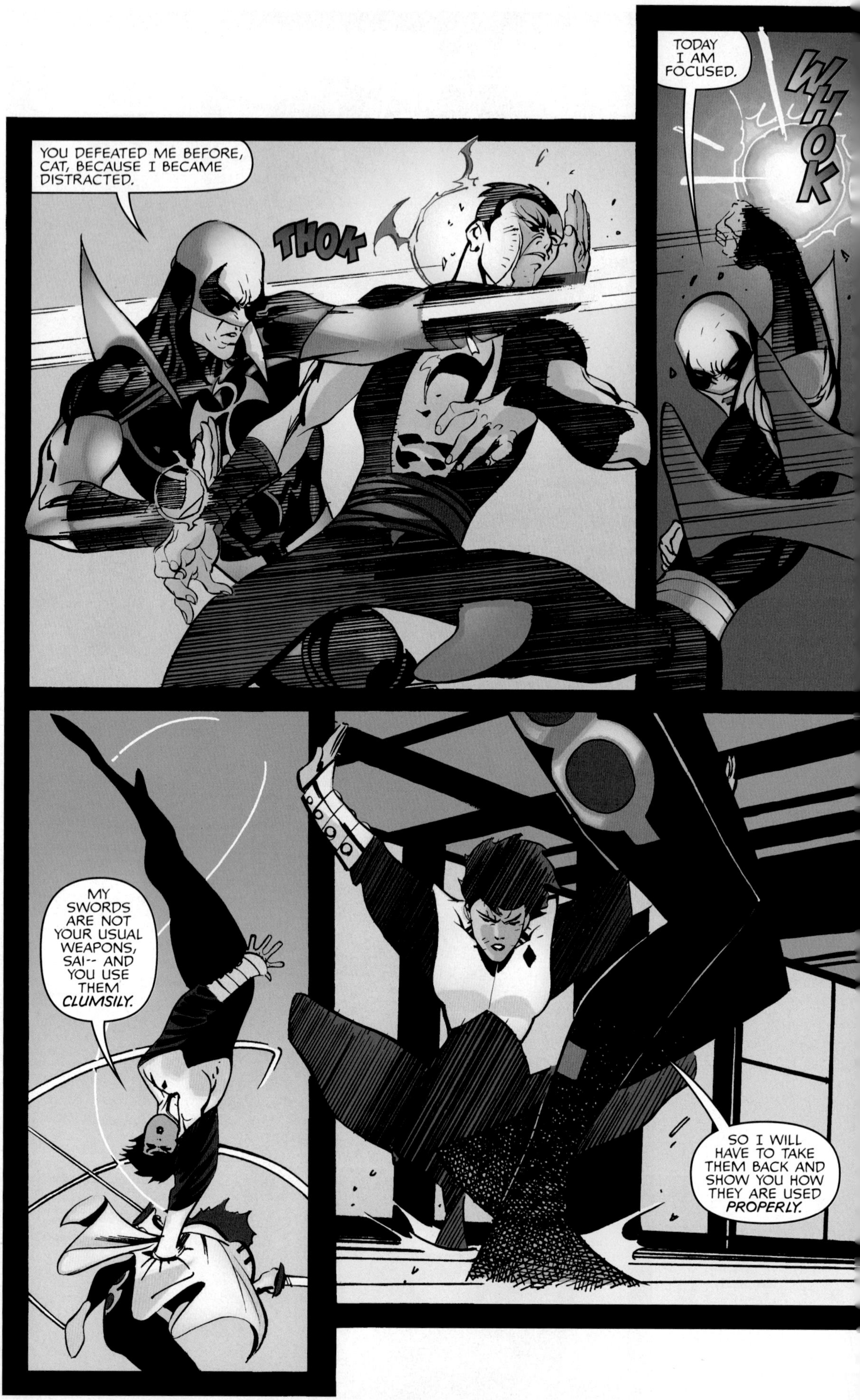
YOU DEFEATED ME BEFORE, CAT, BECAUSE I BECAME DISTRACTED.
THOK
TODAY I AM FOCUSED.
WHOK
MY SWORDS ARE NOT YOUR USUAL WEAPONS, SAI-- AND YOU USE THEM CLUMSILY.
SO I WILL HAVE TO TAKE THEM BACK AND SHOW YOU HOW THEY ARE USED PROPERLY.

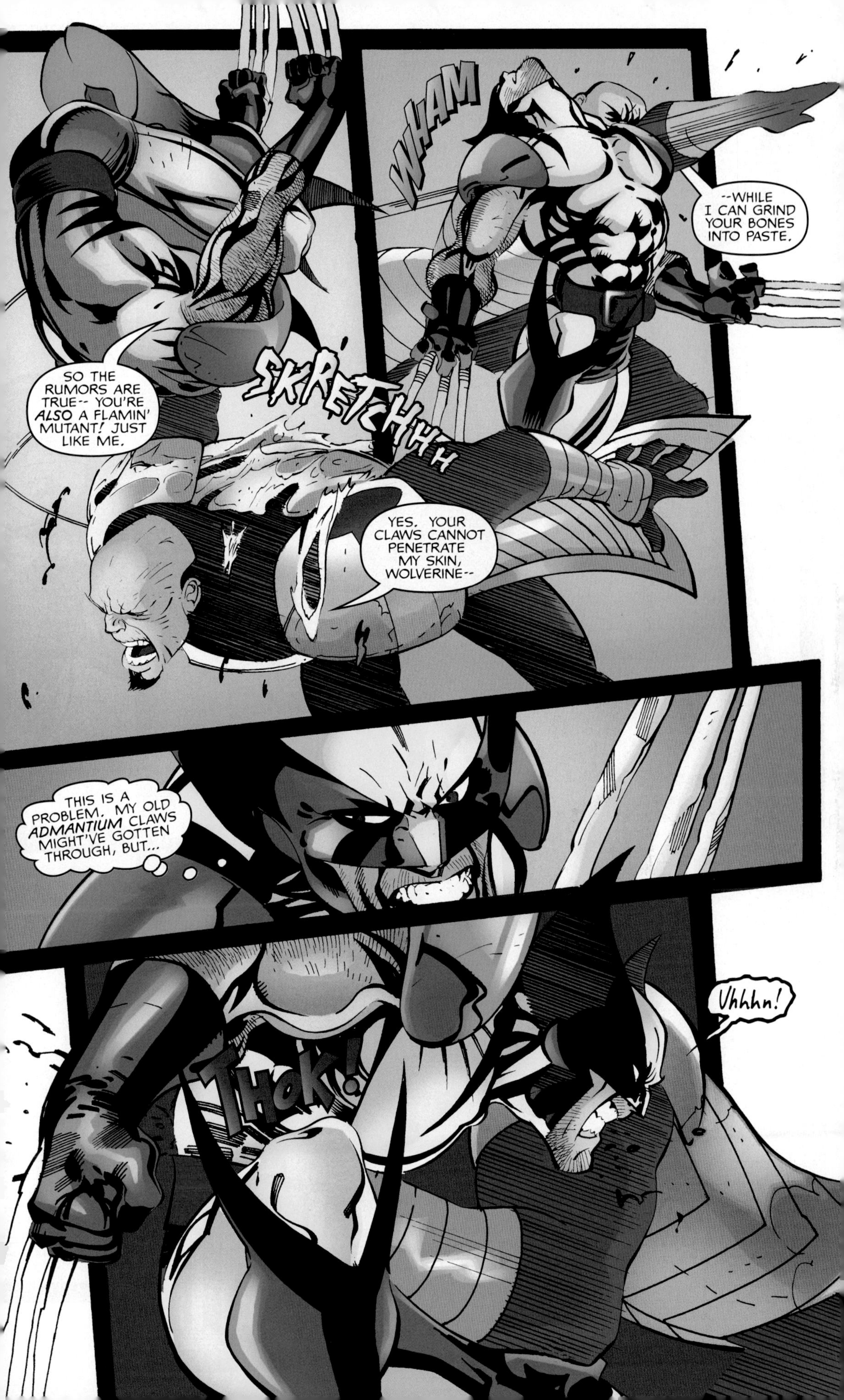
WHAM
SO THE RUMORS ARE TRUE-- YOU'RE *ALSO* A FLAMIN' MUTANT! JUST LIKE ME.
SKRETCHHHH
YES. YOUR CLAWS CANNOT PENETRATE MY SKIN, WOLVERINE--
--WHILE I CAN GRIND YOUR BONES INTO PASTE.
THIS IS A PROBLEM. MY OLD *ADMANTIUM* CLAWS MIGHT'VE GOTTEN THROUGH, BUT...
THOK!
Uhhhn!

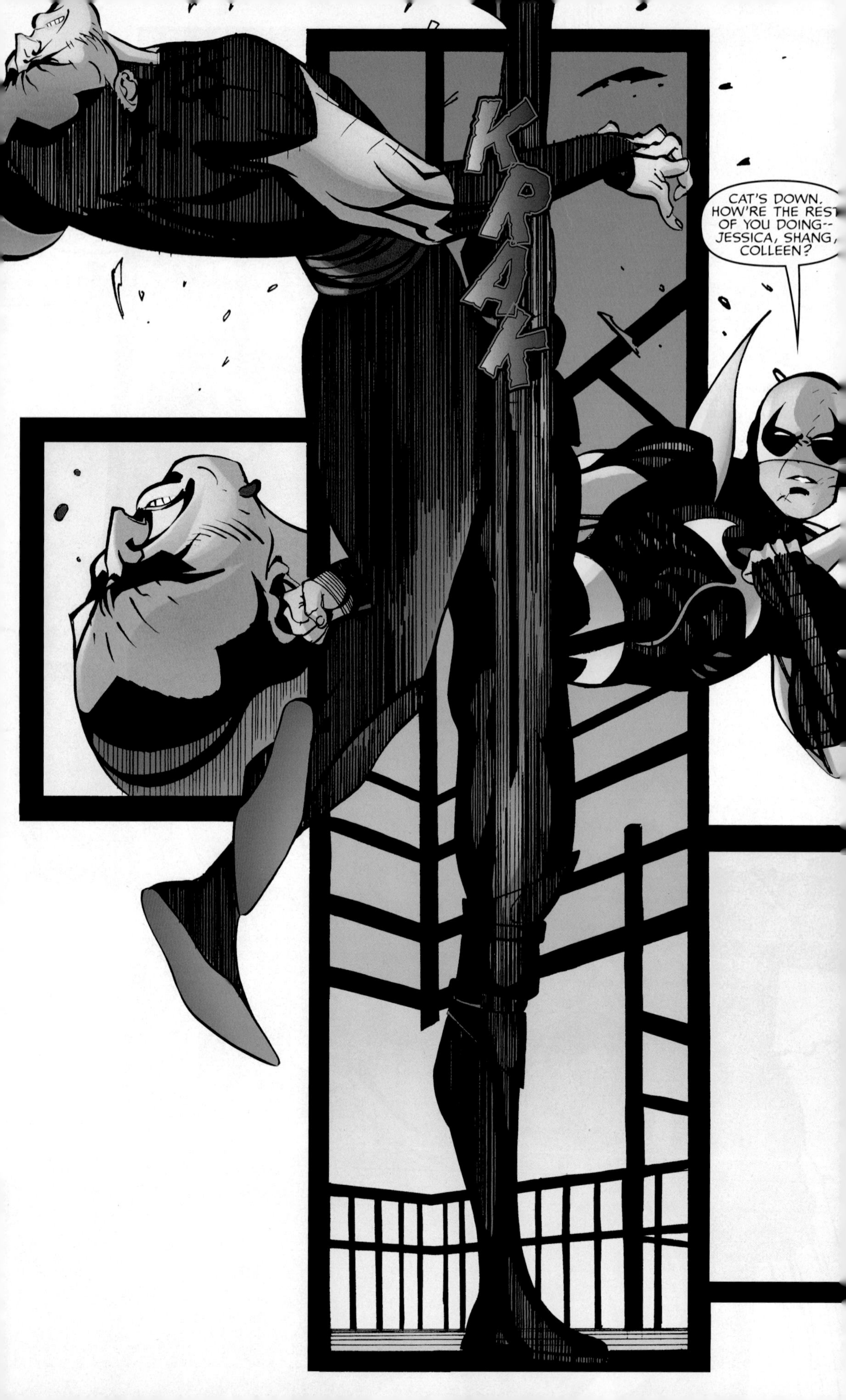
KRAK
CAT'S DOWN. HOW'RE THE REST OF YOU DOING-- JESSICA, SHANG, COLLEEN?

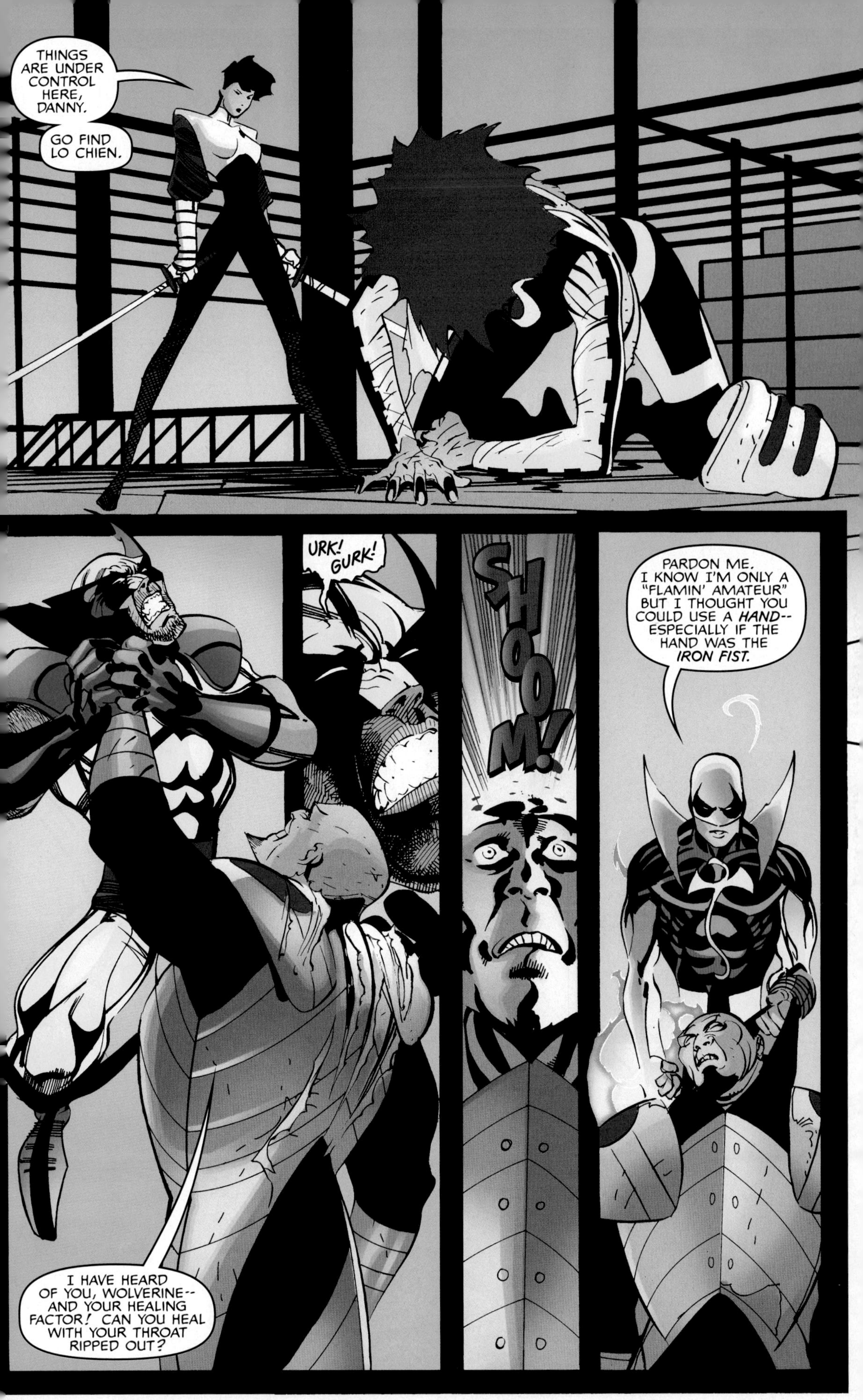
THINGS ARE UNDER CONTROL HERE, DANNY.
GO FIND LO CHIEN.
URK! GURK!
SHOOOM!
PARDON ME. I KNOW I'M ONLY A "FLAMIN' AMATEUR" BUT I THOUGHT YOU COULD USE A HAND-- ESPECIALLY IF THE HAND WAS THE IRON FIST.
I HAVE HEARD OF YOU, WOLVERINE-- AND YOUR HEALING FACTOR! CAN YOU HEAL WITH YOUR THROAT RIPPED OUT?

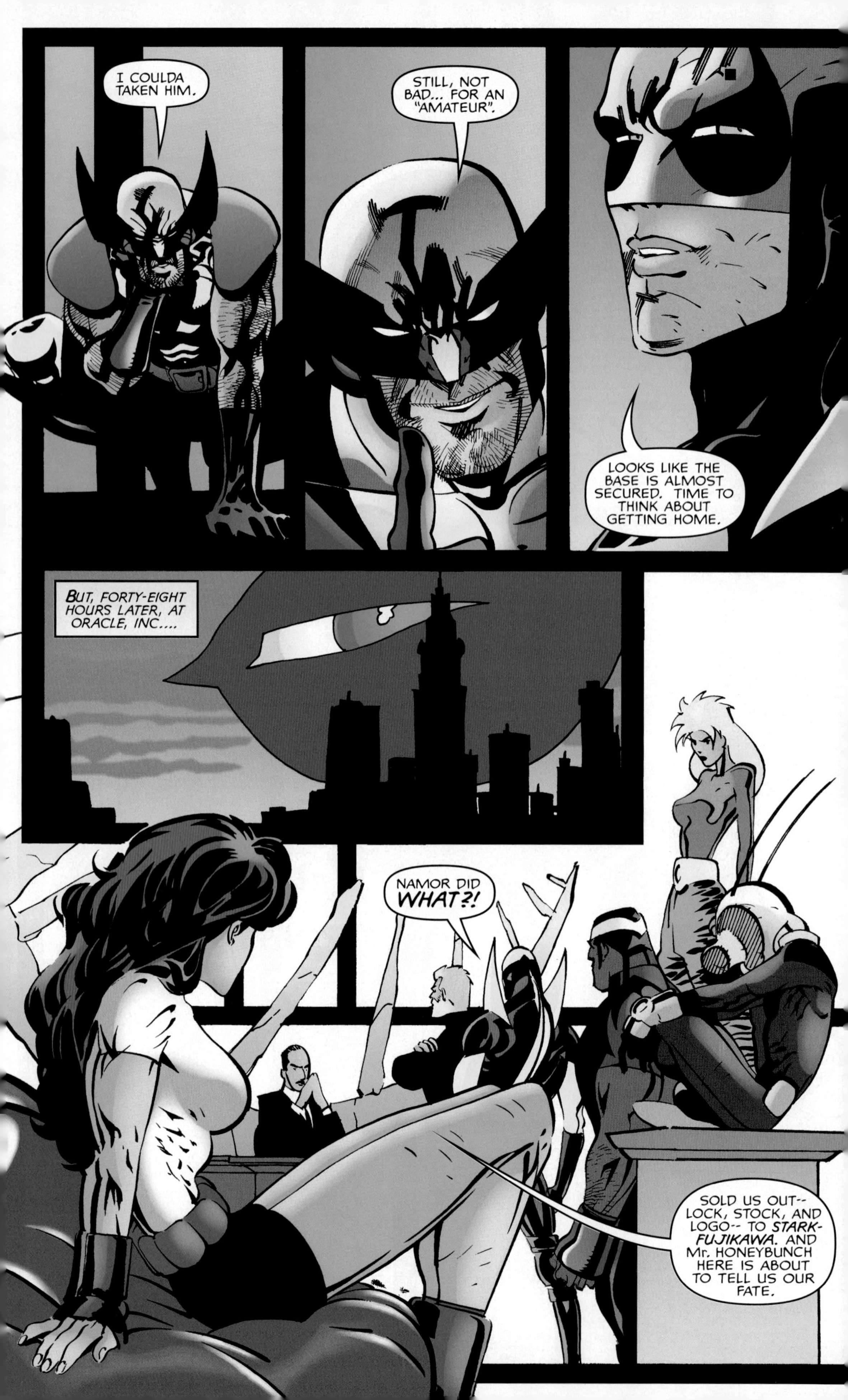
I COULDA TAKEN HIM.
STILL, NOT BAD... FOR AN "AMATEUR".
LOOKS LIKE THE BASE IS ALMOST SECURED. TIME TO THINK ABOUT GETTING HOME.
BUT, FORTY-EIGHT HOURS LATER, AT ORACLE, INC....
NAMOR DID WHAT?!
SOLD US OUT-- LOCK, STOCK, AND LOGO-- TO STARK-FUJIKAWA. AND Mr. HONEYBUNCH HERE IS ABOUT TO TELL US OUR FATE.

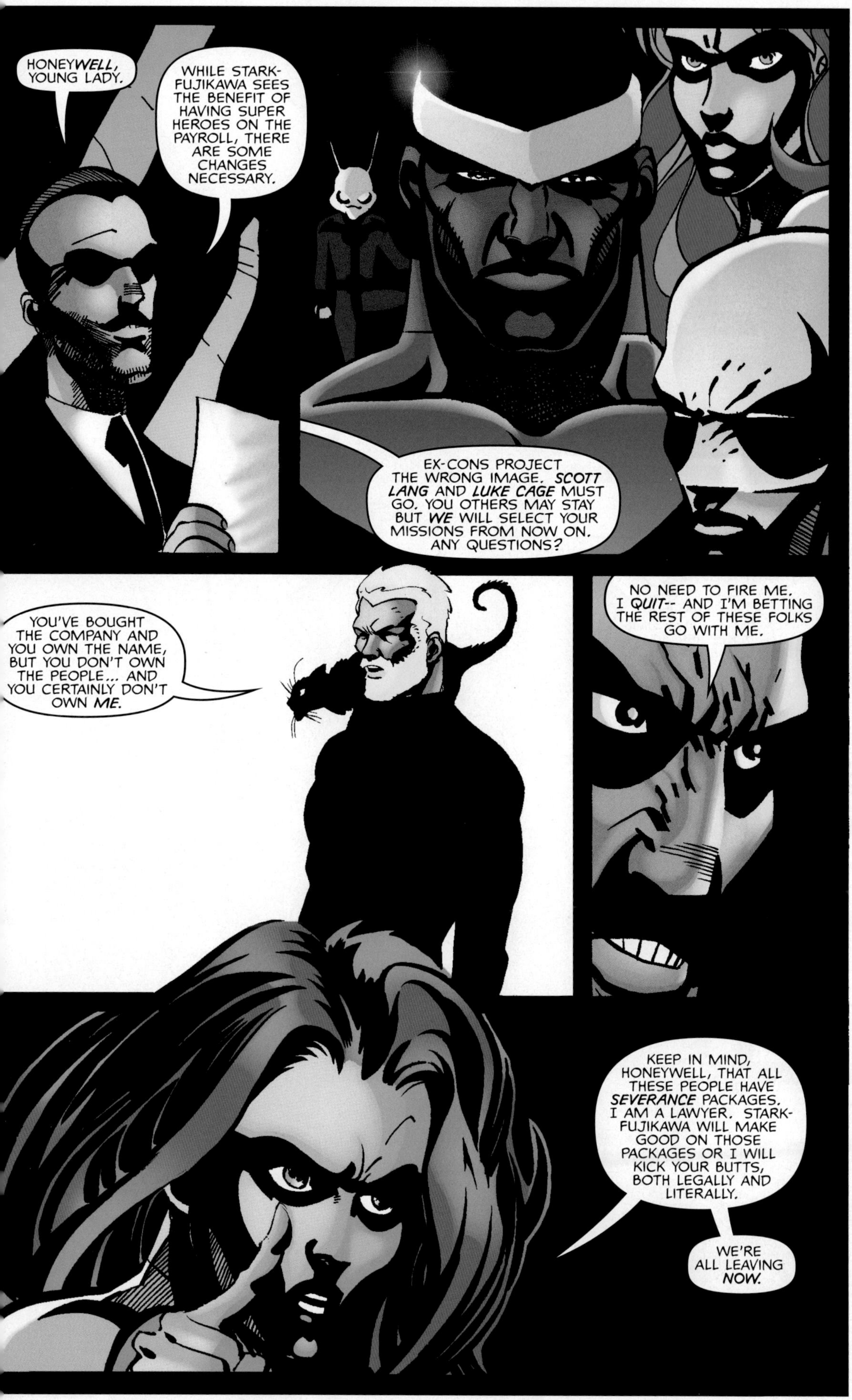
HONEYWELL, YOUNG LADY.
WHILE STARK-FUJIKAWA SEES THE BENEFIT OF HAVING SUPER HEROES ON THE PAYROLL, THERE ARE SOME CHANGES NECESSARY.
EX-CONS PROJECT THE WRONG IMAGE. SCOTT LANG AND LUKE CAGE MUST GO. YOU OTHERS MAY STAY BUT WE WILL SELECT YOUR MISSIONS FROM NOW ON. ANY QUESTIONS?
YOU'VE BOUGHT THE COMPANY AND YOU OWN THE NAME, BUT YOU DON'T OWN THE PEOPLE... AND YOU CERTAINLY DON'T OWN ME.
NO NEED TO FIRE ME. I QUIT-- AND I'M BETTING THE REST OF THESE FOLKS GO WITH ME.
KEEP IN MIND, HONEYWELL, THAT ALL THESE PEOPLE HAVE SEVERANCE PACKAGES. I AM A LAWYER. STARK-FUJIKAWA WILL MAKE GOOD ON THOSE PACKAGES OR I WILL KICK YOUR BUTTS, BOTH LEGALLY AND LITERALLY.
WE'RE ALL LEAVING NOW.

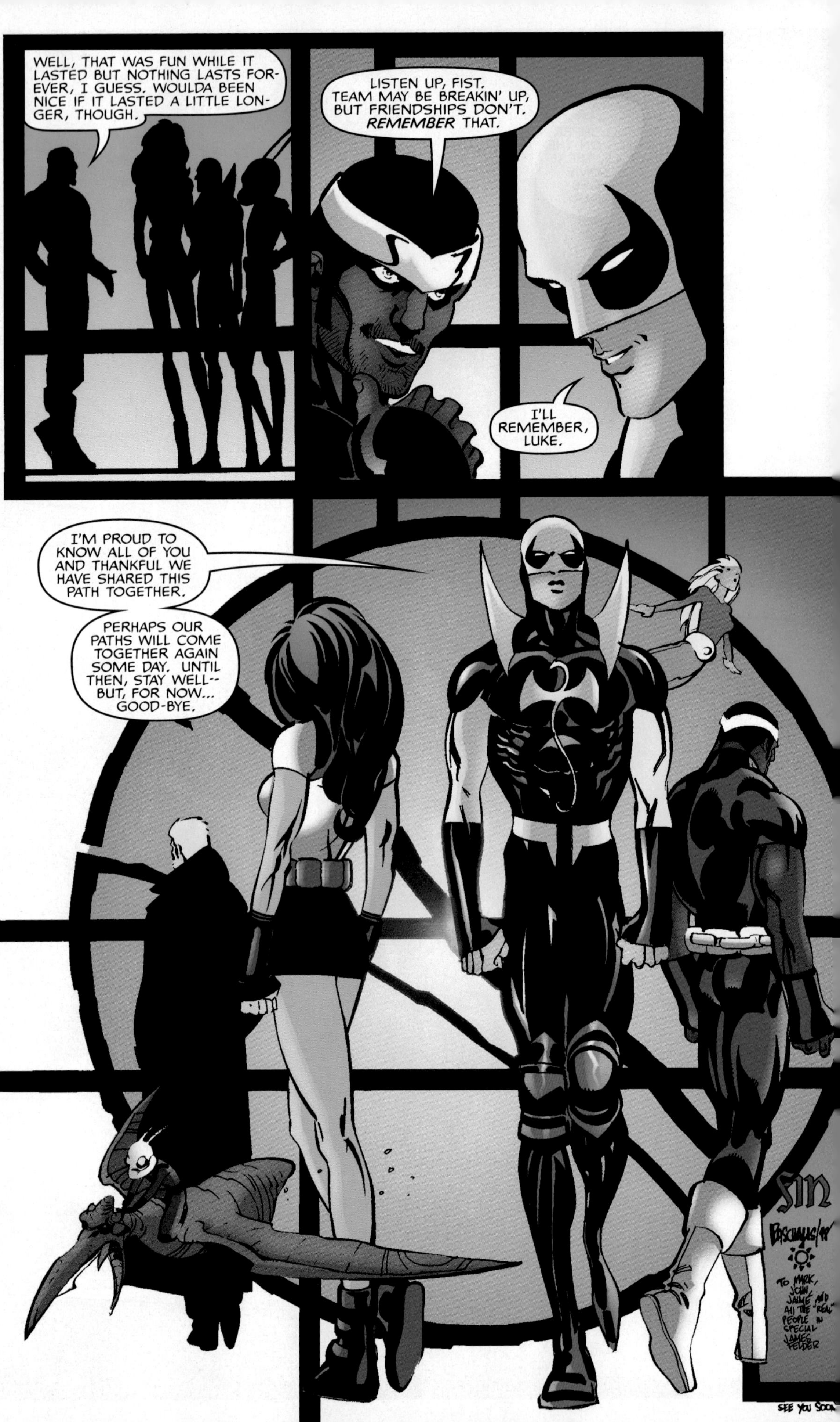
WELL, THAT WAS FUN WHILE IT LASTED BUT NOTHING LASTS FOREVER, I GUESS. WOULDA BEEN NICE IF IT LASTED A LITTLE LONGER, THOUGH.
LISTEN UP, FIST. TEAM MAY BE BREAKIN' UP, BUT FRIENDSHIPS DON'T. REMEMBER THAT.
I'LL REMEMBER, LUKE.
I'M PROUD TO KNOW ALL OF YOU AND THANKFUL WE HAVE SHARED THIS PATH TOGETHER.
PERHAPS OUR PATHS WILL COME TOGETHER AGAIN SOME DAY. UNTIL THEN, STAY WELL-- BUT, FOR NOW... GOOD-BYE.
FIN
TO MARK, JOHN, JAIME AND ALL THE "REAL" PEOPLE IN SPECIAL
JAMES FELDER

SEE YOU SOON

SiEGE!

by Michael Doran

Okay, pop quiz — what do you get when you combine the diverse roster of the super-hero strike team known as Heroes For Hire, the always volatile, sometimes Mighty Avenger Quicksilver, the mutant villainy of Exodus and his Acolytes, and the enigmatic High Evolutionary and his mysterious and powerful Isotope E?

If you said a pretty darn good cross section of the entire Marvel Universe, you wouldn't be too far off. But even more accurately you'd have "The Siege of Wundagore", an ambitious 5-part event running through the July and August issues of HEROES FOR HIRE and QUICKSILVER, and concluding in grand butt-whupping fashion in the HEROES FOR HIRE/QUICKSILVER '98 Annual.

"The Siege of Wundagore is essentially a story that both titles have built up to for quite a while now," says the man with the plan, editor Mark Bernardo. "The QUICKSILVER series started out with the High Evolutionary's homebase Wundagore Mountain being taken over by the evil mutant Exodus, which set up the current status quo with Pietro and the Knights of Wundagore. QUICKSILVER #12, the penultimate issue of this crossover, was always meant to tell the story of the showdown with Exodus and the retaking of the mountain. It's basically the first whole year of the title coming full circle.

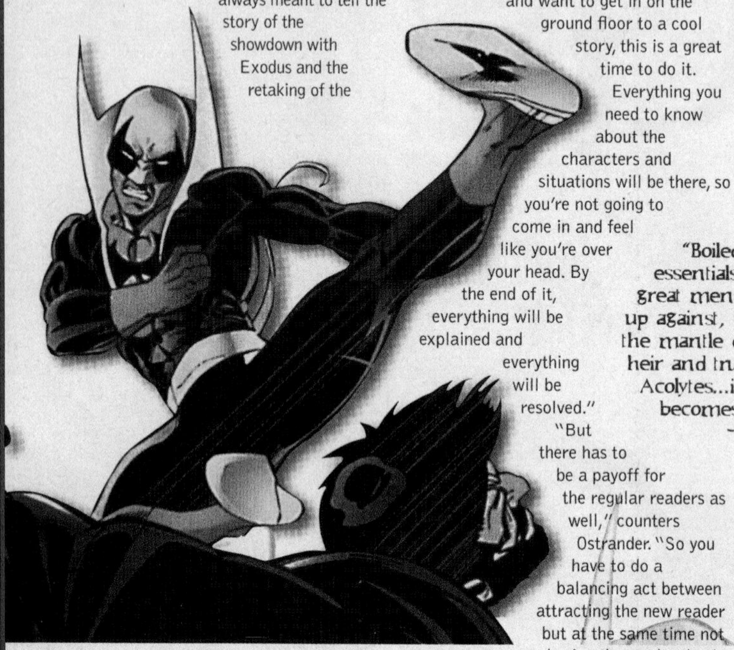

"And as HEROES FOR HIRE went along, and we saw the possible ties to this story develop — White Tiger's connection to Wundagore, the Black Knight's history with Exodus and Quicksilver — a bunch of pieces started to fall into place. And when HEROES FOR HIRE writer John Ostrander came onboard with QUICKSILVER #7 to co-write with Joe Edkin, from that point on we realized that a dual Annual, in the tradition of this year's Annual theme, would be just the perfect opportunity to create an explosive conclusion to storylines significant to both books."

But this isn't some thinly threaded crossover that fans have become wary of in recent years. "I know a lot of readers feel burned with multi-part crossover stories," empathizes John Ostrander. "That's in part because it seems like they aren't really relevant and don't really mesh well together as a story. But given the fact that I'm the regular writer on one book and co-writer on the other, I can guarantee one aspect of the story does lead into the next and that we're using all the page space that we've got to tell a truly mammoth and very epic story."

Despite all the storylines converging on a crash course in this crossover, the creators stress that "The Siege of Wundagore" is a story that can very much stand alone. "Every issue is someone's first, and we're keeping that in mind," say Edkin. "If you have never read either book and want to get in on the ground floor to a cool story, this is a great time to do it. Everything you need to know about the characters and situations will be there, so you're not going to come in and feel like you're over your head. By the end of it, everything will be explained and everything will be resolved."

"But there has to be a payoff for the regular readers as well," counters Ostrander. "So you have to do a balancing act between attracting the new reader but at the same time not boring the reader that's been there for a while. You want to write a story that has a certain amount of characterization, a lot of excitement, something that completely drives you forward, and makes you want to read the next issue. Every cliffhanger is a real cliffhanger and every chapter moves a step forward, and you will not want to miss an issue. Things are constantly changing and you want to keep up with it...you want to know what happens next."

> "Boiled down to its essentials, to defeat this great menace that they're all up against, Pietro must accept the mantle of being Magneto s heir and true leader of the Acolytes...in essence, he becomes his father."
> —Joe Edkin

FIRST BLOOD!

The story hits the ground running in HEROES FOR HIRE #15, in a tale by the title's regular creative team of Ostrander, kinetic penciler Pascual Ferry, and inker Jaime Mendoza. With Quicksilver still off hanging with Earth's Mightiest Heroes in June's "Live Kree Or Die" event, the High Evolutionary makes his return to the Haven to reclaim leadership of the Knights of Wundagore, and decides that now is the moment to his make bid to get Wundagore Mountain back from Exodus. But then Mr. High has never been one to always make rational decisions.

"One of the things that Joe and I have noticed prior to doing this story is that the High Evolutionary's powers and personality really seem to fluctuate," says Ostrander. "On one hand he has the [deep voice] 'powers of a god', but then on the other hand..."

"He can't make tea!" chimes in Edkin.

"Right," continues Ostrander without missing a beat. "And he gets kicked out of his own home by Exodus. Now this is not to put Exodus down and say he isn't powerful...But c'mon, the High Evolutionary is a guy..."

"Who creates planets!" finishes Edkin.

"Yeah, so we've been hypothesizing that there are reasons for that and we hope to explore that and find those reasons."

Chapter 1 finds Mr. Enigma himself sending everyone's favorite cow-woman nanny Bova to retrieve Wundagorian creation the White Tiger to report on her duties (duties that will be revealed in the story). Returning home, she brings along her allies, the core members of H4H, to help take back Wundagore. But when they show up, there is a flare-up between the Knights and H4H, and at this point, the High Evolutionary, smack dab in the middle of one of his "manic phases," uses his powerful Isotope E to devolve the heroes into a Neanderthal state.

"One of the number of mysteries we will be exploring and hopefully resolving in this story is what exactly is Isotope E (which everyone is looking for), as well as, if there is an Isotope E, what the heck were Isotopes A through D? We'll answer that question and it ties into a lot of the history of the Marvel Universe and the High Evolutionary," promises Edkin.

UNMASKED!

The story continues later in July in QUICKSILVER #11, by Ostrander, Edkin, Derec Aucoin and Rich Faber. Pietro returns home to the Haven only to find the High Evolutionary and the Knights gone, and in their place a bunch of devolved H4H, who in this primitive state perceive him as a threat, particularly the Black Knight, with whom Pietro has a long history of antipathy over the affections of Crystal.

"Quicksilver has to deal with getting H4H back to themselves, while at the same time Exodus has noticed that Isotope E has been used and sends the Acolytes to get it," explains Ostrander. "What he's unaware of is that the High Evolutionary and the Knights have returned, are in the vicinity, and ready to make their strike." And as if there wasn't enough going on already, the writers also divulge that at this point, the mysterious Lord Anon gets ready to reveal his agenda and is unmasked in this issue.

THE WAR BEGINS!

Which brings us to Chapter 3, HEROES FOR HIRE #16. "The war begins!" proclaims Ostrander. "H4H has suffered a casualty, but have joined the High Evolutionary at this point to join in the Siege of Wundagore. By the end of this issue, the first attacks have come and gone, and because of some betrayals and defecting sides, the good guys are defeated."

"By the end of this issue, things are looking pretty darn bleak," warns Edkin. "The heroes have been captured, and Exodus has Isotope E." So the bad guys have won, the story should be over, right? Not so fast. Things are just getting warmed up for the fireworks to follow in the double-sized QUICKSILVER #12.

IN HIS FATHER,S FOOTSTEPS?!

Nestor, another mysterious character with an agenda all his own introduced in issue #8, helps Pietro pull his act together and he is the first to escape. But to rescue his fellow heroes, he must make a monumental decision. And according to Bernardo, this may be the most significant chapter in the life of Quicksilver. "Boiled down to its essentials, to defeat this great menace that they're all up against, Pietro must accept the mantle of being Magneto's heir and true leader of the Acolytes...in essence, he becomes his father."

Edkin continues: "One of the things that triggers this is Pietro's exposure to Isotope E. This gives him this huge boost of powers, so that he finally understands what it's like to be Magneto and have all that power. That this must be what it feels like to be Dad! He must face his destiny and lead the Acolytes against Exodus, and in order to do that, he must employ leadership tactics that he learned from his father. But Magneto is not a very even-tempered, kind leader, and the other heroes are going to take note of this. The intent is to leave a very ominous feel for the reader as to what is going on."

By the end of this chapter, you're finally going to get to see Pietro beat the snot out of someone. We figured that would be a good way to wrap up the first year of the book. Unfortunately, that doesn't mean all is fine and dandy. You see, the High Evolutionary has swung into his manic phase again and decides to wipe everyone out. And now not only does Quicksilver have to fight the being who has been a father figure to him, but he's also in conflict with the Knights, whom he is

supposed to be leading but who are back under the rule of their original master. Not only that, but the High Evolutionary has evolved the Knights further, making them less human and more superhuman than they were before."

THE MOTHER OF ALL ANNUALS!

Which leads us into the conclusion, the HEROES FOR HIRE/QUICKSILVER '98 Annual. But this annual won't be in the style readers have become accustomed to in recent years. Explains Ostrander: "I wanted to get back to an old Marvel tradition...that being the annual would always have the biggest event of that book that year." And his partner concurs. "This annual matters," says Edkin. "This is the biggest event for both books this year and what we're really, really striving for is that epic feel, that real sense of the great story."

The writers aren't giving away much about the grand finale, but will drop a couple of hints as to what to expect, including climactic showdowns between Pietro and the High Evolutionary and the Black Knight vs. Exodus. Also, one member of H4H won't be coming back from the mission...and he or she may not be alone. "Yeah, H4H loses at least one member in the Annual," warns Ostrander ominously. "It will be a team somewhat shrunk in size and strength and somewhat demoralized when they get back from this battle. By the end of 'The Siege of Wundagore,' things will not be the same for either book. We know readers have heard that a hundred times before, but we're serious about it."

And they have all the ingredients to make one heck of a convincing case. Ⓜ

> "I can guarantee one aspect of the story does lead into the next and that we,re using all the page space that we've got to tell a truly mammoth and very epic story."
> —John Ostrander

MARVEL SPOTLIGHT: "THE SIEGE OF WUNDAGORE"

On Sale July 15:
HEROES FOR HIRE #15
John Ostrander/Pascual Ferry/ Jaime Mendoza

On Sale July 29
QUICKSILVER #11
John Ostrander & Joe Edkin/ Derec Aucoin/Rich Faber

On Sale In August:
HEROES FOR HIRE #16
John Ostrander/Pascual Ferry/ Jaime Mendoza

QUICKSILVER #12
John Ostrander & Joe Edkin/ Derec Aucoin/Rich Faber

HEROES FOR HIRE/ QUICKSILVER '98

MAKIN' HISTORY WITH JOHN OSTRANDER!

BY POLLY WATSON

John Ostrander is one of the busiest guys we know! Currently writing HEROES FOR HIRE and working as co-writer (with Joe Edkin) on QUICKSILVER, John has instigated an epic crossover between the two books. "The Siege of Wundagore" will culminate in HEROES FOR HIRE/QUICKSILVER '98, which John will also be writing. And before the dust of that project can settle behind him, John will be bringing the Western hero back to Marvel in August in the pages of the limited series entitled BLAZE OF GLORY. Here, he chats about everything from Wundagore to the White Tiger to the Wild, Wild West!

When does the Siege of Wundagore officially start?

June. It covers 3 books, and stretches over 5 issues. It starts in HEROES FOR HIRE #15, and goes on to QUICKSILVER #11, back into H4H #16, goes into QUICKSILVER #12, which is double-sized, and then climaxes in HEROES FOR HIRE/QUICKSILVER '98, which is also double-sized.

The title sounds like an epic tale. What's the basic concept?

In QUICKSILVER, the basic trauma has been that the High Evolutionary got tossed out of Wundagore by Exodus, who's now been hunting for both him and Isotope E. The High Evolutionary has decided that he's got his knights again, and it's time to go back after Wundagore (Editor's Note: Wundagore is a mountain in Transia, which is also the site of a citadel of science erected by the High Evolutionary.) Exodus is out to kick butt, because as far as he's concerned, the High Evolutionary is blasphemous and the Knights of Wundagore are obscene creations. He believes in Homo Superior, but only natural Homo Superior. He wants to use Isotope E for his own purposes, ultimately to destroy the isotope, but also to end the High Evolutionary and the Knights of Wundagore.

What makes QUICKSILVER and HEROES FOR HIRE the ideal forum for this story?

We are going to be concluding major story lines from both books. We'll be explaining what Isotopes A through D are, as well as what Isotope E is and why it's important. Also, we'll explore how the High Evolutionary, who on the one hand can create Counter-Earth, and virtually re-create the Savage Land, on the other hand can be kicked off his own mountain by Exodus. The High Evolutionary is a guy who's basically been up and down the evolutionary scale. Sometimes he has vast power, and then other times he crashes back into a Neanderthal-like state. He's like a physical manic depressive. Isotope E holds the hope of stabilizing him.

There'll be some interesting epercussions in HEROES FOR HIRE. For xample, we've just discovered that the White Tiger is actually a creation of the High Evolutionary. The principle purpose behind her creation will be revealed, and her mission will be completed with astonishing results!

Who will be in the Heroes for Hire lineup at the time of the crossover?

Iron Fist, Luke Cage, Ant-Man, She-Hulk, and of course, the White Tiger. Also the Black Knight, who has a history with Exodus dating back to when he (the man we know now as the Black Knight) travelled back in time, and actually became his own ancestor for a while. Exodus, before he became Exodus, was actually the Black Knight of that time's best friend. It was the Black Knight who wound up sealing him in his tomb after he became Exodus.

Will this crossover change the status quo of HEROES FOR HIRE?

Not only that, but at least one member of the team will not be coming back.

How does QUICKSILVER fit into all this?

Since he got his own book, Quicksilver has been leading the Knights of Wundagore, of whom he was basically left in charge by the High Evolutionary. We should see a major change in that status quo by the time everything's done. Also, Exodus has been set up as his major opponent, and by the end of issue #12, we will see Quicksilver really thumping butt and taking names. He experiences a surge in his powers, and he begins to become aware of what it's like to have all that power. For the first time, he begins to understand what his father, Magneto was all about. In fact, in one desperate stage, he may have to reclaim the mantle of Magneto in order to take the Acolytes away from Exodus. And what happens to him once he does...that is the question!

Will it impact the Marvel Universe beyond these books?

I think eventually it will, because we're redesigning the High Evolutionary's power, and if everything goes right, if the bad guys don't win, the High Evolutionary may wind up with both his power and his position stabilized. Also, a significant number of the Acolytes will be named and numbered. We'll know who they are, and what their names and powers are, and what their agendas are.

Wow! That's a pretty big payoff! Will readers have to buy both books to understand the crossover?

In this case, what we really set out to do was have each issue be a chapter in the story. And you can't just ignore chapters, like try and read only the odd-numbered chapters and think that you've got the whole story. You've got to read the odd and even-numbered chapters. We plan to make use of the broad canvas, the high amount of pages we've got, and tell a really epic story line!

What made you decide to save the finale for an Annual?

I remember when the Marvel Annuals were the biggest event of the year. The marriage of Reed and Sue happened in a FANTASTIC FOUR Annual. The birth of their son Franklin happened in an Annual. The continuity in the monthly books would lead up to the Annual and then lead away from it. I wanted to get away from the idea that the Annual is a stand-alone story, kind of a big story that doesn't fit into continuity. I want people to go, "Yeah, this is a special story." The Annuals should be something special.

If you haven't read any of the other issues, can you still pick up the Annual and enjoy it?

Certainly. But it's a broad-based theme, and there's a lot of players, so it's probably easiest if you buy 'em all!

It sounds like you've got more than enough work to keep you busy! But it's rumored that you're also going to be writing a limited series Western comic for Marvel. Is this true?

Yes! It's called BLAZE OF GLORY, sometimes also referred to as the "Last Ride of the Marvel Western Heroes"! There'll be two 48-page books, with art by Leonardo Manco. He got so excited by the idea of doing a Western with me, that when I was talking to him long-distance, he started playing music over the phone that he was going to be listening to while he drew it!

A lot of the stories that have been printed, like in old issues of RAWHIDE KID and TWO-GUN KID, those are great legends, but not necessarily the truth. We're gonna tell you more of the truth. It's going to have a bit of historical grounding to it. It's not going to be like what I've done on *The Kents*, which I did for DC, I'm going for a different feel here. Look for reinterpretations of classic Marvel characters.

What Marvel Western heroes can fans look forward to seeing?

We're going to be dealing with actual incidents and characters, and then bringing in Marvel Western characters as well. Among the ones we're bringing in are Rawhide Kid, Outlaw Kid, Two-Gun Kid, Kid Colt Outlaw, Red Wolf, Reno Jones, Gunhawk, the original Ghost Rider, and Caleb Hammer, who appeared only once.

Will this be an anthology-type thing, or one big story?

It's one big story, taking place in Montana Territory around 1886. Everyone is gradually pulled together in defense of a town. It's going to be like "The Magnificent Seven" as done by Sam Peckinpah or John Woo. *The Kents* was more like a mini-series; this is going to be like a good western movie!

What drew you to the concept of a Western comic?

Kim Yale, my wife, was always a big Western fan, and she's the one who drew me, sort of dragging my heels, into it.

If you could write any book for Marvel, what would it be?

I've always loved Dr. Strange. He's been created and re-created, and I'd like to get back down to basics with him. Also, I'd like to bring Strike Force Morituri back and put them in the Marvel Universe, but with new characters. I like the concept of it.

But I've got to say, I'm having a ball with HEROES FOR HIRE. It is definitely different from anything I've ever written. And because I came on board at the last minute, we were just making it up as we went, so the narrative voice didn't really begin until issue #5. But once the narrator finally began talking, it was impossible to shut him up!

Are there any artists you've long dreamed of working with?

Jimmy Palmiotti and Joe Quesada keep saying they'd love to do something with me, but it never happens. P and Q: I'd love to, but prove it! Really, I've been very lucky in working with great people across the board. Tim Truman, Tom Mandrake, one of my best friends in the world. Jan Duursema and I are doing some stuff together. I love working with Pascual Ferry and Derec Aucoin. My friend Mary Mitchell is doing issue #14 of HEROES FOR HIRE, it's just beautiful work, and now Leonardo, whom I've already worked with on the WOLVERINE '97 Annual. I've been really lucky. I've just so enjoyed everyone I've worked with for the most part. I've really been blessed in working with such wonderful people.

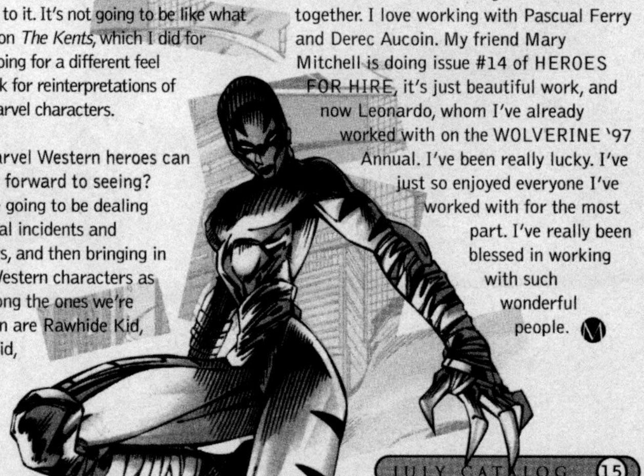

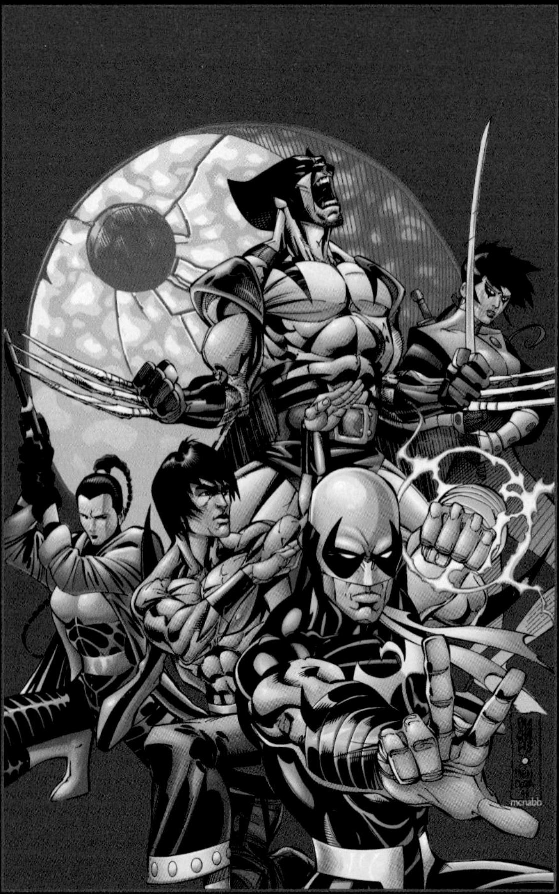

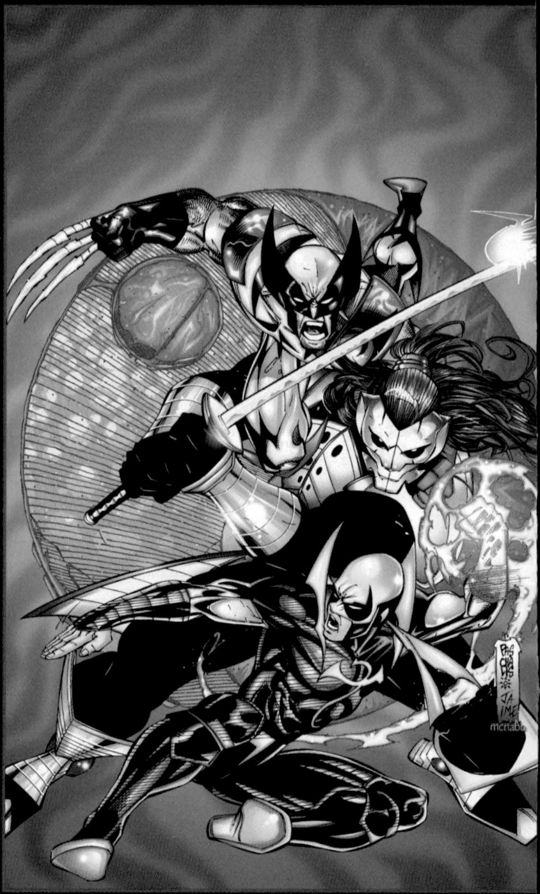

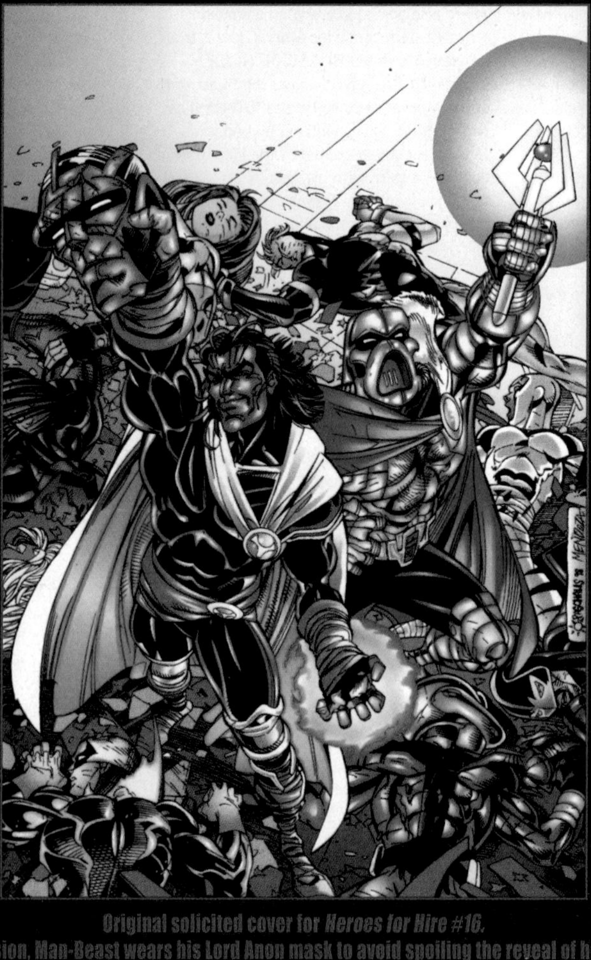

Original solicited cover for *Heroes for Hire #16.*
In this version, Man-Beast wears his Lord Anon mask to avoid spoiling the reveal of his identity.